1973

RUSSELL M. ROSS, Ph.D., University of Iowa, is Professor of Political Science at that institution. He has also taught at San Jose State College. Dr. Ross has held several non-academic positions in the State of Iowa, including Executive Assistant to the Governor, Chairman of the Metropolitan Planning Commission of Johnson County, and Mayor of University Heights. He is the author of a book on the government and administration of Iowa and has contributed to books on urban responses to agricultural change and approaches to the study of urbanization.

KENNETH F. MILLSAP, Ph.D., University of Iowa, is Professor of Political Science at California State College at Long Beach. He is Coordinator of the Public Administration Intern Training Program at that institution. Dr. Millsap has taught at Parsons College and at Michigan State University. He has been City Clerk for Iowa City, Iowa, a member of the County of Los Angeles Charter Study Committee, and a consultant to the Personnel Department of the City of Anaheim, California.

# STATE AND LOCAL

# GOVERNMENT

## AND

# ADMINISTRATION

RUSSELL M. ROSS

University of Iowa

KENNETH F. MILLSAP

California State College at Long Beach

THE RONALD PRESS COMPANY · NEW YORK

Library of Congress Catalog Card Number: 66–20089

PRINTED IN THE UNITED STATES OF AMERICA

# Preface

This text is not an attempt to concentrate exclusively either on the structural point of view or upon the problems of state and local government, but is written from the premise that *both* are important if an understanding of the workings of state and local government is to be attained.

The administrative aspects of state and local government comprise an area that is of great importance to successful government. The functions performed are vital to every citizen. No matter how profound the policy may be, it can be no better than the effectiveness with which it is executed by the administrative personnel.

Although predominant emphasis is on the administrative aspects of state and local governments, the book presents considerable material concerning the structure of governmental units in the United States below the national level. The role the counties play, the position of the municipalities and special districts, and the peculiar problems of metropolitan areas are all examined in detail. The importance of intergovernmental coordination and cooperation is stressed, as is the growing relationship between the national and local governments.

Professor Ross is indebted to the University of Iowa for providing a Research Professorship semester in order that he might complete sections of the manuscript. Professor Millsap is similarly grateful to California State College at Long Beach for having been granted a semester of sabbatical leave to work on the book. Colleagues of the authors at both University of Iowa and California State College at Long Beach were most generous in their assistance, but of course the burden for all errors of omission or commission must be borne by the authors.

University of Iowa
California State College
   at Long Beach
April, 1966

Russell M. Ross
Kenneth F. Millsap

# Contents

**1 Prelude** . . . . . . . . . . .    **1**

Colonial Governments, 1 · Government Under the Articles of Confederation, 3 · Establishment of the United States Constitution, 4 · The Changing Nature of State and Local Governments, 7 · Geography and Population Distribution, 10

**2 Federal—State—Interstate Relations** . . . . .    **22**

The Federal System, 22 · American Constitutional Federalism, 22 · Federal Obligations to the States, 26 · Obligations of the States to the National Government, 29 · Obligations of States to Each Other, 30 · The Merits of Federalism, 32 · The Philosophy of States' Rights, 33 · The Moderate Position, 35 · Interstate Co-operation, 37

**3 The State and Local Units of Government—The Unitary System** . . . . . . . . . . .    **42**

Local Governmental Units in the United States, 42 · Municipal Corporations and Quasi-Corporations, 46 · Home Rule for Local Governments, 49 · State Control over Local Units, 52 · National-local Government Relations, 62

**4 The American County in Local Government** . . .    **66**

Present Position of the County, 67 · County Home Rule, 70 · Organization of County Government, 72 · Proposed Reorganization of the County, 79 · County Officers and Employees, 88 · County Functions, 97 · The Urban County, 104 · The Future of the County, 105 · Special Districts, 106 · Authorities, 109

**5 Municipal Government** . . . . . . . .    **113**

Incorporation of American Cities, 116 · Forms of Municipal Government in the United States, 117 · Municipal Administration, 136 · Municipal Expenditures by Function, 138

**6 Metropolitan Government** . . . . . . .    **146**

Development of the Standard Metropolitan Statistical Area, 146 · Population Trends in Metropolitan Areas, 147 · Future Growth of Metropolitan Areas, 153 · Metropolitan Problems, 155 · Proposed Solutions of the Metropolitan Problems, 157

**7   State Constitutions** . . . . . . . . . . **172**

Evolution of State Constitutions, 174 · Bill of Rights, 177 ·
Separation of Powers and the Structure of Government, 178 ·
Powers of the State Government, 179 · Constitutional Amend-
ment or Revision, 180

**8   The Electorate, Political Parties, and Pressure Groups** . **193**

Requirements for Voting, 194 · Voter Participation, 198 · State
Political Parties, 202 · Political Party Structure and Organization, 205

**9   Nominations, Campaigns, Elections** . . . . . **220**

Nomination of Political Candidates, 221 · State Campaigns, 227
· State Limitations on Campaign Expenditures, 235 · Campaign
Expenditures, 236 · Election Administration, 240

**10   The State Legislature** . . . . . . . . **244**

United States Constitutional Limitations upon State Legislatures,
245 · Organization of State Legislatures, 246 · Qualifications
for State Legislators, 260 · Compensation of State Legislators,
262 · Immunities and Privileges of State Legislators, 267

**11   The Legislative Process** . . . . . . . . **268**

Officers of the Legislature, 268 · Presiding Officer of the Senate, 270 · Other Officials and Legislative Employees, 270 ·
State Legislative Committees, 271 · State Interim Committees,
276 · State Legislative Councils, 277 · Bill-drafting Aids, 279 ·
State Legislative Reference Services, 280 · Legislative Procedure, 280 · State Regulation of Lobbying, 289 · Non-legislative
Functions of the Legislature, 291 · Recommendations for Improving State Legislatures, 292 · Direct Legislation, 294

**12   The State Judiciary** . . . . . . . . . **299**

State and Federal Courts, 299 · The State Court Systems, 301 ·
Judicial Review, 319 · Judicial Advisory Opinions, 320 · Declaratory Judgments, 320 · Conciliation and Arbitration, 321 · Judicial Reforms, 322

**13   The Governor** . . . . . . . . . . . **325**

General Characteristics of the Office, 328 · The Governor as
Head of the Administration, 336 · The Governor and the State
Legislature, 344 · Military Powers, 348 · Judicial Powers, 349 ·
The Executive Office of the Governor, 351

14  **State Administrative Organizations** . . . . . **358**

Constitutional-administrative Officers, 358 · The Secretary of State, 362 · The State Treasurer, 363 · State Auditor, 364 · Attorney General, 365 · Superintendent of Public Instruction, 366 · Secretary of Agriculture, 367 · The Position of the Weak Governor in State Administration, 367 · The Position of the Strong Governor in State Administration, 372 · State Administrative Reorganization, 373 · Standards of Administrative Reorganization, 378 · Types of Administrative Organization, 379 · Growth of the Reorganization Movement, 381

15  **State Personnel Systems** . . . . . . . . **385**

The State Scene, 385 · Selection Process, 390 · Internal Placement of Personnel, 397 · Removal Processes, 400 · Employee Organizations, 401 · Organization for Central Personnel Management, 404 · Current Personnel Trends, 410

16  **State and Local Revenue** . . . . . . . **413**

Trends in State Revenues, 413 · Characteristics of a Sound Tax System, 419 · Major State Revenues, 420 · Federal Grants to States, 430 · Local Revenues, 433 · State Tax Administration, 435

17  **State and Local Expenditures** . . . . . . **439**

Trends in State and Local Expenditures, 439 · Fiscal Management, 443

18  **Law Enforcement and Public Safety** . . . . . **459**

State Agencies, 459 · Local Agencies, 466 · Treatment of Criminals, 472 · Civil Defense, 477 · Organization for Civil Defense, 479 · State and Local Fire Administration, 482

19  **State Educational Systems** . . . . . . . **489**

Trends in the Number of School Districts or Units, 489 · The National Role in Education, 492 · State Organizations for Education, 494 · Education at the Local Level, 498 · Higher Education, 502 · Major Problems in Education, 509 · Library Services, 516

20  **Social Welfare Programs** . . . . . . . **520**

Types of Public Welfare Programs, 520 · Categorical Outdoor Assistance Programs, 521 · State Agencies for Welfare Administration, 528 · Programs for the Aged, 530

21  Public Health  .   .   .   .   .   .   .   .   .   .   537

The Power of Public Health Departments, 538 · Organization
of State Public Health Departments, 539 · Functional Division
of a Public Health Department, 543 · State Public Health Expenditures, 550 · Local Public Health Responsibilities, 551 ·
Hospitals, 553 · Mental Health, 554 · Housing and Public
Health, 557


22  Agriculture and Conservation  .   .   .   .   .   .   564

State Agricultural Organization, 565 · Agricultural Extension
Work, 575 · Conservation Programs, 578 · Parks and Recreation, 579


23  State Highway Administration  .   .   .   .   .   .   584

Local Responsibility for Highway Administration, 594 · Financing of State Highway Systems, 596 · Highway Safety, 603 ·
State Concern for Aviation, 604


24  State Regulation of Business .   .   .   .   .   .   .   607

The Power of the State To Regulate Business, 607 · Administrative Organization for Regulation of Business, 610 · State Regulation of Banking, 612 · State Regulation of Insurance Companies, 615 · State Regulation of Sale of Securities, 617 · State
Regulation of Corporations, 618 · State Regulation of the Sale of
Liquor, 619 · State Regulation of Public Utilities, 620 · Regulation of Professions and Trades, 623 · State Ownership of Business Operations, 626


25  The State and Labor  .   .   .   .   .   .   .   .   630

History of Labor Organizations, 631 · Labor Standards, 632 ·
Labor Union Activities, 640 · State Administrative Organization, 645


26  The States and Their Future .   .   .   .   .   .   .   654

States vs. Regional Governmental Units, 656 · Constitutional
Revisions, 657 · State Legislatures, 659 · The Governors, 660 ·
State Administrative Organization, 660 · Personnel Administra-
tion, 661 · State Judiciary, 662 · Local Government, 663 ·
State and Local Revenues, 664 · Conclusions, 666


Appendix: Model State Constitution  .   .   .   .   .   669

Index .   .   .   .   .   .   .   .   .   .   .   691

# STATE AND LOCAL GOVERNMENT

## AND

# ADMINISTRATION

# 1

# Prelude

## COLONIAL GOVERNMENTS

Before the formation of the United States the thirteen colonies were governed by three different types of government. In the eight so-called Royal Colonies—Georgia, Massachusetts, New Hampshire, New Jersey, New York, North Carolina, South Carolina, and Virginia—the governor was appointed by the King of England. The governor was the supreme ruler and the direct representative of the crown. Many had received their positions due to the fact that they were known to be strong supporters of the King and would execute his mandates. The members of the senior house of the legislature were also appointed by the crown and served in a dual capacity as advisers to the appointed governor and they also constituted the highest judicial body, the court of last resort. The only semi-representative part of the royal colonies was the lower house, whose members were elected by the qualified voters. The enfranchisement was limited to those who owned a certain amount of property, and in some colonies a religious requirement was present. The control of the legislative body by the appointed governor was complete. He was the personification of the King and the distrust of the King was transferred to the governor by the common people. Many of the governors did nothing unless they were certain that it was in conformance with the philosophy of the King. They were indeed the same as puppets. The King of England had one primary motivation, which was to force the colonies to help support England. The royal governor could veto any action taken by the legislature, and his veto was subject only to appeal to the crown, which rarely, if ever, happened.

In Delaware, Maryland, and Pennsylvania the colonies were proprietary colonies with the proprietor substituting his will for that of the King. His goals were in many respects similar since his major objective was to force the colony to make as much money for him as possible. Lord Baltimore and William Penn were the proprietors of these three colonies and had

1

been given the absolute ownership of the territories by the King. The charters granted to the proprietors the authority to appoint the colonial governor and certain other officials and to determine what other governmental agencies should be established. In both Delaware and Maryland Lord Baltimore established a bicameral legislature, with the upper house in each instance known as the council, as in the royal colonies, and the membership was appointed by the proprietor. The lower house was elected by the freemen of the territory. A different and unique unicameral legislature was designed by William Penn for Pennsylvania. Under this arrangement the council was confined merely to advising the governor and had no part in the actual passage of legislation. The veto of the governor could not be overridden by the legislature. Any appeal, except in Maryland, could be taken to the King of England.

The remaining two colonies, Rhode Island and Connecticut, possessed still a third status, that of charter colonies. These charters had been granted to the colonists by King James. Included in the charter was the right of the freemen to select through the popular elective process the governor of the colony on an annual basis. In both charter colonies the bicameral legislature was also subject to annual election by the same electorate. The laws passed by the colonial assembly were not subject to a gubernatorial veto nor were they subject to scrutiny and approval of the crown. The judges were appointed to their positions by the members of the legislature acting in concert with the elected governor. Appeals, technically, could be taken from the verdict of the colonial court to the King but seldom was this resorted to by the colonists. The two charter colonies were by far the most democratically organized of the three types. The charter of Connecticut was retained almost in total as the first state constitution until 1818, and Rhode Island used its charter as the supreme law until 1842 with virtually no changes. The thirteen colonies included eight Royal Colonies, three Proprietary Colonies, and two Charter Colonies. The following colonies are included in the Royal Colony category: Virginia (1607), Massachusetts (1628), New Hampshire (1629), North Carolina (1663), South Carolina (1663), New York (1664), New Jersey (1664), and Georgia (1732). The Proprietary Colonies were Maryland (1634), Delaware (1638), and Pennsylvania (1681). Rhode Island and Connecticut, both established in 1636, were the Charter Colonies.

## The New States and Their Constitutions

During the Revolutionary War the original thirteen colonies followed the suggestions of the Continental Congress and through assemblies or conventions organized themselves into "states." In both Rhode Island and Connecticut the charters were converted into state constitutions while Massachusetts adopted its 1691 charter as its first state constitution.

The ten newly written state constitutions were quite uniform in content and general provisions. All restricted suffrage, all established three branches of government—independent of the others in theory, and seven wrote bills of rights into their constitutions. The governor in each state was to be elected; in four by the electorate and in the others by the legislature. The governor in only one state, Massachusetts, had a veto power, and it could be overridden by a two-thirds vote of the legislature. Annual election of the governor prevailed. The legislatures in eleven of the thirteen states were bicameral, with Pennsylvania retaining its unicameral legislature and Georgia also providing for a single-chamber house in its constitution. The lower house members were elected annually by the franchised voters. Some of the upper houses were elected directly by the people while others were named by the members of the lower house. The upper house, commonly called the senate, became known as the representative of property, while the lower house was known as the representative of the people. Most constitutions allowed only the lower house to initiate tax measures. The judicial branch was made more responsive to the people than it had been under the colonial rule with the judges either elected, as in Georgia, or appointed by the legislature rather than by the governor. Tenure was short and removal at any time by the legislature was ordinarily provided. Three levels of state courts were established—a local justice of the peace, a county court, and a supreme court of last resort.

## GOVERNMENT UNDER THE ARTICLES OF CONFEDERATION

The Second Continental Congress assigned a committee in June of 1776 to draft a document providing for a confederation to be entered into by the new states. The committee report was presented in July and was debated intermittently until approved on November 17, 1777. In the following twelve months, eleven states ratified the Articles of Confederation but, since unanimous approval was required before the new supreme law could go into effect, the Articles were not officially accepted until ratified by Delaware in 1779 and finally by Maryland on March 1, 1781.

Under the Articles of Confederation the thirteen states were joined for their common defense, the security of their liberties, and their mutual and general welfare, with each state retaining its sovereignty, freedom, and independence and every power, jurisdiction, and right that was not delegated to the United States. A league of states was established.

No executive branch was established under the Articles. Congress, a unicameral body, was the only organ of government. It was composed of no less than two nor more than seven delegates from each state. The delegates were paid by the state they represented, and the unit rule prevailed with each state having but a single vote. No delegate could be a member for more than three years of any six-year span. Business was conducted frequently with as few as one-eighth of the entire delegates in attendance.

Congress under the Articles had only those powers expressly granted to it in the supreme law. These included the power to declare war and peace, conduct foreign relations, requisition revenue from the states in proportion to the land values, requisition soldiers from the states in proportion to the number of white residents in each state, borrow money, emit bills of credit, coin money, commission a navy, settle disputes between states, establish a postal service, and regulate weights and measures. Any amendment to the Articles of Confederation had to be agreed to by every state while any other actions required approval by nine of the thirteen state delegations.

The states retained all powers not granted to Congress and therefore were responsible for protecting life and property and promoting the general welfare. They did pledge that they would extend full rights to each state's citizens; give full faith and credit to the records, acts, and judicial proceedings of all other states; deliver fugitives to each other; submit their disputes to Congress; and allow open commerce between states.

The most obvious defect of the Articles of Confederation was the lack of power to levy direct taxes. Faced with an accumulated debt of more than forty million dollars, the Congress tried without success to assess the respective states their fair share. A second major failure became evident when the Congress was unable to regulate commerce among the states, and various state trade barriers arose. A third shortcoming was the necessity of unanimous agreement upon any change in the supreme law. As a result no amendment was ever added. A fourth weakness was apparent in that the Congress could not legislate directly on the people.

By 1785 it became obvious that some drastic changes must occur. The conference at Alexandria, and later at Washington's home at Mount Vernon, in that year began consideration of some major changes. It was not until 1787, however, that Congress provided for the Philadelphia Convention to consider what modifications should be made in the Articles of Confederation.

## ESTABLISHMENT OF THE UNITED STATES CONSTITUTION

A quorom was finally present for the opening of the Philadelphia Convention on May 25, 1787. George Washington was selected as the president of the convention and the rules of the meeting were established. The convention met until September 15 and developed what may well be characterized as a document that embodied the approved principles and provisions of the charters of government with which the authors of the Constitution were familiar.

The Constitution remedied virtually every weakness that had appeared in the Articles of Confederation. It created an executive branch, a judicial branch, and a bicameral legislature. It also provided for the direct power to tax by the central government. Amendments could be approved by a three-fourths vote of the states, and the new Constitution was to go into effect upon the ratification of nine state conventions. The central government was to have full power over interstate commerce. The powers of the national government were delegated, and the residual powers were granted to the states. No bill of rights was included but shortly thereafter the addition of such amendments was assured in order to get the necessary nine state conventions to ratify the Constitution.

The new document placed an emphasis upon the fact that this was a union of the people and not merely of the states. A strong central government was intended, but one possessing limited powers. It provided that the supremacy of the national constitution would prevail when in conflict with state constitutions and state laws.

The first state to ratify the new document was Delaware in a state convention held on December 7, 1787, and the ninth state was New Hampshire on June 21, 1788. Almost two years later, May 29, 1790, Rhode Island became the last of the original thirteen colonies to accept the United States Constitution.

## Governing Territories and Admission of States

In Article IV, Section 3, the United States Constitution asserts that new states may be admitted to the Union by the Congress but that no new state shall be formed or erected within the jurisdiction of any other state; nor any state be formed by the junction of two or more states, or parts of states, without the consent of the legislatures of the states concerned. Congress is also authorized to make all necessary rules and regulations respecting territory belonging to the United States.

After the approval of the legislatures concerned was gained, five new states were created by carving them from original claims or parts of other states and were admitted without going through the probationary period of territorial status. These five were Vermont, Kentucky, Tennessee, Maine, and West Virginia—the section of Virginia that remained in the Union during the Civil War. Each entered the Union upon the approval of its state constitution by the Congress. California also never passed through a territorial period. Texas was unique in that it was an independent nation for ten years before being admitted as a state in 1845. The list of the twenty states that never experienced territorial government is presented in Table 1–1.

TABLE 1–1

States Achieving Statehood Without Territorial Status

| State | Date Admitted as a State |
|---|---|
| Delaware | December 7, 1787 |
| Pennsylvania | December 12, 1787 |
| New Jersey | December 18, 1787 |
| Georgia | January 2, 1788 |
| Connecticut | January 9, 1788 |
| Massachusetts | February 6, 1788 |
| Maryland | April 28, 1788 |
| South Carolina | May 23, 1788 |
| New Hampshire | June 21, 1788 |
| Virginia | June 25, 1788 |
| New York | July 26, 1788 |
| North Carolina | November 21, 1789 |
| Rhode Island | May 29, 1790 |
| Vermont | February 18, 1791 |
| Kentucky | June 1, 1792 |
| Tennessee | June 1, 1796 |
| Maine | March 15, 1820 |
| Texas | December 29, 1845 |
| California | September 9, 1850 |
| West Virginia | June 19, 1863 |

SOURCE: Council of State Governments, *The Book of the States, 1962–1963* (Chicago: Council of State Governments, 1962).

Thirty other states entered the Union after having first served varying periods of time as territories, with Alabama remaining in territorial status for only two years while New Mexico was in this category for sixty-two years. In each and every instance the Territorial Constitution was accepted by the United States Congress. All provided that the President of the United States appoint the governor, the secretary, and usually the members of the territorial supreme court. The parallel between this type of organization and the Proprietary Colonies, and to a degree the Royal Colonies of the pre-Revolutionary era, is significant. The Territorial Constitutions were stereotype documents that exhibited virtually no original thinking and a marked lack of democratic philosophy. Often the governor had never resided in the territory prior to his appointment and frequently spent as little time as possible in the area where he was serving as chief executive. It should be noted that those areas still in a territorial status in the twentieth century were usually able to persuade the President of the United States to appoint the governor from among the residents of the territory. These "native" territorial governors have relieved to a degree the charge that the territories were small dictatorships.

The admission dates of the thirty "new" states and their periods of time under territorial government are listed in Table 1–2.

### TABLE 1–2

#### Period of Territorial Status—Date of Admission

| State | Date of Territorial Status | Years of Territorial Status | Date Admitted as a State |
|---|---|---|---|
| Ohio | 1787–1803 | 16 | 1803 |
| Louisiana | 1804–1812 | 8 | 1812 |
| Indiana | 1800–1816 | 16 | 1816 |
| Mississippi | 1798–1817 | 19 | 1817 |
| Illinois | 1809–1818 | 9 | 1818 |
| Alabama | 1817–1819 | 2 | 1819 |
| Missouri | 1812–1821 | 9 | 1821 |
| Arkansas | 1819–1836 | 17 | 1836 |
| Michigan | 1805–1837 | 32 | 1837 |
| Florida | 1822–1845 | 23 | 1845 |
| Iowa | 1838–1846 | 8 | 1846 |
| Wisconsin | 1836–1848 | 12 | 1848 |
| Minnesota | 1849–1858 | 9 | 1858 |
| Oregon | 1848–1859 | 11 | 1859 |
| Kansas | 1854–1861 | 7 | 1861 |
| Nevada | 1861–1864 | 3 | 1864 |
| Nebraska | 1854–1867 | 13 | 1867 |
| Colorado | 1861–1876 | 15 | 1876 |
| South Dakota | 1861–1889 | 28 | 1889 |
| North Dakota | 1861–1889 | 28 | 1889 |
| Montana | 1864–1889 | 25 | 1889 |
| Washington | 1853–1889 | 36 | 1889 |
| Idaho | 1863–1890 | 27 | 1890 |
| Wyoming | 1868–1890 | 22 | 1890 |
| Utah | 1850–1896 | 46 | 1896 |
| Oklahoma | 1890–1907 | 17 | 1907 |
| New Mexico | 1850–1912 | 62 | 1912 |
| Arizona | 1863–1912 | 49 | 1912 |
| Alaska | 1912–1959 | 37 | 1959 |
| Hawaii | 1900–1959 | 59 | 1959 |

SOURCE: Council of State Governments, *The Book of the States, 1962–1963* (Chicago: Council of State Governments, 1962).

## THE CHANGING NATURE OF STATE AND LOCAL GOVERNMENTS

In 1939, Professor Harold J. Laski, of England, wrote under the title "The Obsolescence of Federalism" that the failure of the federal idea was plain in the United States, Canada, Australia, and Germany. He explained this failure by saying that forty-eight separate units could not seek to compete with the integrated power of giant capitalism for they inevitably would be defeated.[1]

Particularly untrue has been Professor Laski's prognosis that the states would be defeated by the national powers. It is true that between 1950 and 1960 the national governmental expenditures increased from $40 billion to $75 billion, a gain of 92 per cent in a decade. However, almost all of this increase was accounted for directly or indirectly by the department of defense and its allied agencies. During this same decade the state governmental expenditures increased from $13 billion to $32.5 billion, an increase of more than 146 per cent. This meant a jump of from $89 per capita in 1950 to $182 per person in 1960. Similar increases of comparable size occurred in local governments during this same time period. In cities of over 25,000 population the increase for the decade was more than 150 per cent.

In New York State alone, proof of the enormous amount of state activity can be seen from Governor Rockefeller's figures concerning a selected number of state activities. In fiscal 1962, state aid in New York for secondary education amounted to $753 million, which was $87 million more than was even requested by the President of the United States from the Congress for all federal aid to education. New York spent $100 million on civil defense or about one-third of the amount spent by the federal government in civil defense activities. In power development, the State Power Authority of New York built more hydro-electric power generating capacity in the decade from 1950 to 1960 than all of the hydro-electric dams of the TVA system. In public housing the state of New York was considering a $5 billion housing project for New York City alone—the same figure that was suggested for the entire federal housing program.[2]

## Shifts in Functional Activities

State government activity, as Kirk H. Porter has stated, has expanded in three different directions: (1) the states are doing on a larger scale services they have traditionally performed; (2) the states are undertaking entirely new functions; and (3) the state governments are gradually assuming activities that were formerly left to local governments, particularly counties and townships, to initiate and carry forth.[3]

The examples that may be cited of these growths in functions are almost limitless. One of the best illustrations of performing on a larger

[1] Harold J. Laski, "The Obsolescence of Federalism," *New Republic,* Vol. XCVIII (May 3, 1939), pp. 367–9.

[2] Nelson A. Rockefeller, *The Future of Federalism* (New York: Athencum, 1963), pp. 13–15.

[3] Kirk H. Porter, *State Administration* (New York: F. S. Crofts & Co., 1938), p. 8.

scale the traditional state government activities is found in the rapid expansion of state-supported and -controlled higher educational institutions. Today every one of the fifty states maintains a state university, and many states, either in conjunction with the state university or independent thereof, have established a state agricultural or mechanical arts college. In addition, many states have a well-organized system of state colleges and state-supported junior colleges. Nearly 65 per cent of the 2,594,519 full-time students enrolled in higher educational institutions are attending state-supported colleges and universities in contrast with the approximately 35 per cent of all college students attending state schools only twenty years ago. A similar expansion of state services could be cited in the fields of agriculture and public health where the states have greatly increased their activities.

Thirty years ago few states were engaged to any degree in the provision of park and recreational facilities. Today this is an accepted state government service, and all states have an increasingly important role to play in the operation of state parks. The public not only expects this role to be fulfilled by the state but various private groups constantly pressure for expansion and improvement in outdoor recreational systems. Public health laboratories may be listed as another service that the states are now involved with in depth. Three decades ago a few of the more populous states maintained a public health laboratory, but in the second half of the twentieth century every state maintains not only a full public health laboratory but many have branches in various geographical areas of the state. Tests are now run on the water supply and also on various other factors involved in sustaining high public health standards. State public clinics to aid in the treatment and prevention of various types of diseases, not just the contagious ones, are now common among the fifty states. It should be noted that these and other examples of new state governmental activities have originated not at the behest of state government officials but upon the demand of the public.

In the third area of state government expansion—taking over functions that formerly were delegated to local units of government, primarily townships and counties—the most dramatic example probably has been in the field of highways. At the turn of the century the roads within a state were viewed as a completely local responsibility. Each county and each township not only maintained its own road system but also determined what new construction should be undertaken. Today in some states the entire road system within a state comes directly and completely under the state highway department or commission. Even when the county is still allowed to maintain and construct its own roads, prior approval of the plans and specifications must usually be given by the state highway authorities.

The environment in which state government is operating has undergone a tremendous change in the last thirty years, but the governmental machinery has in most instances remained static. Thus the new problems brought about by 70 per cent of Americans living in urban areas are confronting the governmental structure that was designed to handle a rural population.

## GEOGRAPHY AND POPULATION DISTRIBUTION

American state government is big government. It is big in terms of finance, it is big in terms of area, and it is big in terms of population. State government expenditures have now risen to more than $33 billion each year. This is more than twice the rate of expenditures of ten years ago. Likewise, city government expenditures have more than doubled in the same ten-year period. This is true in spite of the growth and power of the national government. The ratio of state and local spending to the total governmental expenditures each year is now approximately 64:40.

### Area and Population Trends

Alaska is the largest of the fifty states, in geographic terms, with more than 571,000 square miles as compared with Rhode Island's 1,058 square miles. Texas is larger than either France or Spain in land area. Even the average American state—Iowa, with 56,000 square miles—is larger than nearly half of the member states of the United Nations.

California with a population of more than 17 millions, according to a 1963 estimate, has nearly as many people as all of Canada. The average state in the United States has more than 2.4 million people, which is larger than such nations as Israel, Jordan, Iraq, Honduras, and Panama.[4]

The worldwide population explosion was evident also in the United States between 1950 and 1960. During this decade the population of the United States increased by 18½ per cent. Nineteen states had a population growth greater than the national average while one, Indiana, exactly equaled the national increase. Several of the states with smaller populations, such as Alaska and Nevada, had tremendous population booms of more than 75 per cent, but other states, including Florida and Arizona, also increased by more than 70 per cent between 1950 and 1960.[5]

[4] The information presented in the two paragraphs above is based on data contained in *The Statistical Abstract of the United States, 1964*, Bureau of Census, U.S. Dept. of Commerce (Washington, D.C.: Government Printing Office, 1964), pp. 10–19; and *The Book of the States, 1962–1963* (Chicago: Council of State Governments, 1962), p. 547.

[5] U.S. Department of Commerce, Bureau of the Census, *U.S. Census of Population, 1960* (Washington, D.C.: Government Printing Office, 1962).

If the United States Census Bureau estimates as of July 1, 1962, are correct, the population increase is continuing at nearly the same rate. Only West Virginia is listed as having fewer people in 1962 than in 1960; during the decade of the fifties both West Virginia and Arkansas lost population and Mississippi barely held its own. The two-year gain from 1960 to 1962 is approximately 3½ per cent, for a total of 185,822,000 individuals. The percentage of growth or decline in population for all of the states from 1950 to 1962, together with area statistics, is contained in Table 1–3. Persons of high school age—fourteen to seventeen—increased

## TABLE 1–3

### The Fifty American States
#### Population Trends and Area Statistics—1964

| State | Population July 1, 1964 (estimated) | Rank 1964 | Percentage of Population Increase, 1950–1960 | Percentage of Population Increase, 1960–1964 | Gross Area | Rank |
|---|---|---|---|---|---|---|
| Alabama | 3,407,000 | 21 | 6.7 | 4.3 | 51,609 | 29 |
| Alaska | 250,000 | 50 | 75.8 | 10.7 | 586,400 | 1 |
| Arizona | 1,581,000 | 34 | 73.7 | 21.4 | 113.909 | 6 |
| Arkansas | 1,933,000 | 31 | − 6.5 | 8.2 | 53,104 | 27 |
| California | 18,084,000 | 1 | 48.5 | 15.1 | 158,693 | 3 |
| Colorado | 1,966,000 | 30 | 32.4 | 12.1 | 104,247 | 8 |
| Connecticut | 2,766,000 | 24 | 26.3 | 9.1 | 5,009 | 48 |
| Delaware | 491,000 | 46 | 40.3 | 9.9 | 2,057 | 49 |
| Florida | 5,705,000 | 9 | 78.7 | 15.2 | 58,560 | 22 |
| Georgia | 4,294,000 | 15 | 14.5 | 8.9 | 58,876 | 21 |
| Hawaii | 701,000 | 42 | 26.6 | 10.8 | 6,424 | 47 |
| Idaho | 692,000 | 43 | 13.3 | 3.8 | 83,557 | 13 |
| Illinois | 10,489,000 | 4 | 15.7 | 4.0 | 56,400 | 24 |
| Indiana | 4,825,000 | 12 | 18.5 | 3.5 | 36,291 | 38 |
| Iowa | 2,756,000 | 25 | 5.2 | − 0.1 | 56,290 | 25 |
| Kansas | 2,225,000 | 29 | 14.3 | 2.1 | 82,264 | 14 |
| Kentucky | 3,159,000 | 22 | 3.2 | 4.0 | 40,395 | 37 |
| Louisiana | 3,468,000 | 19 | 21.4 | 6.5 | 48,523 | 31 |
| Maine | 989,000 | 38 | 6.1 | 2.1 | 33,215 | 39 |
| Maryland | 3,432,000 | 20 | 32.3 | 10.7 | 10,577 | 42 |
| Massachusetts | 5,338,000 | 10 | 9.8 | 3.7 | 8,257 | 45 |
| Michigan | 8,089,000 | 7 | 22.8 | 3.5 | 58,216 | 23 |
| Minnesota | 3,521,000 | 18 | 14.5 | 3.1 | 84,068 | 12 |
| Mississippi | 2,314,000 | 28 | 0.0 | 6.2 | 47,716 | 32 |
| Missouri | 4,409,000 | 13 | 9.2 | 2.1 | 69,686 | 19 |
| Montana | 705,000 | 41 | 14.2 | 4.5 | 147,138 | 4 |
| Nebraska | 1,480,000 | 35 | 6.5 | 4.9 | 77,227 | 15 |
| Nevada | 408,000 | 48 | 78.2 | 43.1 | 110,540 | 7 |
| New Hampshire | 654,000 | 44 | 13.8 | 7.7 | 9,304 | 44 |
| New Jersey | 6,682,000 | 8 | 25.5 | 10.1 | 7,836 | 46 |
| New Mexico | 1,008,000 | 36 | 39.6 | 6.0 | 121,666 | 5 |
| New York | 17,915,000 | 2 | 13.2 | 6.7 | 49,576 | 30 |
| North Carolina | 4,852,000 | 11 | 12.2 | 6.5 | 52,712 | 28 |
| North Dakota | 645,000 | 45 | 2.1 | 2.0 | 70,665 | 17 |

## TABLE 1–3 (Continued)

| State | Population July 1, 1964 (estimated) | Rank 1964 | Percentage of Population Increase, 1950–1960 | Percentage of Population Increase, 1960–1964 | Gross Area | Rank |
|---|---|---|---|---|---|---|
| Ohio | 10,100,000 | 6 | 22.1 | 4.1 | 41,222 | 35 |
| Oklahoma | 2,465,000 | 27 | 4.3 | 5.9 | 69,919 | 18 |
| Oregon | 1,871,000 | 32 | 16.3 | 5.8 | 96,981 | 10 |
| Pennsylvania | 11,459,000 | 3 | 7.8 | 1.2 | 45,333 | 33 |
| Rhode Island | 914,000 | 39 | 8.5 | 6.4 | 1,214 | 50 |
| South Carolina | 2,555,000 | 26 | 12.5 | 7.2 | 31,055 | 40 |
| South Dakota | 715,000 | 40 | 4.3 | 5.0 | 77,047 | 16 |
| Tennessee | 3,798,000 | 17 | 8.4 | 6.5 | 42,244 | 34 |
| Texas | 10,397,000 | 5 | 24.2 | 8.5 | 267,339 | 2 |
| Utah | 992,000 | 37 | 29.3 | 11.4 | 84,916 | 11 |
| Vermont | 409,000 | 47 | 3.2 | 4.9 | 9,609 | 43 |
| Virginia | 4,378,000 | 14 | 19.5 | 10.4 | 40,815 | 36 |
| Washington | 2,948,000 | 23 | 19.9 | 4.6 | 68,192 | 20 |
| West Virginia | 1,797,000 | 33 | − 7.2 | − 3.4 | 24,181 | 41 |
| Wisconsin | 4,107,000 | 16 | 15.1 | 3.9 | 56,154 | 26 |
| Wyoming | 343,000 | 49 | 13.6 | 3.9 | 97,914 | 9 |

SOURCE: U.S. Department of Commerce, Bureau of the Census, *Current Population Reports*, Series P. 25, No. 259 (Washington, D.C.: Government Printing Office, 1964); Council of State Governments, *The Book of the States, 1962–1963* (Chicago: Council of State Governments, 1962); and U.S. Department of Commerce, Bureau of the Census, *U.S. Census of Population, 1960, General Social and Economic Characteristics, United States Summary,* Final Report PC(1)-1C (Washington, D.C.: Government Printing Office, 1962).

more rapidly than any other age group between April, 1960, and July 1, 1962. The number of children under five years of age and the children of elementary school age—five to thirteen—had rates of growth less than the average for all ages. The number of people between eighteen and twenty-four increased slightly while the number between twenty-five and thirty-four declined slightly. The number of persons between thirty-five and sixty-four grew a bit slower than the average of all ages while the number of persons over sixty-five increased more rapidly than any other age group.

The non-white population continues to grow more rapidly than the white population. As of 1961 the non-white population numbered slightly more than 21 millions or about 11.5 per cent of the total United States population. The excess of females to males in the American population continued with 97.7 males for every 100 females, but virtually unchanged from the 1950 figure of 97.8 males to every 100 females.[6]

The mobility of the population is demonstrated by the Census Bureau's estimate that 35.5 million Americans moved at least once during the

[6] U.S. Department of Commerce, Bureau of Census, *U.S. Census Estimates of Population, 1962* (Washington, D.C.: Government Printing Office, 1963).

twelve-month period from March, 1960, to March, 1961. Of these changes, 24.3 millions moved within the same county, 5.5 millions moved from one county to another in the same state, while 5.8 millions changed from one state to another.[7]

In 1961 the average (median) income of families in the United States was $5,700 in a survey conducted in March, 1962. This meant an increase of about 2 per cent over the previous year, but consumer prices rose about 1 per cent during the same period, thus virtually nullifying any increase in earnings.[8]

## Growth of Governmental Employees

One of the best indicators of the growth of state and local government may be seen from an examination of the growing number of employees utilized by these governmental units. The federal government employee census has remained relatively constant during the last ten years, but the number of state and local government employees has increased rapidly. In 1950 the federal employees numbered 2.4 millions while the number of state and local employees, including public school teachers, totaled 4.3 millions. A decade later the federal employees remained at approximately 2.4 millions while the state and local government employees numbered nearly 6.4 millions. Of this latter figure, 2.4 millions were public school teachers, but this number had not increased proportionately during the ten years. Thus of the total civilians employed by governmental units in the United States in 1960 about 73 per cent were paid by state or local units. To state this comparison another way, there were nearly three times as many state and local government workers as there were federal employees, excluding the more than 2 million members of the federal armed forces.[9] A comparison of the growth of public employees and payrolls, both state-local and federal, from 1950 to 1962 is shown in Figure 1-1.

## Diversified State Problems

It has been said that no two state governments are alike. True, they all have separation of powers—an executive branch, a judicial branch, and a legislative branch—but from this point on the differences are much more significant than the similarities.

[7] U.S. Department of Commerce, Bureau of Census, *A Preliminary Report on Mobility and the American Population* (Washington, D.C.: Government Printing Office, 1962), pp. 5–6.

[8] U.S. Department of Commerce, Bureau of Census, *A Sample Survey of Income of American Families* (Washington, D.C.: Government Printing Office, 1962), pp. 2–3.

[9] U.S. Department of Commerce, Bureau of Census, *State Distribution of Public Employment in 1960* (Washington, D.C.: Government Printing Office, 1961), p. 1.

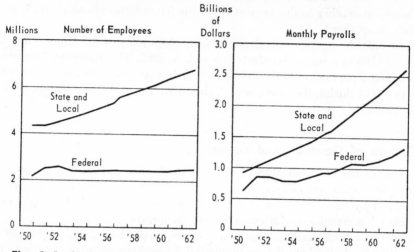

PUBLIC EMPLOYMENT AND PAYROLLS, 1950 TO 1962
(Data for October, Except for 1957 Data, which Are for April)

**Fig. 1–1.** State-Local and Federal Distribution of Public Employment and Payrolls, 1950 to 1962. [Source: U.S. Department of Commerce, Bureau of the Census, *State Distribution of Public Employment in 1962* (Washington, D.C., Government Printing Office, 1963).]

These differences are in a sense necessary because of the different problems that face the fifty states. Some have a tremendous population boom; others are not facing this problem but rather one of an aging population. Over one-half of the counties in the United States had a net population decline between 1950 and 1960.

Variations in per capita income, per capita state revenue, expenditures per pupil in elementary and secondary schools, the number of physicians per 1,000 people, and even the rate of rejections for the draft are all factors with a direct bearing upon the state governmental operations. In each of the above-mentioned categories extreme contrasts can be noted for 1960. The average personal income for the United States was $2,223, but the contrast between Connecticut's $2,863 and Mississippi's $1,173 is reflected in many ways, particularly in the per pupil expenditures for education where Connecticut expended $497 while Mississippi was spending only $220. As might be expected, the median school years completed in Connecticut was 11 years, and Mississippi's was only 8.9 years. The physician-per-patient ratio is also of interest, with Mississippi having only 0.76 physician per 1,000 population while Oregon has 1.27 physicians for each 1,000 people. In rejections for selective service Oregon had, in 1960, only 23 per 100 while Mississippi had nearly 65 of every 100 inductees rejected. Of probably greater significance was the fact that the median school years completed in Oregon was 11.8 years as compared with the 8.9 years in Mississippi.

## Conclusion

There is no question about the fact that great changes have occurred and will continue to occur in the traditional role of the states and local governments in the federal system as it operates in the United States. Tremendous developments have taken place, such as the entrance of the federal government into the regulatory activities which at one time were more or less exclusively lodged in the states but which are now concurrent powers of the states and the national government. While some powers are now shared, other new powers and duties have been assumed by the state and local governments to such an extent that the total picture shows the states and their subdivisions actually performing more services and regulatory activities than ever before in the history of state government.

## BIBLIOGRAPHY

ANDREWS, CHARLES M. *The Colonial Background of the American Revolution,* rev. ed. New Haven: Yale University Press, 1931.
——— *The Colonial Period in American History.* New Haven: Yale University Press, 1938.
CUNLIFFE, MARCUS. *The Nation Takes Shape, 1784–1837.* Chicago: The University of Chicago Press, 1959.
DICKERSON, OLIVER M. *American Colonial Government, 1696–1765,* rev. ed. New York: Russell & Russell, Inc., 1962.
GREENE, EVARTS B. *The Foundation of American Nationality,* rev. ed. Cincinnati: American Book Co., 1935.
FISHER, S. G. *The Evolution of the Constitution of the United States.* Philadelphia: J. B. Lippincott Co., 1900.
KNOLLENBERG, BERNHARD. *Origin of the American Revolution, 1759–1766,* rev. ed. New York: Crowell-Collier Publishing Co., 1961.
MILLER, JOHN C. *The Origins of the American Revolution.* Boston: Little, Brown & Co., 1943.
——— *The Federalist Era, 1789–1801.* New York: Harper & Row, Inc., 1960.
OSGOOD, HERBERT L. *The American Colonies in the Eighteenth Century.* New York: Columbia University Press, 1924.
——— *The American Colonies in the Seventeenth Century.* New York: Columbia University Press, 1930.
PADOVER, SAUL K. *The World of the Founding Fathers: Their Basic Ideas on Freedom and Self-Government.* New York: Thomas Yoseloff, Inc., 1960.
RIKER, WILLIAM H. *Federalism: Origin, Operation and Significance.* Boston: Little, Brown & Co., 1964.
SWISHER, CARL B. *American Constitutional Development,* 2d ed. Boston: Houghton-Mifflin, Co., 1954.
TANSILL, CHARLES C. (ed.). *Documents Illustrative of the Formation of the*

*Union of American States.* House Document No. 398, 69th Cong., 1st Sess. Washington, D.C.: Government Printing Office, 1927.

UMBREIT, KENNETH B. *Founding Fathers: Men Who Shaped Our Tradition.* New York: Harper & Row, Inc., 1941.

VAN DOREN, CARL. *The Great Rehearsal: The Story of Making and Ratification of the Constitution of the United States.* New York: The Viking Press, Inc., 1948.

WARREN, CHARLES. *The Making of the Constitution,* rev. ed. Boston: Little, Brown & Co., 1937.

WILTSE, CHARLES M. *The New Nation, 1800–1845.* New York: Hill & Wang, Inc., 1961.

## BIBLIOGRAPHY BY STATES

### Alabama

KEY, V. O., and HEARD, ALEXANDER. *Southern Politics.* New York: Alfred A. Knopf, Inc., 1949. Chap. iii.

### Alaska

BEBOUT, JOHN. *Local Government Under Alaska Constitution.* Chicago: Public Administration Service, 1959.

SLOTNICK, HERMAN. "Alaska: Empire of the North," in *Western Politics,* ed. F. H. JONAS. Salt Lake City: University of Utah Press, 1961. Chap. ii.

### Arizona

RICE, ROSS R. "Amazing Arizona: Politics in Transition," in *Western Politics,* ed. F. H. JONAS. Salt Lake City: University of Utah Press, 1961. Chap. iii.

VAN PETTEN, DONALD R. *Constitution and Government of Arizona.* Phoenix: John-Tyler Printing & Publishing Co., 1952.

### Arkansas

ALEXANDER, HENRY, M. *Organization and Function of State and Local Government.* Fayetteville: University of Arkansas, 1947.

### California

CRESAP, D. R. *Party Politics in the Golden State.* Los Angeles: John Randolph Haynes and Dora Haynes Foundation, 1954.

CROUCH, WINSTON W., and MCHENRY, DEAN E. *State and Local Government in California,* 2d ed. Berkeley: University of California Press, 1949.

HARRIS, JOSEPH P., and ROWE, L. *California Politics,* 2d ed. Stanford: Stanford University Press, 1959.

### Colorado

MARTIN, CURTIS. "Colorado: The Highest State," in *Western Politics,* ed. F. H. JONAS. Salt Lake City: University of Utah Press, 1961. Chap. v.

MARTIN, CURTIS and GOMEZ, RUDOLPH. *Colorado Government and Politics.* Boulder, Colo.: Pruett Press, Inc., 1964.

## Connecticut

LOCKARD, DUANE. *New England State Politics.* Princeton: Princeton University Press, 1959. Chaps. ix and x.

## Delaware

DOLAN, PAUL. *The Government and Administration of Delaware.* New York: Thomas Y. Crowell Co., Inc., 1956.

## Florida

DOYLE, WILSON K., *et al. The Government and Administration of Florida.* New York: Thomas Y. Crowell Co., 1954.

## Georgia

GOSNELL, CULLEN B., and ANDERSON, DAVID C. *The Government and Administration of Georgia.* New York: Thomas Y. Crowell Co., 1956.

## Hawaii

MELLER, NORMAN, and TUTTLE, DANIEL W., JR. "Hawaii: The Aloha State," in *Western Politics,* ed. F. H. JONAS. Salt Lake City: University of Utah Press, 1961. Chap. vi.

## Idaho

MARTIN, BOYD A. "Idaho: The Sectional State," in *Western Politics,* ed. F. H. JONAS. Salt Lake City: University of Utah Press, 1961. Chap. vii.

## Illinois

GARVEY, NEIL F. *The Government and Administration of Illinois.* New York: Thomas Y. Crowell Co., 1958.

STEINER, GILBERT Y., and GOVE, SAMUEL K. *Legislative Politics in Illinois.* Urbana: University of Illinois Press, 1960.

## Indiana

SIKES, P. A. *Indiana State and Local Government.* Bloomington: The Principia Press, Inc., 1946.

## Iowa

ROSS, RUSSELL M. *The Government and Administration of Iowa.* New York: Thomas Y. Crowell Co., 1957.

## Kansas

DRURY, JAMES. *The Government of Kansas.* Lawrence: University of Kansas Press, 1961.

SMITH, RHOTEN A., and CLARENCE J. HEIN. *Republican Primary Fight: A Study in Factionalism*. Princeton, N.J.: Eagleton Cases in Practical Politics, No. 11. 1958.

## Kentucky

FENTON, JOHN H. *Politics in the Border States*. New Orleans: The Hauser Press, 1957. Chaps. ii and iii.

## Louisiana

HOWARD, P. H. *Political Tendencies in Louisiana, 1812–1952*. Baton Rouge: Louisiana State University Press, 1956.

## Maine

LOCKARD, DUANE. *New England State Politics*. Princeton: Princeton University Press, 1959. Chap. iv.

## Maryland

BOWEN, DON L., and FRIEDMAN, R. S. *Local Government in Maryland*. College Park: University of Maryland, 1955.

## Massachusetts

LATHAM, EARL. *Massachusetts Politics*. New York: Citizenship Clearing House, 1955.

## Michigan

LAPALOMBARA, JOSEPH G. *Guide to Michigan Politics*, rev. ed. East Lansing: Bureau of Social and Political Research, Michigan State University, 1960.

SARASOHN, STEPHEN B., and SARASOHN, VERA H. *Political Party Patterns in Michigan*. Detroit: Wayne State University Press, 1957.

## Minnesota

MITAU, G. THEODORE. *Politics in Minnesota*. Minneapolis: University of Minnesota Press, 1960.

## Mississippi

HIGHSAW, ROBERT B., and FORTENBERRY, CHARLES N. *The Government and Administration of Mississippi*. New York: Thomas Y. Crowell Co., 1954.

## Missouri

KARSH, R. F. *Essentials of Missouri Government*, 2d ed. Columbia, Mo.: Lucas Bros., 1965.

## Montana

RENNIE, ROLAND R. *The Government and Administration of Montana.* New York: Thomas Y. Crowell Co., 1958.

## Nebraska

BRECKENRIDGE, A. C. *One House for Two.* Washington: Public Affairs Press, 1957.

## Nevada

DRIGGS, D. W. "Nevada: The Silver Dollar State," in *Western Politics,* ed. F. H. JONAS. Salt Lake City: University of Utah Press, 1961. Chap. ix.

## New Hampshire

LOCKARD, DUANE. *New England State Politics.* Princeton: Princeton University Press, 1959. Chap. iii.

## New Jersey

RICH, BENNETT M. *The Government and Administration of New Jersey.* New York: Thomas Y. Crowell Co., 1957.

## New Mexico

DONNELLY, T. C. *The Government of New Mexico.* Albuquerque: University of New Mexico Press, 1947.

## New York

CALDWELL, LYNTON K. *The Government and Administration of New York.* New York: Thomas Y. Crowell Co., 1954.

MOSCOW, WARREN. *Politics in the Empire State.* New York: Alfred A. Knopf, Inc., 1948.

## North Carolina

RANKIN, ROBERT S. *The Government and Administration of North Carolina.* New York: Thomas Y. Crowell Co., 1955.

## North Dakota

MORLAN, R. L. *Political Prairie Fire: The Nonpartisan League.* Minneapolis: University of Minnesota Press, 1955.

## Ohio

AUMANN, FRANCIS R., and WALKER, HARVEY. *The Government and Administration of Ohio.* New York: Thomas Y. Crowell Co., 1956.

## Oklahoma

THORTON, H. V., RUSHING, C., and WOOD, JOHN. *Problems in Oklahoma State Government*. Norman: University of Oklahoma, 1957.

## Oregon

SWARTHOUT, JOHN M. "Oregon: Political Experiment Station," in *Western Politics*, ed. F. H. JONAS. Salt Lake City: University of Utah Press, 1961. Chap. xi.

## Pennsylvania

COOKE, E. F., and JANOSIK, G. E. *Guide to Pennsylvania Politics*, rev. ed. New York: Holt, Rinehart & Winston, Inc., 1965.

TANGER, JACOB, *et al. Pennsylvania's Government: State and Local*, 3d ed. University Park: Penns Valley Publishers, Inc., 1950.

## Rhode Island

LOCKARD, DUANE. *New England State Politics*. Princeton: Princeton University Press, 1959. Chaps. vii and viii.

## South Carolina

KEY, V. O. *Southern Politics*. New York: Alfred A. Knopf., Inc., 1949. Chap. vii.

## South Dakota

FARBER, WILLIAM O., GEARY, THOMAS C., and CAPE, WILLIAM H. *Government of South Dakota*. Sioux Falls: Midwest-Beach Co., 1962.

## Tennessee

GOODMAN, WILLIAM. *Inherited Domain: Political Parties in Tennessee*. Knoxville: Bureau of Public Administration, University of Tennessee, 1954.

## Texas

MacCORKLE, S. A., and SMITH, DICK. *Texas Government*, 4th ed. New York: McGraw-Hill Book Co., Inc., 1960.

McKAY, S. S. *Texas Politics*. Lubbock: Texas Tech Press, 1952.

PATTERSON, CALEB PERRY, McALISTER, SAM B., and HESTER, GEORGE C. *State and Local Government in Texas*, 3d ed., New York: The Macmillan Co., 1961.

## Utah

JONAS, FRANK H. "Utah: Crossroads of the West," in *Western Politics*, ed. F. H. JONAS. Salt Lake City: University of Utah Press, 1961. Chap. xii.

LOCAL GOVERNMENT SURVEY COMMISSION. *Local Government in Utah*. Salt Lake City: State of Utah, 1956.

## Vermont

LOCKARD, DUANE. *New England State Politics*. Princeton: Princeton University Press, 1959. Chap. ii.

## Virginia

KEY, V. O. *Southern Politics*. New York: Alfred A. Knopf, Inc., 1949. Chap. ii.

## Washington

WEBSTER, D. H., *et al. Washington State Government*. Seattle: University of Washington Press, 1956.

## West Virginia

FENTON, JOHN H. *Politics in the Border States*. New Orleans: The Hauser Press, 1957.

LAMBERT, O. D. *West Virginia and Its Government*. Boston: D. C. Heath & Co., 1951.

## Wisconsin

EPSTEIN, LEON. *Politics in Wisconsin*. Madison: University of Wisconsin Press, 1958.

## Wyoming

TRACHSEL, HERMAN H., and WADE, RALPH M. *The Government and Administration of Wyoming*, 2d ed. New York: Thomas Y. Crowell Co., 1956.

# 2

# Federal–State–Interstate Relations

## THE FEDERAL SYSTEM

It is popularly believed that the United States invented the federal system of government. This is at best only partially true as a form of federalism had been practiced in ancient Greece. The immediate predecessor of federalism in America was the old Swiss Confederation.

Basically a federal system divides authority between self-governing units and the central government. The fundamental law, usually a written document, is called a constitution and grants to each unit its operating powers. The federal arrangement usually gives authority over matters considered to be of importance to the country as a whole to the central government. These matters almost always include control of foreign relations, defense, foreign commerce, the monetary system, and the postal system while activities of primarily local affairs, such as public education, intrastate commerce, and roads and highways are given to the local units.

The major problem is naturally to establish a division of authority in such a way that it will not be obsolete within a short period of years. With rapidly changing conditions this distribution of powers may be antiquated in a short period of time. It is remarkable that the writers of the United States Constitution were able to devise a document that has remained effective for nearly two hundred years with a minimum number of amendments.

## AMERICAN CONSTITUTIONAL FEDERALISM

The American federal system is a unique phenomenon, partly the product of human purpose, partly of unconscious adaptation to the circum-

stances and the needs of the people. It is now one of the oldest federal systems in existence. It has been tested in many ways: civil war; unprecedented territorial expansion; tremendous population changes; an industrial revolution; and a transition from horse-and-buggy transportation to rockets. During the entire period it has furnished a governmental environment compatible with the unparalleled economic growth and social transitions. It has enabled the people of the United States to enjoy the highest scale and standard of living known to mankind. It has made possible the marshaling of resources to win two world wars.

The framers of the Constitution deemed it wise to include nothing about the rather wide range of powers to be exercised by the states. Alexander Hamilton apparently believed that the functions of the states would be relatively minor and inexpensive. In *The Federalist*, No. 34, he wrote, ". . . in a short course of time the wants of the States will naturally reduce themselves within a very narrow compass" and after the states' war debts had been eliminated, "the only call for revenue of any consequence, which the State governments will continue to experience will be for the mere support of their respective civil lists; to which, if we add all contingences, the total amount in every state ought to fall considerably short of two hundred thousand pounds." Translated into dollars for the early part of the nineteenth century this would have been only about $1 million for all of the thirteen states.

Needless to say, Hamilton's ideas as to the minor activity and role that the states were supposed to play in the total governmental picture have been drastically changed in the last one hundred and seventy years. The states rather than fading into obscurity have continued to be a partner with the national government in making the federal system operate.

## Distribution of Powers by the United States Constitution

The Tenth Amendment declares that "The powers not delegated to the United States by the Constitution, nor prohibited by it to the States, are reserved to the States respectively, or to the people." The Constitution granted only a limited number of delegated powers to the national government.

Every power exercised by the national government must be justified under one or more of the specific powers delegated in Article I, Section 8. The implied powers clause, "to make all Laws which shall be necessary and proper for carrying into execution the foregoing powers, and all other powers vested by this Constitution in the government of the United States, or in any department or officer thereof" has been the basis for the tremendous expansion of the powers of the central government since 1790.

The strict constructionists and the broad constructionists have fought the battle over expansion of powers, with both sides claiming victory at various times in American history. From 1801 to 1835 the United States Supreme Court observed a broad construction of the so-called elastic or necessary and proper clause. Later the interpretation became less elastic but throughout the years the supporters of a strong central government with all necessary powers have basically won the majority of the battles.

The state governments possess an indefinite grant of powers after the exclusive powers have been taken by the national government. Being residual in nature, the state powers are broader than those of the federal government. The major powers of the states center upon the police power under which a great variety of state functions are performed. Some powers, it must be noted, are shared by both the state and national governments and therefore are called concurrent powers. The Constitution of the United States also establishes certain powers that are denied the states and other powers that are denied the national government. Likewise, certain powers are denied to both of the governmental levels.

The supreme law of the land is firmly established as the federal Constitution. It is superior to all other forms of law and none may be in conflict with it. Failure of a state to respect the court decision concerning the unconstitutionality of its acts justifies the use of military force by the federal government. On a few occasions the federal government has been forced to take this final action to uphold the supremacy of the United States Constitution.

Under the powers granted to the national and state governments by the United States Constitution, the following exclusive powers are delegated to the national government:

1. To regulate interstate and foreign commerce
2. To coin money
3. To fix standards of weights and measures
4. To establish post offices and post roads
5. To grant patents and copyrights
6. To define and punish piracy on the high seas
7. To declare war
8. To grant letters of marque and reprisal
9. To raise and support an army
10. To maintain a navy
11. To provide for a militia
12. To conduct foreign relations
13. To govern territories

The following powers are reserved to the states:

1. To conduct elections
2. To regulate intrastate commerce

3. To establish local governments
4. To protect health, safety, and public morals
5. To change state constitutions and state governments
6. To ratify amendments to the United States Constitution

The concurrent powers exercised by both the national and state governments are:

1. To make and enforce laws
2. To tax
3. To spend money for general public welfare
4. To borrow money
5. To establish and maintain courts
6. To charter banks and other corporations
7. To take property for public purposes

According to the United States Constitution certain powers are denied to the national and state governments. Those powers denied to the national government are:

1. May not impose direct taxes disproportionate to population and states
2. May not impose non-uniform indirect taxes
3. May not give preference to one state over another in matters of commerce
4. May not change state boundaries without consent of the states involved
5. May not abridge the rights in the Bill of Rights

The state governments are denied the following powers:

1. May not enter into treaties
2. May not coin money
3. May not keep troops or ships of war in time of peace
4. May not pass laws impairing the obligations of contracts
5. May not tax imports
6. May not deny equal protection of the laws
7. May not prevent persons from voting due to race, color, sex, or failure to pay poll tax
8. May not violate the federal constitution or obstruct federal laws

The following powers are denied to both state and national governments:

1. May not tax exports
2. May not grant titles of nobility
3. May not permit slavery

# FEDERAL OBLIGATIONS TO THE STATES

Under the United States federal system, the national government guarantees to each member state five rights:

1. Territorial integrity, thus assuring each and every state that no part of its territory will be taken without its consent.
2. Guarantees to each state a republican form of government. The exact meaning of this phrase is still uncertain.
3. The protection of each state against domestic violence and foreign invasion.
4. Each state, regardless of its geographic size and population, shall have two members of the United States Senate and no state shall be deprived of this equal representation without its consent.
5. Each state is assured that it will not be sued by individuals in the federal courts without its permission.

## Territorial Integrity of the States

The United States Constitution provides that no state will lose any territory without its consent. A number of states have been carved from existing states and later admitted to membership in the Union. Kentucky, for example, was a part of Virginia but was allowed to join the Union in 1792 as a state when the Virginia state legislature relinquished its control over that territory. Tennessee was formed in 1796 from land that had been granted to the United States by North Carolina. Vermont was granted permission by New York to be separated from that state and was admitted in 1791. The most questionable breach in the territorial integrity clause occurred when West Virginia was granted permission by Congress in 1863 to become a separate state.

The request is frequently heard, with the advent of the large metropolitan areas for the creation of city-states such as Chicago, New York City, Los Angeles, and San Francisco. These plans, if realized, would require the state legislatures concerned to approve the separation of the city from the state and then the Congress could admit the area as a new state. The probability of any such programs is virtually nil since the states involved would undoubtedly never consent to such action.

## Guarantee of a Republican Form of Government

The people of each state may adopt any type of government for their commonwealth that they prefer so long as it is "republican" in form. The United States Constitution assures each state this privilege. The state cannot be established with a hereditary monarchy or create a legalized aristocracy, but it may experiment in almost any other way that the people desire. If a state constitution, which has been accepted by the people, establishes a parliamentary system with the legislature selecting the chief executive officers, this form of government would be legal under the United States Constitution. Likewise, the people are free to determine whether or not they desire a unicameral or bicameral state legislature. In fact, the people are free to develop any type of governmental institutions both state and local that they deem is needed to meet their own special and peculiar circumstances so long as it meets the test of being "republican."

No one can define exactly what a "republican" form of state government really means. A number of interesting theories have been advanced from time to time. The most commonly accepted test is that it means government under popular control. The courts have traditionally regarded the question as being of a political nature and one upon which they have no jurisdiction.

The court's attitude toward answering the question of what is and what is not "republican" government has actually left the matter for the President and the Congress to decide. The President in the case of Dorr's Rebellion in Rhode Island was forced to indicate his choice between the two factions when he sent troops to restore order.[1]

On different occasions the Congress has been urged to refuse to seat or to unseat delegations on the basis that they come from states without a "republican" form of government. The Congress has never taken such action. As recently as 1912 the United States Supreme Court declared that the determination rested with the Congress through its acceptance or rejection of senators and representatives from states charged with not having such a government.[2] Therefore at the present time it would appear that no clear-cut answer is possible to the question as to whether or not a state possesses a "republican" form of government.

## Defense Against Invasion and Domestic Violence

The United States Constitution prohibits the states from maintaining armies and navies and therefore instructs the national government that it must shoulder the responsibility of protecting the states from invasion. Only the federal government has the power to declare war and undertake other military defense actions.

A more delicate point is reached when the determination of the role of the federal government in protecting the states against domestic violence is raised. How, when, and who determines that conditions are such that the national government must step in and put down a domestic up-

[1] *Luther v. Borden* (7 Howard 1, 1849).
[2] *Pacific States Telephone and Telegraph Co. v. Oregon* (223 U.S. 118, 1912).

rising? The judgment falls to the President of the United States but ordinarily he orders federal troops into a state only upon the request of the governor or the legislature. In 1841, President Tyler, upon the request of the Rhode Island authorities, took steps to put down the Thomas Dorr Rebellion, which was attempting to establish what Dorr called a "more representative" state government. The federal troops forced the collapse of the irregular government and restored order. In 1894 President Cleveland sent the federal armed forces into the serious railroad strike in Chicago even though the governor of Illinois did not make any request for federal assistance. Thus the precedent was established that federal forces may be used even though the local authorities protest the action. President Eisenhower federalized the Arkansas National Guard in 1957 and sent in regular army forces, in addition, to enforce the federal court order that commanded the Little Rock schools to be integrated over the protest of the state governor. In 1963 President Kennedy federalized the Alabama National Guard in order to enforce a federal court decision that required the University of Alabama to admit two Negro students. Again, the governor of the state opposed the federal intervention but the judgment of the President prevailed. The President of the United States as the chief executive and the commander of the armed forces must make the decision, aided by any counsel that he cares to consult, as to when federal intervention is necessary to insure domestic tranquillity.

## Equal Senate Representation

The only so-called entrenched clause of the United States Constitution, one that cannot be amended, asserts that no state may be denied equal representation in the United States Senate without its consent. This consent has never been given and all states have at all times had two members in the Senate. This unamendable clause was inserted in the Constitution as the basic portion of the famous Connecticut Compromise which allowed representation in the House according to population but guaranteed even the smallest state, no matter what its population or its territorial size, equality of representation in the upper chamber of the Congress. On a population basis, one United States Senator from Alaska has a constituency of 113,000 while a Senator from California represents nearly 8.5 million residents. Population, however, is not a factor in the composition of the upper house of the Congress.

## State Immunity from Suit in Federal Court

The Eleventh Amendment to the United States Constitution was designed to assure the states that they could be sued only in the state courts and would thereby not be liable to suit in the federal courts on a claim brought by an individual citizen unless the state had consented to the filing of the suit. In 1793, five years before the addition of the Eleventh Amendment, the United States Supreme Court had ruled that a citizen of another state did have the right to bring a suit against a state.[3] Thus states since 1798 have not been required to defend themselves in federal courts against any private suit unless they choose to do so. It should be noted that this does not prohibit individuals from filing suits against state officials. Many states have established claims courts while others require an individual to file a "legislative" claim.

## OBLIGATIONS OF THE STATES TO THE NATIONAL GOVERNMENT

Upon entering the Union certain responsibilities are assumed by each and every state. National elections are conducted by the states. Every state has the right to determine certain portions of the electoral process, but other limits are placed upon the electorate by the United States Constitution. Each state determines the minimum age for voting, which at present has been set in most states at 21. Georgia and Kentucky have established the minimum at 18, Alaska at 19, and Hawaii at 20. Likewise, each state has determined that only citizens of the United States may vote. The minimum residential requirements are also set by state regulations. Federal constitutional amendments require that no state deny a person the right to vote, because of race, color, creed, or sex. Qualifications must be the same as those required for eligibility to vote for the most numerous branch of the state legislature.

Each state's election machinery conducts the national elections. All states use the direct election method with most members of the United States House being elected by the people from single-member districts with only a few states having at-large elections. United States Senators are elected at large with all qualified voters being eligible to vote in the election.

The nominating process to be followed is also a state responsibility. Nominations are made usually by the direct primary, but again the method is determined by the state legislature. Presidential electors also are selected in whatever manner is established by the state legislative body.

The states are also obligated to participate in the amending process of the United States Constitution. This involves action by either the state legislature or a statewide convention. Three-fourths of the states must ratify a proposed constitutional amendment before it becomes effective.

[3] *Chisholm v. Georgia* (2 Dall. 419, U.S. 1793).

## OBLIGATIONS OF STATES TO EACH OTHER

Article IV of the United States Constitution is the basis upon which have been built the interstate relations of the fifty states. Section 1 requires that "Full Faith and Credit shall be given in each State to the public Acts, Records, and judicial Proceedings of every other State. And the Congress may by general Laws prescribe the Manner in which such Acts, Records and Proceedings shall be proved, and the Effect thereof."

The courts have interpreted this section to mean that every state must accept every other state's statutes, charters, deeds, vital records, judicial decisions, and court records. These records must not only be accepted but they must be executed if the persons involved have moved from the state in which the legal action was rendered. A specific illustration could be a civil judgment that is rendered in an Alaskan court requiring Robert O'Conner to pay Jane Jakes the sum of $5,000. If Mr. O'Conner moves to New York the New York State authorities will carry out the judgment of the Alaska court and see that the monetary sum is paid. Similiarly, a will leaving Doris Dakes $1 million is filed in Texas. The will, if properly drawn, will be honored by the courts not only in Texas but in every other state.

Two major exceptions to the "full faith and credit" clause must be noted. The criminal law of one state is not binding upon the other forty-nine states. An individual who commits what is considered a crime in Kansas will not be punished for it in Missouri. The states do cooperate with each other, however, in making arrests of persons who have allegedly committed a crime and in the returning of a "wanted" person through extradition or rendition procedures. The process involved, unless the person held waives extradition, is for the governor of the state in which the fugitive is held to conduct an investigation and usually a hearing before determining that the individual should be returned to face the charges filed against him in the state that has asked for his rendition. The governor is the final authority. If he decides not to release the prisoner to the state authorities, there is nothing that state can do but wait for a change in governor or attempt to extradite him from another state should the fugitive leave the state that has refused to grant extradition. It is most unlikely that such a wanted individual would leave his refuge.

The second exception to full faith and credit among states has developed in recognition of divorce decrees. Occasionally some states refuse to recognize divorces when neither party in the action has established a bona fide residence in the state in which the divorce is granted. A few states have reduced their residence requirements for divorce jurisdiction and grant divorces on many grounds. Both Idaho and Nevada require only a six-week residency, Wyoming only sixty days, Utah just two months, and Arkansas only three months. In both Idaho and Wyoming under special conditions the minimum time requirements may be reduced.[4] The United States Supreme Court has ruled that North Carolina need not recognize a divorce granted two of its residents by Nevada when neither party had established bona fide residence in that state.[5] In another case the Supreme Court ruled that other states must recognize divorces if legal residence has been established by one of the two litigants, if both parties have had an opportunity to contest the jurisdiction of the action, and if the court refuses to allow the action to be attacked by another suit.[6]

The United States Constitution furthermore requires that the citizens of each state are guaranteed the privileges and immunities of citizens of the several states, thus protecting out-of-state persons from being discriminated against by another state. This clause has been used to assure an individual that he may travel, reside, secure due process of law, sue, marry, make contracts, own property, have equal tax assessments, and work in any other state. This does not mean, however, that the rights of resident citizens and of citizens of other states are entirely equal, as might be logically implied. There are at least three major and several minor exceptions. Citizens are not interpreted to include corporations, thus allowing states to legally pass discriminatory legislation involving corporation. This, it might be noted, seldom happens as almost every state is actively seeking new industrial firms and therefore would not discriminate against corporations that are prospective builders of new plants. In addition, the "due process" clause of the Fourteenth Amendment restricts to a degree any discriminatory practices in this area.

States are also allowed to require a residency of "reasonable length" before permitting out-of-staters to engage in the practice of certain professions and businesses. Likewise, out-of-state residents who are members of a profession and licensed in one state may not be able to practice in another state until meeting whatever examinations and qualifications are required for all persons engaging in the profession or business in the state. Similarly, out-of-state residents may be required to pay higher tuition fees at state-supported educational institutions and higher licenses for hunting on the basis that non-residents may participate in the property or proprietary functions of a state on an entirely different basis than local residents. For example, no tuition may be charged to residents attending state schools while out-of-state students will pay fees as high as the state determines.

[4] Council of State Governments, *The Book of the States, 1962–1963* (Chicago: Council of State Governments, 1962), p. 416.
[5] *Williams v. North Carolina* (325 U.S. 226, 1945).
[6] *Sherrer v. Sherrer* (334 U.S. 343, 1948).

## THE MERITS OF FEDERALISM

The proponents of the federal system discern numerous advantages accruing with the use of federalism. It has proved to be useful in that the state governments provide a training ground for national leaders. Both political parties tend to look with favor upon governors or senators as their presidential candidates. Likewise, in many states the route to the United States Senate traditionally leads through the gubernatorial office. Congressmen also have oftentimes served an apprenticeship in the state legislature before running for the lower house of the Congress.

A second way the states have served as a proving ground for improved governmental techniques has been in experimenting with new ideas. Several states had found the executive budget a highly useful administrative tool before the federal government enacted its first executive budget. Similarly, many social welfare activities originally were tried by states before being implemented on a nationwide basis by the federal government. The federal system with its inherent decentralization prevents the overcentralization of power and the infringement of civil rights. It is further claimed that this system tends to bolster the principle of consent of the governed, facilitates participation in government, maintains the habit of initiative with the local people, fosters stimulating competition among the lower levels of government, serves as an outlet for local grievances and for political aspirations as well as an over-all strengthening of the capacity of the electorate for self-government.

The most complete analysis of federalism is to be found in the book written by Studenski and Mort and entitled *Centralized vs. Decentralized Government in Relation to Democracy*. Their findings may be summarized as follows:

MERITS OF WELL-CONCEIVED CENTRAL CONTROL

1. Unifies the nation.
2. Provides for the common or national needs of the population and for the coordinated development of the nation's resources.
3. Safeguards the nation's independence.
4. Safeguards the liberties of the people in a democratic country and provides for an equality of social, economic, and educational opportunities in the various sections of the country.
5. Responds quickly to changed national situations and takes care of national emergencies.
6. Is more efficient and economical in many respects than are local governments.
7. Gives common direction to local governments, impels them to maintain minimum standards of public service, and helps them to operate efficiently.

## MERITS OF WELL-CONCEIVED LOCAL CONTROL

1. Promotes local unity, sense of neighborhood responsibility, spirit of self-reliance, and capacity for group action.
2. Secures close adaptation of public services to local needs.
3. Promotes and safeguards freedom, democracy, and responsible government.
4. Promotes socially beneficial inter-community competition.
5. Permits safe experimentation with new forms and methods of government, thus fostering a gradual improvement in government throughout the country.
6. Promotes political stability.
7. Promotes national unity and national security.
8. Relieves the national government of congestion of business.[7]

The need for the states to share their responsibilities if federalism is to operate is cited by Elihu Root in the following statement:

It is useless for the advocates of states' rights to inveigh against the supremacy of the constitutional laws of the United States or against the extension of national authority in the fields of necessary control where the states themselves fail in the performance of their duty. The instinct for self-government among the people of the United States is too strong to permit them long to respect anyone's right to exercise a power which he fails to exercise. The governmental control which they deem just and necessary they will have. It may be that such control would better be exercised in particular instances by the governments of the states, but the people will have the control they need, either from the states or from the national government; and if the states fail to furnish it in due measure sooner or later constructions of the constitution will be found to vest the power where it will be exercised—in the national government.[8]

## THE PHILOSOPHY OF STATES' RIGHTS

The states' rights theory maintains that the federal system was formed by the uniting of sovereign states and that these states retained their sovereignty with the central government a mere creature of the states. The philosophy holds that the assumption of new functions by the central government is "unconstitutional." It fears "all forms of centralization" and of "big government."

States' rights versus federal control has been an issue in America since the founding of our nation. The Articles of Confederation allowed the states to retain their sovereignty. The Articles did not solve the social,

[7] Paul Studenski and Paul R. Mort, *Centralized vs. Decentralized Government in Relation to Democracy* (New York: Teachers College, Bureau of Publications, Columbia University, 1941).

[8] An excerpt from an Address delivered by Mr. Root before the Pennsylvania Society in September, 1906, as reported by The Commission on Intergovernmental Relations in *A Report to the President for Transmittal to the Congress*, June, 1955, p. 56.

economic, and political problems confronting the new nation. It was necessary to remodel the governmental organization. This was accomplished by drafting the Constitution. The issue of states' rights versus federal control or supremacy was faced. It was, however, only partially resolved in the Constitution itself. The Civil War and a series of judicial decisions have been necessary to resolve this fundamental issue.[9]

One group concerned with the "states' rights" philosophy maintains that the national government was never intended to have or to exercise some of its present powers and functions, particularly in the area of spending for the general welfare and in providing state aid. This group believes that the powers of the national government have become too great with a consequent loss of self-government by the states. As they see it, the federal system as intended by the framers of the Constitution is being lost. It is their desire that the policy decisions, the financing, and the administration of services be left in the hands of the individual states.

Another group has a philosophy that at the surface level would seem to be opposed only to central or national government expansion but is actually opposed to state and local governmental activity also. This group would weaken the national government and revive a system of states' rights to such an extent that the national government would be dependent upon the states for grants-in-aid. Carried to an extreme position this might well eliminate virtually all government at all levels—national, state, and local.[10]

The anti-active-government philosophy looks to the past and those who hold it seem to yearn for smaller, more peaceful, less strenuous and demanding times than what they find in the modern era—something they think must once have existed.

Another opinion along the same line was expressed by a foreign observer, Alexis de Tocqueville, when he wrote:

I am of the opinion that a central administration is fit only to enervate the nations in which it exists, by incessantly diminishing their local spirit. Although such an administration can bring together, on a given point, all the disposable

[9] Included among the major cases which have been involved in the problem are the following: *Marbury v. Madison* (1 Cranch 137, 1803); *McCulloch v. Maryland* (4 Wheat. 316, U.S. 1819); *Gibbons v. Ogden* (9 Wheat. 1, 1824); *Cooley v. Board of Wardens of Port of Philadelphia* (12 Howard 299, 1852); *Scott v. Sandford* (19 Howard 393, U.S. 1857); *Paul v. Virginia* (8 Wall. 168, 1868); *Houston, E & W Texas Railway v. United States* (234 U.S. 342, 1914); *Missouri v. Holland* (252 U.S. 416, 1920); *Schechter Poultry Corporation v. United States* (295 U.S. 495, 1935); *United States v. Butler* (297 U.S. 1, 1936); *Kentucky Whip & Collar Co. v. Illinois Central Railway* (299 U.S. 334, 1937); *National Labor Relations Board v. Jones Laughlin Steel Corp.* (301 U.S. 1, 1937); *Mulford v. Smith* (307 U.S. 38, 1939); and *United States v. South-Eastern Underwriters Ass'n* (322 U.S. 533, 1944).

[10] William Anderson, *The Nation and the States, Rivals or Partners?* (Minneapolis: University of Minnesota Press, 1955), p. 237.

resources of a people, it injures the renewal of these resources. It may insure a victory in the hour of strife, but it gradually relaxes the sinews of strength. It may help admirably the transient greatness of a man, but not the durable prosperity of a nation.[11]

Probably the most outspoken statement made in recent years on the subject of state-federal relationships was the resolution passed by the House of Representatives of the state of Indiana in 1947 in which it was declared:

Indiana needs no guardian and intends to have none. We Hoosiers—like the people of our sister states—were fooled for quite a spell with the magician's trick that a dollar taxed out of our pockets and sent to Washington, will be bigger when it comes back to us. We have taken a good look at said dollar. We find that it lost weight on its journey to Washington and back. The political brokerage of the bureaucrats has been deducted. We have decided that there is no such thing as Federal aid. We know that there is no wealth to tax that is not already within the boundaries of the states.

So we propose henceforward to tax ourselves and take care of ourselves. We are fed up with subsidies, doles, and paternalism. We are no one's stepchild. We have grown up. We serve notice that we will resist Washington, D.C. adopting us.

Be it resolved by the House of Representatives of the General Assembly of the State of Indiana (the Senate concurring), that we respectfully petition and urge Indiana's Congressmen and Senators to vote to fetch our county court-houses and city halls back from Pennsylvania Avenue. We want government to come home.

## THE MODERATE POSITION

All three branches of the national government have maintained varying positions on issues of federalism. The United States Supreme Court has probably taken the most consistently nationalist position. Congress, on the other hand, has continuously extended the sphere of national government power, but has always been mindful of local sentiments and the impact upon state institutions and local governments. Greatest variation has occurred in the attitudes of the various presidents concerning the question of federalism. Some have been strong advocates of strong national action while many others have attempted to protect the powers and responsibilities of the state governments.

During and following all major wars the powers of the national government have been tremendously expanded. For example, in 1862 the first Morrill Act made federal land grants available for agricultural and mechanical colleges in each state and in the same year the office of a com-

[11] Alexis de Tocqueville, *Democracy in America* (New York: Alfred A. Knopf, Inc., 1945), Vol. I, p. 87.

missioner, later to be called secretary of agriculture, was created. In the following year, 1863, a national banking system was created with its federal examination of national banks. A similar expansion of national governmental powers accompanied the Spanish-American War and World Wars I and II.

Periods of economic crises have likewise seen rapid expansion of national powers. The many sweeping powers assumed by the Washington government following the stock market crash of 1929 show most vividly the trends.

In more recent times, The Commission on Intergovernmental Relations has made three observations concerning the overall problems of national-state relations that seem to be most pertinent:

1. The Constitution sets only maximum limits to National action and these are conjectural. The National Government needs not do everything that it can do. It needs some sort of guidelines marking out the conditions and circumstances calling for National action. . . .

2. Where National action is desirable, greater attention should be given to minimizing its extent and to leaving room for and facilitating cooperative or independent State action. . . .

3. The organization of the National Government does not at present afford adequate recognition of the national interest in State and local government. . . . However, some machinery is needed that will help to provide more conscious, continuous, and overall attention to the relation of National action to State and local government.[12]

The Commission recognizes that inadequate administrative coordination at the national level often places formidable barriers in the way of state dealings with national agencies.

Assuming efficient and responsible government at all levels—national, state, and local—America should seek to divide civic responsibilities so that we:

Leave to private initiative all the functions that citizens can perform privately; use the level of government closest to the community for all public functions it can handle; utilize cooperative intergovernmental arrangements where appropriate to attain economical performance and popular approval; reserve National action for residual participation where State and local governments are not fully adequate, and for the continuing responsibilities that only the National Government can undertake.[13]

Economic and physical forces make it necessary to adapt the problem of proper federal-state relations to the changing times. The state is still dominant in many governmental areas:

[12] The Commission on Intergovernmental Relations, *A Report to the President for Transmittal to the Congress* (Washington, D.C.: Government Printing Office, 1955), pp. 60–61.
[13] *Ibid.*, p. 6.

1. Control of political parties and elections
2. Control of education and public health
3. Chartering of corporations
4. Supervision of public utilities
5. Supervision of banking and insurance
6. Regulation of motor vehicles

The national government, however, is assuming an ever increasing interest in many of these areas where the individual states have not carried out their authority with dispatch and efficiency. Government does not work in a vacuum. If the states do not carry out their powers the people will demand that the national government intervene. If Americans desire the states to assume greater responsibilities and the national government less, it will be necessary to build up the states so that they can meet the problems that confront the people.

## INTERSTATE CO-OPERATION

### Interstate Compacts

While not actually a part of the obligations of the states to each other, interstate compacts play an important role in interstate relations. The United States Constitution recognizes the eventual development of interstate compacts by proclaiming in Article I, Section 10, that "No state shall, without the consent of Congress . . . enter into any agreement or compact with another state." Often the procedure has been followed to secure the advanced consent from Congress for two or more states to negotiate an agreement. Following this approval the chief executives of the states involved or their representatives negotiate the desired compact. While more than one hundred such agreements have been authorized by Congress, only about sixty have actually been executed, since many have failed to receive state ratification after the negotiations have been completed. The United States Supreme Court has ruled in *Virginia v. Tennessee* that the consent of Congress is needed only if the compact or agreement tends to "increase the political power in the states which may encroach upon or interfere with the just supremacy of the United States.[14] The New England Corrections Compact, involving Rhode Island, Connecticut, Maine, New Hampshire, and Vermont, and the Interstate Compact on the Placement of Children are two examples of interstate agreements that do not require congressional approval. The United States Supreme Court made another significant ruling in 1951, which declared that state courts cannot terminate a state's participation in interstate compacts.[15]

[14] *Virginia v. Tennessee* ( 148 U.S. 503, 1893 ).
[15] *West Virginia v. Sims* ( 341 U.S. 22, 1951 ).

While originally used primarily to settle such matters as boundary disputes, compacts have now been utilized in almost every conceivable area of interstate relations. The best-known compact is probably the Port of New York Authority. This joint state authority was authorized by Congress in 1921 and governs for the states involved the metropolitan port facilities of the largest harbor in the United States. Included under its jurisdiction are not only the seaport facilities but also the airports, tunnels, bridges, and bus, rail, and truck terminals.

Two compacts that include virtually every state are the Crime Compact of 1934 and the Parole and Probation Compact of 1945, both of which have been ratified by every one of the states. Among the newer fields included in this area of interstate agreements are the Interstate Oil Compact, Southern Regional Educational Compact, the Western Regional Education Compact, Southern Interstate Nuclear Compact, Interstate Sanitation Compact, New England Interstate Water Pollution Control Compact, Pacific Marine Fisheries Compact, Northeastern Forest Fire Protection Compact, and the Interstate Compact on Welfare Services.

Interstate compacts have not always been successful due to a number of limitations inherent within the compact arrangements. Because of their confederate nature the compact activities are subject to a veto by one or more states even though the majority of the participants may desire to carry out a certain function. Any enforcement powers that are utilized by the compact authority must be uniformly granted by all of the states involved, and this often presents a serious problem.

## Cooperation Among the States

A number of agencies have been established that have as their major purpose the achievement of interstate cooperation.[16] The first of these agencies was the National Conference of Commissioners on Uniform State Laws established in 1892. There have been more than forty proposed uniform laws of which the typical state has enacted only sixteen.

The Annual Governors' Conference is an organization established and operated for the purpose of improving state government. These conferences are held at some well-known resort and grapple with the governmental problems that overlap state lines and require interstate cooperation. Most state governors have been very regular in attendance at these meetings.

All of the fifty states support the Council of State Governments. Established in 1935, the Council performs three major services: (1) It serves as a medium to assist in improving state legislative, administrative, and

[16] W. Brooke Graves, *Uniform State Action* (Chapel Hill: University of North Carolina Press, 1934).

judicial practices. (2) It serves as an agency for cooperation among the states in solving interstate problems, either regional or national. (3) It is a means of facilitating and improving federal-state relations. The Council is composed of Commissions or Committees on Interstate Cooperation, or some similar official body in each state, with the typical commission consisting of ten members of the legislature and five administrative officials.[17]

The Council of State Governments, acclaimed by many as the agency that has done the most to promote cooperation among the states, is governed and controlled by the states themselves. The policies are determined by a board of managers that consists of one representative from each of the fifty states, nineteen ex-officio members, ten managers selected at large, and one life member. Each state commission names its own delegate member. The ex-officio managers are the nine members of the executive committee of the Governors' Conference, the presiding officers of the other nine state organizations representing executive, legislative, and judicial branches of the government, and the honorary president of the Council. This board of managers holds an annual meeting and any special meetings as called. The executive committee holds frequent meetings and works closely with the executive director in the administration of the affairs of the Council.

The central office of the Council of State Governments is located in Chicago. Four regional offices are maintained—New York, San Francisco, Atlanta, and Washington, D.C. The first three offices are operated primarily to render services to the state legislatures in their areas, while the Washington, D.C., office is primarily concerned with improving federal-state relations and keeping the states informed on activities of the national government of concern to the states.[18]

The Council attempts to assist the states in their internal problems as well as the problems that cross state lines. Since almost all of the problems of the states are similar, the Council has found that, in assisting one state to solve a particular problem, informing other states of the progress may many times aid in combating the problem elsewhere. Common problems concerning public school education, mental health programs, highway construction and maintenance, highway safety, motor truck regulation, legislative processes and procedures, state and local governmental relationships, and state governmental reorganization are found in almost every one of the fifty states. The Council of State Governments has made studies and surveys on all of these problems and hundreds more.

Five publications are issued by the Council: a quarterly journal entitled *State Government;* a biennial publication, *The Book of the States;* a

[17] Council of State Governments, *The Book of the States, 1962–1963* (Chicago: Council of State Governments, 1962), p. 249.
[18] *Ibid.,* pp. 249–52.

monthly newsletter, *State Government News;* a monthly publication, *States and Nation;* and a quarterly, *Legislative Research Checklist.* The quarterly journal presents relatively short articles of interest to all people working in and studying state government. The biennial *Book of the States* is a comprehensive compilation of material on state activities and officials. The monthly newsletter presents items on developments in all the states, the monthly publication reports on federal activities that bear on state affairs, and the quarterly deals with news and information on legislative organization, procedures, service agencies, and research.

The Council of State Governments serves as the secretariat and cooperates with numerous organizations of state officials including:

The Governors' Conference
The National Legislative Conference
The National Association of Attorneys General
The Conference of Chief Justices
The National Association of State Budget Officers
The National Association of State Purchasing Officials
The Parole and Probation Compact Administrators' Association
The Association of Juvenile Compact Administrators
The National Conference of Court Administrative Officers
The National Conference of Commissioners on Uniform State Laws

## Commission on Uniform State Laws

Every state has a Commission on Uniform State Laws. It is composed of three members who represent the state at the various national conferences on uniform state laws. The commissioners are appointed usually by the governor for four-year terms. The primary duties consist of attending the national conferences on uniform state laws and to promote uniformity in state laws upon all subjects where uniformity may be deemed desirable and practical. Each state commission reports periodically to its legislature on laws that it believes should be passed in order to bring the state laws into conformity with those of the other states.

## BIBLIOGRAPHY

ANDERSON, WILLIAM. *The Nation and the States, Rivals or Partners?* Minneapolis: The University of Minnesota Press, 1955.
————. *Intergovernmental Relations in Review.* Minneapolis: The University of Minnesota Press, 1960.
BENSON, GEORGE C. S. *The New Centralization.* New York: Holt, Rinehart & Winston, Inc., 1941.
BETTERMAN, HENRY J. *State and Federal Grants-in-Aid.* Chicago: Mentzer, Bush & Co., 1938.

CLARK, JANE P. *The Rise of a New Federalism: Federal-State Cooperation in the United States.* New York: Columbia University Press, 1938.

COMMISSION ON INTERGOVERNMENTAL RELATIONS. *A Report to the President for Transmittal to the Congress.* Washington, D.C.: Government Printing Office, 1955.

CONNERY, ROBERT H., and LEACH, RICHARD H. *The Federal Government and Metropolitan Areas.* Cambridge: Harvard University Press, 1960.

COUNCIL OF STATE GOVERNMENTS. *Interstate Compacts, 1783–1956.* Chicago: Council of State Governments, 1956.

ELAZAR, DANIEL J. *The American Partnership: Intergovernmental Co-operation in the Nineteenth Century United States.* Chicago: University of Chicago Press, 1962.

GOLDWIN, ROBERT A. (ed.). *A Nation of States.* Chicago: Rand McNally & Co., 1963.

GRAVES, W. BROOKE. *American Intergovernmental Relations.* New York: Charles Scribner's Sons, 1964.

HAMILTON, ALEXANDER, MADISON, JAMES, and JAY, JOHN. *The Federalist,* ed. PAUL L. FORD. New York: Holt, Rinehart & Winston, Inc., 1898.

KALLENBACH, JOSEPH E. *Federal Cooperation with the State Under the Commerce Clause.* Ann Arbor: University of Michigan Press, 1942.

KEY, V. O., JR. *The Administration of Federal Grants to States.* Chicago: Public Administration Service, 1937.

———. *Administration of Federal Grants-in-Aid.* Chicago: Public Administration Service, 1939.

LEACH, RICHARD H., and SUGG, REDDING S., JR. *The Administration of Interstate Compacts.* Baton Rouge: Louisiana State University Press, 1959.

MAASS, A. (ed.). *Area and Power: A Theory of Local Government.* New York: The Free Press of Glencoe, Inc., 1959.

MACMAHON, ARTHUR W. (ed.). *Federalism Mature and Emergent.* Garden City, N.Y.: Doubleday & Co., Inc., 1955.

MAXWELL, JAMES A. *The Fiscal Impact of Federalism in the United States.* Cambridge: Harvard University Press, 1946.

ROCKEFELLER, NELSON A. *The Future of Federalism.* New York: Atheneum Publishers, 1963.

SADY, EMIL J. *Research in Federal-State Relations.* Washington, D.C.: The Brookings Institution, 1957.

VERNON, RAYMOND. *Metroplis: 1985.* Cambridge: Harvard University Press, 1960.

VILE, M. J. C. *The Structure of American Federalism.* Fair Lawn, N.J.: Oxford University Press, 1961.

WHEARE, K. C. *Federal Government.* Fair Lawn, N.J.: Oxford University Press, 1947.

WHITE, LEONARD. *The States and the Nation.* Baton Rouge: Louisiana State University Press, 1953.

# 3

# The State and Local Units of Government—The Unitary System

The United States Constitution does not explicitly refer to local governmental units. Therefore, each state is allowed to deal with these units as its constitution prescribes. The state may authorize, modify, create, and destroy local governmental units as it sees fit. As a result of this total control over its own local governmental units, each state has created to varying degrees a unitary relationship between the state and the local governmental organizations.

## LOCAL GOVERNMENTAL UNITS IN THE UNITED STATES

### Criteria for Classification as a Governmental Unit

Before a unit may be classified as a governmental entity it must have certain characteristics that have been established by the United States Bureau of the Census. It must first exist as an organized entity: this means that there must be present some form of organization and the possession of corporate powers. Secondly, it must have governmental character: this may be fulfilled if the officers of the entity are popularly elected or appointed by public officials and have a high degree of public responsibility. An easy test for this governmental character is, "Does the unit have the power to levy and collect taxes?" If the answer is in the affirmative, then it certainly meets this test. Third, the unit must possess substantial autonomy, meaning a degree of fiscal and administrative independence. A public agency is classified as an independent unit of government if it has independent fiscal powers and, in addition, has a popularly elected governing body or one representing two or more state or local governments. Even in event the governing body is appointed, the unit is recognized as being autonomous if it performs functions that are essentially different from those of its creating body.[1]

## Enumeration of Local Government Units

The Bureau of the Census conducts a survey of governmental units every five years. In 1962 it listed 91,185 local governmental units, which was the first time this category had been under 100,000 since the turn of the century. This was a reduction of 11,094 local governments from the 1957 enumeration. In only two classifications were more local units listed than in 1957: there were 814 more municipalities, and an increase of 3,918 special districts. All other categories decreased. Counties were reduced by four, in spite of the addition of three counties when Hawaii was added to the Union in 1959. Alaska did not add to the county total since no counties were created in the forty-ninth state. The number of townships and towns decreased by fifty-four; but the big drop occurred in the number of school districts, with a total reduction of 15,768, as school district consolidation continued in many Midwestern states. The historical comparison of the number of governmental units in the various categories is shown in Table 3–1.

### TABLE 3–1

Historical Comparison of Total Number of Governmental Units—1942–1962

| Type of Government | Number of Units | | | | Change in Number | |
|---|---|---|---|---|---|---|
| | 1962 | 1957 | 1952 | 1942 | 1957 to 1962 | 1942 to 1962 |
| U.S. government | 1 | 1 | 1 | 1 | 0 | 0 |
| States | 50 | 48 | 48 | 48 | + 2 | + 2 |
| Counties | 3,043 | 3,047 | 3,049 | 3,050 | − 4 | − 7 |
| Townships and towns | 17,144 | 17,198 | 17,202 | 18,919 | − 54 | − 1,775 |
| Municipalities | 17,997 | 17,183 | 16,778 | 16,220 | + 814 | + 1,777 |
| School districts | 34,678 | 50,446 | 67,346 | 108,579 | −15,768 | −73,901 |
| Special districts | 18,323 | 14,405 | 12,319 | 8,299 | + 3,918 | +10,024 |
| Total Local Governments | 91,185 | 102,279 | 116,694 | 155,067 | −11,094 | −63,882 |
| TOTAL | 91,236 | 102,328 | 116,743 | 155,116 | −11,092 | −63,880 |

SOURCE: Table adapted from U.S. Department of Commerce, Bureau of the Census, *Census of Governments, 1962, 1957, 1952, and 1942* (Washington, D.C.: Government Printing Office). (The figures prior to the 1959 admission of Alaska and Hawaii do not include the governmental units in those two areas.)

[1] U.S. Department of Commerce, Bureau of the Census, *1962 Census of Governments* (Washington, D.C.: Government Printing Office, 1962), pp. 3–5.

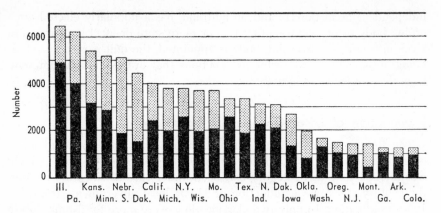

**Fig. 3–1.** Number of Local Governments, by States—1962. [Source: U.S. (Washington, D.C.: Government Printing Office, 1962).]

The average number of governmental units per state, as of 1962, was 1,825. The range was from only 21 governmental units in Hawaii to 6,453 in Illinois. Seven states had more than 4,000 units: Illinois, 6,453; Pennsylvania, 6,202; Kansas, 5,411; Minnesota, 5,213; Nebraska, 5,125; South Dakota, 4,464; and California, 4,023.

Nebraska had more school districts than any other state—3,264—even though its population was less than 1.5 million. Illinois had not only the most special districts—2,126—but also had the largest number of municipalities—1,251. Pennsylvania led in the number of townships with 1,555 and Texas, with 254 counties, had more of these governmental units than any other state. The comparison of the number of units of local government in all of the states is vividly portrayed in Figure 3–1.

## Proposals for Local Reorganization

Professor William Anderson, of the University of Minnesota, has outlined one of the most complete and far-reaching programs for local governmental reorganization and reduction in the number of units.[2] In what he terms "A Rationalization Scheme of Local Government Units in the United States," a reduction of 17,800 local governments is recommended. These would consist of 200 city-county units, each with a core city of at least 50,000 or meaning that every standard metropolitan area as now recognized by the United States Bureau of the Census would be included; 2,100 counties; 15,000 incorporated municipalities; and 500 miscellaneous or special district units. Of the total United States population about 45 per cent would be included in the 200 city-county units, with the remain-

[2] William Anderson, *The Units of Government in the United States* (rev. ed.; Chicago: Public Administration Service, 1945).

Ky.  Miss.  Ala.  Maine  La.   S.C.  Wyo.  Utah  W. Va.  Ariz.  N. Mex.  Nev.  Alaska

Idaho  Fla.  N.C.  Tenn.  Mass.  N.H.  Vt.  Conn.  Va.  Md.  Del.  R.I.  Hawaii

**Department of Commerce, Bureau of the Census, 1962 Census of Governments**

ing 55 per cent of the population distributed among the rural counties. This estimate of the total population living within the city-county areas is probably very conservative and in all probability a reversal of Professor Anderson's population residence would now exist. The plan would attempt to replace the three or four governmental units under which each citizen is governed at the local level by a single governmental body.

The desirability of the plan is beyond question. But the possibility of implementing it in this century appears to be very remote. Other means of improving local government are not as revolutionary and probably have more chance of being realized in the foreseeable future.

Among the possible improvements that may be realized in local governmental units are:

1. Home rule in all fifty states
2. Reallocation of local functions *vs.* state functions
3. Functional consolidation among local units
4. Improved merit type civil service system for local governments
5. Improved state co-ordination of local functions
6. More adequate research and consultive services for local governmental units
7. Contractual agreements for providing functional services among local units
8. Increased state financial assistance to local units
9. Geographic consolidation of neighboring governmental units
10. Greater use of technical experts in all local governments
11. Modernization of structural organization of governmental units

If proposed reorganization efforts fail, another alternative in the effort to find solutions to the complex problems of the relationship between the state governments in America and the local governmental units would be to experiment with methods and practices used in other countries with similar situations. In England the municipalities have much the same re- lationship to the central government as the cities and towns in America have to the state governments. The amount of home rule granted to the English municipality is greater than that allowed in almost any American state. The home rule charters in many instances were granted prior to the year A.D. 1066 and have not been violated by the central government, probably because of political expediency.[3]

The British idea of an administrative department that deals primarily with municipal affairs is a practice that has been considered in several states and instituted in at least three. It has possibilities as at least a par- tial answer to the problem of promoting understanding between the two levels of government. Obviously in some state governments the urban affairs department would be quite small but in other highly urbanized states it might well develop into one of the stronger and larger divisions of the state governmental hierarchy.

The British feature of the so-called provisional order procedure might well be a specific implementation that would be useful in many American states. The English city when it desires to perform a new function does not have to approach Parliament to obtain permission to undertake the activity but goes to the appropriate administrative unit of the central gov- ernment with its request. The administrative branch then acts upon the petition and if favorably received, the city is tentatively allowed to pro- ceed. The order lies before Parliament for a period of time and then if no objection is voiced the permissive order is allowed to become law. This process would save the time of the state legislatures if followed in Ameri- can states. The same effect could be obtained by using the principle that a city has the power to undertake any activity that it considers necessary unless it is specifically denied the authority by the state constitution or by state statute.

## MUNICIPAL CORPORATIONS AND QUASI-CORPORATIONS

### Legal Position of Corporations

The legal position of a local government in most states is determined to a fairly high degree by whether or not it is classed as a public corporation or a quasi-corporation. The municipal corporations are voluntary organ- izations that the state has allowed to be created only upon initiative by the residents in the area, whereas the counties and other quasi-corpora- tions are established by state initiative and prerogative. The legislative

[3] M. E. Dimock and G. O. Dimock, *American Government in Action* (New York: Holt, Rinehart & Winston, Inc., 1951), pp. 75–76.

supremacy in the states that have no constitutional home rule is virtually unchallenged. Quasi-corporations are merely administrative units of the state and as such are much closer to the state government than are the incorporated municipal areas. The quasi-units are at most but local organizations, created by general law for the purpose of civil and political administration of government and are vested with a very limited number of characteristics usually associated with corporation status.

Usually the quasi-corporation has considerably less tort liability than do municipal corporations. It must be noted that the state statutes or the decisions of the supreme court of the state may place tort liability upon the quasi-corporations, and the trend would appear to be in this general direction. Ordinarily the amount of legislative power granted to a quasi-corporation by the state is much more limited than that delegated to the municipal corporations. Similarly, their control over property is more restricted, and their powers of eminent domain in some states is likewise limited in comparison with that of the municipality.

The municipal corporation and the quasi-corporation may be classed as either de jure or de facto. When all of the legal requirements have been complied with in either type of corporation the class of de jure is granted, meaning by right or by law. If for some reason all of the legal requirements have not been met but the corporation has been created and acts "in good faith" it may be recognized as a de facto or an in-fact corporation.

Originally most of the states created each municipal corporation by the enactment of a special legislative act. This is still the prevailing method in Delaware, Florida, New Hampshire, and North Carolina. Oftentimes in at least three of these states alternative methods may be used, but in New Hampshire a special act of the legislature is the only method provided. Most of the states have restricted the authority of the legislature to create municipal corporations because of legislative abuse of this power that frequently occurred during the nineteenth century. In Florida the "only restraints imposed upon the legislative power of chartering and changing municipalities are those dictated by political prudence. . . . In the 1953 session of the legislature, twenty new municipal corporations were chartered."[4] While in Delaware, which has only forty-nine municipalities, the legislature creates towns through the process of incorporation and issues charters to those over five thousand in population. All such charters are issued only "if two-thirds of the entire membership of both houses of the legislature approve."[5] There has not been the necessity of imposing re-

[4] Wilson K. Doyle, Angus McLaird, and S. Sherman Weiss, *The Government and Administration of Florida* (New York: Thomas Y. Crowell Co., 1954), p. 389.

[5] Paul Dolan, *The Government and Administration of Delaware* (New York: Thomas Y. Crowell Co., 1956), p. 332.

strictions upon the Delaware General Assembly as it obviously does not need to spend as much time legislating for municipalities with such a limited number involved.

By far the most widely used form of municipal incorporation is by general law. Usually this incorporation applies to all communities that desire municipal corporation status, but some states may permit "reasonable classification" ordinarily on a basis of population. Most state supreme courts have allowed classification on a population basis on the grounds that such a classification meets the test of "reasonable." A common requirement before incorporation under general law can be initiated is a minimum population. In some states as few as twenty-five qualified voters may be all that is needed to begin incorporation, while in other states at least five hundred may be the minimum population needed. Usually a designated number of residents of the area to be incorporated must sign a petition requesting incorporation. The area must have been platted and maps showing the exact geographical boundaries prepared. Usually after these technicalities have been met, the designated state official will set a date for an election to determine if a majority of the inhabitants of the area to be incorporated are in favor of such action. If at the popular election a majority so indicate, the election results will be promulgated and the state will officially recognize the area as a municipal corporation.

Incorporation under home-rule provisions, the third method now used in the United States, follows much the same procedures as under the general law of incorporation. The additional step of adopting a charter is necessary. Following approval of the charter, which is usually drafted by a charter commission with expert assistance, the document is submitted to the state to check its conformity with state constitutional requirements and state statutes.

Like the creation of a municipal corporation, dissolution is within the discretion of the state legislature unless restricted by state constitutional provisions. If the legislature creates by special act, it may dissolve by a special act. In some states dissolution is left with the state courts. In still other states a popular referendum may be required at which time a majority of the electorate voting must favor the proposal to dissolve the municipal corporation.

Mississippi has a unique dissolution process in that any municipal corporation whose population falls below one hundred persons according to the federal census is dissolved upon notification to the local officials by the secretary of state of the action. Mississippi municipal corporations may be dissolved automatically no matter what their population if they do not hold official council meetings during a year or fail on two successive municipal election dates to hold elections.[6]

---

[6] Robert B. Highsaw and Charles N. Fortenberry, *The Government and Administration of Mississippi* (New York: Thomas Y. Crowell Co., 1954), p. 339.

## Sources of Municipal Powers

A municipal corporation derives its powers from one or more of four sources. These are usually recognized as follows:

1. the constitution of the state.
2. the statutes of the state, including both those applicable to all municipalities or to the class to which the particular city belongs, and special acts of the legislature.
3. the charter, if one has been duly authorized and adopted.
4. in a few states the philosophy of an inherent right of self-government grants power in certain municipal affairs.[7]

A majority of state supreme courts, however, have adopted the rule of strict construction in determination of municipal corporate powers. The famous Dillon Rule is adhered to in which it is asserted that a municipality has and can exercise the following powers and no others:

First, those granted in express words; second, those necessarily or fairly implied or incident to the powers expressly granted; third those essential to the accomplishment of the declared objects and purposes of the corporation—not simply convenient, but indispensable. Any fair reasonable, substantial doubt concerning the existence of power is resolved by the courts against the corporation and the power is denied.[8]

# HOME RULE FOR LOCAL GOVERNMENTS

## Constitutional Home Rule

Some of the state constitutions do not spell out the status of the local governmental units, leaving this authority to the state legislature. Other state constitutions, particularly those written in the twentieth century, do provide for these local units. However, in no instance can it be said that a state constitution creates a true federal relationship between the state and the local governments. In every constitution the state still retains plenary powers of "life or death" over the cities, towns, school districts, counties, and special districts, unless home rule is provided in the state constitution. If a home-rule clause is included in the constitution either in its original form or through constitutional amendment, then it might be regarded by some students of intergovernmental relations that a modified federal relationship is possible.

---

[7] Charles S. Rhyne, *Municipal Law* (Washington, D.C.: National Institute of Municipal Law Officers, 1954), Vol. II, pp. 578–80.

[8] John F. Dillon, *Commentaries on the Law of Municipal Corporations* (5th ed.; Boston: Little, Brown & Co., 1911), Vol. I, sec. 237.

Of the fifty state constitutions, just over half contain a home-rule proviso. The twenty-seven state constitutional home-rule states are listed in Table 3–2.

### TABLE 3–2
#### States with Constitutional Home Rule—1963

| State | Year Adopted | Cities Eligible | Self-executing | Cities Using |
|---|---|---|---|---|
| Alaska | 1959 | 1st class cities and boroughs | Yes | – |
| Arizona | 1912 | Cities of over 3,500 | Yes | 3 |
| California | 1879 | Cities of over 3,500 | Yes | 57 |
| Colorado | 1902 | Cities of over 2,000 | Yes | 12 |
| Hawaii | 1959 | All political government units | Yes | – |
| Kansas | 1960 | All cities | Yes | – |
| Louisiana | 1947 | | Partly | |
| Maryland | 1915/54 | Baltimore/all cities | Yes | – |
| Michigan | 1908 | Each city and village | No | 180 |
| Minnesota | 1898 | Any city or town | No | 81 |
| Missouri | 1875 | Any city over 10,000 | Yes | 3 |
| Nebraska | 1912 | Any city over 5,000 | Yes | 3 |
| Nevada | 1924 | Any city or town | Yes | – |
| New Mexico | 1949 | City-counties over 5,000 | Yes | – |
| New York | 1923 | Every city | No | 7 |
| Ohio | 1912 | Any municipality | Yes | 33 |
| Oklahoma | 1907 | Any city over 2,000 | Yes | 55 |
| Oregon | 1906 | Every city and town | Yes | 107 |
| Pennsylvania | 1922 | Cities over 10,000 | No | 1 |
| South Dakota | 1962 | All cities | Yes | – |
| Rhode Island | 1951 | All cities and towns | Yes | 4 |
| Tennessee | 1953 | Any municipality | Yes | – |
| Texas | 1909 | Cities over 5,000 | No | 99 |
| Utah | 1932 | Any city or town | Partly | 0 |
| Washington | 1889 | Any city over 20,000 | No | 8 |
| West Virginia | 1936 | Any city over 2,000 | No | 8 |
| Wisconsin | 1924 | Cities and villages | No | 0 |

SOURCE: Rodney L. Mott, *Home Rule for America's Cities* (Chicago: American Municipal Association, 1949); and Council of State Governments, *The Book of the States, 1964–1965* (Chicago: Council of State Governments, 1964).

It should be noted from the accompanying table that the eligibility of municipalities to participate under the home-rule provision is greatly restricted in many of the state constitutions. Only Hawaii, Michigan, Nevada, New York, Ohio, Oregon, Rhode Island, South Dakota, Tennessee, Utah, and Wisconsin allow *all* municipalities the opportunity to utilize home-rule powers. However, even in these eleven states the cities have not always accepted this invitation, for in Utah and Wisconsin not a single municipality operates under the home-rule clause of the state constitution. In most of the other states a number of the so-called eligible cities have not elected to participate.

ons are usually considered to be less burden-
detailed legislative enactment dealing with
The constitutional home-rule idea for both
assists these units in escaping the iron hand

outset that some state administrative super-
le but absolutely necessary. Few students of
have the state relinquish all supervisory power

mmission on Intergovernmental Relations, "the
ould not be carried to an extreme. It defeats the
resist needed consolidation of local units by in-
s a right to perpetual self-determination. Self-
plated local unit of a large community often re-
or genuine home rule in the whole community."[12]
ho favor home rule hesitate to see it extended to
this very reason. It has been fairly obvious to
erica has in most of its states a surplus of county
g them home rule may materially reduce the
ernment consolidation.

ment of a degree of uniformity where this is in the
ngthens rather than weakens home rule. There is
nontradictory between home rule and state direction
in spirit and with the proper emphasis. Energetic and
srship can give valuable assistance to local govern-
agencies and especially the state's educational institu-
b assistance to local officials.

sup, again, if used properly can strengthen local govern-
ha appropriate balance of supervision and leadership.
olv certed effort to create the right areas of local govern-
eq m with necessary authority and responsibility.

st ha tury has witnessed an ever-increasing degree of state super-
er th ministrative services performed by government at the county
icipa els. In some areas of governmental activity, such as finance,
trol a e out of the inability of local governments to cope with the
effec of an economic depression.[13]

this ntensified supervision has been resented by some county
icipal officials. At first it was viewed as punitive, but as the state

Commission on Intergovernmental Relations, *A Report to the President for
al to the Congress, June 1955* (Washington, D.C.: Government Printing Of-
), p. 54.
ett M. Rich, *The Government and Administration of New Jersey* (New York:
Y. Crowell Co., 1957), p. 388.

## Legislative Home Rule

Ten state legislatures have extended home rule to their municipalities
without constitutional provisions authorizing such action. This method is
not as favorably viewed as constitutional home rule since the courts
in Michigan and Wisconsin have held such statutes to be unconstitutional.[9] The court rulings in the two cases were based upon the fact that
all legislative power is vested in the state legislature and unless authorized
in the state constitution cannot be legally delegated to local governments.

In addition to the possibility of the legislative home-rule statute being
nullified as unconstitutional by the courts, the stability of the home-rule
powers thus granted is questionable. One session of the legislature may
permit the local governments to assume certain powers, and the following
legislature may withdraw the use of the same power. Another problem
involved in both constitutional and legislative home rule is that of determining exactly what is implied by the term "local affairs." Some matters
are obviously primarily of local concern, and most courts will not question
the local authority's control in these areas. Others are in the so-called "gray
area," which may at one time be considered by a court as local but at another period by the same or a different court as essentially of state-wide importance and therefore not subject to local control. No question is usually
raised as to the local electorates' right to determine the form of government
to be used, but frequently in the "gray area" are such powers as setting civil
service requirements and zoning regulations.

Legislative home rule has not been nullified by the courts in six states.
Florida has employed it since 1915; Georgia, 1948; Connecticut, 1951;
Mississippi, 1900; North Carolina, 1917; and South Carolina, 1899. In these
states the home-rule measure is applicable to all municipalities except in
Mississippi where it applies only to the special-charter cities. Iowa's home-
rule legislation applied only to the special-charter cities from 1858 until
1963 when it was extended by the legislature to all cities and towns, only
to be nullified in a 1964 court decision, which was reversed by the Iowa Supreme Court.

There is little question that the most satisfactory home-rule form is constitutional home rule with self-executing constitutional provisos, wherein
the cities can draft and change their own charters according to prescribed
procedures made explicit in the constitution. However, second best is the
constitutional home rule that requires some legislative action to implement the local authorities' powers. In many respects this is similar to the
pure legislative home rule except it has a constitutional foundation.

The ultimate authority in determining what is to be included in home-

[9] *Elliot v. City of Detroit* (121 Michigan 611, 84 N.W. 820, 1899, and State *ex
rel.*); *Mueller v. Thompson*, (149 Wis. 488, 137 N.W. 20, 1912).

rule powers is the state supreme court. Some state courts have held to a liberal interpretation while others, such as Ohio, has tended to reduce regularly the authority that the local governments may exercise under the home-rule provisions.

There is a continuing interest in many states for home rule both for municipal governments and to a lesser extent for counties. (See Chapter 4 for data supporting home rule.) Although the latter movement has proceeded much more slowly, the centralization trend is present in the state and local government relationship. Everywhere, power, authority, responsibility, and accountability have been shifting from the smaller units to the larger units. There can be no denial of the statement that in spite of home-rule charters and home-rule clauses in state constitutions, the amount of state administrative control and supervision is still on the increase. This is true in virtually every state, in every area of governmental function. Examples of the degree and types of state supervision placed upon local governmental units, including the cities and towns, townships, counties, and special districts will be considered in the latter portion of this chapter. It is probably possible to predict that the likelihood of a reversal of the trend toward centralization appears to be remote since there is no sign that the tempo of technological change will be halted or slowed. Another basic factor that has accentuated the movement from smaller or lower unit to the larger or higher unit is that of cost. It is oftentimes assumed, even though frequently unproved, that the larger the unit of government, the more efficiently and the more economically it can perform the desired functions. In some cases this is true and in other cases it is not evident. Each function and each particular instance must be studied and analyzed in its own perspective before a valid judgment can be made.

## STATE CONTROL OVER LOCAL UNITS

State control over local government usually takes two different forms. In every state both forms of control are exercised. The first type may be classed as constitutional-legislative control. This involves the controls established in the state constitution over the local governments and the plenary powers granted to the state legislature. The second type of control is exercised through the state administrative organization, the governor, and the administrative departments or agencies.

### Constitutional-Legislation Control

It is sometimes assumed that state control over local governmental units is unlimited; but this is, of course, not true. There are several categories of limitations upon the powers of the state government over the local

units in spite of
the limitations ar
quently prohibitin
that all local gove
least must be put
enacted for each gro

Many state consti
counties in the consti
with county boundarie
ment, which must no
become effective. Other
if the county boundaries
the residents concerned t

Most state constitutions
seats, reserving this privil
Still another restriction imp
only the local residents of
local office, thus removing th

### Supervision of Local Gove

"The struggle for home rule
effort on the part of the munici
interference rather than supervi
many states. For some years the
reached a plateau, but in the last
the movement again appears to ha
is still the same as that attributed
thirty years ago—the desire for freed
it would certainly seem that the ad
ernments by the states is continuing u

This supervision may take various
may limit the powers of the local go
which state control is exercised over
state statutes enacted by the legislatur
state administrative agencies power to
tivities, particularly in the fields of finan
public safety. Types one and three have
control has been resisted by the local units.

[10] Kirk H. Porter, *County and Township Gove*
York: The Macmillan Co., 1922), pp. 77–87.
[11] Schuyler Wallace, *State Administrative Super*
*States* (New York: Columbia University Press, 1928)

The cdrict
some in n th
local goions
countiesities
of the sta

It shot th
vision irab
state-locld
and auth

As deCo
principlsh
purposeo
terpretia
determis
stricts tl
Indeed
county
many st
governn
chances

State-
commor
nothing
if given
dynami
mental
tions ca

State
ment b
This inv
ment ar

The l
vision o
and mu
state co
disastrou

Natural
and mu

[12] The
*Transmi*
fice, 195
[13] Ber
Thomas

administrators became oriented to this increased supervisory role the beneficial aspects of the action became apparent even to many of the complaining local officials.

The federal government's expanding financial aid programs to municipal governments has contributed to the increase of state supervision by requiring that the state administer the program and assure conformity by the local governmental units. Similarly, when state assistance in the form of grants to local governments increased, the state demands certain compliances that can be guaranteed only if the state administrative agencies have supervisory authority. Local communities and the state are forced into an ever widening circle of interrelationship from which there is no escape.

## The Governor's Supervision and Control of Local Governments

By and large the governors of the fifty states have not been given either by the state constitution or by the legislature a very large amount of control over local governmental units. The reasons are twofold: (1) the state legislatures do not desire to surrender their authority to the governor's office in most states; and (2) Americans have had a great deal of respect for the unwritten principle of local self-government.

Fewer than ten states authorize the governor to appoint on a regular basis local government officials, and usually these are only minor appointees such as coroners or medical examiners. It is obvious that the appointive power of many state's chief executives in the area of local government is virtually nil. Oftentimes he is authorized to appoint individuals to complete a term in a local post when a vacancy occurs. Municipal judges in Iowa are appointed by the governor whenever a vacancy exists, but at the next general election the position is placed upon the ballot. An unusual example of a governor's power of appointment is found in Missouri, where he appoints a commission that in turn names the police chief in both Kansas City and St. Louis.

The removal power of the chief executive of the state in the realm of local government officials is nearly as restrictive as his appointive authority. In a few states, such as New York, Massachusetts, Ohio, and Michigan, he can remove mayors of municipalities; but in most instances he must be able to prove to the satisfaction of the judiciary that the incumbent is unable to execute the duties of the office. In a few states—Minnesota, New York and Wisconsin—the governor has power to remove county sheriffs. In a number of states the governor may suspend local officials from office when court action against the official is pending. In some states he may request the state attorney-general to institute court proceedings against local officials when he has evidence that leads him to believe that they are incompetent or have committed some illegal action. Florida's state constitution grants such power to its governor.[14]

It must be concluded that it is not the chief executives of the states who interfere with the operation of local governments. However, the governors in most states are not in a position to give any substantial aid and assistance to local governments when they have problems. To be sure in emergency situations, such as a flood or other disaster, the governor may be called upon to order the State or National Guard to render emergency assistance to counties or communities. Most governors, however, do not have financial resources at their disposal to render monetary aid to a stricken area.

## State Control of Local Finance

Since 1890, when Wyoming began its system of supervision of municipal accounts, the trend toward greater state control over municipal financial accounting has been growing. Today more than half of the fifty states furnish to their municipalities either supervisory or advisory services in connection with municipal accounting. In at least fifteen states the supervision is mandatory and in the others it is optional. Some states require only certain classes of their cities to utilize the state supervised accounting while others require all municipalities to comply.[15] The nature of the supervision varies from state to state. Some issue the exact forms that must be utilized. Others merely recommend that certain records be kept and a classification and codification of accounts be followed. A surprisingly small number of states hold instructional schools for municipal accounting officials.

As Kilpatrick suggested, ". . . rather than uniformity in precise forms, procedures, bases, and accounts, the supervision of municipal accounting should be directed toward promoting uniformity in the larger purposes, terminology and classification."[16] The state supervision may be helpful or it may be an actual hindrance to the municipality, largely depending to the degree that the system required meets the criteria established by Professor Kilpatrick.

The second phase of state supervision of municipal accounts involves the post-auditing function. In at least thirty states some provision is made for either state auditing or supervision of audits of its municipalities. Usually the state allows the municipality to choose between the use of

[14] John A. Fairlie and Charles M. Kneier, *County Government and Administration* (New York: Appleton-Century-Crofts, Inc., 1930), pp. 242–45.

[15] T. E. McMillan, Jr., *State Supervision of Municipal Finance* (Austin: Institute of Public Affairs, The University of Texas, 1953), pp. 14–15.

[16] Wylie Kilpatrick, *State Supervision of Local Finance* (Chicago: Public Administration Service, 1941), p. 12.

state auditors or to employ approved private auditors. At least eight states require that the cities utilize the services of the state employees, with the municipality being billed for the services. The states likewise dictate to the municipalities the frequency of the audits, but only about half of them require all municipalities to have an annual audit. Variations are found in the classifications of cities within a state as to how often the accounts must be audited. The necessity of audits is beyond question. However, it may be debated as to whether or not the detail required by some states serves any useful purpose. Every citizen has the right to expect that every precaution will be taken to assure honesty and integrity on the part of the public officials. Likewise, every public official has the right to have the facts openly reported as to the honesty of his records.[17] The auditing of municipal accounts should be made a part of the public record in such a manner as to gain widespread recognition by the citizens.

While it may appear that rather extensive state supervision occurs in the majority of the states concerning municipal accounts it is much more widely practiced in the county government area. Most of the states severely handcuff the county officials, making the state supervision of municipal accounts appear to be quite superficial.

## State Supervision of Local Budgeting

More than half of the states require that a state agency be directly concerned with the municipal budgets. At least twenty-six states have a formal law pertaining to the state supervision of local budgets with an additional six having an informal arrangement which allows state assistance. In some states the state supervision is not universal, as it does not apply to all classes of municipalities. At least four states provide for budget supervision on a voluntary basis—Minnesota, Vermont, Tennessee, and Wisconsin. Municipal compliance with the state control is apparently good, as only eight states report that they have been forced to rigidly enforce sanctions.[18] The devices for obtaining standardization of budgeting techniques include: prescription of the budget forms, installation of budgetary control accounts by the state, preparation of budget manuals and directives, and pre-audit budget review by the state agency.

Of all of the states Indiana has probably the greatest amount of state control over local budgeting and over-all finance. Indiana exercises direct control on an appeal basis over both expenditures and tax levies, but

[17] T. E. McMillan, *State Supervision of Municipal Finance* (Austin: Institute of Public Affairs, University of Texas, 1953), pp. 38–39.

[18] T. E. McMillan, Jr., *State Supervision of Municipal Finance* (Austin: Institute of Public Affairs, University of Texas, 1953), p. 54. Iowa, New Jersey, New Mexico, New York, Oregon, Pennsylvania, Washington and West Virginia.

has no filing requirement.[19] Iowa is another state that has not granted much freedom to its municipalities in the area of finance. The state prescribes the forms, requires the filing of budgets with the county auditor who in turn reports them to the state comptroller, and allows only a maximum tax levy of 30 mills with exceptions made upon petition to the state comptroller. These restrictions were not changed by the legislative home-rule grant in 1963.

## State Supervision of Municipal Indebtedness

The strictest regulation of financial activities of local governments by the state is in the area of indebtedness. Nearly all states impose either by constitution or statute severe limitations upon the borrowing powers of these local units. Almost all states regulate the purposes for which indebtedness may be contracted and also regulate the amount of debt that may accrue. Usually this is in terms of the amount of total assessed valuation of property. The range is rather wide, varying from a low of 2 per cent to as much as 20 per cent of the total property valuation, with the average being about 7 per cent. The length of time that may be used in repayment of the debt is also frequently regulated. More and more the states are limiting the time element to a maximum of twenty years. Likewise a growing number of state regulations concerning the form of the indebtedness are being placed upon the state statute books. The trend is toward requiring the local governmental units to utilize serial bonds rather than allowing the questionable practice of sinking funds. Virtually every state requires that a county or a municipality that desires to issue bonds may do so only after the question has been given an affirmative vote by the residents of the area concerned. Usually an extraordinary majority, frequently of 60 per cent of those voting on the question, must be obtained. There would appear to be little question as to the usefulness of most of the state safeguards in the area of local government debts. The greatest questions center around the maximum amounts permitted as they are based upon the questionable assessed valuations. A few critics contend that the requirement of anything other than an approval by a simple majority before issuance of bonds is detrimental to progressive local governmental programs.

## State Supervision and Control of Personnel

In addition to the power of some governors to appoint certain local government officials there has been increasing supervision by state agencies over many specialized personnel employed by local governments. In a number of states the local assessors are either appointed by a state tax

---

[19] *Burns Indiana Statutes,* Annotated, sec. 64–1331.

commission or must be certified as qualified by having passed a state administered examination before the local authorities may employ them. In Maryland this centralized control over county assessors has been used for more than thirty years, with the local officials submitting a list to the state agency from which the assessor is chosen. In the social welfare area, due primarily to the federal government's influence, county welfare workers in all of the states are under a state merit system, and only the individual who has been certified by the state merit system council or its equivalent may be employed by the county. Much the same control is exercised by a state agency in the field of public health, again because of the federal money involved in the salaries of the local public health officials. State supervision over the teachers employed by the public schools in the states is in most instances very complete. Almost all state departments of public instruction have been vested with the authority to certify teachers who are eligible for employment by the local school boards. Only if the teachers employed are certified can the school be accredited and thus be eligible for the state financial aid.

## State Supervision of Highways

Of all of the administrative areas in which state control and centralization is apparent, highway construction and maintenance would appear to be the one witnessing the greatest degree of impact. A hundred years ago the state as a rule had little if any control over highways, leaving this as an administrative responsibility of the county, the township, and the municipalities. A trend that began at the end of the nineteenth century is continuing by emphasizing greater and greater state control. Beginning with New Jersey in 1891 more and more state supervision and control of highways has evolved. Originally the state vested control over highways with the local units, but the state did support the program financially. The next step, which was taken in North Carolina in 1931, completely centralized the highway function in the state government. Usually this evolution does not directly affect the municipalities but does relieve the counties and townships of their responsibilities. How far this centralization of the control over highways will extend is problematical. Many observers believe that eventually all but the minor streets within the city limits will fall under the control of the state government. Local residents are each year expecting and demanding a higher standard of road construction and maintenance. To achieve this goal the smaller units have in many instances been forced to yield to larger administrative units that can do the job more efficiently and economically.

There is no question that the state government has the power to take over the control of state highways, county roads, and even any city streets that it deems necessary. While originally almost all states used the plan of state supplementary financing for local road construction and maintenance, the trend is now toward state control in a direct construction and maintenance operation.

What has been the attitude of the local officials to this move? Initially many were opposed and objected as strenuously as possible. Others from the very first willingly accepted the state assuming this major financial burden. In the second half of the twentieth century less and less resistance is coming from local officials in most parts of America to this state centralization.

## State Financial Aid to Local Governments

Financial aid to the local governmental units—a major coercive technique—takes three forms: shared taxes, grants-in-aid, and direct grants. Since the end of World War II the states have been increasingly granting support in a financial way to their subdivisions.

Shared taxes usually retain their identity as the money realized from a specific tax or revenue source. The state collects the money from specific levies within a given geographic area and returns the revenue to the local governments. The state acts merely as a collecting agency and often returns all except that part required to compensate the state for its administrative costs in collections and redistribution. The local officials regard the shared taxes as revenue to which they are rightfully entitled.

Grants-in-aid are defined, whether it be between the national and the state governments or between the state and its subdivisions, as a payment of money from a higher governmental unit to a local one on a matching basis for the undertaking of a given function. The matching basis may vary from function to function and certainly from state to state but usually it is expected to be on a fifty-fifty basis. The higher government always stipulates the conditions that must be met if the grant-in-aid is to occur. Usually this involves the higher governmental unit, the state, establishing minimum standards that the local units must meet. It also frequently includes the state holding inspectional or review authority over the execution of the function.

Direct grants from the state are also increasing but probably not at the fast tempo of grants-in-aid. In the direct grant the money involved is virtually a gift to the local unit to use "wisely."

These three sources of local funds are becoming an ever-increasing percentage of the total money available to local governments. The local units are without inherent right to tax and thus are completely at the mercy of the state.

Ninety per cent of the financial aid given to the local units is granted for functional purposes, i.e., highways, schools. Ten per cent of the annual total, which exceeded $9 billion in 1960 and continues to increase each year by more than 10 per cent, was granted for general governmental operations. Education has traditionally been the one function for which at least 50 per cent of all state aid to local units is granted. About one-seventh is annually given for highways, and slightly more is annually allocated for local public welfare activities.

The more than fourfold increase in state-aid payments to local governments between 1942 and 1960, according to selected functions, is depicted in Table 3–3.

TABLE 3–3

State Aid to Local Governmental Units for Selected Years
(Amounts in millions of dollars)

| Year | General Local Government Support | Schools | Highways | Other | Per Capita | Total |
|------|------|------|------|------|------|------|
| 1942 | $224 | $ 790 | $ 344 | $ 422 | $13.45 | $ 1,780 |
| 1944 | 274 | 861 | 298 | 409 | 13.81 | 1,842 |
| 1946 | 357 | 953 | 339 | 443 | 15.90 | 2,092 |
| 1948 | 428 | 1,554 | 507 | 794 | 23.02 | 3,283 |
| 1950 | 482 | 2,054 | 610 | 1,071 | 28.52 | 4,217 |
| 1952 | 549 | 2,525 | 728 | 1,244 | 33.06 | 5,044 |
| 1954 | 600 | 2,934 | 871 | 1,273 | 36.06 | 5,679 |
| 1956 | 631 | 3,541 | 984 | 1,382 | 40.00 | 6,538 |
| 1958 | 687 | 4,453 | 1,167 | 1,637 | 46.87 | 7,943 |
| 1960 | 806 | 5,300 | 1,247 | 1,930 | 51.99 | 9,283 |
| 1962 | 844 | 6,474 | 1,325 | 2,259 | 58.94 | 10,906 |

SOURCE: U.S. Department of Commerce, Bureau of the Census, *Compendium of State Government Finances in 1960 and State Payments to Local Governments,* Vol. VI, No. 2, of the 1962 Census of Governments (Washington, D.C.: Government Printing Office, 1963); and U.S. Bureau of the Census, *Governmental Finance in 1962* (Washington, D.C.: Government Printing Office, 1963).

Most of the state aid comes from the general fund but some states earmark certain taxes, such as sales or gasoline taxes, to be returned to the local governmental units on varying bases, but most frequently the population factor is dominant. Other methods used include some measurement of the local need, which may involve in education the number of students, or in highways the number of miles of highways. Another method followed by some states is the establishment of a floor or minimum amount of aid payable to each local governmental unit.

State supervisory powers over local governmental units are usually divided into two main classes: non-coercive or persuasive measures and coercive or control devices.[20] Reports, inspections, advice and review are

[20] Schuyler Wallace, *State Administrative Supervision Over Cities in the United States* (New York: Columbia University Press, 1928), pp. 27–39.

usually termed as non-coercive. All states utilize these supervisory techniques to some degree. It might appear that some coercion could be hidden beneath mandatory reports and reviews but seldom does this materialize. In direct contrast, orders, ordinances, appointment and removal of local officials are usually supported by a coercive force. The final coercion is a cutting off of financial support for an activity conducted by a local government if state rules and regulations are ignored. This may be followed by what is usually called substitute administration.

New Jersey is one state that authorizes the state administrative agencies to assume control of local government affairs when the subordinate unit commits any one of five offenses: (1) defaults on debt principle or interest; (2) does not make tax payments due to the state or other governmental units; (3) carries a budget deficit for two years in excess of 5 per cent of the tax levy; (4) has excessive floating debt, based on percentage of the budget; (5) has excessive tax delinquency, measured by a percentage of the total taxes levied.[21]

## NATIONAL-LOCAL GOVERNMENT RELATIONS

It is quite clear that the writers of the United States Constitution did not contemplate the degree and amount of interest that the national government has taken in recent years in local governmental activity. If anything, they contemplated complete domination by the state over its subdivisions. Prior to 1930, the contacts between the national government and the local governments were relatively few, very indirect, and most informal. They certainly would have to be characterized as being completely non-coercive. The change since 1932, however, has been almost unbelievable. For example, services performed for the American cities by the federal government before 1875 were only fourteen in number and by 1930 were only seventy-seven.[22] Thirty years later it was impossible to list all of the services rendered to municipalities by the national government because of the expansion. A good estimate would place the number at three or four times that of 1930.

Contacts between the national and local units are no longer informal, no longer indirect, and no longer properly characterized as being totally non-coercive. The cities and even some counties, school districts, and special districts go directly to the federal authorities for assistance with their problems. This is particularly true in a large number of federal

[21] Council of State Governments, *State-Local Relations* (Chicago: Council of State Governments, 1946), p. 27.
[22] National Resources Committee, *Urban Government, Supplementary Report of the Urbanism Committee* (Washington, D.C.: Government Printing Office, 1939), Vol. I, pp. 62–63.

grant-in-aid programs that have been established to aid and assist local governments in solving their problems, particularly when they involve finance. Major examples are to be found in the fields of airport development, hospitals, slum clearance, urban renewal, city highways and free ways, and federal aid for school districts that have become overcrowded because of some nearby federal installation or project.

The oldest service rendered by the national government for the local units involved research, statistic gathering, and informational services. Most of the fourteen services rendered by the federal authorities for subdivisions of the state prior to 1875 would be included in this category. The United States Bureau of the Census is one agency that has for years been prominent in this service function. The United States Office of Education, now a division of the Department of Health, Education and Welfare, is also an established service agency that has for a hundred years or more rendered research, statistical, and general information to local units. A more recent addition are the useful reports on crime statistics published by the Federal Bureau of Investigation. Almost every federal agency puts out a virtual flood of reports that are of some service to cities, school districts, counties, and special districts. Many of these are on a regular basis, others are published when they appear to be of special significance.

A second category of services rendered by the federal agencies includes advice, consultation, conferences, and training programs to assist local units to better perform their various functions. Some of this type of activity was available in the early part of the twentieth century, but the expansion of training services has been notable since 1932. For example, the Federal Bureau of Investigation trains selected local police officers at its National Academy so that these officers can in turn train the members of the local police departments in the new techniques and methods of crime prevention and detection.

The United States Civil Service Commission does not train local personnel officers, but it does make available to them tests and other materials that will enable them to do a more effective job of personnel recruitment, job classification, and placement of employees. Actual assistance in crime detection is given by the F.B.I. through its laboratories to local police units when a particularly baffling crime occurs. Special tests that no local police department could be expected to conduct on bullets, poisons, etc. are performed by the Washington, D.C., laboratory to assist the local police in their investigations. Many other departments and agencies render direct services to local governments of a similar type.

A number of laws passed by the United States Congress since 1932 are directly connected with local governmental units. The 1939 Hatch Act applies to those local government officials who are partially on the federal pay roll. Another national law which has placed federal officials in direct contact and support of local law enforcement officials, is the famous Lindbergh Kidnapping Law of 1932, which allows the F.B.I. and other national law enforcement officers to assist local officers when a kidnapping has been committed. Likewise the 1934 Fugitive Felon Act permits national officers to apprehend fugitives who are charged with a crime by one local jurisdiction when they have crossed a state boundary.

Probably most important to the local units of government has been the trend toward direct financial aid from the national government. Since 1944 the municipalities and counties have been able to secure monetary assistance in connection with highway programs from the U.S. Bureau of Public Roads. Most of the funds were channeled through or required the approval of the state highway commission. Since about 1946 local hospitals have been able to obtain funds from the United States Public Health Service by going through their state department of public health. Financial assistance for building new airports or renovating old airports has at times gone directly to cities, while at other times the state bureau of aeronautics was consulted before action was finalized.

There can be no disguising the trend toward a greater degree of direct contact between the national government and the local units. Almost always this results in the federal government establishing standards that become a form of control over the local governments. Almost all contacts between federal and local officials have tended to give the national government a stronger position than it has ever had before or was envisioned by the framers of the United States Constitution. While the trend has been resisted by many state officials, feeling that they should not be by-passed, the public reaction has been, on the whole, quite favorable. The future relations will undoubtedly see a continuation of the trend toward increased federal control that has been so evident since the outset of the Great Depression.

## BIBLIOGRAPHY

COUNCIL OF STATE GOVERNMENTS. *State-Local Relations.* Chicago: Council of State Governments, 1946.

DILLON, J. F. *Commentaries on the Law of Municipal Corporations,* 5th ed. 5 vols. Boston: Little, Brown & Co., 1911.

FRYE, ROBERT J. *Federal-municipal Relations: An Overview.* University, Ala.: Bureau of Public Administration, University of Alabama, 1963.

GRAVES, BROOKE W. *Uniform State Action.* Chapel Hill, N.C.: University of North Carolina Press, 1934.

GRUMM, JOHN M. *A State Agency for Local Government?* Berkeley: Bureau of Public Administration, University of California, 1961.

INSTITUTE OF LOCAL AND STATE GOVERNMENT. *City-State Relations.* Philadelphia: Institute of Local and State Government, University of Pennsylvania, 1937.

JACKSON, ROBERT H. *Full Faith and Credit: The Lawyer's Clause of the Constitution.* New York: Columbia University Press, 1945.

KILPATRICK, WYLIE. *State Supervision of Local Budgeting.* New York: National Municipal League, 1939.

———. *State Supervision of Local Finance,* Chicago: Public Administration Service, 1941.

LANCASTER, LANE. *State Supervision of Municipal Indebtedness.* Philadelphia: Lane Lancaster, 1923.

McBAIN, H. L. *Law and Practice of Municipal Home Rule.* New York: Columbia University Press, 1916.

McGOLDRICK, JOSEPH D. *Law and Practice of Municipal Home Rule, 1916–1933.* New York: Columbia University Press, 1933.

McQUILLIN, EUGENE. *The Law of Municipal Corporations,* 2d ed. Chicago: Callaghan & Co., 1940.

MOTT, RODNEY L. *Home Rule for America's Cities.* Chicago: American Municipal Association, 1949.

SCOTT, STANLEY et al., *Local Governmental Boundaries and Areas: New Policies for California,* Berkeley: Bureau of Public Administration, University of California, 1961.

TAYLOR, GEORGE R., and OTHERS. *Barriers to Internal Trade in Farm Products.* Washington, D.C.: Government Printing Office, 1939.

THURSBY, VINCENT V. *Interstate Cooperation; A Study of the Interstate Compact.* New York: Public Affairs Press, 1953.

WALLACE, SCHUYLER. *State Administrative Supervision over Cities in the United States.* New York: Columbia University Press, 1939.

WINTERS, JOHN M. *State Constitutional Limitations on Solutions of Metropolitan Area Problems,* Ann Arbor: Legislative Research Center, University of Michigan Law School, 1961.

YLVISAKER, PAUL. *Intergovernmental Relations at the Grassroots,* Minneapolis: University of Minnesota Press, 1956.

ZIMMERMAN, FREDERICK L., and WENDELL, MITCHELL. *The Interstate Compact Since 1925.* Chicago: Council of State Governments, 1951.

# 4

# The American County in Local Government

Local government in the United States has its roots deep in the past and as a result many of the features of county government can be traced to the colonial period. Certain features were pure adaptations of English models while others were inventions to meet the conditions present at that time.

The county, as it is known in the United States, was modeled after an institution of local government with which our English forefathers were very familiar—the shire. History records that the English shire was established in about the ninth century. Its major agent was a court composed of representatives from each township and the individual landowners which met semiannually to administer justice. The important officers of the shire were the earl, the shire-reeve or sheriff, and the bishop. The shire became known as the county soon after the Norman Conquest, and the sheriff, as the representative of the King, became the dominant county officer.

A system of local government, following in many areas a pattern developed in England, was soon installed in the American scene. As early as 1634 the state of Virginia was divided into eight shires or counties. Other states soon followed this example, and counties were established in Massachusetts in 1643, Maryland in 1650, Connecticut in 1663, and Rhode Island in 1703.[1]

The first state constitutions drafted after the American Revolution contained sections relating to county governments, and in some instances these early documents granted a considerable area of self-government to the county. Since many county officials had been appointed by the gover-

[1] An excellent historical development of our institutions of local government is to be found in the following volume: John A. Fairlie, *Local Government in Counties, Towns and Villages* (New York: The Century Co., 1906).

nor, or some other state official, in the period preceding the Revolutionary War, one of the most prominent changes toward local self-government related to the increase of local influence or control in the choosing of county officials. Also, by the end of the first half of the nineteenth century many of our outstanding characteristics of county government as we know them today had taken shape.

During the colonial period four major systems of local or rural government developed: (1) the New England type, where the town was the important unit, with the county serving primarily as a judicial district; (2) the Virginia system, in which the county government was operated by the justices of the peace with the town or township being virtually nonexistent; (3) the New York plan, whereby both county and town were given important duties but were interlocked through the elective county board of town supervisors; and (4) the Pennsylvania system, in which both county and township existed but the latter was a subordinate unit and not represented on the county board. However, not one of these systems was introduced into any of the states formed in the Great Plains, the Rocky Mountain region, and the Far West. In these areas a fifth system was utilized; one that was southern in type in that there were no towns or townships but also emphasized the Pennsylvania type of county board of three commissioners elected at large.[2]

## PRESENT POSITION OF THE COUNTY

### Enumeration of Unorganized County Areas

The county is the almost universal unit of local government and serves as the principal subdivision of the state for many purposes, including electoral, administrative, and judicial activities. Organized county governments are to be found in all states except Alaska, Connecticut, and Rhode Island. There are some "counties" that do not maintain organized governments and in certain sections of the country there are some areas that are not listed as being legally within any county. The 1962 listing of governmental units by the Bureau of the Census records 3,043 independently organized county governments and 88 county-type areas without an independently organized county government. Included in the list of the latter group were the following six major categories:[3]

[2] Paul W. Wager (ed.), *County Government Across the Nation* (Chapel Hill: The University of North Carolina Press, 1950), pp. 7–8.

[3] U.S. Department of Commerce, Bureau of the Census, *Governmental Units in 1962*, Preliminary Report No. 6, 1962, pp. 5–6. As of January 1963 two counties in the state of Virginia were eliminated. Norfolk County was merged with the city of South Norfolk to become the new city of Chesapeake, and Princess Anne County was united with the city of Virginia Beach. For additional details see *National Civic Review*, Vol. LII, No. 4 (April, 1963), p. 220.

1. Three areas that are legally designated as city-counties but operate primarily as cities:
   a. City and County of San Francisco, California.
   b. City and County of Denver, Colorado.
   c. City and County of Honolulu, Hawaii.
2. One area which is designated as a metropolitan government but operates primarily as a city: Metropolitan Government of Nashville and Davidson County, Tennessee.
3. Eleven areas that have specified types of county offices but are counted only as parts of another government such as state, city, or township:
   a. In New York the five counties of Bronx, Kings, New York, Queens, and Richmond are counted as the City of New York.
   b. In Louisiana two parishes are counted as cities: The parish of East Baton Rouge as the city of Baton Rouge and the parish of Orleans as the city of New Orleans.[4]
   c. In Massachusetts two counties are counted under other headings: The county of Nantucket as the township of Nantucket and the county of Suffolk as the city of Boston.
   d. In Pennsylvania the county of Philadelphia is counted as the city of Philadelphia.
   e. In Hawaii the county of Kalawao is listed under the state of Hawaii.
4. Thirty-seven cities that are located outside of any county area but administer functions that are commonly performed by counties:
   a. Thirty-four cities in Virginia.
   b. In Maryland, Baltimore City is distinct from Baltimore County.
   c. In the District of Columbia, the city of Washington.
   d. In Missouri, St. Louis City is distinct from St. Louis County.
5. Sixteen unorganized areas that carry county specifications:
   a. In Connecticut, the eight county areas of Fairfield, Hartford, Litchfield, Middlesex, New Haven, New London, Tolland, and Windham.
   b. In Rhode Island, the five county areas of Bristol, Kent, Newport, Providence, and Washington.
   c. In South Dakota, the three "unorganized" counties which are attached to other counties for governmental purposes: Shannon, Washabaugh, and Todd.
6. Twenty other unorganized county-type areas:
   a. Alaska: nineteen election districts.
   b. Montana: the area of Yellowstone National Park. Those areas of the park located in Wyoming and Idaho are included in county areas in those states.

## Variations in Organized Counties

Certain comparisons can be made between and among the organized counties. The number of counties to be found in each of the forty-seven states possessing this form of local government varies from 3 in Delaware

---

[4] Parishes in Louisiana occupy a legal and political position comparable to that of counties in other states and are considered as counties.

and Hawaii to 254 in Texas. Between 1942 and 1962 only two new counties were formed. In area the counties range from 20,131 square miles in San Bernardino County, California, to 25 square miles in Arlington County, Virginia. Several small city-counties in Virginia have only about one square mile of area each. Approximately one-half of the counties are under 600 square miles, with the smallest ones being located generally in the East and Southeast and the largest ones in the Mountain and Pacific Coast states. Population statistics indicate that, according to the 1960 census, Los Angeles County, California, with the city of Los Angeles, had approximately 6,500,000 inhabitants in contrast with Alpine County, California, which had only 236 people and Loving County, Texas, which accounted for 227 residents. The census reports indicate that the average county had about 42,000 residents but that over four-fifths of all counties had less than 40,000 inhabitants. Population statistics reveal some very interesting trends. First of all, counties serve primarily as units of government for rural populations. While in most instances incorporated municipalities remain a part of the county in which they are located and the property is subject to taxation for county purposes, the county services are still of primary concern to rural populations. Population shifts have increased the governmental problems facing many counties since it has been estimated that during the 1940's about one-half of the counties suffered population losses and as many in the 1950's also declined even in a period that produced an overall increase in the national population. This trend has produced a two-fold problem for counties. On the one hand those counties with an increase in the urban population have had to provide more and more "municipal-type" functions to residents of unincorporated or "open county" areas. On the other hand the rural counties are faced with the prospect of providing the normal county functions and newer activities but with limited resources.

The second major trend indicates that the counties with the largest populations have in many instances relatively small geographical areas. These urban counties, faced with the possibility of additional influx of rural inhabitants, find many of their problems complicated and intensified due to the small geographical areas contained within the counties. These are the areas normally concerned with the creation of a "metropolitan" county or perhaps a city-county consolidation. A third trend arising from population shifts and changes is concerned with the functions to be performed by the county. While in the centralization movement there has been some shifting of duties from counties to states, the counties have lost some functions but have also acquired some new responsibilities. In terms of functions, the American county in many states is of greater importance today than at any time in previous years and the expansion trend is likely to continue.

## COUNTY HOME RULE

The organization of county government has traditionally been a subject over which our state legislatures have exercised a high degree of direct control. As a general rule, state constitutions and legislative statutes have been rather specific with regard to at least five items of county government: (1) listing the officers of the county and enumerating their duties; (2) providing for a definite term of office; (3) indicating the method by which these officers are to be chosen; (4) establishing the salary ranges that can be paid county officers; and (5) stating the services, duties, and functions that will be performed by the county.

While the term "home rule" is subject to many definitions, the general principle attempts to provide for two basic items: (1) to confer more power of self-government upon the counties; and (2) to free the counties from a high degree of legislative control and domination. As a result, home rule usually involves granting to counties the ability to frame, adopt, and change their own charters.

Two possible procedures can be followed by counties in those states that provide for home rule. First of all, some states provide for optional-charter provisions which authorize counties to choose among alternative patterns of organization as set forth in some detail in state laws. Counties in New York and Virginia may select from among four options, North Dakota counties from three, and in three states—Montana, North Carolina, and Oregon—one alternate form to the old established form of organization is provided. The optional-charter laws, while retaining in the state legislature some control over the organizational structure of counties, still permits them to decide upon an organizational pattern which they believe will assist in meeting the services that will be required.

A greater degree of freedom is provided counties in eleven states that provide for constitutional home rule over that afforded by optional-charter laws.[5] The basic purpose of this type of home rule is to allow the county as much freedom as possible in determining by popular referendum the form of government that will be established. Fundamental to the exercising of this freedom is the ability of the county to produce its own charter.

The home rule that has been extended to counties must be distinguished from the type that has been granted to municipalities. Home rule for cities confers, in many instances, not only the ability to determine the type

[5] Constitutional home rule exists for counties in California, Hawaii, Maryland, Michigan, Minnesota, Missouri, New York, Ohio, Oregon, Texas, and Washington. Also in a few states home-rule charters have been granted to a few individual counties by constitutional amendments. Two such examples are Dade County, Florida, and Jefferson Parish, Louisiana.

of organizational structure but permits the municipality some authority to control what is referred to as local affairs as distinguished from those of general state interest. County home rule, as a general principle, has only been concerned with allowing the county to establish its governmental structure but has not increased its ability or freedom to enter certain fields of activities that have generally been forbidden to the county and retained under the authority of the state. Even the choice with respect to determining the structural organization is not complete since some states have required that certain offices must be a part of a county government.[6] Therefore, it must be recognized that home rule for counties includes less freedom than that extended to municipalities.

Home rule has been viewed by some students of public administration as an important method by which the management of county government could be improved. Yet at the present time only sixteen counties have framed and adopted charters as a means of establishing a new structural organization and meeting their local problems. The largest number of home rule counties is to be found in California, the first state to provide for county home rule in 1911, where ten county home-rule charters are in effect.[7] Maryland and Oregon each has two home-rule counties while Missouri and New York each has one.[8] No counties in Minnesota, Ohio, Texas, and Washington have been able to adopt charters since in every instance where these documents have been drafted they have failed to gain the required popular vote. One of the outstanding characteristics that has developed in the adoption of county home-rule charters is the

[6] In California the counties must provide for an assessor, auditor, clerk, coroner, district attorney, license collector, public administrator, recorder, sheriff, superintendent of schools, surveyor, tax collector, and treasurer. The actual method by which these officials are chosen is left to local decision since home rule is present in California. In addition, the California Constitution specifies a number of matters that must be included in each county charter including details with respect to procedure and organization.

[7] Home-rule charters are operating in the following California counties: Los Angeles (1912); San Bernardino (1912); Butte (1916); Tehama (1916); Alameda (1926); Fresno (1933); Sacramento (1933); San Diego (1933); San Mateo (1933); and Santa Clara (1950). In addition, the city-county of San Francisco operates under a home-rule charter but it is considered in most instances as a city rather than a county. Unsuccessful attempts have been made in nine other counties to acquire home-rule charters. California law provides that locally drafted charters must not only be approved by the people but must be accepted by the state legislature. To date no county charter has been denied approval.

[8] In November, 1962, voters in four Oregon counties, balloting on new charters, adopted only two. In Lane County the charter grants the county new lawmaking powers, abolishes several offices, and overhauls administrative functions. The Washington County charter provides: (1) for an administrative officer to be appointed by and directly responsible to the board of county commissioners; and (2) a gradual changeover to a specified departmental structure. International City Managers' Association, *Public Management*, Vol. XLV, No. 3 (March, 1963), p. 67.

provision for a chief executive officer either by popular vote or by appointment on behalf of the county governing body.

Many sponsors of county home rule have also argued by means of analogy that since home rule for municipalities is due recognition of the privilege of local self-government the adoption of county home rule would constitute the same recognition of this fundamental right on behalf of the county. This argument has a tendency to overlook the basic differences that exist between cities and counties. Counties are local units created by the state governments, either by constitution or statute, to perform primarily state functions and have not always been established as the result of local interest, requests, or desires. Until recent times the assignment of purely local affairs to counties has constituted an arrangement of convenience rather than a desire to instill this concept of local self-government. As a result, the validity of the argument loses much of its strength when it is applied to counties.

The adoption by only a few counties of the home-rule system should not in and of itself be viewed as indicating any major flaws within the plan. Many people who have sponsored home rule for cities have evidently become quite indifferent with regard to its adoption within the counties. Where it has been applied in county government the people seem to be well satisfied with the results since we have had few abandonments.

## ORGANIZATION OF COUNTY GOVERNMENT

The organizational structure of county government varies greatly in detail not only from state to state but many times among the counties within the same state. This lack of uniformity within county government is readily apparent when the following items are reviewed: (1) the array of boards, commissions, and officers varying in titles, functions, membership, and mode of creation; (2) the presence of a large number of deputies, assistants, and employees who are frequently chosen on a political basis rather than under a merit or civil service system; and (3) the absence of any one single individual officer capable of coordinating the activities of the various agencies of the county government. In spite of the diversity of organization, most county governments have been organized along two similar principles or concepts: (1) the presence of a general governing body which has limited responsibility in the area of policy making and the supervision of county activities; and (2) the charging, either by constitution or state law, of certain officers with particular responsibilities. While this feature identifies definite areas of functions with certain county officers, it also increases the problem of relating all county operations into a manageable system.

## Types of Governing Bodies

The common type of organization for the governing body of a county is a board composed of a number of individuals varying from three to fifty. The titles of these boards differ among the states and there is no given relationship between the official title of the governing body and the actual work to be carried on by that agency. The Bureau of the Census has identified four major types of governing bodies operating in American counties:

1. Boards of commissioners or supervisors
2. Boards of township supervisors
3. Boards composed of judges and justices of the peace
4. Boards composed of one judge and commission.[9]

The first type of board is composed of members who have been specifically elected to this agency to assume collective responsibility for the functions belonging to the board. The members hold no other public offices, are not responsible to any other local unit, and are not charged with the performance of any other county functions. It has been estimated that about two-thirds of all county governing bodies are of this type. The second classification of boards has a membership chosen from the townships of the county, and in some instances the municipalities, and these members hold responsibilities both as township or municipal officers and as county board members. Boards of the third category have members with dual accountability not only as county governing board members but also as judicial officers. The fourth type of board has a presiding officer who is a judicial officer while the other members function only as members of the county governing board.

## Selection and Terms of Members

Members of county governing bodies are usually popularly elected although in a few counties some form of appointment is present. The direct primary is the most prevalent nomination system with a few instances of petition, convention, or caucus.

The actual methods of final election of members indicate three major variations: (1) the most popular style is to choose members by districts or governmental subdivisions of the county; (2) the election of all commissioners-at-large, though sometimes there is a requirement of residency

[9] U.S. Department of Commerce, Bureau of the Census, *Governing Boards of County Governments, 1965* (Washington, D.C.: Government Printing Office, 1965), pp. 1–5.

within a district.[10] The census bureau estimates that less than 20 per cent of the counties choose all of their governing board members by the at-large process; and (3) a combination of the first two systems providing for some board members at-large and part by the district method. While some students of local government advocate election at large, the selection of county board members by township or district is vehemently defended on the contention that geographical representation will allow local interests or those interests peculiar to a specific locality to be better represented. This claim is not as valid in a homogeneous county as in one having both highly urbanized as well as rural areas. Election from townships or other types of county subdivisions can present a danger in that the governing body will fail to consider problems in the light of general county considerations and will respond more favorably to the politics of the local subdivisions.

Terms of offices for the members of county boards vary from one year for township supervisors in Michigan to eight years for county judges in Tennessee. The great majority are elected for a term of four years with some cases of two, three, or six years. In most instances the same length of term is given to all board members. In just a slight majority of the counties the terms are staggered so that only a portion of the membership will expire in any one year.

## Size of County Boards

The size of the county governing bodies varies considerably. As a general rule, the number of members ranges from three to nine with the largest number of these agencies being composed of either three or five members. There are certain extremes that must be considered. In a few states—particularly in Arizona, Georgia, and South Carolina—it is occasionally possible for a single individual to perform the functions normally assigned to a multimembered organization. In Vermont, and a few other areas, the tasks are carried out by an agency composed of only two members. At the other extreme are some counties where the membership exceeds 30 or even 50 or more individuals. The largest boards are normally found in those counties using the township supervisor system in which each township is represented regardless of size, with additional membership being granted to the populous areas.[11]

[10] In Indiana, where the county is divided into three commissioner districts, all three commissioners are elected at large by all of the county voters but each commissioner must reside in a separate district.

[11] U.S. Department of Commerce, Bureau of the Census, *County Boards and Commissions* (Washington, D.C.: Government Printing Office, 1947), p. 4.

## Organization of County Governing Bodies

Two principal officers are associated with the county board: the chairman, or president, and the clerk. In most situations the chairman or president is elected from among the membership of the board for a one-year term at the organizational meeting of the group which occurs at the board's first regular session of each year. In many counties the election is actually on a "rotation" basis but this system can be interrupted by the interjection of partisan politics. Election of a chairman by the board membership is the system followed by boards of commissioners or supervisors and boards composed of township supervisors which include over two-thirds of all county governing bodies. In those boards having judges and commissioners and judge and justices of the peace, the chairmanship is an ex officio position. In these instances the county judge serves as the chairman as a result of his judicial position. In a few counties the presiding officer is elected to this position by the voters.

The powers of the presiding officer of a county governing body are in general limited to the following activities: (1) serving as the nominal presiding officer and signing official documents on behalf of the board; (2) since in so many situations the chairman is a member of the board he may vote on any issue but then he has no casting vote in case of a tie; and (3) his major influence lies in the prestige status of his position rather than in his ability to appoint and remove administrative personnel or to exercise the veto power. Therefore, the chairman or president of the county board is not in any position to serve as the chief executive officer of the county.

The clerk of the county governing body is normally one of the regular elective county officers who by law serves in this additional post. The position of county clerk or auditor is the most commonly designated officer to serve as clerk of the board. The principal duties of the clerk are: (1) to prepare the agenda for board meetings; and (2) to keep the minutes of board proceedings, including a formal record of all resolutions, ordinances, and other types of official action taken.

In the more populous counties the large governing bodies make extensive use of an elaborate system of standing committees, paralleling to a major degree their utilization in state legislatures and city councils. The board chairman or president is usually granted the power to appoint the personnel of these committees. Although political parties play a lesser role at this level, many committees and committee chairmanships are controlled by the dominant party. The number of committees has a tendency to reflect the actual size of the board which determines the number and type of committees through its bylaws or procedural rules. Among the committees most county boards create are those on ways and means, roads and bridges, salaries and fees, public buildings, jails and county homes, public assistance, public health, and claims.

## Sessions of Boards

The regular sessions of a county board are held at periodic intervals prescribed by constitutional provisions, state statutes, or by rule of the board. As a general procedure many boards will meet regularly once a month, with smaller boards meeting more frequently since in the larger boards much of the administrative work is actually carried on by committees. As an example, the Illinois law provides for five regular meetings per year in the case of three-member boards of commissioners, but only two meetings for those boards composed of township supervisors. Many county boards, those particularly limited to a specific number of meetings, take advantage of the technique of the adjourned session. If a board at a regular session feels that the group should reconvene prior to the next scheduled regular session, this can be accomplished through the adjourned session. Therefore an adjourned meeting is viewed as a continuation of the regular session that began on an earlier date. Special sessions of the board are to be distinguished from regular and adjourned sessions. In the first instance, special sessions may be called in a variety of ways: by the presiding officer, by a designated county officer on his own authority, or by a specific number of the board members. The decision as to when the public interest demands a special session of the board is left to the discretion of the proper officers or the members authorized to call the session. Usually a special session may accomplish any act that is not required to be performed at a regular session, but there are some instances when the board must consider only those items listed in the call for the special session. The general public can usually attend all meetings of the county board but ordinarily few citizens do.

## Powers of the County Board

The powers exercised by county governing bodies, while varying widely among the states, are usually delegated to the board by state statutes although in certain instances some authority is conferred by provisions of the state constitution. County boards, like other creatures of state law, are limited in their legal competence and have only those powers that have been delegated to them by law, either expressed or implied. Many state laws also indicate the methods that must be followed by the board in the exercising of a particular power or duty, and if that procedure is not adhered to the action taken will be held void. While state laws will normally specify those powers to be exercised by the board, the county governing body is also the corporate authority of the county and becomes "the repository of all powers conferred by law upon the county without designation of the officer through which they shall be exercised."[12] The county governing body is an agency of our governmental system that ignores the principle of separation of powers. County boards commonly possess both administrative and legislative powers and in some instances even minor judicial powers.

The county board is popularly referred to as the legislature for the county. This title is a misnomer unless the following two items are observed: (1) while those legislative powers that are possessed by county governing bodies are normally vested in the board, the county is primarily an agent of the state to assist in giving uniformity to the application of state-wide laws and therefore the county, as a quasi-municipal corporation, has only a few full-fledged legislative powers; and (2) the board has been usually viewed by the courts as primarily an administrative unit and not one that is exclusively legislative in nature. The more important legislative powers are those relating to finance and regulatory control. The county board is an agency that levies taxes (determines the tax rate), votes appropriations, and incurs debts for the county, all subject to authority and limitations contained in state constitutions and statutes. In the regulatory area the county board is concerned with the issuance of licenses and permits which control certain business activities in the unincorporated parts of the county such as liquor dispensing establishments, amusement parks, dance halls, carnivals and circuses, and various sporting events. The board may also pass health ordinances and zoning regulations. Frequently counties are authorized to pass and enforce police, sanitary, and other local regulations that are not in conflict with the general laws of the state but in actual practice this has been an infrequently used power.

The administrative powers of the county board, while quite varied and subject to a considerable degree of state control and supervision, constitute the major share of the work performed by this central agency of county government. An important administrative function of the county governing body involves the responsibility for and the control over county property. The board is concerned with the actual administration of the courthouse, the county jail, the county home, the county hospital and many other types of county property. Also the board is responsible for constructing, equipping, and maintaining county facilities, the purchasing of real estate, the leasing of county property, entering into contracts on behalf of the county, and the settling of claims against the county. An-

[12] Clyde F. Snider, *Local Government in Rural America* (New York: Appleton-Century-Crofts, Inc., 1957), p. 132.

other important function of the county board in many areas is the supervision of major county programs particularly in relation to roads and
public assistance. Often county boards are criticized on the point that they
spend too much time in the supervision of the road and highway programs and thereby neglect other important responsibilities. A third major
administrative responsibility of county boards concerns its activities in the
personnel field. Boards quite frequently are given the power to appoint
some county officers, to confirm the appointments of deputy county officers or assistants, and to fill vacancies in certain elective positions. In
addition, the boards may be able to fix the salaries of county officers and
employees within the limitations established by state laws. A fourth activity of the boards is in connection with the county serving as an election
district for the state in which the board is called upon to establish the
boundaries of election districts, appoint officers to conduct the elections,
and provide for polling places and equipment.

The judicial powers of a county board are relatively unimportant. Some
county boards have been designated as courts of record and are empowered to compel obedience to their orders by using a compulsory
power, such as attachment, or by punishing contempt by imprisonment
or fine. Under the Missouri Constitution of 1875 the county governing
body was listed as a constitutional court of record with authority to issue
writs of habeas corpus and hold hearings thereon, to issue injunctions
under certain conditions, and to punish for contempt. With the adoption
of the 1945 state constitution the county governing body in Missouri is no
longer vested with judicial authority and became an agency concerned
with only legislative and administrative functions.

## Compensation of Members

The members of county governing bodies are usually paid an annual
salary or granted a per diem allowance. Either amount is fixed by law or
arrived at by the body itself but within statutory or constitutional limitations. The annual salaries range from about $100 in the small rural coun-
ties to several thousand dollars in a few of the more populous counties.
In the latter situation membership on a board is considered a full-time
job in which members are expected to devote a specific number of hours
to county business. Per diem allowances vary from $5 to $10 for time
actually spent in attendance at board meetings or while on committee
work. In certain states, board members, under the per diem form of compensation, are limited by law to a specific number of days per month or
year for which pay may be given. Members are sometimes allowed mileage for travel to and from board meetings, committee sessions, and other
travel incidental to the conduct of county business.

## PROPOSED REORGANIZATION OF THE COUNTY

### County Consolidation

Consolidation is a proposal for the modernization of county government that has received some attention but one for which little progress can be recorded. While many studies have been made of the possibility of county consolidation, only two such actions involving organized counties have occurred since the turn of the century.[13] In Tennessee, in 1919, James County was united with Hamilton County while in Georgia, in 1932, Milton and Campbell counties were consolidated with Fulton County. In South Dakota two unorganized counties were eliminated when the legislature consolidated the unorganized county of Washington with that of Shannon and annexed the unorganized county of Armstrong to the organized county of Dewey. The voters in Alabama, in 1957, approved a constitutional amendment which authorized the state legislature to eliminate Macon County by dividing it among neighboring counties.

The proponents for county consolidation contend that some counties are inefficient units of local government due, among other things, to their size and inadequate financial resources. While several factors may have contributed to the paucity of county consolidations, the following statement undoubtedly reflects a basic reason for its rare adoption: "Consolidation often seems to be a logical solution, but political decisions are often illogical. The people of one county may be willing to merge with another, providing the *other* county gives up its county seat, courthouse, and officeholders."[14] Local citizens, county officials, and politicians cannot view with favor the possibility of losing their local county identity.

### County Executive

One of the outstanding weaknesses of county government, and perhaps the most serious one at the present time, is the lack of a single chief executive who is vested with the power of supervision or direction over all general county functions. This fact is in direct contradition of almost every other level of government in the United States where the national government has a president as its chief executive, each state has its popu-

---

[13] Some of the more important studies are: S. R. Heckart and G. S. Klemmedson, *County Consolidation in Colorado* (Fort Collins: Colorado Agricultural College, 1933); V. G. Sorrell and J. R. Stuard, *County Consolidation in New Mexico* (Albuquerque: University of New Mexico, 1934; and the Nevada Legislative Counsel Bureau, *County Consolidation and Reorganization in Nevada,* 1948.

[14] Marguerite J. Fisher and Donald G. Bishop, *Municipal and Other Local Governments* (New York: Prentice-Hall, Inc., 1950), p. 627.

larly elected governor, and most municipalities have a mayor or a manager as their executive officer. Yet in the average county there is no single officer who can serve as a counterpart to the above listed officials in the other echelons of government. The general governing body of the county —usually designated as the county board of supervisors—must serve in a dual capacity of exercising legislative and administrative responsibilities. In order to overcome this outstanding deficiency in county government many proposals and plans have been suggested that would perhaps have a tendency to provide for some type of a county executive. While these suggestions vary greatly with respect to details, four definite systems have been advanced and even adopted in certain counties:[15]

1. Strengthen the position of one of the traditional elective county officers, usually the county clerk, by the addition of general supervisory functions.
2. Provide for an elective county chief executive.
3. Provide for an appointive administrative officer who is clothed with administrative authority that is less extensive than a full-fledged manager.
4. Adopt the county-manager plan.

**The County Clerk as County Executive.** A few counties have clothed one of the traditional, popularly elected county officers with some of the powers usually associated with a chief administrator or executive officer. In many instances, the county clerk, where the office exists, is the officer called upon to serve in this new capacity. This is normally the result of the close interrelationship that presently exists between his duties and those of a proposed county administrative officer. Usually the county clerk: (1) serves as the secretary to the county governing body; (2) keeps the record of the financial transactions of the county; (3) frequently performs at least an informal preaudit of claims against the county; and (4) serves as the officer in charge of the position that is viewed by many as the "center of county administration." In this latter situation the county board has a tendency to depend rather heavily upon the advice and opinion of the county clerk, especially with regard to routine county affairs.

The State of Wisconsin has undoubtedly made the greatest progress of any state in establishing the county clerk as a county administrator. Not only does the clerk serve as the secretary to the county board and its committees but he has in many instances been called upon to: (1) prepare the preliminary budget; (2) serve as county purchasing agent; (3) keep the financial records of the county; (4) preaudit all bills coming before the county board for approval or rejection; and (5) serve as the official accountant for the county.[16] The fact cannot be overlooked that

[15] Edward W. Weidner, "A Review of the Controversy over County Executives," *Public Administration Review,* Vol. VIII (Winter, 1948), pp. 18–28.
[16] L. H. Adolfson, "The County Clerk as 'Manager,'" *National Municipal Review,* Vol. XXXIV (March, 1945), pp. 125–28.

even where a county clerk has not been vested with the official title of county executive he can establish for himself a solid administrative position through the mere utilization of the above mentioned financial and administrative functions. In some Wisconsin counties the chairman of the county board, rather than the clerk, assumes these functions and in fact becomes the county administrator.[17]

In some states county officers other than the clerk have had a tendency to serve to a degree as the central county officer or as a limited county executive. In Indiana, the elective auditor serves in many respects as a county administrator if there is no county clerk. These functions of the auditor are: (1) serving as the clerk or secretary to both the board of county commissioners and the county fiscal body, the county council; (2) assisting in the preparation of the county budget; and (3) performing certain tasks with regard to the enforcement of the budget that are usually duties of a comptroller.[18] In North Carolina a few counties have provided for the board chairman to serve as a full-time officer and have granted him the responsibilities of a chief executive.[19] The county judge in Arkansas has been assigned those administrative duties normally given in most states to the central governing body. Even though the Arkansas county judge in this role begins to approach that of a chief executive, a large amount of administrative power is still granted to other elected county officers.[20] In Alabama, the probate judge of some counties can assume, at times, a position virtually equal to that of a county chief executive, but his exact position depends upon a combination of his own personality and leadership abilities and the provisions of the statutes.[21]

**Elective County Executives.** Some counties have established, under varying titles, the position of an elective chief executive. However, this official corresponds more closely to that of a mayor under the mayor-council type of government than that of a city manager. These popularly elected county executives are granted various types of administrative responsibilities and quite frequently can exercise the suspensive veto power over certain types of action undertaken by the county board.

[17] *Ibid.*, pp. 125–28.

[18] Clyde F. Snider and Max M. Sappenfield, "County and Township Government in Indiana," *Report of the Indiana State Committee on Governmental Economy* (Indianapolis, 1935), pp. 103–4.

[19] Paul W. Wager (ed.), *County Government across the Nation* (Chapel Hill: University of North Carolina Press, 1950), p. 410.

[20] Edward W. Reed and Henry M. Alexander, *The Government and Finance of Counties in Arkansas* (Fayetteville: University of Arkansas Bureau of Business and Economic Research, 1953), p. 24.

[21] Karl A. Bosworth, *Black Belt County: Rural Government in the Cotton Country of Alabama* (University: University of Alabama Bureau of Public Administration, 1941), pp. 33–39, 110–11; and *Tennessee Valley County: Rural Government in the Hill Country of Alabama* (University: University of Alabama Bureau of Public Administration, 1941), pp. 21–22.

One of the earliest types of this form of county executive is that of the president of the Cook County (Chicago), Illinois, county board which dates from the late 1800's. The Cook County governing body is a fifteen-member board of commissioners, one of whom is elected to serve dually as a commissioner and as board president. The president not only serves as the presiding officer of the board but he has been granted some additional powers, particularly in the areas of appointments and the use of the veto power. First of all, the president, with the concurrence of the board, appoints many county officers including the attorney, auditor, director of public welfare, and superintendent of highways. However, he appoints on his own the members of the county civil service commission. With respect to fiscal responsibility, every action of the board which creates a contract, appropriates money, or in any way establishes a fiscal liability on behalf of the county must be approved by the president after it has been adopted by the board. The president also exercises a suspensive veto power. When he disapproves a measure he must return the document within five days to the clerk of the board with his written objections. This presidential veto can be overcome by a four-fifths vote by the board. Lastly, the president, in his own discretion, can call special meetings of the county board.[22]

Hudson and Essex counties in New Jersey have provided for popularly-elected executives under the title of county supervisor. The "county executive" in these two counties, while lacking the power of appointment, is nominally charged with the supervision of subordinate officials and employees and may remove or suspend county employees for neglect of duty or insubordination. Aggrieved employees in turn may appeal to the state civil service commission or to the courts. The county supervisor, however, does not serve as a fiscal officer since he has no control over expenditures and plays no part in the preparation of the budget. With respect to the legislative functions, the supervisor has the responsibility of recommending to the county governing body—the board of freeholders—those measures which he believes are necessary. His veto power is also of the suspensive variety and can be overridden by a two-thirds vote of all board members. The supervisor attends the meetings of the board of freeholders and is granted all the privileges of a member of the board but cannot vote.[23]

In the 1930's the counties of Westchester and Nassau in New York adopted special legislative charters that provided for an elective chief

[22] Clyde F. Snider, *County Government in Illinois* (Springfield: Illinois Tax Commission, 1943), pp. 59–60.

[23] James M. Collier, *County Government in New Jersey* (New Brunswick, N.J.: Rutgers University Press, 1952), pp. 16–17; and "Elected County Chief Executives in New Jersey," *The County Officer*, Vol. XX (February, 1955), pp. 47–48.

officer entitled the county executive.[24] A home-rule charter adoption by St. Louis County, Missouri, in 1950 provides for an elective county supervisor to serve as that unit's chief executive officer.[25] The position of the St. Louis county executive is actually stronger than those in New Jersey primarily because of his control and direction over administrative affairs. In 1956 a home-rule charter was adopted by Baltimore County, Maryland, which includes the popularly-elected position of "county executive." The charter stipulated that this officer is to be the "chief executive officer of the county and the official head of the county government." One very interesting item about the Baltimore County arrangement is the fact that this county executive, with the approval of the county council, appoints a county administrative officer, who, in turn, appoints the department heads with the consent of the county executive.

**Appointive Administrative Officer.** The counties of California have been very active in the movement that proposes the creation of a "quasi" manager or of an office that possesses less administrative power than those of an orthodox manager. At the present time over half of the fifty-seven counties in California have established some kind of an appointive chief administrative officer in an attempt to achieve a higher degree of integration in county governmental activities. This official is appointed by and responsible to the elective county board of supervisors. However, in California only charter counties may legally create the post of county manager who is given a large measure of administrative authority including his ability to appoint and to remove the heads of some of the county departments.[26] Both charter and general law California counties may establish the position of chief administrative officer who is primarily an agent of the county board of supervisors. Professor John C. Bollens notes that, in a general sense, there are only two important formal differences between a manager and a chief administrative officer in California counties. First of all, managers are usually authorized to prepare the budget for submission to the county board, whereas the chief administrative officer is ordinarily limited to the mere collection of departmental estimates and the transmission of these details with perhaps a few of his own suggestions to the county governing body. Secondly, managers have usually been invested with the particular power to appoint and to remove department heads and certain other types of personnel. Usually chief administrative

[24] *Laws of New York* (1936), regular session, chap. 879 (Nassau); *ibid.* (1937), chap. 617 (Westchester).

[25] *Charter for St. Louis County, Missouri* (1950), Arts. III, IV.

[26] In 1963 only three counties—Sacramento, Santa Clara, and San Mateo—had county managers. At the present time in California there are ten charter counties, forty-seven standard or general-law counties, and the consolidated city-county of San Francisco, which also has a home-rule charter.

officers can only make recommendations concerning appointments and removals to the county board.[27] While the legal differences between these two types of administrative officers can become rather blurred, managers do exercise a direct legal grant of administrative power with respect to the issues of finance and personnel whereas chief administrative officers have to operate indirectly through their ability to make recommendations to the county governing body.

The first California county to provide for the position of chief administrative officer was that of Los Angeles, where in 1938 the system was adopted and the office was established by ordinance. This post, now popularly referred to under the abbreviated title of CAO, is filled by appointment of the county board of supervisors. In Figure 4–1 the administrative organization of the county of Los Angeles is diagrammatically depicted.

**The County Manager Plan.** By 1963 only twenty-six of the more than 3,000 counties had adopted the county manager form of government. It is now possible in seventeen states for counties to use this form of government either by charter or the permissive laws and constitutional provisions.

County manager government, which began in 1930 in Durham County, North Carolina, is patterned upon the council-manager system used in nearly 2,000 American municipalities. The principle feature is: the county board of supervisors, usually three, five, or seven, serve as the policy-determining body with power to appoint an executive, the county manager, who assumes the responsibility for all administrative activities.

The county board, elected by the residents of the county either at large or by districts, is vested with whatever ordinance-making power that is granted to the county by the state. It makes the determination of what projects shall be undertaken by the county officials and is the final authority on appropriations, taxes, budgetary matters, and personnel, within the limitations set by the state. The major appointment made by the board is that of the county manager. He usually serves without a stipulated term of office with the board being able to discharge him at any time. He is selected solely on the basis of his qualifications as an administrator.

The county manager is ordinarily charged with five major administrative tasks:

1. To enforce the ordinances and resolutions adopted by the board.
2. To appoint and supervise his principal subordinates in the administrative units.
3. To prepare the annual budget for submission to the board.
4. To attend board meetings in order to answer any questions that may arise and advise the members on procedure.

[27] John C. Bollens, *Appointed Executive Local Government: The California Experience* (Los Angeles, Haynes Foundation, 1952), pp. 119–23.

5. To make recommendations to the board concerning administrative matters.[28]

The supervision of the county administration is the responsibility of the county manager. He is permitted to select his own department heads and other personnel in the administrative units, as per any civil service rules and regulations that may apply. Emphasis is placed upon professionally qualified administrative personnel.

The model county manager charter provides that the board shall appoint the manager and have authority to remove him by a simple majority vote after a notice has been presented to the administrator citing the reasons for his dismissal. The charter requires that the manager be given a public hearing before his dismissal is final, assuming that he desires to have such an audience.

There can be little doubt that in most counties there is a need for a single executive to co-ordinate the various administrative activities. The proponents of county manager government believe that this can best be accomplished through an appointed executive. The plan envisions a shorter county ballot, thus reducing the work of the voter in the election and relieving him of the task of selecting administrative personnel.

The statement of the National Municipal League is much to the point as it claims county manager government abolishes overlapping functions and jurisdictional conflicts. "All responsibility is placed on the shoulders of one executive, the manager, whose performance can easily be judged by the commissioners and the public."[29]

Almost every county that has utilized this new form of county government has reported favorably upon the reaction of not only the employees but also the public. Studies in Virginia, New York, and California all tell of greater efficiency and substantial money savings. Stressed by at least one study was the enhancement of popular control and improved governmental reporting that accompanied the change to this format.[30]

It is difficult to explain the reluctance of some 3,000 counties to change to what would appear to be a more efficient, more economical, and more public responsive form of government. One of the most influential arguments raised against the new plan would seem to be that the county is

28 Snider, *Local Government in Rural America, op. cit.*, p. 173.

29 National Municipal League, *The County Manager Plan* (New York: National Municipal League, 1950), p. 10.

30 F. H. Heller, "The Case for a County Manager," *Your Government,* University of Kansas Research Center, Vol. IX, No. 4 (December 15, 1953); James E. Pate, "Virginia Counties Turn Cities," *National Municipal Review,* Vol. XLI (September, 1952), pp. 387–89; George W. Spicer, *Fifteen Years of County Manager Government in Virginia* (Charlottesville: University of Virginia Extension, 1951); and George W. Spicer, "Manager Counties Evaluated," *National Municipal Review,* Vol. XLII (July, 1953), pp. 331–37.

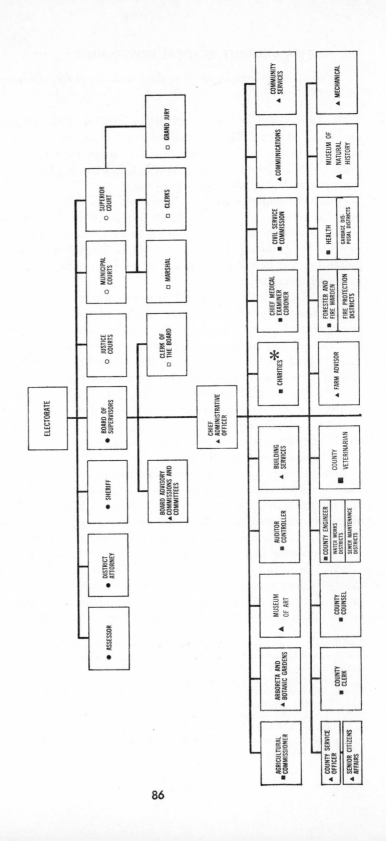

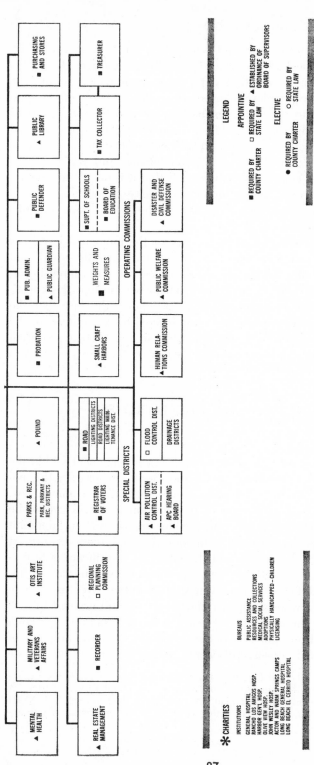

**Fig. 4–1.** Organizational Chart of the County of Los Angeles, 1965. (Source: Office of Chief Administrative Officer, County of Los Angeles, 1965.)

merely a subdivision of the state, and as such it is so closely supervised by state officials that a local administrator is not needed and would result in paying a salary for a service that state government will perform. The vested interests of the popularly elected "row officers" is obviously challenged by changing to the county manager plan and therefore most of this group actively opposes any shift to a new system. The so-called "county court house gang" is usually so well entrenched that any reform organization finds it difficult to bring about change unless the county government has been confronted with a crisis that it is unable to contain. If a scandal, such as embezzlement or a serious misappropriation of funds occurs, the efforts for moving toward a new method of selecting administrators is naturally enhanced.

The manager plan, whether at the county or the municipal level, has been challenged by many opponents as being undemocratic—usually on the basis that it provides for an appointive executive who cannot be directly held accountable by the electorate. This assertion that this constitutes an undemocratic mode of government ignores the fact that the county manager is held accountable by the elected representatives of the people, the board of supervisors, who should be in a much better position than the average voter to ascertain the worth of the chief executive's programs and their execution.[31]

## COUNTY OFFICERS AND EMPLOYEES

### The Sheriff

The most important officer concerned with law enforcement within the county and particularly the rural area is the sheriff. Historically this position is one of the oldest to be associated with English common law. While the exact date of the origin of the position of sheriff cannot be given, it is known that its predecessor, the shire reeve, was an important officer of the English shire as early as the middle of the tenth century. At one time in the early development of the office, the sheriff not only performed law enforcement activities but was also involved in various administrative, judicial, financial, and even military duties. Eventually these latter responsibilities were stripped from the sheriff and granted to new officers, particularly the justice of the peace and the coroner. In England, at the time of American colonization, the sheriff's job was primarily one of preserving the peace, keeping prisoners, and serving as an aid to the

[31] John C. Bollens, *Appointed Executive Local Government: The California Experience* (Los Angeles: Haynes Foundation, 1952), pp. 176–85; and Kirk H. Porter, "A Wet Blanket on the County Manager Plan," *National Municipal Review*, Vol. XVIII (January, 1929), pp. 5–8, for two conflicting views as to the promise of county appointed executive officers.

judiciary. These same functions were placed with the office of sheriff as it was originally established in the United States, and these duties have for the most part been retained to the present time.[32] If the position of sheriff is declining slightly it is undoubtedly the result of two major trends that have been occurring in local law enforcement. First, some general law enforcement activities that were placed in the hands of county sheriffs by state law are now being transferred to the state police units that are in a better position, both in terms of personnel and equipment, to perform these activities. Nevertheless, in a highly urbanized area such as Los Angeles County, the sheriff's office is one of the best trained and highly organized police units in the United States. Secondly, the urbanization movement has actually placed more police responsibilities in the hands of municipal police departments, and sheriffs have been willing to allow city police to carry on all law enforcement and crime control in the incorporated areas. By state law, however, the sheriff is still given in most instances the legal power to enforce state laws and county ordinances in all local units of government within the county.

While the English sheriff was an appointed official, the American sheriff is usually elected for a two- or four-year term. In New York City a single sheriff is appointed by the mayor under civil service provisions for the five counties. The law is normally silent with respect to the qualifications that must be possessed by a sheriff, and choice by popular election does not assure that the sheriff will be an individual who possesses any training, experience, or background for the office. In some states constitutional provisions stipulate that a sheriff may not serve for more than two terms or cannot succeed himself. In actual practice this does not prevent a sheriff and his chief deputy from switching jobs every two or four years! The sheriff may be paid a specified salary, receive certain fees, or a combination of these two methods. The present trend is in favor of giving the sheriff a stipulated salary and requiring him to turn into the county treasury all of the fees he collects.

The present-day activities of the sheriff can usually be placed in three major classifications: (1) he serves as the preservor of law and order within his county; (2) he is the administrator of the county jail; and (3) he acts as an officer or aid to the county court or the courts of record within the county. In some states a collection of varied activities not closely related to law enforcement has been given to the sheriff. One of the most common of these duties relates to the sheriff serving ex officio as the tax collector and the officer who sells property for delinquent taxes.

As previously indicated, the outstanding function of the sheriff is to serve as the conservator of the peace within his county. In this respect he

---

[32] Theodore F. T. Plucknett, "Sheriff," *Encyclopaedia of the Social Sciences* (New York: The Macmillan Co., 1934; Thirteenth Printing, 1959), Vol. XIV, pp. 20–22.

not only maintains law and order but he must find and arrest the law-breakers and suppress disorder of all kinds. When he feels that he and his staff of deputies cannot cope with a situation, the sheriff is given the ability to summon the *posse comitatus,* or "power of the county." Actually the posse consists of those individuals the sheriff calls upon to assist him, and normally penalties can be invoked against any individual who refuses to answer the sheriff's call to duty.

A second major duty of the county sheriff is to serve as the administrator of the county jail. In many cases his custody of the prisoners involves him in providing for the meals of the jail inmates. In some areas he receives a fee or stipulated sum for each prisoner which is viewed by most students of jail administration as a very reprehensible practice since it can result in inadequate care of the prisoners and substandard meals. The custody of prisoners on behalf of a sheriff involves him in a legal duty of protecting their health and life. In some states a sheriff may be removed from office if he permits a prisoner to be taken from his care and lynched. In some counties the fee system for the care and protection of county jail inmates has been abolished and a separate position of county jailer has been created.

The last major responsibility of the sheriff is his role as a court officer. Most of this activity concerns the sheriff in serving legal processes. These include warrants of arrest, summonses to jurors, and subpoenas to witnesses. In some states he conducts tax sales or foreclosures and confiscates illegal and abandoned property, and he may even be called upon to issue certain types of licenses. In criminal cases this usually involves the sheriff in keeping in his custody in the county jail those individuals who have been given short sentences for misdemeanors. He may be called upon to deliver individuals to state penal institutions and in some states the sheriff has to execute the death sentence of a prisoner from his county.

The office of county sheriff is so much a part of our political tradition that its abolition or substantial reduction in responsibilities in the near future is very unlikely. There is always the possibility that certain reforms might be introduced, such as making the sheriff an integral part of a reorganized county law enforcement unit or a member of the state police system. If this should occur, as it has in some urban counties, then the sheriff should be relieved of many of his miscellaneous tasks not basically associated with law enforcement activities.

## County Attorney

The structuring of the law office for the county has tended to present at times a rather complicated and confused picture. This is undoubtedly due to the fact that the duties of the county law office in some states are divided into two major categories which sometimes necessitates the presence of two separate officers while in others the two positions are represented by one individual. These two major duties of the county law officer are: (1) the enforcement of criminal law; and (2) the rendering of legal advice to county officers concerning their duties and powers and conducting civil cases to which the county may be a party, either as plaintiff or defendant. The county prosecuting attorney is concerned with criminal law while a county attorney works with the civil cases and provides the legal advice. Yet in some areas the functions are combined under one officer who is known in the various states as prosecuting attorney, county attorney, state's attorney, district attorney, or even perhaps as solicitor.

The role of the prosecuting attorney in the enforcement of criminal law is very important from the viewpoint of effective law enforcement. When a crime is committed it is the duty of this attorney to investigate, collect evidence, institute formal proceedings, and represent the county or state at the trial. In this phase of law enforcement the prosecuting attorneys must work very closely with county sheriffs, grand juries, and other local police officers. In those states using the technique of a grand jury for indicting persons suspected of serious crimes, evidence is usually presented by the prosecuting attorney. Other times the prosecuting attorney, as an alternative to grand jury indictment, will file an "information," which is an alternative method of bringing criminal charges. It is still, in either situation, primarily the prosecuting attorney who determines what persons will or will not be charged for crimes. After charges have been filed, the prosecuting attorney is responsible for conducting the prosecution.

The second major role of the county law officer is concerned with advising county officers, conducting civil suits on behalf of the county, or defending the county when civil actions are brought against it, examining legal documents particularly those relating to real estate titles, bond forms, and writing contracts.

The position of county law officer is one that is filled by popular election in about three-fourths of the states including even those states that view the position as a state office. Where the position is primarily one of advising county officers and representing the county in civil cases, appointment by the county board is sometimes followed. In many localities the post is held by a young lawyer, only recently graduated from law school, who uses the position to gain experience and to have a source of income until his own private practice is well established. Sometimes older attorneys will accept the post when their private practices have slackened. In some counties the office is used as the beginning step for politically ambitious lawyers.

## County Treasurer

The position of county treasurer is present in most of the states and is popularly elected in approximately three-fourths of the states. In others the position is usually filled by appointment by the county board. The major functions of a county treasurer fall into three classes: (1) receiving county revenues; (2) serving as the custodian of county funds; and (3) disbursing county moneys as required by law. In the receiving of county funds the treasurer collects the general property tax not only for the county but for various governmental subdivisions within the county and also for the state when such a tax is levied. After collecting the tax the county treasurer remits the proper share or portion to the appropriate units of government. In a few states the sheriff serves as the property tax collector while in others a county collector, other than the treasurer, is present. While other officers of the county do collect certain types of revenues, many authorities maintain that the county treasurer's office should become a centralized collection point for all county income and for all governmental subdivisions within a county, including special districts. Such a system could simplify the administration of the financial affairs within the county and aid in the preparation of financial reports. It must be noted, however, that in a few states the position of county treasurer has either been abolished or merged with some other office and in turn banks have been selected to serve as receiving and disbursing officers for county funds.

In order to protect the general public against losses of funds by county treasurers through mistakes, negligence, or dishonesty, two major sets of requirements have been placed in operation in many of our states. First, county treasurers are required to be bonded for an amount that would be sufficient to cover any possible losses. Secondly, states have passed county depository laws which provide that the county board, or a special finance board, select certain banks which will be listed as official depositories. Treasurers are required to deposit public funds in these banks and the county receives a stipulated amount of interest. Before the passage of these laws many county treasurers personally received the interest paid by banks on deposited public funds. In addition, a few states have provided that county treasurers cannot succeed themselves or serve no more than two successive terms. Usually where this provision is present some method of circumventing it has been devised. Often the deputy and the treasurer will trade off running for the office, or the county sheriff, who is often similarly restricted, will trade positions on the ballot with the county treasurer. Evidently these provisions have been established in order to secure accountability on the part of county treasurers since in actual practice in some states a complete audit of the financial books occurs only with a change of officeholder. However, at the present time most states are requiring an annual audit of the treasurer's books.

## County Clerk

The position of county clerk exists in approximately one-half of the states and is typically filled by popular election. The duties, while varying from state to state, have a tendency to follow these lines of responsibility: (1) serving as secretary to the county governing body; (2) issuing warrants against the county; (3) preparing, receiving, and filing various types of documents; and (4) performing certain functions with respect to the administration of elections.

The function of serving as secretary to the county board is viewed by many students of local government as the principal duty of the county clerk. As a result, certain authorities have contended that the clerk should be appointed by the county board. In addition, in some states, the clerk also functions as the clerk of court for many county courts of record. All in all, the position tends to become a clearing agency for general county business. The financial role of the county clerk is a very interesting one. If the county does not provide for an auditor or a comptroller, claims against the county are filed with the clerk for transmittal to the county board. After the claims have been examined and approved by the board, warrants are drawn by the clerk upon the county treasurer for countersignature and payment. The county clerk does not possess or share in any of the legal responsibility in the allowance of claims against the county. It must be recognized, however, that in actual practice the clerk is in a position to make a recommendation to the board that is quite likely to be accepted by that body. This is due to the fact that the clerk will ordinarily go over all the claims before presenting them to the board, and the clerk has all the records available to check the validity of each claim to determine whether the services have been performed or the goods or products delivered. In the third instance, the clerk's office serves as a depository for official records, books, and papers of the county. In addition, the clerk will accept and file papers relating to mortgages, leases, deeds, divorce records, adoption papers, and other similar documents. In some states a separate postion of recorder or register of deeds exists, and all documents pertaining to land and property transactions will be filed in that office. Also in many states the clerk will issue hunting and fishing licenses, marriage licenses, birth certificates, and even citizenship and naturalization papers.

## The Coroner–Medical Examiner

The office of coroner, next to that of sheriff, is one of the oldest in operation in American local government in terms of continuous historical development. Originally known as *custos placitorum coronae,* or guardian of the pleasures of the crown, this title was gradually shortened to "crowner" and then to coroner.[33] In early France the coroner was charged with maintaining the rights of the private property of the crown and as such became an important officer of the royal household. The office was first instituted in England in 1194, actually as a post to aid, and yet at the same time to serve as a check upon, the sheriff. The duties of the first coroners were not too exact and explicit. They assisted sheriffs in the determination of civil cases, in holding inquests, and in presiding over the coroner's jury. In addition, they served as committing magistrates, recording confessions, and performed other civil and law-enforcement functions. Early English coroners also kept records pertaining to criminal justice and collected the goods and chattels of criminals, shipwrecks, and treasure troves for the crown.

The major function of the present-day coroner in America is that of conducting an inquest in the case of a death that occurred under suspicious circumstances, by violence, by accident, or when no physician was in attendance. The inquest is held in an effort to determine the cause of death and to decide whether or not a crime has been committed. If evidence of murder is found, the perpetrator of the crime is sought by the proper authority and all conditions relating to the death are studied and an autopsy may be held. The official findings of the coroner are not usually admissible as evidence before a trial jury, but he is charged to collect and retain all evidence that might aid the prosecuting attorney or a grand jury in determining which criminal charges are to be perferred.

It is permissive in some states and mandatory in others for coroners to convene a "coroner's jury" which is composed typically of six members. The coroner presides over these deliberations and plays a major role in that he actually must combine the talents of a physician and an attorney. As a medical examiner he is supposed to be able to determine the cause of death; as a presiding officer he must conduct the meeting, examine witnesses, and give instructions to the jury. At the end of the inquiry the coroner's jury deliberates and returns its verdict.

In 1953, forty-four of the states filled the office of county coroner by popular election but ten years later only seventeen states called for the election of this official. In many of the states that have turned from the

[33] Harold F. Alderfer, *American Local Government and Administration* (New York: The Macmillan Co., 1956), p. 53.

elective role the requirement is now that the officer, now commonly called medical examiner, must be a qualified physician.[34]

## County Auditor

The position of auditor is found in county governments in about one-third of our states, and while usually an elective position, it is in some instances filled by appointment by either the county board, the courts, or by some other method. The principal function of the county auditor is usually concerned with the preparation of budgets and the maintaining of accounts for the county. A second duty of the auditor is the receiving and examining of claims against the county and subsequently making a recommendation to the board for payment or rejection. This task involves the auditor in what is known as the preaudit since it occurs before the claim is paid. In this type of action the auditor is determining whether such a proposed expenditure has been authorized and if sufficient funds are available. County auditors are not ordinarily charged with the postaudit, which occurs after moneys have been expended. The postaudit in most counties is conducted either by the state auditor's office or by independent auditing firms employed by the county board for this specific purpose.

## The Assessor

In many counties the general property tax remains as the primary source of revenue for county governmental activities. The administration of the property tax involves the determination of the value of property, and this job is usually placed in the hands of the assessor of a county, city, or even a township. As a result, one of the foremost requisites of good administration is the employment of competent personnel in the county assessor's office. Yet it must be recognized that most of the assessors are popularly elected, many of them on a partisan political basis with the possibility that many are untrained and ill-equipped for their jobs. Elected assessors are frequently forced to hire persons who are qualified to do this type of work. As already indicated, the major work of the county assessor is to place a value upon all tangible and intangible property within his jurisdiction. This function becomes all the more important when it is realized that these valuations are usually accepted by local jurisdictions within the county for the purposes of taxation. Some reforms are gradually entering into this area and the appointive method of select-

[34] National Municipal League, *Coroners of 1953* (ed. Richard S. Childs of the New York National Municipal League). See also by Richard S. Childs, "Best State for a Murder," 1963.

ing assessors is receiving increased acceptance among county governmental leaders. A few states have enacted laws that provide that only those individuals who are certified by a state agency as qualified appraisers may set the value of property, and other states are now conducting training schools for county assessors.

## County Superintendent of Schools

The position of county superintendent of schools is to be found in approximately three-fourths of the states. While the office is usually filled by popular election, in those counties operating under the county-unit system the superintendent is selected by a county board of education.

The actual duties of the county superintendent vary considerably not only from state to state but especially between county-unit and non-county-unit states.[35] The major duties of the county superintendent are: (1) serving as an administrative agent of the state department of education to see that general state requirements are met; (2) supervising and directing the county schools with particular regard to administration and finance; (3) visiting school plants; (4) assisting in the development of improved curricula and methods of teaching; (5) making reports to state agencies and keeping records on all teachers in the county; and (6) giving advice to the various school district authorities.

## Miscellaneous County Officers

In addition to the more important county officers who have been discussed in some detail in the preceding paragraphs, various other minor officers can be found in counties throughout the United States.

The *county surveyor* has long served as a traditional county official and the office still exists in most of the states outside the New England area. The position is usually filled by popular election by the county voters and the surveyor is compensated by a fee system in most instances. Two major functions have normally been assigned to this office: (1) to conduct land surveys; and (2) to determine boundary lines. These tasks were carried out either by order of the courts or upon requests from private landowners. This office was an important one while the United States was expanding westward and the opening of public lands engendered many boundary disputes. Today the position has all but disappeared as an active

---

[35] The county-unit system entails the administering and financing of most of the schools by county authorities. City schools are sometimes not placed under direct county supervision and will have their own school boards and superintendents. Therefore, in the approximately fifteen states that use the county-unit system the activities of the county superintendent are particularly important since most of the schools are administered on a county-wide basis.

county office and some authorities are maintaining that the position should be abolished since the functions could be transferred to a section of the county engineer's office or performed by licensed private surveyors.

The post of *county engineer* is still present in many of our counties with the position being filled by appointment by the county governing board, many times only on a part-time basis. The county engineer is normally charged with the location, design, and construction of roads and bridges. In Iowa this office is filled by the county board of supervisors who, by law, are required to fix a term of employment which may not exceed three years but may be terminated at any time by the board. Any person appointed to this position must be a registered civil engineer. The law also establishes the general duties of the engineer by stating that all "construction and maintenance work shall be performed under the direct and immediate supervision of the county engineer who shall be deemed responsible for the efficient, economical and good-faith performance of said work."[36] The salary of the engineer in Iowa is fixed by the county board of supervisors. In some states a position entitled *county roadmaster* supervises the actual construction and maintenance of county roads. In other states an officer referred to as road viewer is given the responsibility of selecting the most feasible route for any new proposed roads within the county.

## COUNTY FUNCTIONS

Counties in general are listed as quasi-corporations and as such are more completely dominated by state legislatures than are boroughs, cities, and other municipal corporations. Since counties are legal agents of the state they have been established as a means of performing state functions within their territorial limits. In some states the courts have declared that counties could be considered the same as municipal corporations in order to perform certain functions. Many of the functions performed by the county were established during the colonial period and have been retained to this day. A discussion of the activities to be performed by a county government has a tendency to attempt to produce a convenient classification system of its functions. Professor Paul W. Wager maintains that counties perform two types of functions: (1) those which the state requires; and (2) those which the state permits but does not require counties to perform.[37] As a result, the mandatory functions almost always include some responsibility for the maintenance of law and order, the care of prisoners, the administration of justice, the conducting of elections, the care and welfare of paupers and dependent children, the

[36] *Code of Iowa 1962,* Chapter 309, section 21.
[37] Wager, *County Government Across the Nation, op. cit.,* p. 18.

construction and maintenance of roads, the recording of important documents, the operation of public schools, and many other related activities. Another type of popular classification divides the county functions on the basis of those that are mandatory and those that are optional in nature, with the latter category constituting the newer activities. These two classification systems merely indicate that the traditional functions are the ones that the state requires of the county, while the newer functions are the ones that the state permits a county to perform. Today the optional functions constitute some of the greatest areas of growth as far as county functions are concerned. This becomes more apparent when it is observed that state governments are gradually assuming functions that traditionally have been county responsibilities, as evidenced in the areas of law enforcement, public assistance programs, highways, and schools. The following discussion briefly describes some of the more traditional activities of county governments and notes some of the newer areas of concern being exhibited on behalf of county governments.

## Administration of Justice

The establishment of courts for the administration of the civil and criminal laws of the state has always been a paramount responsibility of the county. While local courts are usually listed as a part of the state judiciary, their organization, staffing, and financial support rests primarily with the county. In some areas, officers of the local judiciary are also members of county governing bodies. In many rural sections of the United States the justice of the peace court serves as the initial tribunal for settling cases involving minor infractions of the law or receiving small civil suits. For those individuals who have committed a more serious infraction of the law or desire to institute a major civil action, the proceedings are initiated in the so-called general courts. These tribunals are frequently designated as county, district, circuit, or superior courts and their geographical boundaries are many times determined by state law on the basis of county lines. The jurisdiction of these courts may therefore consist of several counties, each of which is called upon to support the court financially. In many states the judges of these courts are popularly elected. In a few states, an intermediate trial court is established between the justice of the peace and the general trial court.

A major criticism of local judicial administration is concerned with the defense that is provided for those individuals who are financially unable to hire adequate legal counsel. Many accused persons do not possess sufficient funds to employ counsel and it becomes necessary for the court to designate a lawyer to represent such individuals. In order to overcome some of the drawbacks to such a system, a few counties and municipalities have provided for the office of public defender who has the responsibility to represent the accused just as the prosecuting attorney is required to conduct prosecutions. The office of public defender was first established in Los Angeles County is 1914.

## Public Welfare

Providing for certain public welfare services has been one of the traditional functions associated with local units of government. Public welfare covers those services that are provided at public expense for certain groups within our society, primarily the delinquent, the criminal classes, those persons suffering from mental or physical handicaps, and the dependent. States have, for the most part, established institutions to care for the dependent poor or those persons unable to support themselves. Although the federal government and the states eventually began to share the responsibility, the county continues to fill an important role in the administering of public welfare services.

The county welfare department is the primary unit for welfare administration at the local level. Before the adoption of the national social security program no agency within county government was responsible for establishing an integrated welfare program. Poor relief, as a function of the county, was normally administered directly by the county governing body or by the "overseers of the poor" who were appointed by the board. Other welfare activities, when they existed, were managed by either the county board or some other county agency. In some states the "mothers' pensions," the predecessor of present-day aid to dependent children, was administered by the county court; county homes were, and still are in many instances, under the supervision of the county board which appoints a steward and matron to operate the institution; and the homes maintained for children were placed under the court or a special board. By 1933 about one-third of the states had provided for the creation of agencies charged with the administration of two or more welfare services on a county-wide basis.[38]

The county's role in welfare activities in many states is concerned with two basic functions. First, it is the unit that administers the outdoor relief which consists of either outright grants of clothing, medical supplies, food, fuel, shelter and utilities or, in some instances, giving funds to the recipient for the purchasing of these items. Secondly, it shares in the administration of assistance to the blind, the aged, and dependent children even though most of the funds for these activities stem from the national and state governments. In recent years there has been an increase in the

[38] Mary Ruth Colby, *The County as an Administrative Unit for Social Work* (Washington, D. C.: Children's Bureau, U.S. Department of Labor, 1933), pp. 23–36.

amount of supervision exercised by the state over the activities of the county welfare unit. Part of this is due to federal law which requires effective administration of national welfare funds in a political subdivision of a state.

## Highways

The building and maintaining of roads in the United States was carried on almost entirely by the counties and other units of local government until almost the end of the nineteenth century. The first major change in this policy was probably the grant-in-aid statute passed by the New Jersey legislature in 1891 but it was not until World War I that all states participated in the construction of highways.[39] At the present time this function is divided between the state and local subdivisions in all but four states—Delaware, North Carolina, Virginia, and West Virginia.

The rural public highways are commonly classified as primary or secondary highways and farm-to-market roads. Primary highways are those that facilitate cross-state or interstate traffic while secondary roads refer to those county highways that are built to link small towns together and feed traffic into the first-class highways. Farm-to-market roads are concerned with the traffic to and from the farms and channels traffic into the roadways of the first two classes.

In some states the county roads are under the direct control of the county governing board while in others they are under a county engineer or highway commissioner. This latter office can either be popularly elected or appointed by the county board. The primary function of the county highway authorities is the construction and maintenance of roads and bridges in the county highway system.

## Law Enforcement

Counties, from the time of their beginnings in England, have had responsibilities relating to the preservation of peace and order. The sheriff and his staff still constitute the only local police force with county-wide jurisdiction. With perhaps the exception of a few highly urbanized counties, the average county sheriff's office is ill prepared to cope with modern crime. Professor Lane W. Lancaster maintains that "We have in reality retained a medieval functionary with almost unchanged status and powers to cope with a criminal class which has completely mechanized itself

[39] Norman Hebden and Wilbur S. Smith, *State-City Relationships in Highway Affairs* (New Haven: Yale University Press, 1950), p. 26; U.S. Bureau of Public Roads, *Highways in the United States* (Washington: Government Printing Office, 1951); and *The Local Rural Road Problem* (Washington: Government Printing Office, 1950).

and taken full advantage of every improvement in transportation and communication."[40] Two important officers, other than the sheriff, concerned with law-enforcement activities are the county attorney and the coroner.

## Education

The actual operation of our public education system has been historically a local function. The determination of educational policies has been the responsibility of local school officials but within those limitations outlined in constitutional, statutory, and state administrative provisions. The local school district, also, has provided a major part of the financial support for public elementary and secondary schools. In addition, the providing of school staffs, buildings, supplies, and equipment has been viewed as a local function. While the state governments have established minimum curriculum standards, local authorities have the power to upgrade the curriculum offerings. Nevertheless, the local residents have the ability to approve or reject proposed bond issues for capital improvements, which in turn can influence to a major degree the school program as it will operate within the local district.

At the present time the county serves as the dominant local government unit in the administration of primary and secondary public education in at least fifteen states.[41] This is referred to as the "county-unit" system under which the schools are administered and financed on a county-wide basis, but even here the city schools may be separately controlled. Even in those areas not under this system, the county school officers still serve an important function in the enforcement of rules and regulations that have been established by the state department of education.

## Newer County Functions

Despite the predictions of some authorities that county governments were diminishing in importance, these units have in recent years been called upon to provide for many new and varied functions. Among the more prominent of these activities are civil defense, parks and recreation, health protection, zoning, and libraries. It must be recognized that the county has assumed these new tasks as a matter of necessity as the result primarily of the rapid growth of population in those areas outside large metropolitan or municipal units.

[40] Lane W. Lancaster, *Government in Rural America* (Princeton N.J.: D. Van Nostrand Co., Inc., 1937), pp. 191–92.
[41] The states are Alabama, Florida, Georgia, Kentucky, Louisiana, Maryland, Mississippi, Nevada, New Mexico, North Carolina, South Carolina, Tennessee, Utah, Virginia, and West Virginia.

Counties in many sections of the country now own and operate parks and other recreational facilities such as swimming pools, golf courses, camping grounds, picnic sites, and playgrounds. In certain sections these recreational areas have been assumed by the county as the result of the failure of municipal governments to provide for these services. In the case of libraries two major lines of development can be noticed. First of all, some counties have signed contracts with city or other county libraries to extend this service to rural residents. Secondly, regional libraries, established cooperatively by several counties, have been used to an increasing degree. Also, state legislatures have recognized that small units of government that are primarily dependent upon the real estate tax cannot maintain adequate library service. As a result, various states have adopted or strengthened state-aid laws. In 1956 the Congress passed the Library Services Act in an attempt to stimulate the development of public library services to rural areas over a five-year period. At that time it was estimated that 319 rural counties had no library services within their areas and that 26 million rural residents were without any library services. At the end of the five year period, after an expenditure of approximately $28 million of federal funds, matched by state and local monies, it was reported that some 4 million citizens had access to library facilities for the first time and that library services were now available in an additional 169 counties and townships. In addition, more than 200 bookmobiles were in use in rural areas.[42]

The development of adequate health programs in county governments is still a problem that confronts many county governing boards. It must be recognized that a large number of rural counties are in no position, as a result of inadequate finances, to establish and maintain complete health departments. The Commission on Intergovernmental Relations in its *Report to the President* in 1955 stated that only 476 counties were able to maintain public health programs. The Social Security Act of 1935 did provide some assistance in that federal funds were made available for the purpose of assisting in the establishing and maintaining of local health services. While on occasion some counties have entered into cooperative arrangements in order to provide for a joint health program, the United States Public Health Service reported in 1952 that only about half of the counties had full time health officers.[43] One of the greatest advances on the county level has been in the field of hospital administration where many counties have established their own hospitals.

[42] Council of State Governments, *The Book of the States, 1962–1963* (Chicago: Council of State Governments, 1962), p. 331.

[43] U.S. Public Health Service, *Report of Local Public Health Resources: 1950* (Washington, D.C.: Government Printing Office, 1952).

Municipal governments have utilized the practice of zoning for many years. This technique, considered by many authorities as an important phase of the planning operation, has provided for the creation of districts regulating the types of buildings that may be constructed and the purposes for which the land may be used. Since the power to zone is inherent with the state governments it must be granted to local units by state legislative action. The primary legal basis for zoning is the state police power which is viewed as the ability of the state to regulate in the interest of public safety, health, morals, and welfare of its citizens.

During recent decades there has been a trend favoring the conferring of the zoning power upon counties and even townships. Under permissive state enabling legislation a county is able to establish a zoning ordinance which can impose regulations upon the use of real property. As in the case of municipal zoning the basic test imposed by the courts in determining the constitutionality of zoning is reasonableness. An unreasonable or arbitrary zoning ordinance could deprive a person of his property without due process of law or deny him equal protection of the law. The first state to provide for actual rural zoning was Wisconsin in 1929. Since that time about three-fourths of the states have passed enabling measures which authorize counties, townships, or both, to engage in zoning activities. However, in only approximately twelve states has the zoning power been extended to open country—land of a strictly rural nature—as well as to suburban lands which are areas of rather dense population.[44]

The major concern of rural zoning relates almost entirely to land use regulation. In this respect rural zoning attempts not only to conserve natural resources but at the same time to encourage a more efficient use of them. Also, this type of zoning is concerned with the possibility of too widespread a distribution of rural population on unproductive land. While the number and types of districts may vary, the accomplishment of the major objectives of rural zoning are realized by the creation of three different types of districts: (1) agricultural; (2) forest; and (3) recreational. The agricultural district, sometimes referred to as the unrestrictive district, permits the land to be used for farming and any other lawful purpose. The land within a forestry district is usually restricted to a long list of specific purposes. The more commonly accepted uses include parks, both public and private, playgrounds, forest industries, recreational camps, summer cottages and cabins, power plants and hydroelectric dams, and the operation of mines and quarries. In most instances these same purposes are allowed also in recreational districts but with the addition of family dwellings so that the owners may be present during the entire

[44] Earling D. Solberg, *Rural Zoning in the United States* (Washington, D.C.: Department of Agriculture, 1952).

year. Farming is normally prohibited in both recreational and forestry districts in an attempt to prevent soil erosion and preserve timber stands.

As counties begin to assume the responsibility for new functions, three major restrictions or limitations must be observed. First of all, many counties cannot assume their new responsibilities without a change in the state laws which would legally permit these units of local government to provide new services. Secondly, the problem of additional finances that can be allocated to the new tasks is one that cannot be taken lightly. Thirdly, there is the very real problem of public apathy or indifference. Some recent studies in local government have arrived at the conclusion that the county is the logical unit of local government to provide many functions in both rural and urban areas. However, many counties are still controlled by the attitude that increased governmental activity can only result in larger taxes without a compensating increase in advantages for the rural residents of the county.

## THE URBAN COUNTY

The county has been traditionally considered as a geographical subdivision of the state in which certain designated officers are elected or appointed to administer state laws. Counties have been created by the sovereign will of the state without any particular consent, solicitation, or concurrent action of the inhabitants. As a result, counties have been contrasted with municipalities which are brought into existence either by the consent of the people concerned or at their direct solicitation. In this respect municipalities have been created mainly for the "interest, advantage, and convenience of the locality and its people" while counties have been established "with a view to the policy of the state at large, for purposes of political organization and civil administration, in matters of finance, of education, of provision for the poor, of military organization, of the means of travel and transport, and especially for the general administration of justice."[45] While these were considered major differences between cities and counties in 1857, the differences today are not as clear and distinct. While the primary functions of counties were to serve as administrative units or agents for the state government, these counties could never operate completely in this atmosphere since the officers were locally elected and received their political tenure of office from the local citizens. Secondly, municipalities have also functioned as agents for the administration of certain state laws. Thirdly, urban counties are engaging in activities for the "convenience and benefit" of local residents.

As the urban or metropolitan county feels the full impact of population growth and finds it necessary to meet the service demands of its residents,

---

[45] *Commissioners of Hamilton County v. Mighels* (7 Ohio St. 109, 118–19, 1857).

Professor Victor Jones finds that such a county must play four different yet interrelated roles:

1. The county is still the traditional local "administrative" agent of the state.
2. Urban and metropolitan counties have in different ways and in varying degrees become, or are becoming, the substitute for a municipal government in providing urban services to people who live outside municipal boundaries.
3. At the same time that urban and metropolitan counties begin to look like suburban governments, they face demands that they act like regional governments.
4. As participants in intergovernmental programs, counties and municipalities are beginning to collaborate in the formulation of intergovernmental urban programs, in the adaptation of such programs to a particular urban area, in regional planning, and in regional administration. In playing this role, the county is not acting as the local "administrative" agent of the state or the national government.[46]

## THE FUTURE OF THE COUNTY

The American county has long been labeled the "dark continent of American politics" and has also been designated by some experts as ready for liquidation as a local unit of government. Yet, with a few exceptions, our counties have successfully resisted such a suggestion even to the point of refusing to consolidate the smaller counties into larger units or to adopt suggested changes that might provide for improvements in organization. As a result, Professor Wager, who has made an extensive study of county government, had to conclude that "It is now apparent that counties are not going to be liquidated."[47] The county is continuing to grow in importance, perhaps as a result of the fact that the national government has "found the county more convenient than the municipality as a base for a number of grant-in-aid programs."[48] The county, even at the present time, remains the center of one of the most concentrated local political power operations this nation has ever experienced. Its offices, still sought by local residents, have steadfastly refused to adopt modern administrative techniques. In metropolitan and urban areas the county is enjoying a renaissance, for in becoming an urban county, it is not only being granted powers that formerly were almost exclusively performed by the municipalities but it is rendering municipal services not only to the unincorporated areas but to the smaller cities within its jurisdiction.

[46] Victor Jones, "The Changing Role of the Urban County in Local Government," *Public Affairs Report* (Bulletin of the Institute of Governmental Studies, University of California, Berkeley), Vol. IV, No. 3 (June, 1963).

[47] Wager, *op. cit.*, p. 32.

[48] Commission on Intergovernmental Relations, *A Report to the President for Transmittal to the Congress* (Washington, D.C.: Government Printing Office, 1955), p. 53.

If the American county is to justify its retention in our scheme of modern local government, certain changes will undoubtedly have to take place. For the highly urbanized regions there must be some movement toward the consolidation of city and county governments. In other areas either more constitutional home rule must be provided for the counties or at least the opportunity provided to choose from optional forms of government. Other proposed changes include the elimination of many popularly-elected county officials, the selection of a county chief executive, the extension of civil service or the merit system among county employees, and an increase in the consolidation of functions or the use of intergovernmental contracts or arrangements.

## SPECIAL DISTRICTS

### Definition of a Special District

No one acceptable definition of what constitutes a special district has been formulated. To different authorities a special district exhibits differing characteristics. The Scott and Bollens study in California defined a special district as "any local government entity which is neither city, county, township, nor village."[49] The Asseff study in Louisiana used the term with reference to units of local government other than parishes and to "districts created only for taxing and/or administrative purposes."[50] The Bureau of the Census in its 1942 and 1952 reports on *Units of Government in the United States* included all units of local government, not administrative or merely a taxing district, except school districts, municipalities, counties, towns and townships. Professor Jewell Cass Phillips notes that a special district usually exhibits the following five characteristics: "(1) a resident population occupying a defined area, (2) a legally authorized governing body, (3) the status of a separate legal entity, (4) the power to provide certain public services, and (5) a substantial degree of autonomy, including power to raise at least a part of its own revenue."[51] One of the most comprehensive definitions has been produced by Professor John C. Bollens who states that special districts are "organized entities, possessing a structural form, an official name, perpetual succession, and

[49] Stanley Scott and John C. Bollens, *Special Districts in California Local Government* (Bureau of Public Administration, University of California, Berkeley, 1949), p. 1.

[50] Emmett Asseff, *Special Districts in Louisiana* (Baton Rouge: Bureau of Government Research, Louisiana State University, 1951), p. 1.

[51] Jewell Cass Phillips, *State and Local Government in America* (Cincinnati: American Book Co., 1954), p. 359.

the rights to sue and be sued, to make contracts, and to obtain and dispose of property. They have officers who are popularly elected or are chosen by other public officials. They have a high degree of public accountability. Moreover, they have considerable fiscal and administrative independence from other governments. The financial and administrative criteria distinguish special districts and other governments from all dependent or subordinate districts and from most authorities which, lacking one or both of these standards, are not governmental units."[52]

## Organization Procedures

The detailed procedures to be followed in the creation of a special district are usually outlined in a general law that has been passed by the state legislature. It is only infrequently that such a local unit of government will be established either by some section of a state constitution or by a special legislative measure. In the main these districts are created as the result of the action taken by local citizens in following the instructions contained within the general law.

Since each state has provided by law for the manner in which a special district can be created, it is extremely difficult to give more than a generalization concerning the procedures that must be followed. Normally the first step is the circulation of a petition which must be signed by a requisite number of legal residents or property owners within the boundary of the proposed district. This petition in most states must identify the type of district that is proposed and indicate clearly the geographical areas to be included. After securing the necessary number of signatures, the second step involves the submission of the petition to the appropriate local governing body which will usually be the county board of supervisors. The action of this board may be very brief and consist of a mere acceptance of the legality of the document, or the board may involve itself in a determination of the desirability or necessity of such a district and on this basis deny or grant the petition. In most instances a favorable decision from the board of supervisors will initiate the third phase, which consists of the submission of the question to create a new district to a popular referendum. In the election all qualified voters participate and normally a simple majority is sufficient to carry the proposition, although occasionally a three-fifths or a two-thirds vote in required. The fourth and last step is the issuance of an official declaration by either the county board of supervisors or a county court bringing the new district into legal existence.

[52] John C. Bollens, *Special District Governments in the United States* (Berkeley and Los Angeles: University of California Press, 1957), p. 1.

## Organizational Patterns

While organizational patterns for special districts will vary from state to state, certain common features or characteristics are present. First, a board composed normally of three, five, or sometimes seven members is established as the governing authority. These members, referred to as trustees, commissioners, directors, or supervisors, are usually elected by the voters of the district for terms ranging from two, four, or six years. Board members in some instances may also be appointed or hold membership ex officio. In California, for example, special districts are governed by one of four possible types of boards: (1) an independent elective board, with the members being chosen from subdivisions within the district or at large; (2) an appointive board, with the members usually chosen by the legal body that supervised the creation of the district; (3) an ex officio board, which consists of the members of a city council or the county board of supervisors; or (4) a board composed of selected members of the governing bodies of the local governments located within the district.[53] A second common feature revolves around the role of the board in the determination of the policy to be followed by the district. Frequently the most important phase of policy determination may be the decision with respect to the tax rate to be imposed upon the residents of the district for the particular service. A third general characteristic involves the appointment by the board of an expert or a staff of trained technicians to supply the function for which the district was established. This is the accepted procedure among school districts which employ a professional superintendent to direct the business of the school district. A fourth feature of many special districts concerns the high degree of informality that is present not only in the organizational structure but also in the use of certain procedures. Also many special districts have very few paid employees, enjoy almost unrestrained freedom in the selection and dismissal of employees, and maintain very few intricate records.

## Functions Performed by Special Districts

Individually the special district performs only one or perhaps two services. Yet when considered as a whole they produce a rather large range of functions or services and will provide more services than one class of governmental units such as townships, small populated towns, and even counties.

[53] Winston W. Crouch, Dean E. McHenry, John C. Bollens, and Stanley Scott, *California Government and Politics*, 2d ed. (Englewood Cliffs, N.J.: Prentice-Hall, Inc., 1961), pp. 270–71.

While the multitude of activities carried out by special districts do not easily lend themselves to a neat classification system, Professor Bollens has established the following eleven categories: health and sanitation; protection to persons and property; road transportation facilities and aids; nonroad transportation facilities and aids; utilities; housing; natural resource and agricultural assistance; education; parks and recreation; cemeteries; and miscellaneous.[54] The functional classification of special districts as produced by the Bureau of the Census is indicated in Table 4–1.

TABLE 4–1

Functional Classification of Special Districts

| Function | Number | Percentage |
|---|---|---|
| Natural Resources | | |
|   Soil conservation | 2,461 | 13.4 |
|     Drainage | 2,240 | 12.2 |
|     Irrigation, water conservation | 781 | 4.3 |
|   Flood control | 500 | 2.7 |
|   Other and composite natural | | |
|     resource purposes | 176 | 1.0 |
| Fire Protection | 3,229 | 17.6 |
| Urban Water Supply | 1,502 | 8.2 |
| Cemeteries | 1,283 | 7.0 |
| Housing | 1,099 | 6.0 |
| Sewerage | 937 | 5.0 |
| School Buildings | 915 | 5.0 |
| Highways | 773 | 4.2 |
| Parks and Recreation | 488 | 2.7 |
| Hospitals | 418 | 2.3 |
| Libraries | 349 | 1.9 |
| Other Single-Function Districts | 862 | 4.7 |
| Multiple-Function Districts | 310 | 1.7 |
|     Total | 18,323 | 100.0 |

SOURCE: U.S. Department of Commerce, Bureau of the Census, *Governmental Units in 1962, Preliminary Report No. 6* (Washington, D.C.: Government Printing Office, 1962).

## AUTHORITIES

The depression of the 1930's fostered to some extent the movement within state and local governments to create units that are popularly referred to as authorities. While resembling special districts because they are established to provide for one major function or sometimes a limited number of related activities, most authorities are not sufficiently autonomous in administrative and fiscal affairs to be recognized as separate and independent units of government. This is undoubtedly the result of two

[54] Bollens, *op. cit.*, p. 21.

very important factors: (1) the functions assigned to authorities are usually in place of or supplement activities ordinarily provided by an already existing unit of government; and (2) in the operation of many authorities the creating unit retains a high degree of administrative supervision and control.[55] Therefore, many students of government maintain that authorities become instrumentalities of state, county, or municipal governments; that they are in the category of a public corporation but cannot qualify as a municipal corporation since they do not possess the characteristic of perpetual existence that is associated with municipal corporations. In addition, these units are not in most instances created as adjuncts or arms of the state government but are established by strictly local units and in many instances already existing municipal corporations.

Many reasons or needs have been advanced for the creation and utilization of authorities.[56] First of all, they have been established in order to provide a method of financing certain types of public works without conflicting with statutory or constitutional debt or tax limitations. Professor Jewell Cass Phillips states that the "most obvious reason for the creation of most authorities is to clear the obstacle of constitutional debt limitations."[57] Historically, in the early 1930's many local units of government were financially unable to match federal grants for public works projects because these units lacked the necessary borrowing power or found themselves confronted with debt or tax limitations. To overcome this deficiency many state legislatures authorized local units to create public authorities. As a result many such units were created to provide for the construction and subsequent operation of toll roads and bridges, port facilities, housing developments, slum clearance, redevelopment projects, utility systems, hospitals, airports, and other types of revenue-producing facilities. While most authorities do not possess any taxing power they may impose a fee or charge upon the service rendered. Initial construction funds are produced by the issuance of revenue bonds which are retired solely from the operating revenues of the authority and not by the imposition of any local tax. There is also some evidence that investors many times will favor revenue bonds over general purpose bonds. An authority that is established for the construction, operation, and maintenance of revenue-producing facilities has been defined as a "governmental business corporation set up outside of the normal structure of traditional government so that it can give continuity, business efficiency and elastic manage-

[55] U.S. Department of Commerce, Bureau of the Census, *Local Government Structure in the United States* (Washington, D.C.: Government Printing Office, 1954), p. 7. It should be noted, however, that some authorities do possess enough autonomy to be listed by the Bureau with the category of special districts.

[56] Council of State Governments, *Public Authorities in the States: A Report to the Governors' Conference* (Chicago: Council of State Governments, 1953), pp. 1, 7.

[57] Phillips, *op. cit.*, p. 361.

ment to the construction or operation of a self-supporting or revenue-producing public enterprise."[58]

In addition to the flexibility of financing, a second reason or need met by the authority involves the establishment of an administrative organization that is flexible enough to manage what is essentially a commercial operation or enterprise. Most authorities are managed by a board of directors or trustees, the members of which are determined in a variety of ways. While such a board is limited by law with relationship to the function or activity to be performed, it is granted a great degree of freedom in determining the methods of managerial operation. As a result the organizational structures of many authorities are modeled very closely upon those of private corporations and therefore in a better position to manage a full-scale business. The third reason for the utilization of an authority lies in the need for some type of an agency that can be effective in the handling of intercommunity problems. Although some authorities have service boundary lines that are coterminous with that of a county or city, many others operate within several local units or cut across traditional boundary lines as the public will or convenience may demand. In recent years some state authorities have been created to provide functions closely related to local governments. An excellent example of this trend is to be found in the field of education. State building authorities are constructing local school buildings, leasing them to local districts, and the rentals thereon are retiring the revenue bonds that were issued to finance the construction of the buildings.

## BIBLIOGRAPHY

ALASKA LEGISLATIVE COUNCIL and the LOCAL AFFAIRS AGENCY. *Final Report on Borough Government*. Juneau: Local Affairs Agency, 1961.

ALDERFER, HAROLD F. *American Local Government and Administration*. New York: The Macmillan Co., 1956.

ANDERSON, WILLIAM. *The Units of Government in the United States: An Enumeration and Analysis*. Chicago: Public Administration Service, 1949.

BEBOUT, JOHN E. *Model County Charter*. New York: National Municipal League, 1956.

BLAIR, GEORGE S. *American Local Government*. New York: Harper & Row, Inc., 1964.

BOLLENS, JOHN C. *Appointed Executive Local Government: The California Experience*. Los Angeles: Haynes Foundation, 1952.

————. *Special District Governments in the United States*. Berkeley and Los Angeles: University of California Press, 1957.

BROMAGE, ARTHUR W. *American County Government*. New York: Sears Publishing Co., 1933.

[58] Luther Gulick, " 'Authorities' and How to Use Them," *The Tax Review*, Vol. VIII (November, 1947), pp. 47–52.

BURCHFIELD, LAVERNE. *Our Rural Communities*. Chicago: Public Administration Service, 1947.

COMMISSION ON INTERGOVERNMENTAL RELATIONS. *An Advisory Committee Report on Local Government*. Washington, D.C.: Government Printing Office, 1955.

FAIRLIE, JOHN A., and KNEIER, CHARLES M. *County Government and Administration*. New York: Appleton-Century-Crofts, Inc., 1930.

KAMMERER, GLADYS. *County Home Rule*. Gainesville: Public Administration Clearing House, University of Florida, 1959.

LANCASTER, LANE W. *Government in Rural America*, 2d ed. Princeton, N.J.: D. Van Nostrand Co., Inc., 1952.

MARTIN, ROSCOE C. *Grass Roots*. University, Ala.: University of Alabama Press, 1957.

NATIONAL MUNICIPAL LEAGUE. *Model County Charter*. New York: National Municipal League, 1956.

———. *Digest of County Manager Charters and Laws*, 7th ed. New York: National Municipal League, 1963.

PATE, JAMES E. *Local Government and Administration*. Cincinnati: American Book Co., 1954.

PORTER, KIRK H. *County and Township Government in the United States*. New York: The Macmillan Co., 1922.

SNIDER, CLYDE F. *Local Government in Rural America*. New York: Appleton-Century-Crofts, Inc., 1957.

SPICER, GEORGE W. *Fifteen Years of County Manager Government in Virginia*. Charlottesville: University of Virginia, 1951.

U.S. DEPARTMENT OF COMMERCE, BUREAU OF THE CENSUS. *County Boards and Commissions*. Washington, D.C.: Government Printing Office, 1947.

WAGER, PAUL W. (ed.). *County Government Across the Nation*. Chapel Hill: University of North Carolina Press, 1950.

WEIDNER, EDWARD W. *The American County—Patchwork of Boards*. New York: National Municipal League, 1946.

WELLS, ROGER H. *American Local Government*. New York and London: McGraw-Hill Book Co., Inc., 1939.

# 5

# Municipal Government

Americans have shown much more imagination in devising forms of municipal government than they have in working out new ways of conducting state government and administration. It might be more proper to state that the people living in the so-called American urban areas have been more willing to experiment with municipal governments than state legislatures have been with state governments. It may be caused by the multiplicity of problems facing the urban governments of America or it may be attributed to the many scandals and corruptions that have been uncovered in our cities. Another possible reason for this willingness to try something new and different is the rapid expansion that has occurred in American cities as contrasted with the more gradual growth in cities throughout the world.

It should be immediately added that in spite of this experimentation that has gone on in the United States, particularly since the beginning of the twentieth century, no completely satisfactory formula or form of municipal government has materialized. It is, however, true that the latest innovation, the council-manager plan, seems to have the greatest potential of any form yet devised, even though it has not been tried in any of our cities of one million or more population. In fact only four of the twenty-one cities above 500,000 population—Cincinnati, Dallas, San Antonio, and San Diego—have city managers.[1] All the other cities in this group except Washington, D.C., still retain the mayor-council form of government, the type that they had when the cities were originally founded. Thus the more radical experimentation has not permeated to any great degree to the cities of the United States with a population in excess of half a million. The cities that have brought about innovations have been usually in the classification between 50,000 and 100,000 population. However, the new forms of municipal government have gradually been adopted and adapted

[1] The International City Managers' Association, *The Municipal Year Book, 1963* (Chicago: The International City Managers' Association, 1963), p. 168.

113

by cities both in the smaller population ranges and to a more limited extent in the cities with greater populations.

The government of American cities or municipalities is usually regarded by most observers as an area which is still in need of great improvement. How many municipalities are there in the United States? An answer which might well be accurate one day would probably be inaccurate the next. The number however appears to be increasing at approximately fifty per year. The term municipalities is used to include all governmentally active units officially designated by the states as cities, boroughs, towns, (except in New England, New York, and Wisconsin), and villages. Under this classification the Bureau of the Census enumerated in 1957 a total of 17,183 municipalities, an increase of 405 over the enumeration of 1952, while the 1962 count listed 17,997 municipalities, an increase of 814. As of 1957 only Illinois had more than 1,000 municipalities, listing 1,181. Pennsylvania was approaching the one thousand figure with 991, while Iowa had 942 incorporated municipalities, and Ohio, 915. By 1962 Illinois had increased to 1,251, Pennsylvania 1,003, Iowa, 944, and Ohio, 932. At the other end of the spectrum, Alaska, Connecticut, Hawaii, Maine, Massachusetts, Nevada, New Hampshire, and Rhode Island each had fewer than fifty governmental units classified as municipalities. It must be noted, however, that in all but Alaska, Hawaii, and Nevada the New England town form of local government exists, and it is not classed by the United States Bureau of the Census as a municipality.

Not all of the more than 17,000 municipalities are included in the Census Bureau's computation which reveals in 1962 that nearly 70 per cent of the entire population of the United States resided in what the Bureau classed as urban areas. The reason for this is, of course, that only those municipalities of 2,500 population or more are termed a part of the urban area. On the other hand the 70 per cent or 125.3 million people does include residents of nonincorporated, heavily populated areas that are not included in the more than 17,000 municipalities. In all probability the two would nearly balance out.

It is well known that between 1950 and 1960 the total population growth of the United States was about 18.5 per cent. The urban population increased by nearly 30 per cent or 28.4 million more people who were in urban areas in 1960 than in 1950. In contrast the rural population decreased during the same period by nearly one per cent.

The rate of growth of urban population exceeded the rate of rural growth in all but three states. More significantly there were at least twenty-eight states in which the urban population increased during the decade while the rural population in those states actually decreased. In only Maine, Massachusetts, and New York did the rural increase exceed the urban increase. This fact can be attributed to the tremendous suburban developments in these three states. Thus the urban population increased in states whose total population declined during the period from 1950 to 1960—Arkansas, Mississippi, and West Virginia.[2]

In actual numbers Table 5–1 gives the best view of the changes that occurred between 1950 and 1960.

### TABLE 5–1

Urban and Rural Residence of the Population of The United States—1950–1960

| | 1950 | | 1960 | | Increase | |
|---|---|---|---|---|---|---|
| Residence | Number | Per-centage | Number | Per-centage | Number | Per-centage |
| Urban | 96,846,817 | 64 | 125,268,750 | 69.9 | 28,421,933 | 29.3% |
| Rural | 54,478,981 | 36 | 54,054,425 | 30.1 | 424,556 | —0.8 |
| TOTAL | 151,325,798 | | 179,323,175 | | 27,977,377 | 18.5 |

SOURCE: The International City Managers' Association, *The Municipal Year Book, 1963* (Chicago: The International City Managers' Association, 1963).

A further breakdown which presents another aspect of the population picture in the United States as of 1960, is shown in the above table of components of the urban population and following Table 5–2 which classes population by incorporated, unincorporated, urban towns and townships, and other urban territory which includes incorporated places of less than 2,500.

### TABLE 5–2

Components of Urban Population—1960

| Component | United States | Inside Urban Areas | Outside Urban Areas |
|---|---|---|---|
| Urban | 125,268,750 | 95,848,487 | 29,420,263 |
| Incorporated places | | | |
| 2,500 or more | 106,308,257 | 79,487,607 | 26,820,650 |
| Unincorporated places | | | |
| 2,500 or more | 5,106,083 | 2,679,492 | 2,426,591 |
| Urban towns and townships | 3,313,559 | 3,140,537 | 173,022 |
| Other urban territory | | | |
| Incorporated places of | | | |
| less than 2,500 | 689,746 | 689,746 | – |

SOURCE: The International City Managers' Association, *The Municipal Year Book, 1963* (Chicago: The International City Managers' Association, 1963).

[2] The International City Managers' Association, *Municipal Year Book, 1962* (Chicago: The International City Managers' Association, 1962), pp. 24–25.

## INCORPORATION OF AMERICAN CITIES

Each state determines the method to be used in the incorporation of its cities and towns. There are still three different procedures followed in the fifty states. The oldest process is the incorporation by a special act of the state legislature. This method is no longer in widespread use because the state legislatures frequently abused the power and also found that it was a time consuming function. The most common procedure is incorporation under general law. This involves following a prescribed number of steps, usually including the filing of a petition signed by a certain per cent of the residents of the area to be included in the corporate limits, an election on the question of incorporation, and the certification of the election by a local district judge if a majority of the voters participating favored incorporation. The incorporation is then proclaimed by a designated state official. The third method employed in America today is incorporation under the self-executing home-rule provisions of the state constitutions in at least seventeen states. Actually the home rule incorporation is more correctly called a re-incorporation of an already existing municipal corporation.

The oldest procedure—incorporation by special legislative act—is used in Delaware, Florida, New Hampshire, and North Carolina. In fact in New Hampshire it is still the only way incorporation may occur. Incorporation under general law predominates in the United States today. The requirements vary from state to state. Minimum population is a typical requirement. Some states will allow incorporation only if at least 500 people are involved in the area. Other states, such as Iowa, allow incorporation with as few as twenty-five qualified voters residing in the area.

Twenty-seven states now use the home-rule concept in determining the relationship of the municipality to the state. Oversimplified, home rule refers to the delegation of authority by the state to the local governmental unit to conduct local affairs with relative freedom from state control. It means that state supremacy will be exercised only with regard to matters of statewide concern.

The objectives of home rule in all of the twenty-seven states now utilizing this concept are threefold: (1) to prevent legislative interference; (2) to permit maximum local self-government; and (3) to give cities adequate powers to meet the problems that they face. The theme is basically to eliminate the constant necessity of judicial interpretation of the powers that the cities possess.

The American Municipal Association model for home rule is based upon the premise that a municipal corporation may exercise any power or perform any function which the legislature has power to devolve upon a city which has not been specifically denied the municipality by state statute. This is a new approach to the home-rule question as the older version of home rule was based upon the concept that a city must obtain specific powers from the legislature by a statutory act.

The advantages usually listed for the new type of home-rule charter are four:

1. The legislature does not have to specifically authorize municipalities by state law to proceed in finding solutions to their individual problems.
2. There is no longer a need for detailed provisions in the state statutes relating to the powers of a municipality.
3. The more generalized state statutes tend to receive a more liberal interpretation by the state courts.
4. There is a decreased need for legislative supervision of the cities and towns.[3]

## FORMS OF MUNICIPAL GOVERNMENT IN THE UNITED STATES

As a direct result of the freedom allowed cities in the United States to try different forms and versions of municipal governments, the following relatively distinct forms are now in existence:

1. New England town government
2. Weak mayor-council government
3. Strong mayor-council government
4. Mayor-administrative assistant government
5. Commission government
6. Council-manager government

In many respects the variations are not great among several of these forms of government. In reality, the mayor-administrative assistant is primarily a modification of the strong mayor system with some utilization made of the experiences of the council-manager plan. Similarly, it is quite difficult to draw a sharp demarcation line between a city with a strong mayor and a city with a so-called weak mayor system, although the differences are marked and significant when they are compared. The International City Managers' Association tri-partite division of forms of municipal governments in the United States is depicted in Table 5–3.

For a complete understanding of the operational use of these six forms of municipal government it is necessary to outline briefly their modus operandi and the extent of their growth and development. Each must be treated separately, but at the same time comparisons with the companion

[3] Harry R. Smith, "Local Government Home Rule," *Iowa Municipalities,* Vol. XVII, Nos. 4, 5, 6 ( 1962).

systems should be noted. Basically the problems that each type faces are of course the same. The methods that they use to solve the problems are not identical. Each form has certain advantages and disadvantages. It must be stated at the outset that no perfect or ideal form has as yet developed to enable a city to use it as a panacea for its problems.

TABLE 5–3

Form of Government in American Cities of more than 5,000 Population

| Population Group | Total Number of Cities | Total in Table | Mayor–Council Number | Mayor–Council Percentage | Commission Number | Commission Percentage | Council–Manager Number | Council–Manager Percentage |
|---|---|---|---|---|---|---|---|---|
| Over 500,000 | 21 | 20 | 16 | 80.0 | 0 | 0.0 | 4 | 20.0 |
| 250,000 to 500,000 | 31 | 31 | 15 | 48.4 | 4 | 12.9 | 12 | 38.7 |
| 100,000 to 250,000 | 79 | 79 | 30 | 38.0 | 10 | 12.6 | 39 | 49.4 |
| 50,000 to 100,000 | 194 | 192 | 70 | 36.4 | 23 | 12.0 | 99 | 51.6 |
| 25,000 to 50,000 | 406 | 393 | 141 | 35.9 | 46 | 11.7 | 206 | 52.4 |
| 10,000 to 25,000 | 1,031 | 1,013 | 484 | 47.8 | 101 | 10.0 | 428 | 42.2 |
| 5,000 to 10,000 | 1,291 | 1,284 | 835 | 65.0 | 62 | 4.8 | 387 | 30.2 |
| TOTAL | 3,053 | 3,012* | 1,591 | 52.8 | 246 | 8.2 | 1,175 | 39.0 |

* Washington, D.C., 14 cities with town meetings, 19 with representative town meetings, and 9 other cities are not included in the tabulation.

SOURCE: The Internatinal City Managers' Association, *The Municipal Year Book, 1964* (Chicago: The International City Managers' Association, 1964).

## The New England Town

The New England town still functions in nearly 1,400 municipalities in the United States; most of these have populations of less than 2,500. In six states —Maine, Vermont, New Hampshire, Massachusetts, Connecticut, and Rhode Island—it is still the primary form of local government. Most of these municipalities are of less than 2,500 population and are therefore classed as rural areas by the United States Bureau of the Census. This form is widely recognized as the oldest type of municipal government in this country. It is also acknowledged to be the last remnant of so-called pure democracy wherein direct citizen participation in the enactment of laws and the setting of taxes is permitted. Even this part of the system has been modified, particularly in Massachusetts, where the municipalities have grown too large for all citizens to participate in the town meeting and has become a representative town meeting.

It must be recognized that in the New England area a "town" is not a small, closely compact geographical area but rather a territory of often twenty or more square miles with a least one small settlement within the designated area. Some authorities contend that geographic factors were most important in the development of the New England town form of municipal government. Originally most New England town boundaries coincided with the area served by the local church.

The most distinctive and the best-publicized feature of the New England town system is the town meeting. This annual affair, held on a date established usually by state statute, is the opportunity for all of the legally qualified voters residing within the boundaries of the governmental unit to gather at the town hall, local school auditorium, church, or other designated meeting place for an all-day session, which shapes the governmental operation for the year. Participation in the smaller populated areas is still surprisingly great, but it is less percentage wise in the more heavily populated regions. This is not due to a lack of interest but because of the difficulty encountered by persons in urban areas to get time off from their positions to attend a day-long session.

  Usually the meeting is called for mid-morning. The first order of business is to elect a moderator, who presides over the town meeting and any special meetings that may be called during the year. The typical moderator is a gentleman of high standing in the community who has the skill of keeping all factions pacified and yet able to execute the announced agenda. Following the election of the moderator, the meeting is opened for nominations for the positions of selectmen, the individuals who wield the executive authority of the town. Ordinarily three are elected each year as the term is commonly three years. In addition to having certain excutive authority the selectmen have a few policy decisions that they are called upon to make during the course of each year. The salary is nominal, usually averaging about $100 per year. One of the three holds the title of chairman of the board of selectmen, but this carries with it no more authority than is given to the other two members of the plural executive body. Some towns have enlarged the number of selectmen to five and a few to as many as seven.

The next order of business again involves the election of the town clerk. The amount of work and the total compensation depends upon the number of people in the town. The pay is usually on a fee basis with some towns augmenting the compensation with a small annual salary. The duties are relatively simply, involving ordinarily the keeping of the town's records. This includes more than just recording the minutes of the town meeting and the meetings of the selectmen; it also includes issuances of various licenses, such as marriage, hunting, and liquor licenses, etc., as well as recording many types of local legal documents—births, deaths, and ownership of real estate. Ordinarily no office is provided for the town clerk and he is forced to operate from his own home or from his place of business. Some town clerks are elected because of the central location of their place of business or home office.

The town treasurer may or may not be the same person who serves as the town clerk. However, the usual practice is for the same person to hold both positions. The treasurer's responsibilities are also quite simple. He is charged with receiving, banking, and expending the funds of the town. He may make payment, however, only upon authorization from two or more of the town's selectmen. At one time he had some discretion as to where he would deposit the funds but often this is preempted by either the selectmen or by a vote at the town meeting directing the treasurer to deposit all funds in a certain banking institution.

Another vote is held to name the town appraisers. From one to three appraisers are elected to establish valuations on all property within the town limits for tax purposes. Both real estate and personal property are assessed by the appraisers. Little difficulty is encountered in the real estate property valuation, but more difficulty is usually found in personal property both tangible and intangible.

One of the characteristics of the New England town government is its reliance upon a long ballot—electing a great number of administrative officials. In addition to the elective offices already listed are a number of other officials, including: one to three auditors, who are not usually qualified to perform a genuine accounting type audit of the town's books; a constable, who is usually paid upon the time-honored fee basis; a town attorney, who prosecutes cases that arise from the activities of the town constable, who is also on a fee basis; and one or more justices of the peace, to conduct the local courts of the town, again with a fee system determining the total compensation received by these officials.

In some of the New England town governments the list of elected officials includes an over-seer of the poor, a sexton, fence viewers, health officer, a road commissioner, water commissioner, and even other officials whose work is almost entirely of an administrative nature. In other New England towns these officials may be appointed.

One other group of universally elected officials possessing primarily policy making powers is the New England school district directors. The boundaries of the town and the school district usually are identical and the town meeting election is used to elect the three or five members of the town school board. These non-paid public servants have complete control over the operation of the schools included within the boundaries of the district. The financial operation of the schools is determined by the school directors but is controlled by the adoption of the town budget, which includes ordinarily the tax levy for schools as well as the municipality. Some check upon the authority of the school board is vested in the state department of public instruction through its certification powers over qualified teachers and its standards that must be met in order for the district to qualify for state aid to secondary and elementary schools.

Following the election of the officials by secret ballot the town meeting turns its attention to policy-making affairs. The major item is the annual adoption of the town budget and its resulting tax levy. The recommendations of a finance committee become the focal point of the discussion. The finance committee may be composed of the selectmen who have just completed the year in office, or it may be an independent body. The entire assembly passes upon all items included in the annual budget. Most items are accepted without question and with a minimum amount of discussion; however, any increase over past allotments may well encounter considerable opposition unless carefully and fully justified by the speakers who present the items. A key feature of the proceedings is that everyone in attendance who is a bona fide voter has the right to speak and make suggestions at any time during the consideration of the budget. The length of the annual town meeting will largely be determined by the opposition that arises to particular items included in the budget. If there is no sizable increase, or if it is less than previous budgets, the meeting may adjourn by the middle or early afternoon. On the other hand, town meetings have been known to be prolonged marathons that continued far into the night.

Frugality is the watchword in the New England town form of municipal government. No high-salaried technical experts are needed or wanted. The fee system prevails in almost every post that carries with it any compensation whatsoever, while most positions are regarded as a part of the civic responsibility of the citizens and the duties are carried out in that spirit. "Where annual elections end, tyranny begins" is truly believed in the New England town.

## Modifications in the New England Town

In most of the areas where the total population of those governed by the New England town has gone beyond the five thousand mark a limited or representative town meeting has replaced the traditional open town meeting. Usually where this occurs a town meeting of more than two hundred is held with each area being entitled to a predetermined number of delegates. These delegates are elected by the residents of the area and perform the same activities as in the regular town meeting already described.

A town manager has relieved the selectmen of the administrative operation in many of the New England towns. A full-time manager is not feasible in the limited population areas. Consequently several towns may frequently join together to employ a manager who in effect "rides the circuit." He handles the affairs for a number of towns, being in one town on Monday and Tuesday, a second on Wednesday and Thursday, and still a third town on Friday and Saturday.

The town auditors in many areas have been replaced with the employment of a professional auditing firm that checks the accuracy of the records of the various officials, particularly the town treasurer and clerk.

These, and other minor modifications, have made it possible for the New England Town government to continue to operate minimum municipal services in the twentieth century. The cost per capita is low but at the same time the services are few and frequently not as adequate as some of the citizens believe desirable. The two hundred years of tradition probably keep this form of government from being abandoned in favor of more modern forms of municipal government in the New England sector.

No student of municipal government seriously suggests that the New England town form of government will ever expand beyond its present regional application. Time will eventually see further changes and modifications that will eventually bring about its total extinction. However, as long as the people of the region are willing to participate in local affairs to the extent required by the semi-pure democracy of New England town government, it will persist.

## Weak Mayor-Council

As was shown in Table 5–3, the most numerous type of municipal government in the United States is still the mayor-council form. In more than 14,000 cities of less than 5,000 population, this form is used by 9 out of 10 municipalities. The exact division between the number of strong mayor and weak mayor cities is not positively known. No one has as yet devised a method for determining in a satisfactory manner a classification for categorizing strong mayor cities as contrasted with weak mayor forms.

Even in the more than 50 per cent of American cities of more than 5,000 population no precise figures are available as to how many cities grant sufficient powers to their mayors to be termed strong as contrasted with those officials with virtually no administrative authority. The best estimates in this second group of cities would probably reveal about an even division between the two classifications.

In spite of the lack of data concerning the precise numerical division between the two systems there is a great deal of agreement among municipal government authorities as to the essential characteristics contained in the two forms. The weak mayor form allocates extensive control over administrative affairs to the council rather than to the mayor. The council usually exercises this power through standing committees. Often a committee is in charge of each major function performed by the municipality, with the department head reporting to the chairman of the standing committee, not to the mayor. Frequently this system has a long ballot with a number of department heads popularly elected. A further variation that occurs is the establishment of independent boards and commissions, which supervise various phases of the administrative process. These groups discharge their duties without any sense of obligation to the mayor but have a sense of responsibility to the council as they must please the policy makers in order to assure continued budgetary support. The mayor's position may be further undermined in some states where state authority over local administrators extends so far as to include his appointment and removal.

Possibly even a more serious defect in the mayor's authority in the weak mayor city, in addition to his restricted appointive power, is his complete lack of influence concerning financial affairs. The budget is drafted by a financial committee and the mayor usually has no role whatsoever in its formulation, consideration, and virtually no power in its execution. The mayor is strictly a figure head. His major responsibility is often limited to presiding at council meetings. Even here he is frequently denied a vote on anything other than procedural matters. Of course he does represent the city on all ceremonial occasions, but this can hardly be regarded as performing a vital municipal function.

It should be noted that the personality of the mayor in the weak mayor system may occasionally make it possible for him to be a real executive in spite of his legally limited authority. This is certainly the exception rather than the rule.

This system is not highly regarded by experts in municipal administration. But it still persists and therefore must be acceptable to the citizens in the municipalities that continue to use this archaic plan. It is perpetuated by inertia in many areas. It is also a relatively inexpensive method of giving minimum municipal services since little salary is paid to the members of the council in spite of the burden of supervising administrative work. Likewise, small compensation is awarded to the members of boards and commissions that further complicate the operation. The big argument always advanced is that this form of municipal government is democratic since almost everyone is popularly elected and accountable to the people. It does include the time-honored check-and-balance system, with no one vested with sufficient power to become dictatorial. It gains the support of those citizens who feel that municipal services should not be increased and extended, because the machinery does not permit the municipality to undertake anything other than the basic functions expected of a local governmental unit.

The serious defects of the plan usually outweigh its merits. The long ballot that inevitably results is viewed as a definite weakness. The voters are not qualified to elect administrative officials because they don't understand the qualifications that these persons should possess and are unable to judge which candidate has the necessary experience in administrative matters. A most important deficit is the lack of a truly responsible head of government. The passing of the buck is a constant and continuous part of the weak mayor system.

The methods employed in municipal administration under a weak mayor system are frequently a generation or more behind the techniques used in cities with more recent governmental innovations. These old techniques may appear on the surface to be inexpensive, but they actually make the minimum services cost the city more than expanded services would with proper procedures. The use of amateurs at all levels of administration to carry out duties that can be more efficiently and economically executed by trained personnel is common practice. It may be characterized as false economy. The schematic arrangement of weak mayor-council government appears in Figure 5–1.

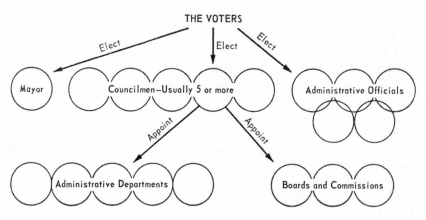

**Fig. 5–1.** The Weak-Mayor Plan of Municipal Government.

There would appear to be no possibility that the weak mayor form of government will increase in number. Annually, cities of all sizes, but particularly those above 5,000 population, are abandoning this form of administration by amateurs for newer systems which emphasize the use of technically trained personnel. Most of the growth in the cities with strong mayor government and a majority of the new council-manager cities has been from the ranks of the municipalities which have never vested sufficient power in any one individual to execute the municipal functions expected by their citizenry. Ordinarily the change results from an awakening of interest in local government stimulated either by a scandal in municipal government or by some citizen groups that demand more services for the tax dollars being expended. State laws may hinder or on rare occasion assist in the change. A few states still circumscribe the cities by forcing them to adhere to an antiquated system, inadequate to meet the demands of the times. However, most states permit a change if proper local interest can be generated.

Lest the mistaken impression arise that within a few years no examples of the weak mayor system will be found, it needs to be added that in all probability the municipalities of less than 5,000 and certainly almost all of those of less than 2,500 population will indefinitely continue to operate under this system. No expert in the field predicts the complete extinction of the weak mayor. As long as the small town in the United States exists, the mayor with limited power and the council with administrative duties will continue to presist.

## Strong Mayor-Council Plan

Dissatisfaction with the weak mayor-council system began to develop in many larger cities in the United States about 1880. As a result, a modification was gradually introduced in many cities using the mayor council form of government in which the mayor was to become the head of the municipal government and the actual chief executive. While the weak mayor system closely follows the pattern established for state government, the strong mayor plan is a replica of the national governmental structure. The new plan solved some of the shortcomings of the weak mayor form and was adopted in many cities of over 50,000 population, but has not been as popular in the smaller cities and towns of the nation.

Under this system the mayor becomes not merely the titular head of the government but the true chief executive with commensurate powers. Administrative authority is concentrated in the hands of the mayor. He is popularly elected as are the members of the council and only one or two other city officials. Thus the ballot is considerably shortened over what is commonly found in the weak mayor type of municipal government. The mayor has the power of appointing virtually all subordinate administrative personnel. He has widespread removal power to accompany his appointive authority. Consequently, he coordinates and supervises the various administrative departments with little or no administrative power in the hands of the council. Likewise, the new plan allows for an executive budget, with the mayor or his finance officer preparing and presenting to the council an annual budget for all administrative functions. The final enactment of the budget and its implementation is vested in the policy-making body, the council, but the initiation and execution of the financial program is the mayor's duty.

The mayor is the center of the municipal government. He speaks for the city, not merely figuratively but literally. His powers are subject to the check of the council in a number of ways in that some of his appointments must be approved by the council; his budget must be passed and enacted into appropriation ordinances by the council, but the public views the actions of the mayor as the image of the city. He is held publicly accountable for governmental actions within the city.

The council under the strong mayor plan is allowed to concentrate its time and energy on the policy-making role that it is best equipped to perform. The amount of time that the individual members of the council need to spend upon city business is greatly reduced from that required under weak mayor council government. The council's size is usually relatively small, often only five or nine except in the very large cities, but even here a marked reduction in the number of members accompanies the switch to strong mayor government. The councilmen are either elected on a partisan or a non-partisan ballot. The larger cities are more inclined to the use of partisan elections. Fifty years ago most city elections were of the partisan variety but a reform movement in the Great Depression days of the 1930's produced a marked decline in the percentage of cities using the partisan ballot for electing the municipal officials, even in strong mayor cities. Some cities use the election by ward method, the larger cities still seem to favor this method, others have modified it with part of the council elected by wards and part at-large. Some cities with strong mayor government have abandoned completely ward elections and have all councilmen elected at-large by all of the voters of the city.

The strong mayor system grants the mayor a veto power that is much more important than under the weak mayor plan. Under the latter plan the mayor usually has a suspensory veto, meaning that if the council passes an ordinance which is then vetoed by the mayor it can be passed again, usually by a mere majority vote, and becomes an ordinance over the veto. In the strong mayor plan the veto of the mayor is subject to being overridden, but only by an extra-ordinary majority, often two-thirds of the council, but in some cities even a three-fourths majority is required. With the focus upon the mayor the veto is supported oftentimes by massive public opinion and thus the council is less likely to attempt to pass the ordinance over the strong mayor's veto.

Usually the only municipal officer not directly under the mayor in this form of the mayor-council government is the city auditor. He is usually either popularly elected or is appointed by and responsible to the city council as his functions are primarily of a postaudit nature.

The key man in the success or failure of this plan is, of course, the mayor. While the council cannot be overlooked, it is the mayor upon whom all attention is centered. It is he who sets the entire tone for the municipal government operation. It is necessary for him to be a true community leader as well as political figure and a ceremonial and administrative head. Obtaining a man of sufficient experience and quality to carry out all of these complex duties is most difficult. Even a superior man may not possess the talent to be an expert in all of these areas. Thus the mayor often finds that he is pressed for time to execute all of his diverse duties. Some provision to assist him is often essential.

Figure 5–2, portraying the strong mayor council form of government, does not vary greatly from the weak mayor system other than the transposition of the departmental officials from accountability to the council to that of the mayor and the elimination of many of the boards and commissions that accompany the weak mayor structure.

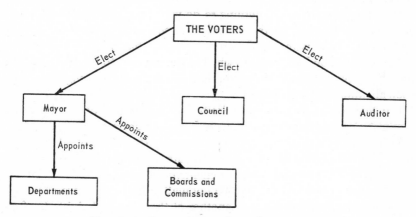

**Fig. 5–2.** Strong Mayor-Council Government.

## Mayor-Administrative Assistant

The newest experiment in the form of municipal governments in the United States is a modification of the strong mayor system. The first major city to employ the so-called mayor-administrator system was probably San Francisco which provided for a chief administrative officer under its mayor-council charter.[4] The administrator is appointed by the mayor in the San Francisco plan, but cannot be removed by him. Removal of the administrator is effected by a recall election or by a two-thirds vote of the council. He is given by the charter both line and staff functions. Under his control are such staff agencies as the purchasing agent and the budget bureau and such line agencies as police, fire, and public welfare. In the San Francisco plan he is independent of the mayor, which may be an asset or a liability. The chief administrative officer is selected by the mayor strictly on the basis of his previous experiences and qualifications

[4] John M. Selig, "The San Francisco Idea," *National Municipal Review*, Vol. XLVI (June, 1957), pp. 290–95.

as an administrator. Naturally, the mayor attempts to get the best possible person, as the success or failure of his administration rests to a large degree on the ability of his administrator. The mayor may find that the administrator's success will mean re-election, but his failure might well make it impossible for the mayor to gain another term.

A more normal organizational arrangement has the administrative assistant appointed by the mayor without confirmation by the council and subject to removal at any time that the mayor desires to relieve him of his duties. This is the pattern followed in Philadelphia. The Philadelphia Home Rule Charter requires the administrator to work closely with the mayor, making appointments only with the mayor's approval. The administrator does not have anything to do with budget preparation, as this function is performed by the mayor's finance director. However, the administrator works with the department heads that he has appointed in preparing their budget requests which are submitted to the budget officer and the mayor. The administrator has the duty of advising the mayor upon all administrative matters.

The New York City mayor-administrator organization does not give the administrator any appointive powers but does charge him with the responsibility of supervising and coordinating the work of all agencies under the jurisdiction of the mayor. The administrator does not have any authority over the budget and personnel departments.[5]

Most of the cities of over 700,000 population in America are at present experimenting with one form or another of the mayor-administrator form of municipal government. In some instances it is a formal arrangement, such as in New York and San Francisco; in others it is on a more informal basis.

Reports of the progress of this new system have almost all been encouraging. Sufficient time to make a detailed analysis of its long-range possibilities has not elapsed. Obviously it is an attempt to combine the good features of both the strong mayor and the council-manager form of municipal government for America's largest cities.

While it is a device used primarily in the largest cities, its value is not restricted to only this group. Duluth, Minnesota, a city of slightly over 100,000, has been using the general plan since 1956. In this city the administrator has full range of administrative responsibilities including budgeting. In many ways the Duluth administrator is a city manager with a different title and with direct accountability to the mayor rather than to the council. He attends council meetings and advises upon policy just as the typical city manager is expected to do. In Duluth, the council as well as the mayor may remove the administrator if they become dis-

[5] Wallace S. Sayre, "The General Manager Idea" for Large Cities, *Public Administration Review*, Vol. XIV (Autumn, 1954), pp. 253–56.

pleased with his actions. Figure 5–3 diagrams the mayor-administrator assistant plan as it operates in many cities.

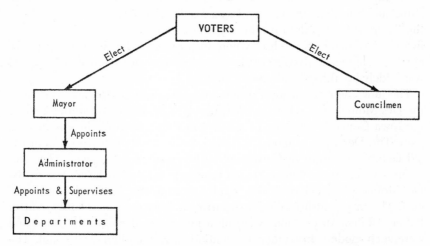

**Fig. 5–3.** Mayor-Administrator Assistant Plan of Municipal Organization.

## Commission Government

Galveston, Texas, in 1901 was the American city which is usually given the credit for the establishment of the unique commission form of government. This is, however, not entirely correct as experiments in this form of municipal government had occurred before the turn of the twentieth century in Sacramento, California, and in other American cities. It is true that the use of the plan in Galveston gave nationwide publicity to commission government which enabled it to spread from Texas to Pennsylvania, New Jersey, and many other states.

The unusual feature of commission government is its complete departure from the traditional checks and balances that has predominated for years in American municipal government as well as in state and national government. In the commission plan the policy-making body serves a dual function of also heading the administrative departments of the municipality. Thus the same men who determine the policy of the city also execute the policy. They pass the appropriation ordinances and then expend the funds through the departments that they head.[6]

In Sacramento, in 1863, the council who individually headed the executive departments consisted of three members. New Orleans in 1870 and

---

[6] T. S. Chang, "History and Analysis of the Commission and City Manager Plans of Municipal Government in the United States" (Ph.D. thesis, University of Iowa, 1918), p. 50.

Mobile, Alabama, in 1873 also used this general format prior to the adoption of the plan in Galveston. Originally the commissioners in Galveston were appointed by state authorities. This was modified because of constitutional questions in 1903, and as a result provisions were approved by the Texas state legislature allowing the commission to be composed of five elected members, each of whom in turn headed a department of the city government and collectively served as the city council. Its success was widely heralded in the American press.

The new commission form of government became popularly known as the Des Moines plan when, in 1907, Des Moines, Iowa, was authorized by the Iowa General Assembly to adopt a modified form of the commission plan. The Des Moines model included the same basic features as in the old commission form in Galveston, with certain improvements. The five commissioners were retained, each popularly elected at large. But in the Des Moines plan each candidate ran for election to a certain departmental post. The mayor also headed a department known as the Department of Public Affairs. All elections were on a non-partisan basis. Also instituted were such modern instruments as initiative, referendum, and recall. The Des Moines plan also included a mandatory civil service system.[7]

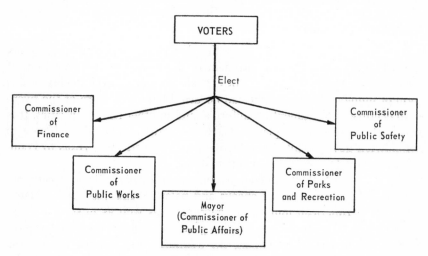

**Fig. 5–4.** Commission Plan of City Government.

Following the Des Moines adoption and modifications nearly five hundred American cities were utilizing the commission plan of municipal government by 1917. In some states all cities in a certain population class were required by the state legislature to use this form of municipal government. World War I marked the date at which this innovation in local

---

[7] Clinton R. Woodruff, *City Government by Commission* (Appleton-Century-Crofts, Inc., 1914), chap. xvii.

government reached its highest peak of popularity. Following the conflict to end all wars the commission form of government began to lose converts.

The advantages afforded under the commission plan were rather obvious to all observers. All power was concentrated in the hands of a relatively few elected commissioners. This naturally assured the voters of a short ballot and at the same time allowed the citizens to fix the responsibility upon the three, five, or seven elected members of the council-administrative unit. It also did away with partisan government in that almost all commission-governed cities held a non-partisan election. With both policy determination and execution in the same hands, very little delay was encountered in putting into effect the policy made by the commissioners. Proponents also proclaimed that accepted corporate business organization principles were followed in the new form of city government.

In spite of these alleged advantages many citizens began to reconsider the wisdom of concentrating both policy-making and policy-executing authority in the same individuals. It was also found that the analogy between the business organization and the municipal organization was not entirely true. Few corporations permit the board of directors to have both policy-making and administrative authority.

It soon became apparent that the voters could not select qualified finance commissioners, public works commissioners, park and recreation commissioners, and other departmental heads. It was also obvious that complete and total abandonment of the check and balance system was not entirely wise. Log-rolling and pork-barreling became almost standard operating procedures in many commission-governed cities, especially during the preparation of the budget and consideration of appropriation ordinances. Many cities found that the rather rigid departmentalization required under the plan did not permit sufficient flexibility to meet their particular problems.

The National Municipal League, which had at first supported the plan, later withdrew its endorsement in favor of an even newer experiment in municipal government—the council-manager plan. This, coupled with the general dissatisfaction encountered in many cities using the commission plan, has led to its abandonment in several cities each year for the last forty years with virtually no movement toward adopting the plan in other cities. This decrease, however, has been very gradual and probably three hundred cities in the United States still use the commission plan. One city in Iowa, Ottumwa, is one of the few if not the only city to abandon commission government in favor of council-manager government, only to return after six years to the commission plan.[8]

[8] The International City Managers' Association, *Municipal Year Book, 1962* (Chicago: The International City Managers' Association, 1962), p. 290.

The position of the mayor is rather unusual in the commission form of government. His department may include a number of administrative units that apparently fit under none of the other commissioners, such as the public health department. He usually has no veto power. He does preside at the meetings of the commissioners but has a single vote just like the other members. His influence will depend more upon his own personality than upon his legal powers. It is true that he frequently receives more publicity than other commissioners. He also appears before the public as the ceremonial head of the city, but his position of leadership is not as strong as most observers believe it should be.

## Council-Manager Government

Council-manager government is the American innovation in municipal government design that has received the most widespread acclaim of all the experiments in the field. It has been considered by many authorities as a major contribution of the United States to the field of municipal government. Not only has it been accepted in America and Canada but also in some European countries. Approximately 2,000 municipalities in America, Canada, Finland, Germany, Ireland, Norway, and Sweden have adopted versions of the American council-manager form of government.[9]

The growth of council-manager government in the United States by 1963 passed the 1900 mark, with nearly seventy-five municipalities being added to the list using this form of government each year since the end of World War II. On the other hand, since 1908 only eighty-one municipalities that adopted the plan either by charter or by popular referendum have abandoned this form of municipal operation.[10]

It is widely accepted that in 1908 the small city of Staunton, Virginia, was the first to institute a city manager. The city council passed an ordinance in that year creating the post of general manager. The first general manager appointed from a long list of applicants was a young civil engineer. The administrative operation of the municipality was entrusted to him with few restrictions. The plan received favorable publicity from the newly created National Short Ballot Organization and was incorporated in the city charter of Sumter, South Carolina, in 1912. Acceptance for the next two years was slow, with only seven cities adopting the system: The only municipality west of the Mississippi was Clarinda, Iowa, which passed a city manager ordinance in 1913. In 1914 the first city of more than 100,000—Dayton, Ohio—installed the manager system. The elements of nature played an important role as Dayton had just experienced a

[9] The International City Managers' Association, *Municipal Year Book, 1964* (Chicago: The International City Managers' Association, 1964), pp. 263–66.
[10] *Ibid.*, p. 264.

disastrous flood and was seeking a government that could handle the situation. The experience in Dayton aroused great interest in the idea and within five years more than one hundred new cities adopted the plan.

State after state authorized their cities to adopt this new innovation. By 1964 only Indiana and Hawaii did not have a single city using the council-manager idea. The basic premises upon which the government operates are very simple. The voters elect a relatively small council, usually only five members but occasionally, in the largest cities, as many as nine or more, who confine their primary function to that of policy determination. The council, usually elected at large on a non-partisan basis, selects a trained professional administrator to "run" the administrative affairs of the municipality, holding him accountable for the success or failure of the administrative programs. The manager is given great freedom in selecting his department heads and staff personnel. He is also given authority to establish modern purchasing and accounting methods. He is required to submit to the council an annual budget for the city as well as make periodic reports on the financial conditions of all city operations. He is usually not given a contract but rather serves only as long as the council has confidence in his administration. His salary is set by the council as are the qualifications that he must possess. The key feature of the plan has been the employment of trained experts in various aspects of municipal administration. The chief ingredients have been compared with the methods used by major corporations of having a board of directors to make policy and then employing an administrator to execute the policy. It has also been likened to the traditional school situation in which the school board turns over all actual administrative operations to a professional school administrator.

It should be stressed that the success or failure of the plan does not necessarily rest with the manager as is popularly believed but rather with the quality of the membership of the city council. The council has the final word in all policy decisions. The manager will be only as good as the city council wants and allows him to be. Some city managers have more talent than others, but the council's role is still the dominant one in the council-manager plan. A council that desires the city manager to be a mere office boy or a cheap politician will in all probability get just such a man. On the other hand a council that is willing to support a dynamic, aggressive, positive administrator will find such a person to fill the city manager's chair.

Many of the early city managers were civil engineers probably because of the need for improvements in streets and other projects that required engineering talents. Today, the trend is toward a trained, general administrator rather than a specialist in one particular phase of municipal administration. To be sure, some knowledge of the principles and basic fundamentals of engineering is valuable to a city manager but more and more this part of the manager's job has been overshadowed by the problems of over-all administration. It has been found that a city engineer is needed as a specialist to work under the direction and guidance of the manager, but this phase of the work should not dominate the over-all operation of municipal government.[11]

It is becoming more common for city managers to exercise a degree of leadership in policy initiation. Factors that determine the exact degree of leadership include: the political climate in the community, the established traditions, the length of time the manager has served the city, the previous experience of the manager, the attitudes of the councilmen, and the attitudes of the citizens. In cities with the right combination of factors the leadership of the manager may approach that of a strong mayor, even in political affairs. No manager can administer a city satisfactorily if he is not free at least to initiate recommendations for legislative action. However, the final decision is the council's policy.

The city manager cannot avoid becoming involved in policy formation merely because it may involve matters that are controversial. It is his duty to present to the council all of the available facts and to encourage the council to weigh these facts when considering their course of action. This information must include technical information as well as advisory statements, accompanied by an interpretation of the technical aspects of municipal operations.

The International City Managers' Association, organized in 1914, has done much to assure a professionalization of the city managers of America. In 1963 a total of 1,609 managers were members, with an additional 1,823 persons holding membership in the organization. The group has a code of ethics, adopted in 1924, to which all members must subscribe. It also provides opportunity for in-service training in more than eleven courses in municipal administration to keep its members and other municipal employees abreast of the latest developments in the field. A management information service is maintained to answer specific questions on management problems and topics.

The trend is continuing toward the appointment of city managers with public administration training. Of those appointed in 1963 with a bachelor's or advanced degree, 52 per cent majored in political science, government, or public administration while 21 per cent hold degrees in engineering, and 13 per cent majored in social sciences other than political science.

A comprehensive profile of city managers shows the average city manager is serving in a city of approximately 10,000 population outside a metropolitan area. He is a college graduate and is in his early 40's. In

---

[11] The International City Managers' Association, *City Management—A Growing Profession* (Chicago: The International City Managers' Association, 1957), pp. 48–51.

college he majored in political science with some public administration
courses. He was upon appointment, a nonresident of the city and is receiving an annual salary of $11,343. He will remain as the city's chief
administrative officer for approximately five years before resigning to accept an appointment in a larger city with greater responsibility and financial reward.[12]

In spite of its many advantages—simplicity, use of experts in all key
positions, concentration of power in an elected responsible body, and
separation of policy determination and policy execution—the plan is not
perfect. One of the most common problems that arises in council-manager
cities is the lack of effective community leadership caused by the failure
of the mayor, usually elected by the council from its own membership on
a year-to-year basis, to assume leadership in policy formation. The vacuum thus created often is at least partially filled by the city manager, but
frequently this leads to involving the professional administrator in partisan community issues that should be settled by the council. There is not
much doubt that the manager is the one man in the community with the
most experience and knowledge of the community's problems, but to what
extent he should aid in creating the policy to be adopted by the council
is still a much-debated question.

Another alleged weakness is the lack of direct popular control over the
chief executive of the city. Actually the use of initiative, referendum, and
recall, which frequently is a part of a city charter that incorporates the
council-manager plan, alleviates this problem.

A charge frequently launched by labor union leaders who are often
opposed to the manager plan is that of dictatorship. They contend that
too much power is placed in the hands of the city manager. This alleged
weakness is based upon the erroneous assumption that because no administrative officials are popularly elected, the system is undemocratic.
This mistakenly links democracy with the long ballot. It also fails to understand that the council has the total power and authority of the city and
is popularly elected in the fullest democratic sense. Figure 5–5 shows the
organizational structure typically found with council-manager government.

A weakness of the council-manager plan that has occasionally appeared
has been the tendency to appoint a home-town boy as the manager once
the system has been operating successfully with outside professional appointees. This may denote a subordination of professional training and
competence to partisan or political expediency.

The organizational diagram would make it appear that there is a sharp
distinction between policy-making and administration. Unfortunately no
such line exists—one merely melts into the other. It is not possible to draw

[12] The International City Managers' Association, *The Municipal Year Book, 1964*
(Chicago: The International City Managers' Association, 1964), pp. 498–507.

the neat distinctions that might appear to be present. Another complicating factor is the presence of boards and commissions that may not be automatically replaced by the adoption of the council-manager plan in some cities. These administrative units continue to operate in their own sphere of power and compound the difficulties of the city manager in operating an efficient municipal administration.

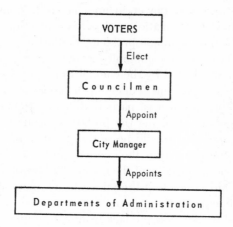

**Fig. 5–5.** Council-Manager Plan of Municipal Government.

Some cities have found that the supply of qualified city administrators is such that no competent manager can be obtained. This problem was probably more intense immediately following World War II than in the 1960's, however, as many universities all over America in recent years have been offering curricula which young men in increasing numbers have been taking to train as city administrators. Likewise the number of assistant city managers has been steadily increasing and most of these men are eager to become city managers on their own.

## MUNICIPAL ADMINISTRATION

The determination of what functions shall be performed by a municipality is a policy decision or series of decisions that is the prerogative of the city council. Not quite all of the local activities carried out by the municipal governments are decisions made at the local level, however, since several of the functions listed by the Commission on Intergovernmental Relations as being locally financed and administered are not voluntarily assumed, but have been forced upon the local unit by a higher governmental authority, usually the state government.

LOCAL FUNCTIONS—LOCALLY FINANCED
AND ADMINISTERED[13]

1. Registration and conduct of elections
2. Fire Fighting
3. Inspectional activities, e.g., building, plumbing, electrical, gas, boiler, elevator, smoke
4. Construction and maintenance of streets and alleys
5. Sewage systems and sewage disposal plants
6. Street cleaning
7. Garbage and refuse collection and disposal
8. Health inspections, including milk, food handlers, water supply
9. Municipally owned public utilities, e.g., water works, gas plants, street railways and bus systems, markets, cemeteries

In order to effectively execute the functions that must be performed by the municipality a structural arrangement whereby the individuals and positions are related in a chain of responsibility is essential.[14] Administrative departments are usually divided into at least three categories: line departments which are the agencies operating to provide services directly to the people; general staff, whose work is dealing with planning and high-policy matters; and technical staff, who combine advisory, control, and service actions, and auxiliary or housekeeping departments, who perform services essential to keeping the line agencies operating, including managing public buildings, providing heat and light for municipal places, stenographic services, maintenance of municipal garage, mailing services, and general record keeping.

The units of administration usually used in municipalities are commonly divided into departments, bureaus, boards and commissions, and authorities. A department is defined as a primary unit of organization dealing with a major field of administration, with the head of the unit in direct contact and supervised by the chief administrator. A bureau is the major internal unit of a department. It is a so-called working unit which performs either a single task or series of related activities. Boards are technically defined as a small group—five, seven, or nine lay citizens paid on a per diem basis who usually perform advisory activities within a department. A commission, in contrast, may be characterized as a smaller group—three or five persons most commonly—who have some degree of expertise, devote full time to the work, and receive a regular salary. Their duties are: administrative, quasi-legislative, and quasi-judicial. Strict adherence to these definitions and delimitations of the duties and responsibilities of boards and commissions is unusual. In some municipal hier-

[13] Commission on Intergovernmental Relations, *Local Government* (Washington, D.C.: U.S. Bureau of the Census, Government Printing Office, 1955), pp. 18–19.
[14] John M. Gaus, "Theory of Organization," *Frontiers of Public Administration* (Chicago: The University of Chicago Press, 1936), p. 66.

archies the boards and commissions are not included within a department but have an independent status. Ordinarily the members of boards and commissions are appointed, but some are popularly elected.

Public authorities utilized in local governmental units have a corporate status which affords flexibility of management, allowing them to undertake public activities of a commercial nature. This independent and corporate position is often used in connection with public housing projects and at times in urban renewal programs.

## MUNICIPAL EXPENDITURES BY FUNCTION

In most cities, public schools are administered by independent school districts, but in spite of this, education takes a larger share of city expenditures than any other single function. Next to the education costs, expenditures were greatest for streets, with $1,700,000,000 being spent in 1962 by the municipalities for this functional activity. About half of this total was for capital outlay. Third, in terms of total expenditures, was the $1,500,000,000 the cities spent for sanitation, including sewage systems, disposal plants, and refuse collection. Two fifths of the total was devoted to capital improvements and investments in sewage disposal plants. Fourth, in terms of total costs for municipalities was the $1,400,000,000 expended for police protection, while fire protection costs amounted to just under one billion dollars—$964,000,000. The sixth most costly function relates to health administration and hospitals, for which $880,000,000 was expended; only $175,000,000 was used for public health administration and the remainder for hospitals.

Personnel expenditures—salaries for the employees of municipalities—constituted in 1962 approximately 44 per cent of the total moneys expended for municipalities. Indebtedness of municipalities totaled $26,-800,000,000, of which $16 billion was of long-term indebtedness, while only $1.7 billion was of the short-term variety, and $9.1 billion was non-guaranteed or revenue-bond indebtedness, not based upon the full-faith and credit of the municipalities.[15]

Per-capita costs of municipal administration tend to increase as the population increases. In cities of more than a million the average per-person costs were 51 per cent larger than those of cities between 100,000 and 250,000 population. In turn, their costs were 100 per cent greater than the cost of services municipalities rendered in cities having fewer than

[15] U.S. Department of Commerce, Bureau of the Census, *Compendium of City Government Finances in 1962* (Washington, D.C.: Government Printing Office, 1963), pp. 1-2.

25,000 people.[16] This per-capita ratio has held relatively constant in recent years and would appear to be stabilized. The same report does reveal an interesting phenomenon in that the four cities in the above one million category, other than New York City, actually had a lower expenditure per person than the cities in the 100,000- to one-million classification.

## Police Protection

The specific purposes of police departments as organized in every American municipality, whether large or small, are crime prevention, apprehension of criminals, protection of property, regulation of traffic, and maintenance of public order. The purposes are expressed in the department's divisions: patrol division, detective division, crime prevention, and traffic. In addition to these purely line activities, auxiliary divisions of identification, records, communications, maintenance of equipment and property, and personnel are usually operative.

Increasing emphasis in recent years has been placed upon the crime prevention activities of American municipal police. This type of police work concentrates upon juvenile delinquency and its causes. Since the predominant age group in criminal offenses continues to be the 16- to 23-year-old group, criminal prevention divisions check upon areas within the city likely to encourage youthful criminal conduct. The aim is not so much to apprehend the young law breaker as it is to prevent continuation of juvenile crime waves. This division works with the character-building agencies of the community.

The traffic division has as its main responsibility the total enforcement of all traffic rules. Everyone is aware that there is a close relationship between traffic law enforcement and the number of accidents. Only if all traffic laws are rigidly enforced will the number of accidents be reduced by 15 to 20 per cent in a single year. No favored treatment, ticket fixing, and other over-looking of violations can be tolerated.

The detective or investigative unit concentrates upon the specialized work involved in the detection and apprehension of criminals. To combat the specialization arising among criminals an equal specialization among the members of the police is necessary.

The uniformed patrol function is the first line of defense against crime. Whether patrol is by car or on foot, the patrolling officer has a multiple number of duties. Included in his job is making arrests of persons who have broken the law, investigating complaints, giving aid and assistance,

[16] U.S. Department of Commerce, Bureau of the Census, *Summary of City Government Finances in 1957* (Washington, D.C.: Government Printing Office, 1958), table 7, p. 13.

reporting and investigating accidents, suppressing disturbances of all kinds, preventing crimes, and in general seeing that law and order—domestic tranquility—is maintained.

## Fire Protection

The basic duties of the fire departments in U.S. municipalities have much in common throughout the country. All are concerned with fighting fires, the prevention of fires, the investigation of fires as to cause, rescue operations, salvage, and the necessary repair and maintenance of fire fighting equipment.

Too frequently fire departments concentrate their attention upon the single purpose of fighting fires. This is particularly true of the volunteer fire department which is on call only if an emergency arises. Many cities have found that rather than confine the fire department work to actual fighting conflagrations, the fire loss record may be most rapidly improved by greater emphasis upon fire prevention operations. Basic to a fire prevention program is an adequate, modern building code and local laws concerning hazardous materials, machinery, and occupations. This combination is often spoken of as the fire prevention code. Responsibility for its over-all enforcement must be placed with the fire department's fire prevention bureau for maximum results.

Most state governments contribute both to local fire and police protection by the enactment of legislation that permits local governments to deal comprehensively with these two functional activities. Both of these divisions of the public safety arm of municipalities are given assistance by many state agencies in training programs, assistance in specialized phases of their activities, and to a more limited extent in other personnel matters. State-wide civil service laws exist in most states that require local jurisdictions to select personnel on a merit system basis. Even the total number of hours that employees in these two departments may be required to work in a week are regulated by many state statutes. Retirement programs also are established under state regulation and in some instances with minor state financial support.

## Public Health

A wide range of municipal activities are involved in the general area of public health. All to a degree are supervised by state authorities and given assistance by state officials. At the demand of the state public health authorities all major cities in most states are required to operate sewage systems and sewage disposal plants. Collection of garbage and refuse is also a part of the over-all sanitation program for the preservation of healthful living conditions in a municipal area. State regulations as to the disposition of garbage and refuse material makes it mandatory for the cities to follow designated procedures. State testing of public water supplies furnished by the municipality is still another example of state and local cooperation for the ultimate purpose of safeguarding public health. Control of contagious diseases, while primarily a state problem, is largely centered in the local municipal or county public health department. Many cities and some counties also maintain hospitals that are in part financially assisted by state and by national programs. Municipal public health clinics and specialized programs are administered locally but under the direct supervision of the state department of public health.

## Public Welfare

Public welfare protects individuals and families against potential or actual social disaster, including economic wants, and helps them find the means to regain economic and social self-sufficiency.[17] While many of the social welfare functions have gravitated toward the larger governmental units—state and national—some activities still are vested in the local municipal governments. Most of these are viewed as "emergency" operations to merely sustain the unfortunate victims until permanent or semipermanent alleviation of their plight can be achieved by established state or national agencies. Poor relief or general assistance and child welfare programs have become quite common in the larger metropolitan areas. Occasionally the cities have been able to delegate a large proportion of the emergency relief cases to privately supported welfare agencies, thus relieving the local public authorities of a major problem, but not of the ultimate responsibility.

## Streets and Street-Related Functions

The major responsibility of a city's public works department is construction and maintenance of a street system adequate to meet the needs of the citizens for transportation. Auxiliary functions include street lighting, street naming, house numbering, sidewalk construction and maintenance, and the establishment of standards for these public works projects. Proper snow removal and street cleaning are other problems that must be economically and efficiently handled.

Both the state and national governments have in recent years given assistance to the municipalities in the construction and maintenance of urban highways and street construction. In a recent year, of all moneys

[17] Fred H. Steininger, "Public Welfare, Developments in 1956," in *The Municipal Year Book 1957*, (Chicago: The International City Managers' Association, 1957), p. 296.

spent on urban highways and streets 16 per cent came from the national government, about 18 per cent from state aid, and 63 per cent from local tax revenues.[18] This ratio, like the over-all costs of municipal services, would seem to have established a pattern which is changed only slightly from year to year. The trend is, however, in the direction of more state aid to the local governments in meeting their street and urban highway problems.

## Parks and Recreational Activities

Even though the national and state governments have moved steadily into the area of providing parks and recreational facilities, the municipalities continue to have a responsibility in this field that consumes more than $600 million each year, or nearly 3 per cent of total municipal expenditures.[19] Parks are the largest single item in a municipal recreational program, even though few cities have the accepted minimum standard of 100 acres of park area for each 10,000 residents. The different types of recreational facilities that may be included in a city's program is almost endless: including playfields, athletic fields, golf courses, baseball and softball diamonds, zoological gardens, zoos, swimming pools, ice-skating areas, picnic areas, archery ranges, horseshoe courts, tennis courts, dance pavilions, stadiums, and aquariums.

Indoor recreational facilities are an even greater financial burden upon many municipal recreational programs. The maintenance and equipment necessary for indoor swimming, basketball, volleyball, wrestling, and other indoor sports require tremendous capital expenditures that can usually be financed only through bond issues.

## City Planning and Zoning

City planning, while primarily defined in terms of directing the physical development of the city, is concerned with all functions of municipal government. It is almost universally agreed that it is impossible to separate physical planning and program planning. It is not enough to plan for only the land area within the city limits, but it must include territory for at least several miles beyond the city boundaries. Edward M. Bassett points to seven principal elements in any comprehensive city development program:[20]

[18] U.S. Department of Commerce, Bureau of the Census, *Statistical Abstract of the United States* (Washington, D.C.: Government Printing Office, 1958), p. 549.

[19] U.S. Department of Commerce, Bureau of the Census, *Compendium of City Government Finances in 1962* (Washington, D.C.: Government Printing Office, 1963), p. 4.

[20] Edward M. Bassett, *The Master Plan* (New York: The Russell Sage Foundation, 1938).

1. Streets and street layouts
2. Parks and recreational areas
3. Sites for public buildings
4. Public reservations
5. Zoning districts
6. Routes for public utilities
7. Pierhead and bulkhead lines

Zoning is the basic tool used to implement the comprehensive municipal plan. It is exercised under the municipalities' police power to protect the public health, welfare, and morals. The best definition of zoning is that it is the dividing of a community into districts according to the permissible use of properties for the purpose of controlling and directing their use and development. Included is the land use, height and size of buildings, the proportion of a lot that may be covered by a structure, thus controlling the density of the population in a zoned area.

## Municipal Public Utilities

The number-one municipal-owned public utility is the water distribution systems. Approximately three-fourths of all American cities own and operate their own distribution systems and two-thirds own their own water supplies. Publicly owned powers systems serve only about 14 per cent of the nation's residential electric consumers. An even smaller percentage of the gas systems of the United States are owned by municipalities, with only 665 such public utilities operated by cities.[21]

Because of financial necessity cities are rapidly assuming most of the responsibilities for urban transit systems, as these have proven to be impossible to operate profitably under the free-enterprise system. Similarly, airports are not financially feasible on a private ownership basis and are a public service supported and operated by most American municipalities of more than 25,000 population.

## BIBLIOGRAPHY

ADRIAN, CHARLES R. *Governing Urban America*, 2d ed. New York: McGraw-Hill Book Co., Inc., 1961.

BANFIELD, EDWARD (ed.). *Urban Government: A Reader in Administration and Politics*. New York: The Free Press of Glencoe, Inc., 1961.

BOLLENS, JOHN C. (ed.). *Exploring the Metropolitan Community*. Berkeley: University of California Press, 1961.

BROMAGE, ARTHUR W. *Introduction to Municipal Government and Administration*, 2d ed. New York: Appleton-Century-Crofts, Inc., 1957.

[21] The International City Managers' Association, *The Municipal Year Book 1963* (Chicago: The International Managers' Association, 1963), pp. 367–69.

Buck, A. E. *Municipal Finance.* New York: The Macmillan Co., 1926.

Fiser, Webb S. *Mastery of the Metropolis.* Englewood Cliffs, N.J.: Prentice-Hall Spectrum Books, 1962.

Greer, Scott. *The Emerging City: Myth or Reality.* New York: The Free Press of Glencoe, Inc., 1962.

Hirsch, Werner Z. *Urban Life and Form.* New York: Holt, Rinehart & Winston, Inc., 1963.

Hodges, Henry G. *City Management.* New York: F. S. Crofts & Co., 1939.

International City Managers' Series, The: Chicago.
*Municipal Fire Administration,* 6th ed., 1956.
*Municipal Public Works Administration,* 5th ed., 1957.
*Supervisory Methods in Municipal Administration,* 1958.
*The Technique of Municipal Administration,* 4th ed., 1958.
*Local Planning Administration,* 3d ed., 1959.
*Municipal Personnel Administration,* 6th ed., 1960.
*Municipal Recreation Administration,* 4th ed., 1960.
*Municipal Police Administration,* 5th ed., 1961.
*Municipal Finance Administration,* 6th ed., 1962.

Jennings, M. Kent. *Community Influentials: The Elites of Atlanta.* New York: The Free Press of Glencoe, Inc., 1964.

Kammerer, Gladys M., *et al. City Managers in Politics.* Gainesville: University of Florida Press, 1962.

Kneier, Charles M. *City Government in the United States,* 3d ed. New York: Harper & Row, Inc., 1957.

Mills, Warner E., and Davis, Harry. *Small City Government: Seven Cases in Decision Making.* New York: Random House, 1962.

Mowitz, Robert J., and Wright, Deil S. *Profile of A Metropolis.* Detroit: Wayne State University Press, 1962.

Municipal Manpower Commission. *Governmental Manpower for Tomorrow's Cities.* New York: McGraw-Hill Book Co., Inc., 1963.

*Municipal Yearbook.* Chicago: The International City Managers' Association. (Published each year.)

MacCorkle, Stuart. *American Muunicipal Government and Administration.* Boston: D. C. Heath & Co., 1948.

Macdonald, Austin. *American City Government and Administration,* 6th ed. New York: Thomas Y. Crowell Co., 1956.

Morlan, Robert. *Capitol, Courthouse, and City Hall.* Boston: Houghton Mifflin Co., 1954.

Pate, James E. *Local Government and Administration.* Cincinnati: American Book Co., 1954.

Pfiffner, John M. *Municipal Administration.* New York: The Ronald Press Co., 1940.

Phillips, Jewell Cass. *Municipal Government and Administration in America.* New York: The Macmillan Co., 1960.

Reed, Thomas H. *Municipal Management.* New York: McGraw-Hill Co., Inc., 1941.

Sayre, Wallace, and Kaufman, Herbert. *Governing New York City: Politics in the Metropolis.* New York: W. W. Norton & Co., Inc., 1965.

Schattschneider, E. E., and Jones, Victor. *Local Political Surveys.* New York: Holt, Rinehart & Winston, Inc., 1962.

SCHULTZ, ERNEST W. *American City Government: Its Machinery and Processes.* New York: Stackpole & Heck, Inc., 1949.

STEEL, ERNEST W. *Municipal Affairs.* Scranton, Pa.: International Textbook Co., 1950.

UPSON, LENT D. *Practice of Municipal Administration.* New York: The Century Co., 1926.

WHITE, MORTON, and WHITE, LUCIA. *The Intellectual Versus the City.* New York: The New American Library of World Literature, Inc. (Mentor), 1964.

WILDAVSKY, AARON. *Leadership in a Small Town.* Totowa, N.J.: Bedminster Press, 1964.

WILLIAMS, O. P., and PRESS, C. *Democracy in Urban America.* Chicago: Rand McNally & Co., 1961.

WOOD, ROBERT C., and ALMENDINGER, VLADIMIR V. *1400 Governments.* Cambridge: Harvard University Press, 1961.

WOODBURY, COLEMAN (ed.). *The Future of Cities and Urban Development.* Chicago: The University of Chicago Press, 1953.

ZINK, HAROLD. *Government of Cities in the United States,* rev. ed. New York: The Macmillan Co., 1948.

# 6

# Metropolitan Government

The governing of the metropolitan areas of America has become one of the major problems confronting the states. Every state except Alaska, New Hampshire, and Wyoming has one or more metropolitan areas. This is not a problem that has come upon the scene overnight, as its growth has been visible for at least forty years; but the flood of Americans into the metropolitan areas in the last fifteen years has staggered the expectations of even the most farsighted planners and population experts.

## DEVELOPMENT OF THE STANDARD METROPOLITAN STATISTICAL AREA

The first recognition given to what are now commonly known as metropolitan areas was by the United States Bureau of the Census in 1910, when population statistics were first listed for metropolitan areas, which in the previous year had been termed industrial districts.[1] In both 1910 and 1920 a metropolitan area was defined as one in which there was a central city of at least 200,000 population, not included in the area of a still larger city, and all of the area within ten miles of the boundary of the core city with a density of at least 150 persons per square mile.

In 1930 the definition utilized in classifying metropolitan areas was changed to the so-called theory of continuous density. The new definition required a core city of only 50,000 and a total area population of at least 100,000. The area outside the core city included all adjacent and contiguous civil divisions having a density of not less than 150 persons per square mile, and usually all contiguous civil districts, even though they did not meet the density criteria, if they in turn were surrounded by densely populated territory that did exceed the minimum population requirements.

[1] Paul Studenski, *The Government of Metropolitan Areas in the United States* (New York: National Municipal League, 1930), p. 9.

In 1950 the definition was slightly altered and the term changed to the standard metropolitan area. The new definition centered upon a county or a group of contiguous counties which contained at least one city of 50,000 or more persons. The United States Census Bureau's comments on the new standard metropolitan area are of interest as they proclaim the new definition to be based on "the criteria of metropolitan character related primarily to the character of the county as a place of work or as a home concentration of nonagricultural workers and their dependents. The criteria of integration relate primarily to the extent of economic and social communication between the outlying counties and the central county."[2] New England is given a special definition with the standard metropolitan areas including the central city of at least 50,000 and surrounding cities and towns having a population density of 150 or more per square mile or 100 persons or more per square mile where strong economic and social integration is present.

Some criticism of the definition has arisen. It is best summarized by Professor W. A. Robson, English political scientist at the London School of Economics, when he wrote:

These criteria are satisfied by a very large number of areas which cannot claim to be metropolitan centers in the proper sense of the term. The figure of 50,000 for the "core" city is so small that it robs the word "metropolitan" of any sociological and political significance; and the definition takes no account whatever of the functions which should be performed by a metropolitan area worthy of the name . . . only metropolitan areas with a central city of at least 400,000 should be regarded as possessing metropolitan status. There were in 1951 about 33 such areas. They would fulfill the functional conditions referred to above.[3]

On the basis of the Census Bureau's definition there were in the United States in 1950, 168 metropolitan areas rather than the 33 that Professor Robson believed merited the connotation. In 1957 the number had risen to 174, had increased to 211 by 1960, and to 212 in 1962. Under the Robson suggestion the 1960 total would have been only 30 metropolitan areas as there were only thirty cities of 400,000 or more population. In Figure 6-1 the 212 Standard Metropolitan Statistical Areas of the United States in 1962 are indicated.

## POPULATION TRENDS IN METROPOLITAN AREAS

The 1960 census revealed that there were still only five cities in the United States with more than 1,000,000 residents within their city bound-

[2] U.S. Department of Commerce, Bureau of the Census, *Local Government in Standard Metropolitan Areas* (Washington, D.C.: Government Printing Office, 1957), pp. 2–3.

[3] W. A. Robson (ed.), *Great Cities of the World* (New York: The Macmillan Co., 1955), p. 31.

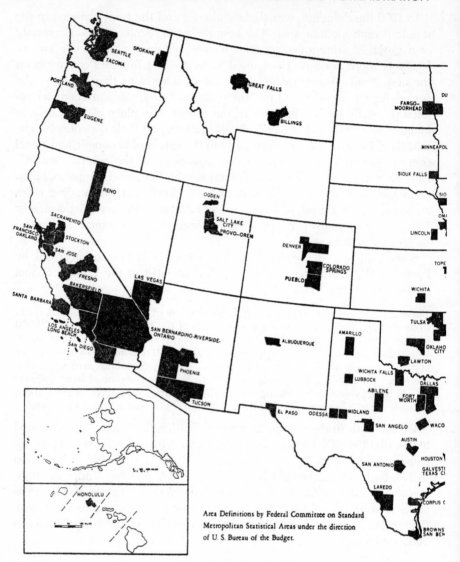

**Fig. 6–1.** Standard Metropolitan Statistical Areas of the United States—1962.

aries. There had been the same five above one million in 1950 and 1940. However, between 1950 and 1960 four of the five largest American cities actually lost population, the only exception being Los Angeles. Of an additional fifteen cities in the population range between 500,000 and 1,000,000, more than half, eight, lost population while the other seven gained. Several of these cities which registered net gains did so because

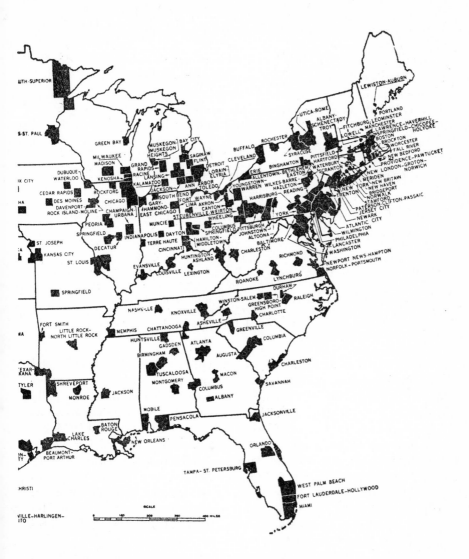

(Source: U.S. Department of Commerce, Bureau of the Census.)

of ambitious programs of territorial annexation. The 1960 census showed that almost 113 million people were living in 212 Standard Metropolitan Statistical Areas.

However, when the metropolitan areas are considered rather than merely the core cities the picture changes drastically. Between 1950 and 1960 the total increase of population in the United States was 26.5 million.

Of this increase 22.5 million occurred in the metropolitan areas with the increase outside of the recognized standard metropolitan areas being only four million.

The areas outside the core cities witnessed the greatest growth in the 1950's. The population in the suburban areas increased at a rate more than six times that of the central city and approximately three times as great as the average for the nation. The population increases for the United States metropolitan areas from 1930 to 1960 are indicated in Table 6-1.

TABLE 6-1

Population Increases for United States Metropolitan Areas—1930–1960
(in percentages)

| Area | 1930–1940 | 1940–1950 | 1950–1960 |
|---|---|---|---|
| Standard Metropolitan Areas | 8.1 | 21.9 | 26.4 |
| Central cities | 5.1 | 13.8 | 9.0 |
| Outlying areas | 15.1 | 35.5 | 48.0 |
| Non-metropolitan Areas | 6.5 | 6.1 | 7.1 |
| United States | 7.2 | 14.4 | 18.5 |

Source: U.S. Department of Commerce, Bureau of the Census, *U.S. Census of Population, 1950,* Vol. I (Washington, D.C.: Government Printing Office, 1952); and *U.S. Census of Population, 1960,* Vol. I (Washington, D.C.: Government Printing Office, 1963).

The standard metropolitan areas grew not only in number but in total population between 1950 and 1960 at a rate nearly 50 per cent greater than the United States as a whole and approximately four times as rapidly as the non-metropolitan areas. The fastest growing metropolitan area was Fort Lauderdale-Hollywood, Florida, which had a phenomenal 297.9 per cent increase. Others with extraordinary increases included Las Vegas, Nevada, 163 per cent; Midland, Michigan, 162.6 per cent; Orlando, Florida, 124.6 per cent; San Jose, California, 121.1 per cent; Odessa, Texas, 116 per cent; and Phoenix, Arizona, 100 per cent. A listing of the metropolitan areas of over one million population according to the 1960 census, together with the populations of the core cities and the number of governmental units, is provided in Table 6-2.

Only eight of the standard metropolitan areas lost population in the decade 1950–1960. Six of these were in the Northeast sector of the United States. The metro area with the largest percentile loss was Wilkes-Barre–Hazelton, Pennsylvania, with a decrease of 11.5 per cent, followed by Scranton, Pennsylvania, −8.9 per cent; St. Joseph, Missouri, −6.4 per cent; Jersey City, New Jersey, −5.7 per cent; Johnstown, Pennsylvania, −3.6 per cent; Texarkana, Texas-Arkansas, −3.1 per cent; Wheeling, West Virginia, −3.0 per cent; Altoona, Pennsylvania, −1.6 per cent. Three of these eight were included within the state of Pennsylvania.

## TABLE 6–2

### Metropolitan Areas of Over One Million Population—1960

| Rank | Core City | Population of Core City | Population of Metropolitan Area | Number of Governmental Units Included |
|---|---|---|---|---|
| 1. | New York, N.Y. | 7,710,346 | 10,602,382 | 555 |
| 2. | Los Angeles–Long Beach, Calif. | 2,450,068 | 6,668,975 | 348 |
| 3. | Chicago, Ill. | 3,511,648 | 6,171,517 | 1,060 |
| 4. | Philadelphia, Pa.–N.J. | 1,971,239 | 4,301,283 | 963 |
| 5. | Detroit, Mich. | 1,654,125 | 3,743,447 | 241 |
| 6. | San Francisco–Oakland, Calif. | 716,276 | 2,725,841 | 398 |
| 7. | Boston, Mass. | 682,303 | 2,566,732 | 125 |
| 8. | Pittsburgh, Pa. | 597,745 | 2,392,086 | 806 |
| 9. | St. Louis, Mo.–Ill. | 747,127 | 2,046,477 | 439 |
| 10. | Washington, D.C.–Md.–Va. | 745,603 | 1,967,682 | 69 |
| 11. | Cleveland, Ohio | 869,728 | 1,786,740 | 137 |
| 12. | Baltimore, Md. | 922,244 | 1,707,462 | 23 |
| 13. | Newark, N.J. | 402,815 | 1,682,882 | 204 |
| 14. | Minneapolis–St. Paul, Minn. | 477,884 | 1,474,149 | 261 |
| 15. | Buffalo, N.Y. | 529,646 | 1,301,604 | 153 |
| 16. | Houston, Tex. | 932,630 | 1,236,704 | 82 |
| 17. | Milwaukee, Wis. | 732,637 | 1,184,806 | 149 |
| 18. | Paterson–Passaic, N.J. | 142,301 | 1,183,514 | 198 |
| 19. | Seattle, Wash. | 551,539 | 1,098,741 | 281 |
| 20. | Dallas, Tex. | 672,424 | 1,098,741 | 60 |
| 21. | Cincinnati, O.–Ky. | 502,484 | 1,067,669 | 131 |
| 22. | Kansas City, Mo.–Kan. | 473,435 | 1,034,150 | 221 |
| 23. | Atlanta, Ga. | 484,825 | 1,010,577 | 84 |
| 24. | San Diego, Calif. | 544,496 | 1,000,496 | 140 |

SOURCE: *Census of Governments, 1962,* Vol. I, U.S. Department of Commerce, Bureau of the Census (Washington, D.C.: Government Printing Office, 1963).

Geographical location apparently is more significant in the change in size of the metropolitan areas than the total population of metropolitan areas. In the Northeast, where the areas are old and many have experienced a depressed economy, the rate of increase is only half that of the national average of the metropolitan areas. In the South and the West the rate of growth is much greater than in the Midwest or East, with the South increasing 38 per cent higher than the average and the West metropolitan areas growing at a rate 83 per cent obove the median.

The shift from the central cities to the suburban regions of the metropolitan areas is evident upon examination of the record from 1900 to 1960. In the 1960 census returns the suburban areas of all of the 211 areas almost equalled the total of the core city areas, the breakdown showing 51.4 per cent being in the core cities and 48.6 per cent in the suburbs surrounding the central cities.

The percentages of metropolitan residents living in the core cities and the suburbs for selected years are listed below:

| | Central Cities Population | Suburb Population |
|---|---|---|
| 1900 | 66.5% | 33.5% |
| 1910 | 66.3% | 33.7% |
| 1920 | 66.2% | 33.8% |
| 1930 | 63.9% | 36.1% |
| 1940 | 61.9% | 38.1% |
| 1950 | 57.5% | 42.5% |
| 1960 | 51.4% | 48.6% |

Because the central cities in many metropolitan regions annexed part of the suburban areas, the suburbs grew only five times as rapidly as the core cities. If there had been no annexations and the central city areas remained the same in 1960 as they were in 1950, the fringe growth would have been forty-one times as great as the central cities.[4] Only in the smaller standard metropolitan statistical areas, those of less than 100,000 population, did the central cities outgrow their suburbs. In the range between 100,000 and 250,000 the rate of growth between the two companion areas was nearly equal. Between 1950 and 1960 the proportion of metropolitan population within central cities declined in 120 of the 174 standard metropolitan statistical areas that were recognized in 1950 with thirty-eight new metropolitan areas added to the list in 1960. Forty-seven per cent of the standard metropolitan statistical areas are classed as either manufacturing or industrial. Only 24 per cent are classed as diversified-manufacturing, 21 per cent in the diversified-retailing category, and only 4 per cent are in the retailing and specialized categories.[5] Over 80 per cent of the manufacturing classed cities are in the Northeast and Midwest and only one, Eugene, Oregon, is in the Far West. The diversified cities are more commonly found in the South and West, and eight of the nine specialized cities are found in these same areas.

A few of the standard metropolitan statistical areas fall into other categories: Washington, D.C., is classed as a governmental city; Champaign-Urbana, Illinois, is listed as an educational city; Colorado Springs, Colo-

---

[4] The International City Managers' Association, *The Municipal Year Book, 1961* (Chicago: The International City Managers' Association, 1961), pp. 40–41.

[5] The International City Managers' Association, *The Municipal Year Book, 1960,* (Chicago: The International City Managers' Association, 1960), pp. 89–90.

Manufacturing City: employment in manufacturing is at least 50 per cent of aggregate employment in manufacturing, trade, and service; and employment in retail trade is less than 30 per cent of aggregate employment.

Industrial City: employment in manufacturing totals more than 50 per cent but is balanced by retail trade employment of at least 30 per cent.

Diversified-retail City: employment in retail trade is dominant and manufacturing accounts for at least 20 per cent of aggregate employment.

Retail-trade City: employment in retail trade is greater than employment in wholesale trade, service, or manufacturing, and employment in manufacturing is less than 20 per cent.

rado, is classed as a service city; and Las Vegas, Nevada, is categorized as a resort or retirement city.

At least seventy-six of the metropolitan areas, or about 36 per cent, have to be classified as low-income areas in that one-fifth or more of their families have incomes of less than $3,000 per year. Only one low-income standard metropolitan statistical area was located in the West, six are in the Northeast, five in the North Central region, and sixty-four in the South. White-collar occupations constitute anywhere from 30 per cent to 59 per cent of the labor force in the 212 United States metropolitan areas, with Washington, D.C., having the highest figure. However, twenty-eight other standard metropolitan statistical areas also have more than 50 per cent white-collar workers.

The standard metropolitan statistical areas in the South have the largest proportion of non-whites. Honolulu, however, has by far the highest proportion, with 64 per cent of the total population being classed as non-white. The non-white population in Atlantic City is the highest of those outside of the South, with 18 per cent. While it is commonly known that the non-whites tend to congregate in the core city, at least forty-nine standard metropolitan areas are equal to the core cities in their division of non-white and whites.

## FUTURE GROWTH OF METROPOLITAN AREAS

The famous philosopher Aristotle limited his ideal city-state to a population of 10,000 on the basis of the difficulty of governing a vast agglomeration of people. Hume, in his essay "On the Populousness of Ancient Nations," placed the maximum population of a city at 700,000, and wrote, "From the past and the present . . . there is a kind of impossibility that any city can rise much beyond this proportion." Another English writer, Sir William Petty, declared in 1688 that the upper limit for London's population was five million as he believed that it would be impossible to secure food for a city if it grew beyond this figure.

These predictions have proved to be completely false. It is significant to speculate upon how large the cities may become and how many there will be in the future. Among the Americans who have suggested that the metropolitan cities have already grown too large was President Franklin D. Roosevelt who advocated the development of many smaller cities instead of the concentration of people in a few great cities when he said, "What America needs is smaller cities and larger towns."

It is well-established that cities, after they reach a certain size, are subject to the law of diminishing returns in proportion to cost in many areas. George Soule illustrated this point in regard to housing:

In large cities it costs more to house people, and they are not housed as well. The more the people, the higher the land values. The higher the land values, the larger the proportion of the cost of housing has to go into land. . . . High land value leads to multi-family construction and over crowding. Families per dwelling and per acre increase as the population grows and open space per person decreases. Up go risks of sickness, death, fire, crime, and accident. Up go costs of sanitation, institutions, police, courts, hospitals, and fire protection.[6]

There is evidence that the costs of city government per capita increase as the number of people in a city increases. Thus in a very large city the difficulty of performing a function increases at a faster rate than the increase in population. For example, the supplying of water will reach a point at which services can be supplied only at an uneconomical rate. Some experts contend that these increased costs are worth paying on the basis that increased advantages keep pace with the growth of the population. These advantages take the form of cultural and educational opportunities.

Lewis Mumford contends that "beyond a certain point, which varies with regional conditions and culture, urban growth penalizes itself. Too large a part of the capital outlays and annual income of the city must be spent in devices for increasing congestion and mechanical relieving its worst results."[7] The question, as yet unresolved, is how to establish this point. The individual is allowed, in the American system, to determine whether or not the cost of living in a city is worth the price. At what point in size does the cost to the individual become so much greater than the advantages he receives that he feels he no longer can afford to pay the costs of being a citizen in a large metropolitan area?

Some observers believed, following the experience of World War II in which large cities proved frequently to be a military liability, that concentrated efforts would be made to keep them from increasing in both number and size. The problem of protecting the people and industries concentrated in large cities, it was frequently asserted, would dictate the limiting of metropolitan areas. However, this has not proven to be true, or at least it has not placed any noticeable brake upon the growth and development of our largest cities. In spite of the governmental problems arising from the congregating in metropolitan areas and the characteristics of urban population, large cities continue to develop.

Some of the characteristics of the social composition of the great cities have little significance to the governmental problems but others are of importance. The large percentage of foreign born, the collecting of the Negro, and the lower percentage of home ownership in the cities present

[6] George Soule, "Will the Cities Ever Stop?" 47 *New Republic* 105, June 16, 1926.
[7] Lewis Mumford, *The Culture of Cities* (New York: Harcourt, Brace & World, Inc., 1938), p. 281.

particular vexing problems for city governments. Many contend that as a
city becomes larger and increases its percentage of foreign born, of Negroes, and of non-home owners, the electoral indifference increases. More
recent evidence tends to refute partially this contention in the metropolitan areas, particularly in those of more than half a million. It is generally
agreed, however, that the economic motivation is of great importance in
getting voters to the polls. The higher the economic status of the population in a metropolitan area the higher will be the percentage of the electorate who exercise their right of franchise. That a large turnout of voters
at municipal elections is desirable is almost universally accepted. Unfortunately, much evidence is presently available that shows people in municipal elections vote in great numbers most frequently when they are
opposed to a policy or administration rather than when in favor. Governmental officials are thus not inspired to perform great positive acts that
will be viewed with favor by their constituents but rather are restrained
from moves that will bring out a negative vote and remove them from
office. The effect is a negative rather than a positive factor in governmental activities.

In spite of the multitude of problems facing the metropolitan areas of
the nation, they continue to be the center of the population migration.
The growth is so great that Charlton F. Chute has come to define them
as urban regions. These consist of two or more contiguous standard metropolitan areas of which the largest is on the Eastern seaboard, stretching
some 600 miles from north of Boston to the southern suburbs of Washington, D.C., in Virginia. Included in this "urban region" are more than
33,000,000 people. The second urban region stretches from Milwaukee,
through Chicago, and around the Great Lakes area to include Cleveland.
The third of these nineteen regions recognized by Professor Chute includes the population agglomeration from north of Los Angeles to the
suburbs south of San Diego.[8] Approximately 40 per cent of the total
United States population is centered in the nineteen areas delineated in
the urban region classification. Every type of municipal governmental
problem is compounded many times in these population clusters.

## METROPOLITAN PROBLEMS

There are at least four major obstacles to any progress in the solution
of metropolitan problems. Probably most significant is the almost unlimited number of local governmental units present in the 212 metropolitan areas of the United States. Each metropolitan area has an average of

[8] Charlton F. Chute, "Today's Urban Regions," *National Municipal Review*, Vol.
XLV (June, 1956), pp. 274–80; (July, 1956), pp. 334–39.

90 governmental units within its arbitrarily determined boundaries. The range of governmental units within standard metropolitan areas for 1962 is indicated in Table 6–3. The range is from two to more than 1,000 units in the New York City metropolitan area. The conflicts caused by this number of governmental units—more than 15,000—result in duplication, conflict of authority, overlapping of jurisdiction, and distrust.

TABLE 6–3

Governmental Units Within Standard Metropolitan Areas—1963

| Type of Government | United States Total | Within SMSA's | Outside SMSA's | Percentage in SMSA |
|---|---|---|---|---|
| School districts | 34,678 | 6,004 | 28,674 | 17.3 |
| Counties | 3,043 | 310 | 2,733 | 10.2 |
| Municipalities | 17,997 | 4,142 | 13,855 | 23.0 |
| Townships | 17,144 | 2,575 | 14,569 | 15.0 |
| Special districts | 18,323 | 5,411 | 12,912 | 29.5 |
| Total | 91,185 | 18,442 | 72,743 | 20.2 |

SOURCE: U.S. Department of Commerce, Bureau of the Census, *Governmental Organization*, Vol. I, of the *1962 Census of Governments* (Washington, D.C.: Government Printing Office, 1963).

Usually little or no direct relationship between the units within the metropolitan area exists. It is quite clear that there is little if any feeling of unity. The citizens living outside the core city have no role in selecting the city officials in the central city. The suburbanites have no voice that can be raised effectively against city income taxes or other tax levies that affect them. Further complicating the governmental picture is the fact that at least one hundred of the metropolitan areas cover more than one county, with some covering two or more states. Thus it is not possible to expect the county to serve as the unit of government for metropolitan purposes.

The second major source of difficulty intimately tied with the superfluity of governmental units is that of lack of financial ability of the metropolitan areas to solve their problems. A few of the areas may have adequate financial resources at their command but many others do not. Most of the central cities have the burden of attempting to perform services for the suburbanites as well as the bona fide residents of the city. The lowering of the average per-capita income of the residents by the exit of the more affluent from the core city places a heavy burden on the central municipalities. Some cities have exploited all of their present resources to meet the rising demands for capital improvements and increased services.

The archaic forms of government used by many American large cities is a further handicap to efficient government in the standard metropolitan statistical areas. The administrative techniques utilized are in many instances outmoded. The selection of administrators on a popular election basis causes the chief executives to lose control of the administrations. In theory the mayor is the head of the city government, but in actuality the authority does not accompany the responsibility. Many of the metro cities are bound by legal restrictions in state constitutions and state statutes. City charters in many of the largest American cities are old and were not designed to meet the problems of the last half of the twentieth century.

The lack of qualified personnel to operate the huge metropolitan city governments is a fourth handicap that faces these areas. With the exodus of the people in the higher economic brackets to the suburbs the vacuum that is left in the core cities has never been filled. Residence requirements on the statute books of every state and in every city charter forbid these "outsiders" from holding any elective public office.

The governmental functional problems that metropolitan areas face include: police protection; fire protection; water supply; sewage disposal; air pollution; traffic and transportation; public health; zoning and planning. Many of these complex functions defy proper performance on a piecemeal basis. Only if they are attacked under a unified metropolitan government will they satisfactorily be handled. For example in the field of public health: in a metropolitan area with two counties, fifty cities, one hundred school districts, and seventy-five special districts, the efforts of one or two may be all that would be needed to nullify the good results of the other governmental units. Similarly, in police work, a weakness in the protection afforded by one governmental unit in the metro area could cause the degradation and failure of the efforts in many if not all of the other governmental jurisdictions.

## PROPOSED SOLUTIONS OF THE METROPOLITAN PROBLEMS

In spite of the herculean tasks confronting metropolitan governments it must be noted that this American political institution has made greater progress than have most of the states, counties, and special districts in adjusting their machinery of government. Greater progress has been made in developing standards of municipal service and administration, in becoming more representative of the needs, interests, and desires of their people; but conspicuously little advance has been made in many states to provide financial means and legal authority to cope with the growing problems.

### Substitute National Administration

A great number of different possibilities must be examined. Some are frankly not too realistic. Some are not politically feasible within the framework of American political heritage with its federal system. A national administration extension has been suggested as one method. Since some of the super metropolitan districts or urban regions cross state boundaries, only a national plan for integration could be effective. But with the limited authority granted by the United States Constitution to the national government it appears unlikely that such a program could be made operative.

In 1962 the national administration attempted unsuccessfully to move at least to a degree into the area of metropolitan government problems. The establishment of a cabinet-ranking department of urban affairs was not passed by the United States Congress. Two attempts were made: in January of 1962 the Rules Committee of the House of Representatives blocked a bill which would have created such a department; this was followed by a Presidential Reorganization Plan based upon the bill that had been sidetracked. Within sixty days the plan would have gone into effect and would have placed in the new department the functions of the Housing and Home Finance Agency, the Federal Housing Administration, and the Federal National Mortgage Association. However, the Congress of the United States moved into the action and the House by a vote of 264 to 150 adopted a resolution disapproving the plan, even though the Senate had defeated a motion to consider the Reorganization Plan No. 1 of 1962. The House action effectively killed the national government's progress in creating a cabinet department to assist the municipal areas. A cabinet post of urban affairs was created in September, 1965, when Congress approved a bill recommended by President Johnson. The eleventh cabinet office includes the same governmental agencies suggested in the 1962 plan.

## Substitute State Administration

A more feasible solution may be direct state action or even substitution of state administration for municipal or metropolitan government administration. A limited degree of this state administration has taken place in a few states wherein the state has taken over certain municipal streets as a part of the state highway system.

While national administration may be legally impossible, state substitution for local governments is certain to be vigorously opposed by the local officials and many of their constituents. They no doubt will defend themselves with the theory that it would weaken the foundations of democracy if there was a shift from the local self-government principle to a higher degree of centralization.

There can be no question that state action directly appears to have advantages. It is simple, should be effective, and can be made compulsory if local cooperation is not forthcoming. It obviously is a logical method to assure the financing of such gigantic problems. A further advantage in prospect is the adequacy of trained, experienced personnel to man such a governmental operation.

In spite of these clear advantages for substitute state administration, the prospects for its utilization on anything remotely resembling a nation-wide scale are dubious. At least four avenues have been followed in state centralization attempts: (1) grants-in-aid to assist local governments in financing important functions; (2) shifts of functions by the state, taking from local units and transferring the responsibility to a larger unit, such as a region; (3) the creation of special governmental commissions or boards to assume new responsibilities for an entire area; and (4) the state's outright assumption of local government functions, as has been previously noted in regard to city streets being amalgamated into the state highway system.

## Municipal Annexation

One of the earliest methods used to solve the problem of the metropolitan area was that of annexation. It is a plan by which the central city extends its boundary lines to cover, in most instances, unincorporated fringe areas and brings all of the territory under one unified control. Through annexation those surrounding areas which undoubtedly have contributed to the problems of the parent city are made to share a part of the responsibility of meeting the problems of the metropolitan area.

While the procedures for annexation of territory vary from state to state, Professor John C. Bollens notes that there were three main methods employed in annexations during the nineteenth century, with no relationship to the amount of territory concerned: (1) general legislation that was applied to each of several classes of municipalities; (2) special legislation; and (3) legislation that authorized annexation on the basis of a favorable vote of the residents of the area seeking to annex the territory and of the inhabitants of the area.[9] The annexation procedures in operation in most states today can be termed "difficult" in contrast to the rather easy methods that were so prevalent before the beginning of the present century. As a result, most of the present-day annexations involve only unincorporated urban fringes and do not provide for consolidation, which is a process normally relating to the unification of incorporated areas. However, consolidation, the joining of two or more separate governmental units, may accomplish the same objective as annexation. Two major requirements have been added to the provisions for annexation which have had a tendency to create a more difficult procedure: (1) an-

[9] John C. Bollens, *The States and the Metropolitan Problem* (Chicago: Council of State Governments, 1956), p. 26.

nexation proposals must initiate from the residents of the area to be annexed; and (2) a majority vote approving the annexation must be achieved in each of the territories to be annexed.

A resurgence of the annexation movement began in 1945, but in a limited sense, with no suggestion that the procedure was being utilized as a means of solving the major problems of a metropolitan region. It has been estimated that in the six-year period from 1948 to 1954 almost one-half of the core cities of metropolitan areas annexing large amounts of area were situated in Virginia and Texas. Both of these states have laws related to the annexation privileges of the central cities that could be classified as being rather liberal. In Texas, home-rule cities were authorized by both a constitutional amendment in 1912 and a state enabling act of 1913 to write into their charters the provisions for annexation procedures. These Texas home-rule cities thus have been granted a degree of wide discretion with respect to annexation procedures. In turn, however, two main types of provisions have been included in Texas home-rule charters: (1) a simple ordinance of the home-rule city council can annex contiguous unincorporated territory without any action necessary by the territory to be annexed; and (2) about forty-five per cent of the home-rule charters require approval by the voters of the area to be annexed and by the city councils. The recent large annexations by Texas cities have occurred in those situations where action by the city council itself authorizes the annexation of territory.[10]

In Virginia, annexations are determined by an annexation court which consists of circuit court judges selected by the Chief Justice of the State Supreme Court of Appeals. This court must function when annexation proceedings have been instituted by any one of four different ways: (1) a petition signed by 51 per cent of the qualified voters of the area seeking to be annexed by a city; (2) passage of an ordinance by the council of the city that seeks to annex the territory; (3) action taken by the governing board of the county in which the annexation will occur; and (4) an ordinance of an already incorporated town that desires to be annexed to another unit. The court, after receiving any one of the above listed documents, must then consider those factors which are listed in state law as being important in considering the annexation problem and arrive at a decision as to whether or not an annexation order will be issued. If the court approves of the annexation it issues a decree which includes, among other things, the following items: (1) a designation of the boundary lines; and (2) a statement of the conditions and terms by which the two areas can adjust their differences and become one unified municipality. A great deal of attention has been given to the Virginia plan since it places responsibility for the ultimate decision in the hands of an impartial tribunal.

[10] Bollens, op. cit., pp. 35–40.

Some authorities have suggested replacing the temporary annexation court with a permanent or continuing administrative agency which could develop a high degree of expertise and provide continuity to the process of deciding annexation proposals.

Several advantages have been cited for the process of annexation as a plan for integration in metropolitan areas. First, it creates, in a very simple style, just one government to solve the problems associated with the metropolitan region. Secondly, it provides for rather complete functional integration and should result in reduced costs.

Certain disadvantages are associated with the procedure of annexation. To many citizens the principal disadvantage is the fact that annexation does not provide a permanent solution to the problems of a metropolitan area. In the rapidly growing suburban areas the population merely spills over the boundary lines and additional annexation must take place if metropolitan integration is to be achieved. Secondly, if the metropolitan area is located in an interstate region, annexation is prevented by legal obstacles, such as state constitutional provisions, from achieving complete unification. Thirdly, many of the annexed communities feel that annexation brings to them increased cost and tax burdens without a commensurate increase in services. Fourthly, many citizens oppose annexation on the ground that it may cause an individual to lose the identity with the community in which he lives. This is an important factor that cannot be overlooked since many suburbanites desire to have identity with their own community.

## Intergovernmental Arrangements—Functional Consolidation

The intergovernmental arrangement or interjurisdictional agreement is the plan that is being used to a greater degree than any other for the solution of the problems connected with the metropolitan region. This technique can be placed with Professor Bollens' general classification of "functional transfers and joint efforts," but it is actually more narrow in outlook. Two systems have been followed in the attempt to achieve some type of functional consolidation. Legislative action has served as a very drastic method. A good example of this occurred in Pennsylvania when a state statute of 1937 removed the public assistance functions from the state's 454 poor districts and transferred this responsibility to the state and to the county boards of assistance. Many other examples could be cited in the fields of highways, assessment, welfare, and other areas where these functions have been changed from small local units to larger ones, such as counties or special districts.

The second type of intergovernmental arrangement that attempts to provide for functional consolidation is the interjurisdictional agreement.

This device, which undoubtedly is used most extensively and effectively to solve particular functional problems of metropolitan regions, can take one of three main forms. First, there is the contract between a governmental unit that possesses ample facilities for one or more specific services and normally a smaller or perhaps weaker unit that is unable to provide satisfactory services of the type involved. The contract stipulates that the larger unit agrees to supply this service to the other unit under certain terms, conditions, or considerations outlined in the document. The second form of the interjurisdictional agreement allows one or more units that are individually unable to provide a service—such as sewage disposal facilities, library facilities, or water supply—to enter into a contract to create or support a special agency or a joint commission that would provide the function to all contracting parties. The two major aspects of such a contract involve the methods to be pursued in choosing the personnel and financing the joint agreement.

The third type of agreement is quite informal in nature by which certain types of functional units of local government exchange their specialized services without requiring any contract or arrangement with precise limitations or stipulations. For example, fire chiefs in the Los Angeles metropolitan area have an oral agreement to assist other fire departments in fighting fires that sweep beyond the ability of one department to combat and might thereby threaten other cities.[11] This type of an informal relationship can do much to increase the cooperativeness of local units of government in many types of specialized local activities even in the absence of any formal agreement or contract for functional consolidation. The most extensive system of intergovernmental arrangements attempting to provide for a degree of functional interrelationship is to be found in Los Angeles County, with its many local governments. However, many other intergovernmental arrangements or city-county contracts can be found throughout the nation concerned with, among other items, public purchasing, police radio systems, welfare functions, and health activities.[12]

Many advantages have been listed for the use of intergovernmental arrangements in an attempt to achieve functional integration. One of the most important is the fact that certain services or functions can be offered under such an arrangement for the residents of those areas that individually could not afford to perform those activities. In addition, these arrangements can be established with a high degree of ease and flexibility. Another advantage stresses the point that these contracts can be set up without the participating units losing their local or separate identity.

[11] Winston W. Crouch, *Intergovernmental Relations* (Los Angeles: The Haynes Foundation, 1954), pp. 80–81.

[12] Council of State Governments, *State-Local Relations* (Chicago: Council of State Governments, 1946), p. 206.

As might be anticipated certain disadvantages have been noted with regard to the possibility of functional consolidation through intergovernmental arrangements. The most prevalent criticism emphasizes the fact that there has not been sufficient use made of this type of arrangement in the metropolitan areas to ascertain whether or not it can be of value in solving the major problems confronting these population centers. Much of this criticism has been summarized by Professor Thomas H. Reed when he wrote that "there has not been enough of it yet to make a dent in the hard shell of the metropolitan problem."[13] Secondly, this system of voluntary contracts or agreements allows the weakest and for that matter the most inefficient units of local government to block a program where some type of functional integration is obviously needed.

## The City-State

The establishment of a city-state is viewed by some authorities as the most extreme plan for solving metropolitan problems. This proposal recommends that large urban areas should be separated from their parent states and admitted into the Federal Union as full-fledged states. Under this arrangement each city-state would enjoy the rights, privileges, and powers granted to all other states and would be in a better position to work cooperatively with the national government in solving the problems peculiar to a metropolitan region. It must be recognized that one of the arguments in favor of the creation of city-states is based upon the supposition that these metropolitan areas cannot receive the necessary assistance from the states in solving their problems since so many state legislatures are under the control and domination of rural interests.

This plan, however, is dismissed by many authorities in the area of metropolitan problems as of no real value because of the constitutional implications. The national constitution provides that a new state cannot be created within an already existing state or established by joining sections of two or more states without the consent of the affected state legislatures as well as the Congress. Therefore, many will maintain that this proposal is just fanciful thinking since no state legislature would agree to such a proposal that would strip the state of such an important economic section.

## City-County Separation

Two methods have been proposed in an attempt to improve the relationships between city and county: city-county separation and city-county

---

[13] Thomas H. Reed, "Progress in Metropolitan Integration," *Public Administration Review*, Vol. IX (Winter, 1949), p. 40.

consolidation. City-county separation, as the title would imply, not only involves the separation of the city's territory from the jurisdiction of the county but consolidates the county and city services within the city limits. County functions continue to be performed in the remainder of the county area with the city taking over almost all previous county functions that were performed by that unit within the city.

In the United States there are only isolated instances of city-county separation. The major examples are Baltimore (1851), San Francisco (1856), St. Louis (1875), and Denver (1903). Virginia is the only state that has made any systematic use of this principle by requiring cities having a population of 10,000 to be almost completely separated from the county. In addition, Virigina cities of over 5,000 population (second-class cities) are partially separated from their counties but continue to make use to a degree of certain county functions and officers.

Certain advantages are cited by proponents of city-county separation. A summary of these advantages include the following points: (1) it eliminates duplicating officers and services; (2) it reduces the problem of overlapping political authority since it places full responsibility for efficient municipal administration squarely upon city officials. City-county separation is usually opposed by the rural sections of the county since the separation of cities from the county would mean a reduction in the assessed valuation and subsequently the revenues of the county. Usually the reduction in county governmental costs will not be commensurate with the loss of revenues. City-county separation could mean that the remaining rural or open county territory might not be able to support a county government without imposing an unreasonable tax load on the county residents. There have been suggestions that should this situation arise it might be necessary for counties, or at least the rural parts of counties, to join a consolidation in order to create a unit that could justify the maintenance of a county government.

## City-County Consolidation

City-county consolidation, while attempting to secure basically the same results as city-county separation, constitutes an entirely different method and must be analyzed separately. Under city-county consolidation the limits of the city are merely extended to the county boundaries and the territories of these two units are consolidated with the result that no open county area exists. As far as the territory of the newly created city-county is concerned, an elimination of two sets of officers for the performance of city and county functions occurs, and the problem of overlapping jurisdictions between the city and county is eliminated.

The stated advantages connected with the consolidation of city and county governments in metropolitan areas usually include the following: (1) the elimination of one layer of government by dispensing with the duplicate sets of officers for city and county; (2) the simplification of the structure of local government; and (3) the improvement of the administrative operations for services to the residents of the metropolitan area. Two difficulties are encountered when city-county consolidation occurs. In the large metropolitan areas the population is continuously spreading out into adjoining counties, and in certain situations into neighboring states, so that the consolidation of just one county with its major internal city will not always solve the problems associated with the metropolitan area. Secondly, certain statutory, constitutional, and political hurdles can be placed in the way of multi-county-city consolidations.

One of the most recent city-county consolidations occurred in June, 1962, when the voters of Nashville and Davidson County, Tennessee, adopted a charter consolidating the city and county governments into one single metropolitan unit. A similar plan had been rejected four years earlier. The unique phase of the Nashville plan is its expandable urban services district, which begins originally with the central city's boundaries but expands with urban growth. All residents are in the general services district and receive and pay for the area-wide services of the metropolitan government. All duplicating county and city officers, boards, departments, and legislative bodies have been consolidated into single metropolitan units. Many of the supporters of the Nashville plan believe that it is the best proposal for the medium-sized or smaller metropolitan areas that are situated completely within single counties.

Several examples of city consolidation can be found throughout the United States. In 1813, in an early recognition of this principle, the state legislature of Louisiana permitted the city of New Orleans to perform certain functions assigned normally to parishes (counties). While many readjustments have taken place over the years with regard to both functions and area, New Orleans still remains as an example of city-county consolidation. In 1822 almost the same arrangement was made for Boston. The boundary lines of the city of Philadelphia were made to coincide with those of the county of Philadelphia in 1854 and twenty-eight local governments in the county became a part of Philadelphia. One of the best examples of city-county consolidation is New York City, where the municipal boundary lines have been extended to cover five counties. While most county functions have been turned over to the city, a unique part of the New York plan provides for local area representation on the legislative body, actually on the Board of Estimate which is the upper chamber of the city council.

Very few consolidations have occurred since the turn of the century. In 1907 the county and city of Honolulu were united, and today the complete island of Oahu is organized as a single unit of local government—the City and County of Honolulu. In Louisiana consolidation was accomplished in Baton Rouge in 1949. A partial consolidation occurred in 1951 between Atlanta and Fulton County, Georgia.

## Metropolitan Federation

To many students of metropolitan government one of the most promising approaches to solving many of its problems is that of metropolitan federation. The plan is also referred to as "municipal federalism" since the application of the principle of federalism becomes quite evident when the features of the system are analyzed.

Under this plan the municipalities in the metropolitan area will not be completely submerged into one single governmental unit but will continue as separate legal units of local government. In the provision of services the authority to administer certain affairs of government that could be classified as of general or regional interest would be transferred to the central or federated city government, which would have jurisdiction or control over the entire metropolitan region. The municipalities would continue to offer those services that are considered local in nature.

This type of federation as a solution to urban problems has been proposed at different times in the United States. As early as 1896 such a proposal was considered for the Boston area, but the legislature failed to take the necessary action with the proposal never coming to a vote. Again, in 1931, the General Court in Massachusetts was reluctant to take the needed action. Popular vote by the local residents defeated attempts to establish a form of federate arrangements in Alameda County (Oakland), California, in 1922 and in Allegheny County (Pittsburgh), Pennsylvania, in 1929. A proposed constitutional amendment that would have authorized the drafting of a federation charter for St. Louis, Missouri, was defeated in a state-wide vote in 1930.

The establishment of the Municipality of Metropolitan Toronto (Canada) in 1954 aroused once again some interest in metropolitan federation. Created in 1953 by an act of the Ontario provincial legislature, this new unit of government consisted of twelve suburban municipalities and the city of Toronto. The federation, in a sense, was a compromise between the concept of annexation (complete amalgamation) as proposed by the city of Toronto and the principle of complete independence which was espoused by the twelve satellite municipalities.

The act which created the new central government specified that it should handle the following region-wide services: water supply, arterial highways, sewage disposal, over-all planning, metropolitan parks, housing, education, and certain welfare and health services. In 1957 the local police forces were taken over by the metropolitan government as the result of an amendment to the original law. The central metropolitan municipality was also granted the power to appoint the governing body of the Toronto Transit Commission, aid in financing education, review and issue bonds for the member cities, establish the uniform assessment rate for all taxable property within the general municipality, and provide for a jail and courthouse. The municipalities are called upon to perform many important functions including law enforcement, fire protection, many public health functions, public relief, building regulations, and libraries.

The second major example of municipal federation is the Dade County (Miami), Florida plan. The experiment started with the creation of a board to study the problems associated with the area and its report recommending a plan of federation. A constitutional amendment which authorized federation was submitted to the Florida State Legislature, which altered it to make the board of county commissioners the governing group for the metropolitan unit. In 1956 the amendment was approved by popular vote along with a home rule charter for Dade County. It was provided that the boundaries of this new metropolitan unit would be limited to Dade County, which does not include all of the heavily urbanized area around Miami. As a result there is some question whether or not the Dade County plan should be classified as a true federation. In spite of this question, this experience in Florida is usually listed as the first instance of federation on the local level in the United States.

The center of the Dade County metro plan is the retention of the twenty-eight local cities (Miami and twenty-seven suburban cities) for the providing of what is referred to as purely local functions, with the granting to Dade County of the responsibility for those governmental activities that are principally metropolitan in nature.

After the voters of Dade County and Miami barely adopted the two-tiered form of government in 1957 (44,404 to 42,619), it was subjected to opposition from many of the municipalities within the county. Shortly thereafter the Dade County League of Municipalities supported an autonomy amendment to the charter which was designed to prohibit the county government from taking any action that would infringe upon the right of the municipalities to "exercise all powers" whether granted by general law, special act, or by the several charters. This amendment, which would have destroyed the effectiveness of the arrangement as a full-fledged metropolitan authority, was defeated by the voters of Dade County in 1958. One of the factors no doubt contributing to the defeat of the amendment was the first annual report of progress that was issued by County Manager O. W. Campbell. In this report he noted that there had been a 6.5 per cent reduction in the county tax rate, a 50 per cent reduction in the number of county departments, the installation of modern accounting and budgeting systems, reorganization of the hospital and welfare programs, a speeding up of the county's highway program, the inauguration of long-range planning, and many other important items.[14]

The Toronto and Dade County successes increased the interest in that type of federation as a possible solution to many metropolitan problems. Professor Victor Jones, an outstanding authority on metropolitan governments, speaking with respect to the solution of their problems, stated, "I doubt that any proposal has much chance of success unless it is based upon the 'federal principle' of allocating metropolitan functions to a metropolitan government and leaving other functions to less-than metropolitan governments."[15] Yet in 1958 the voters of King County (Seattle), Washington, and Davidson County (Nashville), Tennessee, defeated proposals for metropolitan government. However, in that same year, 1958, the Montreal Metropolitan Corporation was established by the Quebec Provincial Legislature. Some authorities maintain that the new Montreal government was just a limited and skeleton form of metropolitan government since insufficient power was granted to the Corporation. In 1959 a charter which would have created the Knoxville-Knox County (Tennessee) Metropolitan Government was defeated by the voters, and that same year witnessed the defeat of similar metropolitan proposals in Cleveland and St. Louis. Yet the year 1960 saw the creation of the third Canadian experiment in metropolitan federation when the Manitoba provincial legislature established the Metropolitan Corporation of Greater Winnipeg.[16] In 1962 a consolidated form of government for the city-county area of Nashville and Davidson County, Tennessee, previously defeated in 1958, was adopted by a vote of 36,978 to 28,105. The metropolitan charter merges city and county governments and absorbs the city of Nashville almost entirely in the consolidated county government. This new governmental unit, serving a population in excess of 400,000 people, has a metro county council of 41 members and a metropolitan county mayor.[17]

[14] While many reports are now being issued on the Miami experiment, some of the more important ones include Gustave Serino, *Miami's Metropolitan Experiment* (Public Administration Clearing Service, University of Florida, Gainesville, 1958); Reinhold P. Wolf, *Miami Metro: The Road to Urban Unity* (Bureau of Business and Economic Research, University of Miami, Coral Gables, 1960); and Edward Sofen, *The Miami Metropolitan Experiment* (Bloomington: Indiana University Press, 1963).

[15] Victor Jones, "Local Government Organization in Metropolitan Areas: Its Relation to Urban Redevelopment," Part IV, *The Future of Cities and Urban Redevelopment*, ed. Coleman Woodbury (Chicago: University of Chicago Press (1953), p. 605.

[16] For an account of this new government see "Greater Winnipeg Agency Created," *National Civic Review*, September, 1960.

[17] The International City Managers' Association, *The Municipal Year Book, 1963* (Chicago: The International City Managers' Association, 1963), p. 60. For a review of

While the period of time for experimentation with the federation plan as a means of solving or attempting to solve certain metropolitan problems has been very brief, we must of necessity note some of the problems apparently inherent in that type of organization. Fundamental to the establishment of the federal principle is the division of power among the units of government. This is also present in this brand of municipal federation. How do you divide the powers or functions of government between the central or metropolitan government and the local units? It is almost instinctive for the local units to fight any reduction in powers. A second major source of controversy revolves around the type of governing body that will be set up for the metropolitan authority. This breaks down into questions involving the actual number of members, the mode of election—by units of government or at large—and how these members shall be distributed or apportioned among the component units. A third major problem is concerned with the type of law that is necessary to create and operate such a form of government. Does it of necessity involve a constitutional amendment, or can it be accomplished by a state law? These few questions indicate immediately some of the major problems that must be faced by any large metropolitan area that desires to create a federation.

## BIBLIOGRAPHY

BIGGER, RICHARD, and KITCHEN, JAMES D. *How the Cities Grew.* Los Angeles: The Haynes Foundation, 1952.

BOLLENS, JOHN C. *The States and the Metropolitan Problem.* Chicago: The Council of State Governments, 1956.

BOLLENS, JOHN C. (ed.). *Exploring the Metropolitan Community.* Berkeley: University of California Press, 1961.

———, and SCHMANDT, HENRY J. *The Metropolis: Its People, Politics, and Economic Life.* New York: Harper & Row, Inc., 1965.

CONNERY, ROBERT H., and LEACH, RICHARD H. *The Federal Government and Metropolitan Areas.* Cambridge: Harvard University Press, 1960.

COTTRELL, E. A., and JONES, HELEN L. *Characteristics of the Metropolis.* Los Angeles: The Haynes Foundation, 1955.

CROUCH, WINSTON W. *Intergovernmental Relations.* Los Angeles: The Haynes Foundation, 1954.

FISER, WEBB S. *Mastery of the Metropolis.* Englewood Cliffs, N.J.: Prentice-Hall Spectrum Books, Prentice-Hall, Inc., 1962.

FISHER, ROBERT M. (ed.). *The Metropolis in Modern Life.* Garden City, N.Y.: Doubleday & Co., Inc., 1955.

the Nashville consolidation see David A. Booth, *Metropolitics: The Nashville Consolidation,* Institute for Community Development and Services, Michigan State University, East Lansing, 1963. For a comparison of the Nashville-Davidson County plan with that of Miami-Dade County, and others, see Daniel R. Grant, "Consolidations Compared," *National Civic Review,* Vol. LII, No. 1 (January, 1963).

ELIAS, C. E., JR., GILLES, JAMES, and RIEMER, SVEND (eds.). *Metropolis: Values in Conflict.* Belmont, Calif.: Wadsworth Publishing Co., Inc., 1964.

*Fortune* (editors of). *The Exploding Metropolis.* Garden City, N.Y.: Doubleday & Co., Inc., 1958.

GOVERNMENT AFFAIRS FOUNDATION, INC. *Metropolitan Surveys: A Digest.* Chicago: Public Administration Service, 1958.

GREENE, LEE S., *et al. The Problem of Government in Metropolitan Areas.* Dallas: Arnold Foundation, Southern Methodist University, 1958.

GREER, SCOTT. *Governing the Metropolis.* New York and London: John Wiley & Sons, Inc., 1962.

————. *The Emerging City: Myth and Reality.* New York: The Free Press of Glencoe, Inc., 1962.

GRUMM, JOHN G. *Metropolitan Area Government: The Toronto Experience.* Lawrence, Kan.: University of Kansas Press, 1959.

GULICK, LUTHER H. *The Metropolitan Problem and American Ideas.* New York: A. A. Knopf, Inc., 1962.

HATT, PAUL K., and REISS, ALBERT J. (eds.). *Cities and Society.* New York: The Free Press of Glencoe, Inc., 1957.

HOOVER, EDGAR, and VERNON, RAYMOND. *Anatomy of a Metropolis.* Cambridge: Harvard University Press, 1960.

JACOBS, PHILIP E., and TOSCANO, JAMES V. *The Integration of Political Communities.* Philadelphia: J. B. Lippincott Co., 1964.

JENNINGS, M. KENT. *Community Influentials.* New York: The Free Press of Glencoe, Inc., 1964.

JONES, VICTOR. *Metropolitan Government.* Chicago: The University of Chicago Press, 1942.

MAY, SAMUEL C., and FALES, JAMES M. *The State's Interest in Metropolitan Problems.* Berkeley: Bureau of Public Administration, University of California, 1955.

MOWITZ, ROBERT J., and WRIGHT, DEIL S. *Profile of a Metropolis.* Detroit: Wayne State University Press, 1962.

OSBORN, FREDERIC J., and WHITTICK, ARNOLD. *The New Towns: The Answer To Megalopolis.* New York: McGraw-Hill Book Co., Inc., 1963.

OWEN, WILFRED. *The Metropolitan Transportation Problem.* Washington, D.C.: The Brookings Institution, 1957.

ROBSON, WILLIAM A. *Great Cities of the World: Their Government, Politics, and Planning,* 2d ed. New York: The Macmillan Co., 1957.

SIMON, HERBERT A. *Fiscal Aspects of Metropolitan Consolidation.* Berkeley: Bureau of Public Administration, University of California, 1943.

STUDENSKI, PAUL, *et al. The Government of Metropolitan Areas in the United States.* New York: National Municipal League, 1930.

TABLEMAN, BETTY. *Governmental Organization in Metropolitan Areas.* Ann Arbor: Bureau of Government, Institute of Public Administration, University of Michigan, 1951.

STEIN, CLARENCE S. *Toward New Towns for America.* New York: Reinhold Publishing Corp., 1957.

SWEENEY, STEPHEN B., and BLAIR, GEORGE S. *Metropolitan Analysis: Important Elements of Study and Action.* Philadelphia: University of Pennsylvania Press, 1958.

U.S. ADVISORY COMMISSION ON INTERGOVERNMENTAL RELATIONS. *Governmental*

*Structure, Organization, and Planning in Metropolitan Areas.* Washington, D.C.: Government Printing Office, 1961.

U.S. DEPARTMENT OF COMMERCE, BUREAU OF THE CENSUS. *Local Government in Standard Metropolitan Areas,* 1962. Washington, D.C.: Government Printing Office, 1962.

————. *Population of Standard Metropolitan Statistical Areas, 1960.* Washington, D.C.: Government Printing Office, 1960.

VERNON, RAYMOND. *Metropolis: 1985.* Cambridge: Harvard University Press, 1960.

WATSON, RICHARD A. *The Politics of Urban Change.* Kansas City, Mo.: Community Studies, Inc., 1963.

WEAVER, ROBERT C. *The Urban Complex.* Garden City, N.Y.: Doubleday & Co., Inc., 1964.

WILLIAMS, OLIVER P., and PRESS, CHARLES (eds.). *Democracy in Urban America.* Chicago: Rand McNally & Co., 1961.

WOOD, ROBERT C. *Suburbia: Its People and Their Politics.* Boston: Houghton Mifflin Co., 1959.

————, and ALMENDINGER, VLADIMIR V. *1400 Governments.* Cambridge: Harvard University Press, 1961.

WOODBURY, COLEMAN (ed.). *The Future of Cities and Urban Redevelopment.* Chicago: The University of Chicago Press, 1953.

# 7

# State Constitutions

A state constitution should be more than a written document setting forth the fundamental principles by which the people are governed. It should be viewed as a symbol of the highest political ideals of the people of the state. It is much easier to write a constitution that merely outlines the framework of the government than it is to prepare a document that will receive the support and respect of all of the people. If the common man is to respect and actively participate in his government he must understand and appreciate the political institutions that are created under the constitution. To establish this needed rapport with the people, the state constitution must be written in such a fashion that the average person, and not just the learned judges and lawyers, can easily understand its meaning and intent. The United States Constitution has served as a true symbol of American political ideology. It effectively reminds all Americans of the vital necessity for agreement on fundamental purposes upon which our nation is based. Unfortunately few of the state constitutions can make the same claim.

Professor William B. Munro, in noting the fallibility of state institutions, wrote:

There has never been an ideal state constitution in America, and perhaps there never will be. Certainly no constitution would be uniformly ideal for all the . . . states. . . . Montesquieu was right when he averred that the best constitution is the one that best suits the genius and the traditions of the people who live under it.[1]

State constitutions in many of our fifty states have, in spite of their inadequacies, gained a sacred position in the minds of many people. Robert Dishman wrote:

One might suppose that the constitution would be equally responsible for some of the "bad" things with which government is charged. But no—inefficiency,

[1] William B. Munro, "An Ideal State Constitution," *The Annals of the American Academy of Political and Social Sciences*, Vol. CLXXXI (September, 1935), p. 1.

waste and confusion are usually blamed on particular men in office and not on the basic law under which they operate. If the House of Representatives is delayed in getting through its calendar, its members are suspected of dragging their feet in order to fatten their mileage allowance. . . . If the chief executive cannot weld the administrative branch into an efficient and responsible team, it is because the governor is weak and not because the constitution keeps him from being strong. . . . If the courts have not always been able to attract and hold the best jurists—politics are again blamed and not the constitution which leaves them vulnerable to political attack. If farmers, merchants and home owners are forced to carry a disproportionately heavy tax burden, it is because government is more costly and wasteful than it used to be and not because the constitution forbids any tax that is strictly geared to the taxpayers' ability to pay. The constitution in short, is given credit for the good which it has helped to make possible but it is seldom blamed for the faults which might be fairly laid at its door.[2]

It was the third President of the United States, Thomas Jefferson, who in 1816 wrote in a similar vein:

Some men look at constitutions with sanctimonious reverence, and deem them like the ark of the covenant, too sacred to be touched. They ascribe to the men of the preceding age a wisdom more than human, and suppose what they did to be beyond amendment. I knew that age well; I belonged to it, and labored with it. It deserved well of its country. It was very like the present, but without the experience of the present, . . . I am certainly not an advocate for frequent and untried changes in laws and constitutions. . . . But I know also, that laws and institutions must go hand in hand with the progress of the human mind.[3]

The fundamental purpose of a constitution is probably best stated by Chief Justice Marshall in his decision of *McCulloch v. Maryland,* in which he wrote:

A constitution, to contain an accurate detail of all the subdivisions of which its great power will admit, and of all the means by which they may be carried into execution . . . could scarcely be embraced by the human mind. It would probably never be understood by the public. Its nature, therefore, requires that only its great outlines should be marked, its important objects designated, and the minor ingredients which compose those objects be deduced from the nature of the objects themselves.[4]

It is universally agreed that there is no such thing as an ideal constitution that will fit or be perfect for all of the fifty states. The scholars who have drafted and redrafted the various editions of the National

[2] Robert B. Dishman, *A New Constitution for New Hampshire?* (Durham: University of New Hampshire, Public Administration Service, April, 1956), pp. 1–2.
[3] Saul K. Padover, *A Jefferson Profile as Revealed in His Letters* (New York: The John Day Co., 1956), p. 281.
[4] *McCulloch v. Maryland* (4 Wheat. 316, U.S. 1819).

Municipal League's model state constitution make no claims that it should be adopted in toto by any state. Each state has its own peculiar problems, its own personality, its own traits and differences that no one supreme document can possibly compensate.

Yet there are certain fundamental functions that a state constitution must perform. The four major functions as listed by John P. Wheeler, Jr., are:

1. To protect the people in the exercise of their civil liberties.
2. To define the powers of government.
3. To establish the more important, the more permanent institutions of government, such as the executive, the legislative and the judicial.
4. To provide a method for changing the fundamental law.[5]

Two guiding principles that should be followed by state constitutional drafters are:

1. Constitutions ought to be written or rewritten in order to facilitate active and dynamic state and local government.

2. Accordingly, it is not appropriate to predetermine decisions with respect to policies and services of state and local governments by writing specific prohibitions, mandates, or prescriptions into state constitutions. Since the evolution of state constitutions, with some notable and fairly recent exceptions, has been largely a matter of imposing more and tighter curbs on the exercise of popular and official discretion, it is suggested that the historic trend in state constitutional revision should be sharply reversed.[6]

## EVOLUTION OF STATE CONSTITUTIONS

State constitutions have nearly completed a full cycle. Early state constitutions were almost always very brief and contained only fundamental law. In contrast, the state constitutions framed in the second half of the nineteenth century and the early decades of the twentieth century were exceedingly long. The assertion is frequently made that the reason for the greater length was largely due to the increasing distrust by the people of their state policy makers. It certainly is true that much of the bulk of the California constitution and the even longer Louisiana document is composed of restrictions upon taxation, public debt, chartering of corporations, and establishing local governmental units. However, in contrast with these lengthy constitutions, three of the latest constitutions, New Jersey (1947), Hawaii (1959), and Alaska (1959) have seen a return to

[5] John P. Wheeler, Jr. (ed.) *Salient Issues of Constitutional Revision* (New York: National Municipal League, 1961), p. xii.
[6] *Ibid.,* p. 166.

a relatively short and basic fundamental law. It must be noted that even these three are much longer than the 3,000 word first constitution of New Jersey, adopted in 1776. The trend, however, is toward brief, concise state constitutions.

The states of Connecticut and Rhode Island merely renamed their charters state constitutions. In the same year, 1776, eight states adopted constitutions, while the eleventh and twelfth state constitutions were drafted in 1777. Massachusetts redrafted its 1691 charter as its first state constitution in 1780.[7] Most of these thirteen constitutions drew heavily upon numerous English sources, e.g., Magna Charta, the Petition of Right, and the Bill of Rights. Likewise, ideas were extracted from the First Charter of Virginia and the Mayflower Compact of 1620. In Table 7–1 a number of the more significant details of the fifty state constitutions now in effect are summarized.

### TABLE 7–1

#### State Constitutions
#### (Selected Items)

| State | Number of Constitutions | Effective Date of Present Constitution | Length in Words | Number of Amendments | Amendments Proposed by Initiative Process | Admitted to Union |
|---|---|---|---|---|---|---|
| Alabama | 6 | 1901 | 80,000 | 212 | | 1819 |
| Alaska | 1 | 1950 | 12,000 | 0 | | 1959 |
| Arizona | 1 | 1912 | 15,000 | 50 | Yes | 1912 |
| Arkansas | 5 | 1874 | 21,500 | 59 | Yes | 1836 |
| California | 2 | 1879 | 75,000 | 350 | Yes | 1850 |
| Colorado | 1 | 1876 | 20,000 | 64 | Yes | 1876 |
| Connecticut | 2 | 1966 | 10,000 | 0 | | 1788 |
| Delaware | 4 | 1897 | 20,000 | 80 | | 1788 |
| Florida | 5 | 1886 | 30,000 | 117 | | 1845 |
| Georgia | 8 | 1945 | 25,000 | 26 | | 1788 |
| Hawaii | 1 | 1959 | 11,412 | 5 | | 1959 |
| Idaho | 1 | 1890 | 13,492 | 68 | Yes | 1890 |
| Illinois | 3 | 1870 | 17,000 | 13 | | 1818 |
| Indiana | 2 | 1851 | 7,816 | 20 | | 1816 |
| Iowa | 2 | 1857 | 7,997 | 21 | | 1846 |
| Kansas | 1 | 1859 | 8,052 | 45 | | 1861 |
| Kentucky | 4 | 1891 | 21,500 | 18 | | 1792 |
| Louisiana | 10 | 1921 | 201,423 | 439 | | 1812 |
| Maine | 1 | 1820 | 9,000 | 89 | | 1820 |
| Maryland | 4 | 1867 | 23,722 | 108 | | 1788 |

[7] Dates of State Constitution adopted:
  1776—Connecticut, Rhode Island, New Hampshire, South Carolina, Virginia, New Jersey, Delaware, Pennsylvania, Maryland, North Carolina
  1777—Georgia and New York
  1780—Massachusetts

TABLE 7–1 (Continued)

| State | Number of Constitutions | Effective Date of Present Constitution | Length in Words | Number of Amendments | Amendments Proposed by Initiative Process | Admitted to Union |
|---|---|---|---|---|---|---|
| Massachusetts | 1 | 1780 | 28,760 | 81 | Yes | 1788 |
| Michigan | 4 | 1964 | 19,203 | 0 | Yes | 1837 |
| Minnesota | 1 | 1858 | 14,991 | 90 | | 1858 |
| Mississippi | 4 | 1890 | 15,302 | 35 | | 1817 |
| Missouri | 4 | 1945 | 30,000 | 13 | Yes | 1821 |
| Montana | 1 | 1889 | 26,000 | 30 | | 1889 |
| Nebraska | 2 | 1875 | 16,550 | 94 | Yes | 1867 |
| Nevada | 1 | 1864 | 16,700 | 56 | Yes | 1864 |
| New Hampshire | 2 | 1784 | 10,900 | 41 | | 1788 |
| New Jersey | 3 | 1947 | 12,500 | 9 | | 1788 |
| New Mexico | 1 | 1912 | 22,400 | 55 | | 1912 |
| New York | 6 | 1894 | 45,000 | 133 | | 1788 |
| North Carolina | 2 | 1868 | 12,000 | 28 | | 1789 |
| North Dakota | 1 | 1889 | 19,797 | 70 | Yes | 1889 |
| Ohio | 2 | 1851 | 15,417 | 88 | Yes | 1803 |
| Oklahoma | 1 | 1907 | 35,940 | 49 | Yes | 1907 |
| Oregon | 1 | 1859 | 25,000 | 249 | Yes | 1859 |
| Pennsylvania | 4 | 1873 | 15,092 | 62 | | 1788 |
| Rhode Island | 1 | 1843 | 6,650 | 36 | | 1788 |
| South Carolina | 6 | 1895 | 30,063 | 251 | | 1788 |
| South Dakota | 1 | 1889 | 24,545 | 71 | | 1889 |
| Tennessee | 3 | 1870 | 9,460 | 10 | | 1796 |
| Texas | 5 | 1876 | 43,000 | 154 | | 1845 |
| Utah | 1 | 1896 | 13,261 | 33 | | 1896 |
| Vermont | 3 | 1793 | 8,000 | 44 | | 1791 |
| Virginia | 5 | 1902 | 23,101 | 92 | | 1788 |
| Washington | 1 | 1889 | 36,422 | 39 | | 1889 |
| West Virginia | 2 | 1872 | 22,000 | 36 | | 1863 |
| Wisconsin | 1 | 1848 | 10,717 | 66 | | 1848 |
| Wyoming | 1 | 1890 | 21,500 | 25 | | 1890 |

SOURCE: Council of State Governments, *The Book of the States, 1964–1965* (Chicago: Council of State Governments, 1964).

The original state constitutions did not have to be approved by Congress before they were effective. However, all of the thirty-seven states that have entered the Union since the original thirteen have been required to submit their proposed state constitutions to Congress for its approval before being admitted to statehood. Ordinarily the process required for admission has involved the following steps:

1. Organization of a territorial government.
2. Petition by a territory to Congress for admission to statehood.
3. Passage of an enabling act by Congress setting forth the conditions for framing a constitution.

4. Framing of a constitution by the territory and gaining approval of a majority of the voters balloting on the proposed state constitution.
5. Passage by Congress of a resolution accepting (thus approving) the Constitution and admitting the territory to full status as a state.
6. Proclamation of admission by the President of the United States.

The contents of modern state constitutions are illustrated by the Michigan Constitution which went into effect in 1964, as it contains the following articles:

*Preamble*

Article I—Declaration of Rights
Article II—Elections
Article III—General Government
Article IV—Legislative Branch
Article V—Executive Branch
Article VI—Judicial Branch
Article VII—Local Government
Article VIII—Education
Article IX—Finance and Taxation
Article X—Property
Article XI—Public Officers and Employment
Article XII—Amendment and Revision
Schedule and Temporary Provisions

## BILL OF RIGHTS

Each state constitution contains a Bill of Rights. In almost every constitution it is the first section as contrasted with the United States Constitution, which added the Bill of Rights as the first ten amendments. At least one state constitution merely copied verbatim these amendments from the United States Constitution. A great deal of uniformity persists in the rights stipulated. Certain safeguards against the powers of the legislative body appear to be almost mandatory in the minds of the writers of state constitutions. Inevitably most of the following items are listed: indictment by grand jury, trial by jury, freedom of worship, separation of church and state, writ of habeas corpus, bill of attainder, prohibition of cruel or unusual punishment, prohibition of excessive bail, compensation for private property taken for public use, freedom of the press, freedom of speech, freedom of peaceable assembly, and the right to petition the government.

In recent years more and more of the state constitutions have been including anti-discrimination clauses in the Bill of Rights. The New Jersey Constitution of 1947 states that no person shall be segregated in the militia or in the public schools because of religious principles, race, color, ancestry, or national origins. A similar declaration was made in a constitutional amendment in New York nine years earlier which stated that "No person shall, because of race, color, creed, or religion, be subjected to any discrimination in his civil rights by any other person or by any firm, corporation, or institution, or by the state or any agency or subdivision of the state."

Some authorities have contended that the Bill of Rights is not necessary in state constitutions. It should be noted, however, that the Alaska Constitution of 1959 includes a listing of twenty-one basic rights of the people of that new state.

Professor Robert S. Rankin, in his publication entitled *State Constitutions: The Bill of Rights,* emphasizes the high esteem placed upon a bill of rights by maintaining that there has been little or no debate over the necessity of including a bill of rights in a state constitution.[8] If there is a debate it occurs only with respect to subject matter. A staff paper prepared for the delegates to the Alaska Constitutional Convention stated that "There can be little question that the Alaska Constitution must have a bill of rights. . . . The basic question . . . is what should and should not be included."[9]

While time has witnessed no lessening in the importance of the bill of rights in a state constitution, Professor James P. Hart asserts:

. . . as the historic conditions that first inspired bills of rights recede further into the dim past, the danger increases that guarantees of personal liberties will not be fully appreciated and that in a constitutional revision they will be weakened or even abandoned.[10]

Professor Rankin further cautions:

The complex social and economic structure of society resulting in new concepts of social and economic democracy, the danger of the improper use of broadening governmental power and the bureaucratic character of the modern state have but increased the importance and necessity of these guarantees in state constitutions.[11]

## SEPARATION OF POWERS AND THE STRUCTURE OF GOVERNMENT

Usually the second section of a typical state constitution sets forth the framework of the state government. Too frequently this establishment of

[8] Robert S. Rankin, *State Constitutions: The Bill of Rights* (New York: National Municipal League, 1960), p. 20.
[9] Public Administration Service, *Civil Rights and Liberties* (Chicago: Public Administration Service, 1955), p. 5.
[10] James P. Hart, "The Bill of Rights: Safeguard of Individual Liberty," *Texas Law Review,* Vol. XXXV (October, 1957), p. 919.
[11] Rankin, *op. cit.,* p. 20.

the governmental organization is in great detail, resulting in a relatively rigid format which lasts for years. Great stress is ordinarily placed upon the importance of separation of powers. The stipulation is frequently included that an individual may serve at the same time in only one of the three governmental branches—executive, legislative, judicial. The executive authority is vested in the governor and certain other constitutional officers; the legislative powers are granted to a popularly elected legislative branch; and the judicial powers are given to a judicial branch consisting of a system of courts often outlined in detail.

No state government has absolute separation of powers. It is recognized that it is impossible to draw a line and stipulate that everything on one side is executive power and everything on the other is legislative. It is not desirable nor possible to so isolate one branch of the government from the other that there is no overlap. Indeed, an integral part of the national and state governmental structure is the theory of checks and balances. Every state constitution writes into the fundamental law this theory, whereby the legislative branch has certain restraining influences upon both the executive and the judicial. Similarly, the judicial has checks upon both the executive and legislative branches, and the executive has certain controls which it can exercise over each of the other two branches of government. The specific powers of each governmental branch will be discussed in appropriate places in later chapters.

## POWERS OF THE STATE GOVERNMENT

In theory the state government has all powers not delegated to the federal government by the United States Constitution or specifically denied to the states. Thus the state constitutions provide for the exercise of the reserved powers that the states possess. Usually the state's basic document enumerates the several types of powers that the various governmental agencies shall exercise. It would probably be more desirable if it would state some definite principle by means of which the powers and their exercise might be determined.

The state constitution may not permit the state to enter into any treaty, alliance, or confederation, nor may a state coin money, make any law impairing the obligation of contracts, grant titles of nobility, or deprive persons of life, liberty, or property without due process of law. The Supreme Court of the United States has held, furthermore, that those powers delegated to the national government which are of such a character that their exercise by a state would be, under any circumstances, inconsistent with the general theory of a national government, may be exercised only by the federal government. It should be noted that those delegated powers not of this character may be exercised by the state until the federal government sees fit to exercise them. An example of this process is found in the field of bankruptcy legislation. During the period between 1878 and 1898 the federal government did not have a national bankruptcy law. Therefore, during this time states were within their rights in enacting state bankruptcy legislation. However, with the passage of the national bankruptcy law all state statutes inconsistent with the federal law on this subject became null and void.

The state constitutions reflect two essential propositions: (1) the doctrine of popular sovereignty and (2) limited government. The people in every state are sovereign and from them must flow the powers of government. All political powers in the United States belong to the people. State government, just as federal government in the United States, is conducted only with and by the consent of the governed. The state constitutions can grant to its governmental agencies only those powers that the people have given through the United States Constitution and the state constitutions.

## CONSTITUTIONAL AMENDMENT OR REVISION

Every state constitution must provide for a method or methods of changing the supreme state law. The methods vary from state to state. Some have had unworkable amending provisions which have constituted a serious barrier to modernizing the state government to meet the changing conditions. It is obvious that government must be dynamic and fluid. It cannot work successfully and be static and passive. An unworkable amending process creates a chaotic situation that causes a great hardship not only on the people working within government but upon the people governed. It is obvious that a defective amending process may be fatal to state government.

### Amendments Proposed by the State Legislatures

All of the fifty states except New Hampshire empower the state legislature to propose constitutional amendments. In twenty-three states, a majority of the members of the state legislature must vote in favor of a constitutional amendment to have it officially proposed. Even within these states some variation in requirements is present. In Vermont only a majority vote in the lower house is required, but a two-thirds majority is necessary in the senate to formally propose such a move. In New Mexico certain types of changes in the constitution must have approval of three-fourths of the legislators, but others require only a simple majority. It is important to note that only nine of the states that allow an amendment to be officially proposed by a simple majority of the legislators permit the constitutional change to go directly to a popular referendum. In fourteen states with this type of requirement for initiating constitutional revision two consecutive sessions of the legislature must give their majority approval. In addition to these fourteen, two states, Delaware and South Carolina, require a two-thirds vote in two consecutive sessions of the legislative bodies. Connecticut has an amending process which requires a simple majority of the lower house in the first session but a two-thirds majority in both houses of the next session. Hawaii and New Jersey are the only states that allow a choice between either one session or two legislative sessions in approving proposed constitutional amendments. In the newest of the fifty states—Hawaii—only one legislative session is necessary for proposing a constitutional amendment if the governor has announced the final form of the amendment ten days in advance of the two-thirds vote in the general assembly; otherwise two separate sessions must grant majority approval of the proposal. New Jersey must have a three-fifths vote in both houses if the proposal is to be passed by a single session of the legislature but requires a majority vote only if it is to be submitted to two separate sessions.[12]

In addition to Hawaii and New Jersey, it is possible to propose a constitutional amendment by the approval of only one session of the state's legislative body in thirty-three states. The majority varies, with seven states, and New Jersey, requiring three-fifths majority, eighteen states and Hawaii, two-thirds majority, and nine states requiring a simple majority vote for the proposal.

Thus it would appear that Delaware and South Carolina have the most difficult requirements for formally proposing constitutional amendments, since both require a two-thirds vote in both houses at two consecutive sessions. Tennessee has nearly as difficult a procedure, with a majority vote in the first session and a two-thirds vote required in the second session. The trend is probably away from the necessity of favorable consideration by two separate legislative sessions or at least to provide different methods for proposing amendments.

## Proposing Constitutional Amendments by Direct Initiative

Fourteen states entrust the power to propose amendments to the state constitution to the people as well as the legislature. This method was first adopted by Oregon in 1902 and has been accepted in thirteen other states. Massachusetts, Michigan, and Ohio are the only states east of the Missis-

[12] The states in this category with the variations mentioned include: Connecticut, Delaware, Hawaii, Indiana, Iowa, Massachusetts, Nevada, New Jersey, New York, Pennsylvania, Rhode Island, South Carolina, Tennessee, Vermont, Virginia, Wisconsin.

sippi River using this plan; all others are in the western area of the nation. It should further be noted that only Missouri and Michigan of the states adopting new constitutions since the close of World War II have accepted the initiative method for proposing constitutional amendments. In thirteen of the fourteen states the number of signers needed on a petition to place a constitutional amendment before the voters is a percentage of the number of voters participating in the most recent state-wide election. Only in North Dakota is a specific number of signatures required (20,000 is the minimum number necessary). The percentage varies from 15 in Arizona and Oklahoma to 3 per cent in Massachusetts. However, a geographic distribution of signers is required in Massachusetts, Missouri, and Nebraska.

Under the initiative plan, any individual or any group may draft a proposed amendment and by securing a sufficient number of signatures to a petition, bring about its submission to a popular vote. The pros and cons of the direct initiative are numerous. Those who regard it as a device for effective popular control are very vigorous in its defense. The opponents contend, equally vigorously, that it can give the opportunity for a small minority group to write into the constitution measures that are not only unnecessary but harmful to the governmental operation.

In the first few years when the opportunity exists for interest groups to propose constitutional amendments by the petition method a great number of proposals are submitted to the electorate, but the record reveals that there is a gradual reduction in the activity in this area. Furthermore, the record of votes on constitutional amendments proposed by the initiative method shows that in nearly two-thirds of the referenda a negative popular vote results. While it appeared that this method might sweep the country in the first twenty-five years of the twentieth century, the momentum has almost completely ceased. Only in California and Oregon does there appear to be continued intense interest in its utilization. The proposal was rejected in the constitutional conventions of Hawaii, Alaska, and New Jersey. In all cases but one where it is used a majority of all those voting on the amendment is necessary in order to place the proposal in the state constitution. In Oklahoma the vote must constitute a majority of all voters participating in the election, whether or not they vote on the constitutional issue. Usually a special election concerned only with the proposed constitutional amendment is held in order to assure fairness to the proposal.

## Approval of Constitutional Amendments

Delaware is the only state that does not provide for a popular referendum on proposed constitutional amendments. New Hampshire requires the amendments proposed by the constitutional convention to be submitted to the electorate. Forty-one states require approval by a vote of a majority of those balloting on the proposed amendment; seven require a majority voting in the election to favor the amendment, while only Rhode Island requires an extraordinary majority of three-fifths of the voters to favor ratification of the proposed constitutional amendment. Submission usually must occur at regular elections, but some states permit special elections to be held for the purpose of determining ratification of constitutional questions.

Very seldom does a constitutional amendment arouse a great deal of interest among the voting population in a state. Most amendments are voted upon by only a minority of the electorate. In many states the statutes require that constitutional amendments must be on separate ballots. In those states with separate paper ballot for the constitutional issue, many discarded ballots are left in the voting booths by voters who are not interested enough to mark the constitutional amendment question. In those states that require a majority of those voting in the election to favor the amendment all voters who do not cast a ballot on the constitutional amendment are automatically voting against the issue. As a result of this lack of interest it is very difficult to get a majority vote if the constitutional question is voted upon in a regular election. In Table 7–2 the

TABLE 7–2

Voter Approval Required of Constitutional Amentment in Referenda

| Majority of Those Voting on the Amendment | | Majority of Those Voting in the Election | Three-Fifths of Those Voting on the Amendment | No Vote Held |
|---|---|---|---|---|
| 1. Alabama | 22. Montana | 1. Illinois | 1. Rhode Island | 1. Delaware |
| 2. Alaska | 23. Nebraska | 2. Minnesota | | |
| 3. Arizona | 24. Nevada | 3. Mississippi | | |
| 4. Arkansas | 25. New Hampshire | 4. New Jersey | | |
| 5. California | 26. New Mexico | 5. Oklahoma | | |
| 6. Colorado | 27. New York | 6. Tennessee | | |
| 7. Connecticut | 28. North Carolina | 7. Wyoming | | |
| 8. Florida | 29. North Dakota | | | |
| 9. Georgia | 30. Ohio | | | |
| 10. Hawaii | 31. Oregon | | | |
| 11. Idaho | 32. Pennsylvania | | | |
| 12. Indiana | 33. South Carolina | | | |
| 13. Iowa | 34. South Dakota | | | |
| 14. Kansas | 35. Texas | | | |
| 15. Kentucky | 36. Utah | | | |
| 16. Louisiana | 37. Vermont | | | |
| 17. Maine | 38. Virginia | | | |
| 18. Maryland | 39. Washington | | | |
| 19. Massachusetts | 40. West Virginia | | | |
| 20. Michigan | 41. Wisconsin | | | |
| 21. Missouri | | | | |

SOURCE: Council of State Governments, *The Book of the States, 1964–1965* (Chicago: Council of State Governments, 1964).

vote required for approval of proposed constitutional amendments by the people is indicated.

## Constitutional Conventions

Most drafters of the state constitutions have realized the ultimate necessity of a total and complete revision of the state's supreme law. Nine of the present fifty state constitutions submit the question, "Shall there be a constitutional convention" to the electorate at regular periodic intervals. Constitutional revision is submitted to voters every seven years in New Hampshire, every ten years in Hawaii, Iowa, and Alaska, every sixteen years in Michigan, and every twenty years in Maryland, New York, Missouri, and Oklahoma. In theory if a majority of the voters ballot affirmatively, a constitutional convention will then be ordered. However, in at least one state, Iowa, the voters have ordered a constitutional convention but no action occurred. In 1920, this question produced 279,652 affirmative votes and only 221,763 "No" votes, but the legislature convening in 1921 failed to provide for the convention which had been voted by the people. Subsequent attorney-general opinions and legislation has assured the people that a convention would be held if a majority voting on the question favored it. It is noteworthy that while the question has been submitted to Iowa voters four times since 1920 no affirmative vote has resulted.

In four states—Indiana, New Jersey, North Dakota, and Vermont—there is apparently no procedure provided in the constitution for calling a constitutional convention. Such a meeting could be ordered only by legislative action based upon custom. In Arkansas, Connecticut, Louisiana, Massachusetts, Pennsylvania, Rhode Island, and Texas there is no constitutional provision—such as statutory provision—for calling a constitutional convention, but in all of these states other legal authority has indicated that the power of calling such a meeting rests with the legislative body of the state.

In only Delaware and Kentucky must the legislature in two consecutive sessions vote in favor of a constitutional convention before the question is submitted to the electorate. In Delaware two-thirds of both houses must favor the calling of a convention but a simple majority is all that is needed in Kentucky. Eighteen states require the convention plan be approved by a simple majority of its legislators in one session before the issue goes to the people. Nineteen states require a two-thirds vote of the legislators, while Nebraska alone requires a three-fifths vote of its unicameral body before allowing the voters to determine if they favor calling a constitutional convention. Twenty-eight of the states require a majority of the voters voting on the question to favor a convention, while twelve states require that a majority of the voters participating in the election must favor calling a constitutional convention before it will be considered officially approved.

It is obvious that several states provide more than one method for calling a constitutional convention to revise or draft an entirely new document. Alaska, Michigan and New York give the voters direct opportunity at periodic intervals, while granting the state legislature authority to initiate the call whenever it deems it necessary.

Calling state constitutional conventions occurs in widely varying cycles. In some decades numerous state constitutional revisions are underway, and then in other decades little if any interest in revising the state constitutions is apparent. So many factors exist that it is impossible to suggest all of the influences that tend to mitigate for and against changing the state's supreme document: economic conditions and war and the threat of war are both major factors.

It is now universally agreed that a constitutional convention must be preceded by a great deal of research and study upon the questions to be considered. Usually this preliminary work is done by some type of a constitutional commission. In Michigan, which held a constitutional convention in 1961–1962, a series of publications on various constitutional sections were produced several months before the convention was convened. These must be carefully and impartially researched documents if the convention is to have the maximum chances of success. The members of the constitutional commission and its staff of researchers usually become technical advisors to the convention itself. Some even may become members of the convention, although the wisdom of this dual role may be open to serious question.

No state constitution outlines specifically the size and composition of the constitutional convention. This matter is apparently left to the discretion of the state legislature. Usually the easiest question to be answered is the qualifications of the delegates. Normally any qualified voter is also a qualified candidate for the position of constitutional convention delegate. It is difficult to determine how many members shall compose the convention since no widespread agreement on this subject appears to exist. Ideally the size must not be so large as to impair deliberative work, yet it must be large enough to represent the various elements of the electorate.

There is agreement that a unicameral body is the form that should be used for the convention. There is no need for a bicameral operation and none of the constitutional conventions in this century has been bicameral. It is hard to envision a successful meeting with many more than one hundred delegates, yet several conventions have had several hundred people.

Election by the people of the delegates seems to be the only method compatible with the American philosophy. Whether they should be selected by districts or at large is another problem. Both methods are employed. Similarly, whether or not they should be elected on strict political party lines or on a non-partisan basis is subject to argument. Students of constitutional conventions appear to favor non-partisan election at large as the means of obtaining the most highly qualified personnel.[13]

Studies of the personnel named as delegates to constitutional conventions would appear to reinforce the belief that the qualifications of persons participating is higher than the average member of the respective state legislatures. This is certainly not too amazing since the constitutional convention work is usually regarded as more important than ordinary sessions of the legislature. Individuals who would not consider being a candidate for a seat in the legislative body will submit to popular election as potential delegates to the convention.

The length of time needed for the deliberation of a convention is virtually unpredictable. Much may depend upon the quality of the pre-convention work done by the researchers. Another factor will be the extent that partisan politics is allowed to enter into the scene. Certainly, the caliber of the membership will influence the time span of the meetings. Most conventions have found it necessary to place some time limit upon their deliberations lest they drag on interminably. Some conventions have been divided into two or more periods. The first part of the convention is generally used to draft a tentative document, then a period of adjournment for the delegates to study the draft and consult with their constitutents, and finally, a period in which the document is completed and approved by delegates.

The conventions are almost always free to establish their own rules and procedure, which includes rules concerned with the percentage of the delegates who must approve the new document before it can be regarded as acceptable to the convention. The typical convention device of committees is normally used. The new term applied to this committee system is appointment of "task forces" to study and propose sections of the new document on the various subjects to be included.

The new trend in writing state constitutions in conventions appears to be a sharp departure from the traditions of the last half of the nineteenth century, when copying either from other state constitutions or adopting sections of previously proposed constitutions was quite common. Since World War II a great deal of time and diligent study of new ideas and concepts has been the accepted procedure among constitutional drafters.

[13] National Municipal League, *The Constitutional Convention—A Manual on Its Planning, Organizing and Operation* (New York: National Municipal League, 1961), pp. 32–33.

This careful examination of new innovations is looked upon with favor by many people but meets with opposition from the more conservative members of the conventions, who accuse the modern ideas as being subversive and un-American. Most observers credit the urbanized American electorate with the prime motivation for the new approaches. The pattern followed in selecting the delegates to the constitutional convention probably will have the most direct effect upon whether the old or the new will prevail in the document that is framed.

The exact method of approving the work of a constitutional convention in twenty states is not provided by the present state constitutions. In some of these states it may be assumed that the present constitution anticipates but does not prescribe that a referendum of the people will be in order. Others certainly imply that the state legislature in the bourbon tradition will have the final voice in determining whether or not the new document shall be implemented. Recent democratic traditions would certainly require that a new supreme document be submitted to the people for ratification. Attorney-general opinions and court decisions in many of these twenty states which have constitutions silent on this issue would probably insist that a popular election be held.

Twenty-two states specify that before a new constitution shall go into effect it must be approved by a majority of the voters voting on the question, "Shall the constitution as drafted by the constitutional convention replace the present state constitution?" In four states, California, Colorado, Illinois, and Montana a majority of the voters in the election in which approval of a new constitution is voted must favor the new document. If this were a special election it would of course be the same as the provisions in the other twenty-two states, but if it were only one of the questions in the general election the requirement is much more difficult. Minnesota requires that three-fifths of the voters voting the proposed constitution must be in favor of it, while New Hampshire has a two-thirds majority requirement. Rhode Island requires a three-fifths majority of all persons voting in the election at which approval is at stake. For ratification of the proposed constitution a summary of the procedures involved in state constitutional conventions and the popular ratification of constitutional proposals is contained in Table 7–3.

## Constitutional Commission

In the last twenty years the constitutional commission has become an important auxiliary and a major addition to the techniques used in remodeling state constitutions. It is not a method of changing or altering a state supreme law but merely an aid to the formal methods of change. No state constitution makes specific provision for such a commission but

## TABLE 7–3

### State Constitutional Conventions

| State | Vote in Legislature | Referendum Vote To Approve Calling Convention | Popular Ratification Convention Proposals |
|---|---|---|---|
| Alabama | Majority of members | M.E.* | No provision |
| Arizona | Majority vote | M.P.† | M.P. |
| Arkansas | Majority | – | M.P. |
| Alaska | Majority/Vote by electorate every 10 years | M.P. | M.P. |
| California | ⅔ | M.P. | M.E. |
| Colorado | ⅔ | M.P. | M.E. |
| Connecticut | Majority | – | No provision |
| Delaware | ⅔ (Two sessions) | M.P. | No provision |
| Florida | ⅔ | M.P. | No provision |
| Georgia | ⅔ | – | M.P. |
| Hawaii | Vote by electorate every 10 years | M.P. | M.P./35% of election |
| Idaho | ⅔ | M.P. | M.P. |
| Illinois | ⅔ | M.E. | M.E. |
| Indiana | No provision | No provision | – |
| Iowa | Legislature may call at any time. Each 10 years voters rate | M.P. | M.P. |
| Kansas | ⅔ | M.P. | No provision |
| Kentucky | Majority/Two sessions | M.P. | No provision |
| Louisiana | Majority | M.P. | No provision |
| Maine | ⅔ | – | No provision |
| Maryland | Voters vote every 20 years | M.E. | M.P. |
| Massachusetts | Majority | M.P. | No provision |
| Michigan | Majority | M.E. | M.P. |
| Minnesota | ⅔ | M.E. | ⅗ M.P. |
| Mississippi | Majority | – | No provision |
| Missouri | Voters vote every 20 years | M.P. | M.P. |
| Montana | Majority | M.P. | M.E. |
| Nebraska | ⅗ | M.P./35% of election | M.P. |
| Nevada | ⅔ | M.P. | No provision |
| New Hampshire | Voters vote on convention every 7 years | M.P. | ⅔ P. |
| New Jersey | No provision | – | – |
| New Mexico | ⅔ | M.P. | M.P. |
| New York | Majority/Voters vote on convention every 20 years | M.P. | M.P. |
| North Carolina | ⅔ | M.E. | No provision |
| North Dakota | No provision | – | – |
| Ohio | ⅔ | M.P. | M.P. |
| Oklahoma | Voters vote every 20 years on convention | M.P. | M.P. |
| Oregon | Majority | M.P. | No provision |

* M.E.—Majority voting in the election.
† M.P.—Majority voting on the proposition.

**TABLE 7–3** (Continued)

| State | Vote in Legislature | Referendum Vote To Approve Calling Convention | Popular Ratification Convention Proposals |
|---|---|---|---|
| Pennsylvania | Majority | – | M.P. |
| Rhode Island | Majority | M.P. | ⅗ E. |
| South Carolina | ⅔ | M.E. | No provision |
| South Dakota | ⅔ | M.E. | No provision |
| Tennessee | Majority/No more than one each 6 years | M.P. | M.P. |
| Texas | Majority | M.P. | M.P. |
| Utah | ⅔ | M.E. | M.E. |
| Vermont | No provision | – | – |
| Virginia | Majority | M.P. | No provision |
| Washington | ⅔ | M.E. | M.E. |
| West Virginia | Majority | M.E. | M.E. |
| Wisconsin | Majority | M.P. | No provision |
| Wyoming | ⅔ | M.E. | M.P. |

SOURCE: Council of State Governments, *The Book of the States, 1964–1965* (Chicago: Council of State Governments, 1964).

all that have been established have been either by state statute or by executive order. The first constitutional commission was organized in New Jersey in 1852, but little use was made of this method of planning and preparing for constitutional change until after World War II.[14]

If a convention or a legislature is to attempt extensively to revise a state constitution, a commission is probably the ideal technique through which to prepare the necessary preliminary plans and research materials. It has been recognized by political scientists for more than forty years that there is a need for a group of experts, appointed usually by the governor upon legislative authorization, to make suggestions for the needed fundamental changes in the supreme law of the state.[15] Included in the states that have utilized this mode of preparing needed amendments or revisions are California, Michigan, Minnesota, New Jersey, New York, and Tennessee. There has been no uniformity of size among the commissions, with some having as few as three members and others more than thirty. The type of personnel appointed has been very high, with a great leaning toward persons of skill in the legal intricacies of constitutional drafting. As might be expected the device has not been universally accepted as the answer to revising antiquated state constitutions. Some critics believe that the commissions have been for the most part dominated by the too progressive members of the body politic.

[14] John P. Wheeler, Jr., *op. cit.*, p. 57.
[15] Bennett M. Rich, "Convention or Commission?" *National Municipal Review*, Vol. XXXVII (March, 1948), p. 133.

It must be emphasized that in no state does the constitutional commission have the power and authority to actually enact or even formally propose constitutional changes. All it can do is make suggestions to the duly constituted authorities, either the state legislature, the constitutional convention, or, in a few states, it might through the initiative process get action upon its recommendations.

The growing use of the constitutional commission as an auxiliary tool is shown by the establishment in 1960–1961 of no less than eight such agencies in Florida, Kansas, Kentucky, New York, North Carolina, Oregon, Pennsylvania, Texas, and West Virginia.[16] The Minnesota Constitutional Commission was appraised by Professor G. Theodore Mitau as follows:

One impression stands out above all others. Minnesota owes this body a profound debt of gratitude for the care with which it phrased its recommendations, for its lively concern for the possible and the practical. Entire sentences in subsequent amendments can be traced back to the language of the Minnesota Constitutional Commission Report; the amendments themselves often serve as substantive implementations of the Commission's prescriptions.[17]

It is quite clear that a constitutional commission may well serve in many states as an ideal agency to assist in the process of continuous constitutional revision which is necessary in this fast-moving age. The commission can be of great value in stimulating public discussion of constitutional issues and may assist in the formulation of needed policy. It should never be thought of as a new agency that can remake the constitution, for this is not its design or its fundamental purpose, but it acts as a catalyst to stimulate and guide the duly ordained agencies of constitutional change.

### Frequency of Constitutional Amendments

Tremendous variance is found in the extent state constitutions have been amended in the fifty states. By far the most frequently amended constitution is the Louisiana supreme law which, in its first forty years of existence, 1921–1961, was amended a total of 376 times. An additional eighty-six amendments were rejected. One might expect that this excessive number of amendments could be attributed to the initiative process, but such is not the case, as Louisiana is not one of the fourteen states with this method of constitutional change. California, which does have the

[16] Council of State Governments, *The Book of the States, 1962–1963* (Chicago: Council of State Governments, 1962) p. 9.

[17] G. Theodore Mitau, "Constitutional Change by Amendment: Recommendations of the Minnesota Constitutional Commission in Ten Years' Perspective," *Minnesota Law Review* (January, 1960), pp. 461–83.

initiative process, has changed its supreme law a total of 350 times since 1879 and rejected a total of 250 amendments, or adopting about two of every three amendments proposed. South Carolina, like Louisiana, requires a revision by a two-thirds vote of each house in two successive sessions of the legislature but in spite of this barrier has changed the constitution 251 times while considering and rejecting 123 other amendments. Other states that have made more than one hundred changes include Texas (1876), 154, Alabama, (1901) 212, New York, (1894), 133, and Oregon, (1859), 111.

At the other extreme of the spectrum the new constitutional document in Alaska, adopted in 1959, has as yet to be changed. New Jersey's new constitution went into effect in 1947 and has been changed only six times. Missouri's post-World War II constitution of 1945 has undergone 13 changes and Tennessee's constitution of 1870 has been amended ten times. The latter went unchanged for more than seventy-five years before its first amendment was added. Illinois' supreme law of 1870 has been altered only thirteen times, while Georgia's constitution adopted in 1945 has already been changed by amendment twenty-six times.[18]

None of the state constitutions with fewer than twenty amendments, except Missouri, allows changes to be made by the initiative procedure. New Hampshire, which allows amendments to be proposed only by a constitutional convention, has had 105 proposed amendments since 1793, of which only 41 have been approved by the necessary popular referendum.

## BIBLIOGRAPHY

ALLEN, TIP H., and RANSONE, COLEMAN B., Jr. *Constitutional Revision in Theory and Practice*. University, Ala.: Bureau of Public Administration, University of Alabama, 1962.

BEBOUT, JOHN. *The Making of the New Jersey Constitution*. Trenton, N.J.: Mac-Crellish and Quigley, 1945.

COLUMBIA UNIVERSITY LEGISLATIVE DRAFTING RESEARCH FUND. *Constitutions of the United States: National and States*. 2 vols. Dobbs Ferry, N.Y.: Oceana Publications, Inc., 1962.

DEALEY, JAMES Q. *Growth of American State Constitutions*. Boston: Ginn & Co., 1915.

DISHMAN, ROBERT B. *State Constitutions, The Shape of the Document*. New York: National Municipal League, 1960.

DODD, WALTER F. *Revision and Amendment of State Constitutions*. Baltimore: Johns Hopkins Press, 1910.

EDWARDS, RICHARD A. (ed.). *Index Digest of State Constitutions*, 2d ed. Dobbs Ferry, N.Y.: Oceana Publications, Inc., 1959.

[18] Council of State Governments, *The Book of the States, 1963–1964* (Chicago: Council of State Governments, 1963), p. 12.

FAUST, MARTIN. *Five Years Under the New Missouri Constitution*. Jefferson City, Mo.: Missouri Public Expenditure Survey, 1950.

GRAVES, W. BROOKE (ed.). *Major Problems in State Constitutional Revision*. Chicago: Public Administration Service, 1960.

HEADY, FERREL. *State Constitutions: The Structure of Administration*. New York: National Municipal League, 1961.

HOAR, ROGER S. *Constitutional Conventions, Their Nature, Powers & Limitations*. Boston: Little, Brown & Co., 1917.

KEITH, JOHN P. *Methods of Constitutional Revision*. Austin, Texas: Bureau of Municipal Research, University of Texas, 1949.

KETTLEBOROUGH, CHARLES (ed.). *The State Constitutions*. Indianapolis: Bobbs-Merrill Co., Inc., 1928.

KUHLMAN, A. F. *Official Publications Relating to American State Constitutional Conventions*. New York: The H. W. Wilson Co., 1935.

MCCARTHY, SISTER M. BARBARA. *The Widening Scope of American Constitutions*. Washington, D.C.: Catholic University of America, 1928.

MCLAUGHLIN, ANDREW C. *A Constitutional History of the United States*. New York: Appleton-Century-Crofts, Inc., 1935.

NATIONAL MUNICIPAL LEAGUE. *State Constitutions: Reapportionment*. New York: National Municipal League, 1960.

———. *Model State Constitution*, 6th ed. New York: National Municipal League, 1963.

———. *Compendium on Legislative Apportionment*, rev. ed. New York: National Municipal League, 1964.

NEVINS, ALLAN. *The American States During and After the Revolution*. New York: The Macmillan Co., 1924.

O'ROURKE, VERNON A., and CAMPBELL, D. W. *Constitution Making in a Democracy*. Baltimore: Johns Hopkins Press, 1943.

POLLOCK, JAMES K. *Making Michigan's New Constitution*, Ann Arbor Mich., George Wahr Publishing Co., 1963.

RANKIN, ROBERT S. *State Constitutions: The Bill of Rights*. New York: National Municipal League, 1960.

STURM, ALBERT L. *The Need for Constitutional Revision in West Virginia*. Bureau of Governmental Research, West Virginia University, 1950.

———. *Methods of State Constitutional Reform*. Ann Arbor, Mich.: University of Michigan Press, 1954.

———. *Constitution Making in Michigan, 1961–62*. Ann Arbor, Mich.: Institute of Public Administration, University of Michigan, 1963.

THORPE, FRANCIS N. (ed.). *The Federal and State Constitutions, Colonial Charters, and Other Organic Laws of the States, Territories, and Colonies Nor or Theretofore Forming the United States of America*. 7 vols. Washington, D.C.: Government Printing Office, 1909.

UHL, RAYMOND, and OTHERS. *Constitutional Conventions: Organization, Powers, Functions and Procedures*. (Constitutional Bulletin No. 1). Columbia: Bureau of Public Administration, University of South Carolina, 1951.

WHEELER, JOHN P., JR., *The Constitutional Convention: A Manual on Its Planning, Organization and Operation*. New York: National Municipal League, 1961.

——— (ed.). *Salient Issues of Constitutional Revision*. New York: National Municipal League, 1961.

———. *The Future Role of the States*. New York: National Municipal League, 1961.

# 8

# The Electorate, Political Parties, and Pressure Groups

There has been very little written and a minimum amount of research completed pertaining to state elections, nominations, and campaigns. Most attention until recent years has been focused upon the activities of the political parties and their candidates for national office, with relatively little study being given to the election problems at the state level. If the nominations, campaigns, and elections at the national level are as important as they appear to be, the state elections, campaigns, and nominations are of equal importance to the governmental process of each of the fifty states.

It is assumed by almost everyone that an informed electorate is an essential ingredient of a successful democracy. If the people are not informed about state issues and policies, even though they are informed about national candidates and issues, the state government will suffer. It is imperative that greater efforts be made to perform the nominating and campaign functions at the state level in such a manner as to assure the securing of qualified candidates and an informed voting public.

The voter turnout in the so-called off-year non-presidential elections is usually quite shameful. In 1962 fewer than 50 per cent of the total eligible voters nationwide participated in the general elections. In spite of the record crowds going to the polls in a few areas, the total picture was still dismal.[1]

---

[1] In California, 78.4 per cent of the qualified voters voted in the 1962 gubernatorial contest. *The Book of the States, 1964–1965* (Chicago: Council of State Governments, 1964), p. 30.

## REQUIREMENTS FOR VOTING

### United States Constitutional Requirments

Only five statements respecting voter eligibility are contained in the Federal Constitution. This document states that any person permitted to vote for the most numerous branch of the state legislature must be allowed to participate in the elections of federal officials. In addition, four amendments to the national constitution pertain to voting. The Fourteenth Amendment establishes a penalty of reduced congressional representation if a state disenfranches any portion of its eligible population. It should be noted that this penalty has never been applied; thus the amendment might be said to be non-operative. The Fifteenth Amendment forbids any state to deny or to abridge the right to vote on grounds of color, race, or previous condition of servitude. The third amendment involved in voter eligibility is the Nineteenth Amendment, which prohibits discrimination because of sex. The Twenty-fourth Amendment prohibits the use of the poll tax as a voting requirement in federal elections.

### State Constitutional Requirements

All other rules and regulations concerning voting are retained by the individual states. The only universal rule upon which all fifty of the states have concurred is the requirement of United States citizenship for all eligible voters. Even this requirement has not always been agreed upon as nearly twenty states only forty years ago did not require United States citizenship as a voter qualification.

Nearly universal agreement is present on the minimum age requirement since forty-six states require a voter to be twenty-one years old. During World War II what was expected to be a trend began to reduce the voting age to eighteen. With the drafting of young men at the age of eighteen strong sentiment was aroused to permit this age group the right to vote. The first state to reduce the age limit was Georgia in 1944, followed in 1955 by Kentucky. No other continental state in the Union has followed this lead, even though it had presidential endorsement in 1956. The two latest additions to the Union, Hawaii and Alaska, both included in their state constitutions new age requirements, Alaska setting nineteen and Hawaii twenty for voter age minimums. It is estimated that if the voter age were reduced to eighteen in all fifty states nearly ten million more eligible voters would be added to the potential voter rolls.[2]

[2] U.S. Department of Commerce, Bureau of the Census, *U.S. Census of Population, 1960* (Washington, D.C.: Government Printing Office, 1962), pp. 1–199.

A third state requirement which varies from state to state but is present in each is a stipulated period of residency. The typical requirement is one year, but variations from six months in several Northern states to two years in a few Southern states are found. In addition residency requirements within the county and within the voting precinct are usually state requirements. Again, the shorter length of residency is found in the North and longer periods in the South. The average would be approximately ninety days in the county and normally thirty days within the voting district.

A fourth requirement almost uniformly demanded is registration. North Dakota and Arkansas have no registration requirements, but all of the other states require registration at least in the urban areas. The purpose served by the registration requirement is to prevent those persons who are not qualified to vote from participating in the electoral process. Registration is the means of proving to an election official in advance of the election that the individual possesses the qualification required of a voter. In most states the registration is of the permanent type which permits a voter to continue to participate, once he registers, for an indefinite period, unless he moves, fails to vote within a certain number of years, or in some other way disqualifies himself. A few states still require periodic registration. In Texas, for example, annual registration is required. To the voter this appears to be an added burden which is more expensive to the government and is regarded by most observers as being unnecessary. A permanent registration, with safeguards for removing names of those who die or move out of the jurisdiction of the voting area, would appear to be preferable.

A fifth voter requirement in nineteen states prior to 1965 was a literacy test in one form or another. Its purpose was often to construct a barrier against the participation of uninformed voters. Too frequently it had been used as a device for denying qualified Negroes the right to vote. A literacy test that requires proof of ability to read and write is defensible in the minds of many people, but when the "proper interpretation of a state statute or state constitution" is a part of the test it obviously becomes discriminatory. The federal Voting Rights Act of 1965 has invalidated the literacy test in some states. South Carolina requires either a literacy test or one may qualify without a test if he owns property. Most states have a sixth requirement for voters which disqualifies all persons convicted of a felony and those who have been declared insane or feeble-minded.

A final requirement which is obsolete is the poll tax. Five states required payment of a poll tax as a prerequisite to voting—Alabama, Arkansas, Mississippi, Texas, and Virginia.[3] However, the Congress of the United

[3] Six states voluntarily removed their poll tax requirements since 1919. North Carolina led the way in 1920; followed by Louisiana, 1934; Florida, 1937; Georgia, 1945; South Carolina, 1950; and Tennessee, 1951.

States in 1962 passed a constitutional amendment which was approved by three-fourths of the states in January, 1964. It nullified the poll tax requirements in the five states that still retained it as a voter qualification. Some view the amendment as still another interference by the federal government into the area regarded as properly the rights of the states.[4]

A summary of the major state qualifications for voting is contained in Table 8–1.

## Negro Suffrage

The Thirteenth, Fourteenth and Fifteenth Amendments to the United States Constitution were designed to assure the Negro the right to vote. Passed in 1865, 1868, and 1870 respectively, they have been, in theory, operative for nearly one hundred years, but no one contends that the Negro has been allowed in the South his exercise of franchise.

At least six different barriers have been used to keep the Negro from the polls. Long residency requirements, often two years in the state and one year in the county, have eliminated many potential Negro voters as they have a high percentage of itinerants. The poll tax, prior to the Twenty-fourth Amendment to the United States Constitution, was used in five states as a primary device for restricting Negro voting. An effective anti-Negro vote device for many years prior to 1965 was the literacy examination. Almost every Southern state has used the test to bar the Negro from voter eligibility. The test is administered in such a way that the Negro, no matter how much education he has received, cannot supply the answers the literacy board requires. The wording involved in the anti-Negro literacy laws usually states that the potential voter must be able to "understand" the law "and interpret" it to the satisfaction of the examining board. The Negro is somehow never able to convince the board that he "understands" the law.

Professor Kirk Porter wrote in 1918 that several Southern states in their constitutions require a voter to prove that he is of "good character" and then make no attempt to conceal the motivation behind this clause— to deny the Negro the right to register and vote.[5]

The famous grandfather clause was a most effective method of barring the Negro from the polls until it was declared unconstitutional in 1915.[6] The grandfather clause was a simple device merely stating that all persons who were eligible to vote prior to January 1, 1866, would be exempt from

---

[4] This section is based on Council of State Governments, "Qualifications for Voting," *The Book of the States, 1964–65* (Chicago: Council of State Governments, 1964), p. 24.

[5] Kirk H. Porter, *History of Suffrage in the United States* (Chicago: The University of Chicago Press, 1918), p. 218.

[6] *Guinur v. United States* (238 U.S. 347, 1915).

TABLE 8–1
## Qualifications for Voting

| State | Minimum Age | U.S. Citizen- ship | Length of State Residence | Literacy Test | No Regis- tration |
|---|---|---|---|---|---|
| Alabama | 21 | x | 2 yr.* | | |
| Alaska | 19 | x | 1 yr. | x | |
| Arizona | 21 | x | 1 yr.* | x | |
| Arkansas | 21 | x | 1 yr. | | x |
| California | 21 | x | 1 yr.* | x | |
| Colorado | 21 | x | 1 yr.* | | |
| Connecticut | 21 | x | 1 yr.* | x | |
| Delaware | 21 | x | 1 yr. | x | |
| Florida | 21 | x | 1 yr. | | |
| Georgia | 18 | x | 1 yr. | x | |
| Hawaii | 20 | x | 1 yr. | x | |
| Idaho | 21 | x | 6 mo.* | | |
| 1Illinois | 21 | x | 1 yr.* | | |
| Indiana | 21 | x | 6 mo. | | |
| Iowa | 21 | x | 6 mo. | | |
| Kansas | 21 | x | 6 mo.* | | |
| Kentucky | 18 | x | 1 yr. | | |
| Louisiana | 21 | x | 1 yr. | x | |
| Maine | 21 | x | 6 mo.* | x | |
| Maryland | 21 | x | 1 yr. | | |
| Massachusetts | 21 | x | 1 yr. | x | |
| Michigan | 21 | x | 6 mo. | | |
| Minnesota | 21 | x | 6 mo. | | |
| Mississippi | 21 | x | 2 yr. | x | |
| Missouri | 21 | x | 1 yr.* | | |
| Montana | 21 | x | 1 yr. | | |
| Nebraska | 21 | x | 6 mo.* | | |
| Nevada | 21 | x | 6 mo. | | |
| New Hampshire | 21 | x | 6 mo. | x | |
| New Jersey | 21 | x | 6 mo.* | | |
| New Mexico | 21 | x | 1 yr. | | |
| New York | 21 | x | 1 yr. | x | |
| North Carolina | 21 | x | 1 yr. | x | |
| North Dakota | 21 | x | 1 yr. | | x |
| Ohio | 21 | x | 1 yr.* | | |
| Oklahoma | 21 | x | 1 yr. | | |
| Oregon | 21 | x | 6 mo.* | x | |
| Pennsylvania | 21 | x | 1 yr. | | |
| Rhode Island | 21 | x | 1 yr. | | |
| South Carolina | 21 | x | 2 yr. | | |
| South Dakota | 21 | x | 1 yr. | | |
| Tennessee | 21 | x | 1 yr. | | |
| Texas | 21 | x | 1 yr. | | |
| Utah | 21 | x | 1 yr. | | |
| Vermont | 21 | x | 1 yr. | | |
| Virginia† | 21 | x | 1 yr. | x | |
| Washington | 21 | x | 1 yr. | x | |
| West Virginia | 21 | x | 1 yr. | | |
| Wisconsin | 21 | x | 1 yr.* | | |
| Wyoming | 21 | x | 1 yr. | x | |

* Fifteen states have reduced the residency required for voting in national elections, from that required for voting in state elections.

† Must owe no past-due taxes.

Source: Adapted from: Council of State Governments, *The Book of the States, 1964–1965* (Chicago: Council of State Governments, 1964).

all poll tax, literacy, and other requirements and furthermore extended the exemption to all lineal descendants.

Following the Supreme Court decision abrogating the grandfather clause the State of Texas enacted in 1923 a white primary law, which declared that only people of the Caucasian race could participate in the Texas Democratic primary elections. This statute remained effective for four years until declared unconstitutional by the United States Supreme Court as a denial of equal protection of the laws.[7] The decision came as a shock to the South as the Supreme Court had ruled in 1921 that the federal government had no control over senatorial primaries, and it was not believed the court would extend federal jurisdiction to any primary election.

A series of cases involving the Negro suffrage question culminated in *United States v. Classic,* which declared the primary election an integral part of the election process and subject to federal regulation.[8]

It is now clear that the federal government is assuming a responsibility for assuring the Negro the right to vote. It is also quite well established that the fight for Negro suffrage is not over.

### Suffrage for Washington, D.C., Residents

Residents of Washington, D.C., were disenfranchised until ratification of the Twenty-third Amendment in 1961. Approval by three-fourths of the state legislatures assured the residents of the nation's capital that in the vote for President and Vice President of the United States they would from 1964 have the privilege of voting and controlling three electoral votes. This still leaves them without voting rights in regard to members of Congress and their own municipal officials. Serious moves are underway to give home rule to the District of Columbia, which would allow them to elect their own mayor and members of the city council. However, it may be some time before Congress will bring itself to releasing its control over the district's governmental operations.

## VOTER PARTICIPATION

An examination of the American voting record since World War I shows several interesting items. It is widely known that voter participation in elections when the United States presidency is at stake is much greater than the so-called off-year elections. Oftentimes the vote in presidential election years is nearly twice that of the off-year elections. However, even

---

[7] *Nixon v. Herndon* (273 U.S. 536, 1927).

[8] *United States v. Classic* (313 U.S. 299, 1941).

in the presidential years voting frequently has been light. In 1924 only 48.8 per cent of the American citizens of voting age bothered to exercise their right of franchise. In more recent years the record of the American voter in participation in presidential elections has been improved. In the 1960 national elections 64.3 per cent of the eligible voters participated in the vote for President. The highest percentage was in Idaho where more than 80 per cent of the eligible electorate voted, but at the other end of the scale only 25.6 per cent of the eligible voters exercised their franchise in Mississippi. In the 1964 presidential election a record number of Americans voted—70,621,490—but this figure was only 62.5 per cent of the eligible voters.

State elections in off-year balloting oftentimes attract less than 50 per cent of the eligible voters. Even more disheartening is the participation in state primary elections, where a 30 per cent vote is often considered quite large. In 1962 and 1963 twenty-four gubernatorial elections were held in states where state-wide registration figures are available. While it must be said that many eligible voters were not registered, the percentage of registered voters that participated in the twenty-four elections was surprisingly high. In California, an unusual election situation pitting former Vice President Nixon against incumbent Governor Edmund (Pat) Brown, a probable record turnout had 98.1 per cent of the registered voters marching to the polls. At the other extreme, in Georgia only 22.8 per cent of the registered voters participated in the gubernatorial election. However, if all twenty-four of the elections are considered, the statistics reveal that in thirteen of these elections more than 70 per cent of the registered voters cast ballots. In only four states—Georgia, Louisiana, South Carolina, and Virginia—did less than half of those registered fail to vote. It must be remembered that these elections were not presidential elections and yet the voter turnout was relatively higher than during some presidential elections.

At the local level a lower turnout is frequent. Municipal elections have probably the widest range in voter participation of any election. Municipal elections occasionally attract as high a percentage of the eligible voters as do presidential elections, while other municipal elections sometimes witness as few as 10 per cent of the electorate participating.

In the voter participation study conducted by the Bureau of Governmental Research at the University of California, Los Angeles, of presidential, state, and municipal elections over an eighteen-year period in forty-five cities, the sample revealed that the voter turnout averaged in municipal elections only 41 per cent of the registered electorate. In contrast, 77 per cent turned out to vote in the average state and national elections. This California study, conducted by Lawrence W. O'Rourke, concluded:

1. Voters tend to vote against candidates rather than for candidates.

2. Voter turnout is dependent upon the degree of opposition that can be generated in the minds of the voters.

3. There is a sizable number of voters who consistently participate in state and national elections but never vote in municipal elections.

4. The percentage of the registered electorate remains constant in each city for most municipal elections.[9]

It would appear that a two-pronged attack is needed. The first effort would be in increasing the voter registration by getting *all* the eligible voters registered and secondly to impress the voter of the importance of each vote in any given election. The paramount question is, how can voter participation in American elections be increased? The suggestion of making voting compulsory as it has been in Australia, Belgium, and Holland, has been virtually rejected in the United States. Two American states have passed laws that if enforced would be similar to the compulsory voting laws in Australia. As of now even where these laws are on the statute book no effort has ever been made to enforce them.[10]

Why do Americans not exercise the right to vote that is so highly prized but not available in many countries? One of the major reasons found in every study of political behavior is inertia.[11] It is also probably true that the frequency of elections in America is a contributory cause of low voter participation. Similarly, the usual lengthy ballot is a deterrent. It has been estimated that as many as 100,000 elections are held annually in the United States. In 1944, for example, major elections were held somewhere in the United States on more than 150 days in the year.

Thirty states attempt to encourage voting by allowing employees to take time off during regular working hours to exercise their right to vote. Although the laws differ, most apply to all workers and in all types of elections. In all but four of the thirty states the laws apply to all workers entitled to vote regardless of occupation or industry. In Arkansas, Indiana, and Massachusetts, the privilege is extended only to employees in factories and other specified industries, while in Alabama the law applies only to those employed in counties with populations of more than 75,000 but less than 130,000. Twenty-five states allow time off for voting in all types of elections. In nineteen states the employer is not permitted to deduct from the employee's wages for time taken from work for the purpose of voting. In a number of states the employee is required to apply in advance for the time off. In other states the employer is permitted to designate the particular hours that may be taken for voting. A number of the

[9] Lawrence W. O'Rourke, *Voting Behavior in Forty-five Cities of Los Angeles County* (Los Angeles: Bureau of Governmental Research, University of California, Los Angeles, 1953).

[10] Henry J. Abrahamson, "One Way to Get Out the Vote," *National Municipal League*, September, 1950.

[11] Charles E. Merriam and Harold F. Gosnell, *Non-Voting: Causes and Methods of Control* (Chicago: The University of Chicago Press, 1924).

state laws allow the time off only if there are insufficient hours either before or after the regular working day for the employee to go to the polls.

The most feasible answer would appear to be to make the task of the American voter easier. The best recommendation would seem to be to reduce the number of elections held every year in the United States. While there are good arguments for not holding national, state, and local elections on the same day, it must be admitted that the burden of the voter would be lessened. Likewise the cost of elections would be reduced by such a procedure.

What types of appeals can and are made to get out the vote? Many civic groups attempt to appeal to the non-voters on the basis that voting is a civic duty of every United States citizen. This non-partisan approach is sometimes sponsored by local units of the League of Women Voters, The American Legion, the American Farm Bureau, and other non-partisan groups. Frequently civic groups such as service clubs attempt to stimulate voter participation, again on a non-partisan basis.

A rank partisan approach to all members of the party is resorted to frequently by the leaders of both major political parties at all levels. The candidates themselves often make last-minute radio and television appearances urging all voters of the party to participate. Voter canvasses by the precinct committeemen and block workers are used in almost every election. Telephone campaigns on the day of elections are also used to increase voter participation.

A great many suggestions have been made as to how increased interest in American elections may be accomplished. The present procedure requires each voter to vote in the precinct polling place in which his residence is located. It has been suggested that it would be more convenient for many workers if the polling places were established in the factories and office buildings in which they work. Another suggestion has been that the day of the election should be changed from the traditional Tuesday to possibly Saturday or Sunday. Much opposition to the Sunday election day, which has been a long standing tradition in many European countries, has arisen from the clergy of America. Indeed so much opposition is present that no state has really given serious consideration to Sunday voting. Saturday voting with the shortened workweek may be a more realistic possibility.

The various political behavior studies that have been undertaken in the last fifteen years have given sufficient evidence to warrant a number of conclusions concerning the voting patterns that usually prevail in American state and local elections.

1. The individual's sex plays little or no role in determining for which candidate he voted. It is however increasingly evident that some candidates have more "sex" appeal than others and are therefore inclined to

get more of the female votes than an opponent who lacks this political sex appeal.

2. The higher the income the more likely the voter will favor the Republican party, with notable modifications in the South.

3. The higher the educational level of the voter the greater the tendency to vote for Republican candidates.

4. The younger voters are inclined to be more liberal and more likely to vote Democratic than the older voters.

5. Catholics are more likely to be Democrats than are Protestants, and members of the Jewish religion are even more likely to be Democrats than the Catholics.

6. People in the upper-income group have a tendency to be more consistent voter participants than those in the lower economic groups.

7. The voters in the upper-age brackets have a greater tendency to go to the polls than the youngest eligible voters.

8. Women traditionally do not exercise their franchise as regularly as do men.

9. Members of labor unions tend to vote traditionally for the Democratic party.[12]

Following the 1962 elections, James Reston of the *New York Times* characterized American voters as having:

1. A tendency to be moderate
2. A tendency to be optimistic
3. A tendency to look forward
4. A tendency to concentrate on the man rather than on the party
5. A tendency to retire old wind-bags
6. A tendency to be skeptical of all politicians and even of their own judgment

## STATE POLITICAL PARTIES

The political party is so essential to democratic government or representative government that its existence in every state in the nation is accepted without question. It is difficult to imagine state government in

[12] See: J. K. Pollock, *Voting Behavior* (Ann Arbor: University of Michigan Press, 1939); P. F. Lazarfeld and Others, *The People's Choice* (New York: Columbia University Press, 1948); R. M. Scammon, *America Votes* (New York: The Macmillan Co., 1956); Eugene Burdick and A. J. Braddeck, *America's Voting Behavior* (New York: The Free Press of Glencoe, Inc., 1958); Angus Campbell and R. L. Kahn, *The People Elect a President* (Ann Arbor: Survey Research Center, University of Michigan, 1952); B. R. Berelson and Others, *Voting* (Chicago: The University of Chicago Press, 1954); Angus Campbell and Others, *The Voter Decides* (New York: Harper & Row, Inc., 1954); Arthur Kornhauser and Others, *When Labor Votes* (New Hyde Park, N.Y.: University Books, Inc., 1956); Samuel J. Eldersveld, *Political Parties: A Behavioral Analysis* (Chicago: Rand McNally & Co., 1964).

America without political parties. What would happen to our governmental framework if there were no political parties? Who would nominate candidates or who would discuss, define, and resolve the public issues? Who or what would tie the processes of government together?

However, political parties have not always been accepted in the United States as a desirable feature of government. No less a figure than George Washington in his famous Farewell Address stated a warning "in the most solemn manner against the baneful effects of the spirit of the party generally." Another President of the United States, John Adams, stated his opinion of political parties as follows: "There is nothing I dread so much as the division of the Republic into two great parties each under its leader."

In every state the entire machinery of representation and popular control is built around the political party system. The legislative branch, the executive branch, and indeed, to a slightly lesser degree, the judiciary in most states depends upon the dynamic drive of political parties.

Three possibilities as to how many political parties may operate within a governmental unit exist. The first type is the so-called one-party state. In America this idea has been at least in theory rejected. In actual practice, however, it must be admitted that in a number of states only one political party really exists in sufficient size and power to be an effective operating device. The American theory has been, since the advent of constitutional government, that the political party is a device through which the people control the government, whether it be the national, state, county, or municipal government. The theory used in Russia is quite the opposite. The political party is the means through which the government controls the people. If the Russian theory is to be utilized, then a one-party rule is desirable. If the American theory is to dominate, then a one-party state is not tolerable.

The second possibility as to how many political parties should exist is the multi-party theory, which encourages as many political parties as there are diverse views as to the proper functioning of government. The ideal multi-party government operation envisions at least four major political parties. The first is a reactionary party, which views everything new and different as bad and resolves all problems by saying, "Now back in the good old days, we did it this way." The second type of political party in the multi-party theory would function as a group that would favor the status quo. These so-called conservatives would resist change and keep things on an even keel. The third political party would be a liberal group that sees need for changing the institutions and would move toward these changes. The fourth political faction would be composed of those who advocate major, immediate changes, who would use all force needed to institute those changes at once. This multi-political party theory has never and probably never will be tolerated in the United States. It makes responsible, representative government difficult to attain and brings about instability.

The third theory is the one that has been most widely advocated and adhered to in most of the states. This is the two-party philosophy which believes that it is essential and vital that two major political parties exist in every state at all times. This is not to eliminate the third parties. These minor parties are not only tolerated but often times encouraged, as it is recognized that the minor parties bring forth excellent reforms that are frequently adopted by one or both of the major parties and eventually are made operative.

As was pointed out in the publication of the American Political Science Association, *Toward a More Responsible Two-Party System,* there is a need for the political parties, an indispensable instrument of government, to be more responsible, more democratic, and more effective.[13] It must be a system that is accountable to the public, respects and expresses differences of opinion, and is at the same time able to handle all of the diverse problems confronting government in the second half of the twentieth century.

A basic need in almost every state is for a party system with greater ability to resist pressure, which is achieved by a unified party. Probably such a party will best be established and thrive if there is a competitive two-party organization. The situation most conducive to responsible government is that of organized party opposition. The second party must act as a critic of the party in power, developing its own program and offering policy alternatives. Both parties in a two-party organization must have sufficient cohesion to carry out the programs that they advocate when and if they become the party in power. This involves the placing of emphasis upon party discipline particularly upon positive measures and general agreement upon policies.

## Party Competition in the States: A Two-Party System?

A serious question is raised by several studies made of political party successes in state elections. Professors V. O. Key and Coleman B. Ransone, Jr., in separate studies of gubernatorial elections in America, present evidence that tends to repudiate the two-party philosophy as it operates in nearly one-third of the states.[14]

There has been in the last thirty years virtually no true second party in fourteen states. Twelve of these are in the South and are strictly Demo-

---

[13] *The American Political Science Review Supplement,* Vol. XLIV, No. 3 (September, 1950), Part 2, "Toward a More Responsible Two-Party System."

[14] V. O. Key, *American State Politics; An Introduction* (New York: A. A. Knopf, 1956), pp. 24, 55, 63; Coleman B. Ransone, Jr., *The Office of Governor in the United States* (University, Ala.: University of Alabama Press, 1956), pp. 13, 40, 75.

cratic states with no Republican candidate for governor given even an outside chance of winning, while two are in New England and the Democratic gubernatorial candidate runs against almost equally great odds. Between 1930 and 1960 the office of governor did not change from one party to another. However, a break appears to be developing in this group of solid one-party states as three, Vermont, New Hampshire, and Oklahoma, have since 1960 elected governors from the second party. No one should assume from these relatively isolated changes that true two-party competition will now be present in these three states or the other twelve. The domination of one party in this group will probably continue for some years unless a national political party realignment occurs, which also seems unlikely.

Table 8–2 lists the fourteen one-party states in gubernatorial elections from 1930 to 1960.

TABLE 8–2

One-Party States in the United States—Based Upon Gubernatorial
Elections from 1930 to 1960

| Democrat | | Republican |
|---|---|---|
| Alabama | North Carolina | New Hampshire |
| Arkansas | Oklahoma | Vermont |
| Florida | South Carolina | |
| Georgia | Tennessee | |
| Louisiana | Texas | |
| Mississippi | Virginia | |

All election studies appear to indicate that in the above-listed fourteen states no effective second 'major party exists. Thus the two-party system does not operate in nearly one-third of the state campaigns during this period. The states of Alaska and Hawaii have not been included since no governors were elected prior to 1960.

SOURCES: Coleman B. Ransome, Jr., *The Office of Governor in the United States* (University, Ala.: University of Alabama Press, 1956); Herbert Jacob and Kenneth N. Vines, (eds.), *Politics in the American States* (Boston: Little, Brown & Co., 1965).

## POLITICAL PARTY STRUCTURE AND ORGANIZATION

The political party structure and organization varies to a degree among the states. Each state legislature controls the form of party organization through the election laws. While there are variations in party structure, these differences are of less importance than the similarities. Some state laws, usually in the one-party states, provide only a general outline of party structure. In the two-party states the laws are usually quite extensive and are modified frequently by the state legislatures. In many states the election laws which involve the political party organization are reprinted and reissued after each session of the state's general assembly.

The typical state party organizational diagram is shown in Figure 8–1.

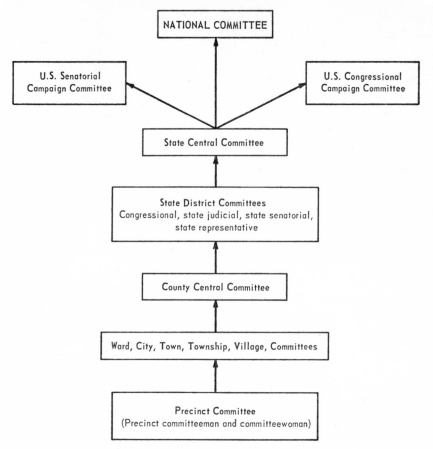

**Fig. 8–1.** A Typical State Party Organization.

## Precinct Committeeman and Committeewoman

The precinct is the smallest voting unit in the United States. The fifty states are divided into approximately one hundred and eighty-five thousand precincts. The number of voters in a precinct varies greatly. In some scarcely populated areas only a handful of people, as few as twenty, may be inhabitants of the voting precinct. In urban areas more than two thousand voters may be residents of a single precinct.[15]

In theory each political party has a precinct committeeman and committeewoman in each and every one of the precincts. Actually it is doubt-

[15] Joseph P. Harris, *Election Administration in the United States* (Washington, D.C.: The Brookings Institution, 1934) p. 207; Sonya Forthal, "The Precinct Worker," *The Annals of the American Academy of Political and Social Science*, Sept., 1948, vol. 259, pp. 30–45; and Samuel J. Eldersveld, *Political Parties: A Behavioral Analysis* (Chicago: Rand McNally & Co., 1964).

ful if there are more than 250,000 precinct committee people in each political party. The Democrats probably have their precincts more completely manned than do the Republicans, as there are many precincts in the Deep South that usually do not have any Republican precinct committeemen or women.

The average precinct in the United States would number about seven hundred voters. Each state has the responsibility for dividing its entire geographic area into precincts. Usually this is delegated to the county governments and to the municipalities.

Three different methods are used in the fifty states for naming the precinct committeemen and women. In some states the accepted procedure is for a caucus in the precinct to convene and name the committeeman and committeewoman. In other states the official selection must be made according to state law at the primary election. In still others the selection is made by appointment by a higher party official, often the county chairman or even the state committee chairman.

The paramount job of the precinct committeeman and his partner, no matter how selected, is to get out the party votes in their precinct. The various ways of performing this task are multitudinous, but all methods normally used inevitably involve the expenditure of some money.

In addition to getting out the party vote on election days, the precinct committeeman has other duties. He is expected in many states to encourage candidates to run for the minor offices, particularly county offices which usually have a scarcity of qualified candidates. His duties in connection with aiding the candidates in the campaign are also numerous. He is expected to assist in the financial drives to ensure a war chest for the campaign. During the days of the campaign he is frequently called upon to stage rallies, arrange dinners, coffee hours, and many other details that include getting the candidates publicity in the local press and placing political advertisements and billboard posters.

In the not too distant past a primary duty of the precinct committeeman, or captain as he is often called, was to bind as many voters to the party as possible by doing all kinds of favors for his people. These ranged from obtaining a government publication, helping a person get before the right judge in a traffic charge, assisting a family in obtaining public assistance or welfare, or securing a government job for a deserving voter. The social welfare function of the precinct captain has diminished in many areas but remains as a primary activity in the lower-income areas of the urban districts.

Many attempts have been made to characterize the individuals who serve their party as precinct leaders. With the vast array it is almost impossible to make a generalization that will properly characterize them. It must be recognized that there would appear to be a distinction between the precinct worker in the suburban area and the slum districts. The suburban committeeman is often a professional person, a lawyer most frequently, who does not desire a governmental job for himself or any of his relatives but does feel an obligation to work for his political party on an active basis. He spends a minimum amount of time in his duties, but usually performs them well. He makes an honest effort to get out the party vote in his district and to raise campaign funds.

The precinct captain in the slum areas has an entirely different problem. It is imperative that he work constantly to aid and assist anyone and everyone in his precinct in any way possible so as to insure their party loyalty at election time. He will probably be a self-made man. Often his background will be similar to everyone else in his precinct. If the district is dominated by members of the labor unions, then it is important that he too be a member of the union. Many of the precinct captains will have at least a part-time job that they have been given as a result of their political activities. The precinct captain may be a part-time city inspector or a part-time recreation director, or he may have a full-time status with some governmental unit. The slum area precinct leader will be well known to everyone in the district. The voters know that he is someone who will intercede in their behalf at every level—from the President of the United States, to congressmen, to the governor and to the local justice of the peace. Many times his influence will be vastly over-estimated by the rank and file of the party, but he must never desert them if his power is to continue.

In a well-organized precinct, in addition to the precinct committeeman and committeewoman, block captains are an important part of the operation. These individuals have the responsibility of contacting every one in their particular block who are members or potential members of the party. The block captains should serve as the eyes and ears of the precinct leaders. They should be able to ring every doorbell in their territory and report the reactions.

In a larger precinct the leader may find it necessary to have a finance chairman to aid in collecting money to support the party's activities. Likewise, a registration chairman and a social chairman may be important positions to aid and assist the precinct leaders. The committeewoman is usually assigned the task of organizing the feminine half of the party's working force. It should never be overlooked that the women normally outnumber the men in most precincts and they have the time to devote to the party's work.

All of these party officials are normally volunteers serving their political party without pay or even remuneration for expenses. As a result, party discipline is frequently difficult to maintain. It must all be based upon party loyalty rather than upon any threat that monetary rewards will be withheld if certain work is not performed.

One of the big problems in precinct organization is the lack of continuous activity. In election years it is relatively easy to get workers to perform tasks, but it is even easier if a constant and continuous program in the off-years is conducted. Political activity must be maintained month by month, week by week and day by day, in every year, not only in the election years, if the best results for the party are to be attained.[16]

## Intermediate Committees

To assert that the relationship between the precinct committeeman and the level of party immediately above him differs from region to region is an understatement. In some jurisdictions it is a ward committee composed ex officio of the leaders of the precincts in the ward. In other areas the committee immediately above the precincts is known as the city committee, which may also be composed of precinct committee leaders or may be elected directly by the party voters in a primary election. It is generally true that no matter how the secondary or intermediate committee is selected, the precinct committeemen and women have a potent voice. In some states this committee level does not even exist.

## The County Committee

In almost every one of the more than three thousand counties in the United States both parties are organized and have a county central committee. The size of the county committees varies just as does the method of selecting the members. A widespread practice is to have a relatively large county committee, composed of two representatives from each precinct. In some states selection as a precinct committeeman and woman automatically confers membership to the county committee.

The key figure in the county party organization is the county chairman. Usually he is selected by the members of the county committee from their group although he may be selected from the outside. This important party official has many responsibilities. If his political party is in control of the state government his patronage powers will be extensive. He is frequently consulted by the governor before political appointments are made from his county. If his party controls the executive branch of the national government he will have great influence by endorsing candidates for postmasters and other political appointments such as federal district attorneys, federal marshals, and collectors of internal revenue.

The county chairman is charged with the responsibility of organizing and conducting the county convention if the state law requires such a meeting. He also is expected to recruit candidates for county offices, the

---

[16] Sonya Forthal, "The Precinct Worker," *The Annals of the Academy of Political and Social Science,* Vol. CCLIX (September, 1948), pp. 30–45.

state legislature, and even state-wide offices. After the primary is completed he is expected to take an active role in the campaign to elect his party's candidates. He may be called upon to organize dinners, meetings, coffee-hours, tours of the county, and to see that a county headquarters is maintained during the campaign period.

Most of the county chairmen serve without pay. Their reward may come in the form of a political appointive post if their party wins the election. They do have an important job to perform in the financial field as it is their responsibility to see that their county contributes its quota to the state party's treasury. Ordinarily the county chairman will turn over the job of soliciting funds to a county finance chairman, or possibly to his vice chairman.

In most counties a vice chairman, inevitably a woman, is also named in the same manner as a county chairman. The vice chairman undertakes to organize the women members of the party, working through the precinct committeewomen and any women's council group that may be instituted. In addition to the women's branch she assists the county chairman in any way that he directs.

## District Committees

Various congressional and state senatorial committees function in the area between the county committee and the state committee. Frequently, where these committees exist, they are composed of the county chairmen and vice chairmen from the counties that are included in the particular district. Sometimes there is a district chairman but often no chairman is selected. The principal work of the committee is to assist the senatorial or congressional candidates to campaign effectively in the district. In many states these committees are only paper organizations and function when situations arise that require their activation, such as filling vacancies for district offices.

## State Central Committee

The party structure in every state is headed by a group called the state central committee, the state executive committee, or the state committee. The membership ranges again from as few as eleven persons to more than five hundred. The methods of naming the committee members also vary, from election in the general primary to selection by convention. Geographic representation of the state is always present on the state committee. The representative district may be the county, the congressional district, or some other area division. The county chairmen are usually influential in shaping the composition and actions of the state central committee, being in a few states ex-officio members of the body.[17]

The top position in every state is occupied by the chairman of the state committee. He is most commonly selected by the members of the state committee but may be chosen by a statewide convention. In some states the gubernatorial candidate has great influence in selecting the state chairman. If the post is a full-time one, as it is in many states, the state chairman may be paid a substantial salary. In many states the chairman serves only on a part time basis but has an executive assistant who devotes all of his time working for the state central committee on an annual salary.

The office of the state chairman is responsible for the over-all operation of the political party's activities throughout the entire state. It is the hub around which the political affairs of the party revolve. Its influence in shaping the party's ticket for the elections is very great. Usually in the primary elections the state chairman plays a watchful, waiting role, encouraging candidates but not actively supporting any particular one. In the general election campaign he plays a very active part. Frequently the state chairman is charged with managing and controlling the finances of the campaign.

Following the general election, if the party has been successful in winning the governorship or the presidency, the state chairman exercises great influence over patronage matters. He is called upon to give political clearance to almost all political appointments made in the state. Ordinarily he will consult with the appropriate local party leaders before endorsing any appointment that affects the area.

In some states the state chairman will receive a post in the governor's administration if he cares to take such a position. In other states he becomes almost automatically the secretary of state under the governor where this post is an appointive one.

## National Committee

The summit of political party hierarchy is the national central committee. Each state is entitled to at least two members of the national central committee in both parties. The Republican party in recent years has allowed the state chairman to be an ex-officio member of the national central committee in those states that have voted Republican. The national committeeman and committeewoman are selected in four different ways. In nearly half of the states the national committee delegates are selected for a four-year term by the state convention. In other states they are se-

[17] Stuart Lewis, "Composition of State and Local Party Committees," *National University Law Review*, 1928; James A. Michener, *Report of the County Chairman* (New York: Random House, Inc., 1961).

lected by the delegates to the national party convention; in others the state committee makes the selection, and in a fourth group the state primary elects the national committeeman and committeewoman.[18]

The highest office in the political organization is the national chairman. He is technically named by the national central committee, but in reality he is selected by the party's candidate for President. If the party's candidate for President is defeated the chairman frequently finds it best to resign, but if he has run a successful campaign he often is rewarded with the cabinet post of Postmaster General and is in charge of all national political patronage. Next to the President he is usually the most important political official.

It should not be assumed that authority flows regularly from one level of the political structure to another. Each set of committees is virtually autonomous. This very loose relationship and lack of discipline arises from a number of causes but mainly from the election laws of the various states. As Professor McKean wrote, "Superficially a hierarchy, in reality the structure of American parties is a loose league or confederation rather than an integrated, or even federal system."[19]

## Bosses and Political Parties

A number of states have been at times dominated by political bosses, and an even greater number of American cities have been under boss rule. No evidence has ever been produced to prove that either national party has been dominated by a boss, but a number of United States Presidents and their campaign chairmen have been alleged to have ruled in a fashion similar to that of state and city bosses.

Huey P. Long was the undisputed ruler of politics in Louisiana during the 1930's. Probably no other one man had as many characteristics usually associated with the American political "boss" or ruled a state more completely. Pennsylvania has had at least two men who dominated their political party organization, Matthew Quay and Boies Penrose. Other states with bosses at one time or another in their political history include, Conkling and Platt of New York, Stephenson of Indiana, and Roraback of Connecticut.

Almost every major city in the United States has been at one time or another under boss rule. Well known to all political historians are the reigns of Tweed and Murphy in New York City, Pendergast of Kansas City, Hague of Jersey City, Big Bill Thompson of Chicago, as well as

---

[18] Wallace S. Sayre, "Personnel of Republican and Democratic National Committees," *American Political Science Review*, Vol. XXVI (April, 1932), pp. 360–63.

[19] Dayton McKean, *Party and Pressure Groups* (Boston: Houghton Mifflin Co., 1949), p. 211.

Kelly and Nash of the same city, Durham, Penrose, and the Vares of Philadelphia, Ames of Minneapolis, and Ruef of San Francisco.

Political bosses rule through domination of a political party in a state or city. They have few similar personal characteristics aside from the one common factor: they control elections and thereby the machinery of government. Seldom does the boss hold a public office. He works from behind the scenes with no public accountability. The boss is removed from control only when his political machine fails to win elections and there is a revolt among the party members. Unlike the true political leader, who is popularly elected to a position of public responsibility, the boss is not handicapped in his operations by a careful observance of state and local statutes. He does anything that is necessary to stay in power, and whether it is in the best interests of the public usually does not concern him. Violence and corruption are used to perpetuate his reign if necessary.[20]

City and state bosses are possible in the United States because the citizens of the particular area are unwilling to take the interest in politics to get responsible men into office. Bosses thrive upon public inertia and apathy. Some bosses have developed their own private political party outside the regular political organizations but most take over an existing party because of the indifference of the members and officials of the party. Only when the citizenry become aroused can proper control of the political party be regained by the citizens.

Other factors that have been present in American politics to make the advent of bosses possible are usually listed as follows: election of too many officials at both the state and local levels of government, the opportunities for graft and corruption in state and local government, the spoils system of appointing personnel, mass ignorance, illiteracy, and lack of participation in both election and nominating processes.[21]

Machines and bosses can be ousted by any number of methods but all require aroused citizen interest and desire to bring about reform even, at times, at great personal risk. Reform movements have taken different forms in almost every city and state where concentrated effort to rid the area of machine politics has been successfully carried out. In some areas fusion parties have been formed, and in other cases new parties have been created that were able to vote out the machine-dominated party.

The machines that are well entrenched gain control of every aspect of government, the law-making process, the judicial branch, the electoral machinery, as well as the various units within the executive-administrative branch. A true civil service–merit system may be a weapon that will tear the machine from control of the powerful tool of public employment.

[20] Harold Zink, *City Bosses in the United States* (New York: The Macmillan Co., 1948).

[21] Richard S. Childs, *Civic Victories* (New York: Harper & Row, Inc., 1952).

A reform in the law enforcement units is also basic to breaking most machine-controlled areas.

Most observers believe that the political machine does not wield the power that it did during the last half of the nineteenth century or during the first decades of this century. Primarily this is due to the reforms in government that have slowly occurred at all levels. Citizen interest in government and politics is still relatively slight. Americans vote in local elections only if aroused by situations that have got so far out of hand that they no longer can be ignored. Then the voter votes against rather than for someone or some project. The boss and his ring, those in the inner circle that form a close working partnership, may be the focus of the "against" voting. The boss will forestall the negative vote by making sure that outward appearances are good. He will have given enough support to new schools, hospitals, roads and bridges to make a good showing until the costs of such improvements are finally brought to light.

Until the American public awakens to the fact that a boss waits for public apathy there will always be the opportunity for new machines to rise. Only when all of the voters are willing to fight for good government by participating actively in it will the possibilities of machine politics be eliminated. Invisible government cannot exist in the full glare of public indignation, but it can flourish if public lethargy continues.

If the average citizen realizes that it is his money that every level of government is spending, he will take seriously his responsibilities as a citizen. Government does not create wealth; only individual initiative and enterprise make is possible to finance governmental operations. The old cliché has much to recommend it: The price of democracy is eternal vigilance.

## Pressure Groups and Political Parties

Both political parties and pressure groups attempt to influence policy. In the United States it is generally accepted that almost all policy making, whether it be at the national, state, or local level, is a matter of compromise.

Any group that has as its objective the influencing of policy-making procedures is a pressure group. Most of the major pressure groups in the United States are organized at the national level and have their counterparts on the state and even local areas. A majority of these pressure groups are organized around an economic core.

Pressure groups are similar to political parties in that both attempt to affect public policy and policy decisions. They are unlike in that the pressure group does not usually have a slate of candidates that it supports for election, while of course the major function of a political party is to present a slate of candidates. The two groups are also separated since the pressure group usually does not take a stand on all of the broad issues confronting government but is concentrating on a very few items with which it is primarily concerned.

While the pressure group does not run its own candidates for public office, it usually finds it necessary to endorse and support the candidates of one or the other of the two major political parties. Furthermore the endorsement often carries with it financial support of the campaigns waged by these candidates. The money that pressure groups put forth is usually given to the individual candidates, rather than the political party, for the obvious reason that this tends to place more directly the responsibility of the successful candidate to the pressure group.

While it is usually accepted that pressure groups do not tie themselves completely to one party or the other, it is universally recognized that the various labor organizations tend to polarize around the Democratic party and usually support nearly the entire slate of Democratic candidates. Seldom does a Republican candidate obtain the endorsement of a labor union when running for office. On the other hand the American Farm Bureau usually finds itself more in sympathy with Republicans and endorses and supports this party's candidates. Similarly the National Association of Manufacturers finds the Republican party's slate more in tune with its thinking and throws its support to this party.

Some pressure groups are large and others are relatively small in total membership. Some are of long duration, others wither after a single year. Some are well financed, others virtually penniless. Some are well organized with groups in every county of a state, while others may have almost no organized operation.

The amount of influence a pressure group wields is almost impossible to measure accurately. Some pressure groups are credited with more power than they actually can muster. The strength of others is underestimated. The total membership of the group is one factor but probably more important is the necessity of its organization being widespread throughout the entire governmental unit, whether it be the state, county, or city. A pressure group that does not have local chapters in most of the counties of the state will not be as effective as one that is statewide in organization.

Pressure groups influence legislation at all levels of government by every means possible. Their first objective is to help to elect candidates to public office that will give their cause a sympathetic hearing. But this, of course, does not end the efforts of the pressure group to gain its own ends. After the election the group continues its campaign to spread its message to all public officials in any position to affect public policy. The initial attack following the election is naturally upon the policy-decision makers, namely the legislators. Every means of persuading the policy makers is used by the pressure group and its lobbyists. Every member of the legislature is studied and his pet projects are known to the lobbyist. The likes and dislikes of the legislator are recognized, and he will be wined and dined by the pressure group. The pressure group is both positive and negative. There are always certain pieces of legislation that they are supporting, but equally important there are certain propositions that the pressure group feels would not be to its best interest and desires to have defeated.

Cases are infrequent in which the pressure groups in the second half of the twentieth century step beyond the bounds of propriety in pushing for their causes. Occasionally, however, some questionable act does come to light. Gifts to legislators who have been particularly friendly or helpful to the pressure group are not unknown. Frequently legislators are invited by the lobbyists to take trips at the expense of the pressure group.

The pressure groups are frequently divided into various types. The methods used are quite standardized but the classification into different groups is based upon the types of people that are included in the membership:[22]

1. Veterans groups: American Legion, Veterans of Foreign Wars
2. Professional organizations: American Teachers' Organization, American Medical Association, American Bar Association
3. Agricultural groups: American Farm Bureau Federation, The Grange, National Farmers Organization
4. Industrial groups: National Association of Manufacturers, U.S. Chamber of Commerce
5. Labor organizations: A.F. of L.–C.I.O.
6. Good government groups: League of Women Voters, League of Municipalities

Pressure groups, as well as minor political parties have often been the source of new policies. It is true that frequently the minor parties are the first groups willing to accept a new idea from a pressure organization and focus attention upon it. Eventually the proposal may be adopted by the major political parties as part of their programs.

[22] For detailed analysis of pressure groups see: D. B. Truman, *The Government Process* (New York: Alfred A. Knopf, Inc., 1951); D. L. Sills, *The Volunteers* (New York: The Free Press of Glencoe, Inc., 1957); R. E. Lane, *Political Life: How People Get Involved in Politics* (New York: The Free Press of Glencoe, Inc., 1958); "Unofficial Government: Pressure Groups and Lobbies," *The Annals of the American Academy of Political and Social Science.* Vol. CCCXIX (September, 1958); C. Wright Mills, *The Power Elite* (Fair Lawn, N.J.: Oxford University Press, 1956); Floyd Hunter, *Community Power Structure* (Chapel Hill: University of North Carolina Press, 1953); V. O. Key, Jr., *Politics, Parties and Pressure Groups* (4th ed., New York: Thomas Y. Crowell Co., 1958).

The current low estate of minor parties is due to various factors, but it may be that one of the most important causes of their eclipse is that more and more of the important pressure groups are formulating policy and taking their proposals directly to legislative bodies and/or to administrative officers.[23]

Some pressure groups on occasion have been able to get policy enacted by legislative bodies, including the United States Congress, even when the program of action advocated by the pressure group has not been accepted by the two major parties in their platforms. Obviously the very largest pressure groups are the only ones that can accomplish this under ordinary circumstances. The pressure groups do not attempt to govern. They are interested in achieving the adoption of certain policies in which they have a vested interest.

Professor E. E. Schattschneider wrote in 1948:

What the parties require is a better morale, a better conception of their potentialities, a more intelligent public support based upon a better understanding of the meaning of party government. Once the parties are aroused, the struggle between the parties and pressure groups is certain to be an unequal one.[24]

This assumes that all pressure groups are evil. Such a blanket indictment is not entirely justified. It cannot be charged that all pressure groups tend to pervert the objectives of democracy.

## BIBLIOGRAPHY

AMERICAN POLITICAL SCIENCE ASSOCIATION. *Toward a More Responsible Two-Party System.* New York: Holt, Rinehart and Winston, Inc., 1950.

BAKER, GORDON E. *Rural Versus Urban Political Power.* Garden City, N.Y.: Doubleday & Co., 1955.

BALDWIN, RAYMOND. *Let's Go Into Politics.* New York: The Macmillan Co., 1952.

BOCK, EDWIN A. (ed.). *State and Local Government: A Case Book.* University, Ala.: University of Alabama Press, 1963.

BONE, HUGH A. *American Politics and the Party System,* 2d ed. New York: McGraw-Hill Book Co., Inc., 1955.

——— and RANNEY, AUSTIN. *Politics and Voters.* New York: McGraw-Hill Book Co., Inc., 1963.

ELDERSVELD, SAMUEL J. *Political Parties: A Behavioral Analysis.* Chicago: Rand McNally & Co., 1964.

FARLEY, JAMES A. *Behind the Ballots.* New York: Harcourt, Brace & World, Inc., 1938.

FENTON, JOHN H. *Politics in the Border States.* New Orleans: The Hauser Press, 1957.

[23] McKean, *op. cit.,* p. 437.
[24] E. E. Schattschneider, "Pressure Groups *v.* Political Parties," *The Annals of the Academy of Political and Social Science,* Vol. CCLIX (September, 1948), p. 22.

FENTON, JOHN M. *The Pollsters: Public Opinion, Politics and Democratic Leadership.* Boston: Little, Brown & Co., 1960.
FISHER, MARGUERITE, and STARRATT, EDITH. *Parties and Politics in the Local Community.* Washington, D.C.: National Council of Social Studies, 1945.
FLYNN, EDWARD J. *You're The Boss.* New York: The Viking Press, Inc., 1947.
FORTHAL, SONYA. *Cogwheels of Democracy: A Study of the Precinct Captain.* New York: William-Frederick Press, Pamphlet Distributing Co., 1946.
GOODMAN, WILLIAM. *The Two Party System in the United States,* 2d ed. Princeton, N.J.: D. Van Nostrand Co., Inc., 1960.
GOSNELL, HAROLD F. *Boss Platt and His New York Machine.* Chicago: The University of Chicago Press, 1923.
HEARD, ALEXANDER. *Money and Politics.* Washington, D.C.: Public Affairs Press, 1956.
HERRING, E. PENDLETON. *The Politics of Democracy.* New York: Holt, Rinehart & Winston, Inc., 1940.
HINDERAKER, IVAN. *Party Politics.* New York: Holt, Rinehart & Winston, Inc., 1956.
JACOB, HERBERT, and VINES, KENNETH N. (eds.). *Politics in the American States.* Boston: Little, Brown & Co., 1965.
KELLEY, STANLEY, JR. *Political Campaigning.* Washington, D.C.: The Brookings Institution, 1960.
KENT, FRANK R. *The Great Game of Politics.* Garden City, N.Y.: Doubleday & Co., Inc., 1924.
KEY, V. O. *Southern Politics in State and Nation.* New York: Alfred A. Knopf, Inc., 1949.
———. *American State Politics: An Introduction.* New York: Alfred A. Knopf, Inc., 1956.
———. *Politics, Parties and Pressure Groups,* 4th ed. New York: Thomas Y. Crowell Co., 1958.
———. *Public Opinion and American Democracy.* New York: Alfred A. Knopf, 1961.
LATHAM, EARL. *Massachusetts Politics.* New York: The Citizenship Clearing House, 1956.
LEISERSON, AVERY. *Parties and Politics.* New York: Alfred A. Knopf, Inc., 1958.
LOCKARD, DUANE. *New England State Politics.* Princeton: Princeton University Press, 1959.
———. *The Politics of State and Local Government.* New York: The Macmillan Co., 1963.
LUBELL, SAMUEL. *The Future of American Politics.* New York: Harper & Row, Inc., 1952.
MARTIN, ROSCOE C. *Grass Roots.* University, Ala.: University of Alabama Press, 1957.
MERRIAM, CHARLES E., and GOSNELL, HAROLD F. *The American Party System, an Introduction to the Study of Political Parties in the United States,* 4th ed. New York: The Macmillan Co., 1949.
ODEGARD, PETER H., and HELMS, E. ALLEN. *American Politics, a Study in Political Dynamics,* 2d ed. New York: Harper & Row, Inc., 1947.
McKEAN, DAYTON. *The Boss: Machine Politics in Action.* Boston: Houghton Mifflin Co., 1940.
PRICE, HUGH D. *The Negro and Southern Politics.* New York: New York University Press, 1957.

RANNEY, AUSTIN, and KENDALL, WILLMORE. *Democracy and the American Party System*. New York: Harcourt, Brace & World, Inc., 1956.
ROCHE, JOHN P., and LEVY, LEONARD W. *Parties and Pressure Groups*. New York: Harcourt, Brace & World, Inc., 1964.
SAIT, EDWARD M. *American Parties and Elections*, 5th ed. by H. R. PENNIMAN. New York: Appleton-Century-Crofts, Inc., 1952.
SORAUF, FRANK J. *Party and Representation*. New York: Atherton Press, 1963.
———. *Political Parties in the American System*. Boston: Little, Brown & Co., 1964.
VAN RIPER, PAUL P. *Handbook of Practical Politics*, rev. ed. New York: Harper & Row, Inc., 1960.
VANDEVANDER, CHARLES. *The Big Bosses*. New York: Howell Soskin, 1944.
WESTIN, ALAN F. (ed.). *The Uses of Power: Seven Cases in American Politics*. New York: Harcourt, Brace & World, Inc., 1962.

# 9

# Nominations, Campaigns, and Elections

As Gunnar Myrdal has said:

Americans are accustomed to being static and receptive. They are not daring, but long for security. They do not know how to cooperate and how to pool risks and sacrifices for a common goal. They do not meet much. They do not organize. They do not speak for themselves; they are listeners in America. They seldom elect representatives from their own midst to Congress, to state legislatures, or to city councils. They rather support friendly leaders from the upper strata, particularly lawyers. . . . Political participation of the ordinary citizen is pretty much restricted to the intermittently recurring elections. Politics is not organized to be a daily concern and responsibility of the common citizen.[1]

There is a great deal of truth in Professor Myrdal's statement, particularly with respect to the selection of officials, but it is not so valid with regard to the amount or number of organizations in America. One of the problems facing political parties with respect to the important role they play in nominating and electing candidates is that too many Americans belong to too many organized groups and as a result do not have the time and energy to participate actively in the nominating and elective processes. The American voter feels he is overworked, that he is all too frequently called upon to exercise his right of franchise. He too often forgets that the nominating process may be even more important than that of the final election, for unless he supports highly motivated candidates in the nominating procedure he will have no opportunity to vote for his candidate in the final election. Likewise, the typical American enjoys watching a good political campaign, but he is reluctant to become a moving part of the action. He prefers spectator sports rather than active participation.

[1] Gunnar Myrdal, *An American Dilemma* (New York: Harper & Row, Inc., 1944), pp. 714, 717.

The importance of participation in the nominating elections, the direct primary, is shown when one considers that the period from 1958 to 1960 in at least seven states, all in the South, the nominating election was the true election. That many voters in these areas realized this was proven by the turn-out in the primary in South Carolina (1958) when more than five times as many voters went to the polls to exercise their franchise as voted in the general election. The contrast in primary voting and general election turn-out is shown in Table 9–1.

TABLE 9–1
Voting Statistics for Selected States—Primary and General Elections

| State | Year | General Election Vote | Primary Election Vote |
|-------|------|-----------------------|-----------------------|
| Alabama | 1962 | 315,776 | 636,403 |
| Arkansas | 1962 | 308,092 | 405,112 |
| Georgia | 1962 | 311,524 | 852,350 |
| Louisiana | 1963 | 506,562 | No primary |
| Mississippi | 1963 | 363,971 | 456,051 |
| South Carolina | 1962 | 253,704 | 328,291 |
| Tennessee | 1962 | 620,758 | 778,759 |

SOURCE: Council of State Governments, *The Book of the States, 1964–1965*. (Chicago: Council of State Governments, 1964).

## NOMINATION OF POLITICAL CANDIDATES

The political parties in the United States perform a governmental function by nominating the candidates who will contest in the general election. The direct primary is the most recent method or device developed for nominating party candidates, but it has not completely replaced two older methods, the caucus and convention. In fact, in some states a combination of methods is employed.

### The Direct Primary

For about one hundred and twenty years the direct primary method of nominating candidates has been utilized in various parts of the United States. It was first tried in Pennsylvania in 1842 in Crawford County with the consequent result that for many years the direct primary was referred to as the Crawford County system. The theory of the direct primary is very simple. It allows the rank and file members of the political party to decide the party's nominee for office by holding a party election at some time prior to the general election. The primary election is held under the same conditions as those prescribed for the general election: secret voting; ballots printed at public expense; the same rules concerning electioneering; and the same machinery for insuring an honest count of the ballots. The objective of the primary is to give all members of the political party an opportunity to participate in the selection of the nominee, thus avoiding any accusation that a small group of key party leaders make the selection of the party's candidates.

In order to avoid the possibility of members of the opposition party helping to select an undesirable candidate, the party primary may by state election law be a closed primary. This is one in which only bona fide members of the party may participate. Thus, only the voter who is registered as a party member, or is otherwise identified with the party, is allowed to vote in the party primary. All but eight of the states employ this type of primary at the present time. Of the continental states, Connecticut, in 1955, was the last one to put into effect the primary system for nominating some of its candidates.[2]

An open primary state does not require party identification. Only Wisconsin, Idaho, Michigan, Minnesota, Montana, North Dakota, Utah, and Washington are recognized as open primary states. However, some experts do not recognize North Dakota as a true open primary state (those in which no request to see party identification is required in order to vote in a primary election). Three other states, Arkansas, Mississippi, and South Carolina, might well be listed as open primary states since they give the voter both a Democratic and a Republican ballot at the primary election, allowing him to participate in the one he desires. The advocates of the open primary method assert that it is the individual's right to keep his political party affiliation a secret and should not be forced to publicly announce his party allegiance in order to participate in the nominating process.

In order to gain a place on the primary ballot in most states it is necessary for the candidate to file a petition with a designated state or county official that is signed by a certain number or certain percentage of the voters who participated in the last general election. In order to assure the good faith of the candidate some states require a filing fee. A few states return the fee if the candidate receives a certain percentage of the votes cast for the office he seeks in the primary election.

In almost every state a candidate who receives a majority of the votes cast is declared the party's nominee in the general election without any further contest. In all but eleven Southern states the candidate with a plurality is declared the winner, but in these states if no candidate has a

<hr/>

[2] Council of State Governments, *The Book of the States, 1954–1955* (Chicago: Council of State Governments, 1954), p. 83.

majority of the votes cast for the office in the primary a so-called run-off primary is held in which only the top two candidates in the first primary participate.[3] This assures in the second primary a majority vote for one candidate. Iowa and South Dakota have a unique rule in that, while not requiring a majority vote for the winner in a primary, a plurality of at least 35 per cent is required. If no candidate polls this portion of the primary vote the primary is said to have failed and the appropriate convention names the party's candidate for the general election ballot.[4]

In two-thirds of the states the cost of operating the election machinery for the primary is entirely borne by the county governments, even though state and national officials may be nominated in the primary as well as county officers. Only about one-third of the states bear a part of the primary election costs. The filing fees are used in some states to pay a part of the cost of operating the primary election machinery.

The dates of the primary contests are established by the election laws in each of the states. Some are held as early as April while others are held in May, still others in June, a few in July and August, and the last occur in September. The arguments over which month is best are inconclusive. Politicians by and large tend to favor later primaries thus avoiding hitting two peaks; one in the primary and a second in the general election. In the South the nomination is tantamount to election and the only real campaign is waged in the primary election. The run-off election in these states is justified because the winner should at least receive a majority of the Democratic votes cast.

A few states have utilized a combination of convention and primary systems for nominating candidates. In Colorado, Massachusetts, New Mexico, Rhode Island, and Utah a party convention is held and proposes a slate of candidates to appear on the primary ballot. This does not eliminate competition on the primary ballot as other candidates may place their names on the ballot by petition. It usually makes it difficult, if not impossible, for the petition nominee to win the primary since the party officials have placed their stamp of approval on his opponent. This modification of the primary election is said to restore the party responsibility which many feared would be destroyed by the installation of the direct primary nominating process.[5]

---

[3] The eleven run-off primary states are: Arkansas, Florida, Georgia, Louisiana, Mississippi, North Carolina, Oklahoma, South Carolina, Tennessee, Texas, and Virginia. The rules differ in each with fewer run-offs in several of the states because not all offices are required to have a majority primary vote and in Tennessee a run-off occurs only in the unlikely event of a tie.

[4] *Code of Iowa, 1962*, State of Iowa, Des Moines, chap. xliii.

[5] Charles E. Merriam and Louise Overacker, *Primary Elections* (Chicago: The University of Chicago Press, 1928).

## Non-partisan Primary

A non-partisan primary is used in a few states and in a majority of municipalities for nominating candidates. The name non-partisan primary is used because no party affiliation of any candidate is permitted on the primary ballot. In this process the candidates all gain positions on the primary ballot by paying a filing fee, filing a petition, or both. Usually the two candidates receiving the highest total of votes for the office are declared the primary winners and face each other in the general election balloting. In a true sense this is not a primary election but rather a preliminary or screening election to reduce the number of hopefuls from an infinite number to two. A few states have election laws that permit a non-partisan primary candidate with a majority of the votes cast to become the winner without the formality of a general election. The primary thereby eliminates the necessity of holding a second election, but in some states this is a rare phenomenon.

## The Convention

While the direct primary is a part of the nominating process in all of the fifty states, in one degree or another the convention system is not entirely obsolete. It is still a part of the nominating process in at least three states for some offices—Connecticut, Indiana, and New York. In another group of states, mostly Southern, where the minority party's cause is usually regarded as hopeless, the convention system may be used by the minority party if it desires. Almost all states allow third or minor parties to make their nominations for state offices by a state-wide convention and permits local conventions to make nominations for local offices.

## By Petition

In most states a place on the general election ballot may be secured by a candidate without any party affiliation. This is achieved by submitting a petition signed by the number of voters as required by the election laws of the state. The candidate is usually labeled as an Independent on the Massachusetts type ballot or is listed under Independent column on the Indiana type of ballot. Seldom does such a candidate appear. Seldom does he either win or materially affect the outcome of the election in our two-party system which is prevalent in the United States.

## Nomination by Self-Announcement

This, the oldest of all of the nominating methods, is for all practical purposes eliminated in most elections. It consists of an individual proclaiming publicly that he is a candidate for an office and thus obtains a place on the ballot. A few municipal, township, or even county offices may still permit such a procedure, but in almost every election for any important position it is now disused.

## Nomination by the Caucus

Limited use is made of the technique of nomination by caucus, the gathering together of a few friends who in an informal meeting nominate a candidate for public office. Only in the most minor elections will this procedure place a candidate's name on the general election ballot. Today it usually is a preliminary step taken by many candidates before they arrange for petitions to place themselves formally on the primary ballot.

To place the nominating processes in historic perspective the self-announcement is the oldest, followed by the caucus, the convention system, and the direct primary. This last system began on a state-wide basis in Wisconsin in 1903 and reached all continental states by 1955, with Alaska and Hawaii providing for it when admitted to the union.

Each system attempts to correct the defects in the one that preceded it in the development or evolution of the nomination process. The caucus broadened the base of the nomination procedure, and the convention idea attempted to make nominations more democratic. However, the convention system proved to be too easily controlled by party leaders and officers and was supplanted by the direct primary.

## Presidential Primary

The value of presidential primary elections is not clearly established. Two types of presidential primaries are in use: (1) election of delegates to the national convention, pledged or unpledged to a certain candidate; and (2) an election in which the voters express their preference among presidential possibilities. Some states even use a combination of these two types of presidential primaries. Table 9–2 lists the presidential preference primary states and indicates the methods of selecting delegates, the use of the preferences, and the voting status of the delegates.

In a presidential election year about one-fourth of the states utilize a presidential preference or presidential primary system. Thirty states normally use a state-wide convention to name their delegates to the national convention; two, Arkansas and South Carolina, allow the state central committee to name the national convention delegates, while Arizona and Kansas usually use a party council in selecting the delegates.

In 1952 in a closely contested race between General Eisenhower and Senator Taft an apparent revival of interest in the presidential primary occurred. However, in succeeding presidential election years this interest

## TABLE 9-2

### State Mandatory Presidential Primaries

| State | How Delegates Are Chosen | Delegates Pledged | Preference Vote | Delegates Bound |
|---|---|---|---|---|
| California | Elected | Yes | Yes | Yes |
| Illinois | Elected | No | Yes | No |
| Indiana | Convention | No | Yes | Yes |
| Maryland | Convention | No | Yes | Yes |
| Massachusetts | Elected | Usually | Yes | No |
| Minnesota | Elected | Yes | No | Yes |
| Montana | Convention | | Yes | Yes |
| Nebraska | Elected | No | Yes | Yes |
| New Hampshire | Elected | Usually | Yes | No |
| New Jersey | Elected | Usually | Yes | No |
| New York | Elected | No | No | No |
| Ohio | Elected | Yes | No | Yes |
| Oregon | Elected | Usually | Yes | Usually |
| Pennsylvania | Elected | Usually | Yes | Usually |
| South Dakota | Elected | Usually | No | Usually |
| West Virginia | Elected | No | Yes | No |
| Wisconsin | Elected | Yes | No | Usually |

SOURCE: Council of State Governments, *The Book of the States, 1964–1965* (Chicago: Council of State Governments, 1964).

was not apparent. Many of the party leaders do not feel that it is a suitable part of the presidential nominating system, even though Woodrow Wilson had urged in 1912 that each state provide for such an election.[6]

The problems caused by presidential primaries are numerous. Often there are few presidential aspirants who will enter very many of the primaries, and usually not in the state where a favorite son will be entered. It is also very difficult to effectively bind the delegates. It is also questionable whether or not it is wise to have the delegates pledged to a particular candidate, especially if he turns out to be an "also ran" in the national convention.

In these states that have a presidential primary only Oregon does not permit the candidates to withdraw from the election if they do not care to participate. As a result, the presidential primary has often become a limited popularity contest that does not prove anything. On the other hand, it is quite widely recognized that President Kennedy gained his nomination by winning key presidential primaries in 1960. One contest in particular, West Virginia, has been credited with catapulting him into the presidential nomination of the Democratic party.[7]

[6] R. S. Baker (ed.), *The Public Papers of Woodrow Wilson* (New York: 1926), Vol. III, p. 76.

[7] Theodore H. White, *The Making of the President, 1960* (New York: Atheneum Publishers, 1961), pp. 112–13.

The presidential primaries begin with the New Hampshire contest in March and end with four primaries in the first week of June, approximately four weeks before the first national convention convenes. Many presidential hopefuls find that it is not only time-consuming to enter many of the presidential primaries but it is also very expensive to wage campaigns in all of the states holding primaries.

## STATE CAMPAIGNS

Political candidates running for state-wide offices in states with large geographic areas have discovered that by judiciously using television facilities they can become known to the electorate more rapidly than by any other means. This does not imply that other types of campaigning can be abolished. Even in the 1962 gubernatorial campaign in California, Republican candidate Richard Nixon used the time honored whistle-stop approach in the latter stages of the campaign. He chartered a special train and traveled the length of the state, making stops at every railroad station. Moreover, a candidate cannot avoid political advertising in the newspapers and billboards, although there is evidence that not as much use of these two techniques is currently being made as twenty and thirty years ago.

Almost every candidate for public office now realizes that it makes relatively little difference how many people attend a particular political rally as long as what he says receives good coverage in the mass communication media. In order to help the members of the press, almost all candidates now have daily or twice daily press releases that are distributed to all of the wire services and to the major news media in the entire state. To be sure, most newspapers, radio stations, and television news programs will not use everything included in the press releases, but at least the highlights of the speech will be carried to all corners of the area. A good press release writer—one who is skilled in the art of knowing what the newsmen will regard as important and what they will spurn as trivial —is an essential part of any state wide political campaign.

The problems presented to the candidate are numerous. How to spend his always limited funds, no matter how much it may be, is a real problem. Should he buy a half-hour program or three ten-minute segments or six five-minute spots or even ten or fifteen two-minute spots? Or should he have a series of telethons, a program that may run one, two, or even three hours, during which time he will inevitably introduce many of the candidates of his ticket from the area covered by the TV station and answer questions called in by listeners? Should he engage in debates with his opponent on television? The answers to these and many other questions concerning politics and the impact of television must be carefully studied.[8]

If the candidate is relatively unknown, a newcomer to the political wars, he may find it necessary to do telethons. However, if he is an established incumbent he probably will not find it as necessary to get this much publicity. If he is the candidate out of office he will be eager to get his opponent to debate the issues with him, but if he is an old pro he will probably avoid drawing an audience for his lesser-known opponent. Most political experts believe that the shorter spot announcements pay bigger dividends than a five- or ten-minute program, which lasts long enough that the uninterested citizen will cease to listen.

A few candidates avoid television because of the image they project on TV. These candidates are, however, few and far between and unlikely to win. Some candidates may avoid the TV screen because of their age, not wishing the voters to be able to observe the obvious age differences. A very few may find that they do not have the voice for either radio or television.

Similar questions are posed for the political candidate as to the best use of advertising in newspapers. Should full-page ads be used in which all of the candidates for state-wide offices are linked with the local candidates? Usually the answer is in the affirmative but may be used near the end of the campaign, usually on the weekend before the election. Should local sponsors be used? Again the answer usually is in the affirmative. The locally sponsored ads will give the voters a feeling that, while they may not personally know the candidates, the influential fellow-townsmen do know them and are endorsing them. Proper placement in the newspapers also is an important factor in the effectiveness of the ad. Few papers will permit the candidate to buy any part of the front page, thus making the back page of the newspaper in all probability the best space available.

House mailings of material concerning the qualifications of the candidate and his position on various issues appear to be decreasing in importance and in the extent of utilization by most state-wide candidates. Local county officials and legislative office seekers seem to find them of some limited value. Too many householders get too many pieces of third-class mail so that the political campaign material finds its way into the waste basket unopened. The expense of printing and mailing of such material does not justify widespread use. It must be personalized in some way to warrant its expense and the time consumed. Frequently this material may be enclosed with a letter from some local citizen whose endorse-

[8] H. A. Simon and Frederick Starr, "The Effects of Television Upon Voting Behavior in Iowa," *American Political Science Review*, Vol. XLIX (June, 1955), pp. 470–77.

ment will entice the householder at least to glance at the picture of the candidate.

Another difficult problem faced by a candidate and his campaign staff is the proper scheduling of his appearances in a state-wide political campaign. Frequently the error is made of placing all of the candidates running for major political offices on the stage at the same time in the same city. Experience has demonstrated that bringing the candidates for the major offices into a city or county separately will usually draw a larger total attendance than bringing them all in for one joint appearance. It may be expedient to have all major candidates on a ticket appear as a team in the major cities which contain a vast majority of the voters in the state. Usually every county chairman will feel that he must have every candidate for state office in his county as least once during the campaign if he is to engender the proper enthusiasm. In a state with more than ninety counties this may be almost a physical impossibility for the candidates.

Probably one of the most common errors made in arranging campaign schedules is what might be called over-scheduling or arranging too tight a timetable for the campaigner. Frequently candidates run from a few minutes to several hours behind the schedule of appearances that has been announced a week or more in advance. Nothing can cause more irritation than to have a crowd assembled and be forced to wait for several hours for a candidate to make his arrival. But even this is better than not keeping the engagement at all. It is much better to allow ample time to make each appearance even if the candidate has a few minutes of free time before his next scheduled speech. This time is often profitably used to do what is commonly called side-walk campaigning which consists of shaking hands with everyone the candidate can meet on the street in the city in which he is making a speech. The effectiveness of this type of person-to-person approach should not be underestimated.

Candidates often complain that they appear too frequently at meetings in which they are talking with their own people only. This is almost inevitable. Many of these occasions are fund-raising affairs at which the party faithful turn out to build up the campaign funds. To be sure, the candidate usually wins no additional votes at these affairs as the people present obviously are in his camp or they would not be present, but with the high cost of waging a major campaign for state office these functions cannot be avoided. It is true that too many such appearances may serious hamper a candidate's vote on election day.

Ideally a candidate will wish to speak to a crowd that is either undecided as to his candidacy or contains a large number of members of the opposition. These are the voters that he may be able to change to his side if he can be persuasive in his presentation. Service clubs frequently offer this type of audience for political candidates. Likewise county fair appearances and similar non-politically sponsored affairs provide an ideal audience.

The importance of the women's vote is now apparent in every state. Frequently a candidate may overlook this important sector of the electorate and neglect appearances before Federated Women's Clubs, National Association of University Women, and the League of Women Voters. This may well be fatal to the candidate's chances of winning the election. The candidate's wife and family also must be judiciously used in the campaign. She may, on occasion, substitute for the candidate. Teas or coffees are occasions at which his family may attract favorable comment to the candidate. Parades, either of the time-honored torch-light variety or the regular parade from the airport down through the heart of the city, are appearances at which the wife and family may brighten the candidate's attractiveness to the average voter. Few bachelors, divorced, or widowed candidates appear to be successful vote getters. The strong family ties are important "plus factors" in the candidate's favor. In the same category is the utilization of the candidate's military record. Few candidates who have not been in military service are able to gain support of the veterans' organizations. This obviously cannot be a vulgar display of decorations and military citations but must be done with tact.

Appearances before each major segment of the population must be carefully arranged. A candidate must make an appearance at the state convention of the various veterans' organizations if they coincide with the months of the campaign. The farm group meetings, such as the convention of the N.F.O., The Grange, and the American Farm Bureau, are likewise important campaign appearances. Oftentimes a corn-husking or a plowing contest will also be an essential appearance before this segment of the state electorate. The state teachers' association will frequently be holding a convention during the campaign and the candidate's appearance and speech here may have widespread influence in all sectors of the state, since the teachers oftentimes influence their students who in turn carry the word back to the home firesides. The meetings either locally or state-wide of labor unions are also occasions at which the candidate has an opportunity to plead his cause. Even though the candidate may believe that he will not have support of the labor group it behooves him to make an attempt for its vote. Similarly, if he feels that the labor support is already his he must take advantage of the opportunity to solidify his position.

Other state occasions that must not be ignored are meetings of the league of municipalities, manufacturers' association meetings, state welfare association conferences, the state bar association convention, truckers' association convention, and many other professional and semiprofessional meetings.

Some new and some old campaign gimmicks should be considered as a normal part of a political campaign. Among the new ideas is the automatic telephone-answering device that has been used successfully in a number of recent campaigns. The candidate makes a minute or even two-minute recording of his position on a particular issue and this may be heard by any one who merely dials a number that is widely advertised. This recording must, of course, be changed regularly so that the caller does not hear the same message week-in and week-out. Among the time-honored pieces of political propaganda are buttons, badges, and stickers, all profusely covered with the candidate's smiling picture, name, and office sought. The effectiveness of these items is subject to question, but a candidate without them is not using all the available means at his command. Therefore, at least a minimum supply of buttons, badges, or even pot holders, yardsticks, and other items, such as nail files, ball point pens, paper hats, and tie clasps is necessary.

Errors in the campaign sometimes can be turned into assets. Examples of this are numerous, but probably not as many errors turn out to be advantages as vice versa. A fairly recent innovation in many states is to fly an airplane or blimp over any large crowd, such as those massed for a major football contest, with the large banner proclaiming "X for Governor." One candidate with such a banner discovered that his aides had misspelled GOVERNOR. However, the publicity that the incident received in the newspapers actually attracted more attention to his candidacy than if the word had been correctly spelled. Another error that received widespread circulation was an ad in an educational association journal urging the teachers to vote for candidate "W" on a given date, which was one day after the election was actually to be held. The wire services spotting the error gave it state-wide attention rather than the limited audience that the ad would have received had it listed the proper date.

Bumper stickers on automobiles, a relatively new campaign device, have both merit and disadvantages, although it would appear to be necessary to have a certain amount of such material available in all sectors of the state. Often the mistake is made of trying to put too much information on the limited area available on a bumper sticker. The name of the candidate and the office sought are nearly always a maximum allowable, yet many candidates crowd additional material into the display, usually losing all effectiveness.

How many campaign headquarters are desirable and where should they be located? Usually the state central committee will have a headquarters in the state's capital city which will be the "nerve center" of the entire campaign. Observers will think it rather strange if all of the major candidates don't have representatives in the central headquarters. This office must be located in an accessible place, yet have sufficient peace and quiet for the staff to accomplish its duties. Ideally it will be located on the street level in or near the heart of the business district of the capital city. If hidden away on the fifth floor it may be peaceful and quiet but it also may not serve the real purposes of the campaign central head-quarters. Party workers will seldom take the effort to climb or even ride elevators up to an office hidden away on an upper floor.

A campaign headquarters for the party is essential in all of the major cities of the state and probably in every county seat. Here, too, the error of locating the center in a hotel room away from the daily traffic is some-times made. It should be on the street level where every citizen and voter can drop in and discuss the issues. Staffing these campaign centers is usu-ally not too difficult a problem. Volunteers are available that make it un-necessary to have a large paid staff. These volunteers are usually more enthusiastic than paid employees and radiate their interest to all visitors. The headquarters should be appropriately decorated, not cluttered and disorganized. Amazing impressions are made just by the physical sur-roundings. Some repel, others attract; some give the air of shabbiness, some of affluence (some too much so); some invite attention, while others rebuff the potential voter.

A cordial relationship between the candidates and the newsmen, includ-ing radio and television, is most important. While the editors of the papers may support the candidacy of a particular nominee, an even more important aspect of the campaign is the attitude of the reporter toward the candidate. This may frequently be heavily colored by the personal re-lationship that exists between the working press and the man running for public office. If he is cool and aloof to the press he will find this image reflected in their reporting of his activities. On the other hand if he is ap-proachable, helpful, and considerate at all times, the reporters will simi-larly reflect a more desirable image to their readers and listeners. If they like the nominee they will do everything in their power to protect him. They will correct his errors, overlook his poor grammar, minimize his blunders, and in general present a most favorable picture. Or on the other hand if the reporters are constantly treated as undesirables they will take every opportunity to destroy the candidate. If he will level with the news-men they will usually reciprocate. When he has an off-the-record session it will be held confidential, but if he plays favorites and gives one reporter or one news media a break he will have alienated all the others, and they will take every opportunity to portray a bad image. Good press coverage of a candidate may properly be listed as the most important factor in a successful campaign. All the editorial support for a candidate can be made meaningless if the working members of the press corps are unfavorably disposed. The editorial endorsement will always be contained on the editorial page in a back section of the paper and read by only a small percentage of the subscribers, but the news stories of the candidate's activities will usually appear on the front page or at least be prominently displayed on a daily basis.

Members of the press desire fair and equitable treatment. They all want the opportunity to work up special stories of human interest. They want both the summarized press releases and at least occasionally a chance to secure the full text of the candidate's major speeches.

It is probably true that no hard and fast rules can be or should be laid down for working relationships with the newsmen. A candidate has to use his intuition. A rule that may work beautifully on one occasion and in one campaign may be a major blunder if adhered to in another situation. Frequently the press can give helpful suggestions to the candidate and his staff. Many of these men and women have covered years of political activity and their opinions should be taken seriously and even solicited. Their judgment of the pulse of the people may well be superior to that of the candidate and his staff. If sympathetic to the cause the press can guide a campaigner around many pitfalls, or if antagonistic they may set traps into which the unwary candidate will fall. The members of the press are usually the first to discern a candidate who is insincere and dishonest. They glory in the opportunity to expose such a false front. Absolute honesty with the news media is no doubt the best policy that a candidate can follow.

Political campaigns are important primarily because of the re-enforcement function they produce in the party faithful. It is commonly recognized that a very small percentage of the voters shift party allegiance during a campaign. The usual estimate is that no more than 10 per cent make the change during any campaign.[9] Thus the party loyalty is sustained by providing congenial propaganda for the party members. However, in exceptional instances, the campaign, if not properly handled, may actually alienate the marginal party member. If the candidate of the party refuses to state a position on critical issues he may antagonize enough of the party's fringe members to bring about his defeat. On the other hand the danger is almost equally great of taking the wrong stand on an issue and thus losing even more votes.

Probably in a majority of political campaigns it may be concluded that a candidate lost the election rather than the other candidate winning the election. The errors made in a campaign by the defeated candidate are

[9] Bernard Berelson, Paul A. Lazerfeld, and William McPhee, *Voting* (Chicago: The University of Chicago Press, 1954), pp. 345–47.

usually the margin of victory for the winner. The campaign that is without error probably has never been conducted, but the campaign that contains the fewest major mistakes is usually the successful campaign.[10]

Far too many elections in America at the local, state, and the national levels are not decided upon the basis of the candidates' stands on the issues in the campaign but rather are decided by the electorate's estimate of the personality and character of the candidates. This fact makes it of vital importance that the image the candidate gets across to the voter is one that will obtain a favorable voter reaction. It is important that he be a "good family man," without any scandal of any type attached to his family background, with a wife and family that are photogenic. His previous public record must be one that can be "pointed to with pride" by all of his supporters. It is ordinarily necessary for him to have a creditable war record or at least a plausible reason for not having been in the military service.

It is impossible to accurately determine in each election how much weight to place upon what Murray B. Levin called "visceral response," or instinctive feelings, but no doubt the consideration must be great.[11] It should not be assumed that no attention is paid to the issues by these people who determine for whom they will cast their vote by this type of reaction. The two are not mutually exclusive but are intertwined. The emotional response may prevail in some cases and the factual evidence available to the voter in another. Entirely too many elections are won by candidates who are regarded by the voters as the lesser of the two evils.

## Public Opinion Polls

The major national and state candidates use public opinion polls to indicate upon what issues and which areas to center their campaign energies. While the polling techniques as developed by George Gallup, Elmo Roper, and Lou Harris are not infallible, they have become relatively reliable and are often an important guide to the candidates.

The polls are frequently utilized to guide the candidates as to which position on a given issue is most acceptable to the majority of the voters. The candidate may then adjust his stand on the issue to conform with the reports from the constituents via the public opinion polls.

Traditionally the candidate who is shown to be trailing in the polls that attempt to determine the relative popularity of the opposing candidates, asserts that he has no confidence in the polls. His opponent how-

[10] H. F. Gosnell, "Does Campaigning Make a Difference," *Public Opinion Quarterly*, Vol. XIV, (Fall, 1950), pp. 1413–18.

[11] Murray B. Levin, *The Alienated Voter* (New York: Holt, Rinehart & Winston, Inc., 1960), pp. 43–46.

ever will probably claim complete confidence in their reliability. Often
the political parties conduct their own polls or employ a private firm to
conduct the research. In most states the leading newspaper of the area
conducts a number of polls and prints them periodically during the
campaign.

The most common criticism of the public opinion polls is that the sam-
pling is often too small to be accurate. A second adverse comment frequently heard is that the polls, when they show one candidate far ahead,
tend to promote the bandwagon idea, thus giving the candidate shown
to be out in front even greater impetus. A third criticism which may or
may not be valid is that the cross section of the population polled may
not be as scientifically determined as might be desirable.

In the 1964 elections the various polls were remarkably accurate. Most
predicted within a fraction of a per cent the vote of President Lyndon B.
Johnson. Similarly most of the polls taken in the state election campaigns
were correct in their predictions of the probable winners and the margin
of victory.

## STATE LIMITATIONS ON CAMPAIGN EXPENDITURES

The Iowa statute concerning the maximum expenditures of money for
political campaigns is quite typical of the forty-five states that have laws
regulating maximum expenditures. The Iowa law states:

It shall be unlawful for any candidate to expend in connection with any primary election campaign more than fifty per cent of the annual salary applicable
to the position for which he is a candidate, and unlawful for him to expend in
connection with his campaign for election (general election) to any office more
than fifty per cent of the annual salary applicable to the position for which he
is a candidate.[14]

Statements of expenditures must be filed in Iowa with the Secretary of
State within thirty days after the primary and the general election. All
candidates for state office, party chairmen of district committees, and the
state chairmen of the recognized political parties, must file a listing of expenditures. County candidates and chairmen of the county central committees file their statements of expenditures with the county auditor.

Failure to file is regarded not as a felony but merely as a misdemeanor.
In most states the filing is followed by a perfunctory examination of the
statements. Most candidates in most states comply with the law rather
than receive unfavorable publicity that might impair their chances in any
future elections. Usually the amount reported is far below the maximum

[14] *Code of Iowa, 1962*, chap. lvi, sec. 7.

allowed. The "normal" limit is 50 per cent of the salary of the office. In most states it is believed that the reports are virtually meaningless and of doubtful value. The laws are so easily circumvented by the establishment of special committees to expend money on behalf of the candidate that it is impossible to control the expenditures.

Five states—Delaware, Illinois, North Carolina, Rhode Island, and Nevada—make no effort to regulate the amount of money expended or received by candidates for state offices. In the first four states, no statutes regulating amounts exist, while in Nevada the statute imposes a limit but no filing report is required. Four other states—Colorado, Idaho, Mississippi, and Vermont—have restrictions which are applicable only to the primary elections with no bars as to expenditures for general election campaigns. In Iowa and Kansas the restrictions are, in theory, only for the state-wide offices, but in Iowa they actually apply to state representatives and to state senatorial candidates as well as to those elected at large.

In Table 9–3 the states with various limitations upon campaign contributions and expenditures are listed.

All states except the five with no restrictions upon campaign contributions and expenditures require candidates and the political parties to file a listing of campaign receipts and disbursements. The filing deadline varies, but it is usually about fifteen days following the election. A few states require these statements to be filed both before and after elections. Some require filing only after the general elections, but most states require a filed accounting after both the general and primary elections.[15]

## CAMPAIGN EXPENDITURES

### State-Wide Campaign Expenditures

How much money does a candidate need to campaign for a state-wide office such as governor? How is the money spent and how is it raised?

The amount of money needed will vary with a large number of factors: the population of the state; the geographic area involved, the previous public positions held by the candidate; the caliber of the opposition; whether or not both a primary and a general election contest is faced; the attitude of the mass communications media in the state toward free political publicity; the amount of apathy existing among the voters; and the number of candidates working as a team.

Obviously, official reports of campaign expenditures are of little help in computing the actual expenditures made in behalf of a candidate seeking a governorship. In only twenty states is there even any attempt made

[15] Alexander Heard, *Money and Politics* (New York: Public Affairs Press, 1956); Louise Overacker, *Money in Elections* (New York: The Macmillan Co. 1932).

## TABLE 9–3

### Various State Limitations Upon Political Campaign Expenditures and Contributions

| Contributions by Corporations Prohibited (34 States) | Contributions by Labor Unions Prohibited (6 States) | Character of Expenditures Restricted (29 States) | Limit on Amount Spent on Behalf of Candidate (20 States) |
|---|---|---|---|
| 1. Alabama | 1. Colorado | 1. Alabama | 1. Colorado |
| 2. Arizona | 2. Indiana | 2. California | 2. Florida |
| 3. Connecticut | 3. Nebraska | 3. Colorado | 3. Idaho |
| 4. Florida | 4. New Hampshire | 4. Connecticut | 4. Indiana |
| 5. Georgia | 5. Pennsylvania | 5. Florida | 5. Kentucky |
| 6. Illinois | 6. Texas | 6. Hawaii | 6. Maryland |
| 7. Indiana | | 7. Indiana | 7. Michigan |
| 8. Iowa | | 8. Kansas | 8. Minnesota |
| 9. Kansas | | 9. Kentucky | 9. Mississippi |
| 10. Kentucky | | 10. Minnesota | 10. New Hampshire |
| 11. Louisiana | | 11. Maryland | 11. New York |
| 12. Maryland | | 12. Massachusetts | 12. North Dakota |
| 13. Massachusetts | | 13. Michigan | 13. Oklahoma |
| 14. Michigan | | 14. Maine | 14. Oregon |
| 15. Minnesota | | 15. Nebraska | 15. South Dakota |
| 16. Missouri | | 16. New Hampshire | 16. Tennessee |
| 17. Montana | | 17. New Jersey | 17. Texas |
| 18. Nebraska | | 18. North Dakota | 18. Vermont |
| 19. New Hampshire | | 19. Ohio | 19. West Virginia |
| 20. New Jersey | | 20. Oregon | 20. Wyoming |
| 21. New York | | 21. Pennsylvania | |
| 22. North Carolina | | 22. South Carolina | |
| 23. North Dakota | | 23. Texas | |
| 24. Ohio | | 24. Utah | |
| 25. Oklahoma | | 25. Virginia | |
| 26. Oregon | | 26. West Virginia | |
| 27. Pennsylvania | | 27. South Dakota | |
| 28. South Dakota | | 28. Wisconsin | |
| 29. Tennessee | | 29. Wyoming | |
| 30. Texas | | | |
| 31. Utah | | | |
| 32. West Virginia | | | |
| 33. Wisconsin | | | |
| 34. Wyoming | | | |

SOURCE: Council of State Governments, *The Book of the States, 1964–1965* (Chicago: Council of State Governments, 1964).

to limit the total expenditures of funds in behalf of a candidate. Some thirty-two states have a limit as to the total amount the candidate may spend, but this is, of course, nearly meaningless.

Few studies are available concerning campaign expenditures at the state level. One of the few that reveals any meaningful statistics was done in Florida in the 1952 primary and run-off primary election for the nomination of the gubernatorial candidates.[16] In this campaign, involving three Democratic aspirants to the Florida governor's post, nearly $565,000 was spent campaigning in the two primary elections. This meant that nearly fifty cents was spent for every voter participating in the first of the two primary elections. This is probably typical of the expenditures on a state-wide gubernatorial campaign. In a large industrial state, expenditure of a million dollars or more is quite common if all of the money used in all phases of the campaign is included.

The division of how the money is spent will vary with the individual candidates and the degree of public familiarity with their experience, background, and public image. Probably more money will be spent for television and radio time than for any other item. However, newspaper advertising will probably be a close second. Unknown candidates, or relatively newcomers to the political wars, may spend more than 50 per cent of their campaign funds on TV and radio time. Newspaper ads probably will get about 20 per cent, other printed material about 15 per cent, with the remainder of the campaign chest spent on various expenditures such as travel, professional consultants, and surveys.

While it is probably impossible to establish a minimum figure that a candidate must have available to launch and complete a successful gubernatorial campaign the figure of $100,000 for even the smallest state, such as New Hampshire, would be a minimum.[17]

In the gubernatorial campaign in Massachusetts in 1962, the two candidates received a total of nearly $865,000 in campaign contributions. The two acknowledged expenditures of approximately $812,000. This means that each candidate expended between $400,000 and $500,000 in his effort to gain the governorship. Because of the new Massachusetts law concerning campaign expenditures it is believed that almost all of the money actually used in conducting the campaign in 1962 was reported. In the same election a hotly contested United States Senatorial race involved only about half as much money, with each of the senatorial candidates reporting only about a quarter of a million dollars expended during the campaign. It is possible that no greater amount of money on a population basis was spent in the gubernatorial campaign in Massachusetts in 1962 than in many other states, but with the new state statute the total amount is revealed for the first time.

Probably an all-time high expenditure for a gubernatorial campaign occurred in the 1962 California contest between Richard Nixon and Ed-

[16] E. E. Roady's "Florida's New Campaign Expense Law and the 1952 Democratic Gubernatorial Primaries," *American Political Science Review*, Vol. XLVIII (June, 1954), pp. 465–76.

[17] Coleman Ransone, *The Office of Governor in the United States* (University, Ala.: Unversity of Alabama Press, 1956), pp. 105–10.

mund G. Brown, the Democratic incumbent. Nixon's campaign expenditures totaled $1,572,664 for the general election alone. According to his campaign finance chairman, Maurice H. Stans, more than 20,000 persons contributed to the campaign fund. Stans called it "California's most successful experience in political fund raising." It is interesting to note that in the report required by the California Registrar of Voters more than $175,000 of the money was contributed by individuals living outside of the state. In spite of this expenditure of money, former Vice-President Nixon was defeated in his race for the chief executive position of California.[18]

The question is often posed, does it cost more or less to campaign in a one-party state than it does in a two-party state? The answer is not an easy one. Probably after all of the qualifying circumstances are considered, the answer is that it makes little difference, particularly in the typical one-party states. Here the candidates will spend as much if not more in a second or run-off primary while his expenditures may be almost nil in the general election, just as the candidates in the two-party states are also forced to engage in the two campaigns.

In a two-party state the candidate normally finances his campaign in the primary from his own resources. If he is successful his party will usually finance the general election campaign.

Thus the big hurdle for the would-be candidate for state office is to find sufficient funds to win the primary election. This is done usually by appointing his own state finance chairman and then securing local finance chairmen to raise the necessary funds. Contributions, of course, are welcomed from all sources. The small contribution by individuals is not refused, but it is not a very dependable source in proportion to the total amount to be raised. The emphasis must be placed upon larger donations from various groups, such as road contractors, building trade groups, manufacturing associations, and similar organizations.

## Non-State-Wide Campaigns

The techniques employed for a localized campaign are quite different from those required of a candidate for governor. In most state representative or state senatorial campaigns the problems are essentially the same but must be approached from a more parochial basis. The campaign usually is concentrated in a shorter time period and is less arduous in

[18] Associated Press Release, and United Press International Release, December 12, 1962. Governor Brown reported expenditurs of $1,482,206. Thus the total spent by the Committees of the Republican and Democratic parties in this 1962 California gubernatorial election was nearly three million dollars. Added to this is about $500,000 spent by each party in the primary elections.

physical effort since fewer miles are to be covered. Ordinarily only a few counties, at most, are involved.

Many candidates for state senatorial and state representative posts in the urbanized areas have found television a great help in contacting a maximum number of people with the greatest ease. Many find, however, the expense of TV time too great a hurdle to overcome. In the future it will probably be mandatory for a successful candidate to make full use of the television stations that cover his area. Candidates for local offices usually make greatest use of the time-honored campaign methods of newspaper space, radio time, and the best of all, personal door-to-door contacts.

## ELECTION ADMINISTRATION

The United States Constitution in Article I, Section 4, requires the states to provide for the election of members of both houses of Congress:

The times, places and manner of holding elections for Senators and Representatives shall be described in each State by the legislature thereof; but the Congress may at any time by law make or alter such regulations. . . .

All states now adhere to the congressional date of the Tuesday after the first Monday of November in the even-numbered years, and most state elections are held on that date as well.

The chief election official in a state is usually the secretary of state. However, in a number of states a state election board is constituted which has the responsibility for the supervision of the state's election machinery. Generally the election administration is diffused among state, county, and municipal officials. Responsibility is not as completely centered in many states as students of elections believe is warranted. Frequently it is possible for one election official to shift to other officers the blame for occasional irregularities.

The county clerk, or some other designated county official, has the job of supervising the actual election-day operation. He must arrange for the polling places, the hiring of the election judges and clerks, arrange for the printing of the ballot and other necessary equipment to be on hand at each precinct, and supervise the collection of the ballots from the various precincts at the end of the day. If voting machines are employed he must see that they are operating properly and are ready for the election.

The Australian ballot is used in all national, state, and local elections in the United States. The ballot is printed at public expense, is available only at the polling places, except for absentee voters, and is marked in secret. The voting machine is widely used in the more urban areas and has the advantages of speed, accuracy, simplicity, but it is expensive and creates storage problems for the administrative officials.

State laws concerned with absentee voting have considerable variety, but in most states it is possible for qualified persons who are away from their legal residences or confined in a hospital for some reason on election day to cast their ballots by mail in advance of the election. The procedure involves obtaining an absentee ballot by applying to the election officials within time limits set by law; marking the ballot, usually within the presence of a notary public or other public official; and returning the ballot by mail before a certain date. The ballot is either counted at the central election office or sent to the precinct in which the voter would ordinarily cast his ballot. In addition, the clerk is required to supervise the printing of the ballots. The state election laws will prescribe the format of the ballot that will be used.

Both the Indiana and Massachusetts type ballots are forms of the so-called Australian ballot and are used in general election but not in the primaries. The characteristics of the Australian ballot include: printing at public expense, available only at the regular polling precincts, all candidates appearing on the same ballot, and voting in secret. In the Indiana party column ballot all members of the same party are listed in a single column. Usually where the Indiana type ballot is utilized the voter is allowed to vote a straight party ticket by merely marking a single "X" in the party circle at the top of the column or by pulling a single lever if voting is conducted on voting machines.

In the Massachusetts block ballot all of the candidates for each office are listed in a group and the voter is ordinarily required to check for his favorite candidate under each office. This does not permit a straight party voting scheme by merely pulling one lever or making one single "X." As a general rule the majority party in a state will prefer the Indiana type ballot while the minority party in a state will prefer the Massachusetts type ballot. The minority party tends to favor the block ballot for obvious reasons.[19]

It is significant to note that while the election may involve federal offices, the cost of the election process is not borne in any part by the federal government. The state or its subdivisions, usually the county, must bear the entire burden of expense. The states differ in this aspect of the election procedure in that some state governments assume almost the entire election machinery expense while others require the counties or the cities to underwrite all or most of the expenditure.[20]

[19] Howard R. Penniman, *Sait's American Parties and Elections* (New York: Appleton-Century-Crofts, Inc., 1948), pp. 616–25.

[20] Spencer D. Albright, *The American Ballot* (Washington, D.C.: American Council on Public Affairs, 1942).

## BIBLIOGRAPHY

ALBRIGHT, S. D. *The American Ballot.* Washington, D.C.: American Council of Public Affairs, 1942.

ALMOND, GABRIEL, and VERBA, SIDNEY. *The Civic Culture.* Princeton; Princeton University Press, 1963.

BARNETT, JAMES D. *The Operation of the Initiative, Referendum and Recall in Oregon.* New York: The Macmillan Co., 1915.

BLAIR, GEORGE S. *Cumulative Voting.* Urbana: University of Illinois Press, 1960.

CAMPBELL, ANGUS, CONVERSE, PHILLIPS, MILLER, WARREN, and STOKES, DONALD. *The American Voter.* New York: John Wiley & Sons, Inc., 1960.

CHILDS, RICHARD. *Civic Victories.* New York: Harper & Row, Inc., 1952.

COUNCIL OF STATE GOVERNMENTS. *Registration for Voting in the United States,* rev. ed. Chicago: Council of State Governments, 1946.

CROUCH, WINSTON. *The Initiative and Referendum in California.* Los Angeles: Haynes Foundation, 1943.

DAVID, PAUL T. *Specifications for a Model State Presidential Primary.* Washington, D.C.: The Brookings Institution, 1956.

―――― and EISENBURG, RALPH. *Devaluation of the Urban and Suburban Vote.* Charlottesville: Bureau of Public Administration, University of Virginia, 1961.

DAVIES, JAMES. *Human Nature in Politics.* New York: John Wiley & Sons, Inc., 1963.

EWING, CORTEZ. *Primary Elections in the South: A Study in Uniparty Politics.* Norman: University of Oklahoma Press, 1953.

HARRIS, JOSEPH. *Registration of Voters in the United States.* Washington, D.C.: The Brookings Institution, 1929.

――――. *Election Administration in the United States.* Washington, D.C.: The Brookings Institution, 1934.

HEARD, ALEXANDER. *The Costs of Democracy.* Chapel Hill: University of North Carolina Press, 1952.

――――. *A Two-Party South.* Chapel Hill: University of North Carolina Press, 1952.

HOLLAND, L. M. *The Direct Primary in Georgia.* Urbana: University of Illinois Press, 1949.

ILLINOIS LEGISLATIVE REFERENCE BUREAU. *The Initiative, Referendum and Recall,* Bulletin No. 2. Springfield: Constitutional Convention.

KEY, V. O., and CROUCH, WINSTON. *The Initiative and the Referendum in California.* Berkeley: University of California Press, 1939.

KURTZMAN, DAVID H. *Methods of Controlling Votes in Philadelphia.* Philadelphia: University of Pennsylvania, 1935.

LANE, ROBERT E. *Political Life: Why People Get Involved in Politics.* New York: The Free Press of Glencoe, Inc., 1959.

―――― and SEARS, DAVID O. *Public Opinion.* Englewood Cliffs, N.J.: Prentice-Hall, Inc., 1964.

LEVIN, MURRAY B. *The Alienated Voter.* New York: Holt, Rinehart & Winston, Inc., 1960.

LIPSET, SEYMOUR MARTIN. *Political Man: The Social Bases of Politics.* Garden City, N.Y.: Doubleday & Co., Inc., 1960.

McGovney, Dudley O. *The American Suffrage Medley.* Chicago: The University of Chicago Press, 1949.

MacKenzie, W. J. M. *Free Elections.* New York: Holt, Rinehart, & Winston, Inc., 1958.

Martin, B. A. *The Direct Primary in Idaho.* Stanford, Calif.: Stanford University Press, 1947.

Merriam, Charles E., and Gosnell, Harold F. *Non-Voting: Causes and Methods of Control.* Chicago: The University of Chicago Press, 1924.

Merriam, Charles E., and Overacker, Louise. *Primary Elections.* Chicago: University of Chicago Press, 1928.

Milbrath, Lester W. *Political Participation.* Chicago: Rand McNally & Co., 1965.

Miller, G. F. *Absentee Voters and Suffrage Laws.* Washington, D.C.: DayLion Co., 1948.

Minault, S. Sydney. *Corrupt Practices Legislation in the Forty-eight States.* Chicago: Council of State Governments, 1942.

Moon, Henry L. *The Negro Vote: Balance of Power.* Garden City, N.Y.: Doubleday & Co., Inc., 1949.

Munro, William B. (ed.). *The Initiative, Referendum and Recall.* New York: Appleton-Century-Crofts, Inc., 1912.

National Municipal League. *Model Election Administration System.* New York: 1930.

————. *Model Registration System.* New York: National Municipal League, 1939.

————. *Model Direct Primary System.* New York: National Municipal League, 1951.

Oberholtzer, Ellis P. *The Referendum in America.* New York: Charles Scribner's Sons, 1911.

Overacker, Louise. *Money in Elections.* New York: The Macmillan Co., 1932.

Porter, Kirk H. *A History of Suffrage in the United States.* Chicago: The University of Chicago Press, 1918.

Price, Margaret. *The Negro Voter in the South.* Nashville: Southern Education Reporting Service, 1957.

Scammon, Richard (ed.). *America Votes: A Handbook of Contemporary Election Statistics.* New York: The Macmillan Co., 1956.

Shannon, Jasper B. *Money and Politics.* New York: Random House, 1959.

Sikes, Earl R. *State and Federal Corrupt Practices Legislation.* Durham, N.C.: Duke University Press, 1928.

Smith, Carl O. *A Book of Ballots.* Detroit: Detroit Bureau of Governmental Research, 1938.

Wilson, James Q. *The Amateur Democrat: Club Politics in Three Cities.* Chicago: The University of Chicago Press, 1962.

# 10

# The State Legislature

Every one of the fifty states has a state legislature, which, in forty-nine instances, is composed of two houses, with only Nebraska using the unicameral system.

In most states the law-making or policy-making body is referred to as the state legislature. Nineteen states, however, call the state policy-making body the general assembly, while Montana, North Dakota, and Oregon term it the legislative assembly and Massachusetts and New Hampshire use the term general court. Following the federal example most states refer to the upper house as the state senate and the lower house the house of representatives. Three states, Maryland, Virginia and West Virginia, use the title house of delegates; California, Nevada, New York and Wisconsin, the assembly, while New Jersey terms the lower house the general assembly. Nebraska's unicameral house is known as the senate.[1]

Irrespective of the title, the major functions of the legislative body of the state are fundamentally the same. The state exists to render services for the citizens, and it is the duty of the policy makers to determine what services the people want and how they shall be rendered. The policy-making powers of the state legislatures may, for purposes of study, be divided into a number of divisions: (1) constitutional revision, (2) law making, (3) supervising administration, (4) executive, and (5) judicial.

In all of the states except New Hampshire, the state legislature has the authority to initiate an amendment to the state constitution. In some states, a minority, it must be approved by two successive sessions of the legislature but in the majority of the states a favorable vote by the members of a single session places the amendment on the ballot for approval by the citizens of the state. (For detailed procedure see Chapter 7.)

The law-making function is certainly the dominant operation associated with the legislative body. It is in this area that the policy-making function

---

[1] Council of State Governments, *The Book of The States, 1964–1965* (Chicago: Council of State Governments, 1964), p. 42.

of the legislature asserts itself. Just how and where to draw the line between policy making and policy execution is a problem that no student of government has ever satisfactorily answered. This law-making function of the legislative process is the basic one in all democratic governments. In America most states have accepted the principle of legislative supremacy. The executive branch, particularly, and the judiciary branch, to a lesser degree, have been subordinate to the legislative. This legislative supremacy is usually accepted as sound and practical. However, a growing distrust of the policy makers has tended to strengthen the authority of the executive branches of many of the state governments. The legislature is viewed as the center of the state government and it sets the tone for governmental action. If it is weak in moral character it will be difficult to have an effective, corruption-free administrative organization. If it is characterized by integrity and honesty, then it is more likely that the same standards will prevail in the other branches of the government. It is the duty of the legislature accurately to reflect the will of the people of the state. It must be responsive to the desires of its constitutents, not too far ahead nor too far behind their wishes and desires. It has sometimes been called the hub of the state governmental machinery, with the executive and administrative units composing the spokes in the wheel, and the judiciary becoming the rim.

The supervision of the administration by the legislature is a function that varies greatly from state to state and from one era to another. There can be little question that the legislature is the most important determinant of the administrator's functions. The legislature allocates emphasis by making appropriations, oftentimes very specific in nature. In most instances the very existence of the administrative agency, unless provided for in the state constitution, is dependent upon the legislature, for the power to create an administrative agency also carries with it the power to eliminate it. The legislature helps to shape executive policy, delegates functions to particular administrative agencies, prescribes and circumscribes administrative activities, and influences many administrative decisions. These have been referred to as the positive legislative controls over administrative bodies.[2]

## UNITED STATES CONSTITUTIONAL LIMITATIONS UPON STATE LEGISLATURES

The United States Constitution places at least twelve major restrictions upon the legislatures of the fifty states. It prohibits these legislative bodies from the following actions:

[2] James C. Charlesworth, *Governmental Administration* (New York: Harper & Row, Inc., 1951), p. 49.

1. Authorizing the coining of money or emiting bills of credit
2. Keeping troops or ships in time of peace
3. Entering into a treaty
4. Passing any law impairing the obligation of contract
5. Denying persons equal protection of the laws
6. Pass any law that conflicts with the U.S. Constitution
7. Obstruct the enforcement of federal laws
8. Enact any law that prevents persons from voting because of race, color, or sex
9. May not tax exports
10. May not tax imports
11. May not permit slavery within the state
12. May not grant titles of nobility

## State Constitutional Restrictions on Legislative Action

Many state constitutions declare that the state legislature shall not have certain powers. Frequently found in this category of limitations upon the state legislatures are:

1. Cannot grant divorces
2. Cannot authorize lotteries
3. Cannot pass local or special laws not of a general nature
4. Cannot change county seats or change county boundaries without the approval of the electors in areas affected
5. Cannot grant extra compensation to any public officer, agent, or contractor after the service is rendered or contract entered into
6. Cannot pass laws violating the rights reserved to the people in the Bill of Rights of the State Constitution
7. Cannot pass a bill of attainder

# ORGANIZATION OF STATE LEGISLATURES

## Bicameral vs. Unicameral

Forty-seven of the fifty states upon their admission to the Union have included a bicameral legislature in their state constitutions. Only Georgia, Pennsylvania, and Vermont provided for a single-house legislative body. All of the other states, probably because of federal bicameralism, have used the two-house idea. Vermont used the single chamber plan for a longer period than any other state, abandoning it in 1836; while Georgia switched to bicameralism in 1790; and Pennsylvania, in 1789. The only state in this century to utilize a unicameral plan is Nebraska, which adopted it after a strenuous campaign headed by Senator George W. Norris. In spite of almost complete opposition by the news media, Senator Norris carried the issue to the people and convinced a majority of the voters to adopt the constitutional amendments that made possible the change in 1937 to a single legislative body.[3] It is significant that no other state has followed the Nebraska lead, and it is particularly noteworthy that the two latest additions to the Union, Hawaii and Alaska, both wrote into their new state constitutions provisions for a bicameral legislature.

An examination of the claimed merits for both the unicameral and bicameral legislatures is presented in the *American State Legislatures,* edited by Professor Belle Zeller. It is obvious from the summary of the report as presented below that the political science profession holds little brief for the bicameral system, but in spite of this academic evaluation the average American appears to be unmoved by the almost obvious superiority of the unicameral system.

## Merits Claimed for a Unicameral Legislature

1. Membership carries greater prestige and opportunity for public service, thus attracting more outstanding citizens.
2. Single chambers operate more efficiently and are thus able to give more thorough consideration to legislation.
3. Eliminated is the jealousy, friction, rivalry and deadlock that oftentimes exists between a two-house chamber.
4. Responsibility can be more definitely fixed as will the accountability of individual members.
5. More effective leadership can be developed.
6. Closer and more effective relationship between the governor and the single-chambered house will be effected.
7. The power of special-interest groups and lobbies is reduced.
8. No longer is there any necessity for conference committees.
9. Public reporting of the work of the legislature is more easily attained and a better informed public results.
10. Substantial economies both in time and money can be achieved.[4]

The proported advantages of the bicameral system, which supposedly prevail in forty-nine of fifty states, are listed as follows:

1. A bicameral legislature prevents hasty and careless legislation.
2. A second chamber serves as a check upon the passions and impulses of the first house.
3. A bicameral organization prevents one chamber from usurping the powers of other branches and invading the rights of the people.

---

[3] Alvin Johnson, *The Unicameral Legislature* (Minneapolis: The University of Minnesota Press, 1937); and John P. Senning, *The One House Legislature* (New York: McGraw-Hill Book Co., Inc., 1937).

[4] Belle Zeller (ed.), *American State Legislatures* (New York: Thomas Y. Crowell Co., 1954), pp. 57–58.

4. The bicameral legislature provides protection against corruption and the control of the legislature by special interest groups.
5. A bicameral legislature permits the use of different bases of representation in the two houses.
6. Bicameral legislatures as used by forty-nine states and the national government are the traditional form of legislatures in America.[5]

The two lists in several respects are contradictory. The merits of the bicameral system are sometimes regarded as more historical than real. It is assumed that a two-house legislative body will agree upon all good legislation but disagree on poor or bad legislative policy. Slow action is apparently regarded by the forces that favor a bicameral system as meritorious in itself. If the arguments for the two houses are sound, then it would behoove almost every city in America to revert to the bicameral system, since less than ten are now using two-chambered policy-making bodies.

The Nebraska experience in unicameral government would appear to give added support to those who favor a single legislative body. Almost all studies of the first twenty-five years of the Nebraska plan appear to show a favorable reaction upon the part of both the citizens of the state and the lawmakers themselves.[6]

The unicameral plan is advocated almost every year by some legislator or group in several states, but no serious effort has been evidenced to follow the plan advocated by the National Municipal League's *Model State Constitution* (see Appendix). Some attention was given to the possibility of a unicameral legislature in Michigan when its state constitution was rewritten in 1962, but the constitutional convention finally decided to follow the traditions of the past and adopt a bicameral body. In undertaking to vitalize the legislature and to render it equal to the responsibilities of its key policy-making and power-distribution role, it is necessary to make a fresh start. The unicameral or single chamber form would be structurally an advance of a dramatic character calculated to fix political and institutional responsibility and to make legislative processes more understandable to the people. The unicameral plan could be expected to add stature to membership. The operation of a bicameral legislature is diffused and dilatory—something we would find quite insupportable in local government and in business organization.[7]

5 *Ibid.,* pp. 51–57.
6 Richard C. Spencer, "Nebraska Idea 15 Years Old," *National Municipal Review,* Vol. XXXIX (February, 1950), pp. 83–86; and Harry T. Dobbins, "Nebraska's One-House Legislature," *National Municipal Review,* Vol. XXX (September, 1941), pp. 511–15.
7 *Report of the Commission on Constitutional Revision,* Statement by Richardson Dilworth and Jefferson B. Fordham (Harrisburg, Pa.: The Commission, 1959), pp. 27–36.

## State Legislative Apportionment

The major problem confronting the fifty state legislatures and state government in general since the famous ruling in 1960 in *Baker v. Carr* (369 U.S. 226) has been the apportionment of the state legislatures in such a way as to satisfy the federal courts. Prior to this historic case, the apportionment situation had been considered as a matter of only state-wide interest and of no concern to the federal government. To be sure, the federal government has always had the right to determine if a state had a "republican form of government" and if declared to be otherwise the delegation of that state to the Congress of the United States could be reduced. The Congress apparently had the power to determine the existence of a republican form of government and it was the duty of the Congress to deny seats to the full delegation from a state whose government was declared to not meet the standards. Prior to the *Baker v. Carr* decision, the majority of the United States Supreme Court and also the lower federal courts had never entered this problem, calling it a political thicket that the court would not enter.

The *Baker v. Carr* decision is well worth some detailed analysis as a case study. The Tennessee State Constitution, as of the filing of the *Baker v. Carr* case, called for the senators to be apportioned among the counties and districts according to the number of qualified electors and "shall not exceed" one-third the number of lower house members. To quote from the state constitution:

In apportioning the senators among the different counties, the fraction that may be lost by any county or counties in the apportionment of the members to the lower house shall be made up to such county or counties in the Senate, as near as may be practicable.

The constitutional requirements in the lower house provided that the number of representatives be apportioned among the various counties or districts according to the number of qualified voters in each, provided that any county having two-thirds of the ratio shall be entitled to one member.

The existing facts of apportionment in Tennessee at the time of the filing of the case were as follows: The last revision of the legislative districts took place in 1901. The 1960 population of the state was 3,567,089, to be divided by 33 senate seats (108,093) and by 99 lower house seats (36,031). The variation in population districts was from the largest senate district of 237,905 to the smallest of 39,727; the population of the largest house district was 79,301, while the smallest had only 3,454 people. The minimum percent of the 1960 population necessary to elect a majority of the state senate was 26.9 per cent and a minimum of 28.7 per cent was needed to control a majority of the house seats.

Robert Brock and David Grubbs of the University of Tennessee's Bureau of Public Administration commented in the 1962 edition of the *Compendium on Legislative Apportionment,*

Under the existing apportionment of legislative seats the Republican Party continues to be discriminated against on both the state and congressional level. Most Tennessee Republicans reside in East Tennessee. Since it is a heavily populated area and is the fastest growing region of Tennessee, it experiences the greatest inequality of representation. This inequality results from failure of the state legislature to reapportion. In short, the Tennessee Republicans fail to receive their fair share of representation due to failure to reapportion.[8]

The problem was both Republican versus Democrat and urban versus rural. The discrimination against the urban population can be seen in that the metropolitan counties of Tennessee contain more than 42 per cent of the 1960 population but were given by the apportionment only 21 per cent of the lower house seats and 20.5 per cent of the senate seats.

The major complaint in the *Baker v. Carr* suit was that discrimination against the urban areas of Tennessee because of the malapportionment also resulted in inequities in the taxing and spending powers of the state. One of the charges brought in the suit was that the formula for dividing the state gasoline tax took virtually no account of the population factor. Likewise, in distributing state educational funds the basic formula took into account each county's and city's ability to contribute to the education of their children but gave little weight to the population distribution factor.

On this evidence the United States Supreme Court determined that federal jurisdiction was present and that federal action to insure reapportionment was necessary. On October 9, 1961, the court considering the case for the second time, again asserted federal jurisdiction and remanded the suit to the Federal District Court for trial on its merits.

Actually the apportionment situation in Tennessee is not much different from that in many of the other forty-nine states. A study of the apportionment prevailing reveals this quite clearly. As of January, 1962, the National Municipal League sponsored a study of each state which showed that only six states had both houses apportioned in such a fashion that 40 per cent or more of the population elected a majority of the members of the state legislature. Only twenty states had apportionment laws that required 40 per cent to elect a majority of one house of the bicameral chamber. In six of these twenty, less than 25 per cent were required to

[8] National Municipal League, *Compendium on Legislative Apportionment* (New York: National Municipal League, 1962), p. 2 (Tennessee).

elect a majority of the second house. The study showed that in at least thirteen states one-third or less of the population could elect a majority of the members of both houses.

Few people would argue the necessity of reapportioning nearly every one of the fifty state legislatures. Just who should do this job and what should be the guide lines for measuring a satisfactory apportionment are two other questions—the answers to which may vary from state to state. Professor James Larson points out that as of April, 1963, the courts had accepted at least seven broad classes into which apportionment decisions may be divided.[9] In summary it might be said that the courts have tried to allow the state legislators to reapportion their policy-making bodies with the minimum amount of guidance. Some people believe that this guidance should be increased and that certain guide lines should be laid down.

Several crucial questions remain unanswered as to what the courts will accept as fair and equitable apportionment. It may be assumed that if both houses are on a strictly population basis, with each legislator representing exactly the same number of people that this would be unquestioned. But how much deviation from this "perfect" apportionment will be tolerated?

Will the federal courts accept as fair and equitable a plan patterned after the representation in the Congress of the United States? Indications are not too clear, as apparently the Court accepted the formula in the Michigan case of *Scholle v. Hare* but refused to even consider this as fair in the Oklahoma apportionment test. Some observers feel that the federal courts are in a sense saying "do not do as we (the federal government) do in apportionment but do as we direct." On the other hand it is certainly true that there is a different relationship existing between the typical state legislature and its counties, which usually are involved as the basis for area representation, than there is between the federal Congress (of the United States) and the fifty sovereign states, the basis for area representation in the Congress.

It was Edmund Burke who suggested that the people are the true legislature. The courts might assume that what is satisfactory with a majority of the voters in a state should be a satisfactory apportionment plan. This, of course, assumes that the voters have the opportunity to express their will on the question and that free, open elections with no voter restrictions exist within the state.

Should the judgment of a federal district judge, or even a panel of federal judges, or even the nine-member Supreme Court of the United States be allowed to usurp the power that some people contend was in-

[9] James E. Larson, "Awaiting the Other Shoe," *National Municipal Review,* Vol. LII (April, 1963), p. 189.

tended by the United States Constitution for the people of the various states? Some people will answer the question in the affirmative without any reservations. Others may question the wisdom of this course of action. It is certainly true that little or no action occurred prior to the *Baker v. Carr* case when the federal courts asserted their authority for the first time in this field. Now action is progressing in almost every state toward the passage of new apportionment amendments by the state legislature.

It may well be a decade or more before the reapportionment of state legislatures is settled and all are apportioned to the satisfaction of the courts. What will be the ultimate guide lines of the courts? Will it be the so-called preferred position doctrine of the First Amendment, that there is a presumption of constitutionality of apportionment provisions which reflect the free exercise of the majority? This would seem to be highly logical and would mean that the test would be whether or not the people of the state possess the means to formulate freely a system of representation or whether they are captives of inflexible constitutional provisions.

The term "invidious discrimination" has been frequently used by the courts in their apportionment decisions. The exact amount of discrimination that this involves has never been defined to the satisfaction of most legislators.

It is quite obvious that resolving the reapportionment problem as of any given date is only the beginning of solving the total apportionment problem. The apportionment machinery must be modernized. The idea of one man and one vote will not prevail indefinitely, as Professor John P. Wheeler and Professor John E. Bebout point out, if the legislatures remain the judges and the juries in their own cases.[10] The apportionment machinery must be changed. A possible answer is to place the power in the governor or in a commission that will be subject to mandamus action.

The United States Supreme Court, in late 1964, refused to accept the judgment of the people of Colorado who had voted in favor of an apportionment plan which had been approved by the state legislature. Instead the court reaffirmed its position that the principle of "one man, one vote" must prevail in establishment of the apportionment of both houses of the state legislature although a majority of the people are satisfied with a less representative legislature. The ultimate answer has yet to be decided since several moves to amend the United States Constitution so as to remove the United States Supreme Court from a position of power over state apportionment have been started. Other congressional action would at least postpone the necessity of a state to reapportion according to the dictates of the Court.

---

[10] John P. Wheeler and John E. Bebout, "After Reapportionment," *National Municipal Review*, Vol. LI (May, 1962), pp. 246–47.

The decision in *Reynolds* v. *Simms* by the United States Supreme Court in 1964 made it definite that it expected the reapportionment of state legislatures to adhere to the one man one vote principle. It did declare that it fully realized that it would not be possible to have each and every legislative district exactly the same population size but gave an unmistakable warning to the state legislatures not to stray too far from the dominant one man one vote idea. The questions that still remain unanswered include: (1) How far from the principle is permissible? (2) How long will the states be given to conform? (3) How many opportunities to conceive apportionment plans will a state be allowed before the federal court will intercede and impose its own plan?

It is still not clear whether an attempt will be made, and if it would be successful, to amend the United States Constitution to declare this area of state legislative apportionment beyond the sphere of power of the United States Supreme Court. The Democratic landslide in the 1964 elections would appear to have weakened the possibilities of the Congress initiating such a constitutional amendment, but a coalition of Southern Democrats and conservative Republicans might be able to start such an amendment. There would appear to be an excellent chance that such an amendment would be ratified by the required number of state legislatures if they were given the opportunity. However, the longer the delay of submitting such an amendment to the states the less the chance of its being approved as more and more reapportionment occurs under the court directive.

If the Supreme Court's ruling on the one man one vote principle remains it is possible that it will give impetus to the consideration in a number of states of the unicameral system and abandonment of bicameralism in some state legislative halls.

## Size and Terms of State Legislatures

American state legislatures range in size from a total membership of forty-three in Nebraska's unicameral system to 424 in New Hampshire's bicameral system. The smallest bicameral legislature is that of Delaware, with fifty-two members, seventeen in the upper house and thirty-five in the second chamber. The number of members in the senates vary from seventeen in Nevada to sixty-seven members in Minnesota. The average number of senators in the typical state senate is fifty.

The range in numbers is greater in the lower house varying from the Delaware low of thirty-five and forty in Alaska to 400 members in New Hampshire, a maximum of 261 in Connecticut, 246 in Vermont, and 240 in Massachusetts.

The ratio of senate to house members averages one to slightly more than three; but this, too, varies greatly from state to state. Idaho has forty-four senators and fifty-nine members of the house, while New Hampshire has twenty-four senate members and 400 house members.

In recent years there has been a slight trend toward increasing the number of members of both the upper and lower chambers in many of the state legislative bodies. For example, during the 1960–1961 biennium, lower houses were increased in Connecticut by forty-five members while Minnesota and Louisiana each added four. Similar increases, but not as great, are also evident in several of the state senates. Ohio and Florida are among the states that have added members to the state senates in recent years. Ohio increased its senate members by five, while Florida added a total of sixteen members to the senate and house in 1962.[11]

State senators are elected to four-year terms in thirty-five of the fifty states, while in the fifteen other states the term for the members of the senate is two years. Included in this latter group are the unicameral senators in Nebraska. Nevada had under consideration, in 1963, a constitutional amendment which would increase the terms of their senators to six years and that of house members to four years: This amendment must be approved a second time by the legislature before being submitted to a popular vote. In a majority of the states with four-year senate terms only approximately half of the senate is elected at any one biennial election, thus staggering the terms of the members of the upper house.

Members of the second house serve only two-year terms in forty-five of the bicameral legislatures. Nevada may be removed from this group if the amendment is approved. Only the house members in four Southern states have four-year terms: Alabama, Louisiana, Maryland, and Mississippi. This makes it possible in forty-five states for the entire membership of the lower house to be changed at a single election.[12]

It is quite apparent that the size and length of the term makes it difficult to attract outstanding men in almost any state to run for the lower house of the bicameral legislature. Oftentimes a candidate, when approached, will ask, "What influence can I have in a legislative body of 400, or of 294, 246, or 240, or even of more than 100?" An honest answer usually will deter the would-be capable candidate from seeking the office. Likewise, a candidate who is forced to run for re-election every two years may find that he spends more time campaigning for the office than he does actually in the legislative halls and will soon decide not to seek the office again.

The question can reasonably be asked, "Why should a state legislature with only 600,000 constituents need 424 members?" Certainly if the entire population of the United States can be properly represented with 435

---

[11] Council of State Governments, *The Book of the States, 1964–1965* (Chicago: Council of State Governments, 1964), p. 43.
[12] *Ibid.*

members in the lower house and only 100 in the senate, it is obviously
unnecessary to have such a large state legislature. While the most extreme case has been used to illustrate the point, many similar situations
are available from the fifty state representative systems.

Likewise, a similar question should be faced, "Is it sensible to elect a
member to attend only one session of the state legislature? Should he not
have at least two sessions included in his term?" The answer to these
queries may be in either of two categories. Assuming the affirmative response is elicited, it means that either the legislature must meet annually
or the term of office, if the biennial sessions are to remain, must be increased to four years, as is the case in four of the states at the present
time. The logical answer may well be to do both: increase the length of
term to four years and have annual sessions of the legislatures. In Table
10–1 the political composition of the state legislature, terms of office, and
total membership are indicated.

TABLE 10–1

Composition of the State Legislatures—1965

| State | Senate Dem. | Rep. | Constitutional Total | Term | House Dem. | Rep. | Constitutional Total | Term | Constitutional Total of Legislature |
|---|---|---|---|---|---|---|---|---|---|
| Alabama | 35 | 0 | 35 | 4 | 102 | 4 | 106 | 4 | 141 |
| Alaska | 17 | 3 | 20 | 4 | 30 | 10 | 40 | 2 | 60 |
| Arizona | 26 | 2 | 28 | 2 | 45 | 35 | 80 | 2 | 108 |
| Arkansas | 35 | 0 | 35 | 4 | 99 | 1 | 100 | 2 | 135 |
| California | 28 | 12 | 40 | 4 | 52 | 28 | 80 | 2 | 120 |
| Colorado | 15 | 20 | 35 | 4 | 24 | 41 | 65 | 2 | 100 |
| Connecticut | 23 | 13 | 36 | 2 | 111 | 183 | 294 | 2 | 330 |
| Delaware | 13 | 5 | 18 | 4 | 30 | 5 | 35 | 2 | 53 |
| Florida | 41 | 2 | 43 | 4 | 102 | 10 | 112 | 2 | 155 |
| Georgia | 44 | 9 | 54° | 2 | 198 | 7 | 205 | 2 | 259 |
| Hawaii | 16 | 9 | 25 | 4 | 39 | 12 | 51 | 2 | 76 |
| Idaho | 19 | 25 | 44 | 2 | 37 | 42 | 79 | 2 | 123 |
| Illinois | 25 | 33 | 58 | 4 | 118 | 59 | 177 | 2 | 235 |
| Indiana | 35 | 15 | 50 | 4 | 78 | 22 | 100 | 2 | 150 |
| Iowa | 35 | 24 | 59 | 4 | 101 | 23 | 124 | 2 | 183 |
| Kansas | 8 | 32 | 40 | 4 | 36 | 89 | 125 | 2 | 165 |
| Kentucky | 25 | 13 | 38 | 4 | 63 | 37 | 100 | 2 | 138 |
| Louisiana | 39 | 0 | 39 | 4 | 103 | 2 | 105 | 4 | 144 |
| Maine | 5 | 29 | 34 | 2 | 81 | 70 | 151 | 2 | 185 |
| Maryland | 22 | 7 | 29 | 4 | 117 | 25 | 142 | 4 | 171 |
| Massachusetts | 28 | 12 | 40 | 2 | 170 | 69° | 240 | 2 | 280 |
| Michigan | 24 | 14 | 38 | 4 | 72 | 38 | 110 | 2 | 148 |
| Minnesota | Non-partisan | | 67 | 4 | Non-partisan | | 135 | 2 | 202 |
| Mississippi | 52 | 0 | 52 | 4 | 121 | 1 | 122 | 4 | 174 |
| Missouri | 23 | 11 | 34 | 4 | 123 | 40 | 163 | 2 | 197 |
| Montana | 32 | 24 | 56 | 4 | 56 | 38 | 94 | 2 | 150 |
| Nebraska | Non-partisan | Elections | Two-year | term | | | | | 49 |
| Nevada | 8 | 8° | 17 | 4 | 25 | 12 | 37 | 2 | 54 |

**TABLE 10–1 (Continued)**

| State | Senate Dem. | Rep. | Constitutional Total | Term | House Dem. | Rep. | Constitutional Total | Term | Constitutional Total of Legislature |
|---|---|---|---|---|---|---|---|---|---|
| New Hampshire | 8 | 16 | 24 | 2 | 176 | 224 | 400 | 2 | 424 |
| New Jersey | 6 | 15 | 21 | 4 | 27 | 33 | 60 | 2 | 81 |
| New Mexico | 28 | 4 | 32 | 4 | 59 | 18 | 77 | 2 | 109 |
| New York | 34 | 24 | 58 | 4 | 88 | 62 | 150 | 2 | 208 |
| North Carolina | 49 | 1 | 50 | 2 | 106 | 14 | 120 | 2 | 170 |
| North Dakota | 20 | 29 | 49 | 4 | 44 | 65** | 113 | 2 | 162 |
| Ohio | 16 | 16 | 32 | 4 | 62 | 75 | 137 | 2 | 169 |
| Oklahoma | 41 | 7 | 48 | 4 | 78 | 21 | 99 | 2 | 147 |
| Oregon | 19 | 11 | 30 | 4 | 28 | 32 | 60 | 2 | 90 |
| Pennsylvania | 23 | 27 | 50 | 4 | 119 | 90 | 209 | 2 | 259 |
| Rhode Island | 30 | 16 | 46 | 4 | 77 | 23 | 100 | 2 | 146 |
| South Carolina | 46 | 0 | 46 | 4 | 123 | 1 | 124 | 2 | 170 |
| South Dakota | 16 | 19 | 35 | 2 | 31 | 44 | 75 | 2 | 110 |
| Tennessee | 25 | 8 | 33 | 2 | 74 | 25 | 99 | 2 | 132 |
| Texas | 31 | 0 | 31 | 4 | 149 | 1 | 150 | 2 | 181 |
| Utah | 15 | 12 | 27 | 4 | 39 | 30 | 69 | 2 | 96 |
| Vermont | 13 | 17 | 30 | 2 | 66 | 180 | 246 | 2 | 276 |
| Virginia | 37 | 3 | 40 | 4 | 89 | 11 | 100 | 2 | 140 |
| Washington | 32 | 17 | 49 | 4 | 60 | 36 | 99 | 2 | 148 |
| West Virginia | 27 | 7 | 34 | 4 | 91 | 9 | 100 | 2 | 134 |
| Wisconsin | 12 | 21 | 33 | 4 | 52 | 48 | 100 | 2 | 133 |
| Wyoming | 12 | 13 | 25 | 4 | 34 | 27 | 61 | 2 | 86 |

* One independent.
† Four independents.

NOTE: Where total of Democrat and Republican does not equal the Constitutional total, a vacancy was in effect.

SOURCE: Council of State Governments, *The Book of the States, 1964–1965* (Chicago; Council of State Governments, 1964); and Americana Corporation, *The Americana Annual, 1965* (New York: 1965).

## Sessions of the State Legislatures

In 1941 only four states held annual sessions of their state legislatures; all of the other forty-four states at that time adhered to the traditional biennial session—once every two years. In the ensuing twenty years fifteen states changed from the biennial session to annual. Actually fourteen states changed, since both Alaska and Hawaii provided for annual sessions in their state constitutions upon being admitted to the Union. The only state trying an annual session and then returning to a biennial meeting schedule was Nevada which tried the annual session for only one year.

From 1864 until 1958 the sessions of the Nevada Legislature were biennial. Under the provisions of Section 1 of Article XVI of the Constitution of the State of Nevada, the Constitution may be amended by the adoption of the amendment by two consecutive regular sessions of the Nevada Legislature and then approval of the amendment by the people at a subsequent general election. From 1864 to 1958, Section 2 of Article IV of the Constitution provided for biennial sessions of the Legislature, but the 1955 and 1957 sessions of the Nevada Legislature approved a constitutional amendment to the aforesaid section so as to provide for annual sessions, and the amendment was approved by the people at the general election in 1958 (Note: The amendment carried by a majority of 11,715 votes.) Consequently, a regular session of the Nevada Legislature was held in the spring of 1959 and again in the spring of 1960.

Shortly after the 1960 session adjourned sine die, a movement was started in the State of Nevada to return to biennial sessions. The movement was spearheaded, financed and propagandized by representatives of the railroads, various public utilities including telephone and power companies, the gambling industry, and other groups. These groups were unhappy with the concept of annual sessions because annual sessions forced them to engage the services of lobbyists to protect their interests once each year instead of once every two years. Their well-organized and well-financed campaign convinced the people of Nevada that biennial sessions were more desirable than annual sessions.

Under the provisions of Article XIX of the Constitution of the State of Nevada, the Constitution may be amended using the second method, namely, the initiative petition. The aforesaid groups circulated the petition to return to annual sessions throughout the State of Nevada, and, consequently, the matter was placed on the ballot of the general election held in November 1960. The vote at the said general election was 48,019 in favor of returning to biennial sessions and 35,397 in favor of retaining annual sessions. (Note: Majority of 12,622.) So, regular sessions of the Nevada Legislature have been biennial beginning in the spring of 1961.

It is the conviction of the Research Division of the Legislative Council, of which I am the Director, that annual sessions are very valuable and would not only pay for themselves but save money even in the small state of Nevada. The only reason that the State of Nevada returned to biennial sessions was because the groups mentioned above sold the voters a bill of goods so that the groups could avoid the expense of maintaining lobbyists annually instead of biennially.[13]

A number of states are giving serious consideration to the desirability of annual sessions, while a few of the annual-session states have had minority groups urging a return to the biennial session under the assumption that a more conservative legislative policy will emerge from biennial sessions than under annual meetings.[14]

New Mexico approved the proposal for annual sessions by a vote of the people in 1964, while South Dakota voters in 1962 voted in favor of the plan. The Iowa lower house has proposed a constitutional amendment in each of the last four sessions that would amend the state constitution to allow annual sessions, but in every session the proposed amendment failed

[13] Letter to Mrs. Donald C. Bryant, from the Director of the Legislative Counsel Bureau of the State of Nevada.
[14] Council of State Governments, *The Book of the States, 1962–1963* (Chicago: Council of State Governments, 1962), p. 36.

to come to a vote in the senate. In spite of these setbacks, the evidence is quite clear that more and more of the states will in the next twenty years accept the necessity of annual legislative sessions. This will actually be only a return to the practice that was quite common when state governments were first formed following the American Revolution. The philosophy of that era dictated that the representatives of the people should meet every year. The Massachusetts Constitution of 1780 stated,

The legislature ought frequently to assemble for redress of grievances, for correcting, strengthening, and confirming the laws, and for making new laws, as the common good may require.

However, the annual session was gradually abandoned during the nineteenth century, the period in which most state legislatures fell into disfavor with the majority of the people. During this century the common saying was that the only good news coming from the state legislature was that it had adjourned. The relatively widespread distrust of the state legislatures led to the favoring of biennial sessions to reduce expenses and to reduce the number of "bad" laws enacted by the policy makers. The twenty states with annual sessions and the thirty with biennial sessions, as of 1966 are listed in Table 10-2.

### TABLE 10–2

#### Sessions of the State Legislatures

| States with Annual Sessions (20) | States with Biennial Sessions (30) | |
|---|---|---|
| 1. Alaska | 1. Alabama | 17. New Hampshire |
| 2. Arizona | 2. Arkansas | 18. North Carolina |
| 3. California | 3. Connecticut | 19. North Dakota |
| 4. Colorado | 4. Florida | 20. Ohio |
| 5. Delaware | 5. Idaho | 21. Oklahoma |
| 6. Georgia | 6. Illinois | 22. Oregon |
| 7. Hawaii | 7. Indiana | 23. Tennessee |
| 8. Kansas | 8. Iowa | 24. Texas |
| 9. Louisiana | 9. Kentucky | 25. Utah |
| 10. Maryland | 10. Maine | 26. Vermont |
| 11. Massachusetts | 11. Minnesota | 27. Virginia |
| 12. Michigan | 12. Mississippi | 28. Washington |
| 13. New Jersey | 13. Missouri | 29. Wisconsin |
| 14. New York | 14. Montana | 30. Wyoming |
| 15. Pennsylvania | 15. Nebraska | |
| 16. Rhode Island | 16. Nevada | |
| 17. South Carolina | | |
| 18. South Dakota | | |
| 19. West Virginia | | |
| 20. New Mexico | | |

SOURCE: Council of State Governments, *The Book of the States, 1964–1965* (Chicago: Council of State Governments, 1964).

## Length of Sessions

Thirty years ago it was evident to some scholars of state government that placing time limits on the length of state legislative sessions had serious repercussions. Professor Robert Luce stated the case this way:

Putting on a time limit is perhaps the most preposterous device men ever conceived for the remedy of political ills. No railroad, banking or manufacturing corporation would be so silly as to try to improve an inefficient directorate by a vote compelling directors' meetings to adjourn after two hours or restricting such meetings to two months in the year. If the administration of justice became conspicuously defective, nobody would risk his reputation for sanity by advising that the courts should sit only from New Year's day to Easter.[15]

In only seventeen of the states is the legislature allowed to meet as long as they believe necessary. Of these, seven are state legislatures that meet every year while ten are state policy-making bodies that convene only once every two years.[16]

Of the nineteen states with annual sessions, nine limit the off-year or odd-year meeting of the general assembly to budgetary matters while the others permit any legislation to be introduced in each annual session.[17]

It might be thought that in states holding annual sessions of their state legislative bodies no special session would be required. However, the constitutions in eight of the nineteen states with such sessions permit not only the governor to call extraordinary sessions but also a certain percentage of the legislators themselves may convene the body. Six other states also permit the lawmakers as well as the chief executive of the state to call for a special session.[18] In the other thirty-six states, however, only the governor has the authority to recall the legislators once the legislature has adjourned sine die.

In a majority of the states, twenty-eight, the members of the general assembly in a special session may consider any type of legislation. In

[15] Robert Luce, *Legislative Assemblies* (Boston: Houghton Mifflin Co., 1924), p. 145.

[16] The seven annual session states without any time restrictions are: Alaska, Massachusetts, Michigan, New Jersey, New York, Pennsylvania, and South Carolina, while the other state legislatures that have no maximum length of sessions are: Illinois, Iowa, Maine, Mississippi, Nebraska, Ohio, Oklahoma, Oregon, Vermont, and Wisconsin.

[17] States with a restriction to only budgetary matters being considered in the odd-year session include: California, Colorado, Delaware, Hawaii, Kansas, Louisiana, Maryland, Pennsylvania, and West Virginia.

[18] Annual session states permitting legislators to call special sessions include: Alaska, Arizona, Georgia, Hawaii, Louisiana, Massachusetts, New Jersey, and West Virginia. The same power is extended in Connecticut, Florida, Nebraska, New Hampshire, New Mexico, and Virginia.

these states the governor may convene the extraordinary session for a specific purpose, but the lawmakers, once they have been called, may take up this subject but also any other matters. It is not unusual for the assembly to completely ignore the governor's request for action on a particular matter and for the policy makers of the state to legislate on many other subjects. In exactly half of the states the length of the special session is unlimited by constitutional restrictions, while twenty-five have a maximum length beyond which the legislature is usually unable to continue in special session.[19]

Most of the state constitutions, either revised or new since World War II, tend to have certain common features: annual sessions, a lessened emphasis upon number of days a session may last, and provision for the legislators as well as the governor to call special sessions.

## QUALIFICATIONS FOR STATE LEGISLATORS

State constitutions usually require that to be eligible for election to the state legislature the candidate for membership in the lower house must be an American citizen, usually at least twenty-one years of age and to have been a resident of the state for a given number of years. In many of the states the constitution establishes a slightly higher age minimum for state senators, usually twenty-five. Most of the state constitutions require that the candidate must be a resident of the district from which he is a candidate for the legislature, while others leave this regulation to statutory enactment. A few states refuse to allow declared atheists to be candidates for the legislature, while most make ineligible anyone convicted of a felony. All states, of course, permit members of both sexes to be candidates. Thus it is obvious that the members of the law-making body are required to have very minimum qualifications from a legal standpoint. They are a typical cross section of the people that they represent. They are, however, different from their constitutents in that they have a sufficient interest in government to become candidates for public office.

Obviously a large percentage of the population of each state possesses the legal qualifications required to become a candidate for the state legislature. However, much more limiting upon the number of potential candidates is the so-called extra-legal requirements oftentimes termed the political availability of the would-be legislator.

---

[19] States with no time limit on the length of the special session include: California, Colorado, Connecticut, Illinois, Iowa, Kentucky, Maine, Massachusetts, Michigan, Missssippi, Nebraska, New Jersey, New York, North Dakota, Ohio, Oklahoma, Oregon, Pennsylvania, Rhode Island, South Dakota, Vermont, Washington, West Virginia, Wisconsin, and Wyoming.

## Members in State Legislative Assemblies

More than 7,600 persons in the United States serve as members of the ninety-nine legislative chambers. While it is often believed that too much emphasis is placed upon the occupation of the members it is significant than when all ninety-nine legislative houses are analyzed the occupation pursued by the largest number is that of law, with farming a fairly close second. The third most important occupational group in terms of numbers is businessmen or merchants.[20] It must be concluded that the occupation of the legislator probably influences his committee assignment more than his voting record, since not all farmers support all farm legislation and not all businessmen in the legislatures support all proposals that are supposed to benefit the business community.

The majority of members of the state legislatures have had some college training. Even in the rural states more and more of the membership are listing college training on their vita. Certainly not a majority have attained a college degree but more than half have at least attended college, varying from a few weeks to seven or more years.

While no such thing as a typical or average state legislator exists, a prototype would be a member of a state senate who is approximately fifty years of age, by profession a lawyer or a farmer or both, a veteran, a Protestant, a member of at least three organizations, such as Rotary, Masons, Farm Bureau or State Bar Association, married with two children, and a record of party loyalty of some ten to twenty years. His counterpart, in the lower house, would be some five or six years younger and of similar background but more likely a farmer by occupation. While at least one-third of the membership of a typical lower house legislature is new every session probably an average state legislator would be serving his second session as a member of the state's legislative body.

Women members of the state legislatures, aside from the New England area, are relatively few in number. In some state legislatures seldom is there a member of the female sex. Probably in any given year fewer than three hundred women are seated as members of the policy making branch of state government. In some states it is not too uncommon to have several women in the house, but seldom will they be elected to the upper chamber. There is, however, a noticeable trend toward more women becoming candidates for the state legislatures than ten, twenty, and thirty years ago. There still remains a visible shortage of women, however, in the typical state assembly. One way of further strengthening the membership would be to have a more active participation of the well-qualified women of a state in legislative affairs.

[20] Zeller, *op. cit.*, p. 71.

In a recent study, which involved the state legislatures in four states, California, New Jersey, Ohio and Tennessee, Professors Wahlke, Eulau, Buchanan, and Ferguson concluded that legislators might be expected to typify the following characteristics when the structure of the political party in a state is competitive:

1. State legislators have had some prior governmental experience on the local level and in a legislative or quasi-legislative capacity.
2. State legislators have held party office or done party work at the local level of politics.
3. State legislators will perceive the political party as a sponsor of their legislative careers.
4. State legislators will recognize the political party as an agency for promoting their candidacies.
5. State legislators will not perceive interest groups and/or friends or associates as agents sponsoring their careers.
6. State legislators will place value on the possession of particular skills thought relevant to a political career.
7. State legislators will have legal training and skills.
8. State legislators will not see an opportunity to combine their private and political careers.
9. State legislators will not stress "opportunity" in general as a factor facilitating their careers.
10. State legislators will not look upon their political careers as a means of achieving personal goals—whether altruistic or selfish ones.[21]

A warning with respect to qualification when too many members compose the legislative body was voiced in the Federalist Papers:

In all legislative assemblies the greater the number composing them may be, the fewer will be the men who will in fact direct their proceedings. In the next place, the larger the number, the greater will be the proportion of members of limited information and weak capacities. . . . The people can never err more in supposing that by multiplying their representatives beyond a certain limit, they strengthen the barrier against the government of a few. Experience will forever admonish them that, on the contrary, after securing a sufficient number for the purposes of safety, of local information, and of diffuse sympathy with the whole society, they will counteract their own views by every addition to the representatives.[22]

## COMPENSATION OF STATE LEGISLATORS

A salary plan rather than a per diem payment for members of state legislatures is gaining in favor among the states. Twenty years ago less

[21] John C. Wahlke, Heinz Eulau, William Buchanan, and LeRoy C. Ferguson, *The Legislative System: Explorations in Legislative Behavior* (New York: John Wiley & Sons, Inc., 1962), p. 120.
[22] *The Federalist Papers*, No. 58.

than half of the states had a regular stated salary for the legislators, but by 1961 thirty-four states were using this plan. The variation in salaries is very great ranging all of the way from a biennial salary in New Hampshire of $200 to New York State's $20,000 as of 1963. The median for the thirty-four states with a salary plan is approximately $3,950 per biennium.[23]

As would be expected, the states with the higher salaries for the legislators are the states with annual sessions. Likewise, the states with high pay programs usually have no limit on length of legislative sessions.

Sixteen states use a per diem, or in some instances, a weekly pay plan. It should be noted that Arkansas, Colorado, and Oklahoma use a combination plan of daily pay and biennial salary, so both may be listed in the two types of pay programs for their legislators. The amounts vary tenfold, from five dollars per day in Kansas, North Dakota, and Rhode Island, to fifty dollars per day in Louisiana. The average daily pay for the per diem plan states is approximately fifteen dollars. Additional living expense allowances are granted in about half of the per diem states; in the states that pay less than fifteen dollars a day this is necessary to allow a legislator to hope to break even. The living expense allowance in such states as Kansas, North Dakota, Alabama, Georgia, Idaho, and Washington is greater than the per diem pay.

There is a discernible trend in almost every state to liberalize the compensation for service in the state legislative body. For example, in the two-year period 1960–1961 at least half of the states increased in one way or another the pay received or the expenses allowed. The only state running counter to this tide was Alaska, which reduced both the salary and the daily expense allowance received.

Another trend reported by *The Book of the States* in the 1962–1963 edition is toward allowing legislators expenses for work performed between sessions, particularly in those states that make only daily payments for the policy makers. Likewise, more and more states are seeing the necessity of removing the salary question from the state constitution and allowing the legislators to determine the pay problem through statutory enactment.

Of interest is the statement made in the final report of the National Legislative Conference Committee:

From the viewpoint of good public service, and in light of the increasing amounts of time that legislators must devote to their duties, both during and between sessions, their compensation in most states is now much too low. Likewise, the pay of legislative leaders, faced with greater demands on their time in most jurisdictions, is notably out of line. Flat salaries rather than a per diem allowance should be paid. Salary and reimbursement of necessary expenses should be provided in amounts sufficient to permit and encourage competent

[23] Council of State Governments, *The Book of the States*, 1962–1963 (Chicago: Council of State Governments, 1962), p. 37.

## TABLE 10–3
### Legislative Compensation—1963

| State | Per Diem | Limit on Days | Biennium Salary | Salary Fixed by | Travel Amount per Mile | Travel Number of Round Trips | Additional Compensation* |
|---|---|---|---|---|---|---|---|
| Alabama | $10 | 36L | – | Constitution | $.10 | One | $ 20 |
| Alaska | | | $ 5,000(A) | Statute | .15 | One | 35 |
| | | | | | | | 300 postage |
| Arizona | | | 3,600(A) | Constitution | .10 | | 10 |
| Arkansas | 20 | 60C | – | Constitution | .05 | One | – |
| California | – | – | 12,000(A) | Constitution | .05 | One | 19 |
| Colorado | | | 6,400(A) | Statute | Actual expense | One | None |
| Connecticut | – | – | 2,000 | Statute | .10 | Each day | $500 expense allowed |
| Delaware | – | – | 6,000 | Constitution | .15 | Unlimited | 25 stationery |
| Florida | – | – | 2,400 | Constitution | .10 | Each week | 15 |
| Georgia | 10 | 40C | – | Constitution | .10 | Four | 40 |
| Hawaii | – | – | 4,000 | Constitution | – | – | 32.50–45.00 |
| Idaho | 10 | 60C | – | Constitution | .10 | One | 15 |
| Illinois | – | – | 12,000 | Statute | .10 | One per week | 50 postage |
| Indiana | – | – | 3,600 | Statute | .06 | One per week | – |
| Iowa | 30 | – | – | Statute | .07 | One | – |
| Kansas | 10 | 120(A) | – | Statute | .15 | One | 7 |
| Kentucky | 25 | 60L | – | Statute | .15 | One | 25 plus stationery |
| Louisiana | 50 | 90C | – | Statute | .10 | Eight Four | 250 per month rest of year |
| Maine | – | – | 1,600 | Statute | .05 | One per week | Postage |
| Maryland | – | – | 3,600 | Constitution | .20 | One | 2,400 per biennium |
| Massachusetts | – | – | 15,600 | Statute | .08 | Each day | 1,200 per biennium |
| Michigan | – | – | 14,000 | Statute | .10 | Two per month | 2,500 per biennium postage |
| Minnesota | – | – | 4,800 | Statute | .15 | One | 8–12 expenses |
| Mississippi | – | – | 3,000 | Statute | .10 | One | 100 per month rest of year |
| Missouri | – | – | 9,600 | Statute | .10 | Two per month | 10 |
| Montana | 20 | 60C | – | Statute | .08 | One | – |

## TABLE 10-3 (Continued)

| State | Per Diem | Limit on Days | Biennium | Fixed by | Travel Amount per Mile | Number of Round Trips | Additional Compensation* |
|---|---|---|---|---|---|---|---|
| Nebraska | – | – | 4,800 | Constitution and statute | .08 | One | 100 postage |
| Nevada | 25 | 60C | – | Statute | .10 | Daily, or $15 | 160 postage |
| New Hampshire | – | – | 200 | Constitution | .20–.05 | Daily | – |
| New Jersey | – | – | 10,000 | Constitution and statute | – | R.R. pass | – |
| New Mexico | 20 | 60C | – | Constitution and statute | .10 | One | Stationery, etc. |
| New York | – | – | 20,000 | Constitution and statute | Actual expense | One per week | $2,500 annually |
| North Carolina | 15 | 120C | – | Constitution | .07 | One per week | 12 |
| North Dakota | 5 | 60L | – | Constitution | .10 | One | 20 |
| Ohio | – | – | 10,000 | Statute | .10 | One per week | Postage and stationery |
| Oklahoma | 15 | 75L | – | Constitution | .10 | One per week | Postage, etc. |
| Oregon | 20 | 120 | 6,000 | Constitution | .10 | One per week | $75 per month/ 150 per month |
| Pennsylvania | – | – | 12,000 | Statute | .10 | One per week | – |
| Rhode Island | 5 | 60L | – | Constitution | .08 | – | – |
| South Carolina | – | – | 3,600 | Statute and constitution | .09 | One per week | 10–40 days |
| South Dakota | – | – | 3,000 | Statute | .05 | One | – |
| Tennessee | 10 | 75C | – | Statute | .16 | One | 5 |
| Texas | – | – | 9,600 | Constitution | .10 | One | 12–120 days |
| Utah | – | – | 1,000 | Constitution and statute | .10 | One per week | 5 |
| Vermont | – | – | 1,750 | Statute | .20 | One | – |
| Virginia | – | – | 1,080 | Statute | .07 | One | 720 per session |
| Washington | – | – | 2,400 | Statute | .10 | One | 25 |
| West Virginia | – | – | 3,000 | Constitution | .10 | One | – |
| Wisconsin | 15 | 110L | 10,800 | Statute | .07–.10 | Actual | 175 per month |
| Wyoming | 12 | 40C | – | Statute | .08 | One | 12 |

* Per day, during the session, unless otherwise noted.

Source: Council of State Governments, *The Book of the States, 1964–1965* (Chicago: Council of State Governments, 1964).

persons to undertake growingly important and time-consuming legislative duties. Actual amounts of salary and expense should be provided by statute rather than specified in the constitution.[24]

The major salary and compensation items for state legislators, as of 1963, are listed in Table 10–3.

## Retirement Compensation for State Legislators

An increasing need for including legislators under state or state and national retirement programs is evident. Only since the end of World War II has any great amount of attention been paid to this particular aspect of the legislative problem. Now nearly one-third of the states have some retirement system that includes the members of the legislative branch. In most of these states the legislators are now included along with other state employees in the state-operated retirement program. In others they have been also included in the social security coverage, e.g., Texas in 1960. In some of the states the retirement benefits are ridiculously small, but in others they may amount to a considerable yearly income upon completion of twenty or thirty years of service to the state. Pennsylvania, for example, has established a maximum annual retirement benefit of $6,000. All plans are basically similar in that the legislator must contribute just as do other state employees. Usually the option is given that the legislator may withdraw his contribution at the termination of legislative service if he so desires. A number of factors, including years of service, age of the recipient, age at retirement, and total amount of contributions, determine the amount of retirement payment. Rules and regulations vary as to what service may be included in accumulated service time. Virtually all of the retirement funds are established upon an actuarial basis and thus the legislators on a per diem pay usually do not have much opportunity to accumulate an annuity fund that will give them much of a retirement payment.

Minimum length of service necessary to qualify varies greatly from one state to another. Georgia at one extreme requires a minimum of thirty-five years while Ohio only five years. The retirement age is much more uniform varying only from fifty-five to sixty-five. Usually time may be accumulated after the minimum retirement age, so if a legislator serves until age seventy his entire length of service to the state will be counted toward his retirement benefit. Some states permit legislators to make back-payments for time served in the legislature prior to the enactment of the retirement program's application to legislators. A few states have started retirement plans for legislators but have abandoned them. These include Massachusetts and Nevada.

[24] *Final Report of the National Legislative Committee* (Chicago: Council of State Governments, 1962).

One of the most severe indictments of state legislatures was made by Patricia S. Wirt when she wrote:

Few American political institutions today enjoy as little prestige as state legislatures. Many are excessively large, most are malapportioned; they are also restricted constitutionally in their powers to legislate, are poorly organized and often hampered by archaic rules and procedures. Theoretically the states' chief policy-making institutions, they have lost much of the respect and support which the people gave in the early days of the republic.[25]

Mrs. Wirt does admit that in spite of the lack of faith of the people in the legislative bodies, serious efforts have gone on for more than half a century to reform state institutions, but she contends that those attempts directed at the policy-making bodies have met with the least success.

## IMMUNITIES AND PRIVILEGES OF STATE LEGISLATORS

Members of state legislatures universally are granted certain immunities and privileges during a legislative session. They are free from arrest, except for treason or major felony, while the legislative body is in session. They are not required to reply to a civil process while the session continues but must respond upon completion of the legislative meetings.

A much more important protection is the one extended to all legislators concerning their remarks when made on the floor of the legislative body. They are not subject to prosecution for any statements even though they would, if made outside of the halls of the legislature, be libelous. This ancient right has great usefulness in that it allows all to express freely their beliefs in the floor discussions. It should be noted that this freedom is seldom abused by members.

Most legislatures are the judges of their own members' fitness to serve. This includes contested elections in which a special committee determines which person has won the election. Likewise, the legislature may usually, by an extraordinary majority (two-thirds, or in some cases three-fourths), censure its own members, or in extreme cases may expel a member for actions that are unbecoming a legislator.

## BIBLIOGRAPHY

See bibliography at end of Chapter 11.

[25] Patricia S. Wirt, *Salient Issues of Constitutional Revision,* ed. John P. Wheeler, Jr. (New York: National Municipal League, 1961), p. 68.

# 11

# The Legislative Process

The legislative process is the method whereby public policies are established in a legal form. Not all laws place new legislation on the statute books; many simply repeal or slightly modify old laws passed by previous legislatures. Every action taken by the legislature in enacting laws may be called policy determination. Some actions are of a negative character while most are positive. In promoting its policy-making responsibilities each legislature has its own peculiar techniques and machinery, with many similarities but also with a vast number of variations. The legislature attempts to reflect the desires and the wishes of the people. How well it does this may be determined by many factors. One of the important factors is the representativeness of its composition. If the rural areas dominate the body it will be a miracle if the urban views are properly reflected in the legislative policy adopted. The reverse of course may also be true since the rural areas will not be given proper attention in a city-controlled legislature. Historically this latter problem has not been of any magnitude in American state legislatures because the over-representation of the rural elements is a well-established fact.

A second factor in the legislature's creation of public policy is the procedural rules and regulations followed. The procedural forms followed are adopted by each legislature but usually with few if any changes from those of previous legislatures. Tradition again has played a heavy hand in dictating the format followed in almost every state general assembly. Customs of years standing are followed even after their value and usefulness have been outlived.

## OFFICERS OF THE LEGISLATURE

### The Speaker of the House

In all of the state legislatures, except Nebraska which has no lower house, the presiding officer is known as the speaker. He is usually selected officially by a vote of the entire membership of the second house.

In reality he is named by the majority party at a pre-legislative session caucus. Normally both parties will nominate a candidate for the post of speaker at the opening meeting of the legislature, but the foregone conclusion is, of course, that the man nominated by the majority party will be elected on a straight party vote. The defeated minority party candidate ordinarily becomes the minority party's house leader. The selection of the speaker is a crucial decision for the majority party. He is usually one of the most experienced members of the body with a long legislative record that marks him as the party's leading spokesman.

One of his most important duties is to appoint the committees of the house. In all but four states the appointments are made solely by the speaker. Naturally, he normally will consult with other party members before announcing the number of committees and their membership. In the four states not granting the power of committee appointment to the speaker various methods are used. A committee on committees may be used to name the committees and in at least one state the minority party is allowed to name its members to the committees after the speaker has determined what committees there will be and the number of members to which the minority party is entitled.

A second major duty and power of the speaker that is almost universally accorded is to refer bills which have been introduced to the appropriate committee. While this may appear to be a mere routine task it can be of utmost significance as referring a bill to an unfriendly committee may be the extinction of the particular bill. In some legislatures it is possible for the author of the bill to protest the assigning of his measure to a particular committee, and he may call for a vote of the entire house to determine which committee shall be placed in charge of the bill. This, however, is not a very common practice.

The speaker as the presiding officer has the authority to rule on all parliamentary questions. Again, this is a power that may be used as a genuine source of authority or merely serve as an academic prerogative. Much depends upon the personality of the speaker and his political ambitions as to what course of action he will pursue in using his power of ruling on parliamentary questions. He is assisted by an appointed parliamentarian who gives him the interpretation which he may accept or reject. His rulings are usually subject to the disapproval of the membership of the house, should a member protest the ruling.

Another most vital role that the speaker plays is in determining, usually with consultation with the minority and majority house leaders, the order of business as it is processed by the house. This allows him to have a measure of control over the course of house debate. He may foster certain actions or may block other bills by the order in which he allows them to be considered by the membership.

The authority vested in the speaker to recognize or refuse to recognize members who seek the floor is also of importance in his control of house action. In this matter most speakers are careful to have an agreement with both majority and minority leaders as to the procedure that will be followed and the allocation of time to the respective sides of the issue under consideration. A few states do not allow the speaker arbitrarily to exercise the power of recognition.

The speakership is viewed as a stepping stone to higher political responsibilities in many states. It is not unusual for speakers to be regarded as potential candidates for state-wide office, and eventually the governorship. Others have used the speaker's office as a springboard for election to the United States Congress.

## PRESIDING OFFICER OF THE SENATE

Not all states in the Union have a position of lieutenant governor; the office does not exist in twelve states. In the other states his primary duty is to preside over the state senate.[1] He is not, however, a member of the body and therefore is not a voting member. He may not even vote in case of ties on substantive matters in most states. On procedural matters he is allowed to cast the deciding vote. Where the office does not exist or the state constitution does not give the lieutenant governor the authority to preside, the senators elect from their own membership a presiding officer in a manner similar to that of the lower house.

In most states the senate's presiding officer has the same powers and authority as the speaker of the house, aside from the voting on substantive matters. This means that he appoints committees, has the power of recognition, controls to a fair degree the conduct of business in the senate with the aid of the majority and minority leaders, rules on parliamentary questions, and selects the committee to which a bill will be referred.

Occasionally the lieutenant governor may be a member of the minority party of the senate, and when this occurs he may find himself stripped of some of the traditional powers granted to a presiding officer. Iowa, for example, in the 1959 session, had a lieutenant governor of the Democratic party while a vast majority of the membership in the senate was Republican. As a result the senate voted to relieve the lieutenant governor of the power to appoint members of the senate committees.

## OTHER OFFICIALS AND LEGISLATIVE EMPLOYEES

In addition to the presiding officers in each of the two houses, there are a number of other officers and employees who play lesser roles in the

[1] The Lieutenant Governors of Kentucky and Massachusetts do not preside over state senates.

legislative process. In the senate, a president pro tem is usually elected from the membership. The majority party on a straight party vote again determines who is selected. His only duty is to preside in case of absence of the lieutenant governor or, in the twelve states without a lieutenant governor, in the absence of the regular presiding officer.

The majority floor leader in each house is a key officer who is responsible for the actual operation of the body. It is his responsibility to maneuver the party's legislative program through the house, in cooperation with the presiding officer. With his assistant, usually given the title of the whip in most legislative assemblies, the majority leader determines the actual day-by-day operations of the policy-making branch. The minority floor leader plays the same role in a reverse fashion in that he is responsible for operating his party's loyal opposition.

In addition to the officers of the legislature each house has a large number of minor officials and employees. A large number of clerks, the most important of whom is ordinarily called the chief clerk of the house, a journal clerk, a bill clerk, and a reading clerk. Their counterparts in the state senate are the secretary of the senate, a journal clerk, a bill clerk, and a reading clerk. Both houses have a number of employees including sergeant-at-arms, a chief doorkeeper and assistants, a postmaster, committee clerks, pages, and in many general assemblies each lawmaker is permitted to select his own private secretary. The employees are in most states hired in the time-honored political patronage method, with the major party making almost all of the appointments. Seldom does the minority party have a voice in the naming of the employees although a few state legislatures do divide the employees along the same percentage lines as the total house membership.

A wholesome trend initiated in Wisconsin and very slowly spreading to other states is the placing of legislative employees under civil service regulations. A well-founded criticism of many of the legislatures is that they have more employees than can be justified. This is particularly true of the number of assistant doorkeepers and pages employed.


## STATE LEGISLATIVE COMMITTEES

It is obvious from the brief examination of the number of members elected to the state legislatures that it is necessary to employ the traditional committee system to expedite the work of the various state policy-making bodies. Seldom does the state constitution say anything about the committee system that must be followed by the legislature. The Model State Constitution provides that "the legislature may establish such committees as may be necessary for the efficient conduct of its business."

Unfortunately most of the state legislatures have been prone to create too many committees. Even in spite of the 1946 Reorganization Act of the Congress of the United States, which materially reduced the number of committees used by Congress, most state legislatures still persist in having more committees than can be justified in order to "efficiently conduct its business." It is an unusual state general assembly that does not have more committees than the Congress of the United States. Even the small senates of Delaware and Nevada appoint more committees than can be economically useful.[2]

Several reasons underly this over-employment of committees. Naturally, each must have a chairman, and in former years some legislatures appeared to be trying to have a committee chairmanship for each member. This is not true in New Hampshire and some of the other states with excessively large lower houses. This allows the legislator to return to his constituents and say, "I was chairman of an important committee"—thus adding prestige to his role in the legislative body. In addition, some legislatures have adopted rules that allow only chairmen of committees to have secretarial assistance, thus the more committee chairmanships available, the more legislators who are empowered to employ a secretary.

While the broad indictment of too many committees is valid, a few state legislatures may be cited as examples where a more realistic number of committees have been established. Georgia has only eight standing committees in the house, Maine only seven, and Massachusetts only five. On the other hand at least three states have more than sixty standing committees.

Not only is the number of committees an important consideration but also the number of legislators serving on each committee is of concern to a student of the state legislative process. The number of members on each standing committee is usually too large. In Iowa, it has been quite common for a member of the lower house to serve on eight or ten committees. Obviously he does not even find it possible to attend the meetings of all of these committees. The legislator may very frequently find that two or more of his committees will be holding meetings at the same time. Again the reason for so many members on each standing committee is readily explained. In an agricultural state every member wants to serve on the agricultural standing committee. In Iowa, this is so true that in almost every session two agricultural committees are appointed in the lower house with every member of the body who comes from any district with a rural orientation being able to serve on an agricultural committee.

A hopeful note may be seen in the gradual increase in the number of joint house and senate committees that are being employed by some state legislatures. Maine and Massachusetts, for example, depend to a large ex-

[2] Council of State Governments, *The Book of the States*, 1962–1963 (Chicago: Council of State Governments, 1962), p. 38.

tent upon joint committees, thus reducing the number of standing committees used in each of the two houses. Connecticut also is among the leaders in the joint committee process, reporting in a recent legislative session thirty-three joint committees. Such a practice is to be encouraged. It reduces the duplication that results from each house having a committee giving consideration to the same bill, holding independent hearings, and other time-consuming considerations.

The Council of State Governments Committee on Legislative Processes and Procedures has called for "a reduced number of committees and their organization according to subject matter should receive further consideration."[3] Unfortunately not as many state legislators have followed their committee's recommendations on committee use as students of the legislative process feel is desirable.

It is interesting to note that in the Nebraska unicameral legislature only fourteen standing committees have traditionally been appointed. Every bill sent to a committee is given a public hearing, a most unusual feature of state legislative process. In contrast with the Nebraska practice many state legislative committees seldom hold public hearings on most of the bills sent to them. A few state legislatures still allow the committee procedure to be cloaked in secrecy, never releasing the vote on the bill under consideration but merely indicating that it was not reported to the house. A few state legislatures keep no committee meeting records, thus allowing the legislators to hide their record on committee actions.

A few state legislatures are now requiring each committee to report on every bill sent to it for consideration. This frequently results in extended sessions, weeks and even months longer than in those states that do not require committee action on every bill, but it does result in more complete deliberation and the assurance of at least some consideration of every measure that is dropped into the legislative hopper.

Assignment to so many committees makes it almost impossible for a legislative member to become an expert in even a limited sense upon the bills presented to his committees. This degree of specialization should be beneficial, particularly in those legislative units that have available so little professional staff assistance.

Professor Zeller as the editor of the American Political Science Association study group concerned with American state legislatures made the following recommendations concerning the use of state legislative committees:

1. A substantial reduction of the number of standing committees and the assignment to each committee of a broad area or related areas of legislation.

[3] Council of State Governments, *Our State Legislatures* (Chicago: Council of State Governments, 1948), p. 10.

2. The utilization of joint committees by the two houses of the legislature.
3. The reduction of the number of committee assignments of members of the legislature.
4. The appointment of committee chairmen who can provide able leadership, and the assignment of members to committees with due regard to their special qualifications.
5. The establishment of rules that provide for advance notice of hearings and adequate records and requiring prompt attention to measures referred to committees.
6. The utilization of permanent legislative council or a limited number of interim committees to investigate the most important subjects of legislation.
7. Adequate and competent committee staffs to assemble data needed by each committee, to aid in the preparation of bills, reports and the scheduling of hearings.[4]

Many of these recommendations are similar to those of the Legislators Committee of the Council of State Governments as contained in the report entitled *Our State Legislatures.*

The legislative committees, their number and size, for the 1960–61 biennium, are presented in Table 11–1.

### TABLE 11–1

#### Legislative Committees—1960 to 1961

| State | Who Appoints House Committees | Who Appoints Senate Committees | Standing Committees House | Standing Committees Senate | Standing Committees Joint | Range in Size House | Range in Size Senate | Range in Size Joint | Open Hearings* |
|---|---|---|---|---|---|---|---|---|---|
| Alabama | Speaker | President | 17 | 30 | 1 | 7–15 | 3–21 | – | Discretion |
| Alaska | Elected | Elected | 10 | 10 | – | 7–11 | 5– 7 | – | Discretion |
| Arizona | Speaker | President | 20 | 21 | – | 15 | 7–14 | – | Discretion |
| Arkansas | Speaker | President | 69 | 25 | 1 | 4–37 | 5– 9 | 12 | Discretion |
| California | Speaker | Rules Committee | 26 | 21 | 4 | 3–22 | 5–13 | – | Yes |
| Colorado | Speaker | Resolution | 17 | 20 | 1 | 3–19 | 3–20 | 6 | Discretion |
| Connecticut | Speaker | President | – | – | 28 | – | – | 26–31 | Yes |
| Delaware | Speaker | President | 22 | 22 | – | 5 | 5 | – | Discretion |
| Florida | Speaker | President | 53 | 38 | 4 | 7–21 | 7–15 | 6 | Yes |
| Georgia | Speaker | President | 24 | 18 | – | 5–48 | 5–18 | – | Discretion |
| Hawaii | Speaker | President | 25 | 12 | – | 3–14 | 8–10 | – | Discretion |
| Idaho | Speaker | President | 22 | 23 | 3 | 3–13 | 5–11 | 9–18 | Discretion |
| Illinois | Speaker | Committee | 25 | 23 | – | 11–45 | 3–33 | – | Yes |
| Indiana | Speaker | President Pro Tem | 28 | 29 | – | 7–16 | 5–11 | – | Discretion |
| Iowa | Speaker | President | 40 | 32 | 2 | 7–46 | 1–27 | 9 | Discretion |

[4] Belle Zeller (ed.), *American State Legislatures* (New York: Thomas Y. Crowell Co., 1954), pp. 97–98.

### TABLE 11-1 (Continued)

| State | Who Appoints House Committees | Who Appoints Senate Committees | Standing Committees | | | Range in Size | | | Open Hearings* |
|---|---|---|---|---|---|---|---|---|---|
| | | | House | Senate | Joint | House | Senate | Joint | |
| Kansas | Speaker | President | 45 | 31 | 1 | 3–23 | 5–11 | 12 | Discretion |
| Kentucky | Comm. | Committee | 43 | 38 | – | 3–33 | 3–18 | – | Discretion |
| Louisiana | Speaker | President | 16 | 17 | – | 16–20 | 6–17 | – | Discretion |
| Maine | Speaker | President | 6 | 3 | 25 | 4–16 | 4–12 | 7–10 | Yes |
| Maryland | Speaker | President | 14 | 15 | 3 | 5–36 | 3–15 | 6–10 | Yes |
| Massachusetts | Speaker | President | 6 | 4 | 31 | 3–15 | 3–8 | 15 | Yes |
| Michigan | Speaker | Committee | 48 | 20 | – | 7–15 | 5–7 | – | Discretion |
| Minnesota | Speaker | Committee | 33 | 20 | – | 5–29 | 15–25 | – | Yes |
| Mississippi | Speaker | Lieutenant Governor | 50 | 46 | 5 | 5–33 | 3–26 | 5–13 | Discretion |
| Missouri | Speaker | President Pro Tem | 47 | 28 | 2 | 5–44 | 5–15 | 15 | Discretion |
| Montana | Speaker | Committee | 18 | 23 | – | 5–17 | 3–11 | – | Discretion |
| Nebraska | – | Committee | – | 14 | – | – | 1–9 | – | Yes |
| New Hampshire | Speaker | President | 25 | 18 | 1 | 5–21 | 3–7 | 8 | Yes |
| New Jersey | Speaker | President | 16 | 16 | 4 | 7 | 5–7 | 12 | Discretion |
| New Mexico | Speaker | Committee | 16 | 7 | – | 7–14 | 7–11 | – | Discretion |
| New York | Speaker | President Pro Tem | 36 | 28 | – | 15–20 | 6–25 | – | Discretion |
| North Carolina | Speaker | President | 45 | 33 | 4 | 8–62 | 6–26 | – | Yes |
| North Dakota | Speaker | Committee | 21 | 18 | – | 3–22 | 3–17 | – | Discretion |
| Ohio | Speaker | President Pro Tem | 20 | 10 | 4 | 7–23 | 8–12 | 4 | Yes |
| Oklahoma | Speaker | Elected | 39 | 34 | – | 3–31 | 3–20 | – | Discretion |
| Oregon | Speaker | President | 20 | 20 | 1 | 9 | 5–9 | 14 | Yes |
| Pennsylvania | Speaker | President Pro Tem | 36 | 23 | – | 10–23 | 9–24 | – | Discretion |
| Rhode Island | Speaker | Rules Committee | 15 | 17 | 1 | 8–17 | 5–10 | 9 | Discretion |
| South Carolina | Speaker | Elected | 8 | 36 | 4 | 5–27 | 5–18 | 6–15 | Discretion |
| South Dakota | Speaker | President | 23 | 18 | – | 3–15 | 3–15 | – | Discretion |
| Tennessee | Speaker | Speaker | 17 | 17 | – | 17–30 | 12 | – | Discretion |
| Texas | Speaker | President | 43 | 24 | – | 5–21 | 5–21 | – | Yes |
| Utah | Speaker | President | 18 | 14 | 1 | 9–17 | 3–5 | 28 | Yes |
| Vermont | Speaker | Special Committee | 18 | 18 | 3 | 5–15 | 3–6 | 6–56 | Yes |
| Virginia | Speaker | Elected | 34 | 21 | 3 | NA | NA | NA | Discretion |
| Washington | Speaker | President | 33 | 25 | – | 5–51 | 2–37 | – | Discretion |
| West Virginia | Speaker | President | 25 | 29 | 3 | 10–25 | 3–18 | 5 | Discretion |
| Wisconsin | Speaker | Committee | 23 | 11 | 2 | 3–11 | 3–5 | 5–14 | Yes |
| Wyoming | Speaker | President | 17 | 16 | 1 | 7–9 | 2–5 | – | Discretion |

* Hearings are open to the public at the discretion of the members of the committees.

SOURCE: Council of State Governments, *The Book of the States, 1962–1963* (Chicago: Council of State Governments, 1962).

## STATE INTERIM COMMITTEES

Prior to the development of the legislative council system, state legislative interim committees were very common. Few states were without this in-between session legislative committee operation. In some states they were permanent installations, while in others they were used intermittently, depending upon the needs of the legislature. When they were permanent or semi-permanent institutions, appointed and reappointed after every legislative session, the duties became quite complex. Usually little attention was given by these interim committees to research, but rather their specific purpose was to supervise the administrative operation. A distinction should be drawn between the permanent interim committee, which was only one agency, and the intermittent interim committee, of which there were often many: as many as eighteen in Michigan, twenty-one in New York, thirty-four in Massachusetts, and fifty-one in California.[5]

Often the interim committee, which still persists in a few states, even with research bureaus or legislative councils, was given authority over funds that could be spent between sessions. In 1963 Iowa's interim committee, composed of five senators and five state representatives, had control of two million dollars that it was allowed to allocate to state agencies during the eighteen months between sessions of the legislature. The agency was required to prepare a requisition, and the interim committee either approved or disapproved the request for funds. Ordinarily only emergency requests for money were granted.

Some question has arisen as to the constitutionality of such sweeping powers being granted to a legislative interim committee. The Iowa Attorney General in June of 1963 declared in his opinion that such a control over money granted to an interim committee was not constitutional. However, no court case has developed either to prove or disprove the attorney general's belief. The legislative interim committee, incidentally, was later given permission by the same attorney general to spend any or all of the two million dollars appropriated by the Iowa General Assembly for the contingency fund.

Unlike legislative councils, the typical interim committee has no permanent staff but merely employs on a part-time basis the employees it deems necessary. Usually the use of interim committees decreases with the advent of the legislative council.

[5] *Ibid.*, p. 137.

## STATE LEGISLATIVE COUNCILS

As of 1963 nearly four-fifths of the state legislatures had either a legislative council or some similar agency assisting in the work of the state policy-making body. In some states the legislative council has replaced the traditional interim committee, while in others the interim committee has continued to function alongside the research agency. In 1933 the first legislative council was created in Kansas. Although Michigan established a similar agency in the same year, it rapidly fell into disrepute and was abolished in 1939. This growth in thirty years is quite remarkable but even more surprising is the fact that no state legislature had seen the necessity of such an agency from 1780 until 1933.

The number of legislators who serve on the council varies. South Carolina has the smallest membership with only five legislators, while Nevada has only eight. Several states permit the entire legislature technically to hold membership on the council.[6]

Where the membership is limited, the appointing authorities, usually the presiding officers of the respective houses, make a special effort to have both parties represented generally on the basis of their strength in the legislature. Likewise, an effort is made to have geographic distribution.

The amount of money spent by the legislative councils varies tremendously. In the 1961-63 biennium the range was from a mere $5,000 for research in Wyoming to nearly $300,000 in Florida, and more than $400,-000 in Ohio. A very small part of the money is paid to the legislative members of the council, with the major expenditure being for the salaries of the professional staff that is the heart of the council's work.

The typical legislative council meets on a monthly or, even more commonly, a quarterly basis. Others will meet only when the chairman issues a call, with some states requiring a minimum number of meetings per year. The council acts as the policy-making board, determining what projects will be undertaken by the professional staff.

All councils have the responsibility for supervising the research of its staff. The councils have varying statutory power and authority. Some are confined to factual studies with no recommendations allowed. Probably a majority are in a second category, however, with the job of preparing and presenting positive positions on the subject under survey. The Kansas legislative council is one of those with this broader scope of

[6] Council of State Governments, *The Book of the States, 1962–1963* (Chicago: Council of State Governments, 1962), pp. 68–69.

power. It is probably true that a legislature gains the most value from its legislative council when it is permitted to make recommendations. Usually this comes gradually, although it did not follow this course in Kansas. Most legislative councils are primarily allowed merely to make factual surveys and then later gradually granted authority for recommending various courses of action.

The amount of the budget will of course determine the size of the professional staff. It is essential that the group be headed by an experienced, trained researcher. He should have a staff of professional personnel suitable to do a thorough job on all of the projects that are approved by the legislative council. In most states only the members of the legislature are allowed to suggest topics for research. In a few, private groups or citizens may ask that studies be conducted. In some, only the members of the legislative council itself determine the research areas to be covered.

Members of the legislative council usually do not directly participate in the conduct of the research. This is probably unfortunate as they are in a position to make genuine contributions. Also not to be overlooked is the advice that the members of the council can give when the recommendations or studies are viewed by the legislature.

Between the legislative sessions most legislative council staffs are responsible only to the members of the council, but once the general assembly convenes, all legislators seek some aid and assistance from them. Almost all such agencies are called upon for spot research and aid in bill-drafting unless the legislature has a separate agency for this purpose. The use of two separate agencies should probably be discontinued. The bill-drafting assistance should be an integral part of the over-all operation conducted by the legislative council's staff. This would inevitably mean that part-time assistance will be added to take care of this specialized function in the months immediately preceding and during the session of the legislature.

The legislative council, if properly used, should be an important aid in shortening the time consumed in the legislative meetings. It should more than offset its cost by reducing the time that the legislature must meet. It should make it possible for a great amount of pre-filing of bills, and the holding of some public hearings on the more important items to be considered by the session. Unfortunately it is probably true that a majority of the state legislatures do not make the maximum use of their legislative councils. This is perhaps the result of a fear that the legislative council will take over the powers and duties that the legislature guards so jealously. This should and will not happen if the legislative members of the council participate actively in legislative research.

## BILL-DRAFTING AIDS

In many states the attorney general's office is the center of the bill-drafting aids for the state legislators. This usually means the addition of several part-time lawyers to the attorney general's staff immediately before and during the legislative session.

Other states use different means. A few have the staff of the legislative council serve as the bill-drafting agency. Others have a legislative research bureau that performs this service. Still others have the state library employ a number of bill drafters to assist the legislators in this task.[7]

New York State has created a bill-drafting commission whose sole job is to draft bills for the members of the legislature. They also assist any committees and other agencies that desire help in the formulating of bills to be presented for legislative consideration.

Every legislator has at his disposal the talents of the lobbyists to assist him in drafting bills of particular interest to a lobbyist. Many of these men are skilled bill drafters, usually with vast legal experience and often times legislative background.

The seven recommendations of the American Political Science Committee on American Legislatures as released in 1954 concerning legislative councils and bill-drafting aids are worthy of examination:

1. There is urgent need for a single legislative service in each state, organized and equipped, adequately financed, and functioning exclusively under legislative control, to provide an integrated service for the members and committees of the state legislature.

2. Legislative councils should be established in every state.

3. Interim committees should be coordinated with the legislative council.

4. Legislative reference services should be established in every state and expanded in many that already have them.

5. There is need in many states for the creation of specialized bill-drafting facilities adequately staffed to provide efficient service to committees and members of the legislature.

6. Every state should have a regular established method of revision of the state statutes and code.

7. Most states need to increase the clerical staffs available to the committees and individual members of the state legislature.[8]

It is obvious that not all seven recommendations apply equally in every

---

[7] E. Witte, "Technical Services for State Legislators," *The Annals of The Academy of Political and Social Science* (January, 1938), p. 140.

[8] Zeller, *op. cit.*, pp. 160–62.

state, as some states have much greater facilities already established to help their legislators. The major principle that has almost universal application is the need for integration of all of these legislative services. Probably no state has as completely integrated and coordinated these services as is possible and desirable.

## STATE LEGISLATIVE REFERENCE SERVICES

Four general purposes are served by the state legislative reference services available to members of the state legislatures. They are universally agreed to be: (1) to collect all available information on any subject that the legislature may take action, (2) to collect and evaluate all of the legislation on a given subject from the other states, (3) to collect general reference material that may be desired by the members of the legislature, and (4) to do research studies on subjects of major importance to either individual legislators or to committees as requested.

Following the lead of Wisconsin and New York, which saw the usefulness of such service early in this century, the other states almost in toto have adopted some form of legislative reference bureau. No two are identical but certainly all have similar aims and purposes. The degree to which these are successfully executed depends upon numerous factors, not the least of which is the financial support that they receive from the general assembly and the personnel selected to man the legislative reference services. While not quite all of the fifty states have official legislative reference services probably all have some facilities available to their legislators. Their status varies in that some are independent, some are merely creatures of the legislature, some are a part of the legislative council, some are recognized as state departments, while others are sections of the state library services.

It is difficult if not impossible to state arbitrarily that one format is better than another. The individual situation may well dictate which form or system will operate for the greatest benefit to the legislators and ultimately the betterment of the law-making process of the state.

## LEGISLATIVE PROCEDURE

### Introduction and Origin of Bills

The privilege of introducing bills is reserved for the members of the state legislature. Each member is equal in his opportunity to introduce legislation. In some states a deadline is set for the introduction of bills which is applied usually well past the half-way mark in the session. After this time only committee bills are accepted. Unless these limits are a constitutional matter, the rules are frequently suspended. In an effort to secure maximum study more and more of the state legislatures are encouraging the members to pre-file their bills.

While each legislature has its own rules of procedure, most allow members merely to file their bills with the clerk of the house. Others require that a legislator be recognized in order to introduce the bill formally to the entire house membership. One or two legislatures still require a petition to be filed with bills that are presented, thus attempting to reduce the number of bills introduced at each session.

No state allows the governor or members of the administrative branch or the judiciary actually to introduce bills in either legislative house. However, this does not prevent many bills from originating with the administrative and judicial branches and being formally introduced by friendly members of the legislature. Likewise, pressure groups through their lobbyists also find eager friendly legislators formally to present bills written by lawyers working for the pressure groups. In addition to individual members of the legislature, legislative committees, both standing and interim committees, have the privilege of formally presenting bills to the two houses of the legislature.

Not to be overlooked is the ability of an individual constituent to draft a proposed bill and convince his senator or representative to introduce it. Usually these bills are written by lawyers or if not they are re-written either by the senator or representative or some legislative reference bureau or bill drafting service.[9]

In most states, unlike the national government where the president and his administrative agencies originate a large percentage of the bills introduced in Congress, the governor and the administrative branch write a small number of the bills filed in the two houses. In some states usually few bills come directly from the governor and his administrative staff. In others, however, the national pattern is beginning to be followed more closely. Some observers believe that it is imperative for a governor who expects to possess genuine legislative leadership to have a large number of bills ready for introduction by his friends in the policy-making body. This is very difficult in states with only a biennial session where the governor is elected only a short time before the beginning of the legislative session. In states with annual sessions and four-year terms for the chief executive the problem is somewhat lessened. But even here until the tradition is well-established some resentment may be expected from the legislature if the governor presses too hard for the bills he has had prepared. The legislative members are usually jealous of their positions and

---

[9] Harvey Walker, "Where Does Legislation Originate?" *National Municipal Review* (September, 1929); *ibid.*, "Well Springs of Our Laws," *National Municipal Review* (October, 1939).

will be quick to inform the governor that he is primarily an executive officer and that they were elected by the people to determine major policy matters. It is obvious that an experienced governor and administrative staff should be in probably the best position of anyone in the state to determine what bills should be written. In spite of this the governor may frequently find his help resented and his efforts rebuffed.

The various administrative agencies should prepare bills that their experience in administering the present laws indicates should be considered. Again, the same jaundiced eye may be cast by the members of the legislature upon these efforts. However, until every state has a large, well-trained staff of legislative research members it is likely that the administratively prepared bills will be one of the best sources of suggested legislation.[10]

## The Governor and the Legislature

As previously noted the governor is not allowed to introduce legislation in any state legislative assembly, but in spite of this provision, the typical governor has become a policy leader. The public expects him to have a legislative program and often regards him as a policy leader rather than the chief state administrator. To be sure, the state legislatures in some states resent the new role of the governor and resist his efforts to guide their policy-making efforts. However, the governor has the means of influencing both the legislature and the public through the mass communications media.

The governor can call upon various state administrative agencies for ideas and data in his attempts to promote a particular program and policy. He can also enlist the assistance of prominent and influential private citizens to innovate policy. Governors' commissions are now common in almost every state. These groups study problems that the chief executive desires examined and make recommendations to the governor which he in turn presses upon the legislature with the full weight of the citizen's committee.

Most successful gubernatorial candidates find that they are elected because they have advocated a particular legislative program rather than because of their promises to be an efficient administrator. Thus it behooves the governor to pursue with vigor the enactment of his legislative ideas that made up the foundation of his campaign.

In almost every state the governor is granted the power of presenting the budget to the legislature. This authority to initiate the budgeting process is an important duty, but every governor soon learns that final

[10] Harvey Walker, "Who Writes the Laws?" *State Government* (November, 1939), p. 199.

authority in budgetary matters resides with the legislative body. It is their decision that ultimately determines the appropriations that will be available for the administrative units of the state and that establishes the tax structure. Obviously one of the most important committees in every state legislature is the appropriations committee which exists in each house. It is their recommendation that is usually the basis for the final appropriations law. The budgetary process is more fully examined in two later chapters.

Every regular session of a state legislature in the United States finds three or four times as many bills introduced as are enacted into law. The range in number of bills introduced is related to a number of factors; probably most important of which is the total population of the state. As would be expected, California and New York normally have more bills introduced in a regular session than the other state legislatures. More than seven thousand bills will be filed in the New York legislature during a normal regular session.[11] On the other hand, such small population states as Wyoming and Nevada may see less than five hundred bills presented for consideration. Of the multitude of bills considered, between 25 and 35 per cent will become law. Most of the other bills will never be reported by committee. This is not true in a few states, however, which require that every bill that is sent to a committee be reported.

The bills considered by the fifty general assemblies in their regular sessions are concerned with every conceivable subject. Most state legislatures have a rule that requires that only one subject may be dealt with in a bill. This may be loosely or rigidly enforced depending upon the presiding officer or in some instances the rules committee, if this is one of the powers that has been delegated to it.

One of the major reasons both for the excessive number of bills introduced and the large number passed is the practice followed by almost all state legislatures, in spite of constitutional limitations, of enacting special legislation. These acts may apply only to one or two counties, or municipalities, or school districts. These bills, which in some states are called enabling acts, for example, allow a bond issue vote that may not have been published the proper number of times, to be legalized by the legislative action. A sizable portion of the bills are usually concerned with local matters. If complete constitutional home rule were allowed, this would not be necessary, and the legislative calendars would not be so cluttered as they are in most sessions.

After being introduced by whatever is the prevailing mode, the bill is given a number by the clerk of the legislative body in which it has been filed; e.g. House of Representatives 556 if in the House or Senate File

[11] Council of State Governments, *The Book of the States, 1962–1963* (Chicago: Council of State Governments, 1962), pp. 56–57.

556 if in the Senate. For speed of action it may be referred to as H.R. 556 from this point until its final passage into law.

The first reading occurs immediately following the assigning of a number to the bill. This is normally by title only and consists of the reading clerk proclaiming the title of the bill and its number. In most legislative halls the bill is then rushed to the printer and within twenty-four hours each member has a copy of H.R. 556 on his desk for his own personal study. Following the reading of the bill the presiding officer designates the committee to which the bill is assigned. In a few legislatures this assigning of bills to committee is a power of the rules committee, but in the majority it is the presiding officer's function. A few legislatures require the speaker to ask the legislator introducing the bill to which committee he desires it to be assigned. Where the legislator does not have this courtesy extended, he may protest to the house the assignment of the bill if he feels the presiding officer has sent it to the wrong committee. Usually the wrong committee is considered to be one that is known to be unfriendly to the bill.

### Committee Procedure

The committee to which the bill is referred is known as a standing committee. These are subject-matter committees established at the beginning of the session and continue usually throughout the duration of the session unless the sifting committee is used. At the time of the appointment of a sifting committee all committees, except possibly the ways and means and the appropriation committee, will be relieved of their unreported bills. The standing committee should in theory take up each bill as it is received, but in actual practice the chairman of the committee will probably determine which bills will be considered at a given time. If the bill is of importance a public hearing may be given, at which time the proponents and the opponents will be heard. In two-thirds of the states the committee may never report the bill. In all houses the bill may be forced out of committee by a discharge petition. Usually this requires signatures of two-thirds of all of the members of the entire house, but it is infrequently used.[12]

If the bill is complex the chairman may decide to have it initially considered by a sub-committee. This group will then report to the entire committee its recommendations. At least seven different alternatives are available to a committee:

1. That the bill be passed. This recommendation is made only when the committee is of the opinion that the bill is as nearly perfect as is possible to make it without change.

[12] Joseph P. Chamberlain, *Legislative Processes: National and State* (New York: Appleton-Century-Crofts, Inc., 1936), p. 92.

2. That the bill be passed with amendment. This action is taken if the members of the committee feel that the bill merits passage but certain changes should be made. The committee usually makes the changes and submits them with its recommendation.

3. Report the bill without any recommendation. If the committee is unable or unwilling to come to any decision it may report the bill to the house without comment and place it on the calendar for consideration.

4. That a substitute bill be prepared and passed. The committee in this instance usually drafts a new bill concerning the same subject and recommends that it be passed in place of the proposed bill sent to them.

5. That the bill be referred to another committee. If the committee believes that another committee should have jurisdiction over the subject matter covered in the bill it may suggest sending the bill to another committee for its consideration.

6. That the bill not be passed. This is a negative report. Rather than make this report, the bill in some legislatures is kept in committee, except in those that require that each bill be reported, and thus never comes to a vote on the floor of the house.

7. That the bill be indefinitely postponed. This recommendation if followed means that the bill is dead for that session and never will come to a vote in the house. The committee recommendation is probably followed in better than 90 per cent of the indefinitely postponed recommendations in a typical session.

Upon being reported by the committee the bill is placed on the regular calendar. When its place on the calendar is reached, the bill is given its second reading. This may be by title only or it may be a full reading of the bill, depending upon the rules of the body. Following the reading, the bill is open for debate by all members of the house. It is also open for any amendments that members may desire to propose. The debate may be very brief or it may be extended, depending upon the importance attached to the measure by the legislators. Rules as to how long each member may speak vary but most legislatures have rather severe limitations upon the time allocation of each member. This custom is carried over from the United States House of Representatives, which also has rigid limits upon the individual members speaking on each bill.

## Debate and Final Passage

Some state legislatures almost automatically go into the committee of the whole while debate is conducted. The only difference between regular procedure and the committee of the whole is that the votes taken during committee of the whole operation are not binding and must be repeated in regular session to become effective.

Upon completion of the debate, either because everyone has said everything he desires to say on the measure or because of time limitations, the chairman of the committee reporting the bill makes his formal report and the question is then called, "Shall the report of the committee be made the vote of the house?" Other legislatures merely have the presiding officer calling for the ayes and the nays on the bill as presented. If a majority of the members vote "yes," the bill is said to have passed and shall proceed for further action.

The next process is the engrossment of the bill. This is simply a retyping of the bill with the amendments that have been attached in order to insure that all members will be fully aware of the entire content of the bill as of the completion of debate.

Again the bill is placed on the regular calendar and awaits its turn for its third reading. When read the third time, which again may be by title only in some legislatures but in others it must be in full, the bill is open for debate only usually upon the merits of the measure as a whole and not as to its individual parts. With unanimous consent it is of course possible even at this point to offer an amendment and have it added to the bill. Few amendments are allowed at this point and those that are permitted are usually corrections of clerical errors.

Upon closing of debate following the third reading the question is, "Shall the bill be enacted into law?" The vote must be a majority of those present and voting in some general assemblies, and in others it must be a majority of the constitutional number of members, meaning it must be one over half of the total membership of the house no matter how many are present. The voting of the ayes and nays is recorded in the journal of the house. Nearly half of the state legislatures are using some type of mechanical voting devices. In some states both houses employ these time-saving mechanisms while in other states only the larger house will utilize them. Upon announcement by the presiding officer of the vote, the vote is said to be official. However, members are usually allowed a certain length of time in which to change their votes following this announcement.

The bill is then messaged to the other house for its consideration. This consists of the clerk hand-carrying it to the presiding officer of the other house who accepts the message, and the procedure is almost completely re-enacted in the second chamber. If the joint committee system is operative the referral-to-committee step is not required as the committee report will already have been prepared in the joint committee.

Following the passage of the bill in the second house, if any amendments have been made or any changes whatsoever have occurred, the bill is sent to the house of origin to see if it will concur in the changes. If the first house to consider the bill refuses to agree to the changes the next move is for the appointment by the respective presiding officers of a conference committee. This committee, actually a special committee, is composed of an equal number of members from each of the two houses. The job of the committee is to attempt to compromise the differences that exist between the two versions of the bill that have passed the respective houses. If the conference committee is able to agree upon a compromise it is returned to each house for its approval. Usually this compromise is agreed to by the two houses if it has been unanimously accepted by the conference committee.

The bill then must be voted upon and passed in identical form by each house and is then duly enrolled. This consists of making a final copy of the bill with appropriate places for the signatures of the necessary officers of both houses. The signatures are usually signed in the presence of the entire house and the certification that the bill is in final form is signed.

## Party Discipline and Voting in State Legislatures

In state legislatures where one-party control is normal the amount of party discipline is frequently lacking. There is in these states no one party line to which all members of the party in the legislative body is required to adhere. In contrast, in states with a genuine two-party legislature, more vigorous attempts are made to force the party members to support the position of the party. However, even this breaks down frequently as the bloc voting that occurs is often along urban-rural or urban-suburban lines.

Party caucuses are used to aid in the attempt to gain party cohesion. M. E. Jewell in his study "Party Voting in American State Legislatures" concludes that there is considerable voting along party lines in the two-party states with the amount "significantly higher in those that are larger and more urban." Similarly, his findings were that a high level of party voting in the legislatures results from party alignments which have largely followed the liberal-conservative urban-rural pattern of national politics.

As would be anticipated, there is a tendency for each political party in a two-party state to move toward a moderate position. A great many legislative roll calls are unanimous and the number of cases of a total one-party alignment against the other is relatively few. This has been found to be true in a number of state legislative studies, particularly in the Pennsylvania legislative studies.

A quasi-non-partisanship would seem to exist in a majority of the state legislatures even though only in Nebraska and Minnesota are the members actually elected on a non-partisan ticket. The study of Wahlke, Eulau, Buchanan, and Ferguson ultimately arrived at the conclusion that "am-

bivalence and uncertainty about the meaning of 'party' is a fact of political life, felt by the legislators themselves."

When the often-expected "bloc" voting does occur it is apparently more
often in connection with the rural legislators combining against the big-
city legislators. In other states it may be the legislators from a certain
area, such as down-state Illinois, voting as a body against the measures
sponsored by the members from the northern section of the state. Likewise the rural legislators may form an allegiance with the law-makers
from the smaller communities. These examples of unit voting appear
more frequent than do straight party voting.

## Gubernatorial Action

The act, formerly known as a bill, is now ready to be sent to the governor for his consideration. When the act is presented to the governor he
has three alternatives and a time limit in which to act. Usually within a
short period, anywhere from three to ten days, providing the legislature
is continuing in session, the governor must determine his course of action.
If he believes the act should become a law he will sign the measure with
the usual formalities of inviting the sponsors to be present and even
follow the accepted Presidential pattern of signing with several pens so
that all responsible for the measure becoming law may have a souvenir.
If he is not sure whether or not the act should become law and the session
is continuing he may not sign but allow it to become a law without his
signature. If he does not want to veto and the session has ended in most
states his lack of signature may constitute a pocket veto, thus preventing
the act from becoming a part of the state code. If he is convinced that
the act should not become law he has the power of veto. (Only in North
Carolina is the governor powerless to veto an act.) This he does by *not*
signing and by sending a message to the presiding officers of both houses
with his reasons for his veto. These may be of great length or may consist
merely of a statement declaring that he believes the act unconstitutional
or he does not think that it is in the public interest or anything else that
he cares to use for his reason for vetoing. In nearly 80 per cent of the
states the governor has an item veto which is usually effective only on
appropriation measures.

If the legislature is still in session, the presiding officer will read the veto
message to the house and ask what action it desires to take. If two-thirds of
both houses believe that the governor was wrong in his veto and are convinced that the law is needed, desirable, and necessary, the veto may be
over-ridden and the act becomes a law over the governor's veto.

Either following the over-riding of a veto or the signing of the measure
by the governor, the act is deposited usually with the secretary of state. It

is his responsibility to see that it is properly handled from this point. In some states acts of "great importance" may be placed into effect immediately upon publication in usually two or more newspapers of general state-wide circulation. In other states no such immediate effectiveness is possible. In some states the acts passed by the general assembly automatically become effective sixty days following the adjournment of the legislature. In others it is quite common for new laws to become effective on the Fourth of July or, if a tax matter, on July 1st.

At the end of the session in most states all of the new laws that have been enacted are printed and made available to all interested parties.

## State Codes and Revision of State Codes

All of the fifty states have a method of permanent statutory publication. Some publish statutes every ten or twenty years while others have a complete revision and publication every two or four years. In those states that use the long interval between complete publication it is usually the custom to publish supplements that bring the code of the state up-to-date. It would appear that frequent publication—every four years—is the most satisfactory method of code revision for most of the states. This permits a fairly large publication at minimum expense both to the state and to the purchasers.

## STATE REGULATION OF LOBBYING

Seventeen states have no laws or legislative rules that require the registration of lobbyists. This means that for all practical purposes no one really knows how extensive the lobbying activities are in these state legislatures. To be sure no one is probably fully aware of the extent of the influence of lobbyists in the thirty-three states that do have either statutory laws or rules in the senate or house requiring registration. Of the thirty-three states, twelve do not require anything more than merely filing of a statement that the individual is working for a certain firm in the role of a lobbyist. The other twenty-one do have regulations that require filing of certain expense statements. However, evidence is abundant that many of these rules are flouted. Often only about one-third to two-thirds of the lobbyists comply with full statements of expenses and how these expenses were incurred. Most of the states have penalties that might be applied if the rules are not met but apparently few prosecutions are made.

A new trend is evident in a few states that are now not only requiring registration but the payment of a fee by all lobbyists. Usually the fee is small, varying from only one dollar to as much as twenty dollars. Alaska is unusual in that the fee varies, with non-residents required to pay as much as one hundred dollars compared with ten dollars for residents.[13]

The validity of the lobbying laws is usually unquestioned. In the few court cases that have occurred the laws have been almost universally upheld. The need for greater control over the activities of the lobbyists in the fifty state general assemblies is evident to all observers. Most lobbyists readily admit that their work is twofold: first, they have certain legislation that they desire favorable action upon; this function is easily recognizable. The second function is not as obvious but may be even more important and that concerns itself with preventing legislation from being enacted that their principals feel might be detrimental to their best interests.

Lest one get the impression that all lobbying is evil it must be stated that many services are provided by lobbyists that are almost indispensable to members of the legislature. Information that might not be available from any other source is frequently presented by lobbyists. It is usually slanted in the way that it will be most beneficial to the concern for which the lobbyist labors.

Publicity is one of the best ways of preventing unwarranted lobbying activities from gaining control of the legislative branch. To make this possible registration is certainly a minimal requirement, which should be followed by expense account filings and penalties for violations. Prosecutions in more states like those made in Wisconsin will probably correct the abuses occurring in the "fourth branch" of government faster than any one method or approach.

Almost every pressure group in every state has a lobbyist or several lobbyists representing it whenever the state legislature is in session. Many of these persons receive salaries that exceed those of the legislators. Almost all of the lobbyists have virtually unlimited expense accounts, if they are to be successful in their major efforts. If all members of the legislature are provided with a list of all lobbyists and the names of the firms they represent and the major interests, they will be forewarned of the efforts forthcoming. An effective lobbyist can make it appear to a naive legislator that all of the state is in favor of the things he proposes and are in opposition to all of the measures that his firm objects to having enacted.

The consumers at both the national and the state level are the one great group that is unorganized and therefore not represented by a lobby. It is essential for the protection of this large group that the lobbyists be kept in their proper role and in proper perspective, not in just

[13] Council of State Governments, *The Book of the States, 1962–1963* (Chicago: Council of State Governments, 1962), p. 80. "The State Lobby Laws," Belle Zeller (ed.).

thirty-three states, where even with their present regulations this is questionable, but in all fifty states.

## NON-LEGISLATIVE FUNCTIONS OF THE LEGISLATURE

The executive function of the state legislatures is in a sense also a positive control over the administrative or executive branch of the state government. Almost every governor must submit his appointments to major state executive offices to the state senate for its approval or rejection. In a few of the states this same body must be consulted before these appointees may be removed from office by the governor.

The judicial aspect of the non-legislative powers of the state legislature centers about the impeachment procedure. Impeachment is a process whereby civil officials of both the executive and judicial branches may be removed from office because of criminal actions or other serious misconduct. The usual procedure in all states except Oregon, which does not provide for the impeachment method of removal, involves the bringing of charges by the lower house, usually after a complete investigation of the alleged misconduct or criminal action has been carried out by an investigating committee. If the articles of impeachment are approved by the lower house it is then incumbent upon the senate to fix a date for trial. The accused must be allowed to present his case with witnesses and legal counsel, while the prosecution is performed by legal counsel of the legislative body of its own choosing, if not by the state attorney general. The most common procedure is for the chief justice of the state supreme court to preside. In New York the justices of the Court of Appeals sit with the members of the senate, while in Nebraska and Missouri the trials are held before the supreme court. Upon hearing all of the evidence, the members of the upper house vote to determine whether the state official is guilty or not guilty. Usually a two-thirds vote is required to cause the individual's removal from office. He is, furthermore, declared to be ineligible in most states to hold office henceforth. The matter is then ended aside from the fact that if the impeachment has been based upon criminal action the impeached official may be tried in regular criminal court and face punishment according to law if convicted.

Supervision of the administrative branch of state government by the legislature is usually performed primarily through the interim committees. This between-session group of legislators is ordinarily given the power to inquire into almost any phase of administrative activity. Special investigating committees may be appointed by the legislature to make studies of a particular governmental agency, usually under the guise that new legislation is needed, and special information on the present administrative practices are necessary before such new enactments can be made. The legislature may follow the practice of requiring an annual report of its activities from each state agency. The rules of each department in some states are required to be submitted to the legislature for its approval before they can be effected. A final check that should be exercised over administration by each legislature takes the form of a post-audit performed by an auditor responsible to the state's general assembly.

## RECOMMENDATIONS FOR IMPROVING STATE LEGISLATURES

Professor Malcolm Jewell has presented one of the most accurate statements on the findings of scholars concerning state legislatures:

> Most studies of American Legislatures . . . center on what is wrong with them. Most observers conclude that few legislatures are doing their job well and that many of the ills of state government result from that fact. The remedy that is prescribed for the legislature usually consists of steps to improve its competence. Legislators should be paid more and serve longer time, there should be more adequate staffs and stronger legislative councils, and the legislature should meet longer and more often in order to give more careful study to legislative proposals. Every one of these suggestions is sound, and each would improve the legislative process. . . . Legislatures often fall short of our expectations largely because at any one time such a two-party system can be found operating well in relatively few states. There is hope for a greater number of responsible legislatures, however, because it is possible to forecast a growth of the two-party system.[14]

The twelve point summary of the Council of State Governments Committee on Legislation Procedures is worthy of serious consideration and implementation.

### Summary of Recommendations

1. Legislative Sessions. There should be no restrictions upon the length of regular sessions. If there is no annual session, then the legislature should be allowed to call itself into special session and discuss any matter they desire.

2. Legislators—Compensation. Annual salaries should be large enough so that competent persons may serve without financial sacrifices. Salaries should not be fixed by the state constitution. Most present salaries are too low.

3. Legislators—Term of Office. The terms of the members should be staggered wherever possible. It is undesirable to have all members of the legislature elected at the same time.

[14] Malcolm E. Jewell, *The State Legislature: Politics and Practice* (New York: Random House, Inc., 1962), pp. 128-29.

4. Legislative Employees. The qualified full-time legislative employees of the legislature should be appointed without regard to political party affiliation but strictly on merit. The tenure should be secure and not dependent upon the political party in control of the legislature. Working conditions and compensation should be comparable to those of the administrative and judicial branches.

5. Legislative Committees—Organization and Procedure. Committees are too numerous in most state legislatures and have too many members serving on most committees. Greater use should be made of cooperative committees between the two house joint committees. Committee should meet at regular scheduled times, with permanent records.

6. Legislative Committees—Public Hearings. All major bills should be given a public hearing by the appropriate committee. Rules of procedure of committees should be made available to the public as should the results of the committee actions.

7. Legislative Councils and Interim Committees. Interim committees and legislative councils should be coordinated with the full time legislative reference bureau and conduct their operations in conjunction with the full time legislative staff.

8. Reference, Research, Bill-Drafting, and Statutory Revision Services. Most state legislatures are handicapped by inadequate reference, research and bill-drafting staffs. Great need is apparent to add competent personnel and increase salaries.

9. Introduction and Printing of Legislation. Greater use should be made of the practice of pre-filing of bills (filing with the full time legislative officials before the formal opening of the session). All bills introduced should be printed and made immediately available to all members of the legislature. Following each session all enacted legislation should be printed and made available to the public.

10. Legislative Rules. Each house should be permitted to adopt its own rules of procedure, but they should be reviewed periodically to insure adequate deliberation on measures and fairness to the second party. Each house should have its own committee on organization and rules.

11. Legislative Finance. The legislature should provide itself with a budget for each fiscal year and employ a fiscal officer to handle the financial affairs of the legislative body.

12. Local and Special Legislation. Settlement of claims against the state should be delegated to a judicial or administrative body. Home rule should be used to avoid special legislation for local units of government where ever possible.[15]

[15] "Our State Legislatures," *Report of the Committee on Legislative Processes and Procedures* (rev. ed.; Chicago: Council of State Governments, 1948), pp. vi–vii.

## DIRECT LEGISLATION

Near the end of the nineteenth century many Americans felt that the state legislatures were not representing their best interests and were not accurately reflecting their desires and needs. As a result, a movement developed to supplement the regular law-making processes by devices for direct popular participation. A forerunner was the Maryland practice in 1825 of allowing the voters to determine whether or not to establish free primary schools.

South Dakota led the way in the field of direct legislation, aside from the Maryland trial run, when the initiative and referendum for state legislation was established in 1898. The South Dakota statute allowed any person or persons to draft a proposed law and upon obtaining the signatures of 5 per cent of the qualified voters of the state on a petition, the proposal had to be given consideration by the state general assembly. If the legislature did not approve the proposed legislation, a second petition, again signed by 5 per cent of the qualified voters of South Dakota, placed the proposal before a popular vote of the people. If, in this election, a majority voted in favor, the legislation, even though it had not gained the approval of the legislators, was enacted into law.

Nineteen states have followed the lead of South Dakota in the direct legislation field. Only Alaska provides for direct legislation in the original constitution, but it was added by amendment in the other states. Of the twenty states with provision for initiative and referendum, two use only the referendum phase, Maryland and New Mexico, while Idaho's state legislature has never enacted the necessary enabling legislation to make direct legislation operative.

In thirteen states not only statutory initiative but also constitutional initiative, amending the state constitution by the initiative process, is possible. The procedure is the same, with the major difference being that in amending the constitution by the initiative process usually a larger percentage of signatures is needed. The range of signatures is from 3 per cent of the number of voters who cast ballots in the gubernatorial election in Ohio to 10 per cent in a number of states, including Arizona, Idaho, Maine, Nevada, and Utah.

Eleven states provide for direct initiative rather than the indirect statutory initiative first enacted in South Dakota. In Alaska, Arizona, Arkansas, Colorado, Idaho, Missouri, Montana, Nebraska, North Dakota, Oklahoma, and Oregon, a measure proposed by initiative is submitted directly to the people without referral to the state legislature. While Maine, Massachusetts, Michigan, Nevada, and Ohio have followed the South Dakota practice of requiring the proposal to be submitted first to the legislature before being voted upon by the public. A third method is used in California, Utah, and Washington, allowing either direct or indirect initiative depending upon the number of signatures obtained. A larger percentage is necessary if the proposal is to be sent directly to the public than if first referred to the general assembly. It should be noted that if the legislature approves the proposal in the states with indirect initiative it is not subjected to the referendum.

The referendum procedure is a method whereby a measure which has been passed by a state legislature may be submitted to a popular vote before it can be put into effect. Three different types of referendums are used to varying degrees in the United States. A mandatory referendum is a compulsory referendum, which must occur in a given situation. Usually, except in Delaware, all proposed constitutional amendments must be approved by the people before they can become effective, as are state bond issues in many states. Thus it can be stated that forty-nine states do have mandatory referendums. In contrast the optional referendum is a permissive procedure, which allows the legislature, if it so desires, to submit a measure which it has approved to popular vote and permits the outcome of that vote to determine whether or not the measure will become effective.

The third class of referendum is called the protest or petition referendum. A proposal that has been approved by the legislature may be made inoperative in twenty states if a petition signed by the necessary number of voters demands a public referendum before the measure can go into effect. If the vote is against the legislation that has been enacted it does not become part of the state code.

As is usually the case, direct legislation has not proven to be the panacea that its proponents have claimed, nor has it been the threat to the legislatures that its opponents insisted it would be. There can be no question that it has been used too much in a few states, and minority lawmaking has on occasion been the result. It has also resulted in some poorly drawn legislation being placed on the statute books. However, this is not unique, since poor legislation has also been drafted by the legislators. There can be little question that it can be an expensive method of enacting new legislation as state-wide elections cost a great deal.

In the final analysis, it must be admitted that a majority of the states have survived without direct legislation, at least of the initiative variety, and therefore it cannot be said to be indispensable. If properly used it probably can make a contribution to democratic state government. It is a useful tool to assure that the legislatures will be in step with the wishes of their constituents.[16]

[16] Winston Crouch, *The Initiative and Referendum in California* (Los Angeles: The Haynes Foundation, 1950); and Joseph G. La Palombara, *The Initiative and Referendum in Oregon, 1938–1948* (Corvallis: Oregon State College Press, 1950).

In Table 11-2 the various types of the initiative and the referendum procedures are outlined.

## TABLE 11–2
### Initiative and Referendum Provisions

| State | Initiative Type | Initiative Size of Petition | Referendum How Submitted Petition | Referendum How Submitted Legislative | Referendum Size of Petition | Both— Vote |
|---|---|---|---|---|---|---|
| Alaska | Direct | 10 per cent in last election | Yes | No | 10 per cent | Majority |
| Arizona | Direct | 10 per cent of Governor vote | Yes | Yes | 5 per cent vote for Governor | Majority |
| Arkansas | Direct | 8 per cent of Governor vote | Yes | – | 6 per cent vote for Governor | Majority |
| California | Direct and indirect | 8 per cent of Governor vote | Yes | Yes | 5 per cent Governor vote | Majority |
| Colorado | Direct | 8 per cent of Secretary State vote | Yes | Yes | 5 per cent Secretary of State vote | Majority |
| Idaho | Direct | 10 per cent Governor vote | Yes | Yes | 10 per cent Governor vote | Majority |
| Maine | Indirect | 10 per cent Governor vote | Yes | Yes | 10 per cent Governor vote | Majority |
| Maryland | | | Yes | | 10,000 | Majority |
| Massachusetts | Indirect | 3 per cent Governor vote | Yes | – | 2 per cent Governor vote | Majority |
| Michigan | Indirect | 8 per cent Governor vote | Yes | Yes | 5 per cent Governor vote | Majority |
| Missouri | Direct | 5 per cent Governor vote | Yes | Yes | 5 per cent Governor vote | Majority |
| Montana | Direct | 8 per cent Governor vote | Yes | Yes | 5 per cent Governor vote | Majority |
| Nebraska | Direct | 7 per cent Governor vote | Yes | – | 5 per cent Governor vote | Majority |
| New Mexico | – | – | Yes | – | 10–25 per cent | Majority |
| Nevada | Indirect | 10 per cent Supreme Court vote | Yes | – | 10 per cent Supreme Court vote | Majority |
| North Dakota | Direct | 10,000 | Yes | – | 7,000 | Majority |
| Ohio | Direct and indirect | 3 per cent Governor vote | Yes | – | 6 per cent Governor vote | Majority |
| Oklahoma | Direct | 8 per cent last election | Yes | Yes | 5 per cent last election | Majority |
| Oregon | Direct | 8 per cent Supreme Court vote | Yes | Yes | 5 per cent Supreme Court vote | Majority |
| South Dakota | Indirect | 5 per cent qualified voters | Yes | – | 5 per cent qualified voters | Majority |
| Utah | Direct and indirect | 10 per cent Governor vote | Yes | – | 10 per cent Governor vote | Majority |
| Washington | Direct and indirect | 50,000 | Yes | Yes | 30,000 | Majority |

SOURCE: Council of State Governments, *The Book of the States, 1964–1965* (Chicago: Council of State Governments, 1964).

# BIBLIOGRAPHY

ABERNETHY, BYRON R. *Constitutional Limitations on the Legislature.* Lawrence: Government Research Center, University of Kansas, 1959.

BAKER, GORDON E. *Rural Versus Urban Political Power.* New York: Random House, Inc., 1955.

―――. *The Politics of Reapportionment in Washington State.* New York: Holt, Rinehart & Winston, Inc., 1960.

BOYD, WILLIAM J. D. *Patterns of Apportionment.* New York: National Municipal League, 1962.

BRECKENRIDGE, A. C. *One House for Two; Nebraska's Unicameral Legislature.* Washington, D.C.: Public Affairs Press, 1957.

BUCK, A. E. *Modernizing Our State Legislatures,* Pamphlet Series No. 4. Philadelphia: American Academy of Political and Social Science, 1936.

BURDETTE, FRANKLIN L. (ed.). *The Legislative Process in Maryland.* College Park: Bureau of Government Research, University of Maryland, 1958.

CHAMBERLAIN, J. P. *Legislative Processes: National and State.* New York: Appleton-Century-Crofts, Inc., 1936.

COUNCIL OF STATE GOVERNMENTS. *Our State Legislatures.* Chicago: Council of State Governments, 1948.

―――. *State Regulation of Lobbying.* Chicago: Council of State Governments, 1951.

―――. *American Legislatures: Structure and Procedures.* Chicago: Council of State Governments, 1955.

―――. *Legal Services for State Legislators.* Chicago: Council of State Governments, 1960.

―――. *Legislatve Reference Bureaus and Library Services.* Chicago: Council of State Governments, 1960.

FARMER, HALLIE. *The Legislative Process in Alabama.* University, Ala.: University of Alabama, 1949.

GRAVES, W. BROOKE. "Our State Legislators," *The Annals of the American Academy of Political and Social Sciences* (January, 1938). Philadelphia, Pa.: American Academy of Social & Political Science, 1938.

GUILD, FREDERIC H., and SNIDER, CLYDE F. *Legislative Procedure in Kansas.* (Governmental Research Series). Lawrence: University of Kansas, 1946.

HAMILTON, HOWARD D. *Legislative Apportionment.* New York, Evanston, and London: Harper & Row, Inc., 1964.

JANDA, D., and OTHERS. *Legislative Politics in Indiana.* Bloomington: Indiana University Bureau of Government, 1961.

JEWELL, MALCOLM E. *The Politics of Reapportionment.* New York: Atherton Press, 1962.

―――. *The State Legislature, Politics and Practice.* New York: Random House, Inc., 1962.

―――, HARVARD, WILLIAM C., and BETH, LOVEN P. *The Politics of Misrepresentation.* Baton Rouge: Louisiana University Press, 1962.

LEE, EUGENE C. *The Presiding Officer and Rules Committee in Legislatures of the United States.* Berkeley: Bureau of Public Administration, University of California, 1952.

LENHOFF, ARTHUR. *Comments, Cases and Other Materials on Legislation.* Buffalo, N.Y.: Dennis & Co., Inc., 1949.

LEWIS, HENRY. *The General Assembly of North Carolina: Guidebook of Organization and Procedure.* Chapel Hill: Institute of Government, University of North Carolina, 1951.

MCKAY, ROBERT B. *Reapportionment and the Federal Analogy.* New York: National Municipal League, 1962.

MCKEAN, D. D. *Pressures on the Legislature of New Jersey.* New York: Columbia University Press, 1938.

NATIONAL MUNICIPAL LEAGUE. *Compendium on Legislative Apportionment,* 2d ed. New York: National Municipal League, 1962.

NEUBERGER, RICHARD L. *Adventures in Politics: We Go to the Legislature.* Fair Lawn: Oxford Unversity Press, 1954.

SORAUF, FRANK J. *Party and Representation.* New York: Atherton Press, 1963.

SCHUBERT, GLENDON. *Reapportionment.* New York: Charles Scribner's Sons, 1965.

SENNING, JOHN P. *The One-House Legislature.* New York: McGraw-Hill Book Co., Inc., 1937.

SIFFIN, WILLIAM J. *The Legislative Council in the American States.* Bloomington: Indiana University Press, 1959.

SMITH, T. V. *The Legislative Way of Life.* Chicago: The University of Chicago Press, 1940.

WAHLKE, JOHN C., and EULAU HEINZ (eds.). *Legislative Behaviour: A Reader in Theory and Research.* New York: The Free Press of Glencoe, Inc., 1959.

———, ———, BUCHANAN, WILLIAM, and FERGUSON, LeRoy. *The Legislative System—Explorations in Legislative Behaviour.* New York: John Wiley & Sons, 1962.

WALKER, HARVEY. *Law Making in the United States.* New York: The Ronald Press Co., 1934.

———. *The Legislative Process.* New York: The Ronald Press Co., 1948.

WEEKS, O. DOUGLAS. *Research in the American State Legislative Process.* Ann Arbor, Mich.: J. W. Edwards Co., Inc., 1947.

WINSLOW, C. I. *State Legislative Committees.* Baltimore: Johns Hopkins Press, 1931.

ZELLER, BELLE (ed.). *American State Legislatures.* New York: Thomas Y. Crowell Co., 1954.

# 12

# The State Judiciary

Professor W. F. Willoughby declared the courts to have nine major functions:

(1) investigate and determine facts, (2) apply the law to the facts thus determined, (3) determine and construe the law, (4) prevent the infraction of the law and the violation of rights, (5) advise the legislature and the executive branch with respect to the law, (6) act as public administrative agencies, (7) administer property, (8) act as agencies to enforce decisions, and (9) determine rules of judicial procedure.[1]

The state courts attempt in one way or another to perform all nine of these activities with varying degrees of success. In the process of dispensing justice a number of important court orders are daily issued by state courts. Included in these are writs of habeas corpus, which direct a jailer to produce a prisoner in court in order to establish whether he is charged with a crime for which he shall be held; a writ of mandamus, which compels an official to perform certain duties required by law; injunctions, which restrain officials or persons from certain actions or mandatory injunctions which compel continuation of activities; subpoenas, which require the presence of an individual in court; subpoenae duces tecum, which force the production in court of documents or records; and writ of certiorari, which orders a subordinate court to send the record of a case to the higher court.

## STATE AND FEDERAL COURTS

In every state in the Union there exists a dual set of courts. Considerable confusion exists as to the relationship that the two courts have to

[1] W. F. Willoughby, *Principles of Judicial Administration* (Washington, D.C.: The Brookings Institution, 1929). chap. xvi.

each other. Many people have the mistaken impression that cases may be shuttled back and forth between the state courts and the federal courts. This ordinarily is not true. In certain types of cases litigants do have a choice between the two sets of courts.[2]

Most cases that begin in the state courts have their final hearing in that system. A few cases that involve U.S. constitutional questions may be appealed from the highest state court to the United States Supreme Court. These cases, however, are rare. There is a limited amount of removal of cases from state to federal courts and federal-court application of state law. The federal courts have exclusive jurisdiction over almost all crimes committed against the United States. In reverse, state courts have jurisdiction over crimes committed against the state, with the only major exception involving federal officials whose cases may be removed to federal courts. In the civil field it is more common for state courts to try matters that are primarily federal in nature.

When citizens of two or more states are involved in a civil matter of more than $10,000 the case is usually tried in the federal courts even though state law is involved. If the amount concerns less than $10,000 the matter is usually handled by the state courts. In a civil case involving more than $10,000, the federal court is serving as another state court for it must apply the state law to the case involved.

Court jurisdiction has one other phase that complicates the picture. A state court ordinarily has no jurisdiction outside the state. A district court or county court usually has none outside its own territorial boundaries. Court jurisdiction is also at times confined to a particular type of case. In some states a special probate court exists which has jurisdiction only over cases of wills, estates, guardianships, and similar matters.

By and large it can truthfully be said that the state courts and the federal courts work side by side in harmony with few arguments concerning jurisdiction.[3]

It should be borne in mind that state courts were organized and in operation prior to the adoption of the United States Constitution. However, no state even considered abandoning its own court system with the advent of the federal courts. It was necessary to allow only the federal courts to interpret the United States Constitution in order to have a uniform interpretation of the supreme United States document. If the state courts had been allowed to interpret the United States Constitution it would have been a limiting factor on the national powers which could not be tolerated.

[2] See Mitchell Wendell, *Relations Between the Federal and State Courts* (New York: Columbia University Press, 1950).
[3] Forrest Talbott, *Intergovernmental Relations and the Courts* (Minneapolis: University of Minnesota Press, 1950).

The parallel nature of the federal and state court systems is diagrammed
in Figure 12–1.

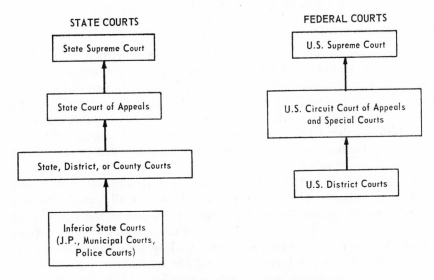

**Fig. 12–1.** Organization of State and Federal Courts.

## THE STATE COURT SYSTEMS

The state courts have the responsibility of applying the state law. This
application requires an interpretation of what the state legislature meant
by the statute. The execution of the law is the responsibility of the executive branch of the state government headed, at least in theory, by the
governor.

The courts have primarily the duty of deciding whether or not the
policy determined by the legislature is in conformity with the state and
national constitutions. If the judges of the courts determine that the state
statute or its method of execution is not in accord, they can and have the
duty of declaring the law null and void—i.e., unconstitutional.

The law has a vital role in directing and adjusting social forces in
American society. It has been properly called the mainstay of our civil
liberties. The role of the court requires the highest kind of integrity and
breadth of human knowledge on the part of those who constitute our
courts. The influence of the judiciary is so great that it is imperative
that it have at its disposal the highest type of person to fill its various
posts. A career in judicial office should offer appealing opportunities to
the young men and women of America.

The court system should be, and to a degree is, traditionally regarded as somewhat apart from the rest of our state government hierarchy.

The tone and demands of the average public sentiment in a given locality rather than the particular system through which such sentiment asserts itself ultimately determine the quality of the personnel.[4]

Three types of laws are used in America. These include public law, private law, and criminal law. Public law regulates the organization of government, the powers and duties of the various governmental agencies and their relations with private citizens. Public law is based entirely upon the formal provisions of the constitutions and legislative statutes. Private law includes that body of rules and principles which regulate the relations of individuals with each other. It has been said that private law is a combination of ruling case law and statutes.[5]

Criminal law is that branch of law which deals with offenses against the safety and order of the state. The most serious of all crimes is treason which may be against the United States or any one of the states. Most state constitutions, like the United States Constitution, defines treason while the other major crimes are determined by legislation. The state is the prosecutor in all such cases. Criminal law by tradition has always included the more serious crimes such as murder, robbery, and burglary. There are two other major divisions of criminal law: felonies and misdemeanors. Felonies involve all cases in which the penalty may be a penitentiary sentence of a year or more. Misdemeanors are crimes which are punishable by a shorter jail term or fine.

Some states still recognize common law as a part of their judicial procedure. Common law is the body of private law that judges have interpreted in the Anglo-American legal system which establishes the foundation upon which the jurisprudence of a state is based.

A few states have distinct chancery courts for equity law. Equity is a remedial branch of justice which developed alongside common law. Equity law grew out of the use of discretion and the so-called rule of reason. It is judge-made law that substitutes for common law where the remedies of common law were not adequate or where such remedies would not result in substantive justice.

## Qualifications of State Judges

In thirty-four states trial judges are required to be United States citizens, while thirty-two have the same requirement for appellate court

[4] W. S. Carpenter, *Judicial Tenure in the United States* (New Haven, Conn.: 1918), p. 212.

[5] Marshall E. Dimock and Gladys O. Dimock, *"American Government in Action"* (New York: Holt, Rinehart & Winston, Inc., 1951), p. 427.

jurists. Another basic legal requirement in approximately three-fourths of the states is residency. Both of these qualifications are probably valueless as are age minimums, which are commonly 21, 25, or 30. Seldom is an individual below the age of 30 chosen for membership on the bench. If an individual is so outstanding that he would be considered at an age of less than 30 there would seem to be no logical reason for refusing to allow him to serve. Thirty-six states have a requirement that all judges above the inferior courts, the most localized such as the justice of the peace, must be "learned in the law." This usually is construed to mean that he must be a qualified lawyer with a minimum in number of years of experience usually five but in some states as high as ten. California and Maryland have established a general requirement of "good character" while North Carolina refuses to allow anyone membership on the bench who does not believe in God.

As is obvious, the statutory or, in some instances, constitutional requirements are minimal and of dubious value. The persons who could technically qualify but who would be unsuitable for other more pertinent reasons are legion. Since a number of states have no minimum age, no citizenship, no residential, or even legal training stipulated, it is possible to maintain a court system of high merit without the legal qualifications being explicitly written down. The various qualifications for membership on state courts are cited in Table 12–1.

### TABLE 12–1

#### Qualifications of State Court Judges

| State | Citizenship L.R.° | T.C.† | Residence L.R. | T.C. | Age L.R. | T.C. | Learned in Law L.R. | T.C. | Legal Experience L.R. | T.C. |
|---|---|---|---|---|---|---|---|---|---|---|
| Alabama | x | x | 5 | 5 | 25 | 25 | x | x | – | – |
| Alaska | x | x | 3 | 3 | – | – | x | x | 8 | 5 |
| Arizona | x | x | 10 | 5 | – | 30 | x | x | 10 | 5 |
| Arkansas | x | x | 2 | 2 | 30 | 28 | x | x | 8 | 6 |
| California | x | x | 5 | 5 | 26 | 26 | x | x | 5 | 5 |
| Colorado | x | x | 2 | 2 | 30 | 30 | x | x | – | – |
| Connecticut | No legal requirements established. | | | | | | | | | |
| Delaware | x | x | | | | | x | x | | |
| Florida | x | x | | | 31 | 25 | x | x | | |
| Georgia | x | x | 3 | 3 | 30 | 30 | | x | 7 | 7 |
| Hawaii | x | x | 1 | 1 | | | x | x | 10 | 10 |
| Idaho | – | x | – | 2 | – | 30 | x | x | – | – |
| Illinois | x | x | 5 | 5 | 30 | 25 | – | – | – | – |
| Indiana | x | – | 5 | – | 30 | 21 | – | – | x | x |
| Iowa | x | x | ½ | ½ | 21 | 21 | x | x | – | – |
| Kansas | x | x | x | x | 30 | 30 | x | x | 4 | 4 |
| Kentucky | x | x | 5 | 2 | 35 | 35 | x | x | 8 | 8 |
| Louisiana | x | x | 2 | 2 | 35 | – | x | x | 10 | 5 |
| Maine | x | x | | | | | x | x | | |

## TABLE 12–1 (Continued)

| State | Citizenship L.R.* | T.C.† | Residence L.R. | T.C. | Age L.R. | T.C. | Learned in Law L.R. | T.C. | Legal Experience L.R. | T.C. |
|---|---|---|---|---|---|---|---|---|---|---|
| Maryland | x | x | 5 | 5 | 30 | 30 | x | x | – | x |
| Massachusetts | No legal requirements established. | | | | | | | | | |
| Michigan | | | | | | | x | x | | |
| Minnesota | | | | | | 21 | x | x | x | x |
| Mississippi | | | 5 | 5 | 30 | 26 | x | x | x | 5 |
| Missouri | x | x | 9 | 3 | 30 | 30 | x | x | – | – |
| Montana | x | x | 2 | 1 | 30 | 25 | x | x | – | – |
| Nebraska | x | x | 3 | 3 | 30 | 30 | – | x | – | x |
| Nevada | x | x | 5 | 5 | 25 | 25 | x | x | – | x |
| New Hampshire | No legal requirements established. | | | | | | | | | |
| New Jersey | x | x | 10 | 10 | 31 | 31 | x | x | 10 | 10 |
| New Mexico | x | x | 3 | 3 | 30 | 30 | x | x | x | 3 |
| New York | x | x | x | – | 21 | 21 | x | x | – | x |
| North Carolina | x | x | 1 | 1 | 21 | 21 | – | – | – | – |
| North Dakota | x | x | 3 | 2 | 30 | 25 | x | x | – | – |
| Ohio | – | x | x | – | – | – | x | x | 6 | x |
| Oklahoma | x | x | 2 | 2 | 30 | 25 | x | x | x | 4 |
| Oregon | x | x | 3 | 3 | 21 | 21 | x | x | – | – |
| Pennsylvania | x | x | 1 | 1 | 21 | 21 | x | x | – | – |
| Rhode Island | x | x | 2 | 2 | 21 | 21 | – | – | – | – |
| South Carolina | x | x | 5 | 5 | 26 | 26 | – | x | 5 | 5 |
| South Dakota | x | x | 2 | 1 | 30 | 25 | x | x | – | – |
| Tennessee | – | – | 5 | 5 | 35 | 30 | x | x | – | – |
| Texas | x | x | x | x | 35 | – | – | – | 10 | 4 |
| Utah | – | – | 5 | 3 | 30 | 25 | x | x | x | x |
| Vermont | x | x | x | x | – | – | – | – | x | x |
| Virginia | x | x | – | – | 21 | 21 | – | – | 5 | 5 |
| Washington | x | x | 1 | 1 | 21 | 21 | x | x | – | – |
| West Virginia | – | x | 5 | 5 | 30 | 30 | – | – | – | – |
| Wisconsin | x | x | 1 | 1 | 25 | 25 | x | x | – | – |
| Wyoming | x | x | 3 | 2 | 30 | 28 | x | x | 9 | 1 |

* "L.R." is the abbreviation for Court of Last Resort.
† "T.C." is the abbreviation for Trial Court.

SOURCE: Council of State Governments, *The Book of the States, 1964–1965* (Chicago: Council of State Governments, 1964).

## State Court Organization

Each state constitution, except New Hampshire, contains a judicial article that is the basis for the state court organization. Usually the legislature is granted considerable authority in organizing the court system below the highest court, usually known as the supreme court or sometimes referred to as the court of last resort. While there are considerable differences in the titles applied to the various levels of courts in different states the skeleton structure is basically similar in all of the fifty states.

**The Court of Last Resort.**   The capstone of the state judicial system is usually known as the state supreme court, a title obviously adopted in many states because of the federal precedent. The title "supreme court" is not borne by all of the highest state appellate courts. The supreme court in New York is actually similar to district courts in most of the states, with the final appellate jurisdiction residing in the court of appeals, which is one step above the supreme court of appeals. Kentucky and Maryland also use the New York terminology, while Connecticut designates its highest court the supreme court of errors, and Virginia and West Virginia term their highest appellate court the supreme court of appeals.

The members of the highest state court are usually selected in the same manner as that used in naming the members of the lower echelons; with nearly three-fourths of the judges of the states' highest tribunals being popularly elected, some on a straight partisan ballot but many on a so-called non-partisan elective ballot. The other states either allow the governor or the legislature to appoint. Table 12–2 lists the methods of selection, number of judges, the terms of the judges of the highest appellate courts of the fifty states, and salaries.

## TABLE 12–2

### State Courts of Last Resort

| State | Selection | Number of Members | Term | Salary |
|-------|-----------|-------------------|------|--------|
| Alabama | Popular election (P)* | 7 | 6 | $16,500 |
| Alaska | Appointed by Governor | 3 | 10 | 22,500 |
| Arizona | Popular election (N.P.)† | 5 | 6 | 19,500 |
| Arkansas | Popular election (P) | 7 | 8 | 15,000 |
| California | Appointed by Governor | 7 | 12 | 27,300 |
| Colorado | Popular election (P) | 7 | 10 | 18,000 |
| Connecticut | Legislature | 5 | 8 | 21,500 |
| Delaware | Appointed by Governor/ Civil Service | 3 | 12 | 22,000 |
| Florida | Popular election (P) | 7 | 6 | 19,500 |
| Georgia | Popular election (P) | 7 | 6 | 22,500 |
| Hawaii | Appointed by Governor/ Senate | 5 | 7 | 23,100 |
| Idaho | Popular election/N.P. | 5 | 6 | 15,000 |
| Illinois | Popular election (P) | 7 | 10 | 30,000 |
| Indiana | Popular election (P) | 5 | 6 | 20,400 |
| Iowa | Appointed by Governor | 9 | 8 | 16,000 |
| Kansas | Appointed by Governor | 7 | 6 | 16,500 |
| Kentucky | Popular election (P) | 7 | 8 | 18,000 |
| Louisiana | Popular election (P) | 7 | 14 | 22,500 |
| Maine | Appointed by Governor | 6 | 7 | 17,000 |
| Maryland | Appointed by Governor | 7 | 15 | 25,000 |
| Massachusetts | Appointed by Governor | 7 | Life | 27,000 |

## TABLE 12-2 (Continued)

| State | Selection | Number of Members | Term | Salary |
|-------|-----------|-------------------|------|--------|
| Michigan | Popular election (N.P.) | 7 | 7 | 25,500 |
| Minnesota | Popular election (N.P.) | 7 | 6 | 22,500 |
| Mississippi | Popular election (P) | 9 | 8 | 15,000 |
| Missouri | Appointed by Governor | 7 | 12 | 22,500 |
| Montana | Population election (N.P.) | 5 | 6 | 16,000 |
| Nebraska | Population election (N.P.) | 7 | 6 | 13,000 |
| Nevada | Population election (N.P.) | 3 | 6 | 20,000 |
| New Hampshire | Appointed by Governor | 5 | Until age 70 | 16,000 |
| New Jersey | Appointed by Governor | 7 | 7/Reappointed Life | 26,000 |
| New Mexico | Popular election (P) | 5 | 8 | 17,500 |
| New York | Popular election (P) | 7 | 14 | 39,000 |
| North Carolina | Popular election (P) | 7 | 8 | 21,500 |
| North Dakota | Popular election (N.P.) | 5 | 10 | 14,000 |
| Ohio | Popular election (N.P.) | 7 | 6 | 20,000 |
| Oklahoma | Popular election (P) | 9 | 6 | 16,500 |
| Oregon | Popular election (N.P.) | 7 | 6 | 19,000 |
| Pennsylvania | Popular election (P) | 7 | 21 | 32,500 |
| Rhode Island | Legislature elects | 5 | Life | 20,000 |
| South Carolina | Legislature elects | 5 | 10 | 19,500 |
| South Dakota | Popular election (N.P.) | 5 | 6 | 14,000 |
| Tennessee | Popular election (N.P.) | 5 | 8 | 20,000 |
| Texas | Popular election (P) | 9 | 6 | 20,000 |
| Utah | Popular election (N.P.) | 5 | 10 | 13,100 |
| Vermont | Legislature elects | 5 | 2 | 10,500 |
| Virginia | Legislature elects | 7 | 12 | 19,500 |
| Washington | Popular election (N.P.) | 9 | 6 | 20,000 |
| West Virginia | Popular election (P) | 5 | 12 | 19,000 |
| Wisconsin | Popular election (N.P.) | 7 | 10 | 24,000 |
| Wyoming | Popular election (N.P.) | 4 | 8 | 15,000 |

* "P" symbolizes that the election is on a partisan basis.
† "N.P." symbolizes that the election is on a non-partisan basis.

SOURCE: Council of State Governments, *The Book of the States, 1964–1965* (Chicago: Council of State Governments, 1964).

Great variation exists in the number of justices that constitute the highest state courts, ranging from only three to as many as nine. Iowa, Oklahoma, Texas, and Washington follow the precedent established for the United States Supreme Court and have a chief justice and eight associate justices. In contrast, Alaska and Delaware have only three judges on their supreme courts. Usually the supreme bench numbers either five or seven members.

Even greater variation is found in the length of term served by the judges of the highest state courts. Only two-year terms are the rule in Vermont, but the typical state that elects its judges allows six years for members of the top court. Two states, Rhode Island and Massachusetts, have followed the United States pattern and appoint judges for life tenure, while Maryland's initial appointment is for seven years with reappointment bringing life tenure. There can be seen a discernible trend toward longer terms for all state court judges but particularly for those on the highest bench.

Judges on the state supreme courts are usually paid nearly as much as the chief executive of the state. While the governor of New York receives $50,000 the judges of that state's highest court receive $36,500. Similar comparisons exist in almost every other state. There can be no question that the salaries of the judiciary are increasing. In spite of this nearly one-third of the state high court judges receive less than $15,000, but in these states the governor is likewise usually paid less than $17,000. About half of the states have elevated the supreme court salaries to the $15,000 to $20,000 range.

Career opportunities in the judiciary are now enhanced since every state has a retirement system for judges which allows them to receive annuities upon reaching retirement age. As might be expected considerable variation exists in the exact requirements that must be met, but most states establish both a minimum number of years that a judge must serve before being eligible for retirement benefits and a minimum age, usually sixty-five or higher. A few states have followed the national government precedent of awarding full salary upon retirement to the members of the supreme court, but most have established a retirement annuity or approximately 50 per cent of the salary received while on active duty. About two-thirds of the programs require the members of the judiciary to contribute to the retirement plan, but only Oklahoma allows the judges to participate in federal social security. The retirement pay received by the supreme court judges is proportionally larger than that received by the lower state court judges.

In all states except Oregon the supreme court judges may be removed from office by impeachment by the state legislature. A simplified version of impeachment is available for removing judges in thirty states, sometimes called legislative address. It involves passage by usually an extraordinary majority of a resolution directing the removal of a judge. The governor upon receipt of the legislative address resolution declares the judicial office vacant. No recourse is available to the judge so removed. Still another form of abrupt dismissal is found in Arizona, California, Colorado, Kansas, Nevada, North Dakota, Oregon, and Wisconsin, where recall by the electorate is possible. Only Alaska and Hawaii have empowered the governor to retire an incapacitated supreme court judge. The governor must in both states appoint a committee to examine the disability of the judge before he can take this action.

In New Jersey and Alaska the supreme court has removal power over judges of the lesser tribunals. New York has a complex arrangement which establishes in a court on the judiciary the power of removing lower court judges. The chief justice and the senior associate justice plus one judge from each of the four intermediate appellate court divisions constitute the court that determines removal of lower court judges.

As the state court of last resort the supreme court, or whatever its title may be, has jurisdiction over any civil cases that may be appealed to it from the lower courts in the state judicial system. Forty-eight of the state supreme courts have similar jurisdiction in all criminal cases in which the state is the prosecutor. Only Oklahoma and Texas vary from this pattern. In both states a separate criminal tribunal of three judges is the final appellate court for criminal cases. The amount of original jurisdiction is limited in virtually every state, but almost all have original jurisdiction in special types of cases. Most supreme courts, except in unusual circumstances, hear very little direct testimony. The court reviews the proceedings of the lower courts and hears any new arguments that the lawyers for the prosecution, plaintiff, or defense believe necessary.

Each of the fifty state courts of last resort records its proceedings in an annual publication usually called the supreme court reports. These annual volumes are ordinarily numbered consecutively from the time the state entered the Union. Included is the title of the case, the litigants, the majority opinion, which may be brief or lengthy, any concurring opinions, and any dissenting opinions. These decisions are printed in full.

**Intermediate Appellate Courts.**   Thirty-six states do not maintain an intermediate appellate court or courts. In the fourteen states that do provide for such a court there is considerable variation as to how many intermediate courts are maintained. In some states a single court exists, while New York maintains a number of intermediate appellate courts. The qualifications for membership on the intermediate appellate courts are usually identical with those required for the supreme court. In eleven of the fourteen states the appellate judges are popularly elected. States with intermediate appellate courts are usually the more populous states.[6] Several others are probably in need of establishing an intermediate appellate court to relieve the state supreme court's docket.

Unlike the lowest courts the intermediate appellate court has no original jurisdiction. Usually the court consists of more than one judge and the cases heard are appeals from the lower courts. Cases may be either civil or criminal. The procedure used is to hear any oral arguments and briefs from the lawyers, to review the record of the case as heard in the lower court, and then to issue a decision by a majority vote of the judges hearing the appeal.

The terms and the compensation granted to the judges on the intermediate appellate courts are usually less than those of the court of last

---

[6] These fourteen states are: Alabama, California, Florida, Georgia, Illinois, Indiana, Louisiana, Missouri, New Jersey, New York, Ohio, Pennsylvania, Tennessee, and Texas.

resort. The terms average about eight years, while the compensation is usually anywhere from $1,500 to $5,000 less than the judges on the supreme court.

**District Courts or General Trial Courts.**   The general trial courts of original jurisdiction are in existence in every state under various titles: state district or county courts; circuit courts; and superior courts. These tribunals usually serve a specific area, a single county, or in some instances, several counties. The courts which serve several counties usually hold sessions in each of the county seats. A resident clerk in each county courthouse serves as a principal agent of the court. He is often popularly elected by the residents of the area, but in other states he may be appointed by the judge or judges of the court.

The judges of the courts of original jurisdiction must in almost every instance be qualified lawyers, having practiced for at least five years. The majority are subject to popular election. The term is shorter than that of the justices in the appellate courts, frequently for only four or six years, with a range of tenure from two years to life. Like the terms, the compensation is less than that for the appellate jurists. The range is from a minimum of $8,400 per year to a maximum, in New York, of $29,000. The generalization that these jurists are paid well in comparison with other state officials is apparent.

The jurisdiction of the district courts is not exclusively original as appeals may be taken in many states from the lowest courts, the justice of the peace courts, and the municipal courts, police, mayor's courts, to the state district court. However, most of the cases are heard for the first time in this level of the state court system. Civil cases usually must involve more than $500, or in some states more than $1,000, to be accepted for trial. If a lesser amount is involved it ordinarily is heard in the inferior courts prior to review by the district courts. Criminal cases usually involve offenses that are in the felony class with a penalty of more than $100 or prison sentences of more than one year.

Decisions by the general trial courts are final as to the facts. The law is applied to the facts and the decision rendered. The defense ordinarily has a choice as to whether the case will be heard by the judge with or without a jury. Either the plaintiff or the defense may appeal the decision to the next higher level, either the appellate court, intermediate, or directly to the supreme court if no intermediate appellate court exists. The general trial court has been called the most important level of the state court system. It certainly is the unit that dispenses the greatest percentage of the justice delivered in the state courts.

**Courts of Equity.**   In most of the state court systems, criminal, civil, and equity cases are all handled by the same court and the same judge. Equity is a preventive type of justice which is usually available only when the litigant can demonstrate to the court that there is no remedy at law. The purpose is to ward off damage where it would be irreparable. The process is usually for the litigant through his attorney to present a bill to the judge stating his case and the action that he believes necessary to prevent irreparable damage. The defendant makes a written reply. The judge then considers both the bill and the defense and makes his decision as to whether or not it is necessary to issue a writ of mandamus compelling a certain action on the part of the defendant, or he may decide to issue a writ of injunction preventing the defendant from taking action. On the other hand, the judge may decide that no action is needed and that the danger of irreparable damage is a figment of the plaintiff's imagination.

In a few states a court of equity is maintained completely separate from the criminal and civil courts. The primary advantages are twofold: first, the judge is allowed to become a specialist in this field; second, the time element is often of vital importance and the equity courts are usually not clogged with cases so that a speedy remedy is forthcoming when needed. Most observers agree that equity procedure as a separate type of process has declined but is now regarded as of increasing importance in all legal procedures and can be effectively executed by the regular courts.

**The Inferior Court System.**    The lowest echelon of state courts, which in a sense are not actually state courts, is properly entitled inferior courts. Technically the lowest courts are a part of the total state judicial system even though the state may, in some instances, not even pay the salaries of the local judiciary.

**Justice of the Peace Courts.**    Since the advent of Jacksonian democracy, the thousands of justices of the peace in the United States, the very lowest level in the state judiciary, have been popularly elected. The original need served by these courts, whose jurisdiction usually does not extend beyond the county in which they are located and are even more territorially limited in some states, was to dispense justice quickly and economically. Few states require the candidate for the office of justice of the peace to have any legal training or background. The cases that he is allowed to hear are usually civil cases involving less than a hundred dollars, or slightly more in some states, and criminal cases that involve fines of $100 or less and no more than thirty days in jail. Thus most of the criminal jurisdiction is concerned with misdemeanors.

The J.P. (justice of the peace) is usually paid on a fee basis. This means that he gets a percentage of the court costs assessed in the cases that come before him. Consequently, the more cases he hears the larger are his total fees. Being popularly elected for ordinarily a two-year term, he is subject to local pressures in dispensing justice. The abbreviation for the court of J.P. has oftentimes been assumed to mean facetiously judgment for the plaintiff, as the plaintiff usually receives a favorable verdict. Speed traps are frequently operated by a joint arrangement between the justice of the peace and the local police officers. Fee splitting between the J.P. and the local police who bring traffic cases to him is not unknown. Tourists passing through a community are the common targets for these operations.

For more than twenty years the American Bar Association has been condemning the justice of the peace system as it operates in almost every state in the nation. In spite of the low prestige associated with the J.P. court it still continues to be the bar of justice faced by more people in America than any other judicial tribunal.

Seldom is the J.P. court one of record. No transcript is kept of the proceedings. In some instances the reporting of the cases heard is so haphazard that no one even has a record of the number of cases heard and the decisions rendered.

The situation has degenerated to such a low point that some states, including Missouri and New Jersey, have abolished the justice of the peace court. Many other states, including Virginia and Maryland, are making modifications. Other states are examining their J.P. courts and contemplating what action to take to accomplish the purposes originally served by this level of the judiciary. The answer to the problem is probably some system similar to that established in Connecticut whereby a state circuit court system with multiple full-time, qualified judges takes over the jurisdiction formerly vested in the justice of the peace courts. It does not seem feasible to attempt to educate the justices of the peace who are now in office. Almost every student of judicial administration condemns the J.P. system. A few justices are probably badly maligned by this indictment, but they work under such handicaps and are apparently so few in number that the system is beyond redemption and must be abolished and replaced by a unified state court judiciary.[7]

The counterpart in the urban areas to the justice of the peace courts that serve the rural areas of America is usually called a magistrate or police court. Other titles borne by this group of courts include mayor's court, municipal court, small claims court, traffic court, night court, family court, and juvenile court. On the whole, these inferior courts are as unsatisfactory as the justice courts. Too frequently the judges are not qualified in the law. Usually they are popularly elected and frequently they depend upon fees rather than upon salaries for their compensation.

[7] W. Brooke Graves, *American State Government* (4th ed.; New York: D. C. Heath Co., 1950), chap. xvii, for one of the most concise denunciations of the justice of the peace system.

The problem is actually more acute in many cities than in the J.P. courts because of the volume of court cases that are annually heard. In the largest cities, for example in Chicago, as many as 50,000 cases a year may be on the docket. A recent newspaper report stated that the municipal courts in that city were approximately two years behind. This would mean that a wait of two years would almost inevitably occur before a case would come before the municipal judge following the charges being filed. However, the vast majority of these cases are civil rather than criminal.

The jurisdiction of the magistrate or police and municipal courts is nearly as restricted as that of the justice of the peace. Territorially it may include the county in which the court is located. In civil cases only matters involving a few hundred dollars are allowed. Criminal cases usually involve fines of less than $100 and jail terms of thirty days or less. However, it must be pointed out that tremendous variations exist in the jurisdiction allowed by the different states.

**The Jury System.**    Criminal law in the United States is based upon the premise that a person is presumed to be innocent until he is proved guilty, usually to the satisfaction of a jury of his peers. Trial by jury has long been regarded as a necessary safeguard of justice. In most states the jury in criminal cases is composed of twelve people. It is impanelled under procedures that vary according to the laws of the states. The list of people called for jury service is usually compiled from the voters in recent elections. However, in many states the list of people that are automatically exempt is becoming increasingly long. Typically and naturally all federal, state, county, and municipal officials are exempt. Likewise for logical reasons all judges and lawyers are barred from jury duty, but usually almost all other professional groups are likewise excused, including physicians, dentists, ministers, educators, and public utility personnel. Members of the national guard and volunteers of fire departments in many states are also excluded. From the list that remains after the exemptions are made a jury is impanelled. They are summoned, examined, and the required number seated to serve in both civil and criminal cases.

Before a criminal case reaches a trial jury an indictment must have been attained by the state prosecutor. This occurs in all states by grand jury indictment. The grand jury is a group of citizens selected in much the same way as the trial jury and hears the evidence presented by the prosecutor, and if they render a "true bill" they have concluded that the evidence in their opinion warrants prosecution. What they have said is that they believe there is sufficient grounds to indicate that the accused may have committed the crime for which he is charged. Indictment in about one-fourth of the states may be by information. This is a newer process which allows the prosecutor to present his evidence to a judge and obtain an indictment without the services of the grand jury. In some states indictment may be only by grand jury. A governor may refuse to extradite a man to another state if the state seeking the extradition has used the information procedure which is not recognized in the state holding the accused. The governor of Missouri refused to extradite a man accused of murder in Iowa until the Iowa authorities got an indictment by grand jury rather than by information, since Missouri did not use or recognize information indictments.

The jury must be an impartial body with either side in both a criminal or civil case having the right to challenge any person drawn as a juryman if his impartiality is in question. In civil cases the plaintiff states his case and the defendant replies. When all of the evidence has been presented the judge instructs the jury as to the rules of evidence, the law applying to the case, and the duties and power of the jury. The jury then is said to take the case for decision and after due deliberation returns its verdict. If the jury cannot agree upon a verdict, a hung jury is said to have occurred, and a new trial is ordinarily ordered by the presiding judge.

The procedure in criminal cases is much the same. The prosecution, the state, presents its case after the jury has been sworn. The counsel for the defense follows. After the closing arguments by both sides the judge instructs the jury. The jury then goes into seclusion and returns with its verdict. If the verdict is innocent the accused is freed. If the verdict is guilty it is in most states the duty of the judge to pass sentence upon the defendant. This in most jurisdictions may be resisted by a motion upon the part of the defense for a new trial. If overruled, the prisoner is sentenced and the sentence carried out by the duly constituted authorities. If the defendant's motion for a new trial is denied, he may appeal to a higher court if any illegality in the proceedings is alleged. This appeal may be allowed or it may be denied depending upon the decision of the higher court after hearing the petition.

**Judicial Administration.** In addition to the increasing use of judicial councils and the establishment of administrative offices, states have been using more and more judicial conferences. The judicial conference is a formal meeting of jurists for the purposes of discussing matters of concern, making rules and recommendations designed to facilitate the administration of justice.

Among the national groups that are organized for the purpose of improving state judicial procedures are: The Conference of Chief Justices, which holds annual meetings devoted to varied aspects of judicial administration; National Association of Attorneys General, which annually meets to discuss various problems confronting the states' chief prosecuting officers; The National Conference of Court Administrative Officers, which has worked on such problems as costs of jury trials and general problems of judicial administration; The National Conference of State Trial Judges, which attempts to work for court reforms and reorganization of the regular trial courts of the states; and The National Association of Municipal Judges, which centers its attention on the multitude of problems of the more localized courts of justice. These groups working with the various committees of the American Bar Association, particularly the Section of Judicial Administration, seek to promote more effective administration of justice in the United States.

Some type of office to assist in the administrative operations of the state court system has been established in twenty-six states. The title, the authority, and the budget allocated to the administrative office varies. In some of the states it is questionable whether or not it is a true court administrative office. In several, such as Missouri and North Dakota, it is merely a part of the judicial council which performs some of the functions ordinarily executed by court administrative officers. The role of the administrative office is usually limited to the so-called housekeeping functions of the court. These include budget preparation, purchasing supplies, preparing payrolls, accounting for funds, and keeping of statistics concerning the case loads of the various divisions of the state court system.

## Criticisms of the State Court Systems

The state courts have been under attack nearly all of this century. The first nationally proclaimed indictment came in 1906 when Roscoe Pound, at the time a young lawyer from Nebraska, leveled an attack upon the entire state court system before the American Bar Association. While Mr. Pound's attack did not result in any immediate action, it certainly must be credited with arousing speculation as to whether or not justice, and particularly prompt justice, was resulting from the state court systems. Many defects have been constantly pointed out by scholars of the American judicial process.

Probably the most frequent criticism has been of the minor courts in the state systems. The justice of the peace court with its lack of trained judges and the fee system has been scrutinized by many state legislative committees and state bar associations.

The popular election of judges is a second major cause of criticism of the state courts. The major role of the courts is to interpret and to apply the law. Too frequently election of judges results in a popular political figure being placed on the bench but not a man who is really qualified to interpret the laws of the state. A better method of selecting members of the state supreme court, circuit courts, appellate courts, county courts, and inferior courts must be found. Many states are trying appointive methods. Some follow the federal government's plan of appointment by the chief executive with confirmation by the senate. Others are establishing judicial commissions that submit a list of qualified persons to the governor from which he must make his judicial appointments.[8]

A third defect in the state courts that has become increasingly apparent is the jury system. Many factors make it almost impossible to get competent jurors. Even when the juries are of high caliber, the increasingly technical details of the law have made it difficult for them to understand the cases that are presented. The rule followed almost universally of unanimous jury decisions makes a single juror disproportionately powerful. The use of usually twelve jurors has also caused difficulty in obtaining true justice in many trials. Many states are now allowing a defendant to waive the right to a jury trial. Forty states have made this provision in misdemeanor cases and nearly one-third allow it in cases of felonies.

Another defect that needs attention is the short terms given to many of the judges. Too frequently a judge is on the bench only for two or four years and then finds, after having learned "the profession," that he is replaced, either because he has lost a political election or has failed to be reappointed because of a switch in the political affiliation of the appointive authority. Many qualified lawyers refuse to consider positions on the bench because of the short tenures of judges in many states. Fortunately, the trend is toward longer terms. Several states, including New Jersey and Massachusetts, are now providing for life appointments. In New Jersey this is true only after a probationary period has been passed. Other states are gradually changing from two- and four-year terms to six, eight, and twelve years.

A fifth major criticism is that the state courts are too often decentralized and therefore inefficient. No one person has the responsibility for supervising the various levels of the court system. Each judge is a king with his own empire. As a result, some courts have crowded dockets while others at the same level in the system have few cases to be heard. Similarly, no one individual is charged with constantly studying the court procedures to keep them up-to-date. New methods of executing courtroom procedure need to be implemented. A lack of statistical studies of the state court system is still a major deficiency in some states.

---

[8] Iowa's Constitution of 1857 was amended in 1962 with this provision for naming judges at both the supreme court and district court levels.

A sixth criticism is that litigation is so very costly that it is financially impossible for many persons of limited means to take their cases into court. This includes the high cost of lawyer fees and the time involved in getting a case into court in many states. Court procedure is so technical that lawyers desiring to win rather than seeking justice may use the court rules to delay a case. A few states have established a companion office to that of the prosecutor—a public defender—under the theory that the state is interested in seeing that justice is rendered—not merely in the number of convictions. Other states allow the judge to name a court-appointed attorney to work with the defendant if he is unable to afford a lawyer.

A seventh charge against the state judicial process concerns the ever increasing number of appealed cases that are allowed. This is a serious problem and one that must be weighed carefully. Some writers contend that "even a somewhat unjust decision may be preferred to uncertainty and delay."[9] This statement, of course, hinges on the phrase "somewhat unjust." Many would hesitate to reduce the number of appeals and the opportunity for appeal if it would in any way deny a "just decision" in even one case. It is probably true that there are many cases in which appeals are allowed that are unwarranted.

## Judicial Reorganization and Reform

The American Bar Association in 1909 reported:

. . . at least for civil cases, the entire judicial power of each state should be vested in one great court, of which all tribunals should be branches, departments or divisions. The business, as well as the judicial administration, of this court should be thoroughly organized so as to prevent not merely waste of judicial power, but all needless clerical work, duplication of papers and records, and the like, thus obviating unnecessary expense to litigants and cost to the public.[10]

In spite of this forthright position taken more than half a century ago, reform and reorganization of the state courts have been appallingly slow. However the movement continues to grow. As the 1962–1963 edition of *The Book of the States* notes:

In state after state, members of the bench, the bar and the general public are showing increased concern about the status of the administration of justice in their states. The congestion of court dockets and the consequent delays in securing trial of cases, particularly noticeable in metropolitan areas, are under increasing attack as evidenced by the growing use of the phrase, "justice delayed is justice denied." Even where these conditions do not exist, there is recognition

[9] William Anderson, Clara Penniman, and Edward W. Weidner, *Government in the Fifty States* (New York: Holt, Rinehart, & Winston, Inc., 1960), p. 293.

[10] *American Bar Association Reports*, 1909.

that continued effective administration of justice may require changes in court structure and organization, selection and compensation of judges, rules and practice and procedure, and other aspects of the judicial system.[11]

Advances have been made in various states on different phases of the court reorganization and reform question. In 1960 Arizona voters approved a constitutional amendment which provides for an integrated judicial system for the entire state. All courts are placed under the direction of the chief justice, with a director to assist the chief justice in all administrative duties. A similar sweeping change was approved in Wisconsin. Illinois voters in the fall of 1962 voted in favor of a constitutional amendment which provides for an integrated court system, comprising the supreme court, an intermediate appellate court, a circuit court, and magistrates with most specialized courts abolished.

Maine completely revised its minor court system in 1961. A district court system with full-time judges replaced the part-time municipal judges. North Carolina voters decided in 1962 to abolish all inferior courts and to establish a supreme court, superior court, and district courts, with the chief justice in charge of the entire system.

Several states, including Iowa and Nebraska, have joined Missouri, California, New Jersey, and Alaska in changing the mode of selecting judges: a key part of the over-all effort to improve the administration of justice. The trend is toward a system which attempts to combine the good points of popular election and appointment. The Iowa system, copied after the Missouri plan, is typical of this new method. Supreme court judges are appointed by the governor from a list submitted to him by a judicial commission, composed of equal numbers of laymen and members of the bar with the senior justice on the supreme court serving as chairman. The appointee serves for at least eight years, but is subject to a vote of the people after serving one year. One year before the end of his first term he again must submit to a vote of the people as to whether or not he should continue on the bench. If the voters approve of the judge's conduct of his office he continues to serve. If they vote him out of office the judicial commission submits a new list of names to the governor. The same method of appointment and popular election or confirmation is used in the Iowa district courts.[12] In Nebraska the same general plan prevails with modifications as to the length of time the judges serve before the popular vote is required.

Another important factor is the recognition in many states during the last ten years of the need for increasing the compensation given to the members of the judiciary. There have been notable advances in most

[11] Council of State Governments, *The Book of the States, 1962–1963* (Chicago: Council of State Governments, 1962), p. 117.
[12] *Amendment of 1962, Constitution of Iowa.*

states, bringing the level of judicial salaries to a point that makes a judgeship almost as lucrative as a good law practice. This is proof that state governments are realizing that low salaries may deter able lawyers from seeking or accepting judicial positions. It is obvious to nearly everyone that the judicial administration can be no better than the personnel that executes the system.

Another aspect of judicial reform that is progressing in many states involves the revision of rules of practice and procedure. Kentucky, Colorado, Michigan, Illinois, and Kansas have been among the states revising their rules of procedure. Kentucky adopted new rules in 1960, designed to reduce the cost of appeals. Illinois adopted a new criminal code, and Kansas revised its rules of civil procedure.[13]

Another feature that is being adopted by many states is improved retirement programs for judges. Retirement benefits have been increased in many states and extended to widows and other dependents of judges. Constitutional amendments within the last four years in Louisiana and Oregon are illustrative of the trends. Louisiana increased retirement allowances of judges from two-thirds to full salary. Oregon established a mandatory retirement age of seventy-five which may be reduced by the legislature to seventy. Iowa's new judicial reform amendment requires the legislature to establish a mandatory retirement age for judges which has been established at seventy-two.

The members of the legal profession are officially officers of the court along with the judges and the members of his staff. It is their responsibility in criminal cases to assure every accused person adequate legal counsel. Probably a majority of the members of the legal profession avoid criminal law practice, and as a result the average legal counsel in criminal cases falls short of the standards maintained in civil actions.[14]

More than half of the fifty states now have what is called an integrated bar. This merely means that no longer in states that have statutes requiring an integrated bar is membership in the state bar association on a voluntary basis. All attorneys who practice before the courts of the state must be members and must comply with the rules and regulations that are promulgated by the bar association. It is claimed that the integrated bar movement in the states where it has been accepted has elevated the standards and ethics of the legal profession and materially aided in the assurance of justice for all.

Another movement still in its infancy on a nationwide basis is the legal aid society. This is a movement that attempts to assure that each person

[13] Council of State Governments, *The Book of The States, 1962–1963* (Chicago: Council of State Governments, 1962), pp. 120–21.
[14] Robert B. Storey, "The Legal Profession and Criminal Justice," *Journal of the American Judicature Society,* Vol. XXXVI (April, 1953), p. 166.

in need of legal counsel even on small matters will be able to afford this technical assistance. In the larger cities the need has been the greatest, and it is in these areas that most of the momentum has been developed.

## JUDICIAL REVIEW

An important function of the state courts is to check the legislative and executive branches of government. They perform their part of the sacred American check and balance system by first determining the meaning of legislative acts when cases come before them; second, by passing on the legality of executive actions; and third, by determining whether statutes and administrative acts are constitutional, more commonly termed the courts' power of judicial review.

National or federal judicial review was established as a basic part of the American system in the decision of *Marbury v. Madison*, 1803, when the United States Supreme Court declared for the first time an act of Congress unconstitutional.[15] While this power of federal judicial nullification is not based on a specific section of the United States Constitution, the authority of the federal judiciary to declare state acts unconstitutional if in conflict with the federal statutes is founded on Article VI of the United States supreme law.

State judicial review is the power of state courts to declare unconstitutional any state statute or state administrative action that is in conflict with the state constitution. While it is technically possible for any state court of record to declare a state law null and void if it finds it to be at variance with the state constitution, ultimately the power is vested in the state court of last resort.

In most states a majority of the court is all that is required to nullify a statute if conflict is shown. However, in a few states, including Nebraska, North Dakota, and Ohio, an extraordinary majority is necessary on exercise of judicial review.

The federal courts have only declared slightly more than eighty acts passed by Congress and administrative orders unconstitutional in the more than one hundred and sixty years the power has been exercised by the United States Supreme Court. The federal courts have been equally prudent since less than nine hundred state statutes have been nullified by judicial actions. State courts have struck down a much larger proportion of state laws on the grounds of conflict with the state constitution. Hardly a year passes without judicial nullification being used to strike down nearly a hundred state laws. No complete count of the exact number has ever been compiled.

[15] *1 Cranch 137*, 1803.

## JUDICIAL ADVISORY OPINIONS

In forty states the judiciary is not authorized to issue advisory opinions. In the remaining ten states the courts may be called upon to issue advisory opinions, but only in Colorado do they have the legal force of a supreme court opinion. Usually if advisory opinions are authorized they are available upon the request of either the governor or the state legislature, but in Florida and South Dakota only the governor may request such opinions.

The device has some merits, but the weight of opinion seems to be that this is a proper function of the attorney general and should not be an added burden upon an already overworked court system. In all probability the attorney general's opinions serve the same purpose as would judicial advisory opinions unless the Colorado practice were followed. Advisory opinions regardless of their source are primarily guides to be followed until the final ruling is made by court decisions. They can be useful in avoiding actions that may prove to be embarrassing because of later declarations of unconstitutionality.

## DECLARATORY JUDGMENTS

While advisory opinions have not been regarded as highly useful adjuncts to judicial administration, the declaratory judgment has been actively supported. At the present time nearly all states by statutory enactment have permitted state courts to render declaratory judgments.[16] The declaratory judgment differs from a regular lawsuit in that the plaintiff does not need to allege an actual or impending legal wrong. There of course must be an actual controversy involved in order for the court to rule on the legal rights of the parties. The declaratory judgment thus saves time and expense by preventing injury and costs that would be brought about by a formal lawsuit.

Only since 1934 has the Federal Declaratory Judgement Act made it possible for similar actions at the federal court level. Several state courts were employing this device prior to this action by the national government. The language of the national statute is similar to that found in most of the states. Since it is available to all citizens and not restricted to the chief executive of the state and the legislature, it has been a step forward in administration of justice for the average person rather than merely for governmental officials, as in the case of the advisory opinion.

[16] Walter H. Anderson, *Actions for Declaratory Judgements* (Atlanta, Ga.: Harrison Co., 1951), Vol. III, pp. 1805–46.

## CONCILIATION AND ARBITRATION

The state courts in most states act in two other capacities: as agents of conciliation and as arbiters in arbitration actions. Conciliation is the process by which a third party attempts to secure an agreement between two parties for the settlement of the controversy. The rules are informal and no verbatim record of the procedure is kept. The court usually acts as the host for the meetings, and the judge may be the actual third party who attempts to negotiate the agreement. It should be noted that the third party's suggestions as to a proper settlement of the dispute are not binding upon either party involved. In some of the integrated court systems a special conciliation court is established, but in the non-integrated courts the regular trial judges are forced to act in the role of conciliators.

In contrast, arbitration requires the two parties in the dispute to accept as firm and binding the decision of the third party, the court, as to the proper disposition of the controversy. Only a few states make it mandatory for the parties involved to arbitrate a dispute.[17] Probably the most famous and definitive statement on this subject is that of Jerome Frank who wrote:

. . . because of the difficulties of precise ascertainment by a court of the actual past facts out of which their dispute arose, it may well be that the best mode of settling it is not a court decision in a law-suit but arbitration. . . .[18]

### State Judicial Councils

Ohio, in 1923, established the first judicial council, although Wisconsin, in 1913, and Massachusetts, in 1919, had agencies of a somewhat similar nature. Only Alaska and California have judicial councils established by constitutional decree. The other thirty-eight are statutory agencies, but in at least ten states they must be listed as inoperative at the present time.

The typical judicial council numbers about twelve members. Its membership includes laymen, judges, lawyers, legislators, and a representative of the state's attorney general office. The function assigned is usually to inquire into the organizational and procedural problems of the state judicial system. Some have been given authority to prepare judicial rules of procedure. In Ohio, the judicial council is authorized to hold public hearings, administer oaths, require attendance of witnesses, and the presentation of documentary materials. The clerks of all the courts in Ohio

---

[17] Clarence N. Callender, *American Courts* (New York: McGraw-Hill Book Co., Inc., 1927), chap. xiv.

[18] Jerome Frank, *Courts on Trial: Myth and Reality in American Justice* (Princeton: Princeton University Press, 1949), p. 377.

are required to submit to the council various reports so that a constant study of the court dockets may be made.[19]

There can be no question as to the desirability of the work performed by most judicial councils. The ten inoperative councils should be reactivated and the ten states that do not use this administrative tool probably should give attention to the creation of a council.

## JUDICIAL REFORMS

A group of prominent Americans of diverse interests and pursuits met in 1965 to examine the judicial systems operating in the United States. The group, under the auspices of the American Assembly of Columbia University, adopted eighteen recommendations which are vital if the civil and criminal trial courts are to be improved. The recommendations, most of them basic legal reforms, can be achieved only by political action in the state legislatures and at the polls. The eighteen are:

1. A state-wide unified court system should be adopted in every state, with effective administrative management to coordinate and supervise judicial business and all related aspects of law administration.

2. A plan of merit judicial selection and tenure should be adopted in every state and made applicable to the selection of all judges, from judges of the courts of last resort to and including the magistrates in lower criminal courts, small claims courts, and the like.

3. Until the enactment of merit judicial selection, state and municipal executives should follow the procedures of the merit selection plan in exercising their appointing powers.

4. Effective judicial performance requires continuing in-service training, particularly for new judges.

5. Judges must be drawn from the more competent members of the legal profession. Judicial salaries and retirement benefits must be made sufficient to enable a person to make a life career of judicial service.

6. Trial judges should be subject to mandatory retirement by age seventy, but should remain subject to call, when needed for judicial work.

7. Cumbersome procedures, e.g., impeachment, should be supplemented by effective machinery for the investigation of complaints against judges and for the removal of those found unfit or guilty of misconduct in office.

8. Provisions should be adopted to keep trial judgeships in line with continuing increases in population.

[19] Francis Aumann and Harvey Walker, *The Government and Administration of Ohio* (New York: Thomas Y. Crowell Co., 1956), p. 197.

9. In most of the great cities of the United States the number of judges now sitting in the lower criminal courts is grossly inadequate and should be increased.

10. Action should be taken to provide effective assistance of counsel to all indigent persons accused of felonies or serious misdemeanors. A tax supported professional public defender office should be created in all judicial areas.

11. Substantial increases should be made to support financially the police and prosecution agencies, and probation and parole services to equip them to handle the heavy burden of effective and fair law enforcement.

12. The existing bail system should be drastically modified. Accused persons should not be held in detention pending determination of charges against them merely for lack of funds to raise bail.

13. Alcoholics and persons addicted to narcotics should not be processed through regular criminal channels but should be committed by court order for necessary medical and psychiatric treatment under court supervision.

14. Minor acts of misconduct, e.g., traffic offenses, should, whenever possible, not be handled by criminal sanctions, but by the employment of administrative penalties with simplified procedures.

15. New measures must be devised to assure prompt relief to the thousands of automobile victims and to reduce court delays caused by the press of personal injury litigation.

16. In civil cases the right of trial by jury should ordinarily be retained, although there is a need for reform in the administration of the jury system.

17. The judicial manpower should be increased to speed up consideration of civil cases.

18. Citizens' committees on the courts should be established in all parts of the country to enlist the informed and active support of the public in the cause of judicial reform.[20]

## BIBLIOGRAPHY

ABRAHAM, HENRY J. *The Judicial Process.* Fair Lawn, N.J.: Oxford University Press, 1962.

BALDWIN, SIMEON E. *The American Judiciary.* New York: Appleton-Century-Crofts, Inc., 1905.

BORCHARD, EDWIN M. *Declaratory Judgements.* Cleveland: Banks-Baldwin Law Publishing Co., 1935.

[20] The American Assembly of Columbia University, *The Courts, The Public, and the Law Explosion* (Englewood Cliffs, N.J.: Prentice-Hall, Inc.), 1965.

BRUCE, ANDREW A. *The American Judge.* New York: The Macmillan Co., 1924.

CALLENDER, CLARENCE N. *American Courts: Their Organization and Procedure.* New York: McGraw-Hill Book Co., Inc., 1927.

COUNCIL OF STATE GOVERNMENTS. *Trial Courts of General Jurisdiction in the Forty-eight States,* Rev. ed. Chicago: Council of State Governments, 1956.

————. *State Court Systems.* Chicago: Council of State Governments, 1962.

ERVIN, SPENCER. *The Magstrates' Courts in Philadelphia.* Philadelphia: Thomas Skelton, Harrison Foundation, 1931.

FELLMAN, DAVID. *The Defendant's Rights.* New York: Holt, Rinehart & Winston, Inc., 1958.

FRANK, JEROME. *Courts on Trial: Myth & Reality in American Justice.* Princeton: Princeton University Press, 1949.

HANNAN, WILLIAM E., and CSONTOS, MILDRED B. *State Court Systems.* Council of State Governments, Chicago: 1940.

HAYNES, EVAN. *The Selection and Tenure of Judges.* Newark, N.J.: National Conference of Judicial Councils, 1944.

JACOB, HERBERT. *Justice in America.* Boston: Little, Brown & Co., 1965.

KEENEY, BARNABY C. *Judgement by Peers.* Cambridge: Harvard University Press, 1949.

LEPAWSKY, ALBERT. *The Judicial System of Metropolitan Chicago.* Chicago: The University of Chicago Press, 1932.

LITKE, WILLIAM W. *Survey of the Minor Judiciary in Pennsylvania.* University Park, Pa.: Pennsylvania State University, Municipal Publications Service, 1942.

LUMMUS, HENRY T. *The Trial Judge.* Brooklyn: Foundation Press, Inc., 1937.

MAYERS, LEWIS. *The American Legal System.* New York: Harper & Row, Inc., 1955.

MITCHELL, WENDELL. *Relations Between the Federal and State Courts.* New York: Columbia University Press, 1950.

MOLEY, RAYMOND. *Our Criminal Courts.* New York: G. P. Putnam's Sons, Inc., 1930.

MURPHY, WALTER F., and PRITCHETT, C. HERMAN. *Courts, Judges and Politics.* Chicago: Random House, Inc., 1961.

ORFIELD, L. B. *Criminal Appeals in America.* Boston: Little, Brown & Co., 1939.

PELTASON, JACK W. *Missouri Plan for the Selection of Judges.* Columbia: University of Missouri, 1945.

VANDERBILT, ARTHUR T. *Judges and Jurors: Their Functions, Qualifications and Selection.* Boston: Boston University Press, 1956.

———— (ed.). *Minimum Standards of Judicial Administration.* New York: Law Center of New York University, 1949.

VINES, KENNETH N., and JACOB, HERBERT. *Studies in Judicial Politics.* ("Tulane Studies in Political Science"). New Orleans: Tulane University, 1962.

WARREN, EARL, BLACK, HUGO L., DOUGLAS, WILLIAM O., and BRENNAN, WILLIAM J., JR. *The Great Rights.* New York: The Macmillan Co., 1963.

WARREN, GEORGE. *Traffic Courts.* Boston: Little, Brown & Co., 1942.

WILLOUGHBY, W. F. *Principles of Judicial Administration.* Washington, D.C.: The Brookings Institution, 1929.

ZEISEL, HANS, KALVEN, HARRY, JR., and BUCHHOLZ, BERNARD. *Delay in the Court.* Boston: Little, Brown & Co., 1959.

# 13

# The Governor

Woodrow Wilson stated that:

The Governor is not *the* executive; he is but a single piece of the executive. There are other pieces coordinated with him over which he has not direct official control, and which are of less dignity than he only because they have no power to control legislation, as he may do by his veto, and because his position is more representative perhaps of the state government as a whole, of the people of the state as a unit. Indeed it may be doubted whether the Governor and other principal officers of the state can even when taken together be correctly described as *the* executive, since the actual execution of the laws do not rest with them but with the local officers chosen by the towns and counties and bound to the central authorities of the state by no real bonds of responsibility whatsoever.[1]

In many of the states the Wilson statement is as true today as it was at the beginning of the twentieth century. However, in others there has been a great change in the relative power and importance of the position of the state chief executive.

The people framing the earliest state constitutions had a great fear of centralized power and particularly of powerful governorships. This was a natural result of the frequent tyrannies that had occurred under the royal governors during the early colonial period. Thus the position began as a mere figurehead with virtually no power. The governor was a ceremonial head with little to do other than preside at public ceremonies and occupy the governor's office in the state capitol. The supremacy of the legislative branch in the nineteenth century was undisputed. During almost all of this period there was in most states a continual movement to make the governor independent of the legislative branch. But by the end of the century legislative dominance was still present in most states.

[1] Woodrow Wilson, *State and Federal Governments of the United States* (Boston: D. C. Heath & Co., 1889), p. 69.

One of the best observations of the relative position occupied by the governors in relationship to the state legislatures of the nineteenth century was made by de Tocqueville:

In America the legislature of each state is supreme; nothing can impede its authority. . . . Its own determination is . . . the only limit to its action. . . . In juxtaposition with it, and under its immediate control, is the representative of the executive power, whose duty it is to constrain the refractory to submit by superior force. The legislative bodies daily encroach upon the authority of the governor and their tendency . . . is to appropriate it entirely to themselves.[2]

The year 1917 marked a major turning point in the role of the governor's office. Frank O. Lowden of Illinois was able in that year to persuade the state legislature to enact the first genuine program for state administrative reorganization and the elevation of the post of governor. While not all of the fifty governorships have been made the chief executive in fact as well as in name many have become offices of not only honor but of power.

Prior to 1917 the men who achieved the position of governor found that this was frequently the end of their political careers. They retired from public life and still were called "Governor" by their friends but had little if any real influence on federal, state, or local affairs. Recent studies have shown that with increased power the office has not only attracted more dynamic and forceful individuals, but also has been utilized as a stepping-stone to other political positions. A more-or-less normal route in many states has been established from the governorship to the United States Senate with as many as one-third of the Senators being former governors.[3]

Samuel R. Solomon's study also reveals a trend toward the election of younger men to the states' chief executive position. Only 21 of the 157 governors in the group surveyed were more than 60 when first elected. During the 1940's the median age was 51, while in the decade from 1950 to 1960 the average beginning age was 47. In the latter period 24 governors began their terms while less than 40 years of age, while only 10 became governor in their 30's between 1940 and 1950. More than half of the 157 men elected governor of a state during the twenty year period under examination were lawyers, while the teaching profession interestingly furnished the second largest number of successful candidates.

Between 1868 and 1952 every United States President elected to two terms had served as a state governor before becoming President. In-

[2] Alexis de Tocqueville, *Democracy in America* (New York: Appleton-Century-Crofts, Inc., 1898), pp. 110–12.

[3] Samuel R. Solomon, "American Governors Since 1915," *National Municipal Review* (March, 1931), pp. 152–58.

cluded in the list of state governors who went on to serve as the chief executive of the United States are: Franklin D. Roosevelt, Calvin Coolidge, Warren G. Harding, Woodrow Wilson, Theodore Roosevelt, William McKinley, Grover Cleveland, Rutherford B. Hayes, James K. Polk, John Tyler, Martin Van Buren, and Thomas Jefferson. Some of these men were among the most successful Presidents while others were less dynamic leaders.

Since 1960, however, no former governor has been nominated for the presidency by either major party, as both parties have centered upon members of the United States Senate for their nominees. Many governors have expected to continue their political careers after their tenure in the state capitol as a United States Senator, but many have found an incumbent, often a former governor himself, that desired to continue in the Senate. Some state chief executives, upon completion of their terms, have become members of the administrative branch of the federal government. Some have been successful members of President's cabinets, while others have held other high level administrative positions.

A few state governors have been named to the federal judiciary. Among the men who have served in both capacities are Earl Warren, Charles Evans Hughes, and James F. Byrnes.

The powers and prestige of governorships in most states are still being increased. The leadership, administrative powers, and political prestige are still in ascendancy in the 1960's. Virtually every state governmental reorganization has witnessed a greater amount of centralization of power in the governor. Even with this increased importance, many governors find that their powers are still much more limited by constitutional and legal restrictions than may be desirable for most efficient administrative and executive action. The average man on the street has little concept of these restrictions. He thinks of the governor as being able to do almost anything that is within the prerogative of the state government. He is frequently held accountable for governmental action or inaction over which he has no control. The statement has been made that the office of governor in a typical American state is one of the least understood offices in the entire governmental structure. The requests made by the constituents upon the fifty governors cover the entire range of governmental activities. Frequently they are called upon to change the state and federal laws since the average citizen does not realize the true role of the state's chief executive. One of the greatest problems facing almost every state governor is the insufficient time available to perform all of the duties associated with the position. Repeatedly, governors have complained that the job has so many aspects that two or more men are needed to fulfill all of the commitments that the chief executive is called upon to make in any one day, week, and year.

The powers, responsibilities, and duties can be classified into certain major categories: executive and administrative, legislative, judicial, military, political, and ceremonial. Each of these classifications must be considered not independently but as an integral part of the position of chief executive in an American state.

## GENERAL CHARACTERISTICS OF THE OFFICE

It is necessary to discuss the general characteristics of the office before consideration can intelligently be made of its powers and duties. These include the qualifications needed by a governor, both legal and political, the method of nomination and election, length of term, compensation, removal from office, and succession to the governorship as established in the fifty states.

### Legal Qualifications

All of the fifty states require that any person seeking the office of governor must be a United States citizen. In some states the constitution specifically denotes this prerequisite while in others the candidate must be a qualified elector. Only Maine stipulates that the citizenship must be attained by being a natural born United States citizen—a statement drawn from the United States Constitution's requirement for eligibility to the office of President. A great amount of variation exists as to the length of residence within a state required of gubernatorial candidates. The extremes are from two years to twenty years. About one-fourth of the state constitutions call for between five and ten years of residency with six specifying seven years. Hawaii and Missouri follow the United States Constitution's lead in requiring that their governors, like the President, must be at least thirty-five years old. Most states that list an age requirement in the state constitution make it mandatory that the candidate for governor shall attain the age of thirty. A few do not mention a minimum age and therefore accept twenty-one.

### Political Qualifications

Obviously more important than the formal legal requirements are the political qualifications necessary to be a successful candidate. It is impossible to categorically state the necessary political qualifications that will hold true in each state. Most successful candidates have a record of previous public or civic service that is highly regarded by the voters. This may or may not be an elective office, but usually having had a successful campaign for a state-wide elected office is regarded as a definite asset. A good candidate must appeal to the entire electorate, not merely to one special segment, and he must have much in common with the voters. This means that in some states being a member of a particular religious group which predominates will be of significance. It should be noted that a particular religious affiliation in the second half of the twentieth century does not appear to carry the same weight either for or against a candidate as it has previously.

Few gubernatorial candidates are successful unless they can work with the party leaders. Candidates who run independently of the regular party leadership are seldom successful. A candidate who is regarded by the regular members of the party as a maverick usually finds his support minimal. Certain patterns are gradually emerging, as was revealed by Joseph A. Schlesinger's study of those who make a successful run for the governor's office. In one group of states previous membership in the state legislature appeared to be almost a mandatory prerequisite. In another group of states the governors usually have held a state-wide elective office, such as attorney general or secretary of state, before becoming a gubernatorial candidate.[4]

The gubernatorial candidate must have a broad knowledge of government and of the problems within his state. He must be able to express himself with a degree of clarity and sincerity that will impress the voter. Obviously he must have a personal appearance that will have a favorable impact upon the electorate. Physical handicaps have on occasion been turned into assets, but normally a successful candidate will be vigorous and forceful both mentally and physically.

Very few women have striven for the office and only two in the first sixty years of this century have campaigned successfully for a governorship. Both Miriam A. Ferguson of Texas and Nellie T. Ross of Wyoming, the first women governors of any state, succeeded their husbands as their states' chief executives. Most states have never had a woman as a serious contender for the governorship. There is no evidence that this situation will be changed in the near future.

The governor in most states is almost automatically the leader or "titular" head of his political party. Normally he speaks not only for the state and is its ceremonial head but also is the voice of his party in the state. His success is the party's success, his failure marks the failure of his political party. The governor usually is the chairman of his party's delegates to the national convention and he is called upon to represent his state and party in the national councils.

The governor is expected to head the party's ticket, and he is supposed to attract sufficient votes to assist in the election of the other candidates

[4] Joseph A. Schlesinger, *How They Became Governor* (East Lansing: Michigan State University, 1957).

of his party. He is the major campaigner and his presence in their districts is requested by almost all of his party's candidates for state legislative positions. The party's candidates for President and Vice President are also assisted in their campaign within the state by the governor. He is expected to greet them upon their entry and to appear with them at virtually every stop. Failure to extend this courtesy is viewed as an affront and an indication of the governor's failure to support the national ticket. As has been stated before, many state governors achieve national stature and head their party's national tickets.

## Nomination and Election Provisions

Each state determines either in its constitution or by state statute the detailed provisions for nominating and selecting the governor. Most states now use the direct primary method of selecting the candidates for the two major parties. In those states, primarily in the South where nomination is tantamount to election, the successful candidate must usually receive a majority of the votes of his party in the primary or face a so-called run-off election at which time the two aspirants who are highest in the primary face each other in a second primary election to determine the party's candidate in the general election. In other states with the direct primary, a simple plurality is all that is required to gain the nomination. A few states require that a certain percentage of the total vote cast in the party's primary election must be attained, or the primary is said to have failed to nominate and a state-wide convention of the party is held to determine the general election candidate.[5] A number of states do not use the direct primary to nominate the gubernatorial candidate, and the nomination is made at a state-wide convention. Yet others use the convention system to show the party preference but then allow a direct primary vote to determine the party's candidate on the fall election ballot. Various attempts have been made to predict the party that will be successful in the gubernatorial races for the states. Coleman B. Ransone, Jr., has made one of the latest studies in this area in which he classifies the states into three categories: one group in which one of the two parties almost always dominates; a second group in which one party usually wins consistently; a third group in which competition is always great and the governorship is won periodically by each party. Constantly changing political issues and complexities make such predictions very interesting but not too reliable, as noted by Professor Ransone.[6]

[5] Iowa and South Dakota are typical of this group requiring 35 per cent of the primary vote be cast for the successful nominee, or the nomination is made at a state-wide convention, which names the party's candidate for the general election ballot.

[6] Coleman B. Ransone, Jr. The Office of Governor in the United States (University, Ala.: University of Alabama, 1956).

The general election for governor in most states is held on the first Tuesday after the first Monday in November. In the states with two-year terms the selection of the governor every other election is at the same time and on the same ballot as that for the President of the United States and therefore is frequently affected by the outcome of the presidential vote. In about half of the four-year term states the gubernatorial election is held in the off-presidential year elections and thus are not as dependent upon the outcome of that contest. Both Kentucky and Mississippi elect their governors for a four-year term in the odd-numbered years. It is only logical that the state issues and the qualifications of the gubernatorial candidates will receive greater consideration if the election is not held simultaneously with the presidential contest.

In forty-six of the states a successful candidate for governor must receive a plurality of the votes cast for the office. In Maine, Vermont, and Georgia, a majority of the votes cast for governor is required. Mississippi uses a complicated electoral vote system. In addition to obtaining a majority of the popular vote the successful candidate must also receive a majority of the electoral vote. Fortunately both usually coincide.

## Term of Office

The last one hundred and eighty years has seen a gradual increase in the length of term allowed the governor by the state constitutions. Many of the original state constitutions of the first thirteen colonies called for annual elections. This gradually was extended to two years and is now giving way to a four-year term. During a transition period some states even provided for a three-year term, but now all states either have two- or four-year terms. Today, thirty-six states grant election for a four-year term with the trend definitely in this direction, while only fourteen cling to the two-year term tradition. Twelve of the latter have no limit upon the number of terms a governor may serve. Sixteen of the four-year term states also have no limitation upon the governors' right to continue in office as long as re-election is achieved. Seven states in their constitutions follow the same pattern as the U.S. Constitution and allow only two successive terms. Five of these states use the four-year term, while two have only two-year terms. Fifteen four-year term states have a limitation which does not permit a governor to succeed himself after completion of his first four years in the governor's chair.[7]

There is almost universal agreement among students of government that a two-year term for the governor is not long enough to allow him to implement any type of an administrative program or get any long-range

[7] Council of State Governments, *The Book of the States, 1964–1965,* (Chicago: Council of State Governments, 1964), p. 142.

plans enacted by the state legislature. There is less universal agreement, however, upon the question of allowing a four-year term governor to succeed himself. Most authorities are inclined to believe that it is unwise for the people to deny themselves the services of an experienced chief executive by not permitting this succession. Few any longer fear that a state governor will become a tyrant and a dictator merely because he is in office for eight or twelve consecutive years. Table 13–1 enumerates the constitutional requirements for the office of governor with respect to terms and tenure.

## Compensation

The salary paid to the governor of a state is actually only a portion of the compensation the position grants. The range in salaries, some of which are written into state constitutions and therefore are frequently much lower than the economic trend of the era would demand, is great. New York pays the largest yearly salary of $50,000, which is closely followed by California with a salary of $40,000. The correlation between population and salary paid the chief executive officer of the state is by no means complete, as Alaska's $25,000 is exceeded by only five states. Arkansas and North Dakota pay only $10,000 yearly. Nine of the states agree upon $25,000 as the appropriate salary. However, in addition to the salary many other compensating features are added. Forty of the governors are given a rent-free executive mansion, with normally a staff to operate the residence. Virtually every governor has at his disposal a tax-free expense account which averages about $7,000 per year. Each state normally provides the governor with an automobile and a driver. The governors usually also have access to a state airplane and the state's National Guard airplanes for official state business.

It should be noted that the governor frequently is not the highest-paid state official. The president of the state university and often deans of professional colleges, as well as heads of some of the special services, such as mental health hospitals, are frequently given a higher annual salary. In some states as many as thirty or forty state employees are more highly compensated on a strictly monetary basis than is the governor.

The trend for increasing the compensation the governors is gradually permitting a larger group of persons to consider running for the office. Fewer persons find that they will have to sacrifice income to accept the position. Certainly it must be said that the compensation does not compare with the responsibilities the office entails. Corporation executives responsible for much smaller budgets frequently receive several times the pay of a state governor. This is one of the facts facing a candidate entering public service.

Table 13–2 indicates the salaries paid the governors.

## TABLE 13–1

### Governors' Terms and Tenure—Constitutional Requirements

| State | Regular Term of Years | Consecutive Terms |
|---|---|---|
| Alabama | 4 | No |
| Alaska | 4 | Two |
| Arizona | 2 | No limit |
| Arkansas | 2 | No limit |
| California | 4 | No limit |
| Colorado | 4 | No limit |
| Connecticut | 2 | No limit |
| Delaware | 4 | Two |
| Florida | 4 | No |
| Georgia | 4 | No |
| Hawaii | 4 | No limit |
| Idaho | 4 | No limit |
| Illinois | 4 | No limit |
| Indiana | 4 | No |
| Iowa | 2 | No limit |
| Kansas | 2 | No limit |
| Kentucky | 4 | No |
| Louisiana | 4 | No |
| Maine | 4 | No limit |
| Maryland | 4 | Two |
| Massachusetts | 2 | No limit |
| Michigan | 4 | No limit |
| Minnesota | 4 | No limit |
| Mississippi | 4 | No |
| Missouri | 4 | No limit |
| Montana | 4 | No limit |
| Nebraska | 2 | No limit |
| Nevada | 4 | No limit |
| New Hampshire | 2 | No limit |
| New Jersey | 4 | Two |
| New Mexico | 2 | Two |
| New York | 4 | No limit |
| North Carolina | 4 | No |
| North Dakota | 2 | No limit |
| Ohio | 4 | No limit |
| Oklahoma | 4 | No |
| Oregon | 4 | Two |
| Pennsylvania | 4 | No |
| Rhode Island | 2 | No limit |
| South Carolina | 4 | No |
| South Dakota | 2 | Two |
| Tennessee | 4 | No |
| Texas | 2 | No limit |
| Utah | 4 | No limit |
| Vermont | 2 | No limit |
| Virginia | 4 | No |
| Washington | 4 | No limit |
| West Virginia | 4 | No |
| Wisconsin | 2 | No limit |
| Wyoming | 4 | No limit |

SOURCE: Council of State Governments, *The Book of the States, 1964–1965* (Chicago: Council of State Governments, 1964).

## TABLE 13–2
### Governors' Salaries—1963

| $50,000 | $44,100 | $35,000 | $30,000 |
|---|---|---|---|
| New York | California | Massachusetts<br>New Jersey<br>Pennsylvania | Illinois |

| $27,500 | $25,000 | $22,500 | $20,000 |
|---|---|---|---|
| Hawaii<br>Michigan | Alabama<br>Alaska<br>Florida<br>Indiana<br>Mississippi<br>Missouri<br>North Carolina<br>Ohio<br>Oklahoma<br>Rhode Island<br>Texas<br>Virginia<br>Wisconsin | Arizona<br>Minnesota<br>Montana ($22,000)<br>Washington | Colorado<br>Georgia ($20,700)<br>Kansas<br>Louisiana<br>Nevada<br>Oregon ($21,500)<br>South Carolina<br>Wyoming |

| $18,500 | $18,000 | $17,500 | $16,587 |
|---|---|---|---|
| Iowa<br>Tennessee | Kentucky | Delaware<br>New Mexico<br>West Virginia | New Hampshire |

| $15,500 | $15,000 | $14,000 | $13,750 |
|---|---|---|---|
| South Dakota | Connecticut<br>Idaho<br>Maine<br>Maryland<br>Utah | Nebraska | Vermont |

| $13,000 | $10,000 |
|---|---|
| North Dakota | Arkansas |

SOURCE: Council of State Governments, *The Book of the States, 1964–1965* (Chicago: Council of State Governments, 1964).

## Removal and Succession

The post of chief executive in a state may become vacant in several ways. Death may cause a vacancy; resignation is not unheard of, particularly if there is a vacancy in the United States Senate from the state; or a vacancy may occur by disability of the governor to perform the duties, usually because of health reasons. Much attention has been given in recent years to this latter problem of deciding when the governor is incapable of carrying out the duties and powers of the office. Various detailed and complicated systems have been devised for determining inability of the governor to continue in office. Some have been written into state constitutions but none seems to be entirely satisfactory. Some states have established so-called medical boards to determine inability while others have allowed the state legislature to declare a vacancy when certain stipulated conditions exist. Prolonged absence of the governor from the state, defined in the Alaska constitution as more than six months, may be evidence that a vacancy exists.

The line of succession also becomes important when the governor is impeached or voted out of office in a recall election. All of the states except Oregon provide that the chief executive may be impeached by the legislative body and upon conviction removed from office. In all but Nebraska, which has only one house, the United States Constitution method of allowing the impeachment proceeding to begin in the lower house is followed.[8] The senators serve as the court. Most states require a two-thirds vote in favor of the indictment before a governor is actually removed from office. Fortunately, few governors have stood trial by the impeachment method. Frequently it develops into political warfare rather than a true judgment as to whether or not the governor has committed offenses that justify his removal from office. Upon conviction of impeachment proceedings the office is vacant, and unless criminal charges are subsequently brought this is the only punishment dealt to the offending officer. It must be admitted that the impeachment procedure has not worked very satisfactorily but is still a device that in theory keeps the governor responsive to the people through their elected legislators. Only four governors have been removed by impeachment, one each in New York and Texas, and two in Oklahoma.

Twelve states provide for recall of a governor.[9] This process involves a petition which must secure a certain number of signatures; usually the number must be a percentage of the votes cast in the last election. The petition is presented to some designated state official, usually the secretary of state. Upon certification that the signatures are proper and in the required number a recall election is held at which time the voter is asked to vote yes or no on the question, "Shall Governor Jones be recalled?" Only one governor has been removed from office by this method. In 1921, Lynn J. Frazier of North Dakota was recalled but later was popular enough with the voters of his state to be elected to the United States Senate.

Thirty-eight states have a popularly elected lieutenant governor, while Tennessee designates the president of the senate as the lieutenant governor, who succeeds the governor whenever a vacancy in the chief executive's office officially exists.[10] In the other eleven states various other

---

[8] The Nebraska unicameral legislature brings the charges, with the Supreme Court serving as the Impeachment Court.

[9] States allowing recall of governors are: Alaska, Arizona, California, Colorado, Kansas, Louisiana, Michigan, Nevada, North Dakota, Oregon, Washington, and Wisconsin.

[10] The following states have no office of Lieutenant Governor: Alaska, Arizona, Florida, Maine, Maryland, New Hampshire, New Jersey, Oregon, Utah, West Virginia, and Wyoming.

officials succeed to the gubernatorial post; most often it is the president of the senate, but in several states the popularly elected secretary of state is next in line to follow the governor into the chief executive's mansion.

It is interesting to observe that in several of the states with popularly elected lieutenant governors it is possible for these officers to be of a different party than the governors whom they may succeed because of death, resignation, or impeachment. However, the latest trend is to have both the governor and lieutenant governor run as a team with a voter not being able to vote for a governor of one party and a lieutenant governor of the other, thus following the national rule used in voting for the President and Vice President.

Succession of the governorship has taken on a more urgent aspect in recent years because of the multiple deaths of state officials in airplane crashes in Oregon and Montana. Some states, fearing atomic attack which might wipe out a large number of state executive officials, have placed in their constitutions detailed provisions for selecting new executives in case of a major disaster.

Disputes over the question of who is the qualified governor have occurred in many states. Rhode Island, Louisiana, South Carolina, North Dakota, and Kentucky are among the states in which this problem has on occasion arisen. In North Dakota, when a governor became involved in a federal trial the lieutenant governor attempted to take over the office but was ousted by the state's supreme court. A somewhat similar situation in Georgia took place when in 1947 Eugene Talmadge, the governor-elect, died on the eve of his inauguration. The lieutenant governor, M. E. Thompson, attempted to assume the office only to be frustrated in his efforts by state troops and legislative action which attempted to install Herman Talmadge as the governor. In this contest the state supreme court resolved the situation in favor of Thompson.

In a more recent dispute over a gubernatorial position, in 1959, Governor Earl Long was committed by state order upon the signature of his wife to a state mental hospital. This dispute ended with the release of Governor Long from the mental institution and the dismissal of a number of state officials involved in the committment. The lieutenant governor, even though vested with the power of governorship, refused to assume the office.

## THE GOVERNOR AS HEAD OF THE ADMINISTRATION

The powers of the governors like those of the President of the United States may be classified into four major categories: (1) executive-administrative; (2) legislative; (3) military; (4) and judicial. The exact amount of authority vested in the chief executive of the state is difficult to determine since so much of it is dependent upon extra-legal factors such as his personality, political factions, and other non-legal and non-constitutional provisions. No two governors have identical powers or find that one method of operation is always successful in the exercise of their powers. Nearly all state governors are severely handicapped in the total execution of their high office by the state constitution, state statute, tradition, or custom and practice. None can compare in total power with that of the President of the United States, even though the attempt to imitate the presidential position is often present.

## Executive-Administrative Authority

It is almost universally agreed that one of the most vital powers of the chief executive is his authority to make appointments. Yet it is also true that in many states the greatest single impediment to executive unity lies in the constitutional and statutory requirement that top administrative officials be popularly elected. The necessity of a clear line of command from the top to the bottom and a return line of responsibility and accountability has been emphasized in virtually every "Little Hoover Commission" report since the conclusion of World War II. In spite of this agreement, few of the state governors are fortunate enough to find this situation prevailing. Forty of the states popularly elect the secretary of state, while an even larger number (forty-two) elect the state treasurer, and the same number allow the voters to select the state's primary legal officer, the attorney general. In twenty-five states popular election is used as the method for selecting the head of the public school organization, usually titled the superintendent of public instruction. As of 1950 the average American state elected thirteen top executive officials.[11] A study of the same offices ten years later reveals that this number has been reduced by nearly 50 per cent but it still remains as a major barrier to executive leadership at the state level. Alaska and New Jersey each elect only two officials who may be classified as top-executive administrators, but in contrast the North Carolina voter is faced with the task of electing 110 state administrative officers. However, this is an isolated case since the next largest list of elected state officials is found in Nevada with forty-two and Texas with thirty-three.[12] The problem facing a governor with a vast array of elected executives is obvious. They may or may not be of his party, and if they are, they may or may not concur with his political

[11] York Willbern, "Administration in State Government," *The Forty-eight States; Their Tasks as Policy Makers and Administrators* (New York: The American Assembly, Graduate School of Business, Columbia University Press, 1955), p. 112.

[12] Council of State Governments, *The Book of the States, 1964–1965* (Chicago: Council of State Governments, 1964), p. 151.

philosophy. In some instances they may have been elected by a larger plurality than the governor himself and therefore believe that he does not have the true support of the people of the state.

Table 13–3 indicates the elected major state officials, both constitutional and statutory.

## TABLE 13–3
### Elected State Officers—1964

| | Governor (50) | Lieutenant Governor (38) | Secretary of State (39) | Treasurer (40) | Auditor (28) | Attorney General (42) | Tax Commissioner (3) | Comptroller (15) | Superintendent of Public Instruction (24) | Agriculture (11) | Labor (7) | Insurance (10) | Utilities (14) | Other Elective Officers | Total Agencies with Elected Officers | Total State Elective Officers |
|---|---|---|---|---|---|---|---|---|---|---|---|---|---|---|---|---|
| Alabama | x | x | x | x | x | x | | | | x | x | | x | | 9 | 11 |
| Alaska | x | None | x | | | | | | | | | | | | 2 | 2 |
| Arizona | x | None | x | x | x | x | x | | x | | | | x | x | 9 | 13 |
| Arkansas | x | x | x | x | x | x | | | | | | | | x | 7 | 7 |
| California | x | x | x | x | | x | x | x | x | | | | | | 8 | 11 |
| Colorado | x | x | x | x | x | x | | | | | | | | x | 8 | 17 |
| Connecticut | x | x | x | x | | x | | x | | | | | | x | 7 | 7 |
| Delaware | x | x | | x | x | x | | | | | | x | | | 6 | 6 |
| Florida | x | None | x | x | | x | | x | x | x | | | x | | 8 | 10 |
| Georgia | x | x | x | x | | x | | x | x | x | x | x | x | x | 11 | 15 |
| Hawaii | x | x | x | | | | | | | | | | | | 3 | 3 |
| Idaho | x | x | x | x | x | x | | | x | | | | | | 8 | 8 |
| Illinois | x | x | x | x | | x | | | x | | | | | x | 8 | 16 |
| Indiana | x | x | x | x | x | x | | | x | | | | | | 7 | 7 |
| Iowa | x | x | x | x | x | x | | | | x | | | | | 7 | 7 |
| Kansas | x | x | x | x | x | x | | | x | | | x | | x | 10 | 15 |
| Kentucky | x | x | x | x | x | x | | | x | x | | | | x | 9 | 11 |
| Louisiana | x | x | x | x | | x | | | x | x | | x | x | x | 12 | 24 |
| Maine | x | None | | | | | | | | | | | | x | 7 | 13 |
| Maryland | x | | | | | x | | x | | | | | | x | 4 | 4 |
| Massachusetts | x | x | x | x | x | x | | | | | | | | x | 7 | 14 |
| Michigan | x | x | x | | | x | | | | | | | | x | 12 | 31 |
| Minnesota | x | x | x | x | x | x | | | | | | | x | x | 8 | 21 |
| Mississippi | x | x | x | x | x | x | | | x | x | | x | x | x | 13 | 17 |
| Missouri | x | x | x | x | x | x | | | | | | | | x | 7 | 11 |
| Montana | x | x | x | x | x | x | | | x | | | | x | x | 8 | 10 |
| Nebraska | x | x | x | x | x | x | x | | | | | | x | x | 9 | 21 |
| Nevada | x | x | x | x | | x | | x | x | | | | | x | 11 | 42 |
| New Hampshire | x | None | | | | | | | | | | | | x | 4 | 8 |
| New Jersey | x | None | | | | | | | | | | | | x | 2 | 2 |
| New Mexico | x | x | x | x | x | x | | | x | | | x | | x | 9 | 20 |
| New York | x | x | | | | x | | x | | | | | | x | 6 | 18 |
| North Carolina | x | x | x | x | x | x | | | x | x | x | x | | x | 11 | 110 |
| North Dakota | x | x | x | x | x | x | x | x | x | x | | x | x | | 12 | 20 |
| Ohio | x | x | x | x | x | x | | | | | | | | x | 7 | 29 |
| Oklahoma | x | x | x | x | x | x | | | x | | x | x | x | x | 12 | 18 |

## TABLE 13–3 (Continued)

| | Governor (50) | Lieutenant Governor (38) | Secretary of State (39) | Treasurer (40) | Auditor (28) | Attorney General (42) | Tax Commissioner (3) | Comptroller (15) | Superintendent of Public Instruction (24) | Agriculture (11) | Labor (7) | Insurance (10) | Utilities (14) | Other Elective Officers | Total Agencies with Elected Officers | Total State Elective Officers |
|---|---|---|---|---|---|---|---|---|---|---|---|---|---|---|---|---|
| Oregon | x | None | x | x | | x | | | | | x | | | | 5 | 5 |
| Pennsylvania | x | x | | x | x | | | x | | | | | | | 5 | 5 |
| Rhode Island | x | x | x | x | | x | | | | | | | | | 5 | 5 |
| South Carolina | x | x | x | x | | x | | x | x | x | x | | | x | 13 | 27 |
| South Dakota | x | x | x | x | x | x | | | x | | | x | x | x | 10 | 12 |
| Tennessee | x | None | | | | | | | | | | | x | x | 6 | 8 |
| Texas | x | x | | x | | x | | x | | x | | | x | x | 12 | 33 |
| Utah | x | None | x | x | x | x | | | | | | | | x | 6 | 14 |
| Vermont | x | x | x | x | x | x | | x | | | | | | x | 8 | 16 |
| Virginia | x | x | | | | x | | | | | | | | x | 6 | 8 |
| Washington | x | x | x | x | x | x | | x | x | | | x | | | 9 | 20 |
| West Virginia | x | None | x | x | x | x | | | x | | | | | | 6 | 6 |
| Wisconsin | x | x | x | x | | x | | | x | | | | | | 6 | 6 |
| Wyoming | x | None | x | x | x | | | | x | | | | | | 5 | 5 |

SOURCE: Council of State Governments, *The Book of the States, 1964–1965* (Chicago: Council of State Governments, 1964).

The typical governor is not allowed to appoint in the average state a sizable number of top executive officials who would be in theory a part of his administrative hierarchy. But he is also confronted with ex-officio memberships on many boards and commissions, thus frequently limiting the governor's control over these agencies.

Statutory and constitutional provisions that require a governor to share executive authority with boards and commissions are all too common. While he may be empowered to appoint the members of the boards and commissions, he is usually required to appoint members of the opposition party as well as members of his own party to the various state agencies. Often he must appoint for terms two and three times as long as the one he is allowed to serve. In some states this means that a governor must be successful in three consecutive gubernatorial elections before he is permitted to appoint the entire membership of all boards and commissions.

There is a trend toward extending the governor's power of appointment and removal. Most of the reorganized state governments, such as New Jersey and Michigan, grant extensive appointive and removal power as compared with the constitutions and statutes of the nineteenth century.

Table 13–4 indicates the major appointments made by the various governors.

## TABLE 13–4

### Major Appointments by Governor—1964

| | Secretary of State | Treasurer | Attorney General | Superintendent of Public Instruction | Comptroller | Auditor | Tax Commissioner | Secretary of Agriculture | Labor | Utilities | Health | Welfare | Insurance | Highways | Conservation | Major Executive Official Departments |
|---|---|---|---|---|---|---|---|---|---|---|---|---|---|---|---|---|
| Alabama | | | | | | | x | x | | | | | x | x | x | 5 |
| Alaska | | x | x | | | | | x | | | x | x | | | | 5 |
| Arizona | | | | | | | | x | x | | x | x | | x | x | 6 |
| Arkansas | | | | x | | | x | x | x | | x | x | x | | x | 8 |
| California | | | | | | | | x | x | x | x | x | x | x | x | 8 |
| Colorado | | | | | | | | | | | x | | | | | 1 |
| Connecticut | | | | | | | x | x | x | x | x | x | x | x | x | 9 |
| Delaware | x | | | | | | x | | | | x | | | | | 3 |
| Florida | | | | | | x | | x | | | x | x | | x | | 5 |
| Georgia | | | | | | | x | | | | x | x | | | | 3 |
| Hawaii | | x | x | x | | | x | x | x | x | x | x | x | x | x | 12 |
| Idaho | | | | | | | x | x | x | x | x | x | x | x | | 8 |
| Illinois | | | | | | | x | x | x | x | x | x | x | x | x | 9 |
| Indiana | | | | | | | x | | | | x | x | x | x | x | 6 |
| Iowa | | | | x | | | x | x | x | | x | x | x | x | x | 9 |
| Kansas | | | | | | | x | x | x | x | | | | x | | 5 |
| Kentucky | | | | | | | x | x | x | | | x | x | x | x | 7 |
| Louisiana | | | | | | | x | x | | | x | | | | x | 4 |
| Maine | | | | | | | | | x | x | x | x | x | x | x | 7 |
| Maryland | | | | | | x | x | x | x | x | | | x | x | x | 8 |
| Massachusetts | | | | | | | x | x | x | x | x | x | x | x | x | 9 |
| Michigan | | | | | | | x | x | x | x | x | x | x | | x | 8 |
| Minnesota | | | | | | | x | x | x | | | x | x | x | x | 7 |
| Mississippi | | | | | x | | x | | | | x | x | | | | 4 |
| Missouri | | | | | x | | x | x | x | x | x | x | x | x | | 9 |
| Montana | | | | | | | x | x | x | x | x | x | | x | | 7 |
| Nebraska | | | | | | | x | x | x | | | x | x | x | | 6 |
| Nevada | | | | | | | x | x | x | x | | | | | | 4 |
| New Hampshire | | x | | | | | | x | x | x | | | x | | x | 6 |
| New Jersey | x | x | x | x | | | x | x | x | x | x | x | x | x | x | 13 |
| New Mexico | | | | | x | | x | x | x | x | x | | | x | | 7 |
| New York | x | x | | | | | x | x | x | x | x | | x | x | x | 10 |
| North Carolina | | | | | | | x | | | | x | x | x | x | x | 6 |
| North Dakota | | | | | | | | | | | x | | | x | | 2 |
| Ohio | | | | | | | x | x | x | x | x | x | x | x | x | 9 |
| Oklahoma | | | | | | | x | x | | | | | | | | 2 |
| Oregon | | | | | | | x | x | | x | x | x | x | x | x | 8 |
| Pennsylvania | x | | x | x | | | x | x | x | x | x | x | x | x | x | 12 |
| Rhode Island | | | | | | | | x | x | x | x | x | | x | x | 7 |
| South Carolina | | | | | | | | | x | | x | | | | | 2 |

## TABLE 13–4 (Continued)

| | Secretary of State | Treasurer | Attorney General | Superintendent of Public Instruction | Comptroller | Auditor | Tax Commissioner | Secretary of Agriculture | Labor | Utilities | Health | Welfare | Insurance | Highways | Conservation | Major Executive Official Departments |
|---|---|---|---|---|---|---|---|---|---|---|---|---|---|---|---|---|
| South Dakota | | | | | | | x | x | | | x | x | x | x | x | 7 |
| Tennessee | | | | | | | x | x | x | | x | x | x | x | x | 8 |
| Texas | x | | | | | | | x | | | | | | | | 2 |
| Utah | | | | | | | x | x | x | x | x | x | x | x | x | 9 |
| Vermont | | | | | | | x | x | x | x | x | x | x | x | x | 9 |
| Virginia | x | x | | x | x | | x | x | x | | x | x | | x | x | 11 |
| Washington | | | | | | | x | x | x | x | x | x | | x | x | 8 |
| West Virginia | | | | | | | x | x | x | | x | | x | x | x | 7 |
| Wisconsin | | | | | | | x | x | x | | | | | x | x | 5 |
| Wyoming | | | | x | | | x | x | x | x | | | | x | | 6 |

Source: Council of State Governments, *The Book of the States, 1964–1965* (Chicago: Council of State Governments, 1964).

One other limitation normally placed upon the governor's appointive power is that all major appointments must in many states be approved by a two-thirds vote in the state senate. This may well mean that the governor's choice of appointees will be circumscribed by a small number of senators.

It has been said that an appointive power is no greater than the power to remove. Yet most state governors are not granted anything resembling adequate removal power. Few governors have been vested by the state constitution with general removal powers. In some states removal is possible only by judicial action, with the attorney general bringing the actual case against the appointee. Many times the governor's only recourse is to out-wait the appointee until his term expires, but frequently the governor's tenure has ended prior to the expiration of the appointee's term. In a situation of this type the appointee's allegiance and loyalty to the governor are often quite slack until the time for renewal of the appointment. In many states reappointment, particularly of members of the opposition party to boards and commissions, seldom occurs; even reappointment of members of the governor's party is not automatic.

Considerable strengthening of the removal power of the governor is needed in many states if the power of appointment is to have its maximum value as a force for making the governor the chief executive in fact as well as in name. Governors in some states must receive the approval of the state senate in removing officials who have been approved by the senate.

## Budgetary Powers

In all states except Arkansas the executive type of state budget is employed. The detailed analysis of the governor's role in the budget-making process is included in the chapter dealing with finance, but a brief examination of this vital power is in order at this point. The formal power and duty of presenting the budget to the legislature is usually lodged with the chief executive. However, the governor finds this to be a very difficult assignment in many states. Frequently he is given only a month after his inauguration to have the budget that he recommends to the legislature completed and printed. This means that the preliminary stages of budget preparation must have occurred before he takes the oath of office. Often he must rely upon the material prepared by a budgeting officer whose allegiance has been to his predecessor. Extended budget hearings for each department and agency may not be possible because of time limitations. In more than half of the states the budget is a biennial budget rather than an annual one and thus demands planning for at least twenty-four months plus the six or more months before the budget actually takes effect. The budget recommendations of the governor are subject to almost complete revision on the part of the legislature. They may adopt his budget in toto or they may completely ignore his suggested figures. The rule concerning the power of lowering and raising budgeted figures varies, but most legislatures have retained a firm hand over budget matters. In spite of these obvious shortcomings the governor's authority to recommend the amount of money to be made available for each state agency gives him a management tool that usually has great persuasive power over these state units. Through his budget recommendations he is often able to place the emphasis that he believes desirable upon certain programs of the state and to cut back on other activities that he feels are not as essential.

## Power To Call for Reports

In approximately three-fourths of the states the governor is empowered to call for periodic reports from the heads of the various state agencies. As Professor Kirk Porter has noted, "the right to call for reports is almost as empty as the right to exercise general supervision."[13] No official is inclined to take very seriously a report that he is requested to make as long

[13] Kirk H. Porter, *State Administration* (New York: Appleton-Century-Crofts, Inc., 1938), p. 45.

as the chief executive is in no position to do anything substantial about it even though the report may be unsatisfactory. Most of the annual, semi-annual, or biennial reports are properly classed as perfunctory, unillu-minating, and largely useless. Even in spite of the lack of authority to do little other than accept the report as submitted, they may give the gover-nor an indication of the work being done by the particular agency. Many do give a great deal of statistical information that may be highly useful in analyzing the over-all operation of the state government and in select-ing areas in which greater emphasis is needed. On the other hand some of the reports may portray a completely erroneous picture of the actual operations. By and large, the reports are received by the governor, noted in the executive journal, placed on file, and then after a suitable interval, deposited in the state archives. Thus the authority to require reports is another power that might appear to be important but in reality is not.

## Ordinance-Making Power

All governors have some degree of ordinance-making power. The exer-cise of this power usually takes the form of executive orders to one or more of the agencies that he nominally controls. Ordinance-making usu-ally involves issuing rules and regulations that fill out the details of the legislation enacted by the general assembly. If the members of the legis-lature do not specifically name the official who is empowered to supple-ment the legislation, the power falls upon the office of governor. How-ever, many legislative bodies are prone to permit the agency head of the unit administering the statute to supplement the law, thus reducing the governor's ordinance-making powers. The attorney general is often also involved in the formulation of rules and regulations, being called upon to check as to their legality. His influence on these matters varies greatly.

## Authority to Investigate

Most governors are given the authority to conduct investigations of the state agencies. This is usually resorted to only when every other supervi-sory authority has failed to bring the results desired by the governor on administrative matters. Some states empower the governor to employ special personnel to check into matters upon which he has been unable to obtain satisfactory information, e.g., the operation of the state liquor control commission. This power may be included under his authority as general supervisor of the state's administrative machinery. In theory, all of the actions taken by subordinates are performed in the name of the governor. Press releases concerning many of the innovations of a depart-ment are issued by the governor's staff, even though all of the actual administrative work has been done by the department. Even though the constitution of the state may proclaim the governor to have general supervision over the various state agencies, the phrase is almost meaningless unless supported by more specific authority. The state courts have not enhanced the governor's authority in this direction by their interpretations of the phrase.

## THE GOVERNOR AND THE STATE LEGISLATURE

Following the example set by Woodrow Wilson in New Jersey, many state governors have attempted to exert leadership over the state legislature. Before 1900 few governors wielded much power in this area of state government. The trend is most easily seen in the types of campaigns the candidates for the governorship have waged in the last sixty years. Most candidates propose a legislative program which they assert they will later recommend to the legislature. Indeed the candidates for the legislature are thereby pressured to identify themselves as either for or against the policies advocated by the gubernatorial candidates. Usually the candidates for the legislature and the governorship are either elected or defeated upon the stands that have been taken upon these strictly legislative issues.

### Veto Power

Prior to 1900 the normal governor exercised only one major power over the state legislature—his veto of statutes enacted by the general assembly. Lord Bryce observed that "the use of his veto, in ordinary times, is a governor's most serious duty and chiefly by his discharge of it is he judged."[14]

Today the veto is still a strong tool used by every state governor, except in North Carolina, where the governor possesses no veto power. The use of the veto, while still important, is only a negative force at the disposal of the governor. Studies show that forty-nine governors hold what might well be called a suspensory veto since it can be overridden by the legislators but it often turns into an absolute veto in many states. Forty-two of the governors possess the item veto. The item veto permits a governor to veto a section of a legislative bill while approving the remainder. Normally this power is restricted to appropriation measures. It is a most useful and desirable device but it is not regularly used. Professor Prescott has summarized its utilization in picturesque terms as "a device that is useful, albeit somewhat rusty 'gun behind the door,' to be

[14] James Bryce, *The American Commonwealth* (London: Macmillan & Co. Ltd., 1899), Vol. II, p. 226.

aimed at an occasional predatory prowler."[15] It is one of the few devices that most governors possess and a number of Presidents of the United States have requested. However, they have failed to obtain action by Congress on the necessary constitutional amendment, since Congress fears further reduction of its powers.

Twelve states have the pocket veto similar to that of the President of the United States which allows these governors to veto a measure sent to their office in the final days of the session by merely failing to sign the bill. Still others, Alabama, Massachusetts, Virginia, and New Jersey, have what is termed an executive amendment power, wherein they may return to the legislature any measure with which they are in agreement but desire certain changes to be made before signing the bill into law.

Varying time periods are given governors to determine what course of action they will take on bills that have been passed by the legislature and sent to them. In some states it is a relatively short period of three days, usually not including Sundays or holidays and not counting ordinarily the day the bill is received by the governor. In other states as long as ten days is granted the chief executive in which to make his decision. Most states allow an extended period, as long as thirty days, for the governor to arrive at his decision if the bills reach his office during the last few days of the session. In theory, the legislature has the opportunity to override the governor's veto. However, if the veto is not made until after the session has adjourned the suspensory veto, in effect, becomes an absolute veto. Typically the constitution will provide for an extraordinary majority vote being required to override the veto. Usually this is two-thirds of the membership of each house.

In most of the Southern states and in some Midwestern states the governor's veto is seldom overridden. For a period of sixty years not a single veto in Iowa was overridden by the legislature; similar records may be found in Illinois and in California. Usually in a "typical session" only about two per cent of all legislation vetoed by the governors becomes law with the veto of the chief executive being overridden. Studies by Frank W. Prescott and Samuel R. Solomon both reveal wide variations in the use of the governor's veto power. However, in one legislative year only five percent of all bills enacted by state legislatures were vetoed.

## Executive Messages to the Legislature

Constitutions in at least 80 per cent of the states require the governor to report to the state legislature concerning the condition of the state.

[15] Frank W. Prescott, "The Executive Veto in Southern States," *The Journal of Politics* (November, 1948), p. 674.

Usually this report is made at the opening of each new session. In some instances it precedes by only a day or two the governor's inauguration, thus it may be the final report of a departing governor or it may be the beginning of a new phase of state leadership. Some messages on the condition of the state are as brief as two pages while others may run as long as two hundred pages. Most state chief executives follow the example of Wilson and deliver the report in person to a joint session. In other states the message is sent to the joint session to be read by a reading clerk.

Ordinarily it is expected that either the report on the condition of the state or the inaugural message, or both, will contain a legislative program that the governor believes should be enacted. The tradition is well-established in many states that the bulk of the legislation that will be passed in a session receives its impetus from the recommendations of the chief executive in his speech to the legislature. After the formal presentation of the governor's view as to the needs for new legislation, the speeches are usually printed and distributed for study by both the legislative members and the general public. In some states actual bills are drawn by the governor's staff to implement his recommendations. These bills are then handed to "friendly" legislators who perform the formality of actually introducing the measures.

Usually within a few weeks of the governor's initial appearance before the law makers he returns to present his budget message. This speech which may be expected to set the tone of the administration pertaining to financial affairs is accompanied by a printed document usually of several hundred pages which sets forth the financial program for the ensuing fiscal period. More details of this budget document will be considered in the chapter on state finance.

Almost all governors are empowered by the state constitutions to request the legislatures for permission to present other special messages during the session. Permission is almost always immediately granted by a concurrent resolution. The range of topics covered in these special appearances of the governor before the general assembly is infinite. The effectiveness of these messages to the legislators is determined by innumerable factors over which frequently the governor may have little or no control. Obviously his reception will be much better if a majority of the members is of his political party, but even this does not insure a cordial reception for the governor's recommendations if they do not coincide with the thinking of the legislative leaders.

Most governors find that it is essential to hold weekly and sometimes daily conferences with key members of the legislature in order to check the progress of the legislative programs they have recommended. Many of these meetings are on a regular scheduled basis with additional conferences called whenever either the legislative leaders or the governor feels they are necessary. Many governors in order to gain rapport with the policy makers entertain all members of the house and senate one or more times during the course of a legislative session.

The extent that the governor is able to lead the legislature and become a positive force in the legislative process varies not only from one state to another but from one period to another. If the tradition of strong legislative leadership has been established within the state it will be much easier for the chief executive to dominate the legislative process than in states in which the tradition of legislative supremacy is accepted. Theodore Roosevelt while governor of New York asserted that he found it necessary and essential to devote a major portion of his time to the problems of legislation. Woodrow Wilson pressed for his legislative program by attending the legislative caucuses of his party, even though not invited.

## Calling Special Sessions

In all of the states the governor is empowered to call a special session of the state legislature. Some states place limitations upon the exercise of this power with three requiring the governor to obtain the agreement of the state executive council before calling an extraordinary session. These are North Carolina, New Hampshire, and Massachusetts. In fourteen states the legislature is allowed to call itself into special session. In the other states the governor is the sole judge as to whether a special session will be held. Nearly half of the state constitutions permit the governor to dictate what subject matters shall be considered by the special session that he convenes, while in the others the legislature may take up any matters that they consider desirable. In at least one-fifth of the state constitutions the governor is allowed to convene the senate independent of the lower house.

The power of calling special sessions has been utilized sparingly in some states but used frequently in many others. Some governors have installed a virtual annual session of the legislature by calling a special session every other year, thus permitting annual budgeting for state finances. Great variation also occurs in the length of the special sessions. Some last for only a day or so while others have remained in session for many months.[16]

The influence of a dynamic governor over the legislative process in a special session is often quite different than during a regular session. Governor Nelson A. Rockefeller in the 1961 special session of the New York state legislature was able to obtain passage of a major reapportionment and a fall-out shelter bill in a matter of a few days. The same legislation if brought forth during a regular session without the assets of a special

[16] Council of State Governments, *Our State Legislatures, 1948* (Chicago: Council of State Governments, 1948).

session probably would have taken weeks to pass. Other strong governors such as George Romney of Michigan and George Wallace of Alabama have found that their leadership in policy matters is enhanced during special sessions of their state general assemblies.

In more than one-third of the states the governor is given what would appear to be an important power over the state legislature in that he is authorized to establish the date for adjournment *if* the two houses of the general assembly cannot agree upon a time for ending the session. In reality, however, this power has been almost meaningless since the two houses seldom become involved in such a deadlock as to allow the governor to have the opportunity of wielding the power of adjournment.

## MILITARY POWERS

In all states the governor is the executive officer charged with the responsibility of organizing and maintaining the National Guard. This includes its training and general well-being. The Guard thus in cases of emergency may be used by the governor for enforcing the law and quelling domestic violence. It is possible for him to call out the Guard and place an area under "martial law" or "martial rule." This is, it should be emphasized, seldom done except in cases of dire emergency. Upon the proclamation of the governor that an emergency situation exists, the National Guard may be ordered to perform a wide variety of duties in addition to merely preserving the peace. They may be asked to preserve order in case of a serious strike involving the threat of violence. The most common usage of the National Guard has been in times of natural disasters, such as tornadoes and floods. The Guard units frequently are called upon to do flood duty, including sandbagging and building of emergency dikes to protect areas from rampaging flood waters. Other unusual circumstances may develop that result in calling out the Guard, such as a massive prison break or rioting.[17]

The chief of the state military force is actually the adjutant general who is appointed by the governor but must be approved by the federal military authorities. The adjutant general is the chief military advisor to the governor. It is upon his recommendation that the governor commissions the various officers of the state's National Guard unit and grants promotions to members of the Guard.

Rarely has the National Guard been used for other than strictly official emergency purposes. Occasionally a governor may attempt to use the

---

[17] Charles Fairman, *The Law of Martial Rule* (Chicago: Callaghan & Co., 1943); and Martha Derthick, *The National Guard in Politics* (Cambridge: Harvard University Press, 1965).

military force to keep his political regime in power, such as was the case in Louisiana in 1934 when Governor Huey Long ordered the Guard to seize the voting lists in New Orleans to ensure the election of his political machine.

The state may lose its control over its National Guard unit if the President of the United States calls up a state unit. It then is said to be "federalized" or "activated" and is no longer under the jurisdiction of the governor. Many states have authorized the governor then to organize a state militia to replace the National Guard units.

## Civil Defense

Civil defense is viewed as a joint responsibility of the national, state, and local governments. The Federal Civil Defense Act provides for federal advice and assistance to the state and local governments in the establishment and operation of civil defense programs. The governor is normally the nominal head of the state civil defense organization but the actual administrative operation is delegated to a director of civil defense named by the governor. The current trend is to place a growing share of the responsibility for civil defense activities under the governor's military commandant, the state's adjutant general.

Because of the continuing tense international situation and with new nations possessing the power of atomic bombs, civil defense functions have assumed a rank of great importance. The civil defense organizations are also charged with the responsibility of dealing with natural disasters, such as tornadoes and floods, aided by the state's national guard.

## JUDICIAL POWERS

The power to grant pardons, commutations, reprieves, and paroles for criminal offenses against the state has been given to the governors in the American states except in Georgia, even though it may be more properly considered a judicial rather than an executive power. The purpose underlying these powers is to provide a mode of correction for any injustices that may have occurred. It is often erroneously believed that this authority pertains to persons convicted of any and all crimes. Such is not the case. Conviction for treason is beyond the authority of the governor just as is the case in which a federal law has been violated.

A full pardon provides release of a prisoner with restoration of all civil rights which he forfeited at the time of his commitment to prison. The United States Supreme Court has defined a pardon as "An act of grace, proceeding from the power entrusted with the executive thereof, which exempts the individual to whom it is bestowed from the punishment which the law inflicts for a crime he has committed." Governors grant pardons for several reasons, with most common justification being to prevent a miscarriage of justice, but several others are frequently cited by governors in granting this form of executive clemency. These include situations where the punishment is disproportionate to the crime, or when the prisoner is serving a sentence for breaking a law which is later repealed, ill health of a prisoner, or the performance of some meritorious deed by the convicted person.

Most state chief executives have used their authority to pardon criminals with great discretion. Extreme pressure by friends and relatives of prisoners has on occasion brought about release when it could not be fully justified. In Georgia the governor has been relieved of any authority concerning the granting of pardons, but in the other states it still remains a power virtually unimpaired.[18]

Commutation is a reduction of a sentence. This may be either merely changing the number of years, or it may involve reducing a death sentence to life in prison. In a number of states prisoners sentenced to life may never be eligible for parole, unless the sentence is commuted to a given number of years.

A reprieve is a stay in the execution of a sentence. This action on the part of the governor does not change the punishment but merely delays carrying it out. Most reprieves involve the death sentence. A prisoner may be scheduled to be executed on a given day, but the date may be postponed by gubernatorial action. There would appear to be no limit to the number of reprieves that an individual may receive. In several states repeated reprieves have been granted to a prisoner but he still is executed.

The power of parole is one that most state governors exercise with great care. State statutes usually direct that paroles are granted in the name of the governor but usually only after they have been recommended by a state parole board. Most state laws give the governor considerable latitude in accepting or rejecting the recommendations of the parole board, but few chief executives find it advisable to disregard the board's suggestions concerning parole matters. Parole releases the convicted individual from prison but ordinarily places him on probation with frequent checks by parole agents as to his activities for a number of years after his release from the state penitentiary.

Very closely associated with the judicial powers of the governor is the action involved in interstate rendition (extradition) of persons wanted to answer for some crime in another state. The governor of the state in which the crime has been committed requests the governor of the state to

---

[18] *Survey of Release Procedures*, Vol. III, *Pardon* (Washington, D.C.: Attorney General's Survey, 1939).

which the accused has fled to return the individual to face the charges as filed. The United States Constitution makes it mandatory that such a request for a person charged with a felony be honored. However, a governor may not be coerced into such action if he feels that there are circumstances that justify his refusal to return the accused. Usually the governor who receives a request from his counterpart in another state for the return of an individual accused of a crime will conduct a hearing to determine whether or not the request should be honored. It is unusual for a governor to refuse such a request but when this does occur the governor making the requested rendition has no recourse.

Most of the judicial powers of the state chief executives are handled in a routine manner by the staff members, with very few coming to the personal attention of the governor for detailed study. Thus most governors do not spend an exorbitant amount of their time on judicial power execution. However in some states, such as North Carolina, the number of pardons granted in a year is so great that countless hours must be spent in giving even cursory consideration to these matters. Between 1941 and 1949, 6,975 pardons were granted.[19]

## THE EXECUTIVE OFFICE OF THE GOVERNOR

The staffs of the governors vary from a minimum of three in some of the small population states to more than fifty people in the largest states. There is some correlation between the population and the staff size, but several other factors appear to be equally important.[20] The customs and traditions that have developed in the state have a great bearing upon how large and extensive the staff of the governor will be. If the governor is expected to know everyone in the state, as he is in such sparsely populated states as Nevada and Alaska, it is out of character to have a large formal staff to act as a buffer between the chief executive and the people. Secondly, the size of the staff is dependent upon the actual power over legislation and administration that the governor is expected to exercise. If he is only the nominal leader of the state, and not the real executive, the size of the staff will be limited.

Another problem is present in actually determining how extensive a governor's staff is. In some states the staff is listed as only those persons working in the governor's office suite. This may not be the total staff, however, as usually other persons such as the budget director and the

[19] Robert S. Rankin, *Government and Administration of North Carolina* (New York: Thomas Y. Crowell Co., 1955), p. 91.

[20] Ransone, Jr., *op. cit.* See chap. x for probably the best discussion of the staffing problems of a governor's office.

adjutant general are not physically located in the governor's suite but usually should be included in the official staff.

A governor's staff should be designed to assist him in executing his basic duties concerned with: (1) policy formation, (2) administrative management, and (3) public relations. In addition to these three major divisions of the staff there will, of course, be the military aide (the state's adjutant general), the budget director, probably the personnel director, and an assistant whose primary duty is connected with various phases of the governor's responsibilities for executive clemency.

The governor's policy assistant, usually called his executive assistant, is ordinarily regarded as his top staff member. It is his responsibility to coordinate the work of the entire staff. This is a small job in some states but a complicated task in others, with forty or fifty staff members. The policy assistant usually has the job of implementing the governor's program. This involves writing many of the major speeches, such as the inaugural message, the state of the state message, the budget message, and other major speeches that the chief executive delivers. He will also have the responsibility of advising the governor concerning bills that have been passed by the legislature, writing vetoes when bills do not conform to the governor's program, and working as general liaison with the legislature.

It is vitally important that the policy assistant and the staff member charged with administrative management work closely together. This is particularly true in dealing with budgetary matters as the budget is both a policy matter and a tool of administrative management. The title of administrative assistant is commonly given to the individual keeping control of the administrative responsibilities of the governor. It is his duty to relieve the governor as much as possible from the day-by-day routine of supervising the many agencies reporting to the head of the state government.

The so-called housekeeping functions of state government, such as purchasing, personnel, accounting, and budget allocations are left to the administrative assistant's supervision. As many of the agency heads as possible should report to him and should have only occasional audiences with the governor on basic policy problems of administering their agencies.

The assistant charged with the responsibility for public relations acts as the governor's eyes and ears in ascertaining the status of all of his programs in the mind of the public. The success of the governor's relations with the various press or communications media will be dependent upon his public relations assistant. Likewise, it should be his duty to see that the governor's interviews are kept at a manageable number. The actual acceptance of interviews is usually done by the governor's personal or confidential secretary but only after consultation with the public relations assistant. Many of the people who come to the state capitol hoping to see the governor can be handled by the public relations assistant and directed to the state agency that is actually involved in the problem the citizen has presented. The routine handling of mail will also fall into the list of duties performed by the public relations assistant. Similarly, this assistant will write many of the so-called minor speeches the governor delivers and will assist the executive assistant in the preparation of major manuscripts for the chief executive.

If a fourth major assistant is employed, his area should probably be that of legal advisor. This is particularly true in those forty-two states in which the attorney general is popularly elected and thus may or may not be of the same political party as the governor. Legal advice that the governor can depend upon is basic to the smooth operation of the chief executive's various roles. This legal assistant will also be involved with the problems of executive clemency. In some states this is a large part of the executive's job and a crucial factor in his success or failure.

In addition to these top assistants, a staff of secretaries, stenographers, and filing clerks is needed. These people should be of the governor's own choosing. It is imperative that they have complete loyalty to the chief executive and not be permanently assigned to the office under civil service rules and regulations. An adequate staff is necessary to reduce as much as possible the governor's work load. Some indication of the hectic pace that confronts almost every state governor is given in the following typical daily and weekly schedules.

The Governor's Day in a Typical
Sovereign State of the U.S.A.

| Time | Activities |
|---|---|
| 8:00– 9:00 | Reviewing staff reports—answering selected correspondence. |
| 9:00–10:00 | Meeting with state treasurer, state auditor, secretary of state, and secretary of agriculture |
| 10:00–10:45 | Press conference—with film on tape for TV stations |
| 10:45–11:00 | Recorded weekly radio report to the people |
| 11:00–11:30 | Conference with the state tax commission |
| 11:30–12:00 | Reviews state financial program with comptroller |
| 12:00– 1:30 | Luncheon with Retail Hardware Dealers of the state—15 minute speech of welcome |
| 1:30– 2:00 | Crowns Dairy Queen—signs two proclamations |
| 2:00– 2:30 | Conference with a county chairman of his political party on county patronage problems |
| 2:30– 3:00 | Interview with honor students from state speech contest on "Problems of Government" |
| 3:00– 3:30 | Answers selected correspondence and reviews speech to be presented in the evening |
| 3:30– 4:00 | Conference with state adjutant general |
| 4:00– | Leaves office for airport |

4:15–        Take-off in National Guard C-47 for speech in northern part of state
6:30– 9:00   Banquet for Industrialists opening new industrial park
9:15–        Take-off for state capital city
11:00        Arrives in capital city
11:15–12:00  Reviews schedule and speeches to be given the next day. . . .

The Governor's Typical Calendar of
Engagements for a Week
(non-legislative)

| Day | Major Engagements |
|---|---|
| 1 (Sunday) | Attends church with family<br>Participates in ground breaking in large city church's educational building |
| 2 (Monday) | Weekly meeting with Executives of major departments<br>Luncheon speech—Retail Hardware Dealers<br>Dinner—Northern City—opening of new industrial park |
| 3 (Tuesday) | Conference with commissioner of public safety on new safety program<br>Luncheon—with members of state Central Party committee<br>Banquet—speech before state Association of Social Welfare Workers |
| 4 (Wednesday) | Conference with state personnel director concerning pay policies<br>Luncheon—with members of the state conservation commission—outlines tourism Program<br>Dinner—speech—State University honoring members elected to Omicron Delta Kappa (honorary leadership fraternity) |
| 5 (Thursday) | Opens Teen-Age Conference on Safe Driving<br>Luncheon—speech before Capital City's Greater Chamber of Commerce<br>Conference with state comptroller on quarterly allocations to various departments<br>Dinner—speech before State Tax-Payers' Association |
| 6 (Friday) | Conference with members of the State Soil Conservation Committee<br>Luncheon—speech before the United Federated Clubs state convention<br>Dinner—speech before a fund raising banquet in a city in the western part of the state |
| 7 (Saturday) | Luncheon speech and dedication of a new wing to one of the State Mental Health Institutes . . .<br>Dinner—with wife and family at their home town country club . . . |

One Midwestern governor reported that in one year he had dinner alone with his family in the executive mansion twenty-two times. All other evenings were spent either entertaining guests in the mansion or attending required functions which inevitably included dinners.

Most state governors carefully plan their speaking schedules to cover the entire state during every year. Some sections and cities will be visited several times depending upon the population of the area and the potential political strength of the governor in that sector of the state. Detailed maps are constantly kept up-to-date showing where the governor has been and where he is scheduled to appear in the future. Acceptance of requests for speaking engagements often are determined by whether or not the place of the meeting fits in with the governor's geographic coverage of the state.

Most state governors find it convenient and necessary to make trips to Washington, D.C., several times during any year. Appearance before Congressional committees in support of a state project is often the motivation.

Many state governors believe that it is essential to make a limited number of out-of-state appearances before meetings of their political party each year. Usually no more than one or two of these trips per month is accepted lest the opposition accuse him of neglecting the state affairs to enhance his own national political position.

Each year virtually every governor takes his family and one or two members of his staff to the week-long Governors' Conference, which is usually scheduled for some vacation wonderland, such as Hawaii.

These annual meetings give the state chief executives the opportunity to explore matters of common interest to all of the states, to exchange ideas, and to promote strong and constructive improvements in state government. Frequently resolutions concerning vital issues of the time are passed which have influence on the course of action taken by both the states and the federal government. The Council of State Governments' staff assists special committees appointed at the annual meetings to prepare reports on a wide variety of subjects which are placed on the agenda for the following year.

Every summer each governor spends several days reviewing the troops at the state's National Guard training encampment. Likewise, almost every university with an Army, Air Force, or Naval Training ROTC program holds a Governor's Day during which the governor is invited to inspect the ROTC units.

During the months that the state legislature is in session the governor finds it necessary to reduce the number of out-of-state speeches and the number of trips that he makes to various parts of the state in order to be available to the legislators. A rule followed by almost every state chief executive is that during the legislative session appointments for nonmembers of the legislature are kept to a minimum and will be either canceled or postponed if a legislator appears in the governor's office and announces that he wishes to have an interview. Often the governor's very carefully prepared schedule for a day will be completely changed by the unexpected appearance in the governor's waiting-room of members of the legislature desiring an opportunity to talk with the governor about legislative matters or patronage problems.

## BIBLIOGRAPHY

ABERNETHY, BYRON R. *Some Persisting Questions Concerning the Constitutional State Executive.* Lawrence: University of Kansas, 1960.

BELLUSH, BERNARD. *Franklin D. Roosevelt as Governor of New York.* New York: Columbia University Press, 1955.

BLACK, HENRY C. *The Relations of Executive Power to Legislation.* Princeton: Princeton University Press, 1919.

BROOKS, GLEN E. *When Governors Convene.* Baltimore: Johns Hopkins Press, 1961.

DEBEL, NIELS H. *The Veto Power of the Governor of Illinois.* Urbana: Univerversity of Illinois, 1917.

FAIRMAN, CHARLES. *The Law of Martial Rule,* 2d ed. Chicago: Callaghan & Co., 1943.

FANNIN, PAUL, and ASSOCIATES. *The Office of Governor in Arizona.* Tempe: Bureau of Government Research, Arizona State University, 1964.

FINLEY, JOHN H., and SANDERSON, JOHN F. *The American Executive and Executive Methods.* New York: Appleton-Century-Crofts, Inc., 1908.

FRIEDMAN, JACOB A. *The Impeachment of Governor William Sulzer.* New York: Columbia University Press, 1939.

GRAVES, W. BROOKE. *The Governors of the States, 1900–1950.* Chicago: Council of State Governments, 1950.

HESSELTINE, WILLIAM B. *Lincoln and the War Governors.* New York: Alfred A. Knopf, Inc., 1948.

HOFSTADER, RICHARD. *The American Political Tradition: And the Men Who Made It.* New York: Alfred A. Knopf, Inc., 1948.

HUTCHISON, W. T. *Lowden of Illinois.* Chicago: The University of Chicago Press, 1957.

JENSEN, CHRISTEN. *The Pardoning Power in the American States.* Chicago: The University of Chicago Press, 1922.

LIPSON, LESLIE. *The American Governor: From Figurehead to Leader.* Chicago: The University of Chicago Press, 1939.

PERKINS, JOHN A. *The Role of the Governor of Michigan in the Enactment of Appropriations.* Ann Arbor: Bureau of Government, University of Michigan, 1943.

RANSONE, COLEMAN B., JR. *The Office of Governor in the South.* Bureau of Public Administration, University of Alabama, 1951.

———. *The Office of Governor in the United States.* University, Ala.: University of Alabama Press, 1956.

RICH, BENNETT M. *State Constitutions: The Governor.* New York: National Municipal League, 1960.

RIKER, WILLIAM H. *Soldiers of the States: The Role of the National Guard in American Democracy.* Washington, D.C.: Public Affairs Press, 1957.

ROHR, CHARLES J. *The Governor of Maryland: A Constitutional Study.* Baltimore: Johns Hopkins Press, 1932.

RUSKOWSKI, CASIMIR. *The Constitutional Governor.* Boston: Bruce Humphries, Inc., 1943.

SCACE, HOMER E. *The Organization of the Executive Office of the Governor.* New York: Institute of Public Administration, 1950.

Schlesinger, J. A. *How They Became Governor.* East Lansing: Bureau of Social and Political Research, Michigan State University, 1957.

Sindler, A. P. *Huey Long's Louisiana.* New Haven: Yale University Press, 1956.

Smith, Alfred E. *Up To Now—An Autobiography.* New York: The Viking Press, Inc., 1929.

Williams, G. Mennen. *A Governor's Notes.* Ann Arbor: Institute of Public Administration, University of Michigan, 1961.

# 14

# State Administrative
# Organizations

In every one of the states the governor is in theory, if not in fact, the head of the state administrative branch of government. The governor's office is always provided for in the state constitution and is at the top of the administrative hierarchy, even though the office may not possess the authority commensurate with the responsibility.

## CONSTITUTIONAL-ADMINISTRATIVE OFFICERS

In addition to the office of governor, in many of the states the constitutions provide for a number of other administrative offices that are popularly elected and thus are to a degree beyond the control of the state legislature and the governor. Thirty-eight of the states have a lieutenant governor specifically provided for in their constitutions. It may be questionable whether many of these number-two men should be considered as officers in the state administrative organization. Usually the primary duties of a lieutenant governor consist of presiding over the state senate and merely waiting for the governor to die, resign, or be so severely incapacitated as to require the lieutenant governor to assume his duties. A more complete discussion of the role of the lieutenant governor in the state governmental picture was presented in the chapter on state legislatures.

The following list indicates the number of state constitutions that provide for certain administrative offices: secretary of state (42), state treasurer (44), attorney general (40), superintendent of education or public instruction (23), state auditor (32), state comptroller (11), secretary of labor (3), commissioner of insurance (5), commissioner of mines (2), land surveyors (9), boards of university regents (5), state boards of education (6) and 18 other miscellaneous constitutional agencies, secretaries of agriculture (9), and public utility commissions (9).[1]

When an office is provided for in the state's constitution, unless the governor is given the power to name the appointees, the official is guaranteed a measure of independence that makes it virtually impossible for the governor to properly supervise or coordinate the work of the agency with the other administrative departments in the hierarchy. Similarly, it makes it difficult to effect any changes in the office or its duties and functions. Each constitutional official, particularly if he is popularly elected, feels that he is conducting his own operation. He will no doubt resent anything that might resemble interference by any other officer in the state governmental chain of command.

It is well-established that all of the state governmental agencies should consider themselves an integral part of the administrative team. The goal which all agencies should have, no matter whether they are constitutional or statutory offices, is to effectively administer the policies that have been determined by the state legislature. If one department fails to execute its work it may impair the efficiency of other state governmental administrative agencies. It is a symptom of poor administrative organization when a number of "empires" are fostered by independent constitutional officers who are not accountable to the chief executive but are basically only responsible to the electorate. Frequently a governor is forced to disregard the lack of cooperation that is so obvious on the part of some of the elected constitutional officers.

Because state administration is growing rapidly it is frequently necessary and vitally important to make changes in the administrative organization and structure; to reorganize agencies, to consolidate agencies and relocate functions and lines of responsibility. When an agency has been made independent and permanent by constitutional decree these changes are either impossible or at best very difficult to make. Not only are the hands of the state legislators tied but also the governors' in bringing about alterations which will promote efficiency and economy. New ideas about purchasing, budgeting, accounting, and auditing may be impossible to institute or at least delayed for years because of the constitutional position of state officials.

It usually is the prerogative of the state legislature to reorganize the state administration. In several states the method of the federal government in granting the chief executive the authority to recommend reorganization plans and submit them to the legislature for its approval has been instituted. Usually this involves the governor sending the plan to the

---

[1] Council of State Governments, The *Book of the States, 1962–1963* (Chicago: Council of State Governments, 1962), pp. 140–41; and *Constitution of Michigan,* effective January 1, 1964.

general assembly which may block the reorganization by a negative vote in either house within a specified time limit, usually sixty days.

It is fortunate that the list of constitutional state agencies does not seem to be increasing. The constitutions written since World War II have all tended to reduce the number of such officers rather than increase them. This is a trend that certainly should be encouraged. The Alaska Constitution provides only for two elective state administrative officers, the governor and the secretary of state, while the Hawaii supreme law provides for a governor, a lieutenant governor, and a state auditor. The New Jersey Constitution of 1948 provides for only a governor and a state auditor. Obviously the state legislature is allowed to establish the other administrative positions that are needed to administer the state's affairs. The Michigan Constitution, effective in 1964, provides for the popular election of the governor, lieutenant governor, secretary of state, attorney general, and state board of education. Table 14–1 indicates the number of constitutional-administrative officers, the total elective administrative agencies, and the total elected administrative officials for the states.

A neglected area of state administration is the qualifications of the individuals serving in major elective and appointive state offices.

The study by Richard L. McAnaw included 950 members of the state administrative hierachy in all fifty states.[2] The findings refuted the notion that state administrative personnel holding major elected and state appointive offices were of second-rate quality. The level of educational attainment of the state officers compares most favorably with that of federal officers. It was found to be slightly higher than that of the municipal office holders and far superior to the educational level of the general population. In his unpublished dissertation Mr. McAnaw compiled a "life model" of a typical state administrator. He found that as of 1963 this typical administrator would be a man of nearly 52 years of age, a product of a small town or farm who had lived the major part of his life since age 18 in a medium-sized or large city. He would be a native born, white, Protestant of Anglo-Saxon origin. He would have had some education beyond the high school level with a great possibility of possessing a college degree. His college work would have been oriented toward the type of function that he is now administering. His first entry into government work was before he was thirty and probably at a lower level of government. His first state government position came five years after his first appointment or election. While his governmental service may not have been continuous he has had fourteen years of experience at the state level. His present salary would be in excess of $10,000. He belongs to four or more fraternal, or service-oriented organizations. He obviously intends to make a career of state government service.

[2] Richard L. McAnaw, "The State Administrators" (Ph.D. dissertation, State University of Iowa Libraries, Iowa City, 1964).

## TABLE 14–1
### Constitutional and Statutory Elective Administrative Officials—1964

|  | Constitutional Officials | Total Elective Agencies | Total Elected Officials |
|---|---|---|---|
| Alabama | 8 | 9 | 11 |
| Alaska | 2 | 2 | 2 |
| Arizona | 8 | 9 | 13 |
| Arkansas | 7 | 7 | 7 |
| California | 8 | 8 | 11 |
| Colorado | 8 | 8 | 17 |
| Connecticut | 6 | 6 | 6 |
| Delaware | 6 | 6 | 6 |
| Florida | 7 | 8 | 10 |
| Georgia | 10 | 11 | 15 |
| Hawaii | 3 | 3 | 3 |
| Idaho | 7 | 8 | 8 |
| Illinois | 7 | 8 | 16 |
| Indiana | 7 | 7 | 7 |
| Iowa | 6 | 7 | 7 |
| Kansas | 8 | 10 | 15 |
| Kentucky | 9 | 9 | 11 |
| Louisiana | 11 | 12 | 24 |
| Maine | 5 | 7 | 13 |
| Maryland | 4 | 4 | 4 |
| Massachusetts | 7 | 7 | 14 |
| Michigan | 5 | 5 | 12 |
| Minnesota | 6 | 8 | 21 |
| Mississippi | 8 | 13 | 17 |
| Missouri | 6 | 7 | 11 |
| Montana | 7 | 8 | 10 |
| Nebraska | 9 | 9 | 21 |
| Nevada | 7 | 11 | 42 |
| New Hampshire | 4 | 4 | 8 |
| New Jersey | 2 | 2 | 2 |
| New Mexico | 9 | 9 | 20 |
| New York | 5 | 6 | 18 |
| North Carolina | 12 | 11 | 110 |
| North Dakota | 11 | 12 | 20 |
| Ohio | 7 | 7 | 29 |
| Oklahoma | 12 | 12 | 18 |
| Oregon | 3 | 5 | 5 |
| Pennsylvania | 5 | 5 | 5 |
| Rhode Island | 5 | 5 | 5 |
| South Carolina | 9 | 13 | 27 |
| South Dakota | 8 | 10 | 12 |
| Tennessee | 4 | 6 | 8 |
| Texas | 7 | 12 | 33 |
| Utah | 6 | 6 | 14 |
| Vermont | 5 | 8 | 16 |
| Virginia | 5 | 6 | 8 |
| Washington | 8 | 9 | 20 |
| West Virginia | 6 | 6 | 6 |
| Wisconsin | 6 | 6 | 6 |
| Wyoming | 5 | 5 | 5 |

SOURCE: Council of State Governments, *The Book of the States, 1964–1965* (Chicago: Council of State Governments, 1964).

## THE SECRETARY OF STATE

Each state has an office entitled secretary of state. In thirty-nine states the position is on the ballot with the people determining the occupant of the post. In Maine, New Hampshire, and Tennessee the legislature appoints, while in Delaware, Maryland, New Jersey, New York, Pennsylvania, Texas, and Virginia he is appointed by the governor. The lieutenant governor in the fiftieth state, Hawaii, acts as the secretary of state thus holding for all practical purposes a dual position. In most states the office is considered, primarily because of federal analogy, next to that of the governor in prestige. In the fifty states the office never has actually held the importance some laymen feel that was intended.

The duties of no two secretaries of state are identical. Technically the official is still the channel for communication with the national government and the governments of the other states. In actual practice even this is no longer followed. Communications are now direct from the governor to the president, from the state commissioner of public health to the secretary of health education and welfare, et cetera. The secretary of state still sends to the proper federal officials the names of duly elected members of Congress and reports the vote of the state's electoral college delegates. His office also plays a minor role in assisting the federal bureau of census in compiling some of its data.

One of the duties commonly designated to the secretary of state is custodian of the state's official records. The acts of the state legislature, the proclamations of the governor, the decisions of the supreme court, and various other public documents are filed with the secretary. It is his responsibility to see that these important official papers are properly filed, available, and promulgated. It is quite obvious that there is little if any discretionary power vested in the secretary as the keeper of the archives. He is strictly a ministerial officer.

The position of the secretary has not changed materially since Walter F. Dodd wrote in 1922:

Few duties are conferred upon the Secretary of State by the constitution, and in most states his duties are prescribed by law. He is the keeper of the states' public records and is frequently custodian of the state capitol. The important duties conferred upon him by statutes usually relate to elections, corporations, and motor vehicles. The laws of many states make him the chief officer with respect to the states' supervision of elections.[3]

The office of secretary of state has in many states become the center for miscellaneous functions that the state legislature decides should be per-

[3] Walter F. Dodd, *State Government* (New York: Appleton-Century-Crofts, Inc., 1922), p. 236.

formed but is reluctant to establish a new agency to carry on the administrative details. It has been said that the office illustrates vividly the chaotic development of state administration.[4]

Professor Kirk H. Porter concludes his discussion of the office by saying:

> There seems no reason for having a department of state. The department could be largely supplanted by the proposed bureau of records. Functions which would not belong in such a department should be located in departments where they do belong. About one point there need be no compromise. The head of this department should certainly not be elected by popular vote. He should be appointed by the governor and be strictly accountable to him.[5]

It is possible the office may become the center of the state's statistical data collection system—headquarters for all of the state's electrical data processing equipment. Certainly in many states the expense of the equipment makes it mandatory that more than one department utilize the same machinery. The secretary of state may well find that the major role of his offices will be in the supervision of this data processing operation.

If new important activities are not found for the secretary of state and his assistants it may well be that the recommendations of a number of eminent authorities in the field of public administration to completely abolish the office and distribute its functions among other departments may be followed.

## STATE TREASURER

The post of state treasurer is a constitutional office in forty-four states and is popularly elected in forty states. Thus he has the independence and prestige that has been attached to the other chief administrative offices. The primary duties of the treasurer in most states are relatively clear cut. He is the custodian for all monies possessed by the state and he may invest, upon proper authority, all money not currently being used. In some states he has discretion as to the selection of banks for depositing state funds while in others this is dictated by legislative action. A few states still center the responsibility for collection of taxes in the state treasurer's office, but the trend is toward establishing a separate tax collecting agency, usually a tax commission or finance department. A major responsibility of a state treasurer is the handling of state bond issues and other borrowing and refunding activities. In the second half of the twentieth century this part of the treasurer's responsibility has been rapidly increasing since more and more states are finding it necessary to issue bonds to supple-

---

[4] Kirk H. Porter, *State Administration* (New York: Appleton-Century-Crofts, Inc., 1938), p. 58.
[5] *Ibid.*, p. 74.

ment the yearly tax revenue, particularly to finance long-range capital improvements. In some states the treasurer has considerable power over local financial transactions of municipalities, counties, special districts, and school districts, but the recent trend is away from centering the authority in a popularly elected treasurer.

Professor Martin Faust of the University of Missouri wrote in 1925, "There is no phase of state financial administration veiled in more secrecy than the administration of public deposits."[6] This is no longer as true as it was formerly. Most states have now restricted the amount of discretion granted the state treasurer in virtually all of his financial actions. The amount of policy making is very low, and the post has become almost completely a bookkeeping, ministerial operation. The same statement that has been made concerning the secretary of state is applicable to the post of state treasurer: there can be no justification of the office being filled by partisan, popular election. The post should be made appointive and integrated with a financial department. This office will be discussed in detail in the chapters on finance.

## STATE AUDITOR

Twenty-nine states popularly elect the state auditor. Six states do not even have such an office or its equivalent. In the other fifteen states the auditor is usually selected by the legislative branch or in conjunction with the governor. The role of the state auditor has been changing drastically in the last twenty years. Originally it was a dual post with both pre-audit and post-audit functions. Today more than two-thirds of the states have removed from the state auditor's authority his pre-audit functions, with this power usually designated to a comptroller. It is believed by most students of financial administration that the roles of post-audit and pre-audit should be performed by two separate offices. The pre-audit should be in a post with direct accountability and responsibility to the governor while the post-audit should be performed by an officer responsible to the legislature. In either position it is quite obvious that the popular election method is an unsuitable method of selecting the state auditor.

There can be no question that all public accounts should be audited either continuously or periodically. Since there are numerous public accounts in every state, the job is of such importance that it should stand alone without being coupled with pre-audit functions. The purpose of the audit which the state auditor makes on the accounts of local government officials should be to insure that all accounts are accurate and balance properly, that the actual funds shown are on hand, and that receipts are

[6] Martin Faust, *The Custody of State Funds* (New York: National Institute of Public Administration, 1925), p. 56.

available to account for all expenditures. Similar checks should be made by the auditor's staff of the debt service funds of local governments. This would be a minimum amount of state supervision that should not be objectionable to any local governmental officials. It may be necessary to facilitate an audit by the state auditor by prescribing some of the accounting forms that are used by the local governmental units.[7]

## ATTORNEY GENERAL

Forty state constitutions provide for an office of state attorney general and the other ten states provide for such a post by statute. In forty-two states, popular election is the method used for selecting the head of the legal department of the state government. In the other states he is appointed, in some by the governor, in others by the supreme court. In many states the position is viewed as a natural stepping stone to the governor's office. While it is usually stated that the primary duty of the attorney general is to prosecute and defend cases to which the state is a party, this, in many states, does not constitute the bulk of the work performed by the attorney general and his staff. Probably the most important aspect of his work is in connection with the legal advice and services that he renders to the governor and all other state administrative agencies, as well as legal assistance given to the state legislature.[8]

Although each state agency usually would prefer to have its own legal staff, in most states the attorney general and his assistants provide the only legal counsel available to the state officials. There is a trend in several states to concentrate the legal officials who have in the past been within separate agencies under the control of the attorney general. This would appear to be desirable.

The major opinions of each state's attorney general are published yearly in a series of volumes entitled "Opinions of the Attorney General." These constitute the official interpretations of state statutes and administrative orders and are the law until they have been ruled upon by court decisions. A very small percentage of the opinions of an attorney general is nullified by any court decision and thus stand as the official ruling. It should be pointed out that even though they are referred to as the official interpretations they do not have the full effect of law.

Representing the various state agencies in litigation also constitutes a large part of the duties of the attorney general's staff. All of the state agencies find themselves involved in court actions at one time or another. The attorney general usually assigns one or more of his assistants to pre-

[7] T. E. McMillan, Jr., *State Supervision of Municipal Finance* (Austin: University of Texas, 1953).

[8] Porter, *op. cit.*, pp. 75–81.

pare the case in which the state agency is involved. It may be a simple matter of preparation of contracts or it may involve a long series of court actions. Best results have usually been attained if the attorney general assigns the same assistant to work with a department on all of its legal problems; thus the assistant becomes more or less familiar with the agency's legal questions and can better solve its administrative technicalities.

Many attorneys general find that their workload is quite unevenly distributed, and it is necessary to employ special assistants during different parts of every year. This is particularly true in extensive highway projects which involve a great deal of purchasing of right-of-way through eminent domain procedures.

Another aspect of the work of the attorney general involves his power to investigate the manner in which any state agency is handling its statutory responsibilities. Often the attorney general will undertake the investigation at the request of the governor, but in most states he is authorized to initiate investigations whenever he has reason to believe that any irregularities exist. Special agents from other state agencies may be assigned to work with the attorney general's staff on these investigations or he may have authority to employ his own special assistants, depending upon the state law and traditions.

Most attorneys general also have a responsibility for coordinating either state district attorneys' or county attorneys' activities. There is a great deal of variation in the amount of authority granted and a great deal of flexibility allowed in the supervision that an attorney general may choose to exercise over these legal officials. Arthur C. Millspaugh has suggested that since

All states have an attorney general's office or a department of justice headed by an attorney general, the way seems open to have the state direct and control prosecuting work. This can probably best be done by abolishing all local prosecutors and by giving the attorney general the necessary staff and funds for the work.[9]

While this suggestion would seem to have merit it should be emphasized that there has been no trend in this direction, probably due to the popular American fear of too great a degree of centralization, particularly in the field of legal prosecution.

## SUPERINTENDENT OF PUBLIC INSTRUCTION

Twenty-three states have established in their constitutions the administrative office of superintendent of public instruction and in the other states

[9] Arthur C. Millspaugh, *Local Democracy and Crime Control* (Washington: The Brookings Institution, 1936), p. 225.

an office is provided by statute. In approximately half of the states the superintendent is popularly elected. It is quite common for the office, however, to be non-partisan rather than appear on the regular partisan ballot. The trend is to have this officer appointed by either the governor or by a state board of public instruction. The importance of the office appears to be increasing at a rate depending upon the additional participation by the state in the financial support of the local public schools. Each year more state departments of public instruction are establishing higher standards for the public schools. Requirements in regard to curriculum, teacher certification, approval of school textbooks, special education programs are all being administered by the superintendent of public instruction's office. A full presentation of the role in education as played by the state is found in the chapter on education.

## SECRETARY OF AGRICULTURE

Only nine of the states have established in their constitutions a department of agriculture but all, except Arkansas, have such an office or its equivalent. In thirteen states the head of the agriculture department is popularly elected. The most common method of selection is by gubernatorial appointment with senate confirmation. The importance of this department is largely dependent upon the extent of agriculture within the state. In some states it is one of the larger state agencies, but in others it lacks stature, power, authority, and financial resources. Ten states have constitutional offices dealing with natural resources and land. Obviously these must be added to the nine constitutional offices of agriculture to gain an insight into the total importance given to this phase of state governmental administration. The importance of this position is discussed in more detail in the chapter on agriculture and conservation.

## THE POSITION OF THE WEAK GOVERNOR IN STATE ADMINISTRATION

While it is obvious that many states still elect too many administrative officials, there is a definite trend away from this mode of selecting these executives who should be under the governor's authority and direction if the chief executive is to be charged with the responsibility for the entire state administrative organization. There is a continuing trend toward fewer separate administrative agencies in most states. New Jersey and Michigan have been the leaders in this area, with their constitutions providing for no more than twenty state administrative departments. This, however, is the exception rather than the rule. A vast majority of the state constitutions still prescribe and provide for a large number of state agencies.

Likewise there is a tendency to abandon the nineteenth- and early twentieth-century custom of having many state functions performed by commissions or boards. Here again it is a slow process, with a few states eliminating a board or commission in favor of a single director. It would appear to be more difficult to end the existence of commissions than boards, since the commission members are full-time, receiving full pay, and in theory have training and experience in the field that they are administering.

As A. E. Buck stated in 1938:

The commission idea was good for its time and is probably still valid in some cases. . . . Even when manned by able and well-intentioned men, boards were not altogether satisfactory. They tended to be slow to act and difficult, if not impossible, for the governor and legislature to supervise.[10]

It is obvious that it will be many years before the slowly developing movement toward single headed administrative units will be complete. A typical state administrative organization, if such exists, would still include a majority of state agencies with multi-headed or plural executives. Iowa's administrative organization is typical of such state administrative organization.

The governor is surrounded by popularly elected executives. The state treasurer is elected, as is the state auditor, secretary of state, secretary of agriculture, and attorney general. All of these elected officials except the attorney general serve on the executive council which is designated as the head of many of the housekeeping functions of state government. If the governor is fortunate the members of the executive council will be members of his party, but occasionally he will find himself completely surrounded by members of the opposite party.[11] The governor has a whole battery of multi-headed state agencies that are in theory under his supervision but whose composition is such that they may or may not be receptive to his directions. The department of social welfare is headed by a three-member board, the state monopoly liquor system by a three-member commission, the highway department by a five-member board, the tax department by a three-member tax commission, and the state's mental health and penal institutions by a three-member board.

The only major state agencies headed by a single director are the department of public safety, department of public health, the banking de-

[10] A. E. Buck, *The Reorganization of State Governments in the United States* (New York: Columbia University Press, 1938), p. 20.

[11] From 1957 to 1961 the Governor of Iowa was a Democrat but all other members of the Executive Council were Republicans. Again in 1963–1964 the same situation existed.

partment, and the insurance and securities department. Even in these offices the governor finds that frequently the term of the appointee is not for two years as he serves, but rather is for four years. Thus the governor may not have the opportunity of appointing the head of the agency during his first term in office.

In addition, a large number of state agencies are headed by ex-officio boards. Here again, Iowa is quite typical. The Iowa governor finds that the real estate commission, the war roster commission, the commission for the blind, the state printing board, the soldiers bonus board, the state fair board, the state geological board, and the state public health board are at least partially, if not entirely, composed of state officials who hold membership on these boards or commissions ex officio.[12] Figure 14–1 depicts the Iowa Administrative Organization with its plural executive structure of organization.

It is unfortunate but still true that

The American state governments until 1910 exhibited almost none of the characteristics associated with the concept of general management. Neither the governor nor any other state officer was in a position to exercise managerial power with reference to state business. The various agencies had no common head and recognized little responsibility to any high executive officer. There was no central planning, no unified command, no administrative program, no coordinating agency, no agency to investigate and report, except ineffective legislative committees, and no fiscal control. American state administration was in short, atomistic and disorganized to an exceptional degree.[13]

Several of these shortcomings have been alleviated. But others still persist.

Good government is keynoted by a sound, efficient administrative organization. Very little will be accomplished, no matter how farsighted and beneficial are the policies of the legislative branch, if these are not faithfully executed by the administrators in their daily operations. Good, sound, faithful performance of administrative responsibilities is often unnoticed. Only when obvious maladministration occurs is the attention of the general public focused upon the administrative agencies.

The first requisite of good and efficient administration is a body of administrative officers of competence, integrity, and dedication. The old cliché that a good workman will do a good job no matter what tools are provided is only partially true. The necessary requisite is a good workman and good tools with which to perform the task assigned. It is quite obvious that many state administrative units are not being provided with the proper tools. As will be noted in the chapter on state personnel ad-

---

[12] Russell M. Ross, *The Government and Administration of Iowa* (New York: Thomas Y. Crowell Co., 1957.)

[13] Leonard D. White, *Trends in Public Administration* (New York: McGraw-Hill Book Co., Inc., 1933), p. 176.

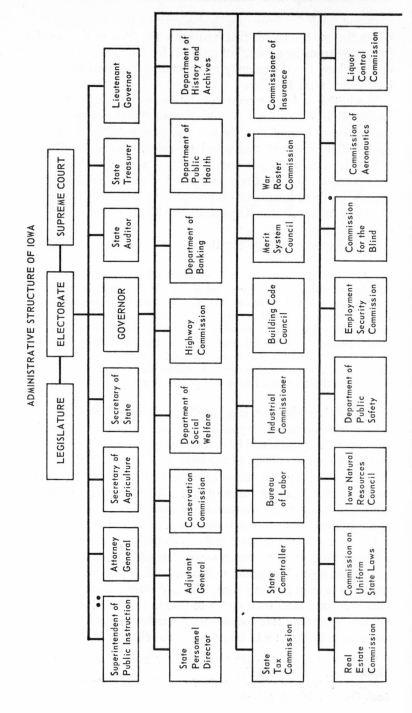

ADMINISTRATIVE STRUCTURE OF IOWA

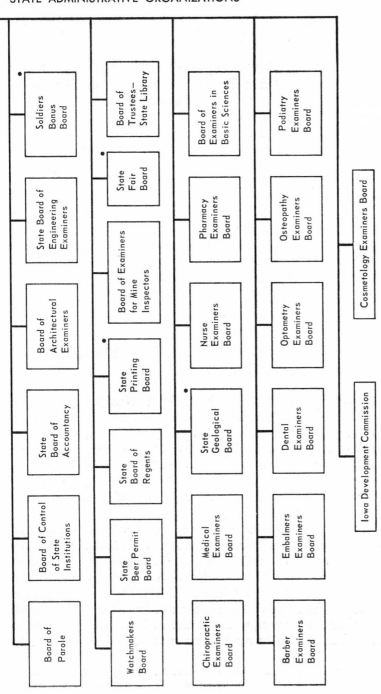

• Membership Ex officio either whole or in part.

•• Appointed by State Board of Public Instruction.

**Fig. 14—1.** Iowa: A Non-integrated State Administrative Organization. [Source: Russell M. Ross, *Government and Administration of Iowa* (New York: Thomas Y. Crowell Co., 1957).]

ministration, it is also true that frequently the good personnel are also missing. When this situation exists good government is purely by chance and not by design.

An important principle that is recognized by all students of administration is that there is a limited number of agencies any chief executive can effectively supervise. In those few states that have reorganized their state governments within the last fifteen years, the governor usually is expected to supervise fewer than twenty administrative agencies. In the majority of states the number is still over fifty and in many it will exceed one hundred.

The total number of state agencies reporting to the governor is usually a fair indicator as to how efficiently the state administration is organized. An exception would be a state that has included in its total number of administrative agencies a large number of examining boards; these obviously will distort the total picture but are not actually major deterrents to effective administrative organization. The difficulty of reorganization may be in part determined by the number of administrative agencies that are prescribed by the state constitution and by statutory enactment.

## THE POSITION OF THE STRONG GOVERNOR IN STATE ADMINISTRATION

The governmental administrative hierarchy in New Jersey under its state constitution of 1947 is in direct contrast with that of Iowa. A four-year term is granted the governor in New Jersey and he is allowed to succeed himself once. The overlapping terms of other constitutional officers in the executive branch have been eliminated. The governor has specific authority to investigate any state administrative agency and to obtain information under oath concerning the official conduct of every agency. The legislature is allowed to appoint only the state auditor.

However, the most important provision is probably the governor's control over the administrative agencies, with such units limited to no more than twenty. Only fourteen administrative agencies have been established. While the constitution states that "the head of each principal department shall be a single executive unless otherwise provided by law," five departments are headed by boards.[14] The members of four of these five boards are appointed by the governor, while the fifth, in theory, is a gubernatorial appointment, but actually the nominations are made by farmers' associa-

[14] Article V., sec. IV, paragraph 2, *Constitution of New Jersey, 1947*. See also Bennett M. Rich, *The Government and Administration of New Jersey* (New York: Thomas Y. Crowell Co., 1957), p. 110.

tions and then forwarded by the governor to the senate for approval. In three of the five multi-headed departments, an administrative officer is also present who is appointed by the governor rather than by the board or commission. Thus in twelve of the fourteen state agencies the governor has a great amount of control over the selection of the heads of the administrative agencies. The removal power of the governor of New Jersey is limited to a lesser degree than his appointive power. The executives of single-headed departments serve at the pleasure of the governor; executive officers of boards may be removed by the governor upon notice and proper hearing. Figure 14–2 diagrams the administrative-hierarchy in an integrated administrative organization—New Jersey.

In addition to his power of appointment and removal of administrative officers a strong governor has a dominant role in both budget-making and budget-execution. Since budget-making includes both the estimation of total requirements of the state government on the expenditure side and calculation of income, it is imperative that the chief executive control this area of activity. Wthout control, the governor would not possess a basic tool for state-wide planning. A governor's administrative power in the field of fiscal management is a key to his total authority.

In the strong governor states the chief executive has the role of supervisor. He not only can make his wishes known but he has supporting authority to secure compliance. In these states the governor is not confronted by an array of administrative commissions and boards through which he operates but rather departments headed by a single individual whose appointment is coterminous with the election of the governor.

The powerful governors are granted both by constitution and statute wide-spread discretionary powers. Ministerial authority is still present but is accompanied by this corollary power of much greater importance to the successful operation of the state governmental machinery. It is possible for some weak governors to become effective leaders in spite of their limited powers, but such is unusual.

## STATE ADMINISTRATIVE REORGANIZATION

Interest in state administrative organization and reorganization began shortly after the turn of the twentieth century. It was only natural that this should occur as a similar movement had taken place in city administration. The city movement can be traced as far back as the 1890's with the New York Bureau of Municipal Research being probably the first formal organization systematically to approach the problems of city administration. At the state level, the People's Power League of Oregon in 1909 was established as the first wedge in the drive for state administrative

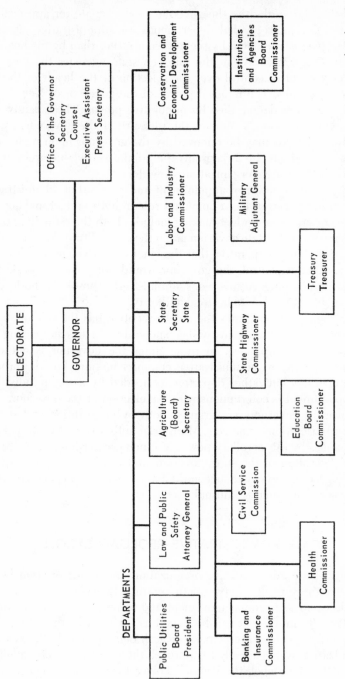

**Fig. 14-2.** The New Jersey State Administrative Organization. [Source: Bennett M. Rich, *Government and Ad-ministration of New Jersey* (New York: Thomas Y. Crowell Co., 1957).]

reorganization.[15] Similar movements were started in Minnesota in 1913 and in New York state two years later.

Reorganization of the national government was inaugurated with the appointment by President Howard Taft of the Efficiency and Economy Commission to study the national administrative picture. As laudable and worthwhile as these studies may have been, very little if any concrete reorganization resulted.

The first actual progress toward the goal of reorganizing state administrative hierarchies occurred in Illinois in 1917 with the establishment of its Civil Administrative Code. The drive did not start and end in 1917 but actually was initiated by Governor Dunne in 1913, when, in his inaugural address, he called attention to specific recommendations for appointing a joint committee of the two houses of the legislature to study certain aspects of the state administrative operations. The Efficiency and Economy Committee was created and after intensive study and public hearings resulted in several major reorganization recommendations. The report recommended the abolition of over one hundred independent officers, boards, and commissions with their functions reassigned to ten major administrative departments. As might be anticipated, the recommendations were not enacted by the legislature of Illinois at that session. However, Governor Dunne's successor, Frank O. Lowden, renewed the recommendations of the Efficiency and Economy Committee and agreed to even "defer making of appointments until the administrative code had been enacted into law."[16] While the legislature of Illinois did not adopt in toto the recommended ten departments, the legislation did follow the main lines of the reorganization proposals.

The constitutional officers were retained and kept their independence of gubernatorial supervision, but the code did achieve sufficient reorganization to enable the governor to exercise supervisory power over the major portions of the state administrative activities. It is interesting to note that both Governor Lowden and his Democratic opponent of 1916 had supported this progressive legislation and had advocated removing from the popular election ballot all the administrative officers except the governor, but to no avail. Four years later in the state constitutional convention that convened in 1920 the proposal was defeated.

The essential features of the 1917 Administrative Code included a direct line of responsibility from governor, directors, and chiefs of bureaus to minor officers, with respect to purely administrative functions. Each department established was provided with an advisory board to assist the director of the department and the governor in matters of broad policy

15 Buck, op. cit., p. 6.
16 Edward F. Dunne, Illinois, The Heart of the Nation (Chicago: The Lewis Publishing Co., 1933), Vol. XI, p. 338.

administration; the civil service commission and a relatively few temporary boards were permitted to retain their independent status.

Between 1917 and 1963 only eight major changes were made in the Illinois Administrative Code; the department of trade and commerce was
abolished in 1933, and seven new departments were created: conservation,
in 1925, insurance, public safety, revenue, aeronautics, personnel, and
financial institutions. The total number of departments now numbers fifteen. Virtually all new agencies and expansion of existing agencies have
been fitted into the framework of the code departments.[17]

As a result of the Illinois reorganization in 1917, added incentive was
apparently given to other states to reconsider their administrative structures. While the Illinois plan must be considered only a partially integrated
administrative hierarchy, it certainly was a vast improvement over what
had preceded it. A number of other states, including California, Idaho,
and Kentucky followed the Illinois lead.

Other states such as Connecticut, Maine, North Carolina, and South
Dakota merely granted the governor stronger power in his fiscal-control.
The purpose was to permit the management of the affairs of the state
through financial supervision to be vested in the governor. A third semi-
reorganization movement in Indiana allowed six constitutional elective
officers to share in the administration of many consolidated departments.
This movement was characterized by Professor A. E. Buck as resembling
the commission form of government familiar to our cities.[18] It retained all
of the shortcomings of the commission form of municipal government and
in general was not viewed as a major step forward in the reorganization
movement.

By 1938 the State of New York had created eighteen constitutional state
administrative departments, that were headed in almost all cases by a single individual and almost all were directly accountable to the governor.
The attorney general as head of the law department was popularly
elected. This was one of the first integrated state administrative hierarchies. The eighteen departments included:

| | | |
|---|---|---|
| Executive | Conservation | Social Welfare |
| Audit & Control | Agriculture & Markets | Corrections |
| Taxation & Finance | Labor | Public Service |
| Law | Education | Banking |
| State | Health | Insurance |
| Public Works | Mental Hygiene | Civil Service |

The new state constitution adopted by Missouri in 1945 was a major
contribution to the reorganization movement. In addition to the governor

[17] Neil F. Garvey, *The Government and Administration of Illinois* (New York:
Thomas Y. Crowell Co., 1958), p. 138.
[18] Buck, *op. cit.*, pp. 28–33.

and lieutenant governor the constitution limits the number of state administrative departments to fourteen. Four elected officers were retained to administer four of the departments: the secretary of state, the state auditor, attorney general, and state treasurer. The departments of revenue, insurance, labor, budget, education, highways, conservation, agriculture, health and welfare were established by the state legislature. The governor was granted power to assign agencies to the departments, thereby allowing a degree of flexibility and integration in the hands of the chief executive.[19]

It is generally agreed that the 1945 Constitution of Georgia did not aid the reorganization program, but the 1947 Constitution of New Jersey did make a major contribution to the science of state government reorganization.

The provisions in Article V, section 4 of the New Jersey Constitution probably establish as near as possible a model integrated state administrative hierarchy:

1. All executive and administrative officers, departments, and instrumentalities of the state government and their respective functions, powers, and duties are allocated by law within approximately twenty principal departments in such a manner as to group them according to major purposes. Temporary commissions for special purposes, may, however, be established by law and such commissions need not be allocated within principal departments.

2. Each principal department is under the supervision of the governor. The head of each principal department is a single executive unless otherwise provided by law. Such single executives are nominated and appointed by the governor, with advice and consent of the senate, to serve at the pleasure of the governor during his term of office.

The laws that have implemented the state constitution have been somewhat short of complete administrative integration. There are apparently some agencies in the New Jersey state administrative system that do not function as integral parts of the departments to which they have been assigned. This is to a degree offset by the need for obtaining gubernatorial approval of budget requests and personnel turnover. As Professor Rich has commented:

The most meaningful feature of the revision-reorganization movement has been the continuing nature of the efforts to improve the state's administrative structure and the efficiency of its operations.[20]

New vitality was given to the study of state government administrative organization with the appointment in 1947 of the federal commission on

[19] Martin L. Faust, *Five Years Under the New Missouri Constitution* (Jefferson City: Missouri Public Expenditure Council, 1950).
[20] Rich, *op. cit.*, pp. 110–11.

Organization of the Executive Branch of the Government of the United States, which became popularly known as the Hoover Commission since it was headed by former President Herbert Hoover. This federal study stimulated a majority of the state legislatures to form study groups to evaluate their own state's administrative structure. The Little Hoover Commissions as they have been termed took four basic forms according to the Council of State Governments:

1. Special interim committees of members of the state legislature, created to study the over-all administrative structure and to report their findings to the next session.

2. Commissions created specifically for the purpose of developing recommendations for reorganizations.

    a. Some commissions were exclusively legislators, others made use of outstanding citizens and others utilized outside experts as advisors.

3. Special legislative committees, on a semi-continuing basis to constantly study the organization problems.

4. Assigning the task to a research agency to make recommendations to the next legislature for needed changes.[21]


## STANDARDS OF ADMINISTRATIVE REORGANIZATION

Six standards based upon experience and supported by actual practice used to measure reorganization efficiency are listed by A. E. Buck as follows: (1) concentration of authority and responsibility, (2) departmentalization or functional integration, (3) undesirability of boards for purely administrative work, (4) coordination of the staff services of administration, (5) provision for an independent audit, and (6) recognition of a governor's cabinet.[22]

Almost every administrative effort has as its keynote the concentration of power commensurate with responsibility in the office of the governor. The chief executive should be held accountable for the entire state administrative operation but can and should be responsible only if he has adequate authority to control all of the various executive agencies. This means that the long list of elected state executives must be eliminated and their positions made subordinate to the governor. This allows the governor to have a cabinet of advisors composed of the men he has appointed to head the various major departments of the state government.

[21] Council of State Governments, *A Progress Report on State Reorganization in 1950* (Chicago: Council of State Governments, 1950).

[22] Buck, *op. cit.*, pp. 14–15.

In order to keep within the span-of-control principle the departments must be based upon a functional organizational procedure. This would produce the consolidation of departments and elimination of overlapping, functional activities. Usually the maximum number of such departments should not exceed twenty at the one extreme and probably ten would be a more manageable number.

No sound administrative reorganization scheme can place boards or commissions in charge of purely administrative operations. The single-headed department is preferable for a number of valid administrative reasons. It focuses authority and responsibility in a single individual who can be held accountable for the department's success or failure. It speeds the administrative process, eliminating "buck-passing," and administrative tie-ups. The only role that a board can properly play in an efficient hierarchy is as a quasi-judicial, quasi-legislative or policy advisory agent.

The coordination of staff services gives recognition to the need for greater use of planning, better methods of budgeting, purchasing, accounting, personnel practices, and pre-auditing. An administrative agency with a state manager is a positive trend in this general direction which is found in Minnesota and slightly modified in Kansas.

The separation of the pre-audit and post-audit functions is recommended in most recent state administrative reorganization reports. The pre-audit should be performed by a comptroller entirely responsible to the governor. This audit is done before money is actually expended and ascertains the existence of adequate funds to cover the expenditure and the legality of the transaction. The post-audit should be performed by an agency entirely accountable to and appointed by the legislative branch. It should be performed immediately after the expenditure of monies so as to be of greatest value to the policy-making branch.

While these are excellent objectives, not all are attainable in one reorganization effort. Continuous studies are often needed to keep the administrative hierarchy in line with the latest administrative practices.

## TYPES OF ADMINISTRATIVE ORGANIZATION

In 1938 A. E. Buck classified the state administrative organizations into four types. While there has been a great deal of effort spent upon changing the administrative structures in many states, the basic classifications are still valuable guides. The type that is closest to the administrative structure designed in the Model State Constitution is called the integrated administrative organization. The second is classed as partially integrated, the third, the fiscal-control type, and the fourth, the commission or plural executive organization.

## The Integrated Type

This form of organization provides complete control of administration in the hands of the governor, with a limited number of departments, each directed by single individuals, appointed, responsible, and removable by the governor at his pleasure. The short ballot is used with only the governor and one or two other executives who are popularly elected. Popular control is continued by the periodic election of the chief executive. The impeachment power is retained in the hands of the legislature, as is the unquestioned right of the policy-making branch to provide tax revenue and make appropriations, and to check upon the accountability of the executive branch through the legislative audit process. The constitutions of Alaska, Hawaii, New Jersey, and Michigan are all directed toward this type of integrated administration. New York, Tennessee, and Virginia have constitutional provisions that strive for the integrated approach but do not attain the completely integrated organization.

## The Partially Integrated Type

This form retains the traditional limitations upon the administration with a long list of popularly elected administrative officers. The governor is in a position to control only a portion of the total administrative hierarchy. The Illinois reorganization of 1917, California, Idaho, Kentucky, Ohio, Pennsylvania, Rhode Island, and Washington are usually called partially integrated state administrative states.

## The Fiscal-Control Type

The governor is given power to manage the administrative affairs of the state through financial supervision rather than through administrative integration. It places under the governor the control of the basic fiscal processes, budgeting, general accounting, centralized purchasing, and some degree of personnel supervision. It is difficult to draw a sharp division between the states with fiscal control and partially integrated administrative structures as many have tended to adopt portions of both systems. Connecticut, Maine, North Carolina, South Dakota, Wisconsin, Alabama, Iowa, and New Hampshire have all adopted fiscal control type systems, but several have also partially integrated the administrative hierarchy under the chief executive.

## Plural-Executive Type

In this plan the governor becomes one of several executives, but usually he is in a slightly more powerful position than the other elected officers.

As a rule several departments are consolidated into a single unit and headed by an elected official, with as many as seven in Indiana comprising the executive administrative group. Colorado is another example of a state with this type of administrative organization.

It is an impossible task to attempt to categorically list many of the states in any one of the four classifications. Many states have drawn heavily from two or more of the systems. The partially integrated type is frequently a transitional stage through which a state passes before the state legislature and the public are prepared to accept a completely integrated hierarchy. Usually the greatest obstacle is the necessity of rewriting or materially amending the state constitution in order to become a truly integrated administrative state.[23] This requires a great deal of aroused citizen participation and interest, and much of this can be done only with years of effort.

## GROWTH OF THE REORGANIZATION MOVEMENT

Following the reorganization efforts in Illinois, Massachusetts in 1918, Idaho and Nebraska in 1919, Washington and California in 1921, and four states, Tennessee, Maryland, Pennsylvania, and Vermont in 1923 made reorganization efforts. By 1935 at least thirty state reorganization plans had been drafted and some changes made in the administrative structure of twenty-six states. Most of these studies were given impetus by the necessity of reduced costs because of the economic depression of the 1930's.

A second reorganization tide followed the Hoover Commission's formula for national administrative reorganization. By 1952, thirty-three states were in the process of studying the need for administrative revision.

In spite of the number of studies, relatively few states have actually made extensive reorganizational progress. Most of the structural changes have been more paper changes than actual administrative reorganization. Why the lack of concrete results? Several factors combine to make the total picture less than might be expected. The groups that oppose change most vigorously, of course, are those with vested interests. These include many incumbents who fear the loss of their positions and influence. On the other side of the reorganization question are the avid reformers who do not lend as much support as might be expected to the reorganization attempts in many states because they do not believe the changes recommended are as great as are needed.

A stream-lined administrative organization does center the concentration of responsibility upon the chief executive but at the same time grants

[23] *Ibid.*, pp. 28–30.

him authority to execute his program. It is important that the governor use wisely the power granted to him and select carefully his important staff and line department heads. He cannot afford to neglect his duties as a leader of the legislature and of his political party. If he does not rely upon his executive aids and attempts to operate the entire state government as a one man operation he inevitably will fail to carry out all of the various aspects of the chief executive's duties in a satisfactory manner.

Reorganization must be a continuous process. It will be constantly underway only if some individual has the power continually to examine the governmental operation. State legislatures have proven that they are not equipped to perform this function in the manner that is needed. The Alaska constitution is the only one which allows the governor to initiate reorganization proposals subject to a veto by the legislature. This plan has worked for the federal government and should be equally effective in the state governments if given a fair trial.

The future of state governmental reorganization depends upon the citizens of the states. The public will achieve the government that they deserve and the government they demand. An interested citizenry will insist on the most efficient, most economical, most effective governmental service possible through the latest administrative techniques and organization. The public's sense of fair play will insist that the governors have the authority commensurate with the responsibility.

The arguments used by those opposed to reorganization are interesting even if only partially true. Probably the most popular argument hinges upon the definition of democracy. The opponents of integration declare that placing full power in the governor's office is undemocratic and therefore un-American. This approach claims that reducing the number of elected officials denies the voter his constitutional rights. Democracy is equated with popular election of a long list of executive officers.

The claim is also pressed that delegating so much authority to the chief executive will allow him to install or reinforce the spoils system. The fear that all power corrupts and absolute power corrupts completely is used to forestall reorganization.

Much value is placed in the work of boards and commissions by the supporters of the status quo. They contend that single-headed agencies cannot give the continuity that public spirited citizens as members of boards and commissions with overlapping terms can accomplish.

Those fighting reorganization contend that in those states which have tried to reorganize, no reduction in the number of agencies and personnel has actually resulted. Therefore the contention is made that it is not worth while to attempt full integration.

The results in the states that have created an integrated hierarchy have admittedly not been as sensational as its proponents have anticipated and led the public to believe would occur. However, increased efficiency has resulted in most instances in more state services, as demanded by the public, rather than in tax reductions.

# BIBLIOGRAPHY

BELL, JAMES R., and DARRAH, EARL. *State Executive Reorganization.* Berkeley: Bureau of Public Administration, University of California, 1961.

BENSON, GEORGE C., and LITCHFIELD, EDWARD H. *The State Administrative Board in Michigan.* Ann Arbor: Bureau of Government, University of Michigan, 1938.

BOLLENS, JOHN C. *Administrative Reorganization in the States Since 1939.* Berkeley: Bureau of Public Administration, University of California, 1947.

BUCK, A. E. *The Reorganization of State Governments in the United States.* New York: Columbia University Press, 1938.

CHARLESWORTH, JAMES C. *Governmental Administration.* New York: Harper & Row, Inc., 1951.

COUNCIL OF STATE GOVERNMENTS. *Reorganizing State Government.* Chicago: Council of State Governments, 1950.

CRENNAN, CHARLES H. *A Survey of State Executive Organization and a Plan of Reorganization.* Menasha, Wis.: George Banta Publishing Co., 1916.

DIMOCK, MARSHALL E., and GLADYS O. *Public Administration,* 3d ed. New York: Holt, Rinehart & Winston, Inc., 1964.

GAUS, JOHN M., WHITE, LEONARD D., and DIMOCK, MARSHALL E. *The Frontiers of Public Administration.* Chicago: The University of Chicago Press, 1936.

GRAVES, W. BROOKE. *Public Administration in a Democratic Society.* Boston: D. C. Heath & Co., 1950.

GULICK, LUTHER, and URWICK, L. (eds.). *Papers on the Science of Administration.* New York: Institute of Public Administration, 1937.

HEADY, FERREL. *State Constitutions: The Structure of Administration.* New York: National Municipal League, 1961.

HEARLE, EDWARD F. R., and MASON, RAYMOND J. *A Data Processing System for State and Local Governments.* Englewood Cliffs, N.J.: Prentice-Hall, Inc., 1963.

LEPAWSKY, ALBERT. *Public Administration.* New York: Alfred A. Knopf, Inc., 1949.

MATHEWS, JOHN M. *Principles of American State Administration.* New York: Appleton-Century-Crofts, Inc., 1917.

MILLETT, JOHN D. *Management in the Public Service.* New York: McGraw-Hill Book Co., Inc., 1954.

MORSTEIN-MARX, FRITZ. *Elements of Public Administration.* New York: Prentice-Hall, Inc., 1946.

NIGRO, FELIX A. *Modern Public Administration.* New York: Harper & Row, Inc., 1965.

PEABODY, ROBERT L. *Organizational Authority.* New York: Atherton Press, 1964.

PFIFFNER, JOHN M., and PRESTHUS, ROBERT. *Public Administration,* 4th ed. New York: The Ronald Press Co., 1960.

PORTER, KIRK H. *State Administration.* New York: Appleton-Century-Crofts, Inc., 1938.

PUBLIC ADMINISTRATION SERVICE. *Proposed Organization of the Executive Branch, State of Alaska.* Chicago: Public Administration Service, 1958.

SCACE, HOMER E. *The Organization of the Executive Office of the Governor.* New York: Institute of Public Administration, 1950.

SIMON, HERBERT A. *Administrative Behaviour.* New York: The Macmillan Co., 1945.

SIMON, HERBERT A., SMITHBURG, D. W., THOMPSON, V. A. *Public Administration.* New York: Alfred A. Knopf, Inc., 1950.

WALDO, DWIGHT. *The Administrative State.* New York: The Ronald Press Co., 1948.

WALKER, HARVEY. *Public Administration.* New York: Holt, Rinehart & Winston, Inc., 1937.

WHITE, LEONARD D. *Introduction to the Study of Public Administration,* 4th ed. New York: The Macmillan Co., 1955.

WILLBURN, YORK. "Administration in State Governments," *The Forty-Eight States.* New York: The American Assembly, 1955.

WILLOUGHBY, W. F. *Principles of Public Administration.* Washington, D.C.: The Brookings Institution, 1927.

# 15

# State Personnel Systems

## THE STATE SCENE

### Public Attitude Toward Government Employment

The prestige value associated with the public service has been, until rather recent times, singularly low. Traditionally, American society has looked upon governmental service with a certain amount of disdain. A few years ago Harry Seligson wrote, "Public service—whether federal, state, or local—seldom evokes admiration, and attitudes toward employees working in public service run the gamut from complete indifference to hostility and contempt."[1] As a result, many well-qualified young people have refused even to consider the possibility of entering upon a governmental career. It is believed that many capable persons currently in the public service took a governmental position in the absence of a better opening. In addition, the vocational advisers in high schools, colleges, and universities for many years did little to encourage their advisees to even anticipate, let alone prepare, for governmental service. One of the best studies of prestige value in the public service was conducted by Professor Leonard D. White who checked the attitudes of some 5,000 individuals in Chicago. His report revealed that "Employment by the city apparently tends to command the respect of the immature, the uneducated, the foreign born, and the laboring people."[2] An additional study under the direction of Professor White of some 7,000 persons in cities located in ten states was equally uncomplimentary to the concept of public service.[3]

---

[1] Harry Seligson, "Bureaucracy in Big Business," *Good Government* (September–October, 1957), p. 41.

[2] Leonard D. White, *The Prestige Value of Public Employment* (Chicago: The University of Chicago Press, 1929), p. 144.

[3] Leonard D. White, *Further Contributions to the Prestige Value of Public Employment* (Chicago: The University of Chicago Press, 1932). See also Morris Janowitz and Deil Wright, "The Prestige Value of Public Employment: 1929 and 1954," *Public Administration Review* (Winter, 1956), pp. 15–21.

More recent studies continue to indicate that the quality of personnel that local governments can recruit and retain is undoubtedly adversely affected by the low prestige of government employment. The Public Personnel Association conducted a survey of local officials and reported that approximately one-half of the responses stated that "low prestige was a major obstacle to recruiting persons to fill key positions in local governments."[4] A similar survey by the American Society for Public Administration of its members—professional public employees not only in all levels of government but also in educational institutions—found that nearly half held similar opinions. The attitude of municipal executives reveals an even more striking manifestation of the effect of local prestige value when a study by the Municipal Manpower Commission of 1,700 local executives indicated that only 17 per cent would "recommend a career in local government."[5]

## Civil Service in the States

At the same time that the Congress of the United States was considering the Pendleton Bill the New York Civil Service Reform Association was drafting the first state civil service law. This piece of legislation was steered through the lower house of the New York legislature by Republican Assemblyman Theodore Roosevelt and signed by a Democrat, Governor Grover Cleveland, on May 4, 1883. Massachusetts, in 1884, became the next state to enact a civil service law. This measure was the work of that state's Civil Service Reform Association but was prepared in consultation with the New York Association. In 1894, New York became the first state to place the merit system in a constitution when the state constitutional convention of that year included a civil service provision in the revised document.[6]

While an "educational program" was conducted by various state and city civil service reform organizations following the steps taken by New York and Massachusetts, no further state action occurred until 1905 when Wisconsin and Illinois accepted the principle of a state merit system. From 1906 to 1918 only five states adopted civil service laws. Maryland passed a civil service law in 1920 which was unique in that for the first time the state personnel operation was to be headed by a single director instead of the usual bipartisan, multi-member civil service commission.

[4] Municipal Manpower Commission, *Governmental Manpower for Tomorrow's Cities* (New York: McGraw-Hill Book Co., Inc., 1962), p. 46.

[5] *Ibid.*

[6] For an excellent discussion relating to the historical development of civil service within the states, see National Civil Service League (H. Eliot Kaplan), *The Law of Civil Service* (Albany, N.Y.: Matthew Bender & Co., Inc., 1958), pp. 22–25.

The adoption of the California civil service constitutional provision in 1934 followed a fourteen year period of inactivity as far as state adoptions were concerned. Then in 1937 state civil service laws were enacted in five states with Connecticut becoming the second state to grant administrative power over personnel matters to a single director, but, unlike Maryland, it provided for an advisory committee of three department heads and two state employees.

The year 1940 marks a turning point in state personnel practices as an amendment to the federal Social Security Act became effective which required the states to place all employees in those departments receiving federal grants-in-aid under the merit system. Most vitally affected were the unemployment security, public assistance, and, in some instances, highway departments or commissions.

Eventually state employees concerned with child welfare, public employment, public health, and vocational rehabilitation activities were placed under the state merit system. All of the states have a merit system in operation for those agencies working in the areas of employment, health, and welfare. In addition, the campaign for complete state-wide coverage has continued. In 1963 Utah became the thirtieth state to adopt a state-wide merit system.[7]

Nevertheless, in twenty states the distribution of some of the state jobs is still determined by a political patronage system. Particularly in some of the Southern and Western states there is a considerable turnover of personnel with the change of administration. The governor's control over patronage can determine to some degree his leadership potential. When compared to the President's power to appoint and remove members of his cabinet and other political executives, the ability of most governors to choose and remove their own subordinates is definitely limited. Rather than being selected by the governor, many officials are appointed by the legislature, picked by boards and commissions, or popularly elected. At the present time it is estimated that governors may appoint, subject to approval by the legislature, approximately one-half of all major state administrators. The governor's control over general patronage is also significant. It must be recognized, however, that the filling of many positions subject to political appointment is not directly handled by the governor since the actual decisions are reached by political party officers and committees which grant political clearance to job applicants. Yet a governor can make many appointments available to deserving politicians while denying patronage to other members of the political party who have not been loyal or faithful to administration policies.

[7] Council of State Governments, *The Book of the States, 1964–1965* (Chicago: Council of State Governments, 1964), p. 174.

## Types of State Laws

Following the example set by New York, the earliest state civil service laws established as bipartisan administrative bodies, civil service commissions or personnel boards composed of three members to be appointed by the governor for fixed, overlapping terms. These boards and commissions were deliberately made semi-independent of the governor in order to be free from any political control or domination. In some states the appointments had to be confirmed by the state senate. The principal administrative employee was usually referred to as the secretary or chief examiner and was appointed and supervised by the commission or board.

The trend toward a single administrator began with the passage of the Maryland law in 1920. Maryland's gubernatorially appointed director, serving without a board or commission to advise him or to act as a buffer zone between the administrator and political forces, constitutes a unique category. Many state civil service laws passed since the 1930's have provided for an administrative officer or director and a multi-member commission or board which is charged with carrying out the quasi-legislative function of rule-making and the quasi-judicial duty of the hearing of appeals. This is the type of organization recommended in the Model State Civil Service Law. The director, who is appointed by either the commission or the personnel board or the governor, is named in some instances following the completion of a civil service examination. In recent years most of the older state laws have been amended to centralize the operating functions in an administrative officer or the president of the commission.

The appointment by the governor of the members of the commission or board continues to be the most popular form. However, in Louisiana the governor appoints the five members of the state civil service commission from a list of fifteen names submitted by the presidents of the five major institutions of higher learning in the state. The present trend is toward giving the governor more authority in the area of personnel matters and a lesser amount of control to semi-independent, appointive boards.

In recent years a few states, including Rhode Island, Kansas, and New Hampshire, have adopted the Connecticut example of making the central personnel agency one of the divisions of a department concerned with administrative or housekeeping staff functions rather than creating an independent agency. The director of civil service in Massachusetts heads the Division of Civil Service which is a part of the Department of Civil Service and Registration.

In general, most state civil service laws have followed the federal laws and rules in providing for competitive examination of initial appointments and promotions, prohibiting political activity and assessments, extending preference to veterans, and removal for cause on written charges, but frequently state civil service commissions have been granted the authority to investigate the charges and make the final decision.

The first county to adopt the merit system was Cook County, Illinois. In 1900, five counties in New York accepted the plan, and ten years later Essex County, New Jersey followed suit. In 1913, Los Angeles County, California, became the first county west of the Mississippi River to operate under a civil service law and the state currently has the largest number of counties with separate and independent civil service systems. In the 1930's the state of Alabama adopted the plan of allowing a county to administer the personnel system for cities contained within that unit of government with Jefferson County–Birmingham serving as the first one of this type. While this system has not received general acceptance it has more recently been adopted in New York. At the present time slightly more than 200 of the 3,043 counties in the United States have some type of a civil service system. In some states—particularly New York and New Jersey—the counties are covered by state law.

Counties and cities are placed under state law in both Ohio and New York. In addition, in the latter state, school districts, villages, and towns are also made subject to state rules and regulations, but the cities and counties are permitted various forms of administration. In New Jersey and Maryland the decision as to whether or not a local jurisdiction will come under the state law and have its personnel plan administered by the state is made by the voters in a referendum. A division with respect to the type of local unit is found in the Massachusetts law which provides for a mandatory system for cities but an operation arrangement for towns and other local subdivisions. In at least thirteen states the laws permit local units to utilize the technical and administrative services of the state personnel agency on a cost basis. In a few states, local subdivisions, primarily cities, are required by the state to establish civil service rules and regulations for their employees despite the fact that in a few of these states a complete state civil service system does not exist.

## State Distribution of Public Employment

The Bureau of the Census reported that in October, 1962, there were 9,400,000 civilian public employees in the United States and that this figure represented an increase of approximately 335,000 workers over the preceding year. The total number of state and local governmental employees for the same date (October, 1962) stood at 6,900,000 while the number of federal civilian employees was 2,500,000. Most of the increase for the period October, 1961 to October, 1962, can be accounted for by the rise in the number of state and local government workers since the number of federal civilian employees increased during this one-year period by only 51,000. However, somewhat over one-sixth of all persons enumerated as paid employees of state and local governments in October, 1962, were working only on a part-time basis. When the number of part-time persons is discounted by applying average full-time earning rates, the full-time equivalent of all state and local government employment becomes 5,945,000. Of this figure approximately 4,467,000 were employees of local governments.

Employment figures indicate a wide range among the state and local governments. New York has a high of 710,000 state and local employees while five states employ fewer than 20,000 state and local officials. State and local government employment in October, 1962, ranged from 261 per 10,000 population in Arkansas to 405 per 10,000 inhabitants in Wyoming. Local government employment on a full-time equivalent basis averaged 240 per 10,000 population which is three times the related average ratio for state government employment of 80 per 10,000.[8] The functional distribution of state and local government employment is indicated in Table 15–1.

## SELECTION PROCESS

### Recruitment

Recruitment has been viewed as the cornerstone of the entire personnel structure. The Commission of Inquiry on Public Service Personnel in its report stated that "No element of the career service system is more important than the recruitment policy."[9] A highly qualified staff cannot be built on ill-conceived recruitment policies.

The first civil service commissions were created to serve primarily as recruiting agencies. In this situation the commissioners were to use a selection process that would minimize or eliminate favoritism and in turn emphasize ability and competence through the use of competitive tests. Historically, however, there developed a tendency to think of recruitment in negative terms. As a result the selection process was concerned with keeping out the "unfit" but did little to encourage the best qualified to enter the public service. This negative philosophy has had a tendency to

---

[8] The information for the above two paragraphs is to be found in the following source: U.S. Department of Commerce, Bureau of the Census, *State Distribution of Public Employment in 1962* (Washington, D.C.: Government Printing Office, 1963).

[9] Commission of Inquiry on Public Service Personnel, *Better Government Personnel* (New York: McGraw-Hill Book Co., Inc., 1935), p. 37. A standard work on this subject is by the Civil Service Assembly, *Recruiting Applicants for the Public Service*, A Report Submitted to the Civil Service Assembly by the Committee on Recruiting Applicants for the Public Service, J. Donald Kingsley, Chairman (Chicago: 1942).

TABLE 15–1

Functional Distribution of State and Local Government Employment

| Function | (October 1961) Employees (full-time equivalent) Number | Percentage |
|---|---|---|
| Education | | |
| Local schools | 2,319,000 | 39.0 |
| Institutions of higher education | 387,000 | 6.5 |
| Other | 30,000 | 0.5 |
| Hospitals | 614,000 | 10.4 |
| Highways | 522,000 | 8.8 |
| Police Protection | 318,000 | 5.4 |
| Financial Administration | 175,000 | 3.0 |
| General Control | 171,000 | 2.9 |
| Local Fire Protection | 153,000 | 2.6 |
| Sanitation | 152,000 | 2.6 |
| Local Utilities Other Than Water Supply* | 130,000 | 2.2 |
| Public Welfare | 133,000 | 2.2 |
| Natural Resources | 123,000 | 2.1 |
| Water Supply | 98,000 | 1.7 |
| Correction | 95,000 | 1.6 |
| Local Parks and Recreation | 90,000 | 1.5 |
| Health | 80,000 | 1.3 |
| All Other | 355,000 | 6.0 |
| Total | 5,945,000 | 100.0 |

* Electric power, transit, and gas-supply systems.

Source: Adapted from U.S. Department of Commerce, Bureau of the Census, *State Distribution of Public Employment in 1962* (Washington, D.C.: Government Printing Office, April, 1963), p. 2.

dominate the field until the Great Depression and World War II when the positive recruitment philosophy received some attention. A positive program of recruitment and selection normally involves the following basic elements: (1) the discovery and subsequent cultivation of the best employment markets for the positions concerned; (2) the use of attractive recruiting materials coupled with ample publicity; (3) utilization of modern tests emphasizing high selectivity and reliability; (4) increased emphasis on seeking candidates from within the service; (5) a placement program that puts the "right man in the right job"; and (6) a follow-up probationary program as an integral part of the selection process.

The methods of recruitment used by public personnel agencies constitute one of the most important phases of the selection process. All too frequently these methods have been confined to the announcement of specific openings by three common techniques: (1) a newspaper announcement or advertisement of specific openings; (2) the posting of announcement bulletins or brochures in public buildings or other centers of congregation; and (3) the sending of announcement lists to individuals, organizations, or institutions that might be in contact with appropriate candidates. Many agencies have also used mailing lists to a major degree.

Sound positive recruitment emphasizes the following points: (1) the entire field of public recruitment must remain as free as possible from those limitations that have little or nothing to do with indicating the ability or competence of an individual; (2) the recruitment staff must make use of the most modern devices and techniques; and (3) the construction and use of the application blank must be such that it will fulfill all of the objectives of the recruitment program by being based on adequate factual research.

## The Classification of Positions

A system of position classification is viewed by many authorities in the field of personnel management as "the starting point for the basis upon which the whole personnel structure must rest."[10] As a result, no phase of a satisfactory personnel program is more important than that of effecting a systematic classification and standardization of all positions included within the system. An understanding of the application of the term "classification" in public service is important. Beginning with the federal Civil Service Act of 1883 the term "classified" was used to include those employees who were placed under the jurisdiction of the civil service commission. In actual practice today the United States Civil Service Commission no longer uses this term but refers to the competitive service, while state and local governments emphasize jurisdictional classification. A second connotation of the word came into usage about 1912 when the city of Chicago established what is now commonly referred to as a duties or occupational classification. This refers to a grouping of positions into classes on the basis of their duties and qualification requirements. Therefore the inauguration of the duties classification constitutes one of the most important steps taken in the field of public personnel administration since it produces influences that can be felt in practically every branch of government. A sound personnel program cannot be instituted without the assistance, to some degree, of the concept of position classification.

Certain conditions present in the American approach to personnel problems have undoubtedly influenced the type and character of the classification of duties developed in this country. In the United States we have

[10] W. F. Willoughby, *Principles of Public Administration* (Baltimore: Johns Hopkins Press, 1927), p. 246. One of the most authoritative and complete works on the subject of position classification is the report prepared by a committee of the Civil Service Assembly, Ismar Baruch, chairman, entitled, *Position Classification in the Public Service* (Chicago: Civil Service Assembly, 1941).

historically been concerned with the selection of already-trained technicians or workers possessing certain skills at the time of appointment. Basic therefore to the duties classification are the terms *position* and *class*. A position is characterized by the presence of two basic items: duties and responsibilities. In turn, a position must clearly be differentiated from its incumbent. A position, because it involves certain specified duties and responsibilities, is assigned a title. A class is a group of positions that are sufficiently alike in respect to responsibilities and duties to justify common treatment with respect to selection, compensation, and other employment processes. While normally defined as a "group of positions," a class may consist of only one position if no others of the same kind exist within the classified service. Typical of classes present within our government services are typists, clerks, carpenters, and statisticians. Each class then contains all of the jobs that are sufficiently alike to be designated by the same descriptive title. Class may be further refined on the basis of rank as indicated by the titles "Typist I," "Typist II," and "Typist III." All members of each class title are expected to possess the same qualifications and assigned similar responsibilities and therefore should receive the same rate of pay.

The central personnel agency is the organization normally charged with the responsibility for initiating a system of position classification. Generally this process of developing a classification plan involves four basic steps: (1) a minute analyzing and recording of the actual duties and any other distinctive characteristics of each position, normally referred to as job analysis and description; (2) separating or grouping the positions in classes upon the bases of their similarities; (3) writing a specification for each class of positions that will reveal its characteristics; and (4) the actual installation of the plan by allocating the individual positions to the classes already created.

The installation of a position classification system will not always eliminate all of the inequities that may be present in a particular jurisdiction or unit of government. Inequities may still exist as the result of inaccuracies being present in the original classification of a position; the absence of adequate reclassification procedures, and the errors present in the exercising of judgment throughout the entire process. Since positions do change as the result of adding or taking away duties, it is necessary to have periodic surveys in order to keep the classification plan current.

## Examinations

The well-designed civil service testing program emphasizes two basic objectives: (1) the examination is given to select those persons who will be efficient in the particular positions to which they are assigned as they enter government service; and (2) the examination should result in the selection of employees who have a capacity to grow and develop not only within a particular position but within the general career service. In the American scene the primary emphasis, historically, has been upon the first objective, by which a person is selected who is well-qualified to perform particular functions associated with a position. As a result, in the United States we have developed the so-called practical or duties examination which in turn has had serious repercussions upon our selection process in that experience has served as the basic criterion for entry into the public service. At the present time, however, there is a trend toward the accomplishment of the second objective which would produce employees exhibiting not only a high degree of native intelligence but a capacity for growth, development, and leadership within the career service.

The examinations used by civil service agencies may be classified in any number of ways. Examinations are sometimes listed as *assembled* and *unassembled,* though in actual practice the testing procedures are usually a combination of the two types. An examination is listed as of the assembled type when the applicants are required to meet in groups for competitive testing purposes. With the unassembled type of examination, the candidates do not appear in groups but the applicants' qualifications are determined on the basis of individual experience, training, and perhaps personal characteristics. The unassembled type is seemingly preferred for positions requiring administrative experience or a high degree of professional background and training.

A second grouping of civil service examinations is on the basis of form and these are usually divided into three major types: (1) written tests; (2) performance examinations; and (3) oral interviews. Written examinations are used by most civil service jurisdictions for the testing of the vast group of intermediary positions in the public service. The performance test has been utilized as a means of measuring occupational skills necessary for efficient performance in certain classes such as skilled tradesmen, typists, and stenographers.

The oral examination is being used increasingly in public personnel testing as an instrument for measuring certain personal traits or attributes since no satisfactory written tests have been devised for evaluating such characteristics as ingenuity, initiative, or the ability to elicit cooperation. There is some public suspicion present that the oral interview is a means by which political influence can enter the appointment process and certain candidates can be "washed out" by this system.[11] The third category

[11] While there is considerable literature available with respect to oral tests, one very important reference is the volume produced by the Public Personnel Association entitled, *Oral Tests in Public Personnel Selection* (Chicago: Public Personnel Association, 1943).

of civil service examinations is concerned with general aptitude tests, health and physical tests, tests of special capacities or aptitudes, personality tests, and achievement tests.

## Veteran Preference

Governments are plagued with the problem of what to do for those who have served in the armed forces. Solutions have historically tended to follow one of two major trends: (1) the providing of a pension; and (2) the granting of a governmental position. It is with the second category that the governmental service has been opened to the veteran on the ground of favoritism. Yet these two solutions provide a dilemma for those officers who are responsible for the determination of public policy. On one hand our legislators are beseiged by many groups who demand that the state must provide some positions for the veterans and especially for those who are disabled. Yet at the same time the concept of good administration demands that these jobs should be filled with the best qualified individuals available. However, most of our governmental jurisdictions have granted to the veteran some additional consideration in the employment process.[12]

A majority of the states have extended by law, rule, or regulation some type of employment preference to veterans. It should be noted that every state operating under a state-wide merit system has established, usually by statute, some provision for veteran preference.[13] Disabled veterans are usually granted ten additional points. There are a few instances where veterans who receive a passing mark are given higher places on eligibility lists than non-veterans regardless of the comparative scores on the examinations.

At the height of the World War II state and local governments not only increased but liberalized their provisions for veterans' preference. By 1949 a movement was underway to reduce the most liberal sections. Those who are opposed to the major aspects of veterans' preference do not deny the fact that society and probably government owes a debt to the veteran. The major question is whether or not this type of preference is the best way to compensate the veteran. On one hand it is recognized that veteran preference can constitute a limiting factor in the effort to build an effective career service since it penalizes the non-veteran and may discourage a qualified individual from seeking a governmental career. At the same time an efficient personnel director will not allow these

[12] For a detailed, historical summary of veterans preference in the federal service see U.S. Civil Service Commission, *History of Veteran Preference in Federal Employment, 1865-1955* (Washington, D.C.: Government Printing Office, 1955).

[13] *Report of the Interim Committee on the Civil Service Program* (St. Paul: State of Minnesota, 1955), pp. 63-69.

preference provisions to remain as an impediment to the establishment of a genuine career service.[14]

## Eligible Lists, Certification, and Appointment

After the applicants have been recruited and subjected to a series of examinations the personnel agency or officer has the responsibility of preparing a register or list of eligible candidates. This register, which is a listing of the candidates who passed according to their relative standings as indicated by individual scores, is usually based on the following items: (1) scores on written and oral tests; (2) records of education and experience; (3) results from personal interviews or investigations; and (4) in some instances the addition of veterans' preference points. The passing mark can be determined either by general law or rule, such as a score of 75, or a passing mark can be assigned by the personnel agency for the particular examination and those who fail to secure the minimum score are eliminated from further competition. Separate eligible lists should be maintained for each class of position for which examinations are given. In those jurisdictions where no classification study has been made it is no doubt possible to find separate eligible lists for two positions that for all practical purposes the duties are the same and the positions could be filled from one rather than two eligible lists.

Appointments are then made from these lists of eligible candidates. In filling a position the department or agency having the vacancy on its staff forwards a requisition or request for certification to the central employment agency which maintains the eligible lists. Upon receiving a requisition the personnel agency then certifies to the appointing officers within the department or agency the names of eligibles from the register. The exact number that is certified depends upon the law or rule of the personnel system. A number of states follow the "rule of three" by which only the names of the three persons receiving the highest scores will be sent to the appointing authority. In some services the personnel agency is required to submit only the highest-ranking name on the list while others allow a larger group to be certified. Many of the jurisdictions permit an appointing authority to reject the first list of certified names "for cause" and to request another group of eligibles.

It is possible for a merit system involving certification to break down, most frequently under the pressure of patronage seekers. The most effective method is the use of provisional appointments which are provided for by law when the appointing officer is informed that no eligible list is available. The appointing officer is authorized to make temporary selections

[14] Leonard D. White, *Veterans' Preference—A Challenge and an Opportunity* (Chicago: Civil Service Assembly, 1944), p. 1.

for a limited period until an eligible register is established from which a permanent appointment should follow immediately. Two other types of appointments must be noted, for in practically all jurisdictions there are provisions for temporary and emergency appointments. Temporary appointments are filling positions for a short time and the length of time for such an appointment is important since in the absence of any restriction it could very well become permanent and undermine the merit system. Emergency appointments are made without regard to eligibility requirements and are normally limited in time. These appointments are to meet sudden emergencies that cannot countenance the time lag that occurs in the regular requisition and certification procedures.

## INTERNAL PLACEMENT OF PERSONNEL

### The Probationary Period

In most governmental jurisdictions a probationary period must be served before an appointment becomes final. The Commission of Inquiry on Public Service Personnel defined probation as the "policy of considering no appointment final until the appointee has demonstrated his capacity in his work."[15] This trial period ranges from three months to one year, with the most common time period being six months. During this period the services of a new appointee may be terminated at any time for any reason. Actually the probationary period is recognition of the need for supplementing the formal examination procedures with another and usually final step in the process of selection and placement.[16]

Certain criticisms have been raised against the use of the probationary period. First, it should be more definitely viewed by administrators as a phase of the total testing program. Secondly, appointing officers have failed, in many instances, to administer in an effective manner the provisions of the probationary period. Many state and municipal civil service laws and rules have recently established a positive probationary period. Under this system an employee is automatically dropped from the service at the end of the period unless the appointing official certifies that his work performance justifies his retention in the organizational unit. Thirdly, sufficient attention is not given by personnel officers to the role of a well-planned orientation program for the new employee during this period.

[15] Commission of Inquiry on Public Service Personnel, op. cit., p. 48.
[16] For additional information relating to probation as a phase of the selection process see Public Personnel Association, Placement and Probation in the Public Service: Reports to the Assembly by the Committee on Placement in the Public Service and the Committee on Probation in the Public Service (Chicago: Public Personnel Association, 1946).

## Promotions

A report of the Civil Service Assembly in 1946 emphasized that promotion was "as important an aspect of the selection process in public personnel administration as original recruitment."[17] Personnel administrators must recognize that promotion offers one of the major opportunities for advancement and the possibility for an employee to make the best use of his capacities. Therefore, good personnel administration must be concerned with determining what positions will be filled by promotion, creating the proper machinery and criteria for selecting the ablest employees for advancement, and instituting programs to assist the employees in developing to their maximum usefulness. Over forty years ago Lewis Mayers emphasized:

The devising of formal methods of selection for promotion which shall effectively pick out the best qualified is one of the most difficult problems in the whole field of personnel administration. The difficulties are far greater than those encountered in devising formal methods of recruitment; and the consequences of improper selection far more serious.[18]

No one single factor is sufficient as a measure of promotability. Other items that demand consideration include test results—written, oral, and performance—length of service, education, and experience, and such intangible values as leadership, personality, and cooperativeness. The major methods and bases used for promotion usually include comparative performance, seniority, examination, and trial on the job. When employees are promoted to higher posts on the basis of their performance or demonstration of potentiality, two essential items must be utilized. First of all, complete and up-to-date records of the performance and qualifications of all employees must be maintained. Secondly, some method must be utilized by the organizational unit to find those candidates that are qualified to fill the higher positions.

The length of service of an employee is viewed by many as the simplest basis for promotion. Those who advocate promotion by seniority argue that long and efficient service is a guarantee that an individual is qualified to handle the duties associated with an advanced position. A vast majority of our public jurisdictions merely provide that seniority will be given some consideration in the promotion process. Some advocates maintain that seniority may justifiably be given considerable weight in promoting

---

[17] Civil Service Assembly, *Placement and Probation in the Public Service,* Report Submitted to the Civil Service Assembly by the Committee on Placement in the Public Service, Samuel Board, Chairman (Chicago: Civil Service Assembly, 1946), p. 80.

[18] Lewis Mayers, *The Federal Service: A Study of the System of Personnel Administration of the United States Government* (New York: Appleton-Century-Crofts, Inc., 1922), p. 317.

from one routine position to another while others insist that it can be the determining factor in selecting between candidates who appear to be equal.

Promotional examinations are commonly used in large jurisdictions functioning under civil service in an effort to discover which candidates possess both the knowledge and the other qualities needed for the higher position. As a result, the promotional examination includes a formal, written section on subject matter, an evaluation of the candidates' records and experiences, and a measuring of such important traits as initiative, judgment, leadership, cooperativeness, and resourcefulness. The testing for knowledge and the review of the record are relatively simple processes but there are problems present in finding a conclusive test relating to personality traits.

The last method relates to actual trial on the job. This is accomplished in some jurisdictions by temporarily assigning an individual to a higher position in an attempt to determine his promotability. While the opportunities for using this device are limited it still remains as a basic means for measuring fitness for a position.

## Evaluation of Performance

The determination and recording of the effectiveness or efficiency of members of an organization is one of the most important aspects of personnel management. These evaluations, which have caused some dissatisfaction among employees, are essential for three major reasons: (1) they serve as the basic guides for the administration as it considers matters of promotion, demotion, transfer, and pay increases; (2) these are the means by which the administration can check, to a degree, the efficacy of its original selection methods; and (3) it is a method by which the working force is literally kept on its toes.

Many devices and methods have been instituted in an attempt to measure job effectiveness. The first commonly accepted technique is that of production records. However, it must be recognized that in almost every working organization there are two types of positions: those in which the work is of a routine, repetitive nature and is quite conducive to the use of unit measurements; and those which are so varied in nature that their contributions cannot be measured in terms of output. The first type is represented by the work of a machine operator, a file clerk, a stenographer, or a typist. As a result, in many areas objective norms for these types of work based on time and motion studies may be established. A guiding principle that should be used insists that objective measurements are superior in most respects to judgments and therefore whenever or whereever the work lends itself to unit measurements it should be utilized.

A second device for measuring the efficiency of the worker is through the administration of periodic tests. This method, much like that of production records, lends itself to routine and repetitive jobs. The third system relates to the use of so-called merit ratings, service ratings, efficiency ratings, or performance ratings. The major problem involved here relates to the value judgments that have to be made by the rating officer.

## REMOVAL PROCESSES

### Dismissal of Employees

The conduct of public employees while on duty should reflect an accepted code of ethics and behavior. The adherence to these standards underlies all of those forces which create morale, self-discipline, and efficiency within the well-developed public service. However, the occasion may arise in the administrative scene when resort must be to punitive measures. Civil service employees are occasionally dismissed at all levels of government even though there is the popular misconception that it is practically impossible to dismiss anyone with tenure. Dismissal or removal from the service constitutes the most extreme penalty since it involves the loss of status, income, and many times the privileges of a pension. In certain situations a person may not only be dismissed from the service but prevented from seeking reemployment with the public authority for a specified period of time.

Many jurisdictions have set forth the procedural requirements that must be present in the removal process including formal written notice stating the reasons for dismissal and the opportunity for a hearing. Civil service laws generally state that dismissal made on allegedly racial, political, or religious grounds requires a review with the authority to make the final decision resting with the employing agency, the central personnel agency, and ultimately the court. If the central agency possesses this authority, the arrangement is popularly referred to as the closed back door, but if final authority rests with the employing agency the open back door policy is said to exist.

### Transfers

In many instances the circumstances surrounding a particular case will not demand that the incumbent be removed from the service but only transferred to another unit. A transfer actually constitutes a horizontal movement of an employee from one position to another of the same class but under the jurisdiction of a different supervisor or executive.

Transfers are usually the result of one of two possible factors. First of all, they may be caused by organizational demands that occur with the expansion or contraction of the organization, changes in work methods, seasonal demands for employees, and perhaps by shifting policies. In these situations transfers are intimately associated with the reassignment of duties and are made by the administrative staff in an effort to adjust the personnel to the work load of the agency.

The second type of transfer is sometimes referred to as adjustment placement and frequently is the result of individual misplacement. Original placement cannot possibly assure that each appointee will be completely fitted for his position. In turn, it is also understood by personnel officers that any employee who is apparently adjusted to his job at any particular time may grow out of harmony with his position at a later date. Good administration demands that placement be a continuing process.

In spite of its recognized role within public personnel administration, transfers in the governmental service are all too infrequent. This is, in part, the result of the existence of very little machinery to aid this type of action and that existing personnel rules in many agencies almost completely limit the process. Nevertheless, a distinction must be made between intradepartmental transfers and interdepartmental ones. The first type is usually made by the department head without requiring any action by the central personnel agency. The interdepartmental transfer ordinarily requires not only the approval of the two departmental heads but also that of the civil service commission. In addition, most rules require that an employee cannot be transferred until he has been in the service for at least six months. Naturally transfers from the exempted to the competitive service can occur only after the successful completion of an examination.

## EMPLOYEE ORGANIZATIONS

### Development of Employee Organizations

In the United States the unionization of public employees did not begin until the decade of the 1880's, although the recognition of some common needs and interests among public employees became evident shortly after the end of the Civil War. Prior to 1880 the only public employee organizations in operation, with the exception of the National Teachers' Association, which was established in 1857, were a few "benevolent societies" found primarily among the police. Beginning in the 1880's, particularly with postal employees, policemen, and teachers, the unionization movement spread rapidly among public employees. Since the movement has seemingly been stabilized in the national service, the largest gains in recent years have been in state and local governments. The organization of state and local government employees was retarded in the beginning no doubt as a result of the greater hold of the spoils system within the states, but extensive unionization has occurred since 1910.

The constitutions of the unions of public employees normally contain statements indicating the reasons or objectives for which such organizations have been established. In spite of the large number of diversified unions now present in the United States there is a considerable degree of uniformity with respect to objectives. Professor Glenn Stahl reports that these goals are normally four in number: "(1) to promote a feeling of solidarity and comradeship among the workers; (2) to protect and extend the merit system; (3) to protect and improve the working conditions, status, and material welfare of the employees; (4) to improve the quality of public administration."[19] The American Federation of State, County, and Municipal Employees lists its major objectives with the preamble of that organization's constitution:

Actuated by the firm conviction that it is a God-given and inalienable right of workers to form into organizations to promote the common good, to improve the social and economic welfare of all employees of state, province, territory, commonwealth, county and municipal governments without regard to sex, color, race, or creed, to promote efficiency in government service, and to give clear evidence of the recognition of our unity with organized labor, we adopt this constitution.

Further, we sincerely believe that it is the purpose of our organization to insure that its membership be guaranteed the recognition of them as human beings, creatures of God, in their dealings with those who are charged with the administration of the business of government service.

The national unions of state and local employees first appeared among the teachers, with the American Federation of Teachers serving as the primary education organization that upholds the trade-union point of view. It is also true that several thousand teachers hold memberships in the National Education Association but this group is viewed usually as more of a professional association than a regular union. The basic national union with general coverage is the American Federation of State, County, and Municipal Employees which is affiliated with the AFL-CIO. After consideration is given to the national organizations covering state and local employees a wide variety of different types of employee organizations are found. In many states there are state-wide organizations of general jurisdiction, but in other instances these are less active than either the national union or the purely local unions. Many of the larger cities

---

[19] O. Glenn Stahl, *Public Personnel Administration* (5th ed.; New York: Harper & Row, Inc., 1962), p. 229.

have also established their own independent local employee associations. In spite of the multiple unionism that is to be found in state and local governments the organization of public workers continues.

## The Right To Strike

The question of the right of governmental employees to strike is one of the most controversial and unsettled issues as far as the general public is concerned. While at one time in this country the question of a strike of such employees was considered almost unthinkable, gradually an attitude has developed in the mind of the general public questioning this possible threat to the cessation of governmental services. As a result, many governmental units have passed legislation forbidding participation in a strike against the government by certain public employees. Strikes of public employees have occurred even where forbidden by law. In New York City in 1962 a considerable number of teachers struck for increased salaries in spite of state legislation (Condon-Wadlin law) which prohibited strikes in the public service. However, it must be noted that prior to statutory prohibition the courts had never passed on the right of government workers to engage in a strike.[20]

In all fairness to unions of governmental employees it must be noted that the constitutions of almost every civil service union prohibit the use of the strike. For example, the constitution of the American Federation of Government Employees states: "We oppose and will not support strikes against the United States government, picketing and other measures which have the effect of embarrassing it." Similarly, the constitution of the National Federation of Federal Employees declares that "under no circumstances shall this Federation engage in or support strikes against the United States government." Despite these assurances, the federal government in 1946 passed legislation to prevent strikes against the national government by attaching clauses to appropriation acts requiring that funds could not be used to pay those employees who refused to sign an affidavit that they did not belong to any organization which asserted "the right to strike against the United States."[21]

The following year the Taft-Hartley Act, the general labor law which was passed over President Truman's veto, provided that it was unlawful for any individual "employed by the United States or any agency thereof including wholly owned Government corporation to participate in any strike."[22] This measure also provided that any individual so employed by the United States who did strike would be immediately discharged from

[20] David Ziskind, *One Thousand Strikes of Government Employees* (New York: Columbia University Press, 1940), p. 233.

[21] P.L. 419, 79th Cong., July 3, 1946.

[22] P.L. 201, 80th Cong., 1947.

his employment, forfeit his civil service status, and not be eligible for re-employment by the United States or any such agency for three years. During 1946 and 1947 at least nine states passed no-strike laws for state and local employees containing sections very similar to the national provisions. Even with public employees exhibiting great restraint in the use of the strike weapon the recent trend has been to prohibit public strikes by legislation.

The basic arguments in support of no strike laws usually center around two major items: (1) the sovereign character of government; and (2) the necessity and urgency of governmental services and administrative operations. Professor Leonard D. White, while maintaining that no categorical answer could be given to the question as to whether strikes should be prohibited by law, did attempt to establish a criterion or rule which was based on the nature and gravity of the consequences involved in a strike, whether by persons employed by government or by a privately owned and operated business. White stated:

A strike that would bring direct, immediate, certain, and serious danger to a primary interest of the community should be prohibited by law, with adequate sanctions, but also with adequate means to secure full public consideration and solution of the issues involved. In other cases the law should remain silent. The criterion of distinction is therefore the consequence of a strike upon the public interest, not the status of the employer.[23]

## ORGANIZATION FOR CENTRAL PERSONNEL MANAGEMENT

### Single Director

The single director arrangement places the entire responsibility for the central administration of personnel matters in one individual who is appointed by and responsible to the chief executive of the state. This organizational arrangement has had only a few adoptions particularly the states of Maryland and Illinois. The following advantages are usually cited for this type of personnel control: (1) all major phases of state personnel management are centralized under the governor who can, when necessary, act quickly and promptly; and (2) personnel leadership is facilitated. The responsibility for personnel operations is placed with the chief executive in that the actual position of the personnel director is strengthened, not only with the general public but with the state legislative body and particularly the members of the governor's party in that body, once the governor has made his position clear with respect to his personnel program. The organization of a state personnel system with a single director is indicated in Figure 15–1.

[23] Leonard D. White, "Strikes in the Public Service," *Public Personnel Review* (January, 1949), p. 6.

## Bipartisan Commission

The responsibility for personnel management in those governmental units operating under general civil service laws is usually divided between a central personnel agency—the civil service commission in many instances—and the operating personnel office. With the introduction of the civil service reform movement of the 1880's, central personnel agencies were established in the national government and in a few states and municipal jurisdictions. As had been previously indicated, the civil service commission from its beginning was viewed as a mere recruiting agency that would eliminate politics from personnel administration and insure that persons of merit would enter the governmental service. It was the popular belief that these goals could be best accomplished by creating a commission that would be organized independent of and largely external to the administrative hierarchy. Through this type of an arrangement it was believed that the commission could successfully ward off the political spoilsmen. As a result, however, the system of civil service control that finally developed was concerned with preventing specific abuses and did not concentrate on other phases of the employment situation. Charles P. Messick wrote that the framers of the early civil service laws devoted most of their attention to "the things that 'shall be unlawful.'"[24] The typical civil service commission became not only the traditional but the dominant organizational pattern for central personnel agencies.

Established in an attempt to "keep the rascals out of office," the commission was composed of members who were normally appointed by the chief executive officer for long, staggered terms and confirmed by the state senate in an effort not only to reduce the possibility of control on behalf of the appointing officer but to provide for some degree of continuity of public policy.

While the bipartisan civil service commission has made its contributions to the improvement of public personnel administration, there are a few specific shortcomings that must be reviewed. One of the major difficulties has grown out of the fact that the commission must exhibit a bipartisan character. In this respect some authorities maintain that too much emphasis has been placed on the political affiliation of the members rather than on their expert knowledge of personnel affairs. Most of the laws provide that not more than two of the three members can belong to the same political party. As a result, the nonpartisanship that was to be achieved by a bipartisan body has actually allowed political pressures to be concentrated upon civil service commissions.

[24] Charles P. Messick, "The Personnel Agency as an Integral Part of Public Administration," *Proceedings*, 19th Annual Meeting of the Civil Service Assembly of the United States and Canada (Philadelphia: Civil Service Assembly, 1926), p. 66.

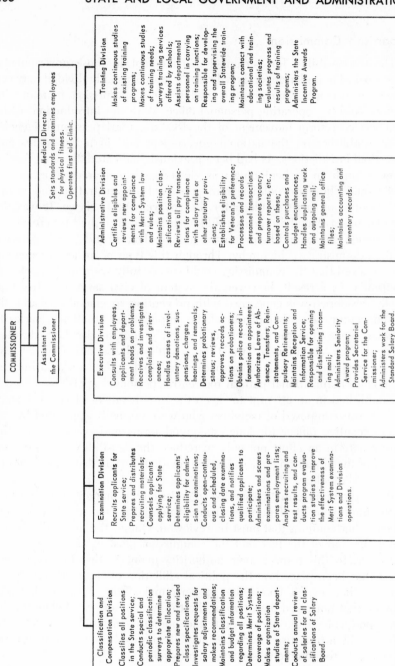

Fig. 15–1. Organization of the Office of the Commissioner of Personnel—State of Maryland. (Source: Office of the Commissioner of Personnel, State of Maryland, 1962.)

A second criticism of the commission form for personnel administration notes this type of organization is "in but not of" the administrative machinery. As far as the prescribing of functions is concerned it is a part of the hierarchy, but in relationship to its practical operations it is generally outside the regular organizational diagram. Since personnel administration is regarded as one of the most important branches of management, the functions of initial selection, promotion, creating morale, maintaining efficiency, and removal must be a part of the administrative processes. Yet when these functions are carried out by an agency that is not placed in the regular chain of command a situation is created that has a tendency to run counter to accepted principles of administration. Even the department heads look with a degree of doubt at this type of extra-administrative agency—the civil service commission.

The amateur character of the membership of many civil service commissions has been listed as an important problem. Some authorities would maintain that in no other area of management has the philosophy of "amateurs in administration" been so apparent. The range of occupations from which commissioners have been drawn varies from journalists and farmers down to professional politicians. In addition, many commissioners, in spite of the widespread provision for a six-year term, do not stay in office long enough to become thoroughly acquainted with their jobs.

## Single Director with Commission

A proposal that would combine the operations of a civil service commission with that of a director of personnel has been produced in the Model State Civil Service Law. Two professional organizations, the National Civil Service League and the National Municipal League, working together, have drafted a Model State Civil Service Law which is an attempt to present the latest thinking in the personnel field based upon past experiences. The document is concerned with the establishment of a merit system of personnel administration within the civil service of any state. While the Model Law covers all responsibilities of a state personnel program, our greatest point of interest in this discussion revolves around the question of the type of organization that is proposed for a state.

First of all, the Model Law would establish a state personnel department which would include both a director of personnel and a civil service commission of three members. The duties of these two major divisions are set forth in the law so that there can be no misunderstanding in the division of duties and responsibilities. The director of personnel is to be the single administrative head of the state personnel department and is granted powers of direction over all administrative and technical operations of the personnel agency. The civil service commission is to be

limited to quasi-legislative functions, such as rule-making and the formulation of general policy, and to quasi-judicial responsibilities concerned
with the hearing of appeals.

The state director of personnel is to be appointed by the governor but
upon the recommendation of the civil service commission. The law requires that this individual be "experienced in the field of personnel administration" and "in known sympathy with the application of merit principles in public employment." The power of removal over the director is
vested within the civil service commission but can be exercised only for
cause after the director has been presented in writing with the reasons for
his removal. The director is given the opportunity to answer any charges
in writing, or he can request a hearing by the commission. The statement
of reasons for removal and the written reply from the director or the
transcript of the hearing is to be filed with the secretary of state as a
public record.

In general terms, the director, as the executive head of the state personnel department, is called upon to administer and supervise all technical
activities of the department. In addition, the law provides that it shall be
the duty of the director:

1. To apply and carry out this law and the rules adopted thereunder
2. To attend meetings of the Commission and to act as its secretary
   and keep minutes of its proceedings
3. To establish and maintain a roster of all employees in the state civil
   service, in which there shall be set forth as to each employee, the
   class title, pay or status, and other pertinent data
4. To appoint such employees of the Department and such experts and
   special assistants as may be necessary to carry out effectively the
   provisions of this law
5. To foster and develop, in cooperation with appointing authorities
   and others, programs for the improvement of employee effectiveness, including training, safety, health, counseling and welfare
6. To encourage and exercise leadership in the development of effective personnel administration within the several departments in the
   state service, and to make available the facilities of the Department
   of State Personnel to this end
7. To investigate from time to time the operation and effect of this law
   and of the rules made thereunder and to report his findings and
   recommendations to the Commission and to the Governor
8. To make an annual report regarding the work of the Department,
   and such special reports as he may consider desirable, to the Commission and to the Governor
9. To perform any other lawful acts which he may consider necessary
   or desirable to carry out the purposes and provisions of this law[25]

[25] A Model State Civil Service Law, section 7. (Prepared by the National Civil
Service League and the National Municipal League, New York: 1953.)

The state civil service commission is to consist of three members appointed by the governor. This technique permits the chief executive to have direct contact with the commission. The governor also appoints the director of personnel upon the recommendation of the commission. These two factors tend to provide for an integrated personnel department and to permit the agency to serve as an integral part of the governor's management team with such other staff aids as finance and planning.

According to the law, members of the commission, in much the same manner as the director of personnel, must be persons "in sympathy with the application of merit principles to public employment." Three political limitations are placed upon the membership. No member of the commission can: (1) be a member of any local, state, or national committee of a political party; (2) be an officer or member of a committee in any partisan political club or organization; or (3) hold, or be a candidate for, any paid public office. The model law also provides for overlapping terms. This technique prevents a governor from naming all the members at any one time and thus makes it unlikely that a patronage-oriented governor could control the commission. The merits of this device have been discussed at great length by students of public personnel administration. There are those who maintain that no obstacle should be placed in the way of a governor who is dedicated to the development of a sound personnel system. On the other hand some personnel authorities insist that even a chief executive who has been dedicated to the principles of a merit system may be tempted when placed in power to introduce the spoils system and perhaps re-establish the patronage system. Members of the commission can be removed by the governor only for cause but after being given a copy of the charges and an opportunity to be heard publicly before the chief executive. A copy of the charges and a transcript of the hearing are to be placed on file with the secretary of state. Members of the commission are to be paid on a per diem basis, but the law includes a stipulation that they cannot earn more than a certain sum in any one month or in any one year. However, they are to be paid travelling expenses and any other expenditures necessitated by the performance of their official tasks.

The duties and responsibilities of the civil service commission are specified in the proposed law as follows:

1. Represent the public interest in the improvement of personnel administration in the state service
2. Advise the Governor and the Director on problems concerning personnel administration
3. Foster the interest of institutions of learning and of industrial, civic, professional and employee organizations in the improvement of personnel standards in the state service
4. Make any investigation which it may consider desirable concerning

the administration of personnel in the state service, and make recommendations to the Director with respect thereto

5. Make an annual report and special reports and recommendations to the Governor[26]

In addition, the commission is required to approve the civil service rules, as they have been prepared and submitted by the director, the classification and compensation plans, and to hear employee appeals.


## CURRENT PERSONNEL TRENDS

### Departments of Administration

The first Hoover Commission made a general recommendation that the use of administrative boards and commissions should be discontinued in all areas of governmental concern. This same principle was repeated by most of the "Little Hoover Commissions" that were created in state governments. Actually all of this has had an impact upon the organization for personnel administration within our states and the trend has been one of concentrating administrative authority in the hands of a single director. Sidney Spector, in his evaluation of the ramifications of these "Little Hoover Commissions," notes that there is a concerted drive within many states to place the personnel function within the executive office of the governor and a preference for the establishment of the position of a single administrator who could rely upon a board or commission within the personnel department for advisory and quasi-judicial functions.[27] Therefore, with respect to the utilization of a single director of personnel and a civil service commission within the same department, the model civil service law is not too advanced of actual practices. There is one area where the law seemingly is ahead of accepted practice. More states allow commissions or boards to select the personnel director than those in which the appointment is made by the governor. In some states an attempt is being made to place all the staff services in one department. In this manner the personnel function is more closely integrated with finance, budgeting, and purchasing. Rhode Island has established a department of administration which is headed by a director who reports to the governor. The director of personnel has been placed in this department and, in turn, is responsible to the director of administration. This arrangement facilitates the coordination of the personnel activities with the other management services and provides for a direct command line from the governor through the director of administration to the director

---

[26] *Ibid.*, section 6.

[27] Sidney Spector, "What the 'Little Hoover Commissions' Say About Personnel," *Public Personnel Review*, Vol. XII, No. 3 (July, 1951), p. 120.

of personnel. Also, in the Rhode Island system an appeals board is present and therefore the creation of a central department of administration under a single director has not eliminated the operation of a multi-member body for quasi-judicial functions. The Model State Law has not provided for a department of administration.

## State Retirement Systems

In 1911 Massachusetts became the first state to provide for a general retirement system, but by 1923 only five other states had adopted similar programs.[28] By 1963 all of the states had adopted plans covering at least certain particular groups of employees and approximately three-fourths of the states had retirement programs covering all employees with many states participating in the national Old Age and Survivors Insurance system. A retirement plan that includes practically all public employees in a particular government jurisdiction is actually the product of the present century and still has many defects to overcome. It was not until 1950, when the Old Age and Survivors Insurance sections of the Federal Social Security Act were amended to allow state and local governments to come under the national law, that states began to establish agreements with the Federal Security Administration to cover state and local employees. These amendments of 1950 did limit the new coverage only to those state and local employees not previously covered by an existing retirement plan.

Certain characteristics should be present in a sound retirement program, and states today are re-examining and re-evaluating their existing pension programs with a view to adopting the most widely accepted standards. The outstanding requisite of a sound retirement system is that it must be based on a sound actuarial foundation. Too frequently the financial planning and the provisions for the establishment of reserves have not been geared to actuarial standards. As an indication of this factor, employees contribute from 1.5 per cent in some jurisdictions to 6 per cent of their salaries and wages in others. The contributions of employees, in many instances, are not sufficient to establish an adequate reserve. As a result, governments are called upon to make annual deficit contributions on the basis of current needs. Another accepted standard is that a sound pension program calls for age 65 or 70 as the basis for retirement rather than years of service, although many state governments while using age as the principal basis also allow the years of service to be a conditioning item. A third standard provides for joint contributions to the retirement fund and a vast majority of state systems meet this requirement.

The administration of the retirement fund calls for the establishment of certain accepted principles. The most common provision requires that the

[28] Connecticut and Maine in 1919; New York in 1920; New Jersey in 1921; and Pennsylvania in 1923.

fund be administered by a board on which government and employees are equally represented. The chief fiscal officer of the state is normally included as a member of such a board. For administrative purposes the retirement plan should be placed in a designated state agency and in many states this has been the state insurance department where a secretarial staff has maintained the records and accounts of the retirement system.

## BIBLIOGRAPHY

BARUCH, ISMAR (ed). *Position-classification in the Public Service*. Chicago: Civil Service Assembly of the United States and Canada, 1941.

CARPENTER, WILLIAM S. *The Unfinished Business of Civil Service Reform*. Princeton: Princeton University Press, 1952.

CHAPMAN, BRIAN. *The Profession of Government*. London: George Allen & Unwin, Ltd., 1959.

Civil Service Assembly of the United States and Canada. *Readings in Public Personnel Administration*. Chicago: Civil Service Assembly of the United States and Canada, 1942.

CROUCH, WINSTON W., and JAMISON, JUDITH NORVELL. *The Work of Civil Service Commissions*. Chicago: Civil Service Assembly, 1956.

FISH, C. R. *The Civil Service and the Patronage*. Cambridge: Harvard University Press, 1920.

GODINE, MORTON R. *The Labor Problem in the Public Service*. Cambridge: Harvard University Press, 1951.

GOODE, CECIL. *Personnel Research Frontiers*. Chicago: The Public Personnel Association, 1958.

International City Managers' Association. *Municipal Personnel Administration*. Chicago: The International City Managers' Association, 1950.

KAPLAN, H. ELIOT. *The Law of Civil Service*. Albany, N.Y.: Matthew Bender & Co., 1958.

MUNICIPAL MANPOWER COMMISSION. *Governmental Manpower for Tomorrow's Cities*. New York: McGraw-Hill Book Co., Inc., 1962.

NATIONAL CIVIL SERVICE LEAGUE AND NATIONAL MUNICIPAL LEAGUE. *A Model State Civil Service Law*. New York: The Leagues, 1953.

NIGRO, FELIX A. *Public Personnel Administration*. New York: Holt, Rinehart & Winston, Inc., 1959.

PAGE, THOMAS (ed.). *The Public Personnel Agency and the Chief Executive— A Symposium*. Chicago: Public Personnel Association, 1960.

POWELL, NORMAN J. *Personnel Administration in Government*. Englewood Cliffs, N.J.: Prentice-Hall, Inc., 1956.

SPERO, STERLING D. *Government as Employer*. New York: Remsen Press, 1948.

STAHL, O. GLENN. *Public Personnel Administration*, 5th ed. New York: Harper & Row, Inc., 1962.

TORPEY, WILLIAM G. *Public Personnel Administration*. Princeton, N.J.: D. Van Nostrand Co., Inc., 1953.

WARNER, KENNETH O. (ed). *Management Relations with Organized Public Employees*. Chicago: Public Personnel Association, 1962.

ZISKIND, DAVID. *One Thousand Strikes of Government Employees*. New York: Columbia University Press, 1940.

# 16

# State and Local Revenue

Taxes are defined as compulsory contributions extracted by a governmental unit for public purposes. A vast portion of the revenue needed to finance governmental activities comes from taxation.

Taxes may be classified in various ways. The most common two categories are progressive and regressive. A progressive tax is one that individuals or corporations pay according to their ability to contribute to the government's financial affairs. A regressive tax is levied without consideration of the amount of income (ability to pay).

Taxes are also classified by what is termed incidence. It may be a direct tax, which is borne by the person on whom it is levied, or it may be shifted to someone else and termed an indirect tax. Excise tax on liquor is an excellent example of a tax that is passed on to the purchaser.

The federal constitution prohibits the states, without the consent of Congress, from levying tonnage duties or placing duties on imports or exports. A state may not use its taxing power to impair the obligations of contract or to violate the equal protection of law clause of the Fourteenth Amendment. As determined in 1819 in *McCulloch v. Maryland* no state can tax federal property that is located within the state's boundaries.

Many state constitutions place numerous restrictions on the state and local taxing powers. Many have a tax uniformity clause, with all property and income being required to be taxed at a uniform rate throughout the entire state. A few refuse permission to the state legislature to levy a progressive income tax, which is prohibited in the 1964 Michigan Constitution. Others set maximum ceilings on various taxes, and the new Michigan Constitution limits a sales tax to no more than 4 per cent.[1]

## TRENDS IN STATE REVENUES

The fiscal year in all states except four begins at the same time as the national fiscal year, July 1st. However, Alabama begins the financial year

[1] *Constitution of Michigan, 1964*, Article IX, section 7.

on October 1st, New York, April 1st, Pennsylvania, June 1st, and Texas, September 1st.[2]

The state governments are not consistent on fiscal year beginnings for their local governmental units as might be expected considering the almost unanimous use of July 1st by 92 per cent of the fifty states. Iowa, for example, uses the traditional fiscal year for the state government and for school districts, but requires the county governments and the more than 945 municipalities to begin the fiscal year on January 1st. The rational for this is unclear even to the state officials most intimately concerned with the problems of finance.

During the ten-year period, fiscal 1951 to 1960, state governmental expenditures exceeded revenue from all sources only three times. In 1959, 1958, and 1955 the total revenue from all sources to the state governments was lower than the expenditures. However, in the other seven years a small surplus was accumulated each year when all of the states are taken as a unit. In both 1958 and 1959 the total expenditures were $1.9 billion more than the state "income," while in 1955 the deficit was only $.7 billion. The largest excess of revenue over expenditures was in 1960 when the states received $1.2 billion more than expended. In both 1953 and 1952 the excess was more than $1 billion.

Table 16–1 records state revenue and expenditures from 1951–1960.

### TABLE 16–1

State Revenue and Expenditures—1951 to 1962 (Fiscal Years)
(in billions of dollars)

| Fiscal Year | Total Revenue | Total Expended | Excess of Revenue |
|---|---|---|---|
| 1951 | 15.5 | 15.0 | +0.5 |
| 1952 | 16.8 | 15.8 | +1.0 |
| 1953 | 18.0 | 16.9 | +1.1 |
| 1954 | 18.8 | 18.7 | +0.1 |
| 1955 | 19.7 | 20.4 | −0.7 |
| 1956 | 22.2 | 21.7 | +0.5 |
| 1957 | 24.7 | 24.2 | 0.4 |
| 1958 | 26.2 | 28.1 | −1.9 |
| 1959 | 29.2 | 31.1 | −1.9 |
| 1960 | 32.8 | 31.6 | +1.2 |
| 1961 | 34.6 | 34.7 | −0.1 |
| 1962 | 37.6 | 36.4 | +1.2 |

SOURCES: U.S. Department of Commerce, Bureau of the Census, *Compendium of State Government Finances in 1960* (Washington, D.C.: Government Printing Office, 1961); and Council of State Governments, *The Book of the States, 1964–1965* (Chicago: Council of State Governments, 1964).

[2] Council of State Governments, *The Book of the States, 1962–1963* (Chicago: Council of State Governments, 1962), p. 195.

It might be expected that the states' indebtedness during the decade would therefore be reduced, but to the contrary, the end of fiscal 1960 saw the total accumulated state debt at an all time high of $18.5 billion. It was primarily due to the fact that each year a greater amount of state borrowing occurred than was retired. In 1960 more than $2.3 billion were borrowed by the states while only $900 million of the debt was amortized.

During this ten-year period the total revenues more than doubled, but at the same time the total expenditures per year likewise more than doubled. The total revenues for all of the states exceeded the total expenditures for the same period by only $300 million in spite of the fact that in seven of the ten years the state budgets were theoretically balanced. But actually the balanced budget in many states was accomplished only by issuing long term bonds, usually for at least twenty years.

In 1960 state and local government tax collections equalled $201 per capita for the nation as a whole. The state average per person showed great variation, ranging from a high of $288 in New York state to a low of only $118 in Alabama.

The per-capita taxes for 1961 fiscal year for state and local governments increased over the previous year. The average of the fifty states was $212 —an increase of $11. California took over the position of the state with the highest tax per person from New York, with the California tax increasing to $298, while New York, in second place, increased only $4 per person over the 1960 tax to $292. Alabama continued as the lowest state with an average of $120.

A more meaningful comparison may be made by considering the percentage of the per person income that is paid in state and local taxes. The average for 1961 in all of the states was 9.4 per cent. Delaware was the state that took the smallest share of the per capita personal income with only 7.1 per cent required to operate state and local governments; closely following were Alaska at 7.2 per cent and Missouri with 7.5.

In addition to the taxes collected by state and local governmental units, the national average of charges per capita for special services was $43.40. In addition, the national government paid to the states and their local units an average of $38.96 per person to assist with governmental costs. In 1961 when all taxes were considered the national average cost of state and local government was $295 per capita.

The revenue of the fifty state governments increased by 8.7 per ⌐ during the fiscal year 1962 over fiscal 1961 and increased by 7.5 ⌐ in fiscal 1963. The total expenditures of $36.4 billion duri⌐ some $1.2 billion less than the revenue received.

This financial picture, however, must be place⌐ by taking into account that during fiscal year 1⌐

amounted to $2.9 billion while debt redemption totaled only $990 million. Thus state debt rose to a new all-time total of $22 billion; an increase of two billion over the figure of the previous year. The net long-term state debt at the end of fiscal 1962 was actually $18.6 billion.

Every state except Colorado had higher tax yields in 1963 than in 1962. The largest increases were in California—up $190 million—and New York with an increase of $177 million. On a percentage basis, however, the highest increases occurred in Wisconsin, up 30 per cent, and Nevada with a 16 per cent increase. Most of the states reported revenue increases more than 5 per cent higher than 1962, with only twelve showing an increase of less than 5 per cent.

California collected more state taxes than any other state in fiscal 1963 with a total of $2,559 million; New York, second with $2,506 million, Pennsylvania, third with $1,268 million; Michigan, fourth, $1,143 million; Illinois, fifth, $1,080 million; and Texas, sixth at $1,041 million. The per-capita amount of state taxes in fiscal 1963 ranged from over $175 in four states to less than $80 for three states.

Trends for state revenue from selected types of taxes from 1959 to 1963 are shown in Figure 16–1:

In 1963 legislatures in thirty-five states passed laws designed to tap new tax sources or to raise effective yields from existing taxes. These changes are estimated to raise annual collections by approximately $1,036 million or about 5 per cent more than has been collected previously.

Seventeen states enacted legislation to tax new sources and thirty-two states expanded coverage or increased major tax rates. Yields from one or more present tax sources were automatically eliminated or reduced by action in nineteen states, but most of the reductions were small. Other proposed tax increases were rejected in twenty-two states.

Indiana was the only state to enact new major taxes when it passed legislation which in effect set up new taxes on corporate income, individual net income, and retail sales taxes. State legislatures acted to increase rates or broaden the base of corporate income taxes in three states, individual income taxes in three states, general sales taxes in ten, tobacco products in fifteen, alcoholic beverages in twelve, and gasoline taxes in three.

In addition to Indiana, sixteen states passed legislation allowing taxes to be placed on new sources of income, which are comparatively insignificant in the revenue structure at the present time. As an alternative to new taxes, New Hampshire adopted a plan to raise an estimated $4 million a year from sweepstake races with the proceeds earmarked for education.

The 1963 trend continued in 1965 with thirty-two of the 47 states with legislative sessions adopting new taxes or increasing existing taxes. These actions should add approximately $1.3 billion a year to state tax revenues.

The 1965 tax hike represented one of the largest increases to be passed in a single year, exceeding the 1963 increase by almost one-third of a billion dollars. Two states, Idaho and New York, adopted new general sales and use taxes. Nebraska adopted new taxes on personal and corporation income, leaving New Jersey as the only state without a personal or corporate income tax if the commuter tax is ignored.

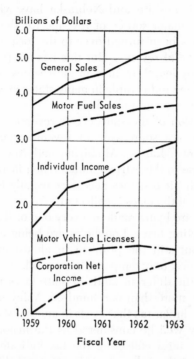

**Fig. 16–1.** Trends in State Revenue from Selected Types of Taxes—1959– 1963. [Source: U.S. Department of Commerce, Bureau of the Census, *Compendium of State Government Finances in 1963* (Washington, D.C.: Government Printing Office, 1964).]

Of the estimated increase in annual state tax revenue enacted by the 1965 legislatures $800 million is derived from increases in sales tax collection; $47 million from additional income tax payments; $282 million from increased tobacco taxes; $2.4 million from increased alcoholic beverage taxes; $98 million from expanded motor fuel taxes; and $91 million from additional revenues of other taxes.[3]

It is true that no two states have tax patterns that are exactly alike. There is becoming, however, a greater similarity in the tax structure of

[3] The information concerning the tax legislation by the 1963 and 1965 state legislatures is taken from: Tax Foundation, *Tax Review*, Vol. XXIV, No. 10 (October, 1963), pp. 39–41, *ibid.*, Vol. XXVI, No. 9 (September, 1965), pp. 35–38.

the fifty states than was true twenty and thirty years ago. Virtually every state has been forced to re-examine in recent years its tax base. Many have created special legislative committees to perform this delicate task while others have employed financial experts to assist the state officials in analyzing the tax structure.

All except New Hampshire and Nebraska have virtually abandoned the property tax as a major source of revenue for the state government. In each instance it has been turned over to the local governmental units as their primary source of revenue. But this has not proven to be a satisfactory answer for any length of time in most states, as the property tax load is rapidly becoming unbearable in many states even without its being used as a source of state government finance.

In every re-evaluation of the state tax or revenue problem the search centers upon finding new sources of tax revenues. Some states, such as Colorado, Illinois, Iowa, Kansas, Michigan, and New York have broadened the state tax base to the extreme limit. When increased revenues are required in these states it becomes necessary usually to increase the rate at which one or more of the taxes is collected.

Constant attempts are being made in every one of the states to improve the method of collecting taxes. Loopholes are being closed at each state legislative session, but still the problem in almost every state remains either unsolved or at best only temporarily relieved.

A listing of all of the different kinds of state taxes now on the statute books would number more than one hundred. Many of these are merely different names for a similar tax that exists in another state.

The following may well be considered as the major state tax sources, with the number of states collecting the tax indicated. The fifty states have certain taxes that they all collect, however, at differing rates. Common agreement is found in taxing motor fuel, motor vehicles, alcoholic beverages, insurance companies, corporations in general, occupation and business licenses, and public utilities. All but one state has some form of tax upon inheritances and gifts and motor vehicle operators.

Once a state collects a particular type of tax it is seldom abandoned. It is also relatively infrequent that the rate at which a particular tax is collected is reduced. On the other hand, many of the tax rates are being periodically increased. This is particularly true of sales, motor fuel, tobacco, and alcoholic beverage taxes. The trend would appear to be toward a definite broadening of the tax base in most states. While the purpose is sold on the basis of distributing the tax burden more equitably, it is also true that with a broader tax base a larger total revenue volume is more easily obtained. Certain pressure groups have at times been in opposition to a broader base which involves new taxes, but usually they have been unsuccessful in their opposition.

## CHARACTERISTICS OF A SOUND TAX SYSTEM

A state tax system is judged in many ways. Obviously it is essential that the taxes included in the system must provide revenue adequate to pay the costs of government at the level that the majority of the people desire. This, to most observers, means that the income and expenditures must be in balance every year. Tradition has dictated that this be so. Many modern day economists are revising this traditional theory and declaring that it is not essential that the income and expenditures be equal every year but that a balance should be forthcoming every "x" number of years when the totals on both sides of the ledger are struck.

The most important standard of judging a tax system is that it must be fair and equitable to the taxpayers. There is basic agreement that ideally each dollar of income should be taxed alike regardless of the manner in which it is spent. Those with the greatest economic capacity should pay larger taxes than those with less. This is the basic concept of taxation on the ability to pay. Obviously not every tax in an acceptable tax system will be strictly on ability to pay. One of the gravest charges against most state tax systems is that too many of them have paid too little attention to having the total tax structure reflecting the ability of the taxpayers to pay. Too frequently the prime state taxes are actually regressive in character, since they take a larger proportion of the income of the people in the lower economic groups than they do of those in the upper economic levels.

A very important aspect of the tax system is the ease of administering the various taxes. Certainly not every tax must lend itself to automatic collection but if many taxes cause difficult problems of collection the costs of administration may become excessive. Likewise, the tax system must be as void of loopholes as possible, so that a minimum number of potential taxpayers are allowed to avoid the taxes that are actually due. No iron-clad rule of how large a percentage of a tax may properly be consumed in the administrative process should be made, but a careful study of administrative costs often will reveal a "worthless" tax—one that is impossible to administer economically and does not produce adequate revenue to justify its existence. A good system avoids too many "ear-marked" taxes.

A good tax system is one that is comprehended easily by the average citizen. The degree of compliance will be enhanced if the taxes within the system are simple. Many times violators do not understand that they actually owe the tax the state demands because of the complications in the tax laws. It should be unnecessary for the average individual to consult a tax lawyer or tax expert every year in order to comply with the state tax system. Unfortunately many of the state tax systems do become so complicated that only people who are constantly studying the state tax laws are in a position to know the exact procedure required of the average tax payer. When this point is reached, the state tax laws should be given a complete and thorough examination with the defective portions remedied.

## MAJOR STATE REVENUES

### Sales Tax

Nearly one-fourth of the total tax revenues of the fifty states annually comes from the general sales tax even though it is not levied in nine states.[4] Massachusetts and Virginia joined the states with a sales tax in 1966; thus forty-one states utilize the general sales tax. West Virginia was the first to levy this regressive type of tax in 1921. In the second half of the twentieth century the states are becoming dependent upon the sales tax as *the* major source of revenue exceeded in some states only by the gasoline tax which is usually earmarked for highway construction and maintenance and thus not a part of the general revenue program. Even though admittedly a regressive tax, it is claimed that if combined with a state personal income tax that its regressive feature is offset. If not applied to food and medicines it also loses much of its regressive character but at the same time loses a large portion of its revenue producing power. The tax is relatively easy for the state to collect as much of the burden is placed upon the local retailer in most states. He is required periodically, in some states quarterly and in others monthly, to pay the amount collected in his establishment to the state collecting agency. Some states allow the retailer to withhold a certain percentage of the collections for his administrative costs, but most states do not give this relief to the retail merchant. The revenue received is relatively stable and inflexible, varying little from year to year unless the rate of collection is changed.

The general sales tax is easily understood and does make the general public aware that it is directly contributing to the cost of government. Most states do not allow it to be a hidden or concealed tax and it must be identified by the merchant.

The basis of the sales tax is gradually being broadened, with several states now including hotels and motels. Other services are also being subjected to the sales tax, with a few states levying it upon legal, medical, dental, and personal services. It is probable that within the next decade every state in the nation will be collecting some form of a general sales tax, with the possibility that greater standardization will occur.

---

[4] The states not resorting to a general sales tax as of September 1, 1966 were: Alaska, Delaware, Minnesota, Montana, Nebraska, New Hampshire, New Jersey, Oregon, and Vermont.

Not only is the tax being broadened but the rate of collection is gradually increasing. At the present time the range is from 2 per cent to a high of 5 per cent. Twenty states collect the sales and use tax at 3 per cent. Most of the states with low sales taxes are bordered by one or more of the states without a general sales tax. On the other hand, Pennsylvania now levies the general sales tax at an all time high of 5 per cent for most retail sales as does Florida on any items classed as sporting goods.

Several states, including Illinois and California, levy a state sales tax and permit their cities also to levy a city sales tax on the same items. In California the state collects on sales at 3 per cent and the cities add an additional 1 per cent tax, while in Illinois the state tax is 3.5 per cent and the cities add an additional one-half per cent. In both cases the state handles the administration and refunds to the cities their share after deducting the administrative costs.

The median sales tax is presently at the 3 per cent figure but there is a definite trend to 4 per cent. The average taxpayer is willing to accept a sales tax in most states with a minimum of complaint. Even an increase in the sales tax appears to be more acceptable to most citizens rather than an increase in other types of taxes if increased revenue is necessary. Public opinion polls consistently show the preference for increasing sales taxes rather than, for example, an increase in the state income tax, where this is the alternative. This lack of resistance to a regressive tax is quite baffling to many economists. Table 16–2 lists the states with sales taxes, the year first levied, the rate, and the major exemption permitted.

## Gasoline Tax

Of all the state taxes, one that every state imposes is the gasoline tax or more properly called the motor vehicle fuel tax. In some states this tax is the largest revenue producer, particularly where no sales tax is levied or if it is at a low rate. Usually the revenue collected from the gas tax is placed in a separate fund and used only for highway construction and maintenance and does not become a part of the state's general fund. It is an excellent example of a tax based upon the benefit theory.

The gas tax rates are never stabilized as one or more states at every session of the legislatures discover the need for more highway construction money and proceed to increase the tax. In 1919 Oregon first levied the tax at a rate of one cent per gallon. The lowest tax per gallon of gasoline now is five cents in Illinois, Kansas, Missouri, Texas, Wyoming, and in parts of Hawaii. The highest tax, eight cents per gallon, is levied in Alaska and in parts of Hawaii. All of these, of course, are in addition to the federal tax.[5]

[5] The gasoline tax or motor vehicle tax is not only levied upon gasoline but also upon diesel fuel, motor oils, and other lubricants used in motor vehicles.

## TABLE 16–2

### State Sales Tax—September, 1966

| State | Year Adopted | Rate | Major Exemption |
|---|---|---|---|
| Alabama | 1936 | 4.0 | Industrial machinery, motor fuel |
| Arizona | 1933 | 3.0 | |
| Arkansas | 1935 | 3.0 | |
| California | 1933 | 3.0 | Food |
| Colorado | 1935 | 3.0 | Prescription drugs |
| Connecticut | 1947 | 3.5 | Food, medicine, motor fuel |
| Florida | 1949 | 3.0–5.0 | Food, medicine, motor fuel |
| Georgia | 1951 | 3.0 | |
| Hawaii | 1935 | 4.0 | |
| Idaho | 1965 | 3.0 | |
| Illinois | 1933 | 3.5 | |
| Indiana* | 1933 | 2.0 | |
| Iowa | 1933 | 2.0 | Motor fuel |
| Kansas | 1937 | 3.0 | Motor fuel |
| Kentucky | 1960 | 3.0 | |
| Louisiana | 1936 | 3.0 | |
| Maine | 1951 | 4.0 | Food, medicine |
| Maryland | 1947 | 3.0 | Food, medicine, motor fuel |
| Massachusetts | 1966 | 3.0 | Food, medicine, clothing |
| Michigan | 1933 | 4.0 | |
| Mississippi | 1930 | 3.5 | Industrial machinery |
| Missouri | 1934 | 3.0 | |
| Nevada | 1955 | 2.0 | |
| New Mexico | 1933 | 3.0 | Coal |
| New York | 1965 | 2.0 | |
| North Carolina | 1935 | 3.0 | Food, medicine, coal |
| North Dakota | 1935 | 2.5 | Medicine |
| Ohio | 1934 | 3.0 | Food, production material |
| Oklahoma | 1933 | 2.0 | Industrial machinery |
| Pennsylvania | 1954 | 5.0 | Food, clothing |
| Rhode Island | 1947 | 3.5 | Food, medicine |
| South Carolina | 1951 | 3.0 | Industrial/Farm machinery |
| South Dakota | 1933 | 3.0 | |
| Tennessee | 1947 | 3.0 | |
| Texas | 1961 | 2.0 | |
| Utah | 1933 | 3.0 | |
| Virginia | 1966 | 2.0 | |
| Washington | 1933 | 4.2 | |
| West Virginia | 1921 | 3.0 | |
| Wisconsin† | 1962 | 3.0 | Selected items |
| Wyoming | 1935 | 2.5 | Motor fuel |

* A combined wholesale, retail, and service tax.
† Transaction tax.

SOURCES: Tax Foundation, Inc., *Tax Review*, Vol. XXVI, No. 1, 1965; and Council of State Governments, *The Book of the States, 1964–1965* (Chicago: Council of State Governments, 1964).

A few states such as Kentucky charge a higher tax rate for gasoline used in heavy equipment and large semi-trailer trucks. Ten states tax diesel fuel at a different rate than gasoline, usually about two cents higher, but in Vermont no tax whatsoever is levied on diesel fuels. The justification for the higher rate is that these heavy vehicles that usually use diesel fuel cause more damage to the roads and highways. The other forty states have the same tax on both gasoline and diesel fuel.

## Cigarette Tax

Forty-eight states have placed a tax on cigarettes with only North Carolina and Oregon not imposing this excise tax. The state tax, which again is in addition to the federal levy ranges, from two cents to as high as eight cents per pack. Arizona has the lowest tax on this form of tobacco product while Washington and Texas collect the cigarette tax at eleven cents.[6]

Seldom does a legislative year occur without some state increasing the tax on cigarettes. However, the increased taxation does not appear to have much effect upon the total consumption. The volume of purchases climbed consistently from 1945 to 1961 but showed a slight decline in 1962, due probably to various medical reports that linked cigarette smoking to lung cancer and other diseases. The increased rate of smoking continued, however, in 1963, with new records established. Thus neither the increased taxes nor the medical assertions of the possible connection between smoking and earlier death has caused any real reduction in the use of cigarettes.

In addition to the federal and state taxes a number of cities have been permitted by their state legislatures to place a city tax on each pack of cigarettes sold within the city limits. Likewise, almost every state and every city requires a retailer of cigarettes to procure a retail cigarette permit for which a sizable fee is assessed.

In spite of this triple taxation on cigarettes in some American cities, the tax does not begin to approach the high rates of many European countries, where rather than being a tax for revenue producing purposes the tax has taken on a public health protection cloak. The United States may in the future adopt this same philosophy.

## Personal Income Tax

In 1964 thirty-six of the states were levying a personal individual income tax, but in two states, New Hampshire and West Virginia, it is based on interests and dividends and not upon regular income. The tax is not a

[6] Twenty-one states collect the cigarette tax at the eight cent figure as of January 1, 1966.

recent innovation as Wisconsin levied a personal income tax on its residents in 1911, even before the first legal federal income tax.[7]

No state followed Wisconsin's lead until 1917, when four states tapped this important source of state revenue. Between 1917 and 1929 no state was added to the list of income tax states, but during the Great Depression the number of states in this tax area rapidly increased.

In 1961 West Virginia was added to the roll of states levying individual income taxes. In the same year the state of New Jersey levied a "commuters" tax which applies only to residents of New York who are employed in New Jersey and New Jersey residents who work in New York.

Most of the state individual income taxes are semi-progressive, with maximum levies never going higher than North Dakota's and Delaware's 11 per cent, except for Alaska which uses a unique plan of taxing the individual at a rate of 16 per cent of the total federal income tax paid. Most states begin their rates at 1 per cent on the first thousand dollars of taxable income and go only as high as 5 or 6 per cent and are not therefore progressive as compared with the federal income tax. Actually Alaska's tax is undoubtedly the most progressive of any of the state income taxes.

In determining how to collect a state individual income tax many problems are confronted. Some states tax only residents of the state, while others tax primarily non-residents. The trend is toward taxing both groups in most states.

A recent movement toward the federal plan of collecting the individual income tax from the employer on a withholding basis has been growing. Five states enacted withholding laws in 1961, and two more were added to the list in 1962, making twenty-six with withholding income tax laws. By 1966 some thirty states were using the withholding feature. However, of these, California withholds non-residents who owe a state income tax but does not withhold residents' income tax payments.[8] The advantages usually cited for using the withholding principle with state income taxes include: the reduction of rate of delinquency; a more effective control of transient workers; elimination of the necessity of lump-sum payments; assures better taxpayer morale as the compliance and equity of the tax is improved; additional revenue is received; a consistent flow of revenue is attained; and the tax may produce a windfall the first year that may be used for capital improvements or other "one shot" budget items.

The opponents of the withholding plan counter with such alleged disadvantages as: the higher expense encountered by employers in book-

[7] The federal income tax levied during and after the Civil War was declared null and void by the federal courts and no legal federal income tax was levied until the passage of the Sixteenth Amendment in 1913.

[8] Council of State Governments, *The Book of the States, 1962–1963* (Chicago: Council of State Governments, 1962), p. 225.

keeping; increases citizen apathy toward government as it becomes more or less a hidden tax; results in refunds and additional staff in the revenue offices; and unless the prior years' taxes are waived the taxpayer is forced to pay two years' taxes in one year.

Another perplexing problem is the determination of what money is or should be subject to the state individual income tax. Some states permit the federal income tax to be deducted from the amount to be taxed by the state; others do not. What other exemptions are to be allowed? The tendency would appear to be toward allowing in most states the same exemptions as are permitted, with modification, by the federal income tax laws.

In spite of the high federal income tax the movement toward every state imposing an individual income tax continues. Many contend that this is a tax field that has been pre-empted by the national government and that the states should not use this particular tax. But the facts are that the typical state cannot afford to take this position without serious impairment of its over-all tax system.

In recent years several states, such as Kansas and Iowa, among others, have completed agreements with the Federal Bureau of Internal Revenue to exchange income tax data. This is an attempt to close the loopholes wherein some individuals report one amount of income to the federal authorities but diminish the figure materially when reporting to the state income tax division.

Forty states do not levy a state tax on income derived from state bonds owned by private citizens. Idaho, Iowa, Montana, and Wisconsin tax income from any bonds issued within their borders, while in Colorado all but bonds issued for sewage facilities and institutions of higher education are taxable. Indiana taxes some but not all of the bonds issued before 1959 while Kansas exempts the bonds issued for construction of the Kansas Turnpike but all others are subject to taxation. In Minnesota individuals holding state and municipal bonds are exempt from tax on these holdings but certain corporations owning state and municipal bonds must pay tax on these holdings. Oklahoma exempts certain bonds but taxes others, and Oregon exempts all bonds issued by the state and its political units after May, 1961.[9] The states with individual income taxes and the rates of collection are listed in Table 16–3.

## Corporation Income Tax

Corporation income taxes levied by thirty-seven states in 1963 brought to the state treasuries 1.5 billion dollars, which amounted to about 50 per

[9] The states that as of January, 1966, did not have a state individual income tax are: Connecticut, Florida, Illinois, Maine, Michigan, Nevada, Ohio, Pennsylvania, Rhode Island, South Dakota, Texas, Washington, and Wyoming.

## TABLE 16–3

### State Individual Income Taxes—January, 1966

| State | Percentage Range | Income Brackets Low | High | Federal Income Tax Deductible |
|---|---|---|---|---|
| Alabama | 1.5 – 5.0 | $1,000– | 5,000 | No |
| Alaska | 16% of U.S. tax | – | – | – |
| Arizona | 1.0 – 4.5 | 1,000– | 7,000 | Yes |
| Arkansas | 1.0 – 5.0 | 3,000– | 25,000 | No |
| California | 1.0 – 7.0 | 2,500– | 15,000 | No |
| Colorado | 3.0 – 8.0 | 1,000– | 10,000 | Yes |
| Delaware | 1.5 –11.0 | 1,000– | 100,000 | Yes (partially) |
| Georgia | 1.0 – 6.0 | 1,000– | 10,000 | No |
| Hawaii | 3.0 – 9.0 | 500– | 30,000 | No |
| Idaho | 2.5 – 9.0 | 1,000– | 5,000 | Yes |
| Indiana | 2.0 gross income | | | No |
| Iowa | 0.75– 5.0 | 1,000– | 5,000 | Yes |
| Kansas | 1.5 – 5.5 | 2,000– | 7,000 | Yes |
| Kentucky | 2.0 – 6.0 | 3,000– | 8,000 | Yes |
| Louisiana | 2.0 – 6.0 | 10,000– | 50,000 | Yes |
| Maryland | 4.0 flat rate | | | No |
| Massachusetts | 3.075 flat rate | | | Yes (partially) |
| Minnesota | 1.0 –10.5 | 500– | 20,000 | Yes |
| Mississippi | 2.0 – 4.5 | 5,000– | 15,000 | No |
| Missouri | 1.0 – 4.0 | 1,000– | 9,000 | Yes |
| Montana | 1.1 – 7.9 | 1,000– | 7,000 | Yes |
| Nebraska | 1.0 – 4.0 | 1,000– | 5,000 | Yes |
| New Jersey° | 2.0 –10.0 | 1,000– | 15,000 | No |
| New Mexico | 1.5 – 6.0 | 10,000– | 100,000 | Yes |
| New Hampshire | 4.25–flat on all interest and dividends | | | No |
| New York | 2.0 –10.0 | 1,000– | 15,000 | No |
| North Carolina | 3.0 – 7.0 | 2,000– | 10,000 | No |
| North Dakota | 1.5 – 8.0 | 3,000– | 15,000 | Yes |
| Oklahoma | 1.0 – 6.0 | 1,500– | 7,500 | Yes |
| Oregon | 2.0 – 7.5 | 250– | 8,000 | No |
| South Carolina | 2.0 – 7.0 | 2,000– | 10,000 | Yes (partially) |
| Tennessee | 6.0 flat interest and dividends | | | No |
| Utah | 2.0 – 6.5 | 1,000– | 4,000 | Yes |
| Vermont | 2.0 – 7.5 | 1,000– | 5,000 | No |
| Virginia | 2.0 – 5.0 | 3,000– | 5,000 | No |
| West Virginia | 1.25– 5.5 | 2,000– | 200,000 | No |
| Wisconsin | 2.0 –10.0 | 1,000– | 15,000 | Yes (partially) |

° Commuters tax—applied only to income derived from sources in New York by New Jersey residents and from sources in New Jersey by New York residents.

SOURCES: Tax Foundation, Inc., *Tax Review*, Vol. XXVI, No. 1 and No. 9 (1965); Council of State Governments, *The Book of the States, 1964–1965* (Chicago: Council of State Governments, 1964).

cent of the amount produced by the states' personal income taxes. The state corporation income taxes are by and large not of the progressive type but rather are flat rates. The low corporation tax of 1 per cent is assessed in Arkansas on income from $1,000 to $3,000 while the highest rate is assessed in Minnesota which charges more than 12 per cent on the income of state and national banks. Until the depression years of the 1930's most states did not resort to taxes on corporation incomes, apparently fearing that such a tax would make the state unattractive to new corporations. Twelve states as of 1966 have not entered this tax field.[10] In 1961 three states, Connecticut, Minnesota, and New Mexico, increased the rates at which corporations pay on earned income, and the trend continued in 1963 when Tennessee, California, and Idaho also increased corporation income taxes.

It is now believed by many economists and experts on plant location theory that a state without a corporation income tax is in no better position than states with such a tax. Apparently the corporation income tax at the rates ordinarily levied by the states is a relatively minor factor far overshadowed by the other elements in the industrial placement plans of companies opening new plants or expanding old facilities.

## Property Tax

Four states have no state-wide property tax of any kind. They are Hawaii, Oklahoma, Tennessee, and Alaska. A number of other states have virtually no state property tax, levying in many instances only a mill or so on all property within the state to assure payment of bond issues floated to pay bonuses for veterans of World War II and the Korean War.

Only New Hampshire and Nebraska depend upon a state-wide property tax levy as the principal base of the state tax program. For the forty-five states with such a tax the fiscal 1963 returns amounted to a total of $687 million.[11]

The property tax has been abandoned by the states, but it has been pushed to a record high by local governmental units in many states to finance new schools, new municipal government operations, and to continue county government activities. It is still the foundation for municipal, county, and school revenue, bringing in usually about 87 per cent of local government revenue annually across the nation.

---

[10] The states without a state corporation income tax are: Florida, Illinois, Indiana, Maine, Michigan, Nevada, New Hampshire, Ohio, Texas, Washington, West Virginia, and Wyoming.

[11] U.S. Department of Commerce, Bureau of the Census, *State Tax Collections, 1963* (Washington, D.C.: Government Printing Office, 1963), p. 5.

## Poll Tax

Only nine states still retain the per capita tax or poll tax.[12] The total received by the nine states in fiscal 1963 was only $8.4 million, with Texas receiving more than $2 million, Virginia, $1.8 million,[13] and New Hampshire $1.4 million. Massachusetts abandoned the poll tax in 1963 and with the Twenty-fourth Amendment to the United States Constitution approved in 1964 it is possible that other states that used the tax to bar Negroes from voting rather than as a tax for revenue will also abandon the per capita tax. It should be noted the Twenty-fourth Amendment does not outlaw the tax but merely the using of it as a voting barrier.

## Severance Tax

Hawaii became the thirtieth state, with its 1963 levy on forest products, to use the severance tax—a tax placed upon minerals, forest products, and oil removed from the ground within a state. In fiscal 1963 more than $188 million were received in Texas, mostly from oil, and $164 million from petroleum in Louisiana. The states with such a tax in 1963 collected the total revenue of $464,537,000—more than half being received by Texas and Louisiana.[14]

While revenue is probably the major purpose served by the severance tax it does have a control factor as it may be raised to such levels as to make certain types of undesirable mining or forest practices unprofitable.

## Motor Vehicle Tax

In all fifty states a motor vehicle tax is collected through the annual sale of either new automobile and truck license plates or inserts for the old plates. In fiscal 1963 a total of $1,642,000,000 was collected from this state revenue source. California collected more than $144 million, followed closely by New York with $141 million, while in contrast Hawaii collected only $36,000.[15]

In the states where the automobile is taxed as a part of the individual's personal property the tax is often a relatively small flat fee. However, in the majority of the states a complicated formula is used to determine the amount each automobile owner will be required to pay for his auto license.

---

[12] The nine states still using the poll tax are: Alabama, Alaska, Indiana, Maine, New Hampshire, Texas, Vermont, Virginia, and West Virginia.

[13] U.S. Department of Commerce, Bureau of the Census, *State Tax Collections, 1963* (Washington, D.C.: Government Printing Office, 1963), p. 5.

[14] *Ibid.*, p. 5.

[15] *Ibid.*, p. 7.

Included in most formulas are the cost of the auto, its weight, the horse-power, model type, and the number of times previously registered. The formula is used in an attempt to force the individual with a more expensive, high-powered car to pay a higher fee. The basic theory of the motor vehicle tax is the benefit or use theory, for in almost every state the tax, like the gasoline tax, is ear marked for highway construction and maintenance.

## Alcoholic Beverage Tax

More money is annually collected by the states on alcoholic beverages than from state-wide property taxes. This amounted to approximately $794 million in fiscal 1963.[16] This includes both taxes on beverages of high alcoholic content and the so-called beer and malt liquor taxes. Tax rates on alcoholic beverages increase by action of one or more state legislatures during any given biennium. In 1961 no less than twelve states increased the tax rate on one or more forms of alcoholic beverages. Sixteen states employ a state monopoly law which permits sale of distilled spirits only through state-owned and operated liquor stores, usually termed the bottle-sale method.[17] Iowa for some years permitted sale only through liquor stores but since 1963 has allowed liquor by the drink, with the clubs, taverns, and cocktail lounges being required to purchase their spirits from the state-owned stores.

There is also a trend toward abandonment of the liquor seal method of collecting taxes on distilled spirits in favor of the usual report by the vendor method of tax collection. The seal method has proven to be expensive and difficult to administer properly.

## Hunting and Fishing Licenses

Every state requires individuals who engage in hunting and fishing within the state to purchase a license. Most states distinguish between resident and non-resident hunters and fishermen, charging much higher fees to the non-residents—sometimes as much as five times the license paid by resident sportsmen. The total revenue raised in the United States from hunting and fishing licenses is annually more than $100 million. In fiscal 1961 it totaled $118 million and rose to $126 million in 1963.[18]

[16] *Ibid.*, p. 2.
[17] The sixteen states using this method of sale of distilled spirits include: Alabama, Idaho, Iowa, Maine, Michigan, Montana, New Hampshire, North Carolina, Ohio, Oregon, Pennsylvania, Utah, Vermont, Virginia, Washington, and West Virginia. Wyoming operates wholesale liquor shops only.
[18] U.S. Department of Commerce, Bureau of the Census, *State Tax Collections, 1963* (Washington, D.C.: Government Printing Office, 1963), p. 7.

Exemptions are often permitted to persons over sixty-five. Also usually exempted are farmers when hunting on their own farms. Most states attempt to gain enough from the hunting and fishing license fees to provide for their game warden costs. In the states that are called a "hunter's paradise," such as South Dakota for pheasants and Wyoming for deer, the revenue from out-of-state license fees defrays a considerable share of the total state conservation and wild-life programs.

## Inheritance and Estate Taxes

Every state except Nevada levies an inheritance or estate tax on moneys and property received by beneficiaries of wills. The federal government allows up to 80 per cent of the state tax to be deducted from the federal inheritance and estate tax. The total is not great but usually constitutes about 2 per cent of the total state revenue. In 1963 it amounted to $594,800,000.[19]

Most states have an accompanying tax which is usually called a gift tax to close the loophole that may arise if rather than willing property or money it is transferred before the death of the donor. This companion tax law is similar to the use tax that accompanies most state general sales tax laws which closes a similar tax loophole.

## FEDERAL GRANTS TO STATES

The fifty states annually receive more than $7 billion from the federal government to assist them in certain functions that the federal government feels a responsibility for partially financing. Most of this money is granted on a matching basis, with the state agreeing to provide an equal amount to finance an approved project. Not all grants-in-aid are on a fifty-fifty basis as the federal government in the interstate highway program has contributed 90 per cent of the money spent.

The extent of federal grants to the states has been rising since 1932, when for the first time federal grant-in-aid programs exceeded the $2 billion mark. Most of the grants during the 1930's were for what might well be classed as emergency relief, which took the form of W.P.A. and P.W.A. projects. By 1946 the grants still totaled only about $2 billion annually but reached the $4.5 billion figure in 1951, nearly $6 billion in 1960, and almost $7 billion in 1961. No longer are the grants considered to be emergency measures and are now included as a regular part of the financial planning of every state.

Rapid expansion of population, urbanization, the technological revolution, and rising living standards have brought about increased demands

19 *Ibid.*, p. 5.

for governmental programs. In most states these expansions can occur only if the state and local subdivisions receive federal grants-in-aid, shared revenues, and commodities.

In fiscal 1962 the increased federal assistance continued unabated. The total amount of money allocated to these three categories for the fifty states totaled $7,651,740,000. The federal amounts received ranged from the $15,599,000 allocated to Delaware while California received $730,-282,000. These figures can be meaningful only if considered as a percentage of the total state expenditures. In Delaware the federal allocation comprised only 13.5 per cent of the total state spending. In direct contrast the $51,128,000 granted to Wyoming made up 49.4 per cent of that state's total expenditures for the fiscal year. A similar high percentage was present in the Alaska budget with the $49,289,000 of federal grants making up 47.3 per cent. The average state depended upon the federal funds for 24.5 per cent of its total expenditures.

The same fiscal year found Alaska's share comprising $200.36 per capita. The only other states that received more than $100 per person in federal assistance were Wyoming ($140.08) and Vermont ($105.07). At the other end of the per capita spectrum was Indiana, whose federal receipts on federal grants-in-aid, shared revenues, and commodities distributed was only $28.53. The average or typical state's per-capita share amounted to $41.35 per person in 1962.

Unless some dramatic change occurs in governmental philosophy, which seems highly unlikely, the importance of federal grants-in-aid, shared revenues, and commodities distributed to the states by the federal government will continue to increase. Without this aid most states would be forced either to drastically curtail their services or to find major new sources of revenue. Raising the present taxes so as to increase state income by one-fourth would appear to be a political impossibility in most states.

The states now budget the anticipated federal grants-in-aid and shared taxes, and if they are radically reduced, the average state budget would be so out of balance that a financial emergency would occur. Periodically the federal government attempts to reduce these programs, but such action is usually resisted by every state governor through the state's Senators and Congressmen.

It should be noted that no state is forced to accept the federal funds if it does not wish to participate. A few states, notably Indiana, have taken this course of action, but a vast majority feel that since their citizens are paying federal taxes they should receive as much federal moneys as possible. The attitude is usually summarized: "If we don't accept our share some other state will receive it and our people will be paying just as much federal taxes."

Grants-in-aid—the term applied to most federal money given to the states—are payments from a higher to a lower unit of government to assist it in financing a particular function. Many states have a similar program between the state and the local units of government. The governmental unit usually attaches a number of conditions to each grant. The lower unit of government, however, does not have to accept the grant if it believes the conditions are too restrictive. The conditions ordinarily establish minimum standards that must be met by the lower government in executing the agreed upon project. The federal government when it is involved in a grant-in-aid project oftentimes reserves the right to conduct on-the-spot inspections. If it discovers violations to the grant-in-aid agreement it may curtail payments on the project.

## State Indebtedness

Few of the fifty states are able to avoid indebtedness for capital improvements. Likewise, frequently because of the irregularity of the flow of revenue into the state treasury, indebtedness must be incurred to finance current operations for short periods of time during any given year. Occasionally an emergency arises which also necessitates borrowing on the part of some state governments.

Most state constitutions place a limit on the total amount of debt that may be accumulated. The range is from a mere $50,000 to $2 million. Obviously these limits are in most cases unrealistic and provision has to be made to exceed the constitutional limit. Most state constitutions make provision for exceeding the maximum figure for certain stipulated reasons. All but two allow the figure to be exceeded if a popular referendum of the voters of the state favor the borrowing.[20]

Various cycles of state borrowing should be noted. No state incurred a debt prior to 1820. Between 1820 and 1860 a number of states floated bonds to excess, particularly in the first twenty years of the period, with a more stringent policy coming about in the decade before the Civil War. The next twenty years again saw an increase in state borrowing with many states getting into financial difficulty as a result. Again restrictions were placed upon indebtedness in many states. The increased borrowing continued into the twentieth century and constantly rose until World War II. During the war many states were unable to continue with road building programs and capital improvements so the over-all state debts declined, only to mushroom in the years following the end of World War II to more than $19 million in 1961 and to $22 billion in 1962—a new all-time high.

Restrictions imposed upon state borrowing include not only the maximum amount figures but also restrictions upon the length of time for which the debt may be contracted. The length varies, with the more conservative

[20] B. U. Ratchford, *American State Debts* (Durham, N.C.: Duke University Press, 1941).

states allowing bonds to be issued for only a period of twenty years, which is, of course, often not the lifetime expectancy of many of the capital improvements that they finance. Other states allow thirty and forty years. Any period over fifty years is normally viewed with skepticism as the improvements may often not continue to be useful for the full length of time needed to pay for them.

Another restriction that is frequently found is concerned with the type of bond that may be issued by the state. Some still allow the familiar sinking fund bond but many permit only the serial type bond with a certain amount of the principal as well as the interest on the entire bond issue being paid off each year. Thus, the total amount expended is greatest in the first year of the bond issue and smallest during the very last year. A few states by outlawing the refunding of bonds do not permit re-borrowing for payment of the same improvement, thereby circumventing the time limitation.

As of the close of fiscal 1960 only Colorado, Florida, Nebraska, South Dakota, Utah, Wisconsin, and Wyoming had no long-term debt supported by the full faith and credit of the state. All of the fifty states had some non-guaranteed bonds outstanding except Alaska, which did have a full faith and credit debt. Only sixteen states had short-term debts as of the end of the same time period.

The state and local indebtedness as of 1960 averaged $388.69 per person. The state with the highest per capita indebtedness was Delaware with $694.65, in contrast with the lowest state per-person debt of $95.89 in South Dakota. The average state debt in the United States was only $103.85 in 1960, but this was a tremendous per capita increase from 1942, when it averaged only $24.61. Thus it is obvious that the local governmental units, including counties, municipalities, special districts, and most important of all, school districts, were in 1960 in debt to a greater degree than the parental state unit.[21]

However, in comparison with the more than $308 billion national debt, the indebtedness of the states and their local units seems small and almost insignificant. But their resources to amortize the debt makes the outstanding bond issues of importance to state and local finance.

## LOCAL REVENUES

Taxes collected by the local units of governments seventy years ago exceeded the taxes collected by the states; in fact they were more than four times the total revenues of the states. During the late years of the

[21] Council of State Governments, *The Book of the States, 1962–1963* (Chicago: Council of State Governments, 1962), p. 219.

nineteenth century the local units of government depended upon the property tax for more than 90 per cent of this total. While it is dangerous to generalize on all local governmental revenues it is still true that more than 80 per cent of all money raised by many of these units is still derived from the tax on property, both tangible and intangible, personal and non-personal. The counties and the school districts are still primarily dependent in most states upon this one tax, while the cities have been forced to broaden the tax base and utilize other taxes wherever possible.

Many of the states have been very restrictive of their local governments in the area of allowing them to broaden their tax base and the total amount of revenue they may raise. No local government may impose a tax without first being authorized to do so by the state legislature. This ordinarily applies, home rule or no home rule. Since almost all of the states are constantly searching for new tax sources, they have naturally been reluctant to grant the local units a taxing area that the state may find desirable.

Growing restrictions even have been placed upon the use of the property tax by local units. These restrictions take many forms but often are limits upon the total millage a unit may impose, a maximum per person levy, or a maximum increase in property tax assessment that may occur in any one fiscal year. With the property tax being used to finance the major share of the costs of county government, municipal government, and schools, it is only to be expected that the property tax has in many states risen to such a point that it is nearly confiscatory.

Part of the property tax problem is undoubtedly the lack of adequate assessment. Frequently the assessments vary from county to county and even within the county itself. No standards have been fully developed and utilized to bring about equality of assessment in many localities. Thus some property bears an unfair share of the property tax while some other may at least partially escape the burden. The belief is growing that state-wide assessment of property of all kinds is the only answer to the tax assessment dilemma. Trained experts in property evaluation must be a part of the solution to this growing crisis.

State legislatures have slowly yielded to the pressure, primarily of the larger municipalities, to allow them certain new taxes. Cities are now authorized in New York, Illinois, California, and Louisiana, to name four, to have a city sales tax. About 1,400 cities now have such a tax in the entire United States. The most satisfactory method of collection is of course for the state to collect the tax for the municipality and then return its share.

Four states, Kentucky, Missouri, Ohio, and Pennsylvania, have permitted the municipalities to levy an income tax. Pennsylvania allows school districts as well as cities to have an income tax, but none of the other states has authorized any governmental unit other than cities to use this form of taxation. The income tax is usually a flat one per cent of gross earnings and is levied on all persons living within the city and all persons who work in the city but live outside of the city limits.[22]

A growing list of cities is now using, following state authorization, city taxes on such items as gasoline sales, tobacco, liquor, and other excise taxes. For years, the cities have been issuing licenses for amusement houses, restaurants, dance halls, pool and billiard rooms, etc. The license fees have been constantly rising and may in some instances provide a sizable source of revenue. Many other types of business are also licensed by the local governmental authorities, but many of them are so small that they barely pay for the costs of inspections and must therefore be regarded as non-revenue producers.

Probably the fastest growing source of local revenue is the payments received in various forms from the higher levels of government, state and federal. The school districts have been more favorably treated in this respect than other local governmental units. Many school districts receive as much as 50 per cent of their total budgets from state funds. Many others, however, are still receiving only 10 to 20 per cent from state sources. Counties have been less fortunate in respect to state aid. Municipalities by and large are in between the school districts and the counties in the degree of support granted from the state.

It is obvious why the school districts have been able to make greater inroads into the state treasury than the other units. Their plea is most effective in order to give every school child equal educational opportunity whether he resides in a wealthy school district with great amounts of assets or in a relatively poor school district with few tax assets.

## STATE TAX ADMINISTRATION

The trend in state tax collection administration is in the direction of a single state department in charge of collection of all state revenues. This system, where it has prevailed, has in general led to a more efficient administrative operation. The most completely centralized revenue system is probably present in New Jersey where an appointed state treasurer is responsible for all tax revenue collection as well as the general fiscal affairs of the state.

A centralized tax administering department would have to have a number of divisions: state income tax, corporations income, sales tax, excise tax (tobacco, beer, liquor, etc.), county tax, liquid fuel, motor vehicle and auto and truck operators license, investigation and accounts, and an administrative division, to name only a part of a complete tax department organization.

[22] Robert Sigafoose, *The Municipal Income Tax: Its History and Problems* (Chicago: Public Administration Service, 1955).

In the past, in some states as many as fifty different departments and agencies acted as tax collectors. This situation apparently prevailed in Michigan as recently as twenty years ago.[23] Such a system divides the responsibility and accountability for collection of public funds in such a way as to reduce efficiency and economy. Likewise, such a type of operation makes it virtually impossible to utilize the latest machine methods for streamlining the collection activities.

An increasing number of states have made agreements with the federal Bureau of Internal Revenue to exchange tax information. This is possible only if the state has placed its tax records on tapes that can be easily and rapidly checked against the federal records. Through the exchange procedure it is possible for the state records to be cross checked against the federal returns of individual taxpayers, corporation, and other tax accounts to assure that the tax records are honestly being reported. It is possible also to ascertain if a taxpayer is failing to file a state return when he should, as most taxpayers apparently have a fear of federal tax prosecution but have little fear of a state violation.

It is patently obvious that the head of the tax collecting agency should be appointed and responsible to the governor. However, the popular election method is still used in at least three states to select the chief of this unit. This practice would appear to be completely indefensible.

If there is any place for a tax commission or board it would be in connection with any quasi-judicial work that the agency may have to perform. This would probably be a part of an appeal situation when the taxpayer believes he has been unjustly charged a higher tax and demands a review, or if the state administrative agency has state-wide tax assessment responsibilities and appeals must be granted from the assessment levy. Little defense can be made for either a board or a commission in a tax-collecting agency as the head of the over-all administrative operations, even though a number of states still retain this archaic method for administration.

An examination of the tax collection administration in the states reveals that using the major state taxes collected—income, sales, gasoline, motor vehicle, tobacco, inheritance, alcoholic beverages—ten states have consolidated these collecting activities into a single agency. Twenty others have reduced the number to two, while fifteen still have taxes collected by three agencies, and five have four different tax units.

## BIBLIOGRAPHY

ALLEN, EDWARD D., and BROWNLEE, O. H. *Economics of Public Finance.* Englewood Cliffs, N.J.: Prentice-Hall, Inc., 1947.

[23] Michigan Public Expenditure Survey, *Save in the State to Save the Nation* (Lansing: State of Michigan, 1944), pp. 3–4.

AMERICAN MUNICIPAL ASSOCIATION. *State-Collected Municipally-Shared Taxes.* Chicago: American Municipal Association, 1946 and 1948.

BLAKEY, ROY G., and GLADYS, C. *Sales Tax and Other Excises.* Chicago: Public Administration Service, 1945.

BLAKEY, ROY G., and JOHNSON, VIOLET. *State Income Taxes.* Chicago: Commerce Clearing House, Inc., 1942.

BUCK, ARTHUR E. *Public Budgeting.* New York: Harper & Row, Inc., 1929.

———— and OTHERS. *Municipal Finance.* New York: The Macmillan Co., 1926.

————. *The Budget in Governments of Today.* New York: The Macmillan Co., 1935.

BUEHLER, ALFRED. *Public Finance,* rev. ed. New York: McGraw-Hill Book Co., Inc., 1945.

BURKHEAD, JESSE. *Government Budgeting.* New York: John Wiley & Sons, Inc., 1956.

COUNCIL OF STATE GOVERNMENTS. *Post-War State Taxation and Finance.* Chicago: Council of State Governments, 1947.

————. *Federal Grants-in-Aid.* rev. ed. Chicago: Council of State Governments, 1949.

————. *Sources of State Tax Revenue, 1940–1949.* Chicago: Council of State Governments, 1950.

CRAWFORD, FINLA G. *Motor Fuel Taxation in the United States.* Syracuse, N.Y.: The Author, 1939.

CRIZ, MAURICE. *The Use Tax.* Chicago: Public Administration Service, 1941.

DUE, JOHN F. *Sales Taxation.* Urbana: University of Illinois Press, 1957.

————. *State Sales Tax Administration.* Chicago: Public Administration Service, 1963.

FEDERATION OF TAX ADMINISTRATORS. *Recent Trends in State Finance.* Chicago: Federal Tax Administrators, 1948.

GROVES, HAROLD M. *Financing Government,* 5th ed. New York: Holt, Rinehart & Winston, Inc., 1958.

HANSEN, ALVIN, and PERLOFF, HARVEY. *State and Local Finance in the National Economy.* New York: W. W. Norton & Co., Inc., 1944.

JENSEN, JENS P. *Government Finance.* New York: Thomas Y. Crowell, 1937.

————. *Property Taxation in the United States.* Chicago: The University of Chicago Press, 1931.

LESTER, WILLIAM M. *A Summary Comparison of State Revenue Systems.* Atlanta, Ga.: Tax Revision Committee, 1949.

LUTZ, HARLEY. *Public Finance,* 4th ed. New York: Appleton-Century-Crofts, Inc., 1947.

NATIONAL ASSOCIATION OF ASSESSING OFFICERS. *Assessment Organization and Personnel.* Chicago: National Assessing Officers Association, 1942.

NATIONAL MUNICIPAL LEAGUE. *Model Accural Budget Law.* New York: National Municipal League, 1946.

————. *Model Cash Basis Budget Law.* New York: 1948.

PENNIMAN, CLARA, and HELLER, WALTER. *State Income Tax Administration.* Chicago: Public Administration Service, 1959.

ROLPH, EARL R., and BREAK, GEORGE F. *Public Finance.* New York: The Ronald Press Co., 1961.

SIGAFOOS, ROBERT A. *The Municipal Income Tax: Its History and Problems.* Chicago: Public Administration Service, 1955.

SMITHIES, ARTHUR. *The Budgetary Process in the United States.* New York: McGraw-Hill Book Co., Inc., 1955.

TAX FOUNDATION. *Facts and Figures of Government Finance.* Englewood Cliffs, N.J.: Prentice-Hall, Inc. (yearly publication).

U.S. ADVISORY COMMISSION ON INTERGOVERNMENTAL RELATIONS. *Coordination of State and Federal Inheritance Estate and Gift Taxes.* Washington, D.C.: Government Printing Office, 1961.

———. *Tax Overlapping in the United States.* Washington, D.C.: Government Printing Office, 1961.

———. *Measures of State and Local Fiscal Capacity and Tax Effort.* Washington, D.C.: Government Printing Office, 1962.

U.S. Department of Commerce, Bureau of the Census. *Historical Statistics on State and Local Government Finances, 1902–1953.* Washington, D.C.: Government Printing Office, 1955.

———. *Compendium of State Finances.* Washington, D.C.: Government Printing Office (yearly report).

———. *Compendium of City Government Finances.* Washington, D.C. Government Printing Office (yearly report).

———. *State Tax Collections.* Washington, D.C.: Government Printing Office (yearly report).

# 17

# State and Local Expenditures

In theory, state and local governments determine what expenditures are necessary during a given year and then proceed to raise the tax levy to a point that will bring in the required revenue to balance the budget. In actual practice, however, most state legislatures, most city councils, and most local unit policy makers probably arrive at their estimate of how high taxes may be placed and then compute the spread of expenditures from this point; determining what per cent of the money available will be devoted to the various functions performed by the particular governmental unit. All possible resources are computed when determining the total revenue available for the budget year.

Two different expenditure pictures present themselves in an analysis of state and local governmental finance. If one considers only the state expenditures, ignoring the local spending, the highway construction and maintenance budget is the largest single item, with education second, public welfare third, and health and hospitals fourth. Major local expenditures rank public education costs first, welfare second, public works (highways, streets) third, and health and hospitals fourth. If the state and local expenditures are combined, education becomes the largest single expenditure item, with highways second, public welfare third and the hospitals and public health administration fourth.

## TRENDS IN STATE AND LOCAL EXPENDITURES

In fiscal year 1962; the fifty state governments' general expenditures were over $31 billion, an all-time high.[1]

While state governments were expending for general purposes just over $31 billion, local governments in the states for the same period were

[1] U.S. Department of Commerce, the Bureau of the Census, *Summary of Governmental Finances in 1962* (Washington, D.C.: Government Printing Office, 1963), p. 20.

spending $39 billion. It should be noted that of this amount at least $11 billion was received by the local governments from the states.

State direct expenditures consisted of:

1. $11.2 billion current operating expenses;
2. 10.8 billion state aid to local governmental units;
3. 7.2 billion for capital outlay;
4. 6 billion interest on debt; and
5. 4 billion insurance trust expenditures.

Local government expenditures consisted of:

1. $31.0 billion current operation expenditures;
2. 9.5 billion capital outlay;
3. 1.5 billion assistance and subsidies;
4. 1.7 billion for interest on debt; and
5. .64 billion insurance trust payments.

Of the more than $70 billion combined state and local government expenditures in 1962, more than one-third of this, 21.921 million, was spent for education—elementary, secondary, and public-supported higher education. Local schools spent $17.4 billion, while higher education costs paid by state and local governments totaled $4.0 billion. An additional $434 million was spent for state supervision and schools for the handicapped.[2]

State governments spent directly only $200 million for local education but provided $6.4 billion or about one-third of the total cost of local school districts. State governments spent $6.6 billion for highways directly while local governments were spending $3.7 billion. About two-thirds of these costs were for capital outlay and the remaining one-third for maintenance. Public welfare and expenditures for health and hospital services were the next largest expenditure items for state and local governments in fiscal 1962. Public welfare totaled $5 billion, while health and hospital expenditures amounted to $4.3 billion, both about equally divided between state and local government expenditures.

State and local government per capita expenditures averaged in 1962 $321. The lowest per-capita expenditure was in South Carolina with a figure of $202, while Alaska was at the other extreme with $551 per person.[3]

The combined state and local government expenditures for education on a per capita basis had a variation of more than $100 from the state spending the lowest to that spending the greatest amount per person. The range was $74 to $176; with capital improvements omitted it ranged from $66 to $144 per person residing in the state. Likewise in highway construction

[2] Council of State Governments, *The Book of the States, 1964–1965* (Chicago: Council of State Governments, 1964, pp. 211–12.

[3] *Ibid.,* p. 219.

and maintenance the variance was more than $100 per person, with $152 in the one extreme to only $38. Not as great a variance appears in the expenditures for public welfare activities, with a range from a low of only $9 per capital to a high of $39. The differences in expenditures for hospitals and public health were similar, a low of $11 to a high of $36 in New York, where the state government gives material assistance to the local units in this area in contrast to many of the states.

It should be noted that the wide differences in state expenditures for education may, to a large degree, be accounted for by the fact that in some states less than 10 per cent of the cost of operating the secondary and elementary schools is borne by the state government, leaving the balance to the local school district. In a number of other states virtually the entire cost has been assumed by the state government.[4]

An examination of state and local government expenditures in 1902 as contrasted with state and local spending in 1960 demonstrates the trend of state and local finance. At the beginning of the century the local governmental units were spending four times as much as the state governments. Now this differential is almost non-existent. Thus the state governments, in most but not all of the states, are assuming a more and more dominant role in monetary policy by controlling the expenditures primarily through different forms of grants-in-aid. Thus the local governmental units are now spending more money than they raise, while the state governments raise more money than they spend directly.

The trend in state expenditures may best be visualized by a survey of the total expenditures from 1942 to 1962 by selected years:[5]

Millions of dollars

| | |
|---|---|
| 1942 — 5,343 | 1957 — 24,235 |
| 1946 — 7,066 | 1958 — 28,080 |
| 1950 — 15,082 | 1959 — 31,125 |
| 1952 — 15,834 | 1960 — 31,596 |
| 1954 — 18,686 | 1961 — 34,700 |
| 1956 — 21,868 | 1962 — 36,400 |

On a per-capita basis these figures indicate these amounts to be an increase of from $40.37 in 1942 to an average state expenditure per person of $176.95 in 1960. This increase is more than four times the per-dollar figure but is not expressed in constant dollars but in actual dollar expenditures.

In 1961 state government expenditures totaled $34.7 billion of which $10.1 billion was distributed to local governments by the states. This total

4 Ibid., p. 219.
5 Council of State Governments, The Book of the States, 1962–1963 (Chicago: Council of State Governments, 1962); and U.S. Department of Commerce, Bureau of the Census, Summary of State Finances, 1962 (Washington, D.C.: Government Printing Office, 1963), pp. 1–3.

increased in 1962 to $36.4 billion, a gain of 8.7 per cent over the previous fiscal year. Of the 1962 total, education accounted for a slightly larger fraction of state spending than any other function, with a total expenditure of $10.7 billion—10 per cent greater than in 1961. State fiscal aid to local governments for support of local schools amounted to $6.5 billion, an increase of one-half billion over the previous fiscal year. Expenditures for higher educational institutions were $3.6 billion.

State expenditures for highways in 1962 increased 6.2 per cent over 1961 and totaled $8.0 billion, of which $1.3 billion were paid to local governmental units for highway purposes. Public welfare expenditures increased by 9.5 per cent and reached $4.3 billion in 1962. State spending for hospitals continued to be the fourth largest expenditure, rising 3.9 per cent and amounting to $2.0 billion. Smaller increases occurred from 1961 to 1962 in state spending for most other general government functions.[6]

Almost one-fifth of all state expenditures are for personal services, totaling in 1962 $7.1 billion. Usually personal services are listed as mainly for current operating expenditures, but some amounts are also for force-account construction.

A number of reasons are obvious for the increase in state expenditures of the last twenty years. The increase in population is of course a major factor in the total increase but cannot be used to account for the rise in per-capita expenditures. The inflation that has occurred since 1946, with its corresponding reduction in the purchasing power of the dollar, must be given as a second major factor and a most important one in the per-person increase. If the constant dollar is used, the percentage of increase in state expenditures is only about half what it would appear to be on a comparison of straight dollar expenditure. A third important factor is the increased number and extent of services that are now provided by state governments.

Even with the increased spending by state governments the ratio of the state and local taxes to the net national product remained virtually unchanged from 1940 to 1962. During no one year has the total amount of revenue taken by the states amounted to more than 8 per cent of the net national product, and it has varied only from 5 per cent to the high of 8.

From the figures already cited it is evident that three functions, education, highways, and public welfare, annually account for more than half of the state expenditures. On the state level considered separately the highway spending is highest, with education second; but when state and local expenditures are combined, education costs exceed the total spent for highways and public welfare together. This pattern has not varied materially for more than a decade, and there are no signs that it will change in the near future.

[6] U.S. Department of Commerce, Bureau of the Census, *Summary of State Finances, 1962* (Washington, D.C.: Government Printing Office, 1963), pp. 1–3.

## FISCAL MANAGEMENT

Professor W. Brooke Graves identifies the basic elements in the fiscal process as follows: (1) the assessment and collection of taxes, (2) the moneys collected must be held for safekeeping, (3) the problem of incurring, managing, and retiring debt, (4) financial planning or budgeting, (5) the problem of fiscal supervision, (6) the procurement or acquisition of necessary property and supplies, (7) paying for the supplies and personal services—disbursements, (8) financial reporting to the public, and (9) ascertaining if the transactions have occurred according to law—auditing.[7] In the previous chapter consideration was given to the first four steps in the fiscal process leaving for consideration in the remainder of this chapter the last five transactions in a typical state financial operation. The agencies usually responsible for the steps involved in fiscal management at the state, county, and municipal levels are contained in Table 17–1.

### TABLE 17–1

#### Divisions of Fiscal Management

| Financial Action | State | County | Municipal |
|---|---|---|---|
| 1. Assessment and Tax Collection | Dept. of Revenue Tax Commission | County Assessor County Treasurer | Department of Revenue City Treasurer |
| 2. Custody of Funds | State Treasurer | County Treasurer | City Treasurer |
| 3. Debt Administration | State Treasurer | County Treasurer | City Treasurer |
| 4. Financial Planning | Budget Bureau | – | Budget Office |
| 5. Financial Supervision | Dept. of Revenue State Comptroller | – | City Comptroller |
| 6. Purchasing | Dept. of Property and Supplies Individual Agencies | – | Dept. of Purchasing |
| 7. Disbursement | State Treasurer | County Treasurer | City Treasurer |
| 8. Auditing | State Auditor | State/County Auditor | City Auditor |
| 9. Budgeting | State Budget Director (Comptroller) | – | City Budget Director (Comptroller) |

SOURCE: Adapted from W. Brooke Graves, *Public Administration in a Democratic Society* (Boston: D. C. Heath & Co., 1950); and Council of State Governments, *The Book of the States, 1964–1965* (Chicago: Council of State Governments, 1964).

### State Budgeting

The budget, often called the most important element in fiscal management, is a comprehensive plan expressed in dollars and cents for operating

[7] W. Brooke Graves, *Public Administration in a Democratic Society* (Boston: D. C. Heath & Co., 1950), pp. 266–67.

a governmental unit for a given period of time. The time element is almost always one twelve-month period. Even those states that have only a biennial session of the state legislature usually make an annual budget and then double it for the biennial figures.

Originally state budgets were most often merely a listing of how much money would be expended for each activity on a line-item basis. Since the Hoover Commission reports indicated the advantages of the performance budget, a few of the states have modified their budgeting techniques to use, at least in part, the performance budget. Some local governmental units have followed the pattern but at a slower pace. Most writers classify the newer types of budgets into a program or activity budget and a performance budget, with the latter carrying the former a step further in the direction of cost accounting and standards of work measurement. Certainly performance budgeting emphasizes that the budgeting process is the most important tool of fiscal management available to the chief executive whether he be the head of a state or a local unit of government.

The importance of the budgeting process is so great that one would expect it to be an old tool of state and local government administration, but actually it has been only during this century that genuine budgets have been used by cities, counties, and state governments. The use of the budgeting device gained a foothold first in the cities and then later in the state governments, with the state of Ohio in 1913 first enacting a state executive budget system.[8] Prior to the adoption of the executive budget system in Ohio, the responsibility of programming financial expenditures and receipts was completely in the hands of the state legislatures, with the governor playing no significant role. Usually the legislature delegated the task to a finance committee which may or may not have prepared a complete budget for all activities.

By 1920 the budget practice of Ohio had spread to forty-three other states.[9] In 1962 the chief executives in forty-four states had been authorized budget-making authority. In other states—Florida, Indiana, North Dakota, South Carolina, and West Virginia—the governor shared the authority with various other elected officials and representatives of the general assembly. Arkansas is the only state that still persists in allowing the legislative assembly to formulate the budget with no assistance of a formal nature from the state's chief executive.

In the forty-four states with executive budgets the governor himself does not prepare the budget but he is authorized to have it prepared by the established budgetary agency which is normally directly accountable to him.

[8] F. R. Aumann and Harvey Walker, *The Government and Administration of Ohio* (New York: Thomas Y. Crowell Co., 1956), p. 142.
[9] Jesse Burkhead, *Governmental Budgeting* (New York: John Wiley & Sons, Inc., 1956), p. 14.

The following types of budgeting systems are in operation in the states:

1. Executive Budget: Used in all but six states, establishes the governor as the authority and with the responsibility of presenting the budget to the state legislature.
2. Administrative Board Budget: Florida and West Virginia vest the authority in the governor and other elected administrative officers to prepare the budget and to submit it to the legislature.
3. Administrative-Legislative Board: Indiana, North Dakota, and South Carolina vest the power in a combined group of elected administrative officers and members of legislative committees.
4. Legislative Type: Arkansas, alone among the fifty states, uses a budget prepared by legislative committee. It employed an executive-type budget from 1937 to 1943 but reverted to the legislative budget.

Professor Harold D. Smith has summarized the major qualities essential for effective budgeting as follows:

1. Responsibility—a single point of final executive decision and responsibility.
2. Comprehensiveness—the entire fiscal program assembled and summarized in one package.
3. Flexibility—the presence of a reasonable degree of policy choice and administrative discretion in execution.
4. Reliability—availability and accuracy of the information provided in sufficient detail.
5. Integrity—the fiscal program may be carried out as intended.
6. Clarity—the budget document must be prepared in such a manner that all interested parties may easily comprehend the fiscal program.
7. Publicity—both the state officials and the public must be informed on the detailed provisions of the budget.
8. Prior authorization—provision must be made by state statute for establishing budgetary power and responsibility.[10]

## Budget Timetable

Ideally, state and local budgeting should be done on an annual basis. Fortunately, most local governmental units do adhere to an annual budget, but a minority of the states are technically able to have an annual budget as only a few have annual sessions of their state legislatures. The first step in the budget sequence is the issuance of budget requests forms to all departments and agencies that receive appropriations. Usually these will be sent out, in a typical state budgeting sequence, in June. The departments or agencies then have usually until either August or September to

[10] Harold D. Smith, "The Budget as an Instrument of Legislative Control and Executive Management," *Public Administration Review* (Summer, 1944), pp. 181–88.

return these forms to the issuing agent, ordinarily the state budget officer. The budget director will work over the requests during September and October and have them reviewed by personnel in his department in order that the governor, or the governor-elect, will have the studied requests ready for his inspection following the November election. After the governor's first study of the requests, most states hold budget hearings at which time each agency is allowed to support its budget recommendations or requests that have been placed in writing. These budget sessions, while they infrequently change or alter the final decision of the chief executive, do give him an excellent over-all view of the operation of state government and allow him to get a briefing on new projects and programs that the various state agencies either are undertaking or believe should be undertaken.

After the governor's budget hearings have been completed, usually by early December, the budget director and the governor arrive at the final decision as to how much money shall be recommended for the entire state operation and the amount each department shall be allocated in the governor's budget.

The entire budget is then sent to the printer and sufficient copies made to supply each member of the legislature, the press, and other interested persons. The governor and his assistants then turn their attention to preparing the budget message which must accompany the printed budget. In this message, often the most important speech of the year for a chief executive, the fiscal program for the state for the next one or two years is outlined. Any great changes that are recommended for a particular function or department are explained in as much detail as the governor believes is necessary. An integral part of the budget and the budget message must be the chief executive's revenue program. This, too, if any major increases or possibly decreases are anticipated, must be explained in detail and justified.

Any well-prepared budget document presented to a state legislature must have at least the following items:

1. A balance sheet by funds or functions
2. A general statement of the general fund operations
3. A summary statement of each and every special fund operation
4. A statement of the current indebtedness
5. A summary of all estimated tax revenue by sources
6. A summary of all non-tax receipts anticipated during the year
7. A summary of all estimated expenditures by function, by agency
8. The necessary bills to enact the recommendations into appropriation laws

A further breakdown of the budget is often given: a comparison of the proposed budget with past budgets for a series of years. The character of expenditures may also be broken into various units, including the cost of capital improvements and personnel.

Most states, assuming the appropriations will be effective the 1st of July, require the governor to present his budget to the general assembly by the first week of February. Following the governor's message the legislative procedure takes over. The budget recommendations are usually divided among a number of committees. The ways and means committee takes the responsibility for consideration of the revenue measures that the chief executive has suggested, while the appropriations committees will turn their attention to the various appropriations recommended by the governor.

## Appropriations

Many state governments have earmarked far too large a proportion of their revenue. This earmarking, which may take various forms, usually provides that all the proceeds from a certain tax will be automatically reserved for a particular function or governmental agency. One of the few justified earmarking of revenues cases may be in the field of highways, wherein some rational can be made for setting aside all state gasoline tax revenue, motor vehicle revenue, and use tax from sale of automobiles for highway construction and maintainence.

Appropriations usually are either lump sum or itemized. The lump-sum appropriation grants a given sum of money to a particular department or for a particular function. The administrator in charge of the unit or the function is then allowed considerable latitude in the expenditure of the funds. Even lump-sum appropriations may be segregated to a degree with a certain portion designated as available for supplies and equipment and another sum for personnel.

The itemized appropriation, when carried to the greatest extremes, may stipulate the exact amount available for every part of the administrative procedure, by designating, for example, the amount that may be spent for typewriters and office furniture. An itemized appropriation establishes the precise amount available for salaries, and frequently ceilings are placed on various administrative positions within the agency. Obviously administrators prefer the lump sum rather than the itemized appropriation. The legislators frequently feel that their control over the administrative activities is retained by a detailed itemized appropriation.

States in which the legislators grant lump-sum appropriations are usually those in which the greatest degree of confidence exists between general assembly and the administration. When the control of the legislature is in the hands of one political party and the administration is of the other, the itemized appropriation is more frequently used. Obviously it is extremely difficult, if not impossible, to draw a hard and fast line between a lump sum and itemized appropriations since many degrees of both types exist and variation may be found within the appropriations made by a state legislature to different governmental agencies in the same legislative session.

In forty-three states the legislative power to change the proposed budget is unrestricted. In the other seven states the following limitations must be noted:

1. California—the state constitution guarantees support of public schools and bond services.
2. Maryland—legislature may decrease but not increase appropriations except for legislative operating expenditures.
3. Nebraska—a three-fifths vote is required to increase an item above that proposed in the budget.
4. New York—may strike out items, reduce items, and/or separate items of expenditure.
5. Oregon—appropriations set by constitutional amendment cannot be altered.
6. Rhode Island—if increases or additions cannot be covered by revenue estimates or surplus, the legislature must provide additional revenue in the same bill.
7. West Virginia—the legislature may not increase items of budget except for judicial and legislative expenditures.

In Maryland, Rhode Island, and West Virginia the governor's proposal is the maximum amount that may be appropriated. In Nebraska the extraordinary majority required to increase an item above the governor's proposal makes such increases unlikely.[11]

Unlike the United States Congress most state legislatures do not utilize authorization acts since the passage of the appropriation for a given department or function becomes both the authorization and the appropriation.

Following the enactment of the appropriation law the responsibility for budget administration passes to the executive branch. Two essential elements of budget execution are (1) a uniform accounting system, and (2) a uniform system of classification of items of expenditure. In most states a state comptroller, usually under the direction of the chief executive, is the responsible officer in charge of the budget administration. His control involves both the problem of keeping the departments and functions within

[11] The governor does not have the item veto in Indiana, Iowa, Maine, Nebraska (partial item veto only), Nevada, New Hampshire, North Carolina, Rhode Island, Vermont, and West Virginia. The governor in the other states does possess an item veto of appropriation measures.

the appropriated funds and the long-range problem of supervision and control of expenditures for the entire fiscal period.

Most states have a system of allotments. This practice, which apparently began in 1917 in Illinois, involves the state comptroller being in charge of each agency's funds until permission is granted for expending a certain percentage of the appropriation during a given time period, usually three months. The process followed is typically one in which the agency requests that a certain amount be made available for expenditures during the quarter. It may be that a more detailed breakdown is required with each agency listing the money requested for each of the functions being performed. In some cases obviously one-fourth of the money will not be spent each quarter. For example, the conservation commission will expend more during the summer quarters than during the fall and winter. As a result, the comptroller will make allowances for so-called "busy" seasons in some agencies.

Many comptrollers require each agency to establish, at least at the beginning of the budget period, a reserve, holding back a certain per cent of the total appropriation before it is divided into the quarterly allotments. Then in case of absolute necessity the comptroller will release funds from the agency's reserve.

Monthly or quarterly reports from each department as to the expenditures of funds during the period are ordinarily required. This gives the comptroller an opportunity to check upon the records of his unit and those of the agency. The unencumbered balance of each agency should be known at all times. With modern data processing machines the comptroller should be able within a matter of hours to give a full report to the governor on the condition of all agency funds.

The actual payment by check is usually centered in the state treasurer's office, but often a check or warrant is issued only upon authorization by the state comptroller. Some states require both the state treasurer and the state comptroller to sign every warrant issued.

It is obviously essential that the state treasurer and the state comptroller work harmoniously. This may not be always possible as the state treasurer is still popularly elected in forty-two states and may be of a different political party than that of the governor and the appointed or popularly elected comptroller.

## Centralized State Purchasing

All but the following five states have centralized purchasing offices: Arizona, Hawaii, Iowa, Delaware, and Mississippi. Even in these states some centralization does exist. Iowa, for example, was once a leader in this field with the establishment in 1897 of centralized purchasing for all mental health and penal institutions; but now, more than sixty-five years later, Iowa still uses the same purchasing procedures. Hawaii has centralized purchasing on some commodities but the other three states allow each agency to do its own buying of all supplies.

In thirty of the states the central purchasing office is a part of an integrated management department. In twenty-two the purchasing officer is a direct appointee of the governor, but in others he is an indirect gubernatorial appointee. In only three states is the purchasing officer under a civil service appointment.[12] The other employees of the central purchasing offices in twenty-eight states are included in the civil service system.

Twenty-five states include every state agency under the central purchasing office, requiring them to make all purchases through this agency. Twenty other states permit only limited exemptions, with usually the state-supported higher educational institutions and the legislative and judicial branches of the state government permitted to purchase for themselves. Highway departments in at least six states, in addition to the five without centralized purchasing, are also free to procure their own supplies and equipment. Table 17-2 indicates the extent of centralized purchasing in the states, the method of appointment of the agency head, and the major units exempt from this procedure.

## TABLE 17-2

### State Centralized Purchasing—July, 1963

| State | Centralized Purchasing | Purchaser Appointed by | Agencies Exempted |
|---|---|---|---|
| Alabama | Yes | Finance Director | State docks and hospitals |
| Alaska | Yes | Commission of Administration | None |
| Arizona | No | – | – |
| Arkansas | Yes | Governor | N.A. |
| California | Yes | Dept. of Finance Director | State universities |
| Colorado | Yes | Governor | State universities |
| Connecticut | Yes | Commissioner of Finance | None |
| Delaware | No | – | – |
| Florida | Yes | Commission | Coast offices, universities, road departments |
| Georgia | Yes | Governor | None |
| Hawaii | No | – | – |
| Idaho | Yes | Governor | None |
| Illinois | Yes | Governor | None |
| Indiana | Yes | Governor | None |
| Iowa | No | – | – |

[12] Council of State Governments, *The Book of the States, 1962–1963* (Chicago: Council of State Governments, 1962), pp. 170–71.

## TABLE 17–2 (Continued)

| State | Centralized Purchasing | Purchaser Appointed by | Agencies Exempted |
|---|---|---|---|
| Kansas | Yes | Civil Service Commissioner | None |
| Kentucky | Yes | Commissioner of Finance | None |
| Louisiana | Yes | Civil Service | Highway department |
| Maine | Yes | Finance Commissioner | University, teachers colleges, Port Authority |
| Maryland | Yes | Civil Service | None |
| Massachusetts | Yes | Governor | None |
| Michigan | Yes | Controller | State universities |
| Minnesota | Yes | Commissioner of Administration | None |
| Mississippi | Yes | – | Printing |
| Missouri | Yes | Governor | University, Highway Departments and Patrols |
| Montana | Yes | Governor | None |
| Nebraska | Yes | Governor | University and state colleges |
| Nevada | Yes | Governor | None |
| New Hampshire | Yes | Comptroller/Governor | University and Liquor Commission |
| New Jersey | Yes | Governor | None |
| New Mexico | Yes | Governor | None |
| New York | Yes | Commissioner of General Service | Legislature and judiciary |
| North Carolina | Yes | Governor | Supreme Court |
| North Dakota | Yes | Governor | Higher education, Highway Department/mills, banks |
| Ohio | Yes | Director of Finance | Highway Department |
| Oklahoma | Yes | Board of Public Affairs | None |
| Oregon | Yes | Governor | None |
| Pennsylvania | Yes | Secretary, Department of Purchasing | Turnpike Authority |
| Rhode Island | Yes | Division of Administration | None |
| South Carolina | Yes | Budget and Control Board | None |
| South Dakota | Yes | Governor | State Cement Plant/Prisons |
| Tennessee | Yes | Governor | University and colleges |
| Texas | Yes | Board of Control | None |
| Utah | Yes | Governor | None |
| Vermont | Yes | Governor | None |
| Virginia | Yes | Governor | None |
| Washington | Yes | Director of Administration | None |
| West Virginia | Yes | Commissioner of Finance | None |
| Wisconsin | Yes | Commissioner of Administration | State University |
| Wyoming | Yes | Governor | University/Highway Department/Fish and Game |

SOURCE: Council of State Governments, *The Book of the States, 1964–1965* (Chicago: Council of State Governments, 1964).

The amount of materials in dollars purchased in 1961 ranged from $1 million in North Dakota to more than $150 million in New York state. Thirty-six states give no preference to in-state bidders, while the others allow as much as 5 per cent higher bids to be accepted from a resident over that of an out-of-state competitor.

The state centralized purchasing offices in eleven states maintain their own testing laboratories. In most of the other states the purchasing agency has access to testing facilities of other state departments, such as the highway commission or department of agriculture. Eight states require bids on all items, no matter what the amount involved may be, while the other states allow non-competitive bidding on purchases of less than a certain amount, ranging from a low of $25 to as high as $3,000 in North Dakota. The general rule that appears to be followed is that items of less than $500 do not have to be purchased with competitive bids.

Centralized purchasing has developed because this staff function can be more efficiently and economically performed by a single agency for all departments. In this one unit the personnel may become specialists in the various phases of purchasing.

Competitive bidding is now required by almost all governmental units in the United States for all major items. When centralized purchasing is instituted it is possible to consolidate purchase orders for the same items in such a way as to obtain lower prices with quantity purchases. Trained personnel in one office for the entire governmental unit will be able to simplify the procedures and expedite purchasing. Standard specifications will reduce the number of different items used and obtain better quality merchandise as well as lower prices. The single purchasing office will be able to maintain a list of vendors and have a better record of their ability to supply material.

Included in the responsibility of the purchasing office are the following:

1. Standardization of specifications—the purchase office working in conjunction with the operating departments should arrive at a concensus of what will be the standard specifications for the hundreds of items purchased each year.
2. Preparation of requisition order blanks—establishing deadlines for receiving purchase orders from the various departments on the different items.
3. Soliciting bids—after the purchase requisitions have been catalogued, the purchase office advertises for bids for the amount of supplies and equipment required.
4. Awarding contracts to the successful bidder—the opening of competitive bids should be a public affair with the contract awarded to the lowest responsible bidder, within whatever state or local restrictions apply. Certain states as noted, do allow the awarding of

contracts to residential bidders even if the price is slightly higher than that submitted by the non-resident.

5. Receiving and testing of material—the purchasing office should have available a testing laboratory for examination of supplies and equipment received from the contractor. All goods received must be checked to insure receipt of exact quantity as well as quality as contracted.

6. Payment or authorization of payment—after all material is received and tested, the invoices are checked and approved, and the purchasing officer signs the authorization for payment upon approval by the state comptroller and treasurer.

In many states with the various institutions geographically scattered it may be necessary for the centralized purchasing office to negotiate for on-demand delivery of contracted material to various locations, rather than call for the entire delivery at one central warehouse. Every purchasing operation inevitably finds that emergency situations arise with great frequency. Provision must be made in the central office to handle these purchases. Usually a system is installed that will enable true emergency purchase orders to be filled within a twenty-four hour period, with the formal procedures shortened by use of telephone contact and informal contract agreements. Some centralized purchasing offices almost automatically allow agencies and institutions to make small purchases of less than $25 or $50 where adequate justification appears to be present.

Central purchasing is oftentimes resisted by departments that for years have been allowed to do their own buying. The principle arguments of merit that are raised by those opposed to centralization of purchasing are (1) the departments are in the best position to know the exact specifications of the supplies and materials that best meet their needs, and (2) the occasional delay that occurs in receiving the supplies and equipment when purchased by a central agency. Both of these disadvantages may be overcome if the purchasing agency is well-operated. The specifications should be drafted with complete consultation with the departments concerned. This is especially true in establishing the standard specifications for technical equipment or supplies. The time element or delay in receiving desired material is sometimes a more difficult problem but may be overcome with proper warehousing and delivery systems. Another objection often times raised is the red tape and surplus of paper work that is involved in requisitioning supplies purchased by the central agency. This, too, is unnecessary and with proper organization needs not be a handicap.

## Post-Audit

The concluding step in financial administration is the post-audit. Its purpose is to ascertain whether or not the administrative operation has

STATE AND LOCAL GOVERNMENT AND ADMINISTRATION

been in compliance with the intent of the legislative body and to assure
that the funds have been legally expended and accounted. For this purpose
it is obvious that the office performing the audit should be independent of
the administration. The accountability should be to the legislative body,
however, but more often than not the audit is conducted by an office
headed by a popularly elected administrative official.

It is, of course, possible to have the post-audit performed by an independent or private firm on a per-diem basis. This, however, is usually
found to be a more expensive method of state auditing than the establishment of a full-time, competent post-auditing unit within the state government. The number of audits performed dictates this latter method as probably the more desirable. Likewise, the state with its own auditing unit can
perform this post-audit service for the local governmental units more reasonably than if they are required to hire, on a per-diem basis, independent
or private certified public accountants. Of course the local governments
will be charged by the state for this service on a cost basis for the number
of days that are required for the state auditing personnel to check the
records and accounts of the unit, which would include the counties, the
municipalities, the special districts, and the school districts in the state.

The post-audit is more than just a check of the accounts to insure their
accuracy. It should include an examination into the efficiency and effectiveness of the work of the administrative unit. This requires that the post-
audit be done either continuously in the major units or immediately following the close of the fiscal year. This may account for the practice of
placing local governmental units on a fiscal year that begins in a different
month than that of the state. In Iowa, the state and the school districts
begin their fiscal year on July 1st, but the counties and the municipalities
begin the year on January 1st, thus the staggered ending of the fiscal periods allows the state auditing department to have a more equitable distribution of its yearly work load.

Mr. R. J. Goldie has summarized the duties of both the pre-audit and
the post-audit as being the following: record, compare, analyze, question,
and forecast.[13] This very concisely enumerates the main responsibilities
performed by the auditing unit and the pre-auditors in any governmental
operation.


### Financial Reporting

The financial reporting done by state and local accounting officials leaves
much to be desired. As Dr. W. Brooke Graves so aptly wrote, "It is clear

[13] R. J. Goldie, "A Managing Executive's Concept of Controllership," *The Controller*
(October, 1945), p. 513.

that among fiscal officers there is no clear understanding of what financial reporting is or why it is necessary to make such reports at all."[14]

Even a cursory examination of these reports reveals that most of them are made merely because the state statute or the local ordinance requires that an annual financial report be published. Many of the reports do not indicate to the average citizen, nor even to the accountant, very much of the important information that should be revealed about the financial operation of all governmental agencies.

Financial reports should be presented in a clear, concise, and understandable fashion. Merely a listing of the funds received and expended without notation of the functional activities involved is not adequate. Likewise, the time element is of great importance in financial reporting. A report that details the financial operations of a year or two years or even more in the past is of little value. It is essential that the reports be issued as rapidly as is possible following the close of the financial books of each time period. Similarly, there can be no defense for time gaps in the reports, for their usefulness is greatly impaired if for a year or more the reports are not issued and therefore not available to students of finance.

In some states the only picture that the general public receives of the activities of the various units of state government comes from the financial reports that are issued each year. Financial reports on a functional basis are just as necessary as having the budget placed on a performance basis. It is very difficult to have the reporting on a functional foundation if the budgeting and accounting are not also on this same standard.

Many municipalities have in recent years done superb jobs of financial reporting to their citizens. Most city managers realize the value to their public relations programs of well-prepared, brief, and illustrated reports, but unfortunately few of the state governments have grasped this medium of public relations and made full utilization of it. There are, of course, some exceptions. Illinois and Michigan may be cited as states that have done noteworthy work in financial reporting.[15]

## Accounting

The responsibility for accounting in some states is shared by as many as three officers—the comptroller, the treasurer, and the auditor. The office of state comptroller, or its equivalent, does not exist in fifteen states. However, the office of treasurer is provided for in every state except Alaska, while six states do not have the office of state auditor, or its equivalent.[16]

14 W. Brooke Graves, *Public Administration in a Democratic Society* (Boston: D. C. Heath & Co., 1950), p. 446.

15 *Ibid.*, p. 449.

16 Council of State Governments, *The Books of the States, 1962–1963* (Chicago: Council of State Governments, 1962), p. 142.

Therefore the accounting performed in some states is not as centralized as other aspects of the financial process. A survey by the National Association of State Auditors, Comptrollers, and Treasurers shows that at least forty-three states do have centralized accounting offices. This centralization certainly does not mean that all accounts are kept in one central office but it does imply that all accounts are unified and coordinated to a relatively high degree. It is obvious that an adequate accounting system at any level of government must be on a double entry basis and preferably on an accrual basis rather than the cash basis. It is necessary to show at any time the current condition of any fund in the entire system and therefore accrual accounting is the only type defensible.

A system of cost accounting is also highly desirable. Thus the cost of various items or operations in a department can accurately be determined. Again this is desirable at any level of government, for the cost account-device makes it possible to have an effective yardstick for management.

### The State Treasurer

The primary duty of the treasurer is connected with the custody of the state funds. Few of the popularly elected state treasurers still have the responsibility for collecting any great number of taxes as either a state tax commission or another division of an integrated finance department has this duty. A good treasurer needs to be a well-qualified accountant and financial expert.[17]

The custody of the state's moneys is in some ways even more complex now than it was twenty or thirty years ago, but in other ways it is much simpler. No longer are the depositories for state funds chosen on the basis of personal and political favoritism in most states. The state legislature oftentimes has established guiding principles that must be followed in the distribution of funds to the approved depositories. Usually the number of depositories is large. A check in Pennsylvania revealed that more than 500 banks were used by the state treasurer as depository agents, while Wisconsin had more than 650.[18] For a long period of time state money was ordinarily not invested and did not draw interest but merely was deposited and the profit was rendered to the depository. This practice is now virtually eliminated, except for a limited amount of funds to pay current operating expenses. The treasurer has an important role in the investment of state funds. He may, in a few states, be solely responsible for this decision, but in many others he is a member of an investment board that makes the actual decision which he is by law required to follow.

---

[17] Kirk H. Porter, *State Administration* (New York: Appleton-Century-Crofts, Inc., 1938), pp. 100–109.

[18] Graves, *op. cit.*, p. 378.

A great deal of the state treasurer's time is often consumed with supervision of the various funds. All states have some type of a general fund and almost all have a variety of trust funds. In addition, special funds for various departments and agencies are maintained by most states. The number of special funds frequently defies proper supervision by the state treasurer. Alabama, between 1900 and 1942, varied from only seven funds to more than one hundred. Colorado apparently has more than 230 special funds, but South Dakota has a record number of between 450 and 530 separate funds.[19]

Such an array of special funds destroys any possible discretion and control over financing. This excessive division of moneys into special funds creates great problems for everyone concerned—the legislature, the treasurer, and even the department or agency. The philosophy should be that all state money belongs to the people of the state and should be available for use where and when the elected representatives of the people see fit. Some trust funds for retirement programs and moneys received from the federal government for certain special projects or functions must be segregated from the general revenues, but the excessive use of special funds has exceeded all reason in many states.

Almost everything that has been said pertaining to the position of the state treasurer and the custody of funds is also true of the city treasurer. In many states the city treasurer has hardly any discretion in the matter of how many funds there shall be as the state statute dictates the number that a city must have. Similarly, state laws have removed much of the power of the city and county treasurers as to where, when, and how they shall deposit the money.

## BIBLIOGRAPHY

CHATTERS, CARL H., and HILLHOUSE, ALBERT. *Local Government Debt Administration*. Englewood Cliffs, N.J.: Prentice-Hall, Inc., 1939.

COUNCIL OF STATE GOVERNMENTS. *Purchasing by the States*, rev. ed. Chicago: Council of State Governments, 1956.

FABRICANT, SOLOMON. *The Trend of Government Activity in the United States Since 1900*. New York: National Bureau of Economic Research, Inc., 1952.

FORBES, RUSSELL. *Governmental Purchasing*. New York: Harper & Row, Inc., 1929.

———. *Centralized Purchasing: A Sentry at the Tax Exit Gate*, rev. ed. New York: National Association of Purchasing Agents, 1941.

——— and OTHERS. *Purchasing for Small Cities*, rev. ed. New York: Public Administration Service, 1951.

HILLHOUSE, A. M., and HOWARD, S. KENNETH. *State Capital Budgeting*. Chicago: Council of State Governments, 1963.

[19] *Ibid.*, pp. 385–86.

KIMMEL, LEWIS H. *Governmental Costs and Tax Levels.* Washington, D.C.: The Brookings Institution, 1948.

NICHOLSON, H. L. *County Purchasing.* New York: National Association of Purchasing Agents, 1940.

RATCHFORD, B. U. *American State Debts.* Durham, N.C.: Duke University Press, 1941.

STUDENSKY, PAUL. *Public Borrowing.* New York: National Municipal League, 1930.

TANNERY, FLADGER F. *State Accounting Procedures.* Chicago: Public Administration Service, 1943.

TAX FOUNDATION. *Rising State Expenditures.* New York: Tax Foundation, 1946.

———. *Recent Trends in State Debt, 1941–1947.* New York: Tax Foundation, 1948.

———. *Postwar Trend in State Debt: A State by State Analysis.* New York: Tax Foundation, 1950.

———. *Constitutional Debt Control in the States.* New York: Tax Foundation, 1954.

———. *The Tax Burden in Relation to National Income and Product.* New York: Tax Foundation, 1957.

U.S. ADVISORY COMMISSION ON INTERGOVERNMENTAL RELATIONS. *State Constitutional and Statutory Restrictions on Local Government Debt.* Washington, D.C.: Government Printing Office, 1961.

# 18

# Law Enforcement and Public Safety

As chief executive of the state, the governor, in the exercising of the supreme executive authority, is charged with the duty of seeing that the state laws are faithfully executed. Most state constitutions have merely copied the phrase from Article II, Section 2, of the United States Constitution that maintains that the president shall "take care that the laws be faithfully executed." To aid the governor in the implementation of this responsibility different agencies, offices, and positions have been established. Since the functions of law enforcement and public safety involve many different programs and activities, states have not been too successful in creating one single department with centralized control over the varying services.

## STATE AGENCIES

### Attorney General

The attorney general is usually regarded as the chief legal officer in each state. In this relationship he is viewed as the governor's main adviser in the areas of law enforcement and public safety affairs. While various state constitutions and legislative enactments may assign varying responsibilities to the attorney general, most of his activities will revolve around the performance of four major functions.

First of all, the attorney general serves as legal adviser to the governor, heads of the departments, the legislature, and various other officers and agencies of the state government. The degree of advising that is carried on between the governor and the attorney general is normally dependent on whether or not the two officers are members of the same political party. In addition, as a service to members of the legislature, the placing of the bill-drafting function in the office of the attorney general was at one time an accepted practice. As recently as 1939, twenty-two states extended such services through this office. Currently only four states regularly use this office for bill drafting services.[1]

The second responsibility of the attorney general is to represent the state in actions not only before state tribunals but also before the United States Supreme Court when the state or one of its officers or agencies is concerned. The third role to be assumed by the state attorney general relates to his ability to exercise supervision over local prosecuting attorneys. Since the attorney general is the state's chief prosecution officer he may have complete control in such matters or he may merely advise and assist, in a limited manner, the district or county attorneys. The fourth activity of the state attorney general concerns his power to conduct investigations. Many attorney generals may investigate, either on their own initiative or at the request of the governor or some other state officer, the activities or actions of state officers and agencies ostensibly to determine whether the law is being observed.

The position of attorney general is filled by popular election in forty-two states. In only six states—Alaska, Hawaii, New Hampshire, New Jersey, Pennsylvania, and Wyoming—is the governor granted the power to appoint the attorney general, with senatorial approval being necessary in four of these states. In New Hampshire this appointment is subject to the approval of an executive council, while in Alaska the gubernatorial appointment of the attorney general is subject to the approval of both houses. In Tennessee the attorney general is appointed by the state supreme court, but in Maine the post is filled by action of the state legislature.[2]

## The State Police

The police power is one of the most important responsibilities that can be granted or assigned to any level of government. Our federal system has attempted to ease the problem of the exercise of the police power. The Tenth Amendment to the Constitution of the United States reserves to the states respectively, or to the people, those powers not delegated by the Constitution to the United States nor prohibited by it to the states. Acting on this basic principle, it is generally recognized that the authority to organize police forces resides with the states and their subordinate units, such as counties, cities, and townships. It is also maintained on this basis that the police power belongs to the state alone. Occasionally the police

[1] Council of State Governments, *The Book of the States, 1964–1965* (Chicago: Council of State Governments, 1964), p. 68.
[2] *Ibid.*, p. 142.

power phrase will be used in conjunction with activities of the national government, but this power has never been recognized by the United States Supreme Court as one of the powers to be exercised by that level of governmental authority. However, it must be noted that the United States Supreme Court has on different instances upheld the exercise of national power so identical to that of the police power of the state that it has become almost impossible to separate the two.

The first recognized form of a state police force appeared in 1835 when the Republic of Texas authorized the creation of three Texas Ranger companies. While placed under the supervision of the military authorities, these Texas Rangers were initially concerned with patrol duty on the Mexican border, with general police work gradually becoming their primary function.

The next major development in the creation of state police forces occurred in Massachusetts in 1865, when a system of state constables was established. While primarily concerned with the problem of commercialized vice, these state constables were also given general police powers effective in any part of the state. For this reason Massachusetts is often cited as being the first state to set up a general state police force. Then followed a long period of inactivity in the establishment of state police forces. Connecticut in 1903 authorized a small force patterned to a considerable degree after the Massachusetts plan as it existed at that time. The Connecticut force was to be concerned basically with the suppression of commercialized vice, the enforcement of gambling and liquor laws, the performance of certain inspectional duties, and the investigation of suspicious fires.

The Pennsylvania State Constabulary was established in 1903—a date that signifies the application of a new philosophy in state police administration. In the period from 1835 to the creation of the Pennsylvania State Police, the state forces were usually established in order to meet one of the following needs: (1) to take over from local police jurisdictions the enforcement of unpopular gambling and liquor laws; or (2) to provide for a border patrol in the new states. These two basic needs apparently did not play any major role in the establishment of the Pennsylvania State Police. Instead, other important motives were recognized as contributing to its creation: (1) the eventual recognition that the old sheriff-constable system was becoming ineffective and thereby placing the rural districts under inadequate police protection; (2) the realization that the chief executive of the state, while invested with supreme executive authority, had not been granted an arm or instrument to aid him in the enforcement of the laws; and (3) the inability of the police forces of local communities to cope with certain problems arising out of conditions present in the iron and coal regions of Pennsylvania.

As has been previously indicated, the establishment of the Pennsylvania State Police introduced new techniques into state police administration and provided for a sharp and distinct departure from established practices. In this respect three major changes can be noted: (1) the superintendent of state police, responsible only to the governor, was given extensive administrative powers, thereby centralizing in the superintendent this type of power; (2) it emphasized a decentralized pattern of organization by using a system of troop headquarters and substations as a basis of operation; and (3) it established a policy of continuous patrol throughout the state, even going into the infrequently traveled rural sections.

In 1917, both New York and Michigan created state police forces, followed in 1919 by the establishment of the West Virginia Department of Public Safety, an organization that, in spite of its rather inclusive title, was concerned only with general police work. However, the West Virginia system did introduce a new feature in providing for a bipartisan board of commissioners to share the responsibility for the control of personnel under the superintendent. Beginning in 1920 several of the older state police forces undertook rather extensive reorganization programs. Massachusetts consolidated all of its public safety functions and, in addition, provided for a uniformed patrol force.

A state police organization is maintained in each state today but under varying titles, ranging from the more commonly accepted term of state police to that of courtesy patrol. At the present time twenty-five states refer to their organizations as state police; twenty-four use the title of state highway patrol, and Hawaii places this responsibility in the sheriff-constable system, particularly in the rural areas.[3] Basically state police agencies are of two types. One group, as typified by the Michigan State Police, is clothed with general police powers and the members can enforce any and all state laws. The other category, like the California Highway Patrol, directs most of its attention to the enforcement of the laws governing the operation of vehicles upon the public highways.

## The National Guard

The state military organization has been provided for by national law since 1792. According to the United States Constitution, states may not maintain troops or warships in times of peace without receiving the consent of the Congress.[4] Yet another section of the Constitution clearly indicates that each state may maintain its own state militia or military force but it is subject to overriding congressional authority.[5] These varying sections give an indication that the militia provided for in the national con-

[3] *Ibid.*, p. 463.
[4] *United States Constitution*, Article I, section 10, clause 3.
[5] *Ibid.*, section 8.

stitution is to be both a national and state force but that substantial control is granted to the Congress and the President. While the state appoints the officers and trains the units under direction from the Congress, the state is powerless to prevent the national government from using these units. State militias have usually consisted of all able-bodied male inhabitants meeting certain minimum and maximum age requirements. The state militias from 1792 to 1916 were kept in varying degrees of preparedness as a result of small federal grants.

The advent of World War I brought about substantial changes in the organization and operation of the state militia. Present-day federal law still provides for a state militia of all eligible male citizens but only active members serve in the organized portion that is now referred to as the National Guard. This new pattern of organization was provided for by the National Defense Act of 1916, in which the old state militia gave way to a National Guard to be supported almost completely by federal funds.

The National Guard unit in a state is ostensibly commanded by the governor, and most state constitutions provide that he is the commander-in-chief of the armed forces of the state except in time of war. The actual operations are commanded by an adjutant general, who is appointed in most instances by the governor, with federal approval, and becomes a member of the governor's staff. In addition, all major gubernatorial appointments to the national guard must be federally approved. The degree of national control over the guard is indicated clearly by the fact that, among other things, the size of the Guard, the nature of the component units, the type of training programs, and the qualifications of officers are all determined by the national government.

Since the primary function of the National Guard is to aid in providing for military security, it may be nationalized and called into service by the President. At that time the units are no longer under state jurisdiction but become a part of the active military forces of the United States. When this situation occurs the state may establish some type of home guard to provide for state security. In addition, the National Guard can also serve as an agency for law enforcement. In this case the governor may call out National Guard troops to serve as a police arm of the state or as an arm of executive authority and power. The vast majority of its functions now occur in times of emergencies, insurrection, industrial disputes or natural disasters, such as fires, floods, hurricanes, or earthquakes. For many years the Guard was called out when strikes occurred, but due to intense opposition from certain groups, particularly labor unions, the Guard is now infrequently used in labor or industrial disputes.

In most instances it is customary for the governor to call out the National Guard to give assistance to local police units and officers, and the governor may even wait for a request from sheriffs and chiefs of police when the latter officers indicate that they are unable to control the situation. At times it may become necessary for the governor to declare martial law, which in effect sets aside the ordinary courts and allows the militia (National Guard) to make arrests, to jail individuals, and to try some cases in military courts. This is a very grave situation since many authorities believe such actions by the National Guard constitute an unconstitutional suspension of the writ of habeas corpus.

The ability of the governor to call out the National Guard is viewed as a discretionary power in that he alone can arrive at the decision to use these troops. Yet there have been some instances in which there was some indication that the governor had acted in a very arbitrary fashion and no doubt abused this power. In 1923 Governor Walton of Oklahoma used the National Guard to prevent the state legislature from convening at the state capitol. Walton was later impeached, convicted, and removed from office. In 1930, Huey Long used the National Guard to prevent the lieutenant governor from taking over the governorship after Long's election to the United States Senate. Long actually ordered the arrest of Lieutenant Governor Cyr, declared the position to be vacant, and installed A. O. King, who had been president pro tempore of the state senate, as lieutenant governor. The state courts refused to intervene since evidently they were under the control of Long. In these instances some authorities have maintained that the governor was using the Guard as a political force.

A major departure from the philosophy of the free ability of the governor to issue a proclamation of emergency and call out the National Guard occurred in 1932 when the United States Supreme Court maintained that a governor's declaration of emergency and his use of the National Guard were subject to judicial review.[6] This reversed an earlier decision of the same court that held that an executive proclamation of an emergency was not subject to judicial review.[7]

The use of the state militia or National Guard should be rather infrequent since states have well-organized police forces that can handle most law enforcement problems. It is to be expected that the National Guard will continue to serve the state as a reserve law-enforcement unit. In the case of an atomic disaster the governor would no doubt be called upon to use the National Guard rather than rely on any type of an emergency organization.

## State Prisons

Several types of penal institutions are operated by individual state governments in order to provide places of confinement that may vary accord-

[6] *Sterling v. Constantin* (287 U.S. 378, 1932).
[7] *Moyer v. Peabody* (212 U.S. 78, 1909).

ing to the seriousness of the crimes. At the end of 1962 approximately 195,000 prisoners were housed in some 300 state facilities. First of all, there are the state penal institutions that are usually referred to as state prisons (penitentiaries) or houses of correction. By some state laws the distinction between these two institutions will often reflect not only the purpose of imprisonment but will also indicate the nature of the offense for which the prisoner is incarcerated. As a result, those individuals guilty of lesser offenses will be sent to houses of correction, while those convicted of major crimes, usually involving at least a one-year sentence, are sent to state prisons. In some states the two separate institutions are maintained, but in those areas where only one prison or house of correction is available, some type of distinction or discrimination usually exists in the assignment of prisoners to cell blocks and to work situations. Secondly, many states operate separate institutions, commonly referred to as reformatories, for women and youthful offenders. In addition, separate institutions are usually maintained for the criminally insane.

The effectiveness of the administrative organization for penal systems depends to a degree not only upon the type of personnel available but also upon budgetary allowances. As can be true of other technical areas of governmental administration, the determination and the execution of sound penal policies can be obstructed by the type of administration present.

Before the Civil War, when the punishment for crime was primarily one of local control, the prisons were operated by a warden and an unsalaried board of inspectors or trustees who were appointed for short terms by either the governor or the legislature. During this time it must be noted that prison office appointments were the source of considerable party patronage with corruption being not uncommon in the correctional field. These abuses led, during the 1860's, to the establishment in many states of central boards of corrections and charities, but these also were composed of unpaid and part-time appointees on behalf of the governor. The next major step in the development of penal administration was the creation of state boards of control, which were composed of members who devoted practically all their time to the management, control, and operation of penal and charitable institutions. These boards, in turn, appointed superintendents and wardens to direct the actual operation of the state penal and correctional plants. The final major move in administrative organization was the creation of a departmental form of organization. In those states adopting such a system the form of administration has had a tendency to follow one of the following three types: (1) penal administration became a section of the department of welfare; (2) it became a subdivision in a department of institutions; or (3) it became a unit in a combined department of institutions and agencies.

## LOCAL AGENCIES

### The Sheriff

The sheriff, whose office dates from the Anglo-Saxon period, is the principal peace officer of the county. While in colonial days the position was one that was filled by appointment from the governor, the nineteenth century saw the rise of a popularly elected officer. Generally the term of office is two years and the remuneration is derived from a stipulated salary, fees, mileage allowance, selling supplies to and boarding prisoners. As a result, sheriffs are among the best paid county officers. The general duties of the sheriff involve: detecting and apprehending criminals, caring for prisoners, administering county jails, executing court orders and processes, making up jury lists and summoning jurors, and in some areas assisting with tax collection. The principal aides to the sheriff are usually deputies, constables, bailiffs, and jailers.

The office of sheriff is frequently the object of severe criticism. In the present-day scene, elective sheriffs are often not qualified to cope with modern crime problems. The appearance of well-trained and equipped federal, state, and municipal police forces has caused many sheriffs almost to abandon their police role and confine themselves to the remaining functions listed above. One leading authority in police administration has written that "In a vast majority of American counties the sheriff system has already collapsed."[8] In some states steps have been taken to terminate the fee system and to stop sheriffs from profitting by selling supplies and providing food to prisoners. In the event the office were abolished, the functions could be transferred to state, municipal, or appointive county police. The responsibilities for jail administration could be given to state officers controlling the correctional institutions. Since this is one of the oldest positions associated with local government, community pride and resistance to such a change will not permit this entrenched office to be abolished. Yet many reforms remain overdue.[9]

### The Public Prosecutor

In most states criminal prosecutions are handled by local officers. In the rural sections this task is performed by county or district attorneys, who are elected usually for two- or four-year terms. This political office is the one from which many prominent political careers have been launched. In urban regions, the prosecutions may be conducted either by the district at-

[8] Bruce Smith, *Police Systems in the United States* (2d rev. ed.: New York: Harper & Row, Inc., 1960), p. 79.

[9] For additional information on the position of sheriff, see Chapter 4.

torneys, special solicitors, or prosecutors appointed by municipal authorities.

The duties associated with the position of public prosecutor are important ones. Not only do they prosecute those accused of crime but many times conduct campaigns in cooperation with local police to uncover organized crime. They defend the county and its officials in actions brought against them. They advise county officers and justices of the peace on questions of law. Upon the public prosecutor rests the decision of whether or not those who have been apprehended will stand trial, and his power of decision with respect to prosecution is almost absolute. His influence over grand juries is usually very great. As a matter of fact his recommendation has considerable weight with the judge as he determines punishment. Therefore, his influence over prosecution is a dominating one. His entire attitude can greatly aid and even stimulate the actions of local police and judicial officers.

## The Public Defender

Every state permits the court to assign counsel to defendants who declare they are financially unable to secure legal assistance. This system usually results in relatively inexperienced lawyers being appointed to defend the indigent. The legal fee involved is paid by the state.

In two states, Rhode Island and Connecticut, and in approximately ninety cities in other states the office of public defender has been created. The post is sometimes an appointive one, but more often it is an elective office. The duty of the public defender is to give legal counsel and court defense for all persons accused of crime who are unable to employ their own attorneys. The quality of the defense provided by the public defender's office is more effective than the court-assigned counsel in that a greater degree of specialization may be attained by the full-time, salaried government attorneys.

The American theory of justice requires that an accused person be given as learned and diligent counsel as is available to the state in its prosecution. In 1965 the Iowa General Assembly created an optional county public defender law which permits counties to establish the office as a counterpart of the county attorney (prosecutor). The movement is slowly growing, with some interest being generated by the Model Defender Act, which was approved by the National Conference of Commissioners on Uniform State Laws in 1959. Most of the larger metropolitan regions are now included in the list of areas with public defenders, but in the rural areas less interest has appeared.[10]

[10] Louis Fabricant, "Voluntary Defenders in Criminal Cases"; and Mayer C. Goldman, "Public Defenders in Criminal Cases," *Annals of the American Academy of Polit-*

## The Constable

The position of constable is another one of the local offices that was brought to the colonies from England and therefore dates back to earliest colonial times. The constable has been identified with the township, town, districts, and even the small incorporated communities, where he is popularly referred to as the town marshal. The constable is usually elected for terms of either two or four years. Most of his compensation comes from fees. While the position is associated with the maintenance of local law and order, most of his time is spent in serving warrants, subpoenas, summonses, and other legal processes utilized by justices of the peace. In some areas the constable, like the sheriff, will assist in the collection of taxes.

The office of constable is one of diminishing prestige. While the position was abolished in England in 1856 it has in many parts of the United States been practically abandoned. Many authorities advocate the abolition of the position by permitting full-time police to take over the small amount of criminal work still remaining and for an administrative officer of a court to perform the assistance now rendered justices of the peace by the constable.

## The Grand Jury

The grand jury is a phase of our judicial system that was inherited by way of the English common law. It has been variously defined as a body selected to perform two tasks: (1) to "inquire" into offenses committed against the state; and (2) to "investigate" both the management of public institutions and the conduct of public officials. At the present time most authorities maintain that its basic function is to determine whether or not the evidence presented against an individual alleged to have committed a crime is sufficient to warrant bringing him to trial. Grand jury meetings take place usually upon the call of the judge holding court in the district, or in some instances by popular petition, and the jurisdiction of the grand jury is the same as that of the court which it serves. Unlike the petit or trial jury, a grand jury is used only in criminal proceedings, and since its activities precede that of the trial jury, it does not decide the guilt or innocence of a person. Almost all of the work of a grand jury is performed in secret, and since its proceedings do not constitute a trial, an accused person has no right to appear before that body.

ical and Social Science (September, 1939); Richard Hartshorne, "Equal Justice for All: The Bar and the Indigent Criminal Defendant," American Bar Association Journal, Vol. XXXVII (February, 1951), pp. 104–6; National Legal Aid and Defender Association, Statistics of Legal Aid Work in the United States and Canada: 1962 Chicago: National Legal Aid and Defender Association, 1963.

After the grand jury has considered the evidence that is presented by the prosecuting attorney and concludes that it is sufficient to justify bringing the accused to trial, it presents a *true bill of indictment* which is a formal charge or accusation, in the name of the state, against the person suspected of committing the offense. This bill must accurately state the name of the accused, list the exact nature of the charges, and note that the crime with which the individual is charged is prohibited by law. In some states if the grand jury rests its accusation upon evidence produced by its own initiative its report is then technically referred to as a *presentment* in order to distinguish it from the usual indictment based upon the recommendation of the prosecutor. Any person so indicted must then stand trial for the crime for which he has been accused. It should be noted that a unanimous verdict is not required in the issuance of an indictment. In several states where the grand jury consists of twelve members, nine must concur in an indictment. Usually the decision of a grand jury is reached by a majority vote with the foreman reporting to the judge in whose court the accused person will be tried. If the jury does not believe that the facts are sufficient for indictment it may report a "no true bill," and the accused person is not brought to trial unless he is charged in a subsequent proceeding.

Gradually over the years certain factors having a tendency to influence the use of the indictment power by the grand jury have become very pronounced. It was at one time, at least in theory, the common belief that the grand jury would conduct its own investigation of the charges brought against an accused person and the jury would determine on its own whether the individual should be held for trial or released. The principal objections to such a system have been summarized by Professor Willoughby as follows:

> The objections to the grand jury, from the standpoint of the prosecution, are: that it is in the nature of a fifth wheel; that real responsibility for the bringing of criminal charges is in fact exercised by the prosecuting attorney, the grand jury doing little or nothing more than follow suggestions; that it complicates by just so much the machinery of criminal administration; that it entails delay which is an evil in itself; that it renders prosecution more difficult through important witnesses getting beyond the jurisdiction of the court, or through memory of facts becoming weakened by lapse of time; that it entails unnecessary expense to the government; and that it imposes a great burden upon the citizens called upon to render jury service.[11]

As a result, many states now provide for an alternate method for the prosecution of criminal cases on the basis of an *information* or *affidavit.* The information is the presentation by the prosecuting attorney of formal

[11] William F. Willoughby, *Principles of Judicial Administration* (Washington, D.C.: The Brookings Institution, 1929), pp. 180–86.

charges against a person accused of committing a crime. The charges are brought by the prosecuting attorney on his official oath, and the basis of his accusation consists of the testimony produced by private citizens willing to make the charges under oath and any other evidence the prosecutor may be able to collect. In many states these charges, when filed with the clerk of the court that possesses competent jurisdiction, have the same effect as an indictment. In other states the information must be approved by the judge. If he disapproves, then the prosecuting attorney must submit his information to the grand jury. This technique places the full responsibility upon the public prosecutor rather than upon the grand jury. Even in those states where the use of the information is permitted, considerable variations exist with respect to the circumstances under which it can be used. As a general rule the indictment must be used for capital offenses and felonies, but the information can be utilized for other grades of crimes.

The controversy over the merits of the *indictment* as over and against the use of the *information* is still current. Some authorities maintain that the grand jury has not only outlived its usefulness but that it is by far too inefficient, too cumbersome, and adds for extra delays and expenses in the enforcement of criminal laws. Apparently in those states that have given the information process a trial its superiority over indictment has been demonstrated primarily through the elimination of the process of criminal fact-finding by amateurs and also by saving time and money.

A second function of a grand jury pertains to that body serving as a general investigatory group. In this relationship the grand jury is called upon to conduct investigations into areas of general public interest ranging from reviewing the conduct of public officials for perhaps alleged neglect, inefficiency, or dishonesty to reports of election irregularities. This type of investigation normally results in the issuance of a public report and perhaps the return of an indictment. In some states in the wake of an unusual crime wave special grand juries may be called into session and indictments will be given to the regular trial courts.

Michigan for approximately thirty-two years used a one-man grand jury, but under pressure from a United States Supreme Court decision that held that the system was incompatible with due process, abolished it in 1949. Two years later, in 1951, the system was reinstituted but in a modified form.[12]

[12] Glenn R. Winters, "The Michigan One-Man Grand Jury," *Journal of the American Judicature Society*, Vol. XXVIII (February, 1945), pp. 137–51; William H. Gallagher, "The One-Man Grand Jury—a Reply," *Journal of the American Judicature Society*, Vol. XXIX (June, 1945), pp. 20–24; William P. Lovett, "One Man Grand Jury in Action," *National Municipal Review*, Vol. XXXIII (June, 1944), pp. 292–94. A historical review of the operation of the Michigan plan is contained in Robert G. Scigliano, *The Michigan One-Man Grand Jury* (East Lansing: Governmental Research Bureau, Michigan State University, 1957).

Members of grand juries are chosen in much the same manner as members of trial juries are selected—by lot or at random—but there is no challenge by opposing attorneys on the ground of qualifications. The term of office for members of the grand jury varies. In many sections, particularly rural states, the members serve for one year, while in other states new juries may be chosen every few weeks and then dismissed when their reports have been issued.

## Municipal Police Departments

The internal organization of a police department has a tendency to vary as the result of the impact of the following three items: (1) the population of the municipality; (2) the character and volume of work to be performed by the department; and (3) the theory of police organization that is accepted by the proper authorities responsible for the operation of such a department.

The problem of organization is quite unimportant in the several thousand incorporated villages and towns that employ only one or two policemen. In these instances the major problem may revolve around the question as to whether the people should elect the police or permit the appointment of the members of the police force. In either instance no major problems with organization, personnel, or equipment are present. However, as the city increases in size, the problems have a tendency to increase, and it becomes necessary to apply principles of administrative organization or management. As a result, the police boards that were so prevalent during the nineteenth century have generally been replaced with single administrators in an effort to provide for quick action that is so essential in police administration.

With the decision to replace police boards with single administrators, the next major problem is one concerned with the selection of the top administrator for the police department. One philosophy of police administration favors the selection of a person who is primarily an administrator but at the same time familiar with the practical aspects of police work, while others prefer an individual who has progressed through the ranks. While even the experts are not in agreement, one factor can be emphasized. As the police organization grows larger, the greater the need for someone who is quite familiar with administration, and less emphasis can be placed on intimate knowledge of police department details. Naturally other members of the department should be selected on the basis of civil service examinations.

In the larger cities the major divisions of the police department may contain as many as fifteen to twenty important types of line, staff, and auxiliary activities. Among the primary line activities would usually be the following items: police patrol, traffic regulation, vice investigation, crime prevention, criminal investigation, and control of juvenile offenders. The principal staff operations are budgeting and program planning and evaluation. The chief auxiliary services normally consist of records management and statistical operations, communications, personnel and training, property and equipment management, jail custody, police laboratory, and public relations. In certain instances some auxiliary services can be classified as staff functions, while budgeting, as an example, many times is viewed as an auxiliary service.[13]

Many large city police departments will group their major activities into three categories: (1) the administrative force, (2) the service force, and (3) the criminal investigation division. Since the administrative and service forces employ more personnel and are responsible for more operations, it is sometimes recommended that each division should be headed by a deputy commissioner, while the criminal investigation division would be placed under the direction of a chief inspector. In this type of an arrangement the administrative division would consist of personnel and training, research, program planning and evaluation, records management, accounting, statistical operations, communications control, property and equipment management, the police laboratory, jail management, personnel management and training, and public relations. The service force would be concerned with the patrol and traffic divisions. The criminal investigation division would contain various specialized investigating units such as robbery, narcotics, homicide, and burglary.[14]

## TREATMENT OF CRIMINALS

### Pardons, Commutations, and Reprieves

Governors have been provided with some powers of a judicial or quasi-judicial nature that will permit them to intervene in the punishment of criminals, particularly with respect to the granting of pardons, commutations, and reprieves.[15] These actions on behalf of a governor are usually classified under the heading of executive clemency. All governors, except in Georgia, may either pardon criminals or share in the process by which a criminal is absolved from legal consequences for his crime. A pardon is actually a remission of penalty and permits a prisoner to go free without any further punishment.

[13] The International City Managers' Association, *Municipal Police Administration* (4th ed.; Chicago: The International City Managers' Association, 1954), chap. ii; see also V. A. Leonard, *Police Organization and Management* (Brooklyn: Foundation Press, Inc., 1951), p. 83.

[14] The International City Managers' Association, *Municipal Police Administration* (Chicago: The International City Managers' Association, 1950), p. 334.

[15] These quasi-judicial powers of the governor are discussed more in detail in Chapter 13.

The power of commutation consists of changing a penalty to a less stringent one, such as the commutation of a death sentence to life imprisonment or the reduction of a five-year sentence to one year. A reprieve is merely a stay of execution of the law and constitutes a temporary postponement of the punishment for some particular reason. It is most commonly used in the postponement of the death sentence to permit additional time for further examination of the case.

## Probation and Parole

Probation and parole, in modern penology, have come to emphasize the reformative rather than the punitive purpose of imprisonment. Probation signifies a conditional suspension by a trial court of the imposition or execution of a prison sentence. In many instances the suspension is granted to first offenders or juveniles. The basic theory behind probation emphasizes the fact that the association by these affected individuals with hardened criminals can be very detrimental, whereas supervision outside a penal institution can be viewed as a major reformative effort. The court in granting probation requires the concerned individuals: (1) to follow all terms of the probation as set down by the tribunal and to exhibit proper conduct at all times, and (2) to be under the jurisdiction of the court. Any probationer who violates the terms of his probation may be arrested immediately and required to serve his sentence.

A parole is a conditional release of a prisoner who has not served all of his original sentence. This release is granted by an administrative agency of the state government—in many instances a parole board—by action of the governor, or a combination of the two preceding methods. This definition points out two major differences that exist between a parole and probation. First, a parole is granted only after the prisoner has served part of his sentence. Secondly, a parole is issued by an administrative agency or an executive rather than by a court.

In some states the exercising of the parole power by the governor constitutes his most important act of executive clemency. The parole system is frequently associated with the indeterminate sentence and has developed in part as the result of the way in which the criminal statutes of a state are written. Many of these laws prescribe a minimum and a maximum term of confinement as punishment for a crime. Judges, in turn, may sentence a man to prison for from six to twelve months for petty larceny or they might give a sentence of two to five years for manslaughter. When the case comes before the governor or the parole board the decision is whether the prisoner should serve the minimum sentence, be retained for a longer period of time, or even kept until he serves his full sentence. Under a parole a prisoner, when released from serving his full term under specified conditions, is usually placed under the supervision of a parole board or officer for the remainder of his original sentence.

To aid the governor in this responsibility most states have created some type of a parole board. This board reviews the records of those persons who are eligible for parole, advises the governor on the cases that come before him, and in many instances the governor accepts the advice of the board. The members of state parole boards are selected in various ways. In some states the members are the same individuals who comprise the membership of the board that selects the heads of various state institutions, such as prisons, reformatories, and sanitariums, with additional members being selected by gubernatorial appointment. The actual operation of a parole board can be regulated by law in that it is required to give its advice and consent to the governor in the issuing of paroles. In other states that function of the board is more of an informal and customary nature. Irrespective of the requirements of the law, most decisions with respect to paroles are in the last analysis made by the parole board.

The Interstate Parole and Probation Compact has been ratified by all states, and in 1945 the Parole and Probation Compact Administrators' Association was organized by the appropriate state administrators and their assistants and deputies. This organization seeks to promote cooperation and the exchange of information among the state administrators. The compact was established in an effort to allow probationers and parolees to leave the state in which they were sentenced and to establish a new home in a different setting yet all the time remaining under the supervision of a parole officer. Before the establishment of this compact most state laws would not permit a parolee or probationer to leave the state without special permission, which in many instances was very difficult to obtain.

In 1960, 48,457 prisoners were paroled from state institutions, which represented only a slight increase over the figure of 48,278 reported in 1959. Also during 1960, a total of 13,586 parole or conditional releasees violated the terms of their release and were returned to state institutions. The figure for 1960 represents a 12.7 per cent increase over the number that were returned in 1959. As a result, it is apparent that in 1960 one out of every four prisoners released by parole or conditional release was returned to prison. This sizable increase reflects the presence of several conditioning factors. First of all, when widespread unemployment is present the parole violation rates have a tendency to increase. Secondly, with the increase in the number of personnel working in parole departments a greater degree of supervision can be present which quite frequently results in more revocations of parole and conditional releases.[16]

[16] Council of State Governments, *The Book of the States, 1962–1963* (Chicago: Council of State Governments, 1962), p. 425.

## County Jails

The county jail is a traditional institution of local law-enforcement that is to be found in all but a few of our counties. While it is viewed as property to be controlled by the county governing board, the jail has in most instances been placed under the immediate direction of the sheriff or a jailer. Two principal classes of prisoners are kept in the county jail: (1) those awaiting action by either a trial jury or a grand jury, and (2) those persons serving short sentences, normally of less than a year. In addition, the county jail will be used to house convicted persons awaiting transfer to a state penal institution, important witnesses who have asked for protective custody or whom the authorities fear might disappear, and insane persons awaiting transportation to mental hospitals. The importance of county jails is emphasized by the fact that approximately one million individuals spend time in these institutions each year.[17]

County jails have long been subjected to widespread criticisms. The most prevelant objection to these institutions is concerned with the unsanitary and filthy conditions that exist. A study of the county jails of California revealed that only 13 out of 54 county jails merited a "good" rating with respect to over-all general sanitation while 26 were classified as "poor."[18] A report on Missouri's jails gave only four a rating of "fairly good" on sanitation and cleanliness with the remainder being rated downward.[19] A survey of West Virginia's 55 county jails indicated that 22 of them could be listed as "bad fire risks" and also reported that some jails that are listed as being fire-resistant perhaps did not deserve that classification.[20]

A second common criticism of jail administration stems from the general lack of appropriate prisoner segregation and classification. All types of individuals—habitual criminals, juveniles, first offenders, healthy or diseased —are all too frequently housed together in very immediate quarters. Also, a large proportion of jail inmates are kept in absolute idleness, which has a tendency to contribute to their physical, mental, and moral deterioration. In some areas a trusty system has been established which permits some prisoners to work in the jail kitchen or to be given various cleaning

[17] James V. Bennett, "The Medieval County Jail," *Forum,* Vol. C (November, 1938), pp. 260–64.

[18] *A Study of the County Jails of California* (Sacramento, Calif., 1949), p. 11. Prepared for the California State Board of Corrections and the Commission for the Study of Adult Corrections and Release Procedures.

[19] Roy Casey, "Missouri Jail Survey," *Proceedings of the Seventieth Annual Congress of the American Prison Association* (New York: 1949), pp. 402–10.

[20] W. T. Hammack, *Survey of County Jails in West Virginia* (Washington, D.C.: U.S. Bureau of Prisons, 1946), p. 38.

jobs in the jail, the courthouse, or perhaps the sheriff's office. A few states provide that county prisoners can be used for road work or on certain types of construction work, such as hospitals and county buildings. A few counties, in addition to maintaining jails, also operate workhouses or industrial farms or work camps. Nevertheless, the general rule is still one of idleness for most inmates of county jails.

A third criticism of county jail administration is concerned with the laxity that is present with regard to jail discipline. In many instances, prisoners that are viewed by jailers as trusties are allowed to come and go much as they please, even to the point of allowing them to spend weekends at home. There are some records of prisoners who have committed burglaries while technically confined to jail. Another deplorable condition to be found in the county jail system is the presence of the famous kangaroo court through which some of the inmates are able to control and even persecute their fellow prisoners. One of the writers on jail administration has stated that, "Fundamentally the presence of this organization within the walls of a jail is a confession of poor prison management, of the inability of guards and officers to keep order and to prevent the stronger prisoners from imposing their will on the weaker."[21] Apparently some jailers are unable to prevent the organization of kangaroo courts while others seemingly welcome the institution as a means of transferring the responsibility for discipline. Most of the kangaroo systems try incoming prisoners for "breaking into jail" while other trials are held for infraction of the rules that have been made under this guise of self-government. A "convicted" prisoner can be required to pay fines to the court or dominant group, to perform certain menial tasks, and, in general, made subject to the will of this controlling group. Refusal to accept the punishment meted out by this "court" can result in vigorous disciplinary action bordering in some instances upon brutality.

Another major criticism of local jail administration has been concerned with the fee system. In somes states the sheriff has been given a dollar, or some similar amount, each time the jail door was locked or opened to receive or release a prisoner. This was popularly known as the "turnkey" fee. Most authorities maintain that such an arrangement can initiate a temptation to cause the arrest and jailing of persons for very slight reasons. The fee system is more damaging when it is applied to the feeding of prisoners. This arrangement gives the sheriff or jailer a fixed sum per day for the board of each prisoner without any regard to the quantity or quality of the food provided. While the available records are seemingly not too accurate in revealing the amount of profit earned by sheriffs, it has undoubtedly been large in many instances. One Missouri sheriff was

[21] Louis N. Robinson, *Jails: Care and Treatment of Misdemeanant Prisoners in the United States* (New York: Holt, Rinehart & Winston, Inc., 1944), p. 27.

reported to have had an income in one year in excess of $13,000 from the feeding of inmates.[22]

Most proposals for improving the management and administration of county jails have a tendency to be concerned with three basic recommendations: (1) the abolition of county jails, except perhaps in the more populous counties, and the establishment of a system of regional detention homes which would be operated either by the state or cooperatively by a group of counties; (2) the adoption of a program for improving the physical condition and management of those jails that are retained; and (3) that fewer persons should be placed in county jails.[23] Some progress can be noted in each of these areas.

A few counties have closed their jails and made arrangements for care of their prisoners in neighboring cities and counties for a stipulated compensation. In Virginia the principle of regional or district jails has been applied to some extent, while in North Carolina, although county jails are still maintained, those individuals who have been given short penal sentences must serve them in state-operated prison camps. The physical condition of jail buildings has also been improved over the years. During the 1930's a number of counties replaced their old jails by receiving federal loans and grants through the Public Works Administration. In other instances, modern sanitary facilities have been installed and fire hazards are gradually being removed. Finally, in many areas the population of our jails is being reduced by the more frequent release of minor offenders on probation. In spite of these gradual improvements in county jails and their management, much work remains to be done. Adequate jail management is dependent upon the utilization of well-trained and experienced personnel. With the elective system of selecting county sheriffs this is highly improbable. Some authorities recommend removing jail management from the sheriff's jurisdiction and placing it in the hands of an individual who would be appointed by, and be responsible to, the courts. Clearly, the improvement of jails and jail management is currently one of the most pressing problems within local government.

## CIVIL DEFENSE

### The Federal Role in Civil Defense

The first major experiences in the United States with civil defense occurred during World War I. At that time the Secretary of War was desig-

---

[22] Casey, *op. cit.*, p. 407. A provision of the new Missouri State Constitution abolished the fee system.

[23] Robinson, *op. cit.*, pp. 273–74. See also Joseph F. Fishman and Vee Terrys Perlman, Let's Abolish the County Jail," *Survey Graphic,* Vol. XXVIII (January, 1939).

nated as the Chairman of the Council of National Defense. Defense councils were created at the state and local levels to direct volunteers working in such fields as welfare, conservation of critical materials, morale, and public health. In 1939 many state and local defense councils were re-established. An Advisory Commission to the Council of National Defense provided for a division of state and local cooperation. The Office of Civilian Defense replaced this division in 1941 and remained in operation until June 30, 1945, when it was abolished by presidential directive.

The National Security Resources Board, in its report in 1950 to President Truman, maintained that the "establishment of adequate civil defense" would complete the national security structure of the nation.[24] The report also noted that civil defense must, along with military defense, be a part of a "sound and well-rounded program" until war is effectually outlawed. As a result, civil defense necessitates a high degree of cooperation among all levels of government. The National Security Resources Board defined civil defense as "the protection of the home front by civilians acting under civil authority to minimize casualties and war damage and preserve maximum civilian support of the war effort."

President Kennedy, in his civil defense message to Congress on May 25, 1961, declared that "one major element of the national security program which this Nation has never squarely faced up to is civil defense." Subsequently the President, under Executive Order 10952 of July 20, 1961, delegated to the Secretary of Defense most of the national functions relating to civil defense. These included: (1) the development and execution of a fallout shelter program and also a chemical, biological, and radiological warfare defense program; (2) the responsibility for warning and communications; (3) emergency assistance to state and local governments in the post-attack period; (4) protection and emergency operational capability of state and local governmental agencies in conjunction with plans for the continuity of government; and (5) the programs for extending financial contributions to the states. The administration of this new program was placed in a specially created office of Assistant Secretary for Civil Defense. As a result, the Office of Civil and Defense Mobilization was replaced by the Office of Emergency Planning. This new agency was to assist and advise the President in coordinating the civil defense operations of the national executive departments, carry out the defense mobilization program and the strategic and critical materials stockpiling programs, engage in planning for the continuity of state and local governments, and administer the natural disaster relief program.[25]

[24] National Security Resources Board, *United States Civil Defense* (Washington, D.C.: Government Printing Office, 1950), p. 3.

[25] Council of State Governments, *The Book of the States, 1962–1963* (Chicago: Council of State Governments, 1962), p. 441.

## ORGANIZATION FOR CIVIL DEFENSE

Much of the effectiveness of a civil defense program rests with the state governments. In 1950 the Council of State Governments and the National Security Resources Board prepared a model civil defense act which has been used by approximately one-half of the states. Local governments are subject to state direction with respect to civil defense. As a result, the governor has the responsibility as the executive head of the state government to appoint not only the members of a defense commission or council but also the executive director, who is to be concerned with administrative details. The role of the state legislature is concerned with the passage of the appropriate legislation that will put into operation both state and local civil defense activities. The responsibility is given to the state civil defense council for the preparation and maintenance of the state-wide program and any other measures that might be needed in the event of disasters or emergencies. In addition, the state under the leadership of the federal government participates in interstate planning for those important target areas contained within more than one state. The state is also called upon to receive and distribute to local areas their portions of federal funds, equipment, and supplies to be used in the support of local activities.

The local governments play a very important role in adapting and executing programs within their communities. Ordinances must be passed, the machinery for civil defense must be provided, and funds must be allocated by the local governments before actual civil defense activities can take place. Once again, following the example set in state government, municipalities and other local political subdivisions in some instances, must create defense councils or commissions that will coordinate local activities in line with the standards established by state and national civil defense agencies.

The Iowa Civil Defense Act of 1959 provides for the creation of a civil defense operation that might be considered typical of many other states. While the Iowa civil defense administration is responsible for the conduct of civil defense matters within the state, it is also required to extend its services in the event not only of man-made disasters but also natural disasters including hurricanes, tornadoes, windstorms, or floods.

The Iowa Civil Defense Administration in 1965 was placed under the supervision of the adjutant general. The management of the administration is under a director who is responsible to the adjutant general. The law provides two major responsibilities for the director: (1) to administer civil defense affairs within the state, and (2) to prepare and execute the civil defense program of the state but under the direction and control of the administration. County boards of supervisors, city or town councils, and school boards are authorized by the law to cooperate with the administration in carrying out the provisions of state law.[26] In accordance with this section of state law, some municipalities in Iowa did establish local organizations as indicated in Figure 18–1 which is the organizational diagram of the Iowa City, Iowa, plan for civil defense.

## Civil Defense Expenditures

Appropriations by the Congress for civil defense have varied considerably over the last decade. In 1950 the Congress appropriated $33,969,999, and by 1957 the figure was increased to $95,760,000, to be followed by decreases in 1958 ($41,514,000), 1959 ($45,285,000), and 1960 ($54,985,000). For the fiscal year 1963, the President requested $695,000,000 for the civil defense functions of the Department of Defense and $11,000,000 for its Office of Emergency Planning.[27] The states spent $20,823,000 for civil defense in 1954, but only $10,132,800 in 1959, while the figure continued to decrease in 1960 to only $7,855,200. During the period from 1951 through 1961, the total spent by the states for civil defense was $142,335,000. During the period 1951–1958 the states expended 77 per cent of their total defense funds for administrative costs and emergency equipment, 21 per cent was contributed to local civil defense, while 2 per cent was allocated for construction or purchase of civil defense facilities.[28]

## Continuity of Government Program

One of the most important sections of civil defense planning that has continued to receive attention is that of the continuity of government program. Four major goals were established for this program: (1) the establishment in the three branches of government of an automatic line of succession for major officers and employees; (2) the safe-keeping and preservation of all essential records; (3) creation of emergency operating centers; and (4) the preparation of plans by which there would be the complete use of government personnel, equipment, and facilities to meet emergency operations.[29]

As of January 1, 1963, constitutional amendments had been ratified in twenty-six states authorizing the state legislatures to provide for the emer-

[26] The Code of Iowa, 1962, chapter 28A, "Civil Defense," pp. 72–73.
[27] Council of State Governments, The Book of the States, 1962–1963 (Chicago: Council of State Governments, 1962), pp. 443–44.
[28] Council of State Governments, The Book of the States, 1964–1965 (Chicago: Council of State Governments, 1964), p. 475. See also same reference for years 1960–1961, p. 405.
[29] Council of State Governments, The Book of the States, 1962–1963 (Chicago: Council of State Governments, 1962), p. 442.

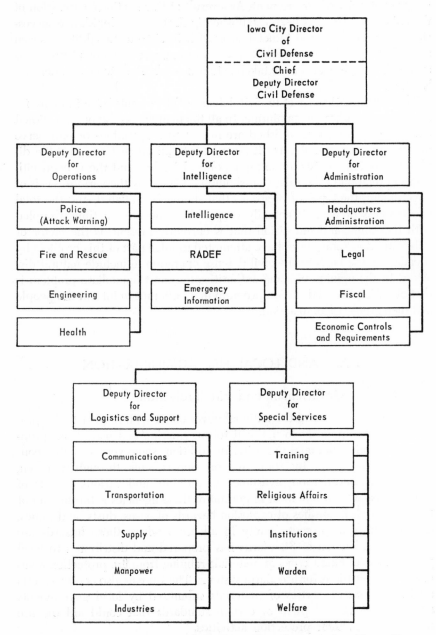

**Fig. 18-1.** Iowa City Civil Defense Basic Plan Organization Chart. (Source: *Iowa City Civil Defense Manual,* City of Iowa City, Iowa, 1960.)

gency continuity of government. As a result of these actions, succession of the chief executive has been established in thirty states, legislative succession in twenty-one, and judicial succession in sixteen. In addition, seven states have provided for records preservation and management programs and twenty-eight states have taken action to establish state government relocation.

The results with respect to civil defense achievements have in many instances been rather disappointing. In all too many areas the organizational units that have been established are mere paper operations or only serve in a perfunctory manner. Yet it must be recognized that considerable division of opinion exists among our political leaders and the general citizenry in relation to the roles that should be played by the various levels of government, the types of programs that should be initiated, and the total effectiveness of what is actually proposed at the present time. Coupled with the doubt and indecision that is currently present, is the factor of public apathy. Some states have attempted to solve part of this problem by broadening the basis of the civil defense operation to include natural disasters. In the opinion of some authorities the most immediate problem is that of an intensive education program in an attempt to inform the people and then arouse them to action.


# STATE AND LOCAL FIRE ADMINISTRATION

## The National Government and Fire Protection

The responsibilities of the national government with respect to fire protection relate primarily to national forests, marine and waterfront properties, and other national property. In addition, some very valuable contributions are made by some federal departments through research, consultation, information, assistance in training, and various aspects of civil defense. One of the most important of these agencies is the Bureau of Mines through its studies of explosion hazards of gases, dusts, and fumes, and its efforts to promote safety in all areas where these hazards are found.[30] The Bureau of Standards has prepared and distributed to local governments different types of materials ranging from fire protection manuals to specifications for fire alarm systems. The Bureau also conducts tests of fire-resistant properties of materials submitted by local governments and proposes the adoption of certain standards that could aid the fire departments in their protection activities.

[30] Office of the Federal Register, *United States Government Organization Manual, 1963–1964* (Washington, D.C.: Government Printing Office, 1963), p. 240.

Also on the national level a Federal Fire Council operates as an official advisory unit in matters relating to the protection of federal employees and property from fire. The agency was organized in 1930 by collective action of governmental departments and agencies and was formally established by an executive order in 1936. In 1949 the council was transferred from the Federal Works Agency to General Services Administration. The Federal Fire Council operates through a governing body composed of eight government officials with the commissioner of public buildings service acting as the chairman.[31]

## State Fire Marshal

Fire protection is a major aspect of any public safety program that is in operation in many of our states. It is a problem of primary concern to the individual citizen as he seeks protection from property losses and personal injuries due to fires. Recent figures indicate that each year in the United States approximately one and a half billion dollars' worth of property is destroyed by fire and nearly 12,000 persons are killed in conflagrations.[32] Some states have expressed their concern with fire prevention measures by the passage of a series of laws dealing with the following important areas: (1) state-wide building codes which have provisions covering fire safety construction features, fire extinguishing devices, building exits, and fire escapes; (2) arson laws; (3) fire hazard legislation dealing with subjects ranging from laws dealing with various flammable liquids to the sale of fireworks; and (4) the creation of the office of state fire marshal with its varied duties and powers.

The principal state office concerned with fire protection is that of state fire marshal. Approximately forty-four states have created this position or its equivalent and in turn established the office of the state fire marshal as a centralized unit for the enforcement of laws relating to fire protection. While the state fire marshal does serve as an important law enforcement officer, the direct participation of his office in actual fire protection activities is somewhat limited since the major responsibilities for fire protection rest with local governments. In twenty-one states this office has been placed for administrative purposes in the state department of insurance with five states placing the fire marshal in the department of public safety. In seven states it is located in the state police while seven states have established a separate department.[33]

[31] *Ibid.*, p. 546.
[32] The International City Managers' Association, *The Municipal Year Book, 1963* (Chicago: The International City Managers' Association, 1963), p. 374.
[33] Council of State Governments, *The Book of the States, 1964–1965* (Chicago: Council of State Governments, 1964), p. 480.

While the duties may vary considerably, most state fire marshals are charged with the following responsibilities: (1) the investigation of fires, particularly those of suspected arson, and the securing of the arrest and prosecution of those individuals so accused; (2) the inspection of buildings to determine the extent of fire hazards and the subsequent issuance of orders to provide for corrections; (3) the exercising of some degree of supervisory control over local fire authorities either in the administering of fire prevention laws or of state building codes; (4) the issuance of both general and specific rules and regulations with respect to fire safety; (5) the conducting of fire prevention educational campaigns and firemen training courses in which state fire marshals, state universities and colleges, and other state agencies cooperate and co-sponsor these activities; and (6) the enforcement of all state fire laws with the exception of those specifically assigned to other state officers. Since the staff of the state fire marshal is usually quite small he must restrict his work primarily to those areas that lack sufficient fire protection and to assisting local authorities when they request his services. The state fire marshal can investigate on his own authority any local fire.

## Municipal Fire Departments

In general, cities of 25,000 population and over have full-time paid fire departments but approximately one-half of the cities in the population range of 10,000 to 25,000 employ more part-time than full-time firemen. Most of the estimated 16,000 public fire departments in the United States and Canada are located in small communities with only part-time personnel, who receive little or no pay for their services. The number of communities with full-time paid professional departments probably does not exceed 1,000 at the present time.[34] Many small communities that cannot individually support fire departments join together to create fire protection districts or arrange for the protection with a larger department. Many such interjurisdictional agreements are now in effect.

The fire departments in most of our large cities are organized as separate administrative units. In some municipalities, however, the fire and police functions are subdivisions of an integrated department of public safety. In many smaller communities this arrangement may perform satisfactorily, but a good brief can be developed for a separate fire department in our larger cities on the ground that the skills and operations that are required for effective fire protection are not the same as those necessary for police protection. As a result, most of our large cities have separate police and fire departments.

[34] The International City Managers' Association, *Municipal Fire Administration* (Chicago: The International City Managers' Association, 1956), p. 42.

Since some authorities have a tendency to classify the function of fire protection as being administrative in character, it is recommended that the fire department should be headed by a single director who is appointed by and responsible to the city manager or mayor. Some support is developing for the selection of the top fire administrator through competitive examination. Subject to civil service rules and regulations, the fire chief should be relatively free in choosing his subordinates. While other personnel should be selected on the basis of civil service examinations, the chief should play the major role in final selections. In spite of this recommendation, some departments still operate under commission or board direction and control. The question is immediately raised with regard to the qualifications for the head of the fire department. Should he be an individual who has advanced through the ranks or a person who has been trained to qualify as a lay administrator? Despite much expert opinion that favors the lay administrator, many fire chiefs are professional men who have been selected from the ranks. Naturally, the ideal chief would be an individual possessing a combination not only of administrative ability but also expert knowledge of the technical operations of a fire department. There is no conclusive evidence that one type is superior to the other, and it remains a decision that must be solved locally.

The actual organization of a fire department is determined, in large measure, by the size of the city, though some variations in structure may be necessary for cities of the same population range due to local problems. As a rule, the well-organized and efficient fire department will group all of its activities into four or five main divisions. Since fire fighting and fire prevention are viewed in most areas as the two major categories of activities for a fire department, the first division would consist of all those activities necessary for fighting fire while the second division would be concerned with those functions relating to fire prevention. Because of the importance attached to these divisions, each should be commanded by an assistant chief. In the larger cities it may be essential that the department establish and maintain its own training schools for firemen which would justify creating a third division, also headed by an assistant chief or a superintendent. A large-city fire department requires many staff and auxiliary functions and the principles of efficient management dictate that all of these activities should be grouped in an administrative unit that is placed either directly under the fire chief or commissioner or in an administrative division under another assistant to the chief. The management functions that would normally be placed in such a division are records, research, public relations, et cetera. In addition, as a fifth division, the size of the city may necessitate the operation of an intricate fire alarm system which because of its technical nature would demand a separate organizational unit controlled by a superintendent.

For so many of our municipal fire departments the organization for fire fighting is all important. The primary unit concerned with fire protection is usually the company. In small municipalities the responsibility for fighting fires will be the responsibility of one small company and its members will also perform whatever fire prevention duties are carried out by the department. In the larger cities the fire companies may be of the following different types: (1) engine, or hose, (2) ladder, or truck, (3) pumper-ladder, (4) rescue squads, (5) salvage squads, (6) fireboat, (7) tank, and (8) special apparatus.[35]

The well-organized fire department will also maintain a fire prevention division in order to carry out what was previously referred to as one of the two major duties of this type of unit. While this function was long neglected in the United States it is now receiving additional consideration. Efficient fire prevention is concerned with four major areas: (1) adequate legislation and administrative regulations, (2) education, (3) inspection, and (4) enforcement.

Education is now being viewed as one of the most important elements in fire prevention. In those cities that can afford it a trained expert, usually in the field of public relations, should be employed. All types of communication media—press, television, radio, movies—and educational techniques should be used. Many communities have found that the programs and campaigns for fire prevention week offer important possibilities. While much leadership can be given by local fire prevention authorities and the state fire marshal, the support of local civic groups is a necessity.

Inspections constitute another important phase of fire prevention activities. As a general rule, a considerable number of the inspections are carried out by the regular firemen who are able to use to good advantage their own personal knowledge of local structures and the physical characteristics of certain neighborhoods. In the larger cities special inspectors make more intensive inspections, and as a result of their expert training and knowledge they are in a position to make policy recommendations to city councils.

Many of the larger fire prevention divisions will include an arson squad which, in many instances, will be composed of a fire prevention officer, a police detective, and sometimes a representative of the prosecuting attorney's office. The National Board of Fire Underwriters also provides some assistance by extending the services of their special agents connected with the arson department. Ideally, the arson squad should be headed by a person who is familiar with the areas of fire fighting, police work, law, and safety engineering. It is now recognized that the use of a well-trained arson squad can substantially reduce fire losses in many communities.[36]

[35] *Ibid.*, p. 49.
[36] *Ibid.*, pp. 333–34.

Governmental administration today is keenly aware of the pressures that are being exerted in the name of efficiency. Fire administration is no exception in that it feels the pressure of organized business, property owners' associations, and insurance and realty organizations.

While no completely objective criteria for measuring the efficiency of fire departments have been developed, certain standards have been established by some groups. The National Board of Fire Underwriters has developed a grading schedule that most cities strive diligently to meet. The schedule is administered by trained engineers and includes the following items: water supply, structural conditions, fire alarm system, fire prevention, building laws, police, and climatic conditions.[37] The rating is performed in terms of deficiency points, with the fewer the deficiencies the higher the classification for the city with respect to insurance purposes. The National Fire Protection Association, with headquarters at Boston, is another organization that is devoted to research and planning for the advancement of fire administration. The International City Managers' Association has reported that satisfactory indexes of efficiency depend upon the development of measurements of performance, effort, results, and expenditures.

The supply of water is a special problem that must be recognized by the fire department. In a city of 20,000 population while the maximum daily consumption may be 3,000,000 gallons, the National Board of Fire Underwriters standards has established a required fire flow rate of 6,500,000 gallons, but for a perfect rating a total delivering capacity of 9,500,000 gallons would be required.[38] In addition, since the ability to deliver water depends upon effective pressure, a standard for pressure must also be met in order for a city to secure a perfect rating on water supply.

Fire insurance classification is determined in cities of more than 25,000 population by rating engineers of the National Board of Fire Underwriters using a grading schedule developed by the board. Other private agencies determine the classification for the smaller cities. A city's classification is determined by the number of points of deficiency assessed against it because conditions are below the prescribed standards. Deficiency points are charged for each defect, and the city with the highest number of deficiency points has the poorest rating. The city in which the fire protection facilities are considered most able to cope with fire and in which the fire hazard is the least receives the lowest number of deficiency points. The total possible number of points of deficiency is 5,000, which can be distributed over nine major items: water supply, fire department, fire alarm, police, hazards, building laws, climatic conditions, structural conditions, and a divergence

[37] *Ibid.*, pp. 26–27.
[38] *Ibid.*, p. 118.

in grading of classes according to the total points of deficiency charged against its fire defenses. If the total number of points of deficiency falls between 0 and 500 points, the city is placed in class 1; between 501 and 1,000 points, in class 2; between 1,001 and 1,500 points, in class 3; and on down the schedule.[39]

## BIBLIOGRAPHY

ALEXANDER, MYRL E. *Jail Administration*. Springfield, Ill.: Charles C Thomas, 1957.

AMERICAN PRISON ASSOCIATION. *Manual of Suggested Standards for a State Correctional System*. New York: American Prison Association, 1946.

CALDWELL, ROBERT G. *Criminology*, 2d ed. New York: The Ronald Press Co., 1965.

CAMP, IRVING. *Our State Police*. New York: Dodd, Mead and Co., Inc., 1955.

FEDERAL BUREAU OF INVESTIGATION. *Uniform Crime Reports*. Washington, D.C.: Government Printing Office. Published annually.

GERMANN, A. C., DAY, FRANK, and GALLATI, ROBERT R. I. *Introduction to Law Enforcement*. Springfield, Ill.: Charles C Thomas, 1962.

HAYNES, FRED E. *The American Prison System*. New York: McGraw-Hill Book Co., Inc., 1939.

HOLCOMB, RICHARD L. *Police and the Public*. Springfield, Ill.: Charles C Thomas, 1957.

International City Managers' Association, *The Municipal Fire Administration*, 6th ed. Chicago: The International City Managers' Association, 1956.

————. *Municipal Police Administration*, 5th ed. Chicago: The International City Managers' Association, 1961.

————. *The Municipal Year Book, 1965*. Chicago: The International City Managers' Association, 1965. Published annually.

LEONARD, V. A. *Police Organization and Management*, 2d ed. Brooklyn: Foundation Press, 1964.

MILLSPAUGH, ARTHUR C. *Local Democracy and Crime Control*. Washington, D.C.: The Brookings Institution, 1936.

PORTER, KIRK H. *State Administration*. New York: Appleton-Century-Crofts, Inc., 1938.

SMITH, BRUCE. *The State Police*. New York: Macmillan, 1925.

————. *Rural Crime Control*. New York: Institute of Public Administration, Columbia University, 1933.

————. *Police Systems in the United States*, 2d ed. New York: Harper & Row, Inc., 1960.

TAFT, D. R., and ENGLAND, ROBERT W., JR. *Criminology*, 4th ed. New York: The Macmillan Co., 1964.

WILLOUGHBY, WILLIAM F. *Principles of Judicial Administration*. Washington, D.C.: The Brookings Institution, 1929.

WILSON, O. W. *Police Administration*, 2d ed. New York: McGraw-Hill Book Co., Inc., 1962.

————. *Police Planning*. Springfield, Ill.: Charles C Thomas, 1958.

[39] The International City Managers' Association, *The Municipal Year Book, 1963* (Chicago: The International City Managers' Association, 1963), pp. 379–80.

# 19

# State Educational Systems

The American people have always adhered to the concept of popular education. During the colonial period and the early days of the Republic the maintenance of schools was assumed voluntarily by religious bodies, secular groups, and the family. However, the public responsibility was recognized early in our history although from that time to the present religious and private schools have continued to supplement publicly supported education.

## TRENDS IN THE NUMBER OF SCHOOL DISTRICTS OR UNITS

The Census Bureau lists the total number of all types of school districts in the United States as 37,019, of which 34,678 are independent school districts and are entered into the count of separate units of government. The other 2,341 dependent school systems are regarded as agencies of other governments. The total figure of school districts for 1952 was 67,346, as contrasted with 108,579 in 1942. This reduction is largely the result of consolidations, although a small measure of it comes from a reclassification of governmental units. As might be anticipated, consolidations or reorganizations have tended to occur in those states where small districts previously existed in large numbers.

In four states—Hawaii, Maryland, North Carolina, and Virginia—and the District of Columbia there are no independent school districts. At the other extreme there are twenty-three states where all local public schools are administered by such governmental units. In the remaining twenty-three states there are some school districts and also some dependent school systems. However, in six of these twenty-three—California, Indiana, Kentucky, Louisiana, Ohio, and South Carolina—all school systems that provide education through grade 12 are independent districts and the additional dependent school systems involve only institutions of higher education operated by city or county governments.

489

The present number of school districts—34,678—is only a little more than one-half of the total of ten years earlier and less than one-third of the 1942 total of school districts as shown by the following statistics:

| School year | Number of school districts |
|---|---|
| 1961–1962 | 34,678 |
| 1959–1960 | 40,054 |
| 1956–1957 | 50,454 |
| 1951–1952 | 67,355 |
| 1941–1942 | 108,579 |

Since the 1956–1957 school year seven states have reduced the number of school districts in each state by more than 1,000. Seven states, as indicated in Table 19–1, account for over two-thirds of the total decrease in the number of school districts during the past five years.

TABLE 19–1

Decrease in School Districts by Selected States

| State | Number of School Districts | | Decrease, 1957 to 1962 | |
|---|---|---|---|---|
| | 1962 | 1957 | Number | Percentage |
| Iowa | 1,336 | 3,665 | 2,329 | 64 |
| Michigan | 1,866 | 3,214 | 1,348 | 42 |
| Minnesota | 2,343 | 3,464 | 1,121 | 32 |
| Missouri | 1,649 | 3,234 | 1,585 | 49 |
| Nebraska | 3,264 | 4,942 | 1,678 | 34 |
| North Dakota | 986 | 1,998 | 1,012 | 51 |
| Wisconsin | 1,752 | 3,758 | 2,006 | 53 |

SOURCE: The International City Managers' Association, *The Municipal Year Book, 1965* (Chicago: The International City Managers' Association, 1965).

Even though there has been a substantial decline in the number of school districts, five states each still had more than 2,000 school districts in the 1961–1962 school year:

| | |
|---|---|
| Nebraska | 3,264 |
| South Dakota | 2,940 |
| Minnesota | 2,343 |
| Kansas | 2,261 |
| Pennsylvania | 2,179 |

These five states collectively account for more than 37 per cent of all school districts in the United States. However, three of these five—Kansas, Minnesota, and Nebraska—have been quite active in the widespread trend toward fewer and larger districts, with each one showing a reduction of more than 50 per cent in the number of school districts since 1942. The other two states—Pennsylvania and South Dakota—have experienced relatively little change during this twenty-year period. It is interesting to note that the number of states having at least 2,000 school districts dropped from sixteen in 1942 to fifteen in 1952, nine in 1957, and five in 1962. As recently as 1952 there were still nine states with more than 3,000 districts, while in 1962 only Nebraska was above this figure.[1]

As used by the Bureau of the Census the term "public school system" includes two types of governmental entities which have responsibilities for providing public schools: (1) those which are administratively and fiscally independent of any other government and are classified for Census Bureau reporting of governmental data as independent school district governments; and (2) those which lack sufficient autonomy to be classified as independent governmental units and are treated as a dependent agency of some other government—a county, municipality, town or township, state government, or, in the case of Pennsylvania joint schools, a group of school district governments. The 2,341 dependent school systems are broken down into the following categories:

| | |
|---|---|
| State | 3[2] |
| County | 449 |
| Municipal | 333 |
| Township (and "town") | 1,141 |
| Other (Pennsylvania "joint schools") | 415 |

The independent-district system prevails in most parts of the nation, but it is particularly prominent in the West. There are only four states in which all public schools are operated through school systems that are adjuncts of other governments—Hawaii, Maryland, North Carolina, and Virginia—and such dependent systems account for a major share of public school enrollment in only six of the twenty-three states that have a composite arrangement, involving both independent school districts and other types of public school systems. These six exceptions are Connecticut, Maine, Massachusetts, Rhode Island, Tennessee, and Vermont. All or a major fraction of all public school enrollment is accounted for by independent school districts in forty of the states.

School systems that operate as adjuncts of counties are to be found primarily in the Southeast but with a few scattered instances elsewhere. School systems that are associated with township, or "town," governments are to be found only in the New England states and New Jersey. There are school systems operated by municipal governments in each of twenty

---

[1] U.S. Department of Commerce, Bureau of the Census, *Census of Governments, 1962, Governmental Organization* (Washington, D.C.: Government Printing Office, 1963), Vol. I, pp. 3–4.

[2] The three state-dependent systems are those of Alaska, Hawaii, and Maine. In Hawaii all public schools are administered directly as part of the state government, while in Alaska and Maine this arrangement applies only to certain sparsely populated areas.

states, but even here some other pattern predominates. In no state are all public schools operated by municipally dependent systems.

## THE NATIONAL ROLE IN EDUCATION

### The National Government and Education

The subject of education is not listed among those powers delegated to the national government by the United States Constitution. As a result, under the Tenth Amendment, the establishment and operation of public school facilities have been a primary responsibility of the state. This does not mean, however, that the national government has not played a role or exhibited any interest in the field of public education. While the advocates of state control of education have emphasized this implied reservation of educational authority to the states, the reference to the general welfare in the United States Constitution could be a means by which the federal government could intervene in the case of an educational emergency. Many reasons have been advanced for the silence of the national Constitution with respect to education. One very plausible explanation emphasizes the fact that at the time the United States Constitution was written education was under the influence of the church and the home.

Early in our history various agencies of government became interested in educational affairs. Even during the pre-Revolutionary period some of the northern colonies adopted policies granting public lands for local schools. In 1785 under the Articles of Confederation one lot in every township was set aside for the maintenance of public schools. The admission of Ohio as a state in 1802 started a pattern of granting of school sections, which was to become an integral part of the system under which many new states entered the Union. These land grants in time were to reach a total of 121,130 square miles with an estimated value of approximately $1 billion.[3] In addition, in all states where the national government owned land, grants totaling millions of acres have been made to the states, usually to be used for higher education under the discretion of the individual states.

The next important national measure was the Morrill Act of 1862, by which the United States Congress awarded to each state 30,000 acres of government land for each member of Congress to which the state was entitled, to be used for the erection of land-grant colleges. The grants under the Morrill Act were conditional in that the states had to provide for the buildings and equipment out of state funds in order to qualify for

[3] H. R. Douglass and C. Grieder, *American Public Education* (New York: The Ronald Press Co., 1948), p. 190.

the gift. At the present time there are sixty-nine land-grant institutions accommodating one out of every five college students in the United States. The national government has continued to provide aid to these colleges through the second Morrill Act of 1890 and supplementary grants in 1907 and 1935. These grants now total over $5 million a year.

The Smith-Hughes law of 1917 was another step taken by the national government for the aiding of education. This basic measure, together with the supplementary acts of 1929 and 1934, supported the teaching of agriculture, home economics, and the mechanic arts trades on the high school level. Those states desiring to participate under the Smith-Hughes law had to match the national funds. In 1937 the George-Deen Act was passed to aid in subsidizing education for distributive occupations, and in 1946 the George-Barden Act increased the amounts previously allotted for agriculture, home economics, and trade and industrial education.

Following World War II the national government, which previously had assisted education through certain indirect financial methods, began to work directly in conjunction with local school districts and, occasionally, to educate directly. Public Law 874 was passed to reimburse schools for the education of children who were present in the school district only as the result of the location of a federal installation or defense project. Public Law 815 was enacted to aid these impacted areas for school buildings and capital outlay. Under the GI Bill of Rights funds were made available to veterans for educational purposes. In 1956 the Congress considered but failed to pass proposals for federal aid in the construction of public school buildings, but in 1958 the Congress passed the National Defense Education Act which allotted slightly more than $1 billion in federal aid to schools.

All of these examples indicate that the additional extension of the interest on behalf of the national government in public education can occur at any time, but particularly if emergency circumstances exist. Nonetheless, the providing of education remains a primary function of the state with local subdivisions assuming the responsibility for elementary and secondary schools.

## The United States Office of Education

The United States Office of Education was established in 1867 and has functioned for almost a century under different titles and with varying responsibilities. The first period of development for this office covers the years from 1867 to 1906. This historical period witnessed the development of three major responsibilities on behalf of the Office of Education: (1) the production of biographical and historical research which was followed by considerable publication, (2) the assumption of the task of providing for the education of Indian children in Alaska, and (3) the administration of the national subventions of approximately five million dollars annually to the land-grant colleges.

The second era, 1906 to 1933, saw an increase in the activities as well as in the number of personnel. A new departure in the duties of this office occurred in 1911 when for the first time the services of its experts were made available for the purpose of surveying school districts. Internal reorganization of the office established new divisions, particularly in the areas of higher, rural, and Negro education. New publications included the issuing of the monthly magazine *School Life,* and in 1918 the *Biennial Survey of Education* was distributed for the first time. The increase of annual appropriations from $300,000 to $1,600,000 noted the added developments within the Office.

In 1939, by Reorganization Plan I, the Office and its functions were transferred from the Department of the Interior to the Federal Security Agency which, in 1953, became the Department of Health, Education, and Welfare. At the present time the Office of Education is the primary agency of the national government that is responsible for the formulation of educational policy and the co-ordination of educational activities at the federal level. In order to carry out its functions the Office works in close relationship with other governmental agencies, state governments, professional groups, and institutions, and interested citizen organizations. Its major functions are: (1) to conduct studies and provide services of a national character with respect to education; (2) to collect and disseminate information relating to education in other countries and the states; (3) to evaluate those trends that might affect education; (4) to identify some of the major problems in education that necessitate the introduction of action programs and call for immediate research; (5) to provide national leadership for education and to serve as an impetus for educational research; (6) to extend professional educational advisory service and to assist in improving educational practices; and (7) to administer grants-in-aid in the field of education.[4]

## STATE ORGANIZATION FOR EDUCATION

### State Board of Education

In every state an educational department has been established with one or more state boards dealing with varying phases of educational functions. In forty-eight states one central unit, commonly referred to as the state board of education, exerts some degree of control over elementary and

[4] *United States Government Organizational Manual, 1963–1964* (Washington, D.C.: Government Printing Office, 1963), pp. 347–48.

secondary schools. Within a single state, however, many special boards may be concerned with different phases of educational functions, such as teacher retirement, library, and vocational education.

The members of the state board of education are chosen in a variety of ways but the predominant method in thirty states is by gubernatorial appointment.[5] The method of selecting the members usually can be related to the functions to be performed by the board or to the historical beginnings of the agency. The ex-officio membership of the attorney general and the state treasurer on some state boards, for example, continues from an earlier period when the boards had as their major responsibilities the control of state aid funds and the supervision of public school lands. Some students of educational administration seem to prefer the method of gubernatorial appointment with legislative approval for the selection of members of the state board of education. Other methods involve popular election, selection by the state legislature or by conventions of school board members.[6] The number of members on the boards range from three to twenty-one with seven or nine being the usual number. The term of office varies from one to twelve years with an average of a little over five years.[7] Some states have established certain requirements for membership on state boards of education. These vary from a requirement that all congressional districts in the state be equally represented to one that prohibits a member from being a professional educator. No state requires what might be classified as an educational qualification for membership, but a vast majority of state board members are college graduates.

State boards of education possess differing powers and exercise varying degrees of supervision and responsibility. Yet a survey of the activities of the boards reveals certain common responsibilities, particularly with respect to supervising the state-operated schools and administering the general state educational statutes, selecting courses of study and the adopting of textbooks, and the making of general policy for state education. Most of the activities of a state board of education can be placed in three categories: (1) directing the activities of the state department of education, (2) providing expert advice to the state legislature, and (3) surveying and studying the problems associated with state education.[8] The survey by the

[5] Council of State Governments, *The Book of the States, 1964–1965* (Chicago: Council of State Governments, 1964), p. 336. The 1964 Constitution for the state of Michigan provides for an eight-member elected state board of education which subsequently appoints the state's chief school officer.

[6] W. D. Cocking and C. J. Gilmore, *Organization and Administration of Public Education*, Staff Study No. 2, Advisory Committee on Education. (Washington, D.C.: Government Printing Office, 1938), pp. 66–67.

[7] W. G. Reeder, *Fundamentals of Public School Administration* (3d ed.; New York: The Macmillan Co., 1951), p. 60.

[8] Emery Stoops and M. L. Rafferty, Jr., *Practices and Trends in School Administration* (Boston: Ginn & Co., 1961), p. 29.

Council of State Governments entitled *The Forty-Eight State School Systems* listed the following as the most important responsibilities of state boards of education: (1) adoption of rules and regulations which have the effect of law, (2) regulation of teacher certification, (3) prescription of minimum standards in specified areas, (4) determination of educational policies, (5) adoption of courses of study, (6) determination of regulations governing the apportionment of state school funds, (7) regulation of teacher education other than by certification, (8) determination of the plan of organization for the state department of education, and (9) adoption of textbooks.[9] In three-fourths of the states, the state board of education serves as the state board for vocational rehabilitation. In one-third of the states the board has certain responsibilities for junior colleges, teachers colleges, and other institutions of higher learning. Only thirty-three states have boards with general responsibility for elementary and high school education, while boards in six states have limited or specialized responsibilities for "below" college education.

## The Superintendent of Public Instruction

Each state has established a position that is responsible for directing and supervising public education. This administrative officer is usually referred to as the superintendent of public instruction, but in other states he is given the title of commissioner of education, director of education, or state superintendent of schools. In 1812 the State of New York pioneered this office by appointing an individual whose primary duties related to the management of the funds that were granted to local districts. The State of Maryland created a similar position in 1826, but both of these offices were subsequently abolished and then later re-established. Nevertheless, these two early experiments provided our first attempts to create a director for state-wide public education.[10] From these inauspicious beginnings this position has developed into one for which there is great potential for the "unification and leadership of education in each of the states. . . ."[11]

The position of state superintendent of public instruction in 1964 was filled in each state by one of the following three methods: (1) popular election (21 states), (2) appointed by state boards (24 states), and (3) appointed by the governor (5 states).[12] While in practice most of these

[9] Council of State Governments, *The Forty-eight State School Systems* (Chicago: Council of State Governments, 1949), p. 37. Each function listed above was performed by boards of education in from 21 to 37 states. See also Table 9, p. 183, of this report by the Council.

[10] Douglass and Grieder, *op. cit.*, pp. 148–49.

[11] Lee M. Thurston and William H. Roe, *State School Administration* (New York: Harper & Row, 1957), p. 113.

[12] Council of State Governments, *The Book of the States, 1964–1965* (Chicago: Council of State Governments, 1964), p. 336. Under the new Michigan constitution

chief state educational officials have been individuals who possess backgrounds emphasizing extensive training and qualifications, slightly less than half of the states require specific educational qualifications. Most of the requirements are of a legal nature, relating to residence and age rather than to particular educational prerequisites.[13] The term of office is usually established in state law at either two or four years. When state boards of education make the appointment it is more common to prescribe an indefinite term, allowing the superintendent to serve at the pleasure of the board. There are some instances where definite terms are provided when state boards select the superintendent. The median salary of state superintendents is approximately $14,000 annually, which is still low in comparison with the salaries paid superintendents in large cities.

The functions of the state superintendent of education are anything but uniform and range in nature from only advisory in New York, New Hampshire, and Maryland to extensive direction and supervision in Michigan, Colorado, and Massachusetts. This is perhaps due to two important factors: (1) this position is provided for in state constitutions in approximately two-thirds of our states and, in turn, the duties and powers of the office are contained within these documents; and (2) the superintendent serves as a member of the state board in about half of the states and in many others he serves as secretary to the board. As a result, the superintendent may serve both as an administrator and as a policy maker, but such a combination has a tendency to deter qualified persons from seeking such an office particularly where popular election is involved.

## State Departments of Education

In most states, in addition to a board of education, there will be present a state department of education. Depending upon the accepted practice within each state, these departments may have primarily administrative responsibilities concerned with executing the policies contained within state school laws or formulated by the state board of education. In other states the department will be responsible for carrying out many of the duties granted to state boards. As a result, a state department of education, as the organic unit of state administration for educational matters, may be headed by either the state board of education or the state superintendent of public instruction.

The Wyoming State Department of Education is an example of a state department that exercises general supervision over the public school sys-

---

the superintendent of public instruction is appointed by the state board of education which is popularly elected.

[13] Council of State Governments, *The Forty-eight State School Systems* (Chicago: Council of State Governments, 1949), p. 40.

tem and assists the work of the schools, particularly those in the rural districts. Within the department there are nine divisions: administration;
teacher retirement; high schools, certification and equalization; deaf and
blind service; elementary and special education; school lunch; finance;
vocational rehabilitation; and vocational education. The department of
education is composed of the state superintendent of public instruction,
the deputy superintendent, the state board of education, and the commissioner of education. The deputy superintendent heads the division of
administration. The commissioner of education supervises the divisions
concerned wtih elementary and high schools, certification and equalization, and school finance. The remaining divisions are manned by other
officers in the department. Responsibility for the educational program of
the state is divided among the superintendent of public instruction, the
state board of education, and the commissioner of education.[14]

The Texas Education Agency is an example of a unit that has been
created to assist the state commissioner of education in the performance
of his duties. This agency, headed by the commissioner and a deputy commissioner, is divided into seventeen divisions each of which is managed by
a director. The names of the following divisions give a clear indication of
the broad responsibilities of this education agency: textbooks; vocational
rehabilitation; research; administrative services; finance; school audits;
curriculum development; special education; school accreditation; teacher
education and certification; agricultural education; distributive education;
home and family life education; industrial education; veterans education;
civil defense education; adult education; and guidance and supervision. In
addition to these divisions, three major administrative areas are in operation: vocational education, junior colleges, and the Texas School for the
Blind and the School for the Deaf.[15]

## EDUCATION AT THE LOCAL LEVEL

The operation of public schools has been basically a local function. As
a result, school authorities at this level have been called upon to exercise
a major responsibility in the actual determination of educational policy but
within the limitations provided by constitutional, statutory, and state administrative provisions. Three principal types of local units have been
established in different sections of the nation: (1) the common school district, (2) the town or township type, and (3) the county-unit system.[16]

[14] Herman H. Trachsel and Ralph M. Wade, *The Government and Administration
of Wyoming* (New York: Thomas Y. Crowell Co., 1953), p. 172.

[15] Caleb Perry Patterson, Sam B. McAlister, and George C. Hester, *State and Local
Government in Texas* (New York: The Macmillan Co., 1961), p. 187.

[16] B. F. Pittenger, *Local Public School Administration* (New York: McGraw-Hill
Book Co., Inc., 1951), p. 26.

## The District System

The responsibility for providing elementary and high schools under the district system resides primarily upon small school districts which are organized and operated under state law. In 1952 more than 67,000 district units were in operation in the United States with many Midwestern states among the leaders.[17] While some of the districts in urban areas did serve large school populations, many such units were of the small rural variety.

The governing authority in the typical school district system is an elective board normally composed of three or five members. This group exerts general administrative control over district school affairs, hires teachers, and exercises custody over all school property. In some states the school finances are controlled by a board, while in others the voters in an annual school meeting decide the answers to the financial problems of the district.

Where the district serves as the principal unit for local school administration it is organized separately from, and generally independent of, any other unit of local government. This organization becomes the basic unit, in administrative and financial matters, for providing elementary and secondary education. The area concerned is separately incorporated as a school district.

Where once the district was utilized as a means of making education available to all children, its inadequacies are well recognized today. First of all, the building facilities consist in so many rural areas of only a one-room structure which lacks the proper facilities for lighting, ventilation, heating, and sanitation. Secondly, the teacher, who in many instances is both inexperienced and underpaid, must provide instruction in many areas. Under these conditions high-quality teaching cannot be expected. A third major disadvantage of the district system rests in the inequality of financial resources that are available for the support of schools in the various districts. As a result, when the financing of schools is left to individual districts some children will have much better educational opportunities than others. These same weaknesses, but in different form, can be found in many of our smaller high schools in rural areas.

## The Town or Township Unit

The town serves as the principal unit for school administration in the New England states, while the township is the primary unit in New Jersey, Pennsylvania, and Indiana. Educational matters under the New England town system are placed in the hands of a board of school directors or

[17] Minnesota and Nebraska each had more than 6,000 districts, while Illinois, Iowa, Kansas, Michigan, Missouri, South Dakota, and Wisconsin each contained more than 3,000 such units.

trustees, which is selected by the local voters at school or town meetings. As a general rule, this board manages not only the schools within villages but also those in strictly rural areas. A few of the larger municipalities do have city boards of education. In Pennsylvania and New Jersey each township constitutes a school district that has a board of education for administering all schools except those within areas, for the most part municipalities, which are separately incorporated for school purposes. In Indiana every civil township is incorporated also as a school township and an elective township trustee is charged with management of the rural schools therein.

The utilization of the town or township as a fundamental educational unit does not necessarily mean the elimination of the small one-room school. One-room schools, serving small attendance areas, still exist where state laws permit and local school authorities desire. Nonetheless, this type of educational administration, using the town or township as the basic unit in contrast with the district, "tends to encourage use of larger attendance areas and the operation of larger, better-equipped, and better-staffed schools. . . ."[18]

## The County Unit

The county-unit plan of school administration is used in approximately fifteen states, primarily in the South but also in Nevada, New Mexico, and Utah. This system emphasizes an arrangement under which the schools are financed and managed on a county-wide basis. While the administrative organization varies, two basic elements are usually present: (1) a county board of education, and (2) a county superintendent of schools who is appointed by and responsible to the county board of education. The superintendent serves as the executive officer of the board and is charged with the management of the county rural schools. While in some instances the city schools are placed under the jurisdiction of the county unit, in many others they are separate units with their own school boards and superintendents.

## The Consolidation Movement

The disadvantages present in a small school district system can usually be remedied by providing for larger financing and administrative units. As a result, some educational authorities propose the consolidation of the smaller districts into a smaller number of larger districts. A number of states have established various types of consolidation programs. Some of

[18] Clyde F. Snider, *Local Government in Rural America* (New York: Appleton-Century-Crofts, Inc., 1957), p. 443.

these have been voluntary in nature, emphasizing the role to be played by the local inhabitants. Others have been compulsory in character. Whether merger is to be accomplished by measures that are compulsory or voluntary, several states have established on the county level various committees emphasizing survey or reorganization activities. These committees have been charged with the responsibility of preparing plans emphasizing school reorganization and consolidation. The plans may take various forms. In some instances they have been mere recommendations and the voters have been free to accept or reject them. In other instances, after public hearings, the county committees have been authorized to put the plans into operation by means of a compulsory order.

Kansas is one state where compulsory consolidation has been utilized. Although the Kansas law was eventually declared unconstitutional, a significant number of consolidations did occur under its provisions.[19] The 1945 Kansas consolidation act created within the state department of education a division of school reorganization and established in each county a school reorganization committee which was to be appointed by the board of county commissioners. The county committees were not only authorized to prepare plans for reorganizing the elementary school districts but were directed to issue the necessary orders putting these plans in operation after holding public hearings. An appeal could be made by dissatisfied individuals to the district court for a review of the county committee's procedures and plan. The state division of school reorganization was directed to become familiar with all items relating to the determination of boundary lines for elementary school districts and to provide the county reorganization committees with advice and counsel. The Kansas Supreme Court declared this law unconstitutional in 1947 on the ground that it attempted to delegate legislative power to the various county committees.[20] The consolidation orders that had been issued before this court decision were subsequently validated by action of the state legislature which was upheld by the court.[21]

A program of school reorganization emphasizing the voluntary approach was created by an Illinois statute in 1945. A state advisory commission on school reorganization was established by this law. In addition, at the discretion of local school boards, school survey committees could be created in the counties. The members of these committees, while selected by the members of school boards, were to work under the dual supervision of the state superintendent of public instruction and the state advisory commis-

---

[19] *Kansas Session Laws* (1945), chap. 291. A subsequent amendment provided that a county could replace its appointive reorganization committee with one consisting of members elected by a convention of delegates chosen at a special school-district meeting.

[20] *State v. Hines* (163 Kan. 300, 1947).

[21] *State v. Common School District No. 87* (163 Kan. 650, 1947).

sion. The studies of the county committees of existing districts were to provide recommendations that would achieve at least the following three objectives: (1) provide better educational opportunities, (2) create a more efficient and economical administration for the public schools, and (3) secure a more equitable distribution of revenues for the public schools. Any final recommendation of such a committee had to be approved by the voters of the areas concerned before it could become effective.[22] In approximately two years' time practically every Illinois county had established such a school survey committee. The number of Illinois districts had been reduced from more than 12,000 to fewer than 4,000 by 1952 through reorganization plans approved by the local voters. The United States Census Bureau in 1962 listed the number of school districts in Illinois at 1,540.[23]

## HIGHER EDUCATION

### State Universities and State Colleges

The first state university established in the United States was the University of Virginia in 1819. The prime motivating force was Thomas Jefferson, who personally supervised and planned many of the original buildings. Early colonizers had a great faith in the benefits of higher education, but these were usually private institutions with strong church affiliations and ordinarily received no public financial assistance. There can be little doubt that with Harvard, Princeton, Yale, and the other fine private institutions the need for state-supported schools of higher learning in the Eastern states was not as pressing as in the South and along the frontier.

The Morrill Act of 1862 made possible state colleges of agriculture in all states and gave assistance to the formation of state universities either in conjunction with the agricultural schools or as separate entities. By 1954 all of the states maintained a state university and in many instances two or more. The last states to establish a state-supported university or university system were New York, New Jersey, and Vermont. Both Alaska and Hawaii had government-supported state universities upon their entry as states in 1959.

The American philosophy of education that has been the foundation of the public-supported institutions of higher education is tied very closely to the idea of free public education through the elementary and secondary

---

[22] *Laws of Illinois* (1945), p. 1608.
[23] U.S. Department of Commerce, Bureau of the Census, *Census of Governments, 1962, Governmental Organization* (Washington, D.C.: Government Printing Office, 1963), Vol. I, p. 279.

school levels. It is now assumed that each state has a responsibility for providing relatively low-cost higher educational opportunities for its citizens with the tuition charged being only a fraction of the total cost of extending the higher education instruction. The second aspect of the philosophy is the responsibility of the state to provide certain types of training considered essential to the progress of the state. Included in most state universities are schools, colleges, or departments that provide vocational and professional education in the fields of medicine, dentistry, law, education, engineering, and nursing, as well as liberal arts courses.

The state university or university system is handled and operated slightly differently in almost every state. In some it may include several campuses under one president with a chancellor in charge of each separate center. In other states separate institutions have been established, each with its own responsible administration and chief executive. In some states the college of agriculture is a part of the university, but in others it has its own separate management. A recent trend has been for almost every state agricultural college to expand and become a university, as has occurred in Michigan, Iowa, and Kansas.

The higher educational institution that has even in many states preceded the state university is the state teachers' college. Most states now have one or more of these schools in addition to the college of education located in the state university. The original purpose of the teachers' college was to train teachers mainly for the elementary grades rather than the high schools. Eventually the curriculum was expanded and the teachers' college trained for both the elementary and secondary levels. Most of these colleges were and are smaller in the number of students enrolled and are geographically scattered throughout the state. Few state legislatures have withstood the political pressures to have a number of these colleges strategically placed within the state. As the enrollments increase the courses offered are expanded, and the trend is toward the dropping of the teacher-training emphasis and to organize these schools into a state college system.

The original control mechanism favored by most state legislatures was to establish a board of trustees for each state-supported institution of higher education. Thus, if the state maintained a state university it would have its own board, the state college of agriculture a separate governing board, and still others for each one of the state teachers' colleges financed by the state revenues.

The trend in this century has been away from separate boards for each higher education institution. Iowa, in 1909, organized a state board of education and placed all of the state-supported institutions of higher education under this single nine-member board, appointed by the governor with the consent of the state senate. At least a dozen states have followed this pattern of a single board for state-supported higher education government. The arguments for consolidation of boards administering state universities and colleges within a state is well-founded and has the active support of many professional educators and public administrators. A number of states still have a popularly elected board, such as Illinois, Michigan, and Colorado. Professor Kirk H. Porter has written, in relationship to elective boards of higher educational institutions:

> Not only does the elective board not thus conform, but at its best it tends to perpetuate and aggravate certain undesirable conditions. They spring from the spirit of aggressive independence. . . . Where there are several (institutions), and where each is under a separate board, the trouble is sure to become a major problem for the legislature. The institutions inevitably become rivals for legislative support. Those in charge are compelled to resort to political tactics that are most distasteful to them in order to win the support which they truly believe their institution deserves; thus the vicious circle of degeneration begins.[24]

All boards of trustees of higher educational institutions are vested with a great amount of power over their unit or units. Ordinarily they are empowered to appoint the chief executive who has the responsibility of the actual operation of the college or university. The ultimate authority is still retained in the board with all major decisions requiring board approval before being implemented. Decisions made by the governing board include such subjects as admission requirements, curricula, faculty salary scales, promotional policies, retirement programs, degree requirements, as well as the vitally important questions concerning the fiscal affairs of the institutions. In some states the board of trustees may fix the tuition and fee rates, but at others the state legislature must approve of matters of this importance. Capital improvements are also subject to differing authorities with the legislatures usually believing that this major policy matter should be retained with the popularly elected representatives rather than being delegated to the governing board.

The board of regents or trustees has the responsibility for submitting their budget requests usually to the governor, who in turn makes his recommendations to the state legislature as to how much support the institutions should receive. A governor friendly to the cause of higher education can wield a great deal of influence over the appropriations received by the state universities, state colleges, and teachers' colleges in any session of the state legislature. On the other hand, it is sometimes possible for the board of regents to sell the legislature on the necessity of greater support for higher education than a conservative governor has been willing to suggest in his budget document.

[24] Kirk H. Porter, *State Administration* (New York: Appleton-Century-Crofts, Inc., 1938), pp. 244–45.

## Community and Junior Colleges

The local level has seen the development of two types of educational institutions: the junior and community colleges. The junior college is a two-year institution that provides for two categories of training: (1) terminal vocational and sub-professional training beyond the secondary level, and (2) college preparatory training for those who intend to continue at a four-year institution. The junior college is actually a product of the twentieth century with 634 such institutions in operation in 1950.[25] Most junior colleges, while locally controlled, also receive some of their support from the state. The major advantage of the junior college is the fact that it brings an educational opportunity to those individuals who might otherwise not be able to financially afford higher education. The community college is usually referred to as a junior college that offers an adult education program.

In recent years the states have given increased attention to the establishment and support of junior or community colleges. In Arizona a state-wide junior college system has been established which provides for a separate state board to assist in the creation of junior colleges but in accordance with certain minimum standards as to the number of potential students, assessed valuation, and population. The system also authorized the junior college districts to issue bonds, while state aid was provided for operations and capital outlay. Kansas has inaugurated a system of state aid for junior colleges and municipal universities and authorized junior colleges to issue revenue bonds for certain purposes. In Massachusetts the development of regional community colleges continues, with four in operation in the fall of 1961 and others planned for the near future. The State of Colorado has not only increased its state aid to junior colleges but has permitted counties operating such schools to charge tuition for those students coming from other counties and required those counties not maintaining junior colleges to levy taxes to pay the cost of the tuition charges. In Missouri any school district or combination of districts meeting certain minimum standards is authorized to establish junior colleges and levy taxes for their support. The state board of education in Missouri has been vested with the responsibility for promoting the creation of these institutions and determining the appropriate standards. Many other states have passed legislation increasing not only the level of state support but providing for the creation of junior college districts.[26]

[25] Council of State Governments, *Higher Education in the Forty-eight States* (Chicago: Council of State Governments, 1952), p. 25.
[26] Council of State Governments, *The Book of the States, 1962–1963* (Chicago: Council of State Governments, 1962), p. 322.

## Municipal Colleges and Universities

A few cities maintain municipal colleges and universities in an effort to bring that phase of higher education to their residents. Only thirteen such schools were in operation in 1952.[27] In the past when a small college was forced to close its doors the local authorities, in several instances, have taken over the management of the educational institution and created a municipal educational institution. The College of Charleston, South Carolina, which is usually listed as the first municipal college in the United States, changed from private to public control in 1837. Some of the larger city or municipal colleges are to be found in New York City; Akron, Cincinnati, and Toledo, in Ohio; Omaha, Nebraska; and Louisville, Kentucky.

Local funds, student fees, and in recent years, veterans' fees from the federal government have served as the primary sources of income for municipal colleges and universities. In 1918 local funds provided 89.7 per cent of the income, but by 1950 the proportion was only 44.8 per cent. The share provided by student fees increased from 7.9 per cent in 1918 to 25.7 per cent in 1942 before experiencing a sharp drop to 15.4 per cent in 1948. The payment was 19.6 per cent in 1950. The federal payments for the GI fees provided 8.7 per cent of municipal college income in 1946, 28.6 per cent in 1948, and 18.5 per cent in 1950. While other sources of income have been relatively insignificant, the municipal colleges in 1950 received 9.3 per cent of their income from state government sources, but in no previous year had the figure reached more than 2 per cent from state funds.[28]

The municipal universities in Ohio of Akron, Cincinnati, and Toledo are classed as agencies of those city governments. Each university is governed by a board of directors appointed by the mayor, and the sponsoring city government may levy an annual tax for maintenance and for service of bonded indebtedness. Washburn University of Topeka, Kansas, is governed by a board of regents, with four members appointed by the governing body of the city, four by the board of education of the city school district, with the mayor serving in an ex officio capacity. When the state furnishes financial assistance a member of the state board of regents also serves on the municipal university board.

A general law providing for the establishment of municipal universities in first-class cities after local referendum is the basis for the operation of the University of Louisville, Kentucky. The university is administered by

---

[27] Council of State Governments, *Higher Education in the Forty-eight States* (Chicago: Council of State Governments, 1952), p. 18. Wayne University, which was included in this total, is now under state control.

[28] *Ibid.*, p. 110.

a board of trustees, who are appointed by the mayor and the board of aldermen. The city governing body is authorized to levy a tax for the support of the university and may issue bonds with the approval of the electorate. The general law also provides for municipal universities in second-class cities with similar legal provisions. A municipal college support district may be established by a Kentucky county in which a municipal university is located to provide for a tax levy outside the city area.

## California: A Case Study

The state educational pattern in California presents some unusual and peculiar arrangements. The superintendent of public instruction is the only major state executive officer who is elected on a non-partisan basis for a four-year term. Though popularly elected, he is actually responsible to a ten-member state board of education which is appointed by the governor. The superintendent serves as secretary and executive officer of the state board and as the administrative head or director of the state department of education, in which capacity he executes the educational policies established by the board of education, which is designated as the governing and policy-determining body of the department of education. In addition, the superintendent sits ex officio on the Board of Regents of the University of California and the Board of Trustees of the State Colleges. The superintendent is charged with the general responsibility for administering the state laws relating to public schools, including the junior colleges, and provides, through the department of education, professional assistance to these units. Within the state department of education he appoints the commissions and boards, of which the two most important ones are concerned with credentials and curriculum.

The organizational unit that is charged with general supervision over California's immense educational operation is the state department of education. This unit is charged with the supervision of education from the primary grades through the junior colleges. The internal management of this department is divided into five divisions: (1) departmental administration, which has the general responsibility for the management of the department's personnel, financial, legal, informational, and research affairs; (2) school administration, which is concerned with regulating the apportionment of school funds and maintaining school records, the supply of elementary textbooks, pupil transportation, school-lunch program, schoolhouse planning, child-care centers, and district organization; (3) instruction division, which supervises the content of education at the various school levels; (4) division of special schools and services, which has general control over schools for the physically handicapped; and (5) the division of libraries, which maintains the state library and the legislative reference service for the state legislature. In California, as in some other states, not all of the agencies of the state department of education are contained within the divisional organization. This is the situation with respect to the boards and commissions named by the superintendent of public instruction.

The University of California is composed of several campuses all under the control of the Board of Regents, consisting of sixteen members who are appointed by the governor for terms of sixteen years. The superintendent of public instruction, an ex officio member, serves as the official liaison between the state department of education and the board of regents. Other ex officio members of this board are the governor, the lieutenant governor, the speaker of the state assembly, the president of the state board of agriculture, the president of the Mechanics Institute of San Francisco, the president of the university alumni association, and the president of the university. The board of regents selects the president of the university, who serves as the chief administrative officer for the entire university system and its various campuses.

On July 1, 1961, the fifteen state colleges, which previously had been under the state department of education, were transferred to the jurisdiction of the newly created board of trustees of the state college system. It is anticipated that this sixteen member board, appointed by the governor for eight-year terms, will supervise these institutions in much the same manner as the university system is managed by the board of regents. The executive officer of the state college system is selected by the board of trustees and serves as the chief administrator. Each college is headed by a president, who is also chosen by the board of trustees.

Since 1899 various studies and recommendations have been made with respect to the California state educational program. The state legislature, responsive to the problem of mounting enrollments in the state's institutions of higher education and fearful of the possibility of unnecessary duplication among the various educational institutions, created in 1959 a liaison committee to develop a "master plan for higher education." This committee, composed of representatives of the state board of education and the university regents, established a study committee to develop a proposed master plan. The study committee consisted of a representative of the state colleges, the junior colleges, the university, the independent colleges, and three joint staff members. In turn, technical committees were established to investigate and study practically every aspect of the higher education program within the state.

After seven months of intensive study and deliberations a plan was submitted which proposed a constitutional amendment which would define the duties and functions of the three state systems of public higher education. In brief the plan proposed that: (1) the junior colleges should offer a wide variety of two-year terminal and transfer courses; (2) the primary function of the state colleges would be to provide instruction for undergraduate and graduate students through the master's degree in the sciences and liberal arts and applied fields and in the professions, including teaching; and (3) the University of California was to provide work in the liberal arts and sciences and in the professions, exclusively in dentistry, law, medicine, veterinary medicine, and graduate architecture. While the University of California was to retain the sole authority to award doctoral degrees, it could arrange with the state colleges to award joint doctoral degrees in certain selected fields. In addition, the university was to be the principal state-supported academic organization for research purposes.

Other segments of the master plan reaffirmed the philosophy of free tuition for residents of the state to all public colleges; an expansion of a state program of loans and scholarships to worthy and needy students; the maximum utilization of existing educational facilities; the creation of new college and university campuses; and the establishment of guide lines for the state program in adult education.

The California state legislature was called into extraordinary session in 1960 by Governor Brown to consider the findings and rcommendations of the master plan. While the lawmakers could not agree upon a constitutional amendment they did pass a bill incorporating such items as the functions and organizational structure recommended for the junior colleges, state colleges, and the University of California.[29]

## MAJOR PROBLEMS IN EDUCATION

### School Finance

American schools have historically depended for their funds on local property taxes. At one time the proceeds from this source constituted almost the entire support for public schools, and even at the present time this tax, viewed nation-wide, still provides the largest single amount of local school revenue. In recognition of increased state interest in elementary and secondary education the states, during the past few years, have assumed a substantial share of the burden of school finance. Every state now provides some state aid for schools, and the trend is toward an increase in the amount. During the school year 1951–1952 nearly 39 per cent of all local school revenues in the United States came from state sources as compared with less than 17 per cent in 1929–1930. The per-

[29] For additional details see California Liaison Committee of the Regents of the University of California and the State Board of Education, A Master Plan for Higher Education in California, 1960–1975 (Sacramento: California State Department of Education, 1960).

centages of total school revenues derived from state sources vary widely. In 1951–1952 the range was from less than 10 per cent to more than 70 per cent, with the schools of a dozen states deriving more than half of their revenues from state sources.[30]

Financial grants have been given by the states to local school districts or units in an effort to accomplish in most instances the following items: (1) to alleviate the load placed upon the local property tax for school revenues, and (2) to assist local school districts in improving their facilities. Usually these grants are made on one of the following bases: (1) according to need, or (2) a fixed basis or rate which in many instances emphasizes per pupil in average daily attendance. If the apportionment is according to need, the term equalization grant is used, since the major purpose of the grant is to provide for a degree of equalization for educational opportunities between the more wealthy and the poorer school districts. In some states this arrangement provides that the state will assist a district in meeting or maintaining state-established standards when that district has levied the required minimum rate of property taxation for school purposes. In most states these funds are distributed by the state department of education in accordance with state law and the county superintendent of schools serves as a local intermediary.

It has been reported that for 1951–1952 approximately 58 per cent of all local school income was derived from local sources, basically the local property tax, while only 3 per cent came from the national government.[31] For the year 1960–1961 revenue receipts for public schools totaled nearly $15 billion, of which about 56 per cent came from local sources, approximately 40 per cent from state sources, and 3.6 per cent from federal sources. It is interesting to point out that the source proportions have not changed radically from those that have prevailed since the early 1950's since the state and federal governments have assumed only a slightly larger percentage of school costs. Internally, however, the share of the support that comes from the federal and state governments varies significantly. With respect to the federal government, its contributing share varied from .9 per cent of the operating funds in Vermont to more than 17 per cent in Alaska. State sources supplied almost 80 per cent of the school revenues in Delaware but only 4 per cent in Nebraska.[32] It can

---

[30] Rose Marie Smith, "Statistical Summary of Education: 1951–1952," *Biennial Survey of Education in the United States: 1950–1952* (Washington: U.S. Office of Education, 1955).

[31] *Ibid.*

[32] Council of State Governments, *The Book of the States, 1962–1963.* (Chicago: Council of State Governments, 1962), p. 307. An excellent study of state aid to education in the northeast region of the United States is to be found in the volume written by Stephen K. Bailey, Richard T. Frost, Paul E. Marsh, and Robert C. Wood, *Schoolmen and Politics; A Study of State Aid to Education in the Northeast* (Syracuse: Syracuse University Press, 1962).

be noted that in 1959 the inhabitants of nine states were paying more than one-tenth of their income for state and local governmental services. In that year the national average of state and local tax collections for all governmental purposes per $100 of personal income was $8.49. Of this amount approximately $3.25 was spent for education: $1.85 by the local districts and $1.40 by the state.[33]

The educational needs of the state of California serve as a good example of the problems facing many other states in this field. In the 1960–1961 school year California had approximately 90,000 unhoused pupils in its elementary and high schools. In many districts the half-day sessions were the result of classroom shortages or the lack of teaching personnel. Despite the large number of teachers being trained within the state, and augmented by the qualified teachers moving into the state, an estimated shortage of elementary school teachers will average about 5,000 per year during the 1960–1970 period. The demand for high school teachers will also exceed the supply until at least 1970. The financial demands to support adequately the four million persons now attending state-supported schools is tremendous. Yet with the state expecting 660,000 full-time college and university students by 1975 and five million elementary and high school pupils, the new building costs alone will total over $2 billion between 1960 and 1970. In 1961 the state's growing population added 430 new students to the elementary and high school classrooms each day.

The units of educational administration in California are the more than 1,700 local school districts. The local educational policies are usually set by locally elected boards of education, who appoint superintendents to carry on the day-to-day supervision of curriculum and finances. However, with the tide of students increasing at the rate of 190,000 each year the state government has been compelled to share continually larger portions of local district expenses. The legislature sets aside about $200 for each unit of average daily attendance—about half the total cost of educating a public school student. Concurrently with greater state expenditures has come a large state government role in setting standards and requirements for students, personnel, and plant. Local districts must meet state requirements to qualify for state aid.

The State of California spends a billion dollars annually—approximately 42 per cent of its total budget—on education. By 1970, when the public school enrollment is expected to exceed five million, the educational budget will be easily twice its current figure, which does not include the junior colleges, state colleges, and the University of California. It must be remembered that the state budget figures do not portray the entire magnitude of the educational operation in California. When the combined state-

[33] Ibid. The nine states were Kansas, Louisiana, Minnesota, Mississippi, Montana, North Dakota, South Dakota, Vermont, and Wyoming.

local educational effort is reviewed the bill for the 1955–1970 period will have approached $20 billion.[34]

## Interstate Agreements

The interstate compact, while used in other areas of governmental activities for many years, has only recently been applied to the field of education. Two types of the interstate agreement have been established and placed in operation. First of all, one system provides for a regional compact by which the states in one part of the nation pool their resources in an effort to provide the best of educational facilities for their students. The first arrangement of this type was the Southern Regional Education Compact of 1948. The purpose of this compact is to "assist states, institutions and agencies concerned with higher education in their efforts to advance knowledge and to improve the social and economic level of the Southern region."[35] The compact created the Southern Regional Education Board which is composed of the governors from the sixteen member states and four persons appointed by each governor.[36] Under the plan any member state that is unable to provide for quality professional training enters into an agreement with the board to place certain of its residents seeking specialized training in, for example, dentistry or medicine. Another participating state accepts the students and receives a stipulated sum from the first state to defray the costs of the education.

In 1951 an arrangement entitled the Western Regional Education Compact was ratified by Colorado, Montana, New Mexico, Oregon, and Utah. Since that time the states of Alaska, Arizona, California, Hawaii, Idaho, Nevada, Washington, and Wyoming have joined the pact. The purpose of this new interstate agreement is to "expand professional and higher educational facilities in the West through cooperative and regional use of facilities; to make surveys of basic needs of the West and to implement such surveys with the necessary action."[37] The members of the Western Interstate Commission for Higher Education are appointed by the governors of the participating states.

[34] The information contained in the above paragraphs dealing with California is taken from the following document: Budget Division, Department of Finance, *Projected Enrollment in California's Schools, 1956–1970* (Sacramento: State of California, 1956), pp. 1–3.

[35] Council of State Governments, *The Book of the States, 1964–1965* (Chicago: Council of State Governments, 1964), p. 286.

[36] The member states are Alabama, Arkansas, Delaware, Florida, Georgia, Kentucky, Louisiana, Maryland, Mississippi, North Carolina, Oklahoma, South Carolina, Tennessee, Texas, Virginia, and West Virginia. Headquarters of the board are maintained in Atlanta, Ga. *The Book of the States, 1964–1965*, p. 286.

[37] Council of State Governments, *The Book of the States, 1964–1965* (Chicago: Council of State Governments, 1964), p. 287. Commission headquarters are established in Boulder, Colo.

In 1955 the New England Higher Education Compact established the New England Board of Higher Education. The purpose of this organization, much like those previously mentioned, is to provide residents of New England with increased educational opportunities and services. The board also aids states, institutions, and agencies that are concerned with higher education in their efforts to advance the academic, economic, and social levels in New England. Members of the board are appointed according to resolutions adopted by the individual states, and as a result some are appointed by the governors while others serve ex officio.[38] While such educational interstate arrangements are still in the experimental state, the brief past experiences would indicate the possibility that the number of such compacts may be increased and the scope of the present ones extended.

A second approach to the use of interstate agreements or compacts in the field of education emphasizes the ability of two states to agree to the utilization of specified facilities. The University of West Virginia in 1944 was authorized to enter into a contract with the Medical College of Virginia to admit a number of West Virginia students. In 1950, before any state had ratified the Western Regional Education Compact, the legislature of Wyoming, meeting in special session, passed legislation in an effort to assist in the training in the "professional health services." The law authorized the University of Wyoming to enter into contracts with out-of-state institutions for the training of Wyoming students in the fields of medicine, dentisty, veterinary medicine, and nursing. The University of Wyoming, following the enactment of the legislation, negotiated a contract with the University of Colorado School of Medicine to accept five students from Wyoming at the beginning of the fall quarter of the academic year 1950–1951. The students were to be selected by the president of the University of Wyoming with the assistance of the Wyoming State Medical Board. The students were required to meet all of the Colorado requirements and qualifications for admission into the School of Medicine, and Wyoming was to pay the full cost of the training, which was estimated to be $2,655 per student for the nine-months academic year. Since, however, Wyoming only charged $218.33 per quarter, the student was paying only $655 per year and the state of Wyoming paid $2,000. Actually the state was advancing a grant-in-aid of $8,000 per student for the four-year training program.[39]

In 1961 the Universities of Missouri and Nebraska established a cooperative program which, in particular programs of study, waived out-of-

[38] *Ibid.*, p. 276. The member states are Connecticut, Maine, Massachusetts, New Hampshire, Rhode Island, and Vermont. Board headquarters are maintained in Winchester, Mass.

[39] Trachsel and Wade, *op. cit.*, pp. 354–56.

state tuition for students from the two participating states. The following year the University of Missouri established a similar program with the University of Arkansas. Also, in 1962, the Universities of Wisconsin and Minnesota provided for a joint venture in the field of audio-visual education. Many other developments with regard to formal and even informal educational arrangements could be noted. The most important point is the fact that some type of regional education activity is today an accepted institution and will undoubtedly continue to expand in the future.

## Segregation in Public Schools

The famous separate but equal doctrine was officially pronounced by the United States Supreme Court in 1896.[40] In this decision the doctrine was applied to public transportation but was soon interpreted as also being applicable to public educational institutions. The Supreme Court did not change the status quo as segregated schools, public transportation, and other facilities had traditionally been accepted in the South and even in other areas as the only tolerable means of providing such services. The philosophy of the nineteenth century and the first half of the twentieth was basically that facilities, particularly educational, did not need to be integrated to be equal. It is interesting to note that in 1903 a candidate for the governorship of Mississippi expressed the belief that if the Negro public schools of the state were to be closed, as one candidate suggested, the federal government might require that Negroes be admitted to the white schools.[41]

Even before World War II the first indications of the possibilities of the desegregation of educational facilities and the final demise of the separate but equal doctrine appeared in the Supreme Court's decision in *Missouri ex rel. Gaines v. Canada,* wherein the state of Missouri was ordered to admit a Negro to its law school since it had no other such facilities within the state.[42] The decision did not outlaw segregation but did focus attention on this problem, only to have it submerged by the crisis of World War II.

The United States Supreme Court in 1954 set aside a precedent of more than a century when it declared that segregation in public schools was a denial of the equal protection clause of the United States Constitution. In its opinion, which was unanimous, the court maintained that segregation created educational facilities that were inherently unequal. The court ordered that desegregation should proceed "with all deliberate speed."[43]

[40] *Plessy v. Ferguson* (163 U.S. 537, 1896).
[41] A. D. Kirwan, *Revolt of the Rednecks* (Lexington: University of Kentucky Press, 1951), p. 151.
[42] *Missouri ex rel. Gaines v. Canada* (305 U.S. 337, 1938).
[43] *Brown v. Topeka Board of Education* (347 U.S. 483, 1954).

"Deliberate speed" meant different things to different school districts. Some integrated promptly while others refused to take action until court cases specifically involving them were filed. The seventeen Southern and border states have a total of about 6,600 school districts, of which some 2,800 have both white and Negro children. About 645 of these districts had at least token integration by 1957, and this number had increased to 824 by 1961 and to more than 976 by 1963. In most districts the action has taken place quietly and without fanfare, but in others open violence resulted when integration was attempted. The most famous case occurred in Little Rock, Arkansas, when Governor Faubus defied the federal court orders and President Eisenhower was forced to send in regular army troops to enforce the desegregation orders.

All states had desegregated by 1963 if the entry of one student into a college in South Carolina and one in Mississippi can be classed as such. More than 300 state laws have been enacted to facilitate or, in the majority of cases, to oppose desegregation. Many of these laws have been held unconstitutional by both state and federal courts.[44] The public schools at the elementary and secondary levels were still completely segregated in 1963–1964 in Alabama, Mississippi, and South Carolina. The situation was little different in Georgia and Louisiana as all schools with the exception of the city schools in Atlanta and New Orleans were completely segregated.

The segregation problem is not limited to the South and the border states but confronts many of the large metropolitan cities of the North and West. School segregation problems have not been solved in such large cities as New York City, Chicago, and Los Angeles, at least not in the minds of many of the desegregation leaders who feel the de facto segregation brought about by the organizing of school districts on strictly residential boundaries is as inherently unfair as many that exist in the South. In 1962–1963 voluntary school desegregation occurred in eight public school districts in Northern and Western states. Unknown to many people the following cities had previously maintained separate facilities for Negro and white children: Elroy, Arizona; Stamford, Connecticut; Mount Vernon, Illinois; Jersey City, Montclair, Morristown, and Newark, all in New Jersey; and Coatesville, Pennsylvania.

## Religion and Education

In the case of *Engel v. Vitale* the United States Supreme Court held that state officials could not compose an official state prayer and require

[44] Council of State Governments, *The Book of the States, 1962–1963* (Chicago: Council of State Governments, 1962), pp. 304–5.

that it be recited in the public schools.[45] The Court ruled that even though the prayer was denominationally neutral and even though pupils were not actually required to recite it or even remain in the room while it was recited, it still infringed upon the religious freedom of the students and the law was unconstitutional. The decision was based upon an interpretation prohibiting the enactment of any law "respecting the establishment of religion" as contained within the first amendment to the United States Constitution. The Supreme Court was not unanimous in this decision—the vote being six to one—as it had been in the case concerning segregation.

The parents of ten students in the New Hyde Park schools (New York) objected to the prayer on the grounds that it was contrary to their beliefs and violated their civil liberties. The opinion of the court was written by Justice Hugo Black who wrote, "When the power, prestige, and financial support of government is placed behind a particular religious belief, the indirect coercive pressure upon the minorities to conform to the prevailing officially approved religion is plain." The decision was met with immediate waves of protest. Several members of the Congress proposed constitutional amendments to overturn the ruling. Churchmen and others denounced the ruling in terms ranging from "scandalous" to "disappointing." However, other members of the clergy endorsed the statements as did a number of leading newspapers.

While the ruling in *Engel v. Vitale* outlawed only an officially endorsed prayer, the decision will undoubtedly have a broad impact on practices in the schools of America. A few states require that each day's session begin with a recitation of the Lord's Prayer. It would now seem to be unconstitutional for this regulation to be enforced by the states. Likewise, the requirement in many states of the reading of the Bible as part of the opening morning exercises in schools would appear to be of questionable constitutionality. Thus the public school systems are beset by not only the problems of overcrowding, understaffing, and finances but also by two emotionally packed issues—segregation and religion. Both hold potential crises for many states.

## LIBRARY SERVICES

Education and library services are two closely associated functions of government, yet they are usually administered by different governmental units. The first libraries in this country were organized by private citizens who formed voluntary associations that were supported by individual contributions. The first beginnings of the public library system are associated

---

[45] *Engel v. Vitale* (370 U.S. 421, 1962).

with the New York state law of 1835 that provided for school-district libraries that were tax-supported. Gradually, however, public libraries have become parts of municipal, county, or other types of local governments. Almost every city of 10,000 or more population provides for a library, while over 350 libraries are operated by special districts. In some instances school districts and counties maintain libraries or cooperate with other governmental units to establish regional library facilities. Yet the United States Office of Education conducted a survey in the spring of 1962 and reported that more than 12 million children attend schools without centralized school libraries. This figure constitutes about 47 per cent of the public elementary school membership, approximately 50 per cent of the non-public elementary school membership, and 4 per cent of the public and non-public secondary school membership.[46]

The states have also been concerned with the maintenance of libraries. In many instances, however, state libraries have been established to preserve historical materials or for use by state officials. As a result, some states have very specialized units designated as legislative-reference libraries. At the present time every state has some agency that is responsible for library-extension activities. Whatever its type of organization, the library-extension unit is concerned with the expansion of library coverage within the state. This may include providing book service or the giving of advice to local libraries. In 1963 a new Interstate Library Compact was enacted by the legislatures of Maine, Massachusetts, New Hampshire, New York, Rhode Island, and Vermont. In the Midwest some states have authorized interstate library agreements.

The American Library Association sets a minimum standard of 10,000 library volumes for communities with fewer than 2,500 people. However, the Library Association believes that 69 per cent of the 7,260 public libraries in the United States are substandard. A former United States Commissioner of Education, Francis Keppel, called the fact that in 80 per cent of the 8,000 elementary schools only 40 per cent have a central library a national disgrace.

The record is only slightly better in college libraries. The statistics reveal that only 17 per cent of the nation's college libraries meet the 100,000 volume standard which is considered as minimal for a liberal arts college. Only twenty-five graduate colleges claim to have more than the one and a half million volumes considered minimal for graduate college training.

The national government played only a small role in the public library movement until 1956. In that year the Congress passed the Library Services Act in an effort to provide more public library service to rural areas and to those communities where there was minimum library service. The

---

[46] Ruth M. White, "Libraries," *The Americana Annual, 1964* (New York: Americana Corp., 1963), p. 391.

act was so successful that the Congress extended it until July, 1966. Yet in spite of the impressive results, there were still in 1960 approximately 22 million rural residents with no library facilities, 18 million others with inadequate service, and 150 rural counties without any library service.[47]

## BIBLIOGRAPHY

ALLEN, HARRY K. *State Public Finance and State Institutions of Higher Education in the United States.* New York: Columbia University Press, 1952.

ALVES, HENRY F., and MORPHET, EDGAR L. *Principles and Procedures in the Organization of Satisfactory Local School Units.* Washington, D.C.: Office of Education Survey, 1938.

AMERICAN ASSEMBLY. *The Federal Government and Higher Education.* Englewood Cliffs, N.J.: Prentice-Hall, Inc., 1960.

AMERICAN ASSOCIATION OF SCHOOL ADMINISTRATORS. *School District Organization.* Washington, D.C.: American Association of School Administrators, 1958.

AXT, RICHARD G. *The Federal Government and Financing Higher Education.* New York: Columbia University Press, 1952.

BAILEY, STEPHEN K., FROST, RICHARD T., MARSH, PAUL E., and WOOD, ROBERT C. *Schoolmen and Politics: A Study of State Aid to Education in the Northeast.* Syracuse: Syracuse University Press, 1962.

BENSON, CHARLES S. *The Economics of Public Education.* Boston: Houghton Mifflin Co., 1961.

BURKE, ARVID J. *Financing Public Schools in the United States.* New York: Harper & Row, Inc., 1957.

BURKHEAD, JESSE. *State and Local Taxes for Public Education.* Syracuse: Syracuse University Press, 1963.

BUTTS, R. FREEMAN, and CREMIN, LAWRENCE A. *A History of Education in American Culture.* New York: Holt, Rinehart & Winston, Inc., 1953.

COUNCIL OF STATE GOVERNMENTS. *The Forty-eight State School Systems.* Chicago: Council of State Governments, 1949.

———. *Higher Education in the Forty-eight States.* Chicago: Council of State Governments, 1952.

DOUGLASS, HARL R., and GRIEDER, CALVIN. *American Public Education.* New York: The Ronald Press Co., 1948.

GLENNY, LYMAN A. *Autonomy of Public Colleges.* New York: McGraw-Hill Book Co., Inc., 1959.

GOOD, H. G. *A History of American Education.* New York: The Macmillan Co., 1956.

GRIEDER, CALVIN, and ROMINE, STEPHEN. *American Education—an Introduction to the Teaching Profession,* 3d ed. New York: The Ronald Press Co., 1965.

HAGMAN, HARLAN L. *The Administration of American Public Schools.* New York: McGraw-Hill Book Co., Inc,. 1951.

HALES, DAWSON. *Federal Control of Public Education.* New York: Bureau of Publications, Teachers College, Columbia University, 1954.

---

[47] Eleanor A. Ferguson, "Library Services and Legislation," *The Book of the States, 1962–1963* (Chicago: Council of State Governments, 1962), p. 331. See also, White, *op. cit.,* p. 427.

KEEZER, DEXTER M. (ed.). *Financing Higher Education, 1960–70.* New York: McGraw-Hill Book Co., Inc., 1959.

KNEZEVICH, STEPHEN J. *Administration of Public Education.* New York: Harper & Row, Inc., 1962.

MARTIN, ROSCOE C. *Government and the Suburban School.* Syracuse: Syracuse University Press, 1962.

MASTERS, NICHOLAS A., SALISBURY, ROBERT H., and ELIOT, THOMAS H. *State Politics and Public Schools.* New York: Alfred A. Knopf, Inc., 1964.

MILLETT, JOHN D. *Financing Higher Education in the United States.* New York: Columbia University Press, 1952.

MOEHLMAN, ARTHUR B. *School Administration.* Boston: Houghton Mifflin Co., 1951.

MOOS, MALCOLM, and ROURKE, FRANCIS. *The Campus and the State.* Baltimore: Johns Hopkins Press, 1959.

MORLAN, ROBERT L. *Intergovernmental Relations in Education.* Minneapolis: University of Minnesota Press, 1950.

MORT, PAUL R., REUSSER, WALTER C., and POLBY, JOHN W. *Public School Finance,* 3d ed. New York: McGraw-Hill Book Co., Inc., 1960.

MUNGER, FRANK J., and FENNO, RICHARD F. *National Politics and Federal Aid to Education.* Syracuse: Syracuse University Press, 1962.

PITTENGER, B. F. *Local Public School Administration.* New York: McGraw-Hill Book Co., Inc., 1951.

REEVES, FLOYD W. (ed.). *Education for Rural America.* Chicago: The University of Chicago Press, 1945.

RIVLIN, ALICE M. *The Role of the Federal Government in Financing Higher Education.* Washington, D.C.: The Brookings Institution, 1961.

RUDOLPH, FREDERICK. *The American College and University.* New York: Alfred A. Knopf, Inc., 1962.

THURSTON, LEE M., and ROE, WILLIAM H. *State School Administration.* New York: Harper & Row, Inc., 1957.

WAHLQUIST, J. T. (ed.). *The Administration of Public Education.* New York: The Ronald Press Co., 1952.

# 20

# Social Welfare Programs

The term "welfare" has either been omitted or only briefly referred to in the Constitution of the United States, and the same is true of practically all of the state constitutions. In some of these documents, particularly the national constitution, the phrase "to promote the general welfare" has been regarded only as a justification for the creation of government. Yet all of our governments have given considerable attention to the welfare needs of their citizens. However, in just the last two decades a gradual change has occurred in the attitude of much of our citizenry with respect to their philosophy toward government and the role it should play in providing for certain welfare functions. The Constitution of Hawaii, in emphasizing this changing opinion, contains the following sections:[1]

Sec. 1. The State shall provide for the protection and promotion of the public health.

Sec. 2. The State shall have power to provide for treatment and rehabilitation, as well as domiciliary care, of mentally or physically handicapped persons.

Sec. 3. The State shall have power to provide assistance for persons unable to maintain a standard of living compatible with the decency and health.

Sec. 4. The State shall have power to provide for or assist in slum clearance and the development of rehabilitation of substandard areas, including housing for persons of low income.

## TYPES OF PUBLIC WELFARE PROGRAMS

Public assistance activities have a tendency to fall into two major categories. The first classification distinguishes between *indoor* or *institutional* relief and *outdoor* or *home* assistance. Indoor assistance is the means by which the doors of public institutions are opened for the benefit of needy or poor persons. The indoor system is an essential operation on behalf of the government for those individuals who, because of illness or some type of physical or mental handicap, require constant treatment. This system is

[1] *Constitution of Hawaii*, Article VIII.

widely accepted because it is less expensive for the state to care for several persons in one institution rather than to provide individual care in homes. In addition, it is easier to provide the proper care and attention for those persons in an institution that is adequately equipped and maintained. Historically, indoor assistance has been viewed as the primary means of caring for those individuals who are deemed to be permanent charges for the government. Welfare departments in many states have direct responsibility for the operation of hospitals for the feeble-minded, the insane, and epileptics; for managing homes for the veterans, the deaf and dumb, the blind, dependent children, the cripples, and the poor; and for supervising various types of penal institutions, reform schools, and sanatoria.

Outdoor assistance is provided for normally within the home of the recipient and possesses an advantage of greater flexibility. In this situation an able-bodied person who may not have sufficient income is permitted to maintain the home environment for the family with the supplementary funds being furnished by the state or local government. In this way the stigma of pauperism is removed as over and against that connected with the person who is sent to the county home. While there is always the possibility that the absence of this stigma may encourage some "raids" on outdoor aid, a vigilant administration can prevent, to a degee, such padding of the public support rolls. Traditionally, outdoor aid has been viewed as a means of assisting those who will require such support only temporarily, and therefore the recipient should be permitted to lead a normal, home-oriented life.

The second category of public-assistance measures produces a distinction between *general* and *categorical* aids. General assistance is made available to all individuals needing aid and whose support has been labeled as a public responsibility, but who cannot qualify for aid under any one of the special or categorical programs. Categorical assistance has been created to aid needy individuals who can be placed in limited, special, or specific groups, such as the blind. At the present time many states are providing for four categorical outdoor assistance programs: (1) old-age assistance, (2) aid to the blind, (3) aid to families with dependent children, and (4) aid to the permanently and totally disabled. These programs are administered by the state governments or by local agencies under state supervision and are financed partially by national aid.

## CATEGORICAL OUTDOOR ASSISTANCE PROGRAMS

### Old-Age Assistance

Assistance to the needy aged is by far the most extensive and costly of any one of the categorical assistance programs. This type of aid will continue to be important as the proportion of older people within our total population becomes larger and larger. In the early 1950's there were more than 13,000,000 individuals in the United States sixty-five years of age or over and this group constituted more than 8 per cent of the total population.[2] It has been estimated that by 1980 there will be at least 22,000,000 such persons.[3] These individuals in this high age group have a tendency to possess certain characteristics that, in turn, seemingly create certain problems for society. Dependency, many times, is the key word, since a large number of older persons do not have an income, possess little savings, and may have no close relatives to support them. Frequently chronic illnesses plague many such individuals, and even those who are surprisingly able-bodied cannot secure jobs because of their advanced age.

States began to provide for some type of pensions for the needy aged almost forty years ago. Montana established a pension program in 1923 and by 1935 thirty states had created some type of arrangement for pensions or assistance to those who could qualify under state laws. However, adequate systems were not in force, with particular respect to benefits and coverage, until the states were able to take advantage of the public assistance provisions of the national Social Security Act. The national government established certain conditions that must be met by the states before they became eligible to receive old-age assistance funds. The more important of these were: (1) assistance was to be given to those persons over sixty-five years of age on the basis of need; (2) the national funds granted to the states must be matched by state funds according to a ratio determined by the national government; (3) the program within the state was to be administered by a single agency whose employees were to be selected on the basis of merit; and (4) any applicant denied assistance was to be given a fair hearing. Every state is now participating with the national program and has met these stipulations.

The national government previously paid approximately 80 per cent of the $31 per month paid by the state to each individual. As of October 1, 1962, the federal share was increased to $29 of the first $35 of the grant, with the average monthly maximum being increased from $66 to $70 exclusive of vendor payments for medical care. A state is given the freedom to pay whatever it desires over the $70 per month figure, but any sum over that amount must be paid entirely out of state funds. The District of Columbia in 1963 was paying the highest average at $113.72, followed by Minnesota with $109.28, while Mississippi was paying slightly less than $36.[4]

[2] Federal Security Agency, *Annual Report: 1952* (Washington, D.C.: Government Printing Office, 1953), p. 42.
[3] Ollie A. Randall, "The Aged," *Social Work Year Book: 1947* (New York: National Association of Social Workers, 1948), pp. 41–45.
[4] Council of State Governments, *The Book of the States, 1964–1965* (Chicago: Council of State Governments, 1964), p. 416.

In 1954 more than 2,500,000 individuals—nearly one in five of the population age sixty-five or over—were receiving old-age assistance, with the average monthly payment of about $51.[5] Some authorities in this area are predicting that the number of persons requiring old-age assistance should show a decline as the coverage of the OASI is extended to additional classes of workers, as more and more workers, upon reaching retirement, have been employed for a sufficient period of years to qualify under the old-age and survivors insurance. Nevertheless, old-age assistance will continue as one of the primary means of providing aid to those individuals who need this type of support and cannot qualify under the national system.

Old-age assistance must not be confused with the program of old-age and survivors insurance, which was also created by a provision within the national Social Security Act. This latter program is not in the strict sense a public or social welfare project, since the benefits are based upon the contributions paid into the national government by each individual recipient and his employers. The OASI program, financed by a federal payroll tax, is administered entirely by the national government, and the states play no role whatsoever.[6] On the other hand, the old-age assistance program receives its funds from both the national and state governments, and this payment is actually a form of relief and is paid only to an aged, needy person in the form of a gratuity. The OASI program now covers the vast proportions of employed individuals in the United States with the only major groups of workers not covered being those federal employees who are under the United States civil service retirement program, employees of state and local governments that have not chosen OASI coverage for their workers, persons with incomes not adequate to qualify for benefits, and ministers who do not choose to be covered. The benefits from this program are paid when the employees reach the age of sixty-five, or when they reach the age of sixty-two if the recipients are willing to accept reduced payments. Surviving dependents, such as a widow and children under eighteen, are entitled to the benefits the worker would have received.

## Aid to the Blind

Another category of persons receiving assistance under social welfare programs is that of the blind. This type of aid has been established to provide support for those persons who are either completely blind or whose sight is impaired to the degree that they cannot hold a job. States

[5] U.S. Department of Health, Education and Welfare, *Annual Report: 1954* (Washington, D.C.: Government Printing Office, 1955), p. 41.

[6] The tax was originally set at 1 per cent and during 1963 employer and employees were contributing 3⅝ per cent.

have had a tendency to vary their definitions of blindness that must be met by applicants desiring to participate in the assistance program. Some states, as in the case of old-age assistance, have set no limit with regard to the maximum amount of individual awards for aid to the blind. For those states that have established a maximum payment that will be permitted, the range varied, as of October, 1962, from a high of $325 per month in Washington, which can be exceeded to prevent undue hardship, to the payment of only $40 per month in Mississippi.

As of June, 1963, 98,385 individuals were given assistance through the various state programs, with the individual monthly payments averaging approximately $81.30. Of this average figure approximately 46.6 per cent was derived from federal funds, while 53.4 per cent was contributed by state and local sources. In the state of Mississippi only 23.8 per cent of the funds came from state and local sources, with the federal government contributing 76.2 per cent. In contrast, in the State of Pennsylvania, the federal government provided only 18.6 per cent, while the state contributed 81.4 per cent. The highest average payment per recipient, as of June, 1963, occurred in Massachusetts with the figure of $136.95, with the lowest being paid by Mississippi—$37.98.[7] The matching ratios for aid to the blind were changed by an act of the Congress in 1962 so that the federal government, beginning October 1, 1962, provided for $29 of the first $35 of the grant.

The aid to the blind program is administered in many states by the state department of public or social welfare or an equivalent department. In Ohio, beginning in 1941, the Division of Social Administration became responsible for the general program of services for the blind. Previously, the Ohio Commission for the Blind had conducted the program, but continued to serve in an advisory capacity. The general purposes of the blind program in Ohio are: "(1) to prevent unnecessary blindness; (2) to furnish instruction and employment for blind adults in workshops, factories, and homes; and (3) to ameliorate the conditions of the aged and infirm blind."[8] In addition, the program includes the maintenance of a trade training school where various skills and trades are taught and assistance in securing employment when the course is completed; employs teachers who visit blind adults and give them instruction in reading and writing the embossed types, and in mending, sewing, and other skills; maintains a complete register of the blind in the state which indicates, among other items, each individual's capacity for education and vocational training; and makes arrangements for the sale of articles produced by the blind.

[7] Council of State Governments, *The Book of the States, 1964–1965* (Chicago: Council of State Governments, 1964), p. 418.

[8] Francis R. Aumann and Harvey Walker, *The Government and Administration of Ohio* (New York: Thomas Y. Crowell Co., 1956), p. 273.

Typical of other state action is the pattern that developed in New Jersey. In 1909 the state created a Commission for the Amelioration of the Condition of the Blind. This commission was to prepare a register of the blind and later was authorized to make loans to the blind for the establishment of businesses. The commission recommended the actual assistance funds that were made available by the county and determined their use. This function was relinquished when the commission, in 1922, was placed under the general supervision of the Department of Institutions and Agencies.[9]

## Aid to Families with Dependent Children

For some time it has been the accepted custom to provide for needy, neglected, and dependent children through one of the following three methods: (1) placing the children in the county homes where they received care alongside adults; (2) placing them in orphanages that are maintained by fraternal, social, or religious institutions; and (3) by state and county governments.[10] At the present time the trend is away from the use of institutional care, and every attempt possible is made to permit the children to be reared in a normal home environment by foster parents, near relatives, or by granting financial assistance to the mother to maintain her own home. This latter method is particularly desirable when the mother can demonstrate that she is the proper person to care for her dependent children. While this is a subject that should not be dominated completely by fiscal concerns, it has usually been more economical to assist the mother than to break up the home and place the children in an institution.

Before the passage of the Social Security Act, aid to dependent children was usually referred to as mothers' aid or mothers' pensions. The Social Security Act stipulated that a dependent child is one who is a needy child: who (1) is under the age of eighteen; (2) has been deprived of parental support as the result of the prolonged and continued absence from the home, the mental or physical incapacity, or the death of one of the parents; or (3) is living with one of his parents or anyone of a detailed list of relatives. The national government has provided funds to the states, but under this program each state has enacted and administered its own child welfare laws. In 1962 the Congress of the United States adopted the so-called "Public Welfare Amendments" which contained some of the most extensive changes in the Social Security Act since its

[9] Bennett M. Rich, *The Government and Administration of New Jersey* (New York: Thomas Y. Crowell Co., 1957), p. 252.

[10] Martha P. Falconer, "Institutions for the Care of Children," *Encyclopaedia of the Social Sciences* (12th Prtg.; New York: The Macmillan Co., 1957), Vol. III, pp. 410–12.

passage in 1935. One amendment changed the name of the program for needy children to that of "aid to families with dependent children." In addition, the provision for aid to dependent children of families in need due to the unemployment of a parent was extended for five years, until June 30, 1967, and the assistance to certain dependent children in foster family care was made a permanent part of the program. Before this time, only one parent of dependent children could be included in the grant, but the amendment of 1962 made it possible to include the second parent living in the home if incapacitated or unemployed.[11] In July, 1962, recipients of aid to dependent children totaled 3,640,900, of whom 45,400 were in families of unemployed parents, with the average payment of $31.40 per individual receiving aid to dependent children.[12] By June of 1962 only fifteen states had adopted the new program of aid to dependent children of unemployed parents. These states reported a total of 51,843 families, including 188,349 children in the case load for that month. However, thirteen states had adopted the new program of aid for dependent children in foster care and reported 639 cases with 1,516 children as of June, 1962.[13] Currently the national government contributes $14 of the first $17 paid monthly in support of a dependent child and one-half of the remainder up to a total of $32. The national government also limits its support for additional children in the family group or in a foster parent's home to $23. Individual states are free to raise these limits with their own resources. As of June, 1963, payments were being made for approximately 2,952,385 dependent children embracing 962,686 families, with the average monthly payment per family being $126.50.[14]

## Aid to Permanently and Totally Disabled Individuals

One of the most recent additions to the categorical aid programs was established to extend support to individuals who are permanently and totally disabled. The Social Security Act was amended in 1950 to extend national aid to state programs, but the federal money could be used by states to aid only those individuals who are fifty years of age or older. State laws may provide for a younger eligibility age, but in this situation the state must provide for the full support of these individuals until they reach the age of fifty. Many states have established provisions regulating the amount of the assistance payments that are quite similar to, and in

[11] Ellen Winston, "Social Welfare," *The Americana Annual, 1963* (New York: Americana Corp., 1963), p. 598.

[12] Robert M. Ball, "Social Security," *The Americana Annual, 1963* (New York: Americana Corp., 1963), p. 598.

[13] Winston, *op. cit.*, p. 598.

[14] Council of State Governments, *The Book of the States, 1964–1965* (Chicago: Council of State Governments, 1964), pp. 414–15.

some instances identical with, those pertaining to old-age assistance. Almost half of those persons granted disability payments are suffering from paralysis, arthritis, or heart disease, and a substantial group of amputees is also included.

By June, 1962, the number of individuals receiving disability payments was 417,000, with an average monthly payment of $72.00.[15] In 1963, with all fifty states participating in the national program, disability payments were being made to 461,538 individuals, and the average monthly payment had increased to $74.82.[16] The range in the average payment to the permanently and totally disabled in June, 1963, varied from a high of $131.89 in Massachusetts to a low of $34.23 in Mississippi. In the state of Mississippi for the calendar year 1962, the federal government provided for 75.6 per cent of the funds for these payments with the state contributing only 24.4 per cent. However, in Massachusetts, at the other extreme, the federal support was only 33.6 per cent, with the state supplying 66.4 per cent for the payments to this category of individuals.[17] As of 1962, twenty-seven states had provided maximum limitations for monthly payments, ranging from $325 in Washington to a maximum of $45 per month in Mississippi.[18] The matching ratios for aid to this category of individuals were liberalized by congressional action in 1962, so that instead of the federal government providing 80 per cent of the first $31 of the grant, the federal share, as of October 1, 1962, was increased to $29 of the first $35 of the grant, with the average monthly maximum increased from $66 to $70 exclusive of vendor payments for medical care.

## Medical Assistance to the Aged

The Congress in 1960 passed the Kerr-Mills Bill which provided for from 50 to 80 per cent matching grants to states that established programs of medical assistance for aged persons who are medically indigent. The national law established certain requirements that must be followed by the states: (1) no state may set an age limit higher than sixty-five, (2) any United States citizen is eligible and no residence restrictions may be imposed, and (3) the property of any applicant is not subject to lien before his death, and recovery from the estate may await the death of the surviving spouse. The states have been granted an area of discretion in determining the actual scope of the program, but it must include some institutional and non-institutional care.

[15] The figures for June, 1962, are taken from Winston, *op. cit.*, p. 599.
[16] Council of State Governments, *The Book of the States, 1964–1965* (Chicago: Council of State Governments, 1964), p. 419.
[17] *Ibid.*
[18] *Ibid.*

Appropriate legislation to make states eligible for participation in the program, but varying considerably in scope, was in operation in twenty-nine states by the fall of 1963.[19] Programs of medical assistance for the aged, serving over 101,000 persons were reported in twenty-seven jurisdictions as of June, 1962, with more than two-thirds of the individuals under these programs, as authorized by the 1960 Kerr-Mills legislation, residing in California, Massachusetts, New York, and West Virginia.[20]

The Kerr-Mills Act, which established a cooperative federal-state medical care system, actually placed in operation two programs. The first plan is in essence a mere extension of the old-age assistance program by which only those individuals are eligible to participate who are receiving public assistance. Depending upon the level of per capita income within a state, the national government will support a part of the costs through a matching ratio, varying from 50 to 80 per cent. The legislation provided that the national contributions to a state could not exceed a sum equal to $12 per month multiplied by the number of persons receiving assistance under the program.

The second program aids those elderly persons who are not on the assistance rolls, but who need some financial aid with respect to medical care. In this situation, while state funds are matched on the same basis as in the assistance program, no limit is placed on the total amount that may be granted by the federal government. The major limitation rests with the state legislatures as they indicate their willingness to appropriate funds for medical care purposes. In 1965, the Medical Care for the Aged statute passed by the 89th Congress replaced much of the Kerr-Mills legislation.

## STATE AGENCIES FOR WELFARE ADMINISTRATION

Historically, outdoor assistance or home relief was the most prevalent type of aid extended to needy individuals. During the colonial period, the construction and maintenance of public institutions for the poor were beyond the abilities and resources of most communities, and, in addition, outdoor assistance was cheaper. Since "poor relief" at that time was a responsibility of local government, many of these units resorted to such practices as indenture, banishment of the unsettled poor, contracting out, and even the sale of the poor as means of solving their relief problems.[21] Local authorities actually retained a large amount of control over both

19 *Ibid.*, p. 424.
20 Winston, *op. cit.*, p. 599.
21 Paul T. Stafford, *Government and the Needy* (Princeton: Princeton University Press, 1941), p. 24.

indoor and outdoor assistance until almost 1935. Some states, however, began to assume a limited amount of responsibility for welfare administration by the middle of the nineteenth century by providing for certain types of institutional care.

The great surge on behalf of the states to provide for rather thorough public aid programs came in 1935 with the passage of the federal Social Security Act. That law, among other things, made provisions for grants-in-aid to states for four different types of public assistance: (1) old-age, (2) dependent children, (3) the blind, and (4) the permanently and totally disabled. Immediately four states—Idaho, Pennsylvania, West Virginia, and Wisconsin—noting the emphasis of the national law on public assistance, established separate departments under the specific title of public assistance. Prior to the passage of the Social Security Act, state welfare organizations were a haphazard operation of boards, commissions, and agencies. Since there had been no major movement emphasizing centralized administration, it was accepted practice to establish a separate board as a new welfare function was added by the state legislature. Illinois, in 1917, unified its welfare functions into a single administrative authority, and while some states followed this example, the major part of unification occurred after 1935.

While the first state welfare activities were under the direction of boards and commissions, by 1952 the over-all welfare administration was under the control of boards in only five states. At that time thirty-seven states had welfare departments with single directors; Maine and Missouri had highly integrated departments of health and welfare; and the remaining four states had single-director departments that were similar in most respects to welfare departments in other states, though not having precisely that title.[22]

The various activities or functions to be placed within the welfare department have a tendency to vary. However, the Council of State Governments reported that in seventeen states the following five basic welfare responsibilities were concentrated in a single department: (1) over-all welfare administration, (2) general assistance, (3) old-age assistance, (4) maternal and child welfare, and (5) blind welfare. In twelve states, four of the above five duties were centralized within a single department, but in at least a dozen states the welfare responsibilities were dispersed among three, four, or even more agencies. It is therefore apparent that while more than one-half of the states have integrated their welfare functions within a single department, at least one-third have not followed

[22] Council of State Governments, *The Book of the States, 1952–1953* (Chicago: Council of State Governments, 1952), pp. 664–65. Nebraska had a Department of Assistance and Child Welfare; New Jersey, a Department of Institutions and Agencies; West Virginia, a Department of Public Assistance; and Washington, A Department of Social Security.

recommended principles of public administration in providing for their public welfare activities.

## A Typical Department of Public Welfare: Delaware[23]

After a decade of consistent and constant pressure upon the general assembly, an administrative department with extensive jurisdiction in the field of public welfare was created. In 1931 there were twenty-three separate agencies providing for welfare services on either a quasi-public or full state or county basis. The establishment of a single department became a possibility in 1944 with the creation of the Delaware Council of Welfare Agencies, but the central organization was not established until 1951.

The State Board of Welfare is the governing body of the Department of Public Welfare. The twelve members are appointed by the governor for staggered terms of three years, and bipartisanship is provided on the board, since no more than six members may come from one of the major parties. Since the matching of state and county funds is present in the Delaware system, the custom has been for the governor to give each county representation by naming a member of each county levy court, which is the county governing body, to the commission. While the members of the board receive no stated compensation, they are reimbursed for actual expenses incurred in attendance at their meetings. The primary duties of the welfare department consist of administering all programs of public assistance and all the services that are specifically related to these programs.

The department is divided into two operating divisions: child welfare and public assistance. Each division is broken down into a county office for each of the three counties. In addition to the operating bureaus, there exists a division of business administration, a medical consultant, and a staff agency that is concerned with research and information. The internal organization of the department, as indicated in Figure 20–1, has been vested in the board and the director by state law. The personnel of the department are appointed upon a merit basis. The position of the director is the key to the successful operation of this agency, since he must not only coordinate the work of several welfare activities, but he must satisfy the demands of certain public elements who may have a different view with respect to the administration of welfare activities.

## PROGRAMS FOR THE AGED

The problems associated with the elderly segment of our population are becoming of more concern, not only to the national government, but also

[23] The above information is taken from Paul Dolan, *The Government and Administration of Delaware* (New York: Thomas Y. Crowell Co., 1956), pp. 222–23.

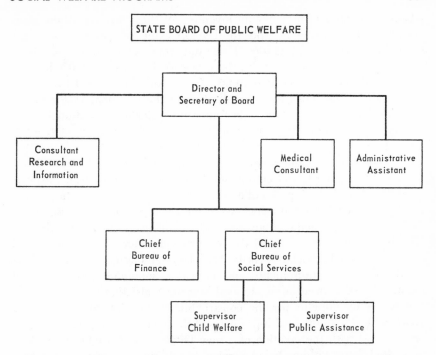

**Fig. 20–1.** Organization of the Department of Public Welfare in Delaware. [Source: Paul Dolan, *The Government and Administration of Delaware* (New York: Thomas Y. Crowell Co., 1956).]

to state legislatures, which during the decade of the 1950's gradually increased state services for the aging. In 1900 there were three million Americans over the age of sixty-five. At the present time there are nearly sixteen million, and it has been estimated that the figure will increase to at least twenty million by 1970. Only 4 per cent of the population were sixty-five and over at the turn of the century, while at the present time this age group composes approximately 9 per cent of our population. In addition, the inadequacy of income for the majority of our senior citizens is emphasized by the report that, in 1958, some three-fifths of the men and women over sixty-five had a monetary income of less than $1,000 per year. The national government exhibited its interest in the problems of the aged by passing, in 1958, a measure calling for a White House Conference on Aging to be held in January, 1961. The principal purpose of the conference was to provide an impetus for the further development of policies and services of governmental agencies at all three levels, as well as public agencies, that would create an atmosphere and environment in which these individuals could realize a greater potentiality. Each state was invited by the act to collect information concerning its older population, make an inventory of those resources now present to meet their needs, and to develop some recommendations for improving services and facilities. These state reports were to be submitted to the Secretary of Health, Education, and Welfare as the basis for discussion and action at the conference. Grants of from $5,000 to $15,000 were made to the states for the collection of the pertinent material and for holding at least one state-wide conference prior to the national meeting. As a result, committees or commissions on aging were created in all of the states.[24]

The White House Conference on Aging was held in Washington, D.C., January 9 to 12, 1961, and comprised twenty sections on various aspects of problems of the aging. A policy statement and recommendations were produced by each section which were widely distributed and discussed by appropriate agencies of government at all levels. Subsequently, the Congress, in its efforts to assist the fast-growing older population, passed amendments to the Social Security Act which, among other things, liberalized eligibility requirements and increased minimum payments and widows' benefits. In addition, federal housing legislation was broadened to serve as an impetus for the construction of housing for the elderly. Efforts to deal with the health problems of the aged were stepped up at the federal level with the creation of a new Division of Chronic Diseases in the United States Public Health Service. In addition, programs of medical assistance to aged people were established by the Kerr-Mills measure.

## Action Within the States

The section on state organization of the 1961 White House Conference on Aging recommended that each state should establish a permanent unit to be concerned with the problems of the aging. Twenty-seven states have now created committees, commissions, or separate units by legislative action. Also, at least nine states have established active agencies by executive orders.[25] While many of these agencies pre-date the White House Conference, some of them have been created since 1961. Some of the typical actions by state legislatures are revealed by the following examples. The Texas legislature established a new permanent position entitled state coordinator on aging and placed it under the direction of the governor. In Oklahoma, gerontological services were established within the Family Life Institute of the University of Oklahoma Extension Services.

[24] This paragraph is adapted from information presented in Council of State Governments, *The Book of the States, 1962–1963* (Chicago: Council of State Governments, 1962), p. 376.
[25] Council of State Governments, *The Book of the States, 1964–1965* (Chicago: Council of State Governments, 1964), p. 422.

In Utah, a council on aging was created with provision for a full-time director.

Other actions by the states to assist the aging are concerned with the areas of employment, income maintenance, health, and housing. Since 1961 several legislatures have considered various proposals for prohibiting discrimination in employment on the basis of age, and measures to this effect were passed in some states. Laws prohibiting employment discrimination of older workers are in operation in fourteen states.[26] During the legislative sessions that met during 1960 and 1961, five states passed new laws prohibiting employers from refusing to hire, from discharging, or otherwise discriminating against older workers because of age unless founded upon some bonafide occupational qualification. The Ohio law prohibits employers from refusing to interview applicants and from discharging employees because of age. The age protections differ in the various states; the law in Alaska applies to individuals over forty-five, in California to those persons between forty and sixty-four, in Delaware those between forty-five and sixty-five, while the Ohio and Washington enactments protect those between forty and sixty-five. The New York law was changed to protect those from forty to sixty-five rather than from forty-five to sixty-five.[27]

Other efforts to aid the elderly in the area of employment are concerned with the training or retraining of older workers in an effort to improve their employment possibilities. In California a cooperative program between the California State Department of Employment and the Adult Division of the San Francisco Unified School District has been established for the short-term training of large numbers of people in skills required in the employment market. In addition, some states are permitting the payment of unemployment compensation to eligible persons during the period of occupational retraining. Other states have instituted flexible retirement policies for their own employees. As an example, the Louisiana State Board of Education authorized institutions under its control to extend employment beyond the age of sixty-five on a year-to-year basis, but dependent on the fitness and health of the individual employee. The Public Employees Retirement Act of 1961 in Kansas, while providing for a retirement age of sixty-five, also included the possibility of extended employment at the option of the employer on an annual basis until the age of seventy. The New Jersey Highway Authority, in 1960, began hiring retired men over sixty-five to serve as part-time collectors on the Garden State Parkway.

[26] Council of State Governments, *The Book of the States, 1962–1963* (Chicago: Council of State Governments, 1962), p. 494. These states are Alaska, California, Colorado, Connecticut, Delaware, Louisiana, Massachusetts, New York, Ohio, Oregon, Pennsylvania, Rhode Island, Washington, and Wisconsin.
[27] *Ibid.*

In the last few years, some of the states have enacted laws to allow tax exemptions that would benefit older persons. California exempts drugs prescribed for treatment of human beings from sales and use tax. In Hawaii, the state income tax exemptions for older persons was increased from $800 to $1,200. Property tax exemptions for elderly persons with limited income are provided in eight Maryland counties. Several states, including Kansas, Tennessee, Utah, and West Virginia, in an effort to insure more adequate income after retirement, passed laws either establishing or improving state retirement systems. Some states established or expanded programs of medical care in addition to the Kerr-Mills program of medical aid for the aged. In South Dakota, the Department of Public Welfare assumed responsibility for paying for hospital and physicians' services received by old-age assistance recipients. The legislature in Indiana provided that any medically indigent person who had been a resident of the state for three of the last nine years was eligible for medical care. Also, since 1960, several states have improved their public assistance grants. In California, the basic old-age pension has been raised from $95 to $100 per month, assistance to the needy blind from $104 to $115, and the allowance for special need cases among both of these groups from $115 to $165. The Arizona legislature appropriated monies to provide single individuals with a minimum of $100 per month and a couple with $155 per month.

In several states recent legislation has been enacted to provide better health services for our aging population. The use of nursing homes is becoming more prevalent. In Minnesota, approximately 2,500 beds have been added in some fifty-four homes in the past two years. States are also increasing the standards required in the conducting of these homes. In Maryland, the law regarding the licensing of hospitals used as nursing, convalescent, or care homes was strengthened by requiring certain minimum standards as well as the approval for the alteration or construction of facilities. In an effort to encourage the development of additional homes, the Arkansas legislature authorized cities to develop and operate nursing homes and to use the proceeds from revenue bonds and available revenue for this purpose. A state debt of $1.5 million was authorized by the Maryland legislature to supplement loans for the construction of public or non-profit nursing homes. With the construction of additional nursing homes, some public mental hospitals are attempting to place geriatric patients in such facilities as a means of relieving over-crowded conditions in hospitals.

In some states the public housing authorities have been setting aside sections of new structures or constructing separate buildings for elderly tenants, which are especially equipped and designed to meet their problems. In Indiana, the chairman of the state commission on aging has been authorized to investigate the possibility of creating a state-wide housing council on the aging. This organization, which would include representatives from construction, finance, and health interests, could draw up the standards for materials and give advise to those organizations interested in developing housing for the aged.

## BIBLIOGRAPHY

ABBOTT, EDITH. *Public Assistance*, Vol. I. Chicago: The University of Chicago Press, 1940.

ABBOTT, GRACE. *From Relief to Social Security*. Chicago: The University of Chicago Press, 1941.

BRECKINRIDGE, SOPHONISBA P. *Public Welfare Administration in the United States*, 2d ed., Selected Documents. Chicago: The University of Chicago Press, 1938.

COMMISSION ON INTERGOVERNMENTAL RELATIONS. *A Study Committee Report on Federal Aid to Welfare*. Washington, D.C.: Government Printing Office, 1955.

COUNCIL OF STATE GOVERNMENTS. *The States and Their Older Citizens*. Chicago: Council of State Governments, 1955.

CORSON, JOHN J., and McCONNELL, JOHN W. *Economic Needs of Old People*. New York: Twentieth Century Fund, 1956.

DRAKE, JOSEPH T. *The Aged in American Society*. New York: The Ronald Press Co., 1958.

LEIRFALLOM, J., and DRAKE, R. P. *Organization and Administration of Local Public Welfare Services*. Chicago: American Public Welfare Association, 1943.

LEYENDECKER, HILARY M. *Problems and Policy in Public Assistance*. New York: Harper & Row, Inc., 1955.

McMILLEN, WAYNE. *Community Organization for Social Welfare*. Chicago: The University of Chicago Press, 1945.

MERIAM, LEWIS, et al. *The Cost and Financing of Social Security*. Washington, D.C.: The Brookings Institution, 1950.

MILES, ARTHUR P. *An Introduction to Public Welfare*. Boston: D. C. Heath & Co., 1949.

MILLSPAUGH, ARTHUR C. *Public Welfare Organization*. Washington, D.C.: The Brookings Institution, 1935.

PERKINS, ELLEN J. *State and Local Financing of Public Assistance*. Washington: D.C.: U.S. Department of Health, Education and Welfare, Bureau of Public Assistance, 1956.

RAUP, RUTH. *Intergovernmental Relations in Public Welfare*. Minneapolis: University of Minnesota Press, 1952.

STAFFORD, PAUL T. *Government and the Needy*. Princeton: Princeton University Press, 1941.

STEVENSON, MARIETTA. *Public Welfare Administration*. New York: The Macmillan Co., 1938.

STREET, ELWOOD. *The Public Welfare Administrator*. New York: McGraw-Hill Book Co., Inc., 1940.

TURNBULL, JOHN G., WILLIAMS, C. ARTHUR, JR., and CHEIT, EARL F. *Economics and Social Security—Public and Private Measures Against Economic Insecurity*, 2d ed. New York: The Ronald Press Co., 1962.

VASEY, WAYNE. *Government and Social Welfare: Roles of Federal, State, and Local Governments in Administering Welfare Services.* New York: Holt, Rinehart & Winston, Inc., 1958.

WHITE, R. CLYDE. *Administration of Public Welfare*, 2d ed. Cincinnati: American Book Co., 1950.

WHITE HOUSE CONFERENCE ON AGING. *Aging in the States—a Report of Progress, Concern, Goals.* Washington, D.C.: Government Printing Office, 1961.

# 21

# Public Health

The state's authority in the field of public health comes from the fact that it is regarded as a reserved power of the states rather than one delegated to the federal government by the United States Constitution. This does not mean that the national government is uninterested in the field of public health because related delegated powers have been used as the authority for considerable health work on the part of the national government. Of great importance, in addition to the financial assistance, is the collection of vital statistics, the dissemination of information concerning health subjects, public health planning, research, and consultative services.

The first work of the federal government in this field began in 1798 with the establishment of the hospital for American seamen, which was the forerunner of the Public Health Service now a part of the Department of Health, Education, and Welfare. There can be little doubt that the work of the United States Public Health Service has served as a tremendous impetus and incentive for activities in this field by the various states. Without the leadership of this agency the status of public health work in the United States would even be more neglected than it is at the present time. In addition to the United States Department of Health, Education, and Welfare a number of other federal agencies deal directly and indirectly with public health matters, mostly in cooperation with state activities.

Some of the progress in the field of public health is revealed by a study of a few vital statistics concerning health trends in America. The birth rate in the years 1960, 1961, and 1963 has been quite constant, approximately 4.2 million live births, with the birth rate per thousand people dropping slightly since the fifties, being 23.3 per thousand in 1961 and 24.5 per thousand in 1960. The average length of life for the entire population is now 70.2 years as compared with 68.4 in 1951. There has been an even greater amount of progress in the percentage of infant deaths, with the rate dropping from 28.4 per thousand in 1951 to 25.3 per thousand ten years later, and even more amazing is the 50 per cent drop in maternal death rate in the same span of years, 1951 to 1961.

The decrease in communicable diseases is also significant in examining the total public health picture: the principal communicable diseases are usually considered to be scarlet fever, diphtheria, whooping cough, and measles. In 1900 these four accounted for 243 deaths per 100,000 children. Fifty years later the death rate from these four contagious diseases was only 5 per 100,000 and in 1961 had dropped to an amazing 1 per 100,000. Death rates in the total population from tuberculosis declined from 20.1 to 5.7 per 100,000 in the 1951-1961 decade, and syphilis deaths dropped in the same period from 4.1 to 1.8 per 100,000 American citizens.

On the other hand areas where greater emphasis is needed is the record of deaths caused by cancer and cardiovascular-renal diseases. In 1951, heart diseases of all types caused 513 deaths per 100,000 and increased by one in the next ten years. Cancer was the cause of 140.5 deaths in every 100,000 residents in 1951 and increased to 147.5 in 1961. Yet cancer in a number of states is not a reportable cause of death, and thus the exact death toll due to cancer may never be known.[1]

## THE POWER OF PUBLIC HEALTH DEPARTMENTS

A department of public health is primarily a control agency. The state department of public health must issue orders, compel people to refrain from doing certain things, and force them to do things they would not do voluntarily. At times a state department of public health may find it is forced even to destroy property against the wishes of the owner. It must establish standards that may be considerably higher than those currently existing. These are all control or regulatory operations and not service functions. Frequently they are not cordially received and are resisted by the general public.

Many of the activities of a department of public health border upon exercise of quasi-judicial powers. Whenever the department orders an individual to comply with a certain regulation or inspection rule its action is subject to review by the state court system. If the courts believe that the administrative rule has been arbitrary or discriminatory, it may nullify such an order. The department must prove to the court that the state statute authorizes the action that it has ordered. The presumption is usually against the department's right to take action. Thus it is obvious that the representatives of the public health authorities have a large measure

[1] The above discussion of health trends is based upon information contained in an article written by the surgeon general of the United States, Luther L. Terry, "Public Health," *The Americana, 1963* (New York: American Corp., 1963), pp. 551–52.

of discretionary power, but they are held in check by the state courts. As a result most departments of public health are relatively slow to develop their full potentialities. It is important that the courts take a more liberal position in interpreting grants of powers, and the individual officer must be able to shift the ultimate responsibility to the department and not be personally held accountable for the actions taken.

The police power is the principal source of state authorization for much of the work that is done in the area of public health. It is under this power that a wide range of restrictions, rules, and regulations pertaining to public health are promulgated by the state health departments. Similarly, the licensing of drugs, and their sales, as well as the licensing of the personnel in the field of health, are founded upon the police power of the state governments.

## ORGANIZATION OF STATE PUBLIC HEALTH DEPARTMENTS

While the first organized governmental efforts in the area of public health can be traced to the presence of local boards of health in Massachusetts in 1797, Louisiana, in 1855, created a state health board with state-wide power and authority. Its single purpose was to enforce quarantine regulations that were necessary because of a yellow fever epidemic. Some fourteen years later the first truly state-wide effort in the field of public health developed in Massachusetts with the establishment of a state board of public health with powers much greater than merely that of enforcing quarantines. A year later, 1870, California developed a state health department, followed by Minnesota and Virginia in 1872, Michigan in 1873, Maryland in 1874, and Alabama in 1875. The need for such a state agency was so apparent that by the time Arizona was admitted to the union (1912) all states had such an administrative unit.[2]

The first health departments in state government were dominated by the board type of organization. Even today almost every state has a board of health which is composed of members appointed by the governor for overlapping terms of from four to six years. However, the functions of these boards are normally related to advisory duties or the determination of policies for those programs that will be carried out by the state department of health. As recently as 1952 the basic health organization in thirty-three states was a department headed by a single administrator or director; Missouri and Maine had combined health and welfare departments with single directors; and in thirteen states boards or commissions were the principal health agencies, but these usually had a health officer who

[2] Wilson G. Smillie, *Public Health Administration in the United States* (2d ed.; New York: The Macmillan Co., 1940), p. 369.

was subject to the board's control and responsibility for the administrative actions. By 1963 all states listed a chief health officer in charge of such a department, but most retained an advisory state health board.[3]

The governor appoints the commissioner of public health in 34 states while he is appointed by a board in 12 states and by a combination of these two methods in Arkansas, North Carolina, and Utah. Only in Colorado is the director of the department of public health selected through civil service procedures. Every state requires the public health director to be a medical officer usually with special public health training. As a result, the salaries are in most states higher than other state administrative officials. In Table 21–1 the salaries of the fifty state commissioners of public health are outlined.

TABLE 21–1

Salary of State Commissioners of Public Health—1963

| $10,000–<br>$12,500 | $13,000–<br>$15,000 | $16,000–<br>$20,000 | Over $20,000 |
|---|---|---|---|
| Arizona | Alabama | Alaska | California |
| Iowa | Delaware | Arkansas | Connecticut |
| Kansas | Maine | Colorado | Idaho |
| Louisiana | New Hampshire | Florida | Illinois |
| Mississippi | New Mexico | Georgia | Maryland |
| Nebraska | South Dakota | Hawaii | Massachusetts |
| —6— | Vermont | Indiana | Michigan |
| | Wyoming | Kentucky | New York |
| | —8— | Minnesota | Oklahoma |
| | | Missouri | Tennessee |
| | | Montana | Virginia |
| | | Nevada | Wisconsin |
| | | New Jersey | —12— |
| | | North Carolina | |
| | | North Dakota | |
| | | Ohio | |
| | | Oregon | |
| | | Pennsylvania | |
| | | Rhode Island | |
| | | South Carolina | |
| | | Texas | |
| | | Utah | |
| | | West Virginia | |
| | | Washington | |
| | | —24— | |

SOURCE: Council of State Governments, *The Book of the States, 1964–1965* (Chicago: Council of State Governments, 1964).

The state health office is charged with the administration of the health department and the enforcement of the health laws of the state. Directors

[3] Council of State Governments, *The Book of the States, 1962–1963* (Chicago: Council of State Governments, 1962), p. 145.

of health departments are, as a rule, chosen for a term of office that usually coincides with that of the chief executive of the state. Public health authorities seem to favor the establishment of a state department of public health that is headed by a single director, appointed by the governor for an indefinite term. The department would consist of major divisions or bureaus with the exact number to be determined by the importance and the volume of the public health work undertaken. Health boards or commissions should be restrained to rule-making, advisory, and quasi-judicial activities. Only under special circumstances should such a board be granted any administrative duties. This type of organization is depicted in Figure 21-1 which diagrams the structure of the New Jersey Department of Health.

Professor Kirk Porter asserts:

A department of public health should be under the control of a board. The need for geographical representation on the board is not apparent and there are no clearly defined elements of society that need be represented. Moreover, this is one board usually not dominated by laymen. . . .

The board of health should appoint a full-time executive officer of high professional qualifications. In many states the principal health officer is appointed by the governor, even though there is a board of health. This is not a good arrangement. It definitely tends to deflate the board and to undermine its interest in the work of the department. It also impairs the sense of responsibility of both the board and the officer himself.[4]

While Professor Porter believes in the importance of professional personnel—doctors, nurses, and dentists—on the board of public health, Professor Wilson G. Smillie contends that the professional qualification is not as important:

The most essential qualification for membership on the State Board of Health is that the member shall be a representative, public spirited citizen, who is interested in, and familiar with public health affairs. Many states have designated specific qualifications for membership on the State Board of Health; for example, the requirements that a certain number must be physicians, or sanitarians, or engineers, pharmacists, educators, veterinarians, etc. . . . It is much more important that the members are representative and intelligent persons who have a real interest in, and knowledge of, public affairs.[5]

Another expert in the field, Ira V. Hiscock, has stated that in his opinion a "board of health or an advisory council is considered an essential factor in the administrative plan."[6] It may be concluded that a board is a useful

[4] Kirk H. Porter, *State Administration* (New York: Appleton-Century-Crofts, Inc., 1938), pp. 287–88.

[5] Wilson G. Smillie, *Public Health Administration in the United States* (3d ed.; New York: The Macmillan Co., 1947), p. 450.

[6] Ira V. Hiscock, *Community Health Organization* (4th ed.; New York: Commonwealth Fund, 1950), pp. 29–30.

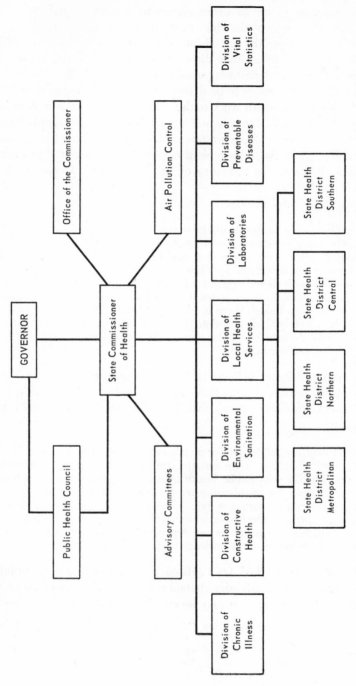

**Fig. 21–1.** New Jersey State Department of Health. [Source: Bennett M. Rich, *Government and Administration of New Jersey* (New York: Thomas Y. Crowell Co., 1957).]

administrative adjunct of the department of public health if properly used. None of the authorities contend that it can be of any great value as an administrative unit but place it primarily in the role of an advisor and consultant.

Professor Smillie wrote, nearly twenty years ago:

No one can predict what the future trend in state health administration will be. It probably will not follow the same trend in all states. As local health services become more adequate and effective, state health department activities should be less extensive. The normal function of a state health department would seem to be consultative and advisory. . . . But the important, in fact the essential, function of a state health department is leadership. For a long time to come, supervision of local health activities, demonstration of good health practices, and actual direct aid to certain local health departments by subsidy or otherwise will be required of state departments in the slow and gradual betterment of local health service.[7]

Unfortunately, too many of the state departments of public health are still in this transitional stage, with really very little progress being made in the smaller municipalities and the rural areas to attain acceptable public health programs. Probably a major obstacle to progress in addition to the lack of adequate financial support is the number of local governmental units with public health boards that seldom meet and public health officers who are unable to gain support for their public health activities.

## FUNCTIONAL DIVISION OF A PUBLIC HEALTH DEPARTMENT

There has been considerable discussion concerning the activities that should be assigned to the state health departments. An outstanding public health authority has asserted:

. . . the chief activity of the state health department is one of advice and aid to the local health organizations, which in turn render direct service to the people. The state should give few direct services.[8]

It is well-established that there is no completely uniform pattern of functions performed by state departments of public health. Some states may have all of the major functions while others may have only a few of the different divisions ordinarily associated with a complete departmental organization. At least ten different functional divisions are usually associated with a department: (1) public health education, (2) communicable disease control, (3) sanitation, (4) vital statistics, (5) public health nursing, (6) industrial public health, (7) dental health, (8) maternal and child care, (9) public health laboratories, and (10) pure food and drug

[7] Smillie, op. cit., p. 480.
[8] Ibid., p. 454.

inspectional activities. Many state departments have other functional activities not included in these major divisions but certainly agreement is fairly wide-spread that at least these units should exist in a total public health program operated by a state department.

## Public Health Education

A good sound educational program operated by the department of public health is essential. Even though the funds available may not be adequate to promote some of the ten major functions this can to a degree be off-set by a superior educational program that will get the populace to co-operate in the prevention of disease and other menaces to the public health of the people within the state. It is obviously highly important that the department maintain excellent relations with the communication media, for it is through these agencies that the general public will be made aware of the necessity for good public health practices and the methods to be followed. Many successful public health educational programs have been based upon getting the information to the parents via the school-age children of the state.

Each department of public health devotes considerable attention to presenting training courses, publications, conferences and, with the help of citizen advisory committees and civic groups, acquainting the public with what is being done in the field of public health. An even more important aspect is the planning that should be done in the future to safeguard the health of the population.

## Communicable Disease Control Division

Sometimes called the division of preventable diseases, this is often the nucleus from which the entire state department of public health has developed. It is in most states still a major work of the department. The types of communicable diseases upon which this operation is focused changes as these diseases become controlled. Originally the major emphasis was upon such common diseases as typhoid, diphtheria, small pox, scarlet fever, and malaria. Today in most states these five have been virtually completely eradicated through the use of modern sanitation methods and vaccination, although periodically a state will be confronted with an outbreak of one of these five diseases.

Greatest stress today is now placed on a different group of communicable diseases: brucellosis, particularly in the agricultural states; meningoccal meningitis; whooping cough; pittacosis; catarrhal jaundice; and trichinosis. In all states, and particularly in the heavily urbanized areas, the emphasis upon control of venereal disease has been intensified. Many state departments either have a separate division or bureau within the communicable disease division in this area. State departments have encouraged and oftentimes sponsored local venereal disease clinics. Federal funds along with the state funds have made it possible to charge minimum fees for this type of testing and treatment. Included in the activities in this phase of public health are often three operations: (1) supplying drugs to physicians and clinics for use in reported venereal disease cases, (2) consultation services to physicians concerning new methods of diagnosis and treatment, and (3) emphasis upon the need for early treatment of syphilis and gonorrhea.

## Sanitary Engineering and Enivronmental Sanitation

One of the first divisions usually established in most state departments of public health is a bureau of sanitary engineering or, as it is now more commonly called, a bureau of environmental sanitation. Usually headed by a sanitary engineer this unit has the responsibility of developing programs and regulating activities in the area of water pollution, sewage disposal, garbage and refuge collection, water and milk supply inspections, and other related subjects. No two states probably include the same set of inspections and regulations under the sanitary engineering division. Most states require that local authorities must receive approval by this division before any changes or new operations in this field may be undertaken.

Since 1948 federal funds have been made available to state departments of public health to aid and assist in the establishment of campaigns to control water pollution. This includes not only the drinking water supply used by the cities and towns in the state but also stream pollution. Regulations concerning swimming pools are also frequently administered by the division of sanitary engineering. Another activity that has been turned over to this unit is the supervision of sanitary facilities for trailer parks and camp ground sites.

Because of the ever-increasing problem of pollution of American rivers and streams many divisions of environmental sanitation or sanitary engineering divisions have established special water pollution units. Oftentimes mobile units with laboratory equipment are used to collect and analyze stream samples, municipal and industrial water samples. Ohio and other states with large industrial plants have in the last decade passed legislation which severely limits the amount and controls the quality of wastes discharged into streams, rivers, and lakes. Usually a permit by a board which has conducted extensive surveys is required before any waste material may be so deposited.[9]

[9] Francis Aumann and Harvey Walker, *The Government and Administration of Ohio* (New York: Thomas Y. Crowell, Co., 1956), p. 252.

## Division of Vital Statistics

One of the routine functions of every state department of public health is its record-keeping division—a bureau of vital statistics. The U.S. Public Health Service has encouraged better record keeping in each of the states as the only means of evaluating the success or the failure of various health department activities. Unfortunately no uniform system has been installed in every state, and the records are not as comparable as would be desirable. The state departments are forced to rely upon the reporting of the local health units, usually the county public health agent, for the raw data. In many counties this is carefully compiled, but even a few counties not complying can invalidate the entire statistical report for the state. Reporting of births has been standardized to a relatively high degree, but the cause of death and the diseases that must be reported leave much to be desired in this statistical area. For example, while it is believed that cancer is a major cause of death in Iowa no one knows positively since the state department of public health does not require Iowa physicians to list cancer as the cause of death unless they choose in their reporting to the county health officer.[10]

## Public Health Nursing

The division of public health nursing, found in virtually every state department, is concerned with the full-time supervision of the public health nurses who are employed by the local governmental health programs. A seven-fold program is often times used:

1. Aiding in the recruitment of nurses for this service
2. Directing the supervision of the nurses employed in the state by local health units
3. Planning programs involving nursing agencies or related services
4. Consulting with non-official public health nursing agencies
5. Assisting in studying the nursing needs of the state as a whole
6. Providing advice and counsel on health problems in local areas
7. Rendering direct health services, usually in cases of emergencies

In recent years several states, including New Jersey, have directed much of their work in the public health nursing area toward providing leadership, educational, and consultative services of a generalized nature for all of the full-time and part-time public health nurses employed by various agencies and governmental units within the state. New Jersey is one of the

[10] Russell M. Ross, *Government and Administration of Iowa* (New York: Thomas Y. Crowell Co., 1957), p. 195.

states that has developed a grant-in-aid program to encourage municipalities to employ public health nurses directly rather than rely upon state-paid employees.[11]

## Industrial Public Health

The division of industrial hygiene, as it is titled in most state departments, consists chiefly of engineering investigations of potentially hazardous operations in various industries located within the state. A major problem in many highly industrialized states is the pollution of the atmosphere by industrial plants. Likewise the presence of explosive gases in sewers and carbon monoxide gas in both industrial plants and residences constitute other problems confronting the unit. Most industrial hygiene divisions work closely with the state's labor agency or department in its plant inspections, oftentimes making a joint inspection. Special emphasis is also given to the promotion of industrial health programs with agency personnel working with the executives of the manufacturing plants in establishing plans.

Almost every state law requires, as does the New Jersey statute, that the department of public health, "encourage the establishment of medical, dental, environmental engineering and nursing services in all industrial plants."[12] In New Jersey the division is making fewer visitations than in the past, placing emphasis upon investigations and control of atmospheric pollution. Most health departments provide consultative, educational, and training services in the field of radiological health, with the programs including detection, use, and disposition of radiological materials.

## Dental Health Care

Nearly every state has a unit in the department of public health dealing with dental health. The work is primarily designed to teach the principles of dental health through motivating acceptable habits of adequate nutrition, to improve the oral hygiene practiced by the children, and in general to promote proper dental care. Tremendous amounts of printed material are ordinarily distributed each year. In many states each elementary school student is urged to have at least one yearly dental examination and a record of the completion of necessary dental work is kept. Some assistance of a professional nature is usually offered, although most state staffs are so small that this can be only of limited extent.

Dental problems involving tooth decay have been called "the most com-

---

[11] Bennett M. Rich, *The Government and Administration of New Jersey* (New York: Thomas Y. Crowell Co., 1957), p. 230.
[12] *Laws of the State of New Jersey*, 1947, chap. 117, p. 807.

mon of all our afflictions."[13] In order to lessen the effect, most states have their division of dental health care give demonstration dental treatment programs throughout the state. The state dental health units have been active in assisting cities in planning for water fluoridation. This program, while still controversial in many areas, has been accepted by most dental authorities as one of the best methods for preventing tooth decay and associated dental problems.

## Maternal and Child Care Division

Since 1921 the federal government has subsidized maternal and child health care and every state department of public health has placed a considerable amount of emphasis on this phase of its program. It is true that the flow of federal money to the state departments has not been constant, and often the programs in certain states have been de-emphasized only to be reactivated in years when more public health funds from the federal government for this area were available. The ideal program consists of establishment of clinics in various sections of the state to assist the pre-natal cases in the area. These clinics serve also as outposts for other phases of child care, nutritional programs, health supervision for preschool children, and those afflicted with crippling childhood diseases. In states where permanent clinics have not been feasible, temporary clinics manned by specialists from the state universities often render an important service. The division in most states distributes a great amount of serums for diphtheria immunization, whooping cough, tetanus, vaccines to prevent various other diseases, and silver nitrate for treatment of the eyes of newborns. Probably the largest function of the division in most states is directed toward the educational measures designed to inform the citizens concerning the problems of maternal and child care.

The effectiveness of the states' maternal and child health care programs is reflected in the falling mortality rate from maternal causes. In 1961 it was 25.3 deaths per 1,000 live births, a new low. The decrease in maternal mortality is shown by the following record: 1920-1924, 76.7 per 1,000 births; 1930-1934, 60.4; 1940-1944, 42.4; 1950, 29.2; and in 1960 only 26.0 per 1,000.[14]

## Public Health Laboratories

Every state now maintains a public health laboratory with various degrees of modern facilities. Oftentimes the state laboratory is closely con-

[13] New Jersey's *Seventy-third Annual Report of the Department of Public Health, 1951* (Trenton: State of New Jersey, 1952), p. 9.

[14] Oswald K. Sagen, "Death, Causes of," *The Americana Annual, 1963* (New York: Americana Corp., 1963), p. 198.

nected with the state university. In other states it is a separate installation and may have assumed the responsibility of supervising the training of laboratory technicians. Some state laboratories may supervise private health laboratories and also those operated by the larger local governmental units.

The original laboratories established in 1890 in Minnesota and in 1894 in Rhode Island confined their work primarily to diagnosis of communicable diseases, and this remains a major part of the work. Specific services now commonly performed include examination of water supplies, air, drugs, and food samples. Some state laboratories do a small amount of manufacturing of antitoxins, vaccines, and other drugs for use by state agencies; none, of course, are marketed commercially. The state laboratory in many instances may be regarded as a reference laboratory to which all of the public health units of the state refer problems.

The Ohio Division of Laboratories is typical of the more modern state laboratories, concentrating its three sections, bacteriology, chemistry, and serology on three activities: (1) the inspection and approval of public health laboratories for performance of serologic tests for syphilis in the pre-marital and pre-natal examinations; (2) the examination of samples of public water supplies and the effluent of sewage treatment plants; and (3) the examination of specimens for the diagnosis of diphtheria, typhoid fever, hydrophobia, glanders, and other diseases, and of food suspected to be the cause of disease.[15]

## Pure Food and Drug Division

Many states include a unit within the department that has the responsibility of inspecting food and drug material produced within the state. In other states this function may be either completely outside the department of public health or shared with another agency, usually the department of agriculture. Much of the job of this division is done by the federal government, for a high percentage of the drugs, and even to a slightly lesser degree the food stuffs, produced in any given state are subjected to federal pure food and drug inspections as they become a part of interstate commerce. The division must maintain a close working relationship with the federal officials to insure an adequate inspectional program.

The purposes of the New Jersey food and drug inspections, which cover nearly 40 per cent of the foods, drugs, and cosmetics consumed in the state since they are not in interstate commerce, are two-fold: (1) to protect the public from misbranded products, and (2) to protect the individ-

[15] Francis R. Aumann and Harvey Walker, *The Government and Administration of Ohio* (New York: Thomas Y. Crowell Co., 1956), p. 254.

ual conducting a legitimate business from the competition of those dealing in fraudulent merchandise.[16]

Usually the responsibility for enforcing the drug laws of a state is shared not only by the pure food and drug division of the department of public health but by all peace officers of the state as well. Most states have a separate board of pharmacy which cooperates with the health department in enforcing laws concerned with the handling of drugs by pharmacies.

The department of public health is one of the most difficult agencies to integrate in the administrative structure. Its activities are so diverse that while it might appear that a common purpose exists, it may well be hidden by the types of functions actually performed by the department officials.

Added to this integration problem is the number of different state agencies that have jurisdiction over activities that are directly related or actually a part of a complete public health program. Professor E. Pendleton Herring wrote:

To list its (the department of public health) cooperative activities would be to call the roll of the departments and some of the independent establishments.[17]

## STATE PUBLIC HEALTH EXPENDITURES

State expenditures for public health, including state hospitals and institutions for the handicapped, amounted to only $311 million in fiscal 1942 but had increased seven-fold by 1960 to $2.072 billion.[18] The per capita expenditures amounted to only $2.35 in 1942 but increased to $11.60 in 1960. The greatest surge in expenditures for public health came between 1946 and 1950 when more than twice as much money was devoted to public health than was expended in 1946.

While the total figures expended for health activities by the fifty states in 1960 is impressive, a breakdown of the statistics reveals that the departments of health expended only $255 million of state funds. The hospitals operated by the states, on the other hand, used a total of $1.7 billion.[19] This figure includes administering programs for mental health hospitals, construction of mental hospitals and other medical facilities, water pollution control, and crippled children services but does not include the con-

[16] Rich, op. cit., p. 227.

[17] E. Pendleton Herring, Public Administration and the Public Interest (New York: McGraw-Hill Book Co., Inc., 1936), p. 342.

[18] Council of State Governments, The Book of the States, 1962–1963 (Chicago: Council of State Governments, 1962), p. 198. The expenditures for selected years were as follows: 1946, $447 million; 1950, $1.042 billion; 1952, $1.258 billion; 1954, $1.402 billion; 1956, $1.602 billion; 1957, $1.905 billion; 1958, $1.909 billion; and 1959, $2.012 billion.

[19] Ibid., pp. 368–69.

struction and operation costs of general hospitals and tuberculosis sanato-
riums. The increase of expenditures over the previous fiscal year was
approximately 9 per cent. Local contributions increased by 12 per cent,
while the amount of federal funds varied from less than 14 per cent of the
total expenditures in some states to more than 24 per cent on others.[20]

In 1962 the states expended $2 billion for state hospitals and institutions
for the handicapped. This was an increase of almost 4 per cent over the
previous year and was the fourth ranking major state functional expenditure. The money spent for departments of public health by the states totaled only 378 million dollars; less than was spent on natural resources by
approximately 60 per cent; slightly over half as much as was spent on state
correctional institutions; less than was expended on employment security
administration; but slightly more than the money expended for state police and general control administration. The amount spent on public health
activities by the state was only slightly more than one-half that expended
for interest on state indebtedness during the same fiscal year, 1962. New
York was by far the largest spender in the field of public health, with more
than $62 million, while California was second in this category with only
$40 million, Pennsylvania was third, with $32 million, and Florida fourth,
with $19 million.[21]

## LOCAL PUBLIC HEALTH RESPONSIBILITIES

Professor Wilson G. Smillie emphasized the fact that it has only been in
this century that complete awareness of the importance of state and local
public health work has been recognized when he wrote:

Beginning about 1900, communities began to interest themselves in a pur-
poseful way to provide facilities for the promotion of health of the individual.
The initial activities were undertaken almost entirely by voluntary, and not by
official health agencies.[22]

The importance of the local public health units is often overlooked by
the public. Professor Mustard pointed to the importance of these units in
his statement, which emphasizes the role of the local health officials:

. . . The state health department is concerned with the whole state and in most
instances renders its service to the people indirectly, through city, county district, or township health agencies. In ordinary circumstances the responsibility
is that of the local government concerned. In event a locality fails or refuses,

20 *Ibid.*, p. 359.
21 U.S. Department of Commerce, Bureau of the Census, *Summary of State Government Finances in 1962* (Washington, D.C.: Government Printing Office, 1963), p. 15,
Table 6.
22 Smillie, *op. cit.*, p. 70.

or is otherwise unable, to cope with its health problems, the state may either lend assistance or assume control. . . . Though the state may assume control in health matters, it seldom does. To do so would be somewhat comparable to the situation where the state militia supersedes the local sheriff or police, under martial law.[23]

## Local Public Health Organizations

The United States has nearly 18,000 local public health units performing health services of various descriptions. Many of these are purely paper units that do not actually exist. Employed by these units are approximately 40,000 persons—two-thirds on a full-time basis and the other one-third on a part-time basis. Obviously many of these units have neither the population ordinarily believed necessary to support a public health program and many do not have the economic base to carry out a successful operation. The Committee on Local Health Units of the American Public Health Association has studied intensively these 18,000 units. After considering these organizations, the Committee recommended that there be a reduction to approximately 1,200 public health units in the entire United States. The proposed units would average about 110,000 people—approximately the number advocated by many public health experts as the size unit needed to give greatest assurances of success. The Committee suggested that best results could be achieved by having some 821 multi-county health units, 36 county units, and 22 city units.[24]

This recommendation presents a gigantic contrast to the present situation. One state, Iowa, with a population of 2,700,000, has nearly as many statutory health units as are proposed for the entire nation. Iowa law provides that each of the 99 counties shall have a public health agency and that each of the 945 municipalities be likewise charged with the creation of a public health unit. The mayor, the city or town council, and the appointed city physician are automatically members of the municipal board of health. A vast majority of these municipal health boards do not have a public health program in operation. Several of the municipalities have full-time health officers, but many do not have even a part-time paid health officer. Few of the municipal health boards ever convene to consider their responsibilities in spite of the fact that the law states that they shall have at least two meetings each year.

Under the committee on local health units' program probably all of the Iowa public health units that now exist primarily on paper would be eliminated and in their place approximately twenty-five multi-county units would be created. These public health units would have sufficient popula-

[23] Harry S. Mustard, *Government in Public Health* (4th ed.; Cambridge: Harvard University Press, 1959), pp. 51–52.

[24] Haven Emerson and Matha Luginbuhl, *Local Health Units for the Nation* (New York: Commonwealth Fund, 1945), Forward, v. p. 4.

tion and potential economic resources to undertake a true public health program with a full-time staff and basic laboratory facilities.

The larger American cities have in recent years slowly awakened to the problem, often stimulated by state assistance, and have established public health units with qualified personnel.

In 1962 America had in actual operation 914 single-county health departments, 324 city departments, 233 local health districts, and 120 state health districts. The northeast sector of the United States tends to depend upon independent city health departments, while single county and local health districts are more common in the southeastern and southcentral states; state health districts predominantly are found in the northcentral and northeast states as supplementing services of local health units.[25]

The number of local major health organizations and the populations they serve are listed in Table 21-2.

## TABLE 21-2
### Number of Local Health Organizations—1960

| Type of Health Organization | Health Organizations | | Counties | | Populations | |
|---|---|---|---|---|---|---|
| | Number | Percentage | Number | Percentage | Number | Percentage |
| Total number of counties and population | – | – | 3,047 | 100.0 | 177,021,000 | 100.0 |
| Total number of health organizations | 1,557 | 100.0 | 2,425 | 78.9 | 167,150,351 | 94.4 |
| Single county health units | 902 | 58.0 | 902 | 29.4 | 69,702,064 | 39.4 |
| City health departments | 307 | 19.7 | 7 | 0.2 | 49,913,173 | 28.2 |
| Local health units (districts) | 237 | 15.2 | 665 | 21.6 | 15,648,281 | 8.8 |
| State health districts | 111 | 7.1 | 851 | 27.7 | 31,886,833 | 18.0 |
| Total number of counties and population with no health units | – | – | 647 | 21.1 | 9,870,649 | 5.6 |

SOURCE: Adapted from The International City Managers' Association, *Municipal Year Book, 1962* (Chicago: The International City Managers' Association, 1962).

## HOSPITALS

Each year one of every eight Americans is admitted to a hospital. These nearly twenty-six million patients are treated in approximately 6,923 hos-

[25] The International City Managers' Association, *The Municipal Year Book, 1963* (Chicago: The International City Managers' Association, 1962), p. 344.

pitals. While all levels of government—national, state, county, and municipal—operate hospitals, the majority of these institutions in America are private. Of the nearly 1,700,000 hospital beds about half are devoted to the care of mentally ill. Of the total annual admissions 67 per cent are to the voluntary, short-term hospitals, which comprise about 50 per cent of the total number of such institutions but have only a little over one-fourth of the total of all hospital beds. Total expenditures for hospitals rose 11 per cent in 1961 over the previous year, and total number of hospital beds increased by 12,000. Although about 63 per cent of the nation's hospitals are small, containing fewer than 100 beds, most of the patient-days of care were provided in the larger hospitals, since those with over 100 beds accounted for over 77 per cent of the nation's total hospital beds.

Many general hospitals, which include nearly three-fourths of all such institutions, are adding psychiatric units to the already relatively large number of services offered. This is an excellent trend as it encourages the patient suffering from a mental disturbance to seek early treatment. There is less social prejudice attached to mental illness if the person is treated in a hospital that is located in the vicinity of the patient's home. Treatment of mental patients in general hospitals has proven so successful that the United States Veterans Administration has decided to use its general hospitals for this purpose rather than building additional neuropsychiatric hospitals.

Area-wide planning is obviously necessary if the problem of needed hospital facilities is to be met in the United States. Planning on at least a state-wide basis is necessary. Interstate compacts, which have proven valuable for specialized problems of mental illness, may be the ultimate answer to the hospital bed shortage found in many areas.[26]

## MENTAL HEALTH

It is commonly believed that one person of every ten in the United States at one time or another needs mental treatment. The rejection rate of young men inducted into the armed forces during World War II focused attention upon this hitherto neglected area of public health as mental and nervous diseases were the most important single reason for disqualification for service.

The mentally ill for many years were treated in much the same manner as criminals, because the nature of their problems was unrecognized. Until this century it was commonly believed that the family of the unfortunate victim of mental illness should be held responsible for any treatment

[26] James K. Hamilton, "Hospitals," *The Americana Annual, 1963* (New York: Americana Corp., 1963), pp. 307–8.

and care that was needed. It was only with the development of the theories of Sigmund Freud that it was realized that mental disorders were subject to treatment and eventual cure just as other physical diseases. Following World War II the development of the new tranquilizing drugs gave some promise of relief.

There is no indication that the future rate of mental illness affecting the American public will decline and it will probably increase. Thus the problem of treatment and care for the mentally disturbed is one of the ever-growing areas of service that the state and local governments must solve.[27]

The National Mental Health Act of 1946 marked the beginning of the modern era of the treatment of mental illness. The National Institute of Mental Health was established in Bethesda, Maryland, to administer federal grants to the states and to assist in developing community health programs and to aid the states in modernizing their mental health treatment methods. This agency was granted the power to conduct research and to make special studies in the field as well as to make grants to states and colleges for training in the mental health professions. The national grants were orginally to be on an equal matching basis, with the federal government starting the program with an initial appropriation of $3.5 billion to be matched by a similar amount by the states.

Three general types of administration are used to handle the mental health programs that are operated by the states. The oldest type of administrative organization still views the mentally disturbed in the same general category as criminals and has a department or board of state institutions which governs both the mental health and the penal institutions. About one-third of the states include the mental health activities as a regular part of the state public health department, usually with a division of mental health. This is commonly viewed as a transitionary stage which is already utilized in about fifteen states, with independent departmental status being given to the mental health programs.

The magnitude of the problem is evident from a brief examination of the statistics of a recent year which showed approximately 600,000 patients in state-maintained mental hospitals. This meant that nearly one of every two hospital beds available in the United States is required for mental patients. Of all of the mental patients hospitalized each year nearly 85 per cent are in state and local hospitals, 13 per cent in hospitals operated by the United States Veterans Administration, and only 2 per cent in private sanitariums.

[27] B. C. Bosselman, *The Troubled Mind* (New York: The Ronald Press Co., 1953); L. P. Thorpe, *The Psychology of Mental Health* (2d ed.; New York: The Ronald Press Co., 1960); G. S. Stevenson, *Mental Health Planning for Social Action* (New York: McGraw-Hill Book Co., Inc., 1956); and Gilbert Cant, *New Medicines for the Mind* (Washington, D.C.: Public Affairs Press, 1955).

The change from custodial care to treatment has occurred in most states within the last twenty years. The need for continued emphasis upon treatment was stressed in the policy statement of a Special Governors' Conference on Mental Health held in Chicago in 1961:

In the light of new knowledge and treatment potentials, a balanced state program for mentally ill should include: prevention and early case-finding and treatment; a complete range of community-based services, emphasizing continuity of treatment; active treatment rather than custodial care during necessary periods of hospitalization; rehabilitation and aftercare services; specialized services for patients suffering from conditions closely related to mental illness, such as mental retardation, alcoholism, delinquency, drug addiction, deterioration connected with old age; research, recruitment, training and imaginative utilization of paid staffs and volunteers; effective centralized responsibility for all state supported services; and involvement of professional associations and voluntary mental health and social agencies in the basic planning and provisions of the highest quality of care for all mental patients.

Administrative reorganization, as implied in the policy statement, has been taking place in a number of states in recent years. For example, Georgia, in 1959, changed the over-all responsibility for administration of its state mental hospitals from its department of welfare to the department of public health. In 1961 New Hampshire created a department of health and welfare, which included the mental health units; Nebraska replaced the board of control with a department of welfare and a department of Institutions, each with its own head; and the Illinois mental health program became a responsibility of a newly created department of mental health.[28]

State mental hospital budgets have in almost every state continued to rise, but the increase is not as great in the last three years as in similar previous periods following 1946. The most significant rises have been in the expenditures for professional services. From 1961 to 1962 increases from 10 per cent to 18 per cent were common.[29]

A few states charge according to the services rendered in the mental health hospitals, assuming the patient or his family has the ability to pay. New York now charges $10 per day for the first 150 days or longer if extensive treatment is continued and reduces the rate to $5.50 per day for further hospitalization. Texas charges $300 for the first month and $117 for each succeeding month. In contrast, Ohio, which at one time had similar charges, has reverted to the basis of average cost, about $5.00 per day.[30]

[28] Council of State Governments, *The Book of the States, 1962–1963* (Chicago: Council of State Governments, 1962), p. 379.

[29] Georgia salaries increased by 18 per cent; Texas, 13 per cent; New Hampshire, 12 per cent; Arkansas, Missouri, Nevada, New York, and Wisconsin all reported increases of at least 10 per cent between 1961 and 1962 for personal services at mental health hospitals.

[30] Council of State Governments, *The Book of the States, 1962–1963* (Chicago: Council of State Governments, 1962), p. 376.

Intensive care for newly admitted patients, of which there are nearly 300,000 each year, is increasingly provided by a team approach. In many state hospitals treating the mentally ill, the new patient is placed in an intensive treatment building while continued treatment is continued in other buildings set aside for long-term patients. As a result of the new methods and the generally excellent results obtained, in a majority of the states the average resident patient population has continued to decline. This has helped to reduce the overcrowding of many state mental hospitals, but most states still have a larger patient load than the facilities were designed to accommodate. Apparently between 60 and 95 per cent of the patients are now being discharged in one year or less.

The problem that has plagued many states is the increasing number of geriatric cases that are included in the mental hospital rolls. In order to control this rising tide, several states are establishing foster, family, and nursing homes for those who no longer can benefit from hospital care and are well enough to adjust to these community facilities. States using this approach include California, which had more than 1,500 patients in the program, Missouri, which appropriated $500,000 for this new approach for 1961–1963, and Ohio, which spent $739,254 on its foster care program in 1960.

Several states are in the process of constructing new schools and hospitals for the mentally retarded children. Other states have attempted at least to relieve the problem of the mentally ill child by developing day programs. Special classes for retarded children are now available in most states, at least for the educable. Classes for the emotionally disturbed children still are not found in many states although several have made advances in this field, including Connecticut, New Jersey, Washington, Wisconsin, and North Dakota.

The Interstate Compact on Mental Health is operative in twenty-four states with the main theme being to provide hospitalization and treatment of mental patients on the basis of therapeutic considerations and benefits, regardless of the residence requirements.

## HOUSING AND PUBLIC HEALTH

In America, the wealthiest country in the world and with the highest standard of living, at least 20 per cent, one of every five individuals, is living in what would be classified by the U.S. Census Bureau as sub-standard housing. Sub-standard is defined as housing that contains one or more of the following four factors; (1) no private toilet, (2) no running water, (3) having only cold running water, and (4) being in such a di-lapidated run-down condition as to endanger the health and safety of the people living in the dwelling.

The connection between sub-standard housing and health problems is probably best stated by Charles Abrams when he wrote:

In almost every community surveyed, the high death and disease rates correspond with the areas of poor housing. Among the factors responsible are lack of sun, overcrowding, dampness, filth, poor water, and decay of buildings. In these areas, too, there will be found a high concentration of suicides, mental disorders, and infant mortality. . . .[31]

To assist and to encourage private enterprise in the field of housing the government philosophy has been to work in areas where private contractors have either thought it unprofitable or ill advised to operate extensively. Some contractors feel as do some realtors that the competition with public housing has been detrimental to their welfare, but a study of the statistics involved in public housing vs. private housing does little to substantiate this fear.

The stimulus for public housing has basically come from the national government with the first national housing act passed in 1937 by the United States Congress. The 1937 United States Housing Act had as its major purpose the beginning of a slum clearance program and implementation of a low-cost, low-rent housing construction program.

This action by Congress was followed by the National Housing Act of 1949 which enlarged the original public housing programs. The Public Housing Administration by 1951 was cooperating with nearly 1,000 communities in participating in the public housing aspects of the program and had another 600 cities constructing nearly 102,000 new units.[32]

The public housing development came under Congressional fire in 1951 and 1952, and a severe reduction in the number of authorizations were made in the name of defense economy. Until the passage of the 1954 and 1956 Housing Acts the public housing programs continued at a relatively slow pace with minimum assistance from the federal government. However, with the creation of the Urban Renewal Administration the pace again increased with renewed emphasis upon slum clearance, now known as urban renewal.

A major new concept was introduced which included the so-called workable program. Congress required that a city demonstrate to the satisfaction of the Urban Renewal Administration that it had a program for the prevention and elimination of slums and blight before financial assistance would be available for public housing, urban renewal, or special mortgage insurance for new building or rehabilitation in renewal areas. The city was required to have an up-graded building code, effective en-

[31] Charles Abrams, *The Future of Housing* (New York: Harper & Row, Inc., 1946), p. 30.
[32] The International City Managers' Association, *The Municipal Year Book, 1952* (Chicago: The International City Managers' Association, 1952), p. 328.

forcement machinery, a general plan for orderly growth and development, and show that it had made provisions for relocation of individuals moved from urban renewal areas, and assurance of general citizens support and participation. By the end of 1954, 23 projects had been finished and an additional 279 were in progress.[33]

The role assumed by the state governments in the public housing program varies. To allow the local communities and local agencies to participate in the federal aid, enabling legislation must be passed by the state legislature. By 1962, 47 states had passed laws enabling their municipalities to participate in federally aided public housing programs. Only Oklahoma, Utah, and Wyoming had taken no action on enabling legislation or had defeated attempts to pass such legislation.[34]

The 1961 Governors' Conference revealed the increased state interests in the public housing programs by the passage of a resolution underlining the recognition of urban and regional development programs. Governor Gaylord Nelson of Wisconsin in 1961 stated,

Most of our states have been content to allow the federal government to direct unilaterally the hugh task of urban renewal. If we continue to abdicate to the federal government in this area, the states will have lost the opportunity to respond to one of the great challenges of our time—the battle against slums, obsolescence, and flight from the city. . . . It is imperative that in the states' plan for the future, this enormous job of urban renewal be given priority attention.

The number of communities participating in urban renewal or public housing programs took a tremendous jump in 1961. In the previous year only 1,000 cities were included in the program but in 1961, 1,850 cities were actively working on public housing and urban renewal programs. The Federal Housing Act of 1961 gave renewed impetus behind the federally aided renewal programs, and in 1962 a similar increase was evident. The 1961 program allowed federal grants to assist local public bodies in acquiring land to be used as permanent open spaces and combined loans and grants for comprehensive planning for mass transportation.

This new phase of the federally assisted programs added still another dimension to the city rebuilding programs which had begun in the 1930's as slum clearance and straight public housing functions, the neighborhood conservation emphasis of 1954, and the subsequent inclusion of industrial and commercial areas in the slum clearance authorizations.

From 1954 to the beginning of 1962 all but five states provided funds to match federal money for urban planning in some 1800 small communities.

[33] The International City Managers' Association, *The Municipal Year Book, 1955* (Chicago: The International City Managers' Association, 1955), p. 336.

[34] Council of State Governments, *The Book of the States, 1962–1963* (Chicago: Council of State Governments, 1962), p. 460.

This aspect of urban renewal—public housing, popularly known as the "701 program" because it was authorized in section 701 of the 1954 Housing Act—included in fourteen states state-wide planning as well as local government planning.

By 1963 about 1,800 municipalities were participating in the federal low-income housing program while another 170 localities were participating solely in state or locally sponsored public housing programs. The total number of dwelling units in federally aided low-rent housing programs under the jurisdiction of the Public Housing Administration was over 646,000. Of this figure, 525,000 were completed and being utilized while 42,000 units were under construction and 78,000 units were in the so-called preconstruction phase. The Housing Act of 1961 authorized the Public Housing Administration to place under annual contribution contracts an additional 100,000 units.[35]

In 1963 five states were directly participating in urban renewal operations and four other states were making loans for veterans' housing, in addition to the seven states that had prior to 1962 backed veterans' housing loans or some other form of renewal operations. The five states authorizing state moneys for the renewal operation were Connecticut, Louisiana, Massachusetts, New York, and Pennsylvania. The eleven states in the second category included California, Mississippi, Oregon, Wisconsin, Hawaii, Illinois, New Hampshire, New Jersey, North Dakota, Ohio, and Washington. Numerous other state legislatures were discussing the need to participate directly with state funds, and additional states are being added annually.[36]

Few individuals would argue that public housing has become a threat to private enterprise in the housing construction industry. In any given year less than 5 per cent of the housing units started are financed through public housing authorities. For example, in 1962 in the entire United States the number of private housing starts numbered about 1,429,000 and the number of public housing units begun in the same year was 28,800. This was a reduction, however, from about 51,000 public housing units completed in the previous year, 1961.

In spite of what would appear to be an obvious need for as much housing as can be produced both through public housing authorities and private enterprise, much opposition has developed to public housing. The most vocal opposition has been, as would be expected, from realtors and private contractors. Disagreement also exists as to how much housing is needed in the United States. As far back as 1948 the National Association

[35] The International City Managers' Association, *The Municipal Year Book, 1963* (Chicago: The International City Managers' Association), p. 353.

[36] Council of State Governments, *The Book of the States, 1962–1963* (Chicago: Council of State Governments, 1962), p. 456.

of Housing Officials estimated a need for as many as 1.7 million houses each year between 1950 and 1960. Other authorities, usually closely aligned with private housing contractors, have denied that the need is as large as that estimate. Several have predicted that anything in excess of one million units per year would result in a housing surplus. The facts do not appear to support their position; as already cited the 1962 starts included nearly 1.5 million housing units.

The legality of the public housing and urban renewal legislation at both the state and national levels has been consistently upheld by both the federal courts and the various state courts. For example, in 1958–1959, courts in no less than seven states ruled in favor of its constitutionality, including the highest courts in Florida, Georgia, Indiana, Kansas, Kentucky, Minnesota, and Texas.

One of the major problems involved in public housing has always been a question concerned with civil rights. In 1962 this point was at least temporarily resolved when the President of the United States issued an executive order which barred discrimination in the sale and purchase of housing financed through federal assistance. For several years public housing had been available under the same rules and regulations which were applied by the President's executive order to publicly financed or assisted housing.

The prediction that this regulation would depress the housing starts has not proven to be true, as the spurt of home construction in 1962 and 1963 continues to expand the number of housing units started in each year.

In future years it would appear that there will be a widening of urban renewal into metropolitan and regional areas through programs of open space control and transportation planning. This will undoubtedly pull the states into a closer working relationship with renewal and call for more state funds to be used in the process. The continued interest of the 1962 and 1963 Governors' Conferences gives credence to this belief of greater state participation.

New York State has been a leader in the state participation in both urban renewal and public housing. The total expenditure from state funds in New York reached $44 million following a 1961 referendum. The state housing finance agency of New York has become a vehicle for financing middle-income housing with loans to private builders of as great as 90 per cent of the total cost per unit. This agency has an authorized capital of over $500 million which was raised by the sale of bonds to private investors with the mortgages as security. In one year alone (1962) it committed $237 million for housing projects that were under private owner-

ship.[37]

[37] Nelson A. Rockefeller, *The Future of Federalism* (New York: Atheneum Publishers, 1963), p. 49.

## BIBLIOGRAPHY

ABRAMS, EDWARD C. *Forbidden Neighbors: A Study of Prejudice in Housing.* New York: Harper & Row, Inc., 1955.

AMERICAN PUBLIC HEALTH ASSOCIATION. *Evaluation Schedule for Use in the Study and Appraisal of Community Health Programs.* New York: American Public Health Association, 1947.

————. *Guide to the Evaluation Schedule.* New York: American Public Health Association, 1948.

————. *Keystones of Public Health for Pennsylvania.* New York: American Public Health Association, 1948.

BANFIELD, EDWARD C., and GRODZINS, MORTON. *Government and Housing in Metropolitan Areas.* New York: McGraw-Hill Book Co., Inc., 1958.

BLUM, HENRIK L., and LEONARD, ALVIN R. *Public Administration: A Public Health Viewpoint.* New York: The Macmillan Co., 1963.

COUNCIL OF STATE GOVERNMENTS. *The Mental Health Programs of the Forty-eight States.* Chicago: Council of State Governments, 1950.

EHLERS, VICTOR M., and STEEL, E. W. *Municipal and Rural Sanitation.* New York: McGraw-Hill Book Co., Inc., 1943.

EMERSON, HAVEN, and LUGINBUHL, MARTHA. *Local Health Units for the Nation.* New York: Commonwealth Fund, 1945.

FREEMAN, ALLEN W. (ed.). *A Study of Rural Public Health Service.* New York: Commonwealth Fund, 1933.

GOLDMANN, FRANZ. *Public Medical Care: Principles and Problems.* New York: Columbia University Press, 1945.

HANLON, JOHN J. *Principles of Public Health Administration.* St. Louis: The C. V. Mosby Co., 1950.

HISCOCK, IRA V. *Community Health Organization,* rev. ed. New York: Commonwealth Fund, 1950.

INTERNATIONAL CITY MANAGERS' ASSOCIATION, The. *Administration of Community Health Services.* Chicago: The International City Managers' Association, 1961.

LUCKETT, GEORGE S., and GRAY, HAROLD D. *The Elements of Public Health Administration.* New York: Blakiston, A Division of McGraw-Hill Book Co., Inc., 1923.

MEYERSON, MARTIN, TERRETT, BARBARA, and WHEATON, WILLIAM L. *Housing, People, and Cities.* New York: McGraw-Hill Book Co., Inc., 1962.

MOUNTAIN, JOSEPH W., and FLOOK, EVELYN. *Distribution of Health Services in the Structure of State Government.* Washington, D.C.: U.S. Public Health Service, 1943.

————. *Guide to Health Organizations in the United States.* Washington, D.C.: U.S. Public Health Service, 1947.

MOUTAIN, JOSEPH W., and GREVE, CLIFFORD H. *The Role of Grants in Aids in Financing Public Health Programs.* Washington, D.C.: Government Printing Office, 1949.

MUSTARD, HARRY S. *Rural Health Practices.* New York: Commonwealth Fund, 1936.

————. *Government in Public Health.* New York: The Commonwealth Fund, 1945.

————, and STEBBINS, ERNEST L. *An Introduction to Public Health,* 4th ed. New York: The Macmillan Co., 1959.

OSBORN, BARBARA. *Introduction to Community Health.* Rockleigh, N.J.: Allyn & Bacon, Inc., 1964.

PATTERSON, RAYMOND, and ROBERTS, BERYL. *Community Health Education in Action.* St. Louis: The C. V. Mosby Co., 1951.

PAUL, HUGH. *The Control of Diseases,* 2d ed. Baltimore: The Williams & Wilkins Co., 1964.

ROSSI, PETER H., and DENTLER, ROBERT A. *The Politics of Urban Renewal.* New York: The Free Press of Glencoe, Inc., 1961.

SIMMONS, JAMES S. (ed.). *Public Health in the World Today.* Cambridge: Harvard University Press, 1949.

SMILLIE, WILSON G. *Public Health Administration in the United States,* 3d. ed. New York: The Macmillan Co., 1947.

TOBEY, JAMES A. *Public Health Law,* 3d ed. New York: Commonwealth Fund, 1947.

WHITE HOUSE CONFERENCE ON CHILD HEALTH AND PROTECTION. *Public Health Organization.* New York: Appleton-Century-Crofts, Inc., 1932.

# 22

# Agriculture and Conservation

In the early part of the 1800's the promotion of the agricultural interests of most states was vested with voluntary societies, some local and others state-wide in scope. The custom and practice of granting public funds to these organizations to assist them in carrying out their work began at an early date. By the middle of the nineteenth century a number of states had created boards of agriculture composed of representatives of the local agricultural societies. In 1853 Massachusetts established by law certain state officers as ex-officio members of the agricultural board. The same general plan was followed in a number of Midwestern states with the semi-public boards being subsidized by state funds. Four major purposes were set for these early boards: (1) to foster interest in agriculture, (2) to encourage the breeding of better animals, (3) to promote the introduction and use of better seeds, and (4) to promote better methods of cultivation. It soon became obvious that greater financial resources than were available to the voluntary societies and the semi-public boards were necessary if the burden for improving agriculture was to be consummated. Therefore, the states were obligated to play a more direct role in assuming the financial support necessary.[1]

Currently many state and county governments carry on programs designed to promote agricultural production and improve the welfare of the farmer. Most of the programs are heavily underwritten by the federal government, with the states cooperating with the United States Secretary of Agriculture and his department. The state governments' agricultural activities are primarily of a regulatory and inspectional nature designed to control plant and animal diseases and insects. Inspections of food, dairy herds, and meat are made by state employees but often in conjunction with federal officials.

[1] Edward Wiest, *Agricultural Organization in the United States* (Lexington: University of Kentucky, 1923), chap. xiv.

564

The basic problem of agriculture is the adjustment of the supply of farm commodities to the demand. As a basic industry, agriculture produces the foods and raw materials upon which the American population and manufacturers depend. It is such a problem that only the federal government has the finances, the power, and the jurisdiction to solve it. The states can cooperate, but the basic decisions on farm policy matters are made by the national government and not by the individual states.

## STATE AGRICULTURAL ORGANIZATION

### The Secretary of Agriculture

The office of secretary of agriculture, or its equivalent, is to be found in every state with the exception of Arkansas. In twelve states the position is filled by appointment from the governor with the approval of the state senate. In Virginia, while the post is filled by gubernatorial appointment, the secretary must be approved by both houses of the legislature. In both Massachusetts and New Hampshire the office is under the appointing power of the governor and the council. In Connecticut this officer is appointed by the governor and approved by either house.[2]

Popular election of the secretary of agriculture is the method used in only thirteen states. Of this number, the lieutenant governor of Indiana serves as the chief administrative official in charge of this function, while in North Dakota the responsibility for agricultural activities belongs to the officer in charge of labor. In ten states a departmental board or commission is charged with the responsibility of appointing the secretary of agriculture. The legislature of Maine is the only one charged exclusively with the selection of the agricultural secretary. The impact of civil service is to be felt in only one state, Colorado, where the office is filled by civil service appointment following competitive examination. A slight twist of an old accepted form of filling public office is in operation in New Jersey where the agricultural head is appointed by a departmental board with the approval of the governor.[3]

### The State Department of Agriculture

The administrative organization that is present in the states for the operation of the various agricultural programs is quite varied. While most states have created a central agency for agriculture and its related functions, there is still present some dispersion of these activities among

[2] Council of State Governments, *The Book of the States, 1964–1965* (Chicago: Council of State Governments, 1964), p. 148.
[3] *Ibid.*, p. 148.

many departments or agencies. Even in some of the states that have undergone extensive reorganization movements in recent years, not all of the agricultural and conservation functions are located in one single department.

The primary agricultural agency in most of the states is the department of agriculture. This department may be headed by a board or commission, a secretary, a commissioner, or a director. The trend is seemingly in the direction of a single director, appointed by the governor, serving as head or executive officer of the state department of agriculture. In some instances this department is provided for by constitutional provision and as a result the secretary, director, or commissioner of agriculture may be a popularly elected state official.

Since the states vary with respect to agricultural conditions, the functions of a state department of agriculture also differ. Inasmuch as the State of Iowa is recognized as one of the leading agricultural states, it undoubtedly has one of the most extensive administrative organizations dealing with the state's role in agriculture, and therefore it would seem appropriate to analyze its agricultural activities.

When the state department of agriculture in Iowa was reorganized by the General Assembly in 1923, a single administrator known as the secretary of agriculture replaced the multi-member board. The legislative act also established three primary objectives:

1. To encourage, promote, and advance the interests of agriculture, including horticulture, livestock industry, dairying, cheese making, poultry raising, beekeeping, production of wool, production of domesticated fur-bearing animals, and other kindred and allied industries.

2. To promote and devise methods of conducting these industries with a view of increasing production and facilitating an adequate distribution of the same at the least cost to the producer.

3. To administer efficiently and impartially the inspection service of the state as is now or may hereafter be placed under its supervision.[4]

The secretary of agriculture in Iowa is popularly elected on a partisan basis. The qualifications as provided by law are indeed very meager, with the principal ones being prescribed or dictated by the political parties. The three mandatory qualifications are: (1) a minimum age of twenty-one, (2) United States citizenship, and (3) state residence. The salary as of 1964 was $12,000 per year. The assistant secretary of agriculture is appointed by, and is responsible to, the secretary. The assistant secretary assumes the responsibility for the work of the department in the absence of the secretary and performs additional duties as they are delegated to him by the secretary.[5]

[4] Code of Iowa, 1962, chap. 159, section 2.
[5] John H. Haefner, "Iowa State Department of Agriculture—Its Evolution," Iowa Journal of History and Politics, April, 1943, pp. 113–75.

The current organization of the Iowa department of agriculture, as indicated in Figure 22–1, consists of eight major functional divisions and one miscellaneous unit. Each division is headed by a single director who is appointed by the secretary of agriculture. The administrative organization for agriculture in Iowa is rather unique in one respect. The state has an unusually large number of state-wide organizations of agricultural producers in dairying and plant and animal industry. These societies actually antedate the establishment of the department of agriculture but perform major functions that are closely linked with the work of the department and therefore are listed as affiliated societies.

## Weather Division

The state weather bureau, a section of the department of agriculture since 1923, has been known as the weather division since 1937. This unit is headed by a chief who is a member or officer of the United States weather bureau when such a person is available. The state division is aided in its work by approximately 285 volunteer observers in each of the ninety-nine counties. The weather division is required by state law to collect and disseminate not only weather and phenological statistics but also meteorological information.

The division works in close relationship with the United States Weather Bureau in making the following services available to the residents of the state:

1. Two daily weather forecasts (four at airports)
2. Special storm, flood, and frost warnings when necessary
3. Weekly crop and weather summaries
4. Monthly weather summaries
5. Corn phenology and corn moisture information
6. Storm reports from towns and townships within the state

The division establishes volunteer weather stations in one or more places in each county, appoints observers at each of these stations, supervises their activities, receives reports of meteorological events, and tabulates all of the data for the permanent record. The division issues from April 1 to October 1 weekly crop and weather bulletins. In addition, it prepares and publishes monthly weather reports, containing meteorological data of particular importance to agriculture, commerce, and transportation, and other items of interest to members of the general public.

## The Dairy and Food Division

This division, headed by a chief, is charged with a large number of inspectional functions that are closely related to the problems associated

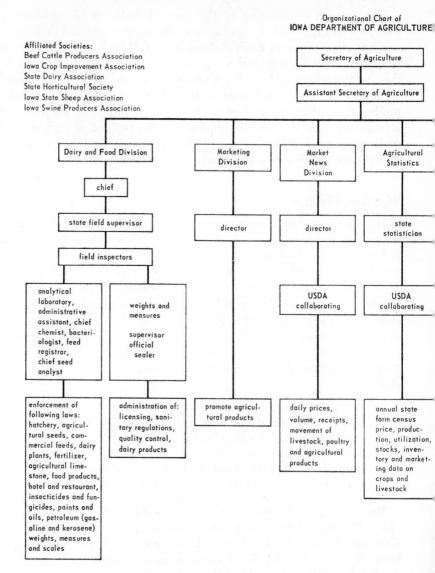

**Fig. 22–1.** Organizational Chart of Iowa Department of Agriculture, State of Iowa, 1962.)

with public health. Of the more than fifty laws enforced by the state department of agriculture at least thirty are administered by this division. In addition, the state chemistry laboratory is affiliated with the dairy and food division, with the state chemist, who is appointed by the governor, being included in the personnel of the division. Also under the direction

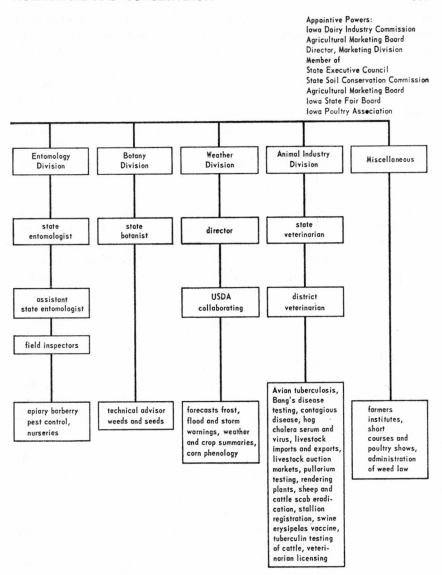

Appointive Powers:
Iowa Dairy Industry Commission
Agricultural Marketing Board
Director, Marketing Division
Member of
State Executive Council
State Soil Conservation Commission
Agricultural Marketing Board
Iowa State Fair Board
Iowa Poultry Association

| Entomology Division | Botany Division | Weather Division | Animal Industry Division | Miscellaneous |
|---|---|---|---|---|
| state entomologist | state botanist | director | state veterinarian | |
| assistant state entomologist | | USDA collaborating | district veterinarian | |
| field inspectors | | | | |
| apiary barberry pest control, nurseries | technical advisor weeds and seeds | forecasts frost, flood and storm warnings, weather and crop summaries, corn phenology | Avian tuberculosis, Bang's disease testing, contagious disease; hog cholera serum and virus, livestock imports and exports, livestock auction markets, pullorum testing, rendering plants, sheep and cattle scab eradication, stallion registration, swine erysipelas vaccine, tuberculin testing of cattle, veterinarian licensing | farmers institutes, short courses and poultry shows, administration of weed law |

of Agriculture. (Source: Office of the Secretary of Agri-

of the chief of this division are the state bacteriologist and five supervisors who are assigned various inspection duties.

The division inspects and supervises all food processing or distributing establishments and all cold storage plants, including fixtures, utensils, machinery, furniture, and other items of equipment in an attempt to prevent the preparation, packing, production, storage, or transportation of food in any manner which might be detrimental to its character or quality. A rather large inspection force of approximately thirty individuals serves under a chief inspector. Included in this group are special restaurant and hotel inspectors, heavy scale, motor fuel, and regular inspectors. It is the policy to make three inspections a year of the more than 1,600 hotels and 6,200 restaurants in the state.

Another responsibility of this division, though not directly inspectional in nature, is in relationship with local milk supplies and dairies. The division assists cities in the preparation of model milk ordinances and in conducting inspections of the milk sheds.

A further major inspectional area relates to the enforcement of the pure food laws, labeling laws, weights and measure laws, and the regulation of other commodities. This form of inspection primarily involves testing an article against certain standards that have been specifically defined by state law. Among the commodities subject to this type of inspection are commercial feeds, agricultural seeds, commercial fertilizers, insecticides, gasoline, petroleum, paints, turpentine, and certain foods. The pure food laws establish standards for such items as butter, certain types of cheese, ice cream, other frozen milk products, and oysters.

## Animal Industry Division

The division of animal industry, sometimes popularly referred to as the division of animal husbandry, is the section of the state department of agriculture that is charged with safeguarding the health of the livestock industry within the state. The division lists its official duties as follows:

1. Enforce all laws and regulations governing the control and eradication of animal diseases.
2. Control the importation of all livestock to make certain that the health standards of the state are met.
3. Approve health certificates for all interstate movement of livestock. The division certifies that all animals listed for exportation meet the health requirements of the state of destination.
4. Issue permits and licenses for the manufacture and sale of all biologics.
5. Inspect and license all garbage processing plants. Routine inspections are made every thirty days by state and federal inspectors of the sixty-one garbage cooking plants now under license within the state.
6. Inspect, license, and supervise all livestock auction markets. Iowa has 174 auction markets operating under state permit, and these markets are divided into three classifications according to the extent of compliance with state and federal regulations.

7. Inspect and license all rendering plants.
8. Enforce the Stallion Registration Law.
9. Conduct annually veterinary examinations for eligible applicants and issue all new and annual renewal licenses.
10. Cooperate in a voluntary state meat inspection program. This proposal was inaugurated in 1954 on a strictly voluntary basis and at the end of 1961 only 35 voluntary meat inspection seals had been issued. The program falls far short of giving the consuming public the protection to which it is entitled.
11. Cooperate with the United States Department of Agriculture in all disease control and eradication programs involving animal health.[6]

The Iowa division of animal industry employs ten graduate veterinarians, with one of them serving as state veterinarian or as chief of this division. The remaining nine work as district veterinarians with each being assigned to an area consisting of eleven counties. Their activities are closely coordinated with that of the animal disease eradication division of the United States Department of Agriculture. In addition to the staff of veterinarians, the division includes a superintendent of law enforcement and four inspectors who are concerned with law enforcement work in matters relating to disease control. The federal government employs in Iowa twelve law enforcement inspectors and trained technicians who work in close harmony with the state force in all animal disease and law enforcement matters.

This division could be called upon to assume additional duties if the United States should become involved in an all-out war in which a defense against biological and chemical agents would be as important as a defense against nuclear weapons and fallout. In conjunction with the state civil defense operation, the division of animal industry would be capable of assuming a high degree of responsibility for community sanitation, waste disposal, and providing for a wholesome milk, meat, and water supply.[7]

## State Botanist

The secretary of agriculture appoints the head of the botany and plant pathology section of the Iowa agricultural experiment station to serve as state botanist. His primary duty is to cooperate in developing a constructive weed eradication program. The work is primarily one of an educational nature with annual demonstrations of proper methods of weed control being given in almost every county in the state. In a typical year

[6] *Iowa Book of Agriculture, Fifth Biennial Report, 1960–1961* (Des Moines: State of Iowa, 1962), pp. 76–83.
[7] *Ibid.*, p. 77.

more than 10,000 farmers attend the meetings sponsored by the extension service. The secretary of agriculture may, upon the recommendation of the state botanist, temporarily declare noxious any new weed appearing in the state which possesses the characteristics of a serious pest.[8]

## Bureau of Agricultural Statistics

The bureau of agricultural statistics, in cooperation with the United States Bureau of Agricultural Economics, collects, compiles, and publishes statistical information concerning such items as the condition and progress of crops; the production of livestock, livestock products, poultry, and other related farm statistics that will increase the knowledge of the agricultural industry in the state. These published statistics serve as the official agricultural statistics for the state. The person in charge of these activities is the state statistician, and he is appointed by the secretary of agriculture, but he is also an officer of the United States Bureau of Agricultural Economics.

The bureau, after compiling statistics in a large number of different areas, publishes and issues monthly, quarterly, and yearly reports. The following list indicates the wide coverage of the statistics gathered by this bureau:

1. Livestock inventories, production, and marketing
2. Dairy manufacturing production
3. Crop acreage, production, and value
4. Poultry inventories, production, and marketing
5. Milk and egg production
6. Prices of commodities purchased by farmers
7. Prices of commodities sold by farmers
8. Grain stocks in storage
9. Farm income and farm tenancy
10. Farm population
11. Land values

## The Market News Division

The marketing news service division, in collaboration with the federal market news and grading division of the United States Department of Agriculture, collects and disseminates information and data relating to the market prices and the conditions of agricultural products raised and handled in the state. In past years this division has performed four major reporting functions in an attempt to keep the farmers informed on the latest market conditions: (1) the daily prices of hogs at a certain number

[8] *Code of Iowa, 1962*, chap. 317, sections 317.2 and 317.8.

of packing plants and major buying stations; (2) total daily volume of hogs received at these points; (3) daily prices of lambs and sheep and the total receipts daily, including out-of-state shipments; and (4) quotations twice weekly on poultry and eggs purchased and the weekly volume received by dealers within the state. The director of the division is appointed by the secretary of agriculture and is an officer of the federal market news and grading division of the United States Department of Agriculture if one can be detailed for that purpose by the federal government.

## The Marketing Division

The agricultural marketing division is one of the newest sections of the Iowa department of agriculture, being formed as the result of legislation passed by the general assembly in 1959. While other states had preceded Iowa in the establishment of such a division, many of the activities now placed under this new division were handled by other sections of the department.

The state law maintains that it is the duty of this division to do those things designed to lead to a more advantageous marketing of the agricultural products of the state. As a result, the division is authorized to: (1) investigate the subject of marketing farm products; (2) promote their sales, distribution, and merchandising; (3) furnish information and assistance concerning these items to the general public; (4) study and recommend efficient and economical methods of marketing; (5) cooperate with the division of agriculture of the Iowa State University of Science and Technology in its farm marketing education and research and to avoid all unnecessary duplication; and (6) gather and distribute information relating to all phases of the marketing of farm products in cooperation with other public or private agencies.[9]

The first program devised by the division, in close cooperation with the Iowa Development Commission, emphasized market development in which a specific target area was chosen. The target area—the New England states and Pennsylvania and New Jersey—is one in which approximately 30 per cent of the United States food dollar is expended and includes many specific items common to Iowa production. As specific activities under the new market development operations, the division developed and issued an Iowa agricultural quality product directory entitled "A Buyers Guide—1961 Edition" which contained the names of Iowa firms and the volume of production available for sale.

The director of the division is appointed by the secretary of agriculture but with the approval of the Iowa agriculture marketing board. The mar-

[9] Ibid., chap. 159, section 20.

keting board, provided for in the same legislation that established the division, consists of seven voting members who represent the Iowa statutory producer associations for swine, beef, sheep, dairy, horticulture, crops, and poultry. The dean of agriculture at the Iowa State University and the state secretary of agriculture are both ex officio and non-voting members. The voting members of the board are appointed by the secretary of agriculture from a list of three members submitted by the president of each producer association. The terms of the board members are for two years, with four being appointed one year and three the following year. The appointive members of the board are entitled to receive necessary expenses.

The director, while serving under the general supervision and direction of the state secretary of agriculture, is required to perform the following activities: (1) to appoint competent and experienced persons to assist him in the performance of his duties and to delegate to these individuals any of the powers and duties conferred upon the director; (2) to investigate into methods and practices in connection with the processing, handling, standardizing, grading, classifying, sorting, weighing, packing, transportation, storage, inspection, and merchandising of farm and food products; (3) to ascertain sources of supply of Iowa farm and food products and publish the names and addresses of the producers; (4) to perform the acts of inspection and grading of any farm and food products of the state when requested by any person, group, or association engaged in the production of farm products. The person or persons requesting the inspection or grading must be willing to pay for these services under the rules to be established by the director; (5) to cooperate with the Iowa State University of Science and Technology extension service in the dissemination of pertinent information; and (6) to make rules and regulations necessary to carry out the provisions of the law relative to the operation of the division.[10]

## The Entomology Division

The division of entomology is primarily concerned with activities in the field of plant pathology. The section is headed by the state entomologist who has his headquarters at Iowa State University at Ames and his salary is paid by the university. The division, while possessing varied responsibilities, is charged with the inspection for insects, plant diseases, and the supervision of their control in the nurseries throughout the state. As a result, the entomology division is concerned with the control of crop pests such as cinch bugs, grasshoppers, and hessian flies, the inspection of nursery stock audits, interstate shipment of plants, establishment and en-

[10] *Ibid.*, section 21.

forcement of plant quarantines, barberry eradication, insect identification, and control of pests that are found in stored materials such as grains.

## AGRICULTURAL EXTENSION WORK

### Farmers' Institute

The Farmers' Institute was undoubtedly the forerunner of the present-day agricultural extension service. The institute idea probably started in Massachusetts where the secretary of the state board of agriculture, starting in 1852, was instructed to deliver lectures in the agricultural regions of the state. These talks were to emphasize not only the science but the practice of agriculture. It was not until approximately 1864 that the Massachusetts agricultural board made arrangements for annual meetings to which the leading farmers of the state were invited. These sessions were to be concerned with the mutual problems facing the farmers of that day.

These conferences became known as farmers' institutes and gradually the movement expanded until by 1910 almost every state was participating in the one- to two-day meetings at which crowds numbering in the hundreds of thousands appeared. The zenith of the farmer institute system was probably reached around 1914 when it was estimated that over three million people attended sessions in the various states. About this time, however, it became apparent through discussions at these meetings, that the farmer was desirous of having his problems reviewed personally by an expert in agriculture. From this point on, the farmers' institute lost much of its effectiveness and at the present time is actually an insignificant force in American agriculture.

### The County Agent

The county agent system was established in Texas in 1906 in an effort to assist the farmer with his agricultural problems. Prior to this time the national government had set up in different Southern states what were referred to as demonstration farms. The primary objective of these farms was to provide techniques that could lead to better methods of farm cultivation in an effort to increase crop production. As a result, many farmers in the South were actually cultivating their lands under the supervision of national agents who were assigned the responsibility of overseeing these farms.

The success of the experiment with the demonstration farms motivated the farmers of one county in Texas to request the assignment of an agent from the national government on a full-time basis. The county even offered to share in the payment of the county agent's salary. In 1914, when approximately 900 county agents were providing technical assistance to farmers, the Congress passed a measure that granted several million dollars to the states for the purpose of assisting persons who could not attend the state agricultural colleges. These funds were to be used in an effort to afford some type of practical demonstrations not only in the field of general agriculture but also in the area of home economics. This piece of legislation required the following actions from the states: (1) the grant of national money had to be "matched" by sums from either the state or local sources, and (2) that all plans or programs for local action had to be reviewed and accepted by the national government.

The county extension agent is normally classified as an employee of the county. This is in spite of the fact that his salary is paid for out of a combination of national, state, and local funds. In addition, he must meet the qualifications that are established by the state but approved of by the national government. His work as a county agent is in turn supervised by the state agricultural college in order to provide for a uniform system throughout the state. In the selection of a county agent, the director of the state extension service in most instances will submit to the county a list of eligible appointees and the final selection is made from that listing. However, he may be removed from his position by the supervisors for any reason.

Wherever possible, the county agent attempts to assist by using the technique of an actual demonstration on the farm. The agent today must accomplish this through a wide variety of functions. The improvement of the land is a major phase of this program. This ranges from the agent recommending the use of new fertilizers, top quality seeds, and nitrogenous crops. They must constantly advocate the improvement of livestock strains and introduce preventive measures to combat animal diseases. Recently the programs of the county agents have emphasized not only production methods but also marketing practices. Many states have involved themselves in actions leading to cooperative marketing associations. All of these activities culminate in the agent instructing the farmer how to keep accurate farm records and therefore general instructions in "farm management" have become a necessity.

The county extension agent does not find his activities restricted only to problems of an agricultural nature. It has been pointed out by Professor Wallace Ogg that the educational activities of the cooperative extension service are actually threefold: (1) those concerned with making a livelihood, (2) those accentuating "living" in the home, and (3) those depicting the role to be played by the citizen in a democratic society.[11]

In the present-day work load of all county extension agents, much attention is given to the creation of programs that will provide some training

[11] Wallace E. Ogg, "The Cooperative Extension Service in Today's World," *State Government*, Vol. XXV (September, 1952), pp. 211–15.

of the rural youth and their families for active participation in governmental activities. It is a well recognized fact that the citizen can no longer be concerned only with the activities of his government at just the local and state levels. He must also be interested in international affairs. As a result, county agents have been called upon to develop adult education programs in the areas of international relations and foreign affairs. In an endeavor to present materials relating to diseases and the techniques by which they might be controlled, county agents have also produced major health programs. Many other programs covering social, economic, and cultural aspects are presented through the agricultural extension service.

## The Home-Demonstration Agent

The co-worker of the county agent is the home economics agent whose task is to teach farm women how to make their homes attractive and safeguard the health of their families. The academic training of the home-demonstration agent has particularly fitted her for this work since she is usually a college graduate, possessing a bachelor of science degree in home economics. As a part of her collegiate training, she has included many subject matter courses that closely relate to her demonstration work. In many instances there have been courses ranging from poultry management to landscaping.[12]

The services provided farm women by the home economics agent are both numerous and diversified.

They provide advice and instruction concerning food selection and preparation; canning and preservation of fruits and vegetables; the nutritional value of different foods and the balancing of diets, textiles, sewing, and the operation and care of sewing machines; the care, repair, and remodeling of clothing; household sanitation; child care; home and community recreation; improved methods of gardening and poultry raising; and a wide variety of related subjects. In addition, they assist in the organization and work of home-demonstration clubs composed of farm women, are responsible for girls' club work where there is no special 4-H Club agent, and work with the agricultural agents on numerous projects of civic and health education. On the more strictly cultural side they encourage good reading, often through special reading courses conducted by home-demonstration clubs, and sometimes organize study courses in music and art appreciation.[13]

## Agricultural Experiment Stations

Agricultural experiment stations are operated in conjunction with the state agricultural colleges or universities. Initially these stations were set up as the result of national grants, but at present they are maintained

[12] U.S. Department of Agriculture, *The Home Demonstration Agent* (Washington: Government Printing Office, 1946), p. 5.
[13] Snider, *op. cit.*, p. 454.

primarily by state appropriations. This has had a tendency to release the states from a large degree of national controls.

The experiment station is concerned with two major types of activities. First of all, a wide range of experiments is conducted. The topics vary from various kinds of plant diseases to different types of fertilizers for field crops. Secondly, the station publishes the results of the more important experiments in bulletins and reports. In this manner as wide a distribution as possible is made of this information to the farming communities of the state.

## CONSERVATION PROGRAMS

### Soil Conservation

The United States has historically exhibited little concern with respect to the problem of soil conservation. The years of the droughts during the early 1930's eventually impressed the American people with the fact that the problem of soil depletion was one that had to be faced immediately. The United States Congress enacted the Soil Conservation Act of 1935, and subsequently the states passed legislation which established conservation agencies and provided for the creation of local soil conservation districts.

These local districts, established by application of interested farmers to the state agency and upon receiving a favorable vote in a public referendum, are headed by an elective board of from three to five members with a total of approximately 14,500 men and women serving on these boards without pay. As of July 1, 1963, there were, in the fifty states, 2,942 soil conservation districts organized under state laws as units of state governments. The districts include 3,653,001 farms and ranches with a total area of 1,719,000,000 acres.[14] An important newer aspect of the soil conservation work has been emphasized by national legislation passed and signed into law in 1961. As amended, the law now permits any irrigation or reservoir company, water users' association, or similar organization to sponsor watershed projects if the authority has been granted by the state for such activity.

Between 1955 and 1960 the legislatures of forty states enacted laws to provide for further cooperation between state and local agencies and the national secretary of agriculture in those activities authorized by the Watershed and Flood Prevention Act, Public Law 566. The objective of the majority of the state legislation was to speed up soil and water conservation and to encourage individuals and groups to plan for more extensive programs in the future. Some states have authorized districts to

[14] Council of State Governments, *The Book of the States, 1964–1965* (Chicago: Council of State Governments, 1964), p. 496.

borrow money, and others have authorized the districts to issue bonds. In addition, several states have given counties, cities, and towns the authorization to participate in watershed protection. Since water conservation is an urgent problem in many states, many districts are changing, not only in name but in character, from soil conservation districts to soil and water conservation districts. During 1962 and 1963, thirty-six states passed new legislation in recognition of this changing development.

## Forests

State actions in forestry administration began in 1885 when four states —California, Colorado, Ohio, and New York—each created organizations for forestry activities. By 1910 twenty-five states had established some administrative unit in this field, and currently forty-nine states have administrative organizations working in state forestry.[15] Seven major functions are undertaken by most of these state agencies. They include (1) fire control, (2) reforestation, (3) administration of state forests, (4) woodland management assistance, (5) insect and disease control, (6) supervision and administration of forest practices acts, and (7) watershed protection and flood prevention.

As recently as 1960 the United States Department of Agriculture's Forest Service estimated that 424,770 acres of forests needed fire protection, while about 402,740 acres were under some type of fire control action. Total expenditures in this field accounted for more than $56 million, with the federal government, under the Clarke-McNary Act, contributing about $9.4 million while the remainder was raised from state and private funds. In the same year (1960) a total of nearly $4 million was expended by the federal and state governments in the cooperative forest management program. A total of 81,283 woodland owners was involved, with more than 4 million acres of forest land.

## PARKS AND RECREATION

### Federal Activity

In 1962 the federal government took a new step in the field of parks and recreation with the creation of the Bureau of Outdoor Recreation as recommended by the Outdoor Recreation Resources Review Commission. Even before the establishment of this new agency the national government had some twenty departments, divisions, and bureaus with programs concerned in one way or another with the administration of national laws relating directly or indirectly to recreation. The more important ones include the United States Forest Service, The Fish and Wild-

[15] *Ibid.*, p. 510.

life Service, National Park Service, Veterans Administration, Office of Education, and the Children's Bureau of the Department of Health, Education, and Welfare.[16] It is believed that the new agency will be able to coordinate better the progressive expansion of national activities.

Each year an increase in the number of persons using the national parks is recorded. The numbers may be in part accounted for by the rapid growth in population, but the increased percentage of the public visiting the national parks and monuments far exceeds the population expansion. Americans having more leisure time and affluence are taking an ever-growing interest in these scenic areas. For much of our population, however, the parks operated by the federal government are too great a distance from their homes, forcing this large segment to depend upon state or municipal parks and recreational areas for their leisure-time outings.

## State Parks

By 1961 there were 2,664 state parks with an area of more than 5.6 million acres. In the two-year period from 1959 to 1960 more than 320,-000 acres were added to the state park systems through large gifts, acreages acquired from other state agencies, surplus properties acquired from the federal government, and purchases. The expanded park system was necessary as is evidenced by the increased utilization by the public. During 1960 more than 259 million visits were reported by state authorities. Five states—California, Michigan, New York, Ohio, and Pennsylvania—each claimed more than eighteen million visitors. The totals represented an increase in the two-year period of approximately 8.3 per cent. Overnight camping in the state parks also rose to an all-time high of twenty million campers.

With increased use the expenditures also continued to rise. In 1960 more than $87 million were devoted to the operation of state parks. Of this figure $12 million were spent for new land acquisitions. In addition, other state agencies, primarily highway commissions, expended about $8 million dollars for improvements in the parks, an increase of 33 per cent over the annual expenditures for the preceding two years. Revenues from the parks likewise increased, reaching a new high in 1960 of $22.6 million, a rise of some 24.2 per cent from 1958. The total expenditures by state park agencies for operation and maintenance, if prorated on a number-of-visit basis, amounts to only 34 cents, and if the revenue is deducted the net cost per visit is only 12 cents.

Full time employees of state parks increased by nearly 11 per cent from 1958 to 1960 to a total of 7,412. Part-time or seasonal employees increased

[16] Harold D. Meyer and Charles K. Brighthill, *Community Recreation* (Boston: D. C. Heath & Co., 1948), chap. iii.

only 1.4 per cent to a total of 10,125. The increase in number of employees is about at the same rate, percentage wise, as the increase in visitations.[17]

## Municipal Parks and Recreation

The recreation services of the state park systems and the federal efforts in this area afford only a part of the facilities desired by the American public. The responsibility of the municipalities for parks and recreational activities is probably greater than either of the other two levels of government. A number of state governments have in recent years worked directly with municipalities to develop a well-rounded, comprehensive recreational program. State health departments have assisted the local communities in the enforcement of certain regulations concerning swimming pools, beaches, and other recreational facilities that may involve a health problem. Other state agencies in a few states have sponsored state-wide training courses for state and municipal recreational personnel.

The expenditures for recreational activities by municipal governments have been contantly increasing. In 1961 American cities spent approximately $604 million for this function. This was about 4 per cent of the total municipal expenditures.[18] It should be noted that the more than $600 million does not include expenditures for other purposes which contribute incidentally to recreational activities.

Municipal parks are much smaller in total area but larger in number than those operated by the state governments. It has been observed by George D. Butler that "municipal parks and other dedicated recreation areas, not including school sites, number 20,417 and have a combined area of 748,701 acres."[19] In spite of the number of municipal parks and recreational facilities most authorities assert that few cities have adequate recreational areas. The widely accepted standards of one acre for each 100 persons is attained by only a handful of cities in the United States. Unfortunately there would appear to be a trend toward a slowdown in the expansion of areas devoted to recreational parks at the very time that the urban population is rapidly expanding.

A national personnel and salary study conducted in 1962 by the National Recreational Association included 880 of the larger cities. It reported that over 10,000 professional full-time, year-round recreational personnel were employed. This would be in addition to the maintenance

[17] Council of State Governments, *The Book of the States, 1962–1963* (Chicago: Council of State Governments, 1962), pp. 486–88.

[18] U.S. Department of Commerce, Bureau of the Census, *Summary of City Finances in 1961* (Washington, D.C.: Government Printing Office, 1962), p. 6.

[19] George D. Butler, "The Structure of Public Leisure Agencies," *The Annals of the American Academy of Political and Social Science,* Vol. CCXIII (September, 1957), pp. 122–23.

employees. The national median salary paid to municipal recreational executives was $7,200, an increase of 40 per cent in ten years.[20]

## BIBLIOGRAPHY

BENEDICT, MURRAY R. *Farm Policies of the United States, 1790–1950.* New York: Twentieth Century Fund, 1953.

———. *Can We Solve the Farm Problem?* New York: Twentieth Century Fund, 1955.

BENNETT, HUGH H. *Elements of Soil Conservation.* New York: McGraw-Hill Book Co., Inc., 1955.

CALLISON, C. H. (ed.). *America's Natural Resources.* New York: The Ronald Press Co., 1957.

COMMISION ON INTERGOVERNMENTAL RELATIONS. *Federal Aid to Agriculture, A Study Committee Report.* Washington, D.C.: Government Printing Office, 1955.

———. *Natural Resources and Conservation, a Study Committee Report.* Washington, D.C.: Government Printing Office, 1955.

CIRIACY-WANTRUP, S. V. *Resource Conservation: Economics and Policies.* Berkeley: University of California Press, 1952.

CLAWSON, MARION, HELD, R. BURNELL, and STODDARD, CHARLES H. *Land for the Future.* Baltimore: Johns Hopkins Press, 1960.

COUNCIL OF STATE GOVERNMENTS. *State Water Legislation, 1955.* Chicago: Council of State Governments, 1955.

———. *State Administration of Water Resources.* Chicago: Council of State Governments, 1957.

DEWHURST, J. FREDERIC, and ASSOCIATES. *America's Needs and Resources; A New Survey.* New York: Twentieth Century Fund, 1955.

GABRIELSON, IRA N. *Wild Life Conservation,* 2d ed. New York: The Macmillan Co., 1959.

GULICK, LUTHER H. *American Forest Policy; a Study of Government Administration and Economic Control.* New York: Duell, Sloan & Pearce, Inc., 1951.

HARDIN, C. M. *Freedom in Agricultural Education.* Chicago: The University of Chicago Press, 1955.

JOHNSON, V. W., and BARLOWE, RALEIGH. *Land Problems and Policies.* New York: McGraw-Hill Book Co., Inc., 1954.

McCONNELL, GRANT. *The Decline of Agrarian Democracy.* Berkeley: University of California Press, 1953.

McCUNE, WESLEY. *The Farm Bloc.* Garden City, N.Y.: Doubleday & Co., Inc., 1943.

MAASS, ARTHUR. *Muddy Waters.* Cambridge: Harvard University Press, 1951.

NETSCHERT, BRUCE C. *The Future Supply of Oil and Gas.* Baltimore: Johns Hopkins Press, 1958.

NIXON, H. C. *The Tennessee Valley: A Recreation Domain.* Nashville: Vanderbilt University Press, 1945.

ORDWAY, SAMUEL H., JR. *Resources and the American Dream.* New York: The Ronald Press Co., 1953.

[20] The International City Managers' Association, *The Municipal Year Book 1963* (Chicago: The International City Managers' Association, 1963), p. 452.

PINCHOT, GIFFORD. *Breaking New Ground.* New York: Harcourt, Brace & World, Inc., 1947.

SOTH, LAUREN. *Farm Trouble.* Princeton: Princeton University Press, 1957.

WENGERT, NORMAN. *Natural Resources and the Political Struggle.* Garden City, N.Y.: Doubleday & Co., Inc., 1955.

# 23

# State Highway Administration

## The State Role in Highway Administration

The national, state, and local governments all carry certain responsibilities and obligations with respect to the building and maintaining of highways. Until the last decade of the nineteenth century these two tasks were primarily performed by local governments. The usual form of national participation in general road building is the grant-in-aid in which the state is called upon to perform the actual job of road construction. Those states participating in such a project must match or supplement the national funds and meet certain minimum standards imposed by the central government, usually in the areas of inspections, auditing, use of funds, and type of state administrative organization.

In the decade of the 1890's the states began to develop some type of highway organization, but it was primarily for the granting of state funds to local units for road construction or improvement. In 1891 the state of New Jersey pioneered the movement, and by 1917 every state had created some type of a highway agency or was providing for a grant-in-aid program to local governments. During the period from 1891 to 1917 the states gradually accepted the general responsibility for road building as the result of the national grant-in-aid programs and with the eventual realization that the local units of government could never develop an integrated highway system. Slowly states began to assume certain already established highways, to construct their own roads, and to establish a state highway system. It was during the decade covering the period from 1910 to 1920 that the number of states with established highway systems increased from seven to forty-two. All states have now created highway departments and assumed the responsibility for the construction, maintenance, and control of certain roads that are collectively referred to as state highway systems.

The centralization movement in highway administration, by which the responsibility for the construction, maintenance, and administration of roads changed from local units to state governments, exhibited considerable variations within several states. On one hand only four states have relieved local governments of the responsibility for or control over roads and placed virtually all highways, other than city streets, under state control. In 1931 the state of North Carolina made the switch of highway control from local to state, followed by Virginia (1932), West Virginia (1933), and Delaware (1935). At the other extreme there are eight states in which the state controls less than 10 per cent of the total highway mileage in 1949.[1]

The responsibility for highway construction and maintenance is dispersed rather widely throughout the states. The responsibility for what is referred to as rural road building generally rests in most of our states with the counties, but in some sections it is a joint function of the counties and townships. In New England the town performs the local road functions. It is estimated that there are almost 2.5 million miles of rural roads in the United States that are under local control. However, states may exercise some supervision which ranges from merely giving advice and recommendations to the point where the local agency does little more than carry out instructions received from the state highway agency. In most instances city streets are controlled by the proper municipal authorities except when the streets constitute an extension of the state highway. Even when a highway goes through an incorporated place the control of the street is shared by the city and the state highway agency. In Table 23–1 the mileage of state-administered roads as divided among the primary, secondary, county, municipal, and other state roads is indicated for each state.

The building of toll roads has been proposed to states as a partial means of solving the problem of highway building costs. Tolls are usually charged on the basis of the number of miles traveled, and the revenue received is used to pay the original costs of constructing the road. Present-day state-operated toll roads date from 1940, when Pennsylvania opened the first section of a 400-mile turnpike. Since that time approximately 2,300 miles of toll highways have been built and financed by a variety of methods: (1) state borrowing, (2) appropriations from state tax sources, and (3) aid from the national government. In some instances a combination of these methods has been used by states. While these roads have been built on the assumption that the motorist will use them because they

[1] U.S. Department of Commerce, Bureau of Public Roads, *Highway Statistics*, 1950, p. 126.

## TABLE 23-1

### Mileage of State Administered Roads: January 1, 1961

| State | State Primary System | State Secondary System | County System (State Control) | Municipal | Other State Roads | Total |
|---|---|---|---|---|---|---|
| Alabama | 7,327 | – | 9,231 | 1,285 | 53 | 17,896 |
| Alaska | 4,212 | – | – | 62 | – | 4,274 |
| Arizona | 4,595 | – | – | 238 | – | 4,833 |
| Arkansas | 10,380 | – | – | 769 | – | 11,149 |
| California | 12,338 | – | – | 1,686 | 1,931 | 15,955 |
| Colorado | 7,832 | – | – | 399 | 18 | 8,249 |
| Connecticut | 2,550 | – | – | 714 | 118 | 3,452 |
| Delaware | 460 | 1,352 | 2,192 | 170 | – | 4,174 |
| Florida | 9,084 | 4,355 | – | 1,710 | 109 | 15,258 |
| Georgia | 14,372 | – | – | 1,865 | 55 | 16,292 |
| Hawaii | 472 | 584 | – | 34 | 2 | 1,092 |
| Idaho | 4,518 | – | – | 264 | 8 | 4,790 |
| Illinois | 10,970 | – | – | 2,256 | 193 | 13,419 |
| Indiana | 9,792 | – | – | 963 | 157 | 10,912 |
| Iowa | 8,797 | – | – | 1,099 | 283 | 10,179 |
| Kansas | 9,612 | – | – | 563 | 237 | 10,412 |
| Kentucky | 19,511 | – | – | 829 | 89 | 20,429 |
| Louisiana | 3,698 | 10,336 | – | 1,194 | 32 | 15,260 |
| Maine | 3,270 | 7,344 | – | 610 | 206 | 11,430 |
| Maryland | 1,729 | 2,778 | – | 267 | 29 | 4,803 |
| Massachusetts | 1,781 | – | – | 604 | 297 | 2,682 |
| Michigan | 8,113 | – | – | 1,126 | – | 9,239 |
| Minnesota | 10,169 | – | – | 1,671 | 1,050 | 12,890 |
| Mississippi | 9,820 | – | – | 752 | – | 10,572 |
| Missouri | 7,860 | 20,204 | – | 1,345 | 2 | 29,411 |
| Montana | 5,571 | 5,167 | – | 227 | 23 | 11,168 |
| Nebraska | 8,890 | – | – | 392 | 27 | 9,309 |
| Nevada | 2,113 | 3,495 | 508 | 108 | – | 6,225 |
| New Hampshire | 1,552 | 2,152 | – | 309 | 108 | 4,121 |
| New Jersey | 1,273 | – | – | 509 | 822 | 2,684 |
| New Mexico | 11,349 | – | – | 569 | – | 11,918 |
| New York | 12,209 | – | – | 1,115 | 1,256 | 14,580 |
| North Carolina | 11,293 | – | 56,668 | 2,955 | 180 | 71,096 |
| North Dakota | 6,033 | – | – | 230 | 28 | 6,291 |
| Ohio | 15,801 | – | – | 2,616 | 241 | 18,658 |
| Oklahoma | 10,972 | – | – | 694 | 189 | 11,855 |
| Oregon | 4,490 | 2,511 | – | 449 | 1,262 | 8,712 |
| Pennsylvania | 12,920 | 25,593 | – | 3,283 | 4,652 | 46,448 |
| Rhode Island | 655 | – | – | 281 | 64 | 1,000 |
| South Carolina | 8,232 | 16,811 | – | 3,295 | 149 | 28,487 |
| South Dakota | 7,008 | – | – | 219 | 112 | 7,339 |
| Tennessee | 7,680 | – | – | 854 | 358 | 8,892 |
| Texas | 53,298 | – | – | 4,354 | 30 | 57,682 |
| Utah | 5,005 | – | – | 621 | – | 5,626 |
| Vermont | 1,949 | – | – | 185 | 60 | 2,194 |
| Virginia | 7,593 | – | 41,190 | 1,588 | 71 | 50,442 |
| Washington | 3,786 | 2,304 | – | 522 | 132 | 6,744 |
| West Virginia | 4,577 | – | 26,141 | 618 | 201 | 31,537 |
| Wisconsin | 10,020 | – | – | 1,474 | 271 | 11,765 |
| Wyoming | 5,094 | – | – | 135 | – | 5,229 |
| TOTAL | 402,805 | 104,986 | 135,930 | 50,158 | 15,175 | 709,054 |

SOURCE: Council of State Governments, *The Book of the States, 1962–1963* (Chicago: Council of State Governments, 1962).

are fast and more convenient, it must be noted that since 1956 there have been no new authorizations of toll roads, and some states have canceled projected plans for such highways. This undoubtedly is the result of the passage of the Federal-Aid Highway Act of 1956, which established the interstate expressway systems. Several very populous states have constructed toll roads, usually without federal funds, but the yields from such systems have in many instances been very discouraging.

## State Highway Department Organization: Two Case Studies—Delaware and Texas

The actual organization of the state highway departments varies considerably. In 1948 fifteen states had such agencies or departments under the administrative control of single directors, and in five others the single directors were at the head of the highway department, but provisions were present for highway commissions to act in an advisory capacity. Four states made provision for a division of responsibility for highway department control between commissions and single executives.

The states of Delaware and Texas illustrate two approaches to state highway administration. Delaware is one of the states in which virtually all highways, except city and town streets, have been brought under state jurisdiction. Texas, however, uses the more traditional plan of dividing the responsibility among state, county, and municipal governmental units. The administrative organizations used in these two states for highway operations are analyzed in the following pages.

**State Highway Administration in Delaware.**    The administrative organization of the state highway department in Delaware follows a rather common pattern. The department is headed by a commission of twelve members appointed by the governor for staggered six-year terms on a bipartisan basis. Each of the three counties is given three representatives and three members are appointed at large. The commission selects one of its members as chairman. No compensation is granted for the services of the members, but actual expenses incurred are paid.

The commission appoints a chief engineer who is the administrative officer of the highway department in charge of construction and maintenance. In addition to the chief engineer the department employs a secretary who acts as the accountant of the commission. This officer is placed in charge of the highway budget, and he is in a position to countermand the suggestions and requests made by the chief engineer in the matters of staffing and purchasing of supplies. No one person is usually named to serve as the executive director of the department and consequently the chairman of the commission has acted as the chief executive officer. While the chief engineer coordinates surveys, maintenance, and construction, there is no one officer, with the exception of the chairman, who can bring all staff and line operations together so that the entire department operates as an effective unit.

The state highway department since 1935 has been charged with the determination, the laying out, the construction, and maintenance of all highways in the state. When a highway runs through a town or city the department has jurisdiction as to its construction and maintenance, but it does not have control of the other streets in the town. Since there is no county road system in Delaware, many suburban streets and roads have come under the jurisdiction of the highway commission largely because there is no local governmental unit that can be charged with construction. In addition to its powers and duties relating to the construction and maintenance of highways, the state department is charged with the maintenance of the state police, the registering, licensing, and issuing of titles of all motor vehicles operating under state license, together with the examining and licensing of drivers. Other duties relate to the charge of all bridges within the state, the maintenance of groins and jetties along the waterfront, the control of beach areas, and the regulation of outdoor advertising.[2]

The department has been organized into eight main divisions to perform its varied functions: (1) state police, (2) motor vehicle division, (3) roads and bridges, (4) Delaware River crossing division, (5) administration and accounting, (6) motor fuel, (7) outdoor advertising, and (8) the Delaware interstate highway division. This last division is an anomaly in the administrative arrangements of the highway department. The state legislature in 1955 provided that this section would consist of three individuals, two from one of the major political parties, to be named by the highway commission for a term of six years. The division is actually an autonomous unit within the state highway department and is charged with making the rules and regulations for the control of traffic using the approaches to the Delaware River Bridge and traffic on all limited access roads leading to the bridge. Figure 23–1 shows diagramatically the internal organization of the Delaware State Highway Department.

**The Texas State Highway System.**   The Texas highway system, exclusive of the streets located in cities of over 2,500 population, is composed of four different types of roads and highways: (1) federal-aid highways, (2) state highways, (3) farm-to-market roads, and (4) the system of local and county roads not supported by state or federal funds. At the

[2] For a more complete report on the organization of the Delaware State Highway Department see Paul Dolan, *The Government and Administration of Delaware* (New York: Thomas Y. Crowell Co., 1956, chap. xviii.

beginning of 1960, the mileage of these four groups in Texas totaled 197,-756. Of this figure, 55,468 miles were under the federal and state system, of which 32,349 miles were farm-to-market roads. Local roads under county commissioners' jurisdictions totaled 142,288 miles.

The state highway department is headed by the highway commission and highway engineer. Internally, there are eighteen central divisional administrative units, one engineer manager for Houston's urban expressways, and twenty-five district or field units. The division heads are as follows:

Assistant state highway engineer
Director of equipment and procurement
Bridge engineer
Construction engineer
Engineer of aid projects
Chief engineer of highway design
Materials and tests engineer
Planning survey engineer
Accounting director
Motor vehicles director
Director of personnel
Engineer of secondary roads
Right-of-way engineer
Engineer of information and statistics
Claims director
Chief engineer of maintenance operations
Insurance director
Engineer-director of operations

Each of the twenty-five district engineers is responsible for all preliminary construction and maintenance work in his area. Each district on an average includes slightly more than 2,200 miles of road. Resident engineers under the supervision of the district engineers are charged with the responsibility for carrying out the plans and specifications of the department.

The administrative control of the state highway department is vested in a highway commission, a policy-making body composed of three members appointed by the governor with senatorial approval for six-year terms. The chairman is designated by the governor. The duties and powers of the commission are as follows:

1. To formulate plans and policies for the location, construction, maintenance, and operation of a comprehensive system of state highways
2. To collect information and statistics relative to the mileage, character, and condition of the public roads of different counties

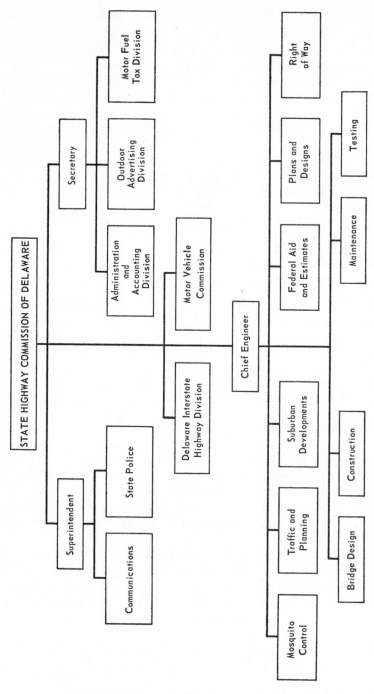

**Fig. 23-1.** The State Highway Commission of Delaware—Organizational Chart. [Source: Paul Dolan, *The Government and Administration of Delaware* (New York: Thomas Y. Crowell Co., 1956).]

3. To confer with local authorities concerning general plans for road development
4. To cooperate with the United States Bureau of Public Roads in receiving and applying federal road grants
5. To let all contracts involving the construction and maintenance of the roads in the state highway system
6. To prepare quarterly statements and biennial reports showing the detailed activities of the department
7. To select a state highway engineer as administrative head of the department

The highway commissioners are customarily selected from different parts of the state. Meetings are held at the state capitol once a month and the commissioners are paid annual salaries.

The position of state highway engineer is the most important one in the department, since the millions of dollars spent on the state highways are largely directed from his office. This official must be a graduate civil engineer of an accredited engineering school and licensed to practice civil engineering by the state board of registration for professional engineers. In addition, he must be experienced in highway construction and maintenance prior to his appointment. One of his primary duties is to act in an advisory capacity with the highway commission and to prepare, with its approval, the plans for the state highway system. Personnel and procedural changes in the department are subject to the supervision and control of the state highway engineer.

*Locating the Highway.* One major duty of a state highway commission is to conduct public hearings in order that the viewpoints of the general public with respect to needs and desires relating to a highway system may be known. These needs and wishes are studied at the local and regional levels by engineers of the state highway department. During these preliminary investigations the officials of local government agencies are contacted in order to determine their reactions to the proposed plans. The highway projects are included on the programs prepared by each district engineer as funds become available. The state highway engineer reviews the district programs and after approval forwards them to the state highway commission for study. It is then up to the commission to grant authorization for the project on the basis of the need exhibited for the facility. Approval by the commission activates the initial phases of work: establishing the location of the highway, acquiring the right of way, and the gathering of the engineering data for design and specification.

*Highway Design.* In the designing of a highway one of the first steps is concerned with the determination of the control points or the points between which the road is to be constructed. All possible routes must then be investigated, and if federal aid is to be used, the federal engineers must concur with the state engineers in deciding the location. The next step is related to the engineering design of the road. Highways that are designed for speed and volume must also be concerned with appearance, comfort, convenience, and safety, all of which must be within justifiable construction and maintenance costs. Whenever the legislature provides for heavier legal road limits different design standards must be included in the design plan for pavements and bridges. In those areas concerned with the density of traffic it may be necessary to provide for divided highways with controlled or limited-access features. The following three items must be recognized in the designing of a highway with a view toward convenience and safety: width, sight distance, and passing distance requirements. The location of a highway necessitates a detailed study of topography, soils, construction materials, possible traffic requirements, routing, and economics.

*Right of Way.* In 1956 the Texas legislaure passed the fifty-fifty right-of-way purchases law by which the counties and the state share equally in the cost of right of ways. This law applies only to the federal-aid primary and state-numbered highways but not to the farm-to-market roads or interstate highways.

The Federal Aid Highway Act of 1956, concerned with interstate and freeway highways, provided that the national government would pay for 90 per cent of the cost and the state cover the additional 10 per cent. The United States Bureau of Public Roads must approve of the routes for these highways prior to acquisition of right of way. Public hearings must be held on any proposed interstate, federal, and state routes and the transcripts evaluated before the actual purchasing of the right of way. The width of the right of way depends on two major items: (1) the class of the highway to be constructed, and (2) the type of design. Most right of ways range from 120 to 200 feet, with farm-to-market roads calling for 100 feet, while some interstate highways necessitate 300 feet.

*Bridges and Culverts.* The design and construction of bridges and culverts constitute two very important phases of the construction of a highway. Some of the more important factors involved relate to the stability of the foundation, load capacity, drainage requirements, safety, and general appearance. In Texas four types of drainage structures are used: span bridges, multiple-box culverts, concrete-box culverts, and culvert pipes.

*Highway Contracts.* All contracts for the construction of highways or for the purchase of materials to be used in maintenance work are let by competitive bids. Any contractor who desires to be placed on the list of those eligible to bid on highway construction contracts must fill out a required data sheet concerned with certain financial, equipment, and experience items. Through this form the commission determines the value of work on which each contractor may bid or have under contract at any one time. Quality control of the contractor's work and materials used on each job is maintained by the state through the use of field engineering test laboratories and by tests of samples furnished from each project. The construction division of the highway department maintains construction control elements from the time that the project is proposed until the job is finished.

*Highway Maintenance.* Traffic wear and tear on the highways and the forces of nature combine to make necessary the use of large maintenance operations. All of the ordinary maintenance of the roads—patching, repairing, and sealing top surfaces—is carried out by state highway personnel. All of the materials, supplies, and equipment required to maintain the highway system is purchased on a low-bid basis. All requisitions must be approved by the board of control, which acts as the purchasing agent for the state. The state operates one central warehouse and a few regional store depots.

*Financing the Texas Highway System.* The financing of the Texas highways offers a prime example of cooperation among the three major levels of government—nation, state, and county. At the same time there is probably no better example than highways to indicate the shift in function that has occurred from the local to the national level, while more and more local highways have come under the supervision of the state and the construction and maintenance of both local and state highways have been influenced by the grant of federal funds.

Almost all of the money used in highway construction and maintenance in Texas comes from three sources: (1) gasoline tax, (2) registration fees, and (3) the federal government. The gasoline tax revenue is divided five ways: (1) about 1 per cent is placed in an enforcement fund for collection expenses; (2) approximately 5 per cent is credited to the county and road district indebtedness fund; (3) about 9 per cent is returned to consumers on refund requests based on claims that the gasoline was not used on the highways; (4) approximately 20 per cent is placed in the state available school fund; and (5) the remainder is placed in the state highway fund. The registration fees are received by the county tax assessor-collector, with the amount of the registration fee being determined by the weight of the vehicle. Each county is permitted to keep all registration fees up to $50,000 and one-half of additional net fees to $175,000, but anything above this figure belongs to the state. Under this plan the state receives approximately three-fourths of all registration fees collected.

Since 1916 the federal government has aided in the improvement of public highways in the form of federal aid. Texas was allotted $43.5 million for primary highways, $30 million for farm-to-market roads, and $13.5 million for urban routes through metropolitan areas under the provisions of the Federal Highway Act of 1944. The state matched these sums on a forty-sixty basis. The Federal Highway Aid Act of 1956 modified this state-federal money ratio to ten-ninety for interstate freeways and highways.[3]

## LOCAL RESPONSIBILITY FOR HIGHWAY ADMINISTRATION

### The Role of Municipal Governments

In American cities the primary responsibility for the construction and maintenance of streets is commonly placed in the department of public works, which in many instances has become a catch-all department of municipal administration. In the largest cities this department is placed under the control of a director as recommended by many authorities in the field of public administration. A second system of organization, which places a board or commission in charge of the street or public works department, is not viewed with too much favor by public administration authorities, particularly when the board is made directly responsible for administration. A third plan is actually a combination of the two preceding patterns in that it provides for a board or commission to determine the departmental policies but creates an executive officer of the board who is to direct the administrative operations and carry out the policies established by the board.

While all the activities associated with streets—construction, maintenance, lighting, location, design—are undoubtedly the most common functions of a municipal public works department, there are other important functional responsibilities placed in such a department. These normally include: sidewalk construction and maintenance, garbage and refuse disposal, sewer construction and maintenance, operation of the water supply system, property management, general maintenance shops, traffic engineering and management of the traffic signal system, operation of the airport, maintenance of the city cemetery, and management of any other municipalities utilities. Many other activities could be listed, but this would merely reveal that while some functions of the public works department are obviously related to streets, many of them are not. The Fifth Edition of *Municipal Public Works Administration* contains five chapters and more than 150 pages that are concerned with a discussion of "Streets and Street-Related Activities."[4]

Streets can be classified on the basis of the primary function that they perform for the local unit of government. On the basis of a classification

[3] The information contained in this section has been based upon Caleb Patterson, Sam B. McAlister, and George C. Hester, *State and Local Government in Texas* (New York: The Macmillan Co., 1961), chap. xiii.

[4] The International City Managers' Association, *Municipal Public Works Administration* (5th ed.; Chicago: The International City Managers' Association, 1957).

by function four major categories of streets are: (1) expressways, (2) major arterials, (3) collectors or arterial connectors; and (4) local streets. Such a classification of streets facilitates the selection of paving materials and contributes to more effective administration of other street-related functions.

General expenditures by American cities, not including the spending for utility and employee-retirement purposes, totaled $13.2 billion in 1962. Of this amount, $1,710 million was expended for highways. Almost one-half of the total was for capital outlays, which include the direct expenditures for contract or force account construction of buildings, roads, and other improvements and for the purchases of equipment, land, and existing structures. It also includes the amounts for additions, replacements, and major alterations to fixed works and structures but expenditures for repairs is classified as current operation expenditures.[5]

### The Role of the County

The county is the governmental unit that controls many miles of roads where the quality of construction and maintenance is of utmost importance to the local citizen. Since counties possess a highly disintegrated form of administrative organization, the major administrative responsibilities usually reside with a county governing body composed of from three to five members. As a result, one of the major duties of such a board relates to that of road construction and maintenance. In some of the larger counties a road superintendent, commissioner, or supervisor is placed in charge of the administration of the county highway system. In many states the county road program must be submitted to the state highway department for approval before it can be implemented.

Since road construction and maintenance has become a very technical and extremely costly operation in recent years, many counties have been forced to re-evaluate their position with respect to providing efficient road services. Some counties cannot afford to have a staff composed of trained engineers and to purchase the expensive equipment that is so essential to road operations.

### The Role of the Town and Township

The New England town still possesses some responsibility for the administration of local highways. In some towns the board of selectmen assumes the responsibility for this function, while in others a town man-

[5] U.S. Department of Commerce, Bureau of the Census, *Compendium of City Government Finances in 1962; City Finances:* 1962 (G-CF62-No. 2) (Washington, D.C.: Government Printing Office, 1963), p. 4.

ager, a commissioner of highways, or a road agent is appointed by the board and given the responsibility for street and highway activities.[6] A number of other patterns of highway administration is present in local government. In many of the township states the highway function has been given almost completely to the county. Two major reasons have been given as to why the township has been able to retain some of its road functions. First of all, it has been defended on the ground that it preserves home rule and secondly, on the score that the township has been kept alive by the use of road work for which perhaps as high as 40 per cent of township budgets have been expended.[7]

## FINANCING OF STATE HIGHWAY SYSTEMS

Governments at all levels are constantly striving to increase the funds available for the operation of the network of highways. As a result, these governments have found it necessary to increase present tax rates, tap new sources of revenue, and stretch the dollars in their budgets to provide for additional highway services. In 1959 the nationwide receipts for highway purposes totaled $10,326 million, while it was estimated that the receipts would reach $12,226 million in 1962. Of the estimated total figure for 1962, federal funds were expected to reach $3,373 million.[8] The further expansion of federal-aid highway funds is shown by the apportionment of federal aid for this purpose in 1964 fiscal year for each state in Table 23-2.

The funds collected within the states for highways, excluding federal payments, show a steady rise from $5,678 million in 1959 to an estimated figure of $6,533 million for 1962. These funds are derived primarily from motor fuel and vehicle taxes, although miscellaneous taxes and fees, appropriations from the general fund, tolls, investment income, and bond issue proceeds account for approximately $1 billion annually. Local government funds, excluding intergovernmental payments, climbed from $2,220 million in 1959 to an estimated figure of $2,460 million in 1962. At the same time it was expected that the funds collected by local rural governments would decline from $895 million in 1959 to an estimated income of only $882 million in 1962. However, highway funds collected by municipalities were to experience a steady rise from $1,325 million in 1959

[6] Paul W. Wager (ed), *County Government Across the Nation* (Chapel Hill: University of North Carolina Press, 1950), pp. 75, 97, 127, 128, 130, 143, 145.

[7] Lane W. Lancaster, *Government in Rural America* (2d ed.; Princeton, N.J.: D. Van Nostrand Co., Inc., 1952), pp. 213-14.

[8] The highway figures contained in this and the following three paragraphs are based on information contained in Council of State Governments, *The Book of the States, 1962-1963* (Chicago: Council of State Governments, 1962), and the U.S. Department of Commerce, Bureau of Public Roads, *Highway Statistics, 1961*, issued on January 7, 1962, p. 334.

# TABLE 23–2

## Mileage of Federal-Aid Highway Systems by State—December 31, 1962

| State | Interstate Highway | Federal Aid Primary System | Federal Aid Secondary System | Total Federal Aid Systems |
|---|---|---|---|---|
| Alabama | 891 | 5,403 | 21,770 | 27,173 |
| Alaska | – | 1,730 | 2,544 | 4,274 |
| Arizona | 1,161 | 2,537 | 4,045 | 6,582 |
| Arkansas | 527 | 3,326 | 14,486 | 17,812 |
| California | 2,161 | 8,403 | 11,603 | 20,006 |
| Colorado | 935 | 4,050 | 4,048 | 8,098 |
| Connecticut | 273 | 1,176 | 1,128 | 2,304 |
| Delaware | 38 | 534 | 1,416 | 1,950 |
| Florida | 1,183 | 4,362 | 12,663 | 17,025 |
| Georgia | 1,107 | 7,677 | 19,676 | 27,353 |
| Hawaii | 50 | 521 | 579 | 1,100 |
| Idaho | 610 | 3,140 | 5,304 | 8,444 |
| Illinois | 1,667 | 10,807 | 13,786 | 24,593 |
| Indiana | 1,096 | 4,849 | 16,712 | 21,561 |
| Iowa | 688 | 9,744 | 33,059 | 42,803 |
| Kansas | 790 | 7,582 | 23,502 | 31,084 |
| Kentucky | 677 | 3,869 | 15,086 | 18,955 |
| Louisiana | 695 | 2,693 | 7,675 | 10,368 |
| Maine | 300 | 1,715 | 2,299 | 4,014 |
| Maryland | 304 | 1,984 | 7,033 | 9,017 |
| Massachusetts | 329 | 2,149 | 2,221 | 4,370 |
| Michigan | 967 | 6,593 | 24,853 | 31,446 |
| Minnesota | 921 | 8,045 | 30,296 | 38,341 |
| Mississippi | 686 | 5,782 | 13,593 | 19,375 |
| Missouri | 1,095 | 8,406 | 23,037 | 31,443 |
| Montana | 1,236 | 5,913 | 5,232 | 11,145 |
| Nebraska | 492 | 5,461 | 17,108 | 22,612 |
| Nevada | 540 | 2,199 | 2,791 | 4,990 |
| New Hampshire | 203 | 1,219 | 1,626 | 2,845 |
| New Jersey | 294 | 1,772 | 2,126 | 3,898 |
| New Mexico | 1,004 | 3,901 | 5,436 | 9,394 |
| New York | 1,207 | 8,772 | 18,666 | 29,380 |
| North Carolina | 766 | 6,899 | 25,618 | 35,517 |
| North Dakota | 587 | 4,159 | 13,187 | 17,365 |
| Ohio | 1,451 | 7,920 | 17,871 | 25,791 |
| Oklahoma | 798 | 7,567 | 12,647 | 20,214 |
| Oregon | 695 | 3,935 | 7,492 | 11,427 |
| Pennsylvania | 1,611 | 7,602 | 13,417 | 21,019 |
| Rhode Island | 69 | 461 | 469 | 930 |
| South Carolina | 746 | 4,818 | 16,875 | 21,691 |
| South Dakota | 718 | 5,498 | 12,426 | 17,924 |
| Tennessee | 1,096 | 5,622 | 10,910 | 16,532 |
| Texas | 3,025 | 15,967 | 30,822 | 46,789 |
| Utah | 904 | 2,280 | 3,700 | 5,980 |
| Vermont | 343 | 1,263 | 1,836 | 3,099 |
| Virginia | 1,062 | 4,767 | 18,511 | 23,278 |
| Washington | 672 | 3,765 | 10,248 | 14,013 |
| West Virginia | 398 | 2,471 | 10,721 | 13,192 |
| Wisconsin | 480 | 5,984 | 18,833 | 24,817 |
| Wyoming | 1,006 | 3,420 | 2,377 | 5,797 |
| TOTAL | 40,610 | 243,317 | 594,625 | 837,942 |

SOURCE: Council of State Governments, *The Book of the States, 1962–1963* (Chicago: Council of State Governments, 1962).

to an anticipated $1,478 million in 1962. The major sources of local highway funds are property taxes and assessments, general fund appropriations, and bond issue proceeds.

In 1959 the federal-aid reimbursements to the states totaled $3,059 million and was expected to reach $3,277 million in 1962. The states in 1959 diverted to local governments $1,176 million, while a transfer of $1,312 million was expected for 1962. It was anticipated that the states would expend or administer about two-thirds of the total highway funds in both 1961 and 1962.

The total long-term debt that was outstanding for highways at the end of 1959 was $12,700 million, and it was estimated that by the end of 1962 the total outstanding debt would reach $14,400 million. Of this last total the obligations of the states would account for $10,200 million and those of the local governments the remaining $4,200 million. This total debt was almost equally divided between toll and toll-free facilities.

The continued demands upon state highway budgets have forced many states to increase already existing taxes. The gasoline tax has been a favorite source and several states in recent legislative sessions have raised this tax. Alaska increased its gasoline tax from 7 to 8 cents; Missouri from 3 to 5 cents; Delaware and New Jersey from 5 to 6 cents; Pennsylvania from 5 to 7 cents; California from 6 to 7; Washington from 6½ to 7½; and Arizona from 5 to 6 cents. The average gas tax in most states at the present time is between 6 and 7 cents per gallon. Some state legislatures recognize that they cannot raise this tax too often or too much at any one time without encountering considerable public opposition, particularly since the federal government also levies 4 cents per gallon gas tax.

A few states have recently acted to divert highway funds into the general fund or to some other state activities. The motor fuel tax increase of two cents in 1960 in Alaska was placed in the general fund while the one cent raise in New Jersey was to be used for general budget-balancing and to subsidize rail commuter service. Proposals to allow highway fund diversion were rejected by the legislatures of California, Idaho, Massachusetts, and Texas. A two-year diversion of highway funds to school purposes was ended in Connecticut.

The states do not always finance their highway construction programs on a pay-as-you-go basis. Frequently they are forced to resort to the issuing of bonds to pay for highway construction. In one two-year period (1960–1961) nearly one-fourth of the states had bond issues for various highway purposes. The bond issues during that period ranged from $300 million in Pennsylvania for interstate highway systems to $4 million in Oregon for state highways.

In 1960 the direct general expenditures of state and local governments for total highway expenses was $9,427.7 million. Alaska spent the smallest

amount for highways—$7.4 million—while New York expended the largest
sum—$920.2 million.[9] For the same year the per capita direct general ex-
penditure of state and local governments for highways was $52.38 through-
out the United States, with the per capita expenditure being lowest in
Alaska—$32.46 and with Wyoming spending the top figure of $140.06.[10]

## Federal Participation in Highway Operations

The construction and maintenance of highways were originally a responsibility of local units of government, but since about the last decade
of the nineteenth century the states have shared in these activities. The
national government, early in the nineteenth century, did establish a policy of giving to new states the proceeds from the sale of public lands for
the purposes of building roads.[11] The Congress in 1806 approved an initial
appropriation of $30,000 for the Cumberland Road, which was to serve as
a national highway connecting Cumberland, Maryland, and Steubenville,
Ohio. This important road was eventually to extend as far as southern
Illinois and to account for construction appropriations of nearly $7 mil-
lion. For many years this roadway was under national control and was
referred to as the Great National Pike. This phase of highway construction
by the national government was halted with the development of railroad
transportation in the 1840's.

The next important federal action in the area of highway transportation
occurred in 1893, when the office of road inquiry was established in the
department of agriculture. This agency was eventually to become known
as the bureau of public roads and remained a part of the agriculture department until 1939, when it was transferred to the Federal Works Agency.
Ten years later, in 1949. the bureau became a part of the Department of
Commerce. The bureau's functions from 1893 to 1912 were restricted to
research and investigation, but in the latter year the Congress authorized
$500,000 for an experimental project in rural post-road construction.

The national participation in the development of highway programs
was re-established with the passage of the Federal-Aid Road Act of 1916.
This measure provided for a five-year highway grant-in-aid appropriation
of $75 million that was to be allocated on the basis of population, area,
and post-road mileage within each state, with each factor being given
equal weight. As a result, the sparsely populated states benefited under
the item of area while states like New York gained under the population

[9] Council of State Governments, *The Book of the States, 1962–1963* (Chicago:
Council of State Governments, 1962), p. 217.

[10] *Ibid.*, p. 218.

[11] John A. Fairlie and Charles M. Kneier, *County Government and Administration*
(New York: Appleton-Century-Crofts, Inc., 1930), p. 351.

factor.[12] The mileage of post roads was included on the basis that the national government should pay for its use of the highways and that this type of aid would fulfill to a degree the constitutional obligation of the national government to maintain post offices and post roads. This act also aided the secretary of agriculture, in extending the federal funds for highway construction, to cooperate with the state highway departments, and a later statute maintained that these state departments must possess "adequate powers" and be "suitably equipped and organized." This was a definite attempt on behalf of the national government to ensure that the states would establish a central highway agency that could be capable of coping with various road problems. As a result, within one year after the Act of 1916 became effective, sixteen states established state highway departments.

The next major federal grant-in-aid measure for roads was the Highway Act of 1921, which provided for several important items. The law stated that future federal road grants and the matching state funds must be used upon a connected highway system that was limited in the beginning to 7 per cent of the total road mileage in each state, but additions of 1 per cent were permitted as the accepted program neared completion. The net result was the development of a network of main roads now referred to as the federal-aid system with standard route numbers. In addition, the act provided that each state should receive at least one-half of 1 per cent of the total highway grants to the states. Also it was made mandatory for those states receiving this type of federal highway aid to administer directly the nationally-assisted projects and not delegate the work to local governments with the state merely supervising its administration. This measure of 1921 extended a phase of national control over state decisions regarding highway construction when it was provided that the states must submit the plans designating those portions of their highways for federal aid and that these plans must be approved by federal authorities before the funds could be allocated. The approval was formerly made by the secretary of agriculture but is now given by the bureau of public roads in the Department of Commerce.

For several years the annual federal subsidy to the states of $75 million dollars, as provided for in the Act of 1916, continued unchanged. The annual grant in 1931 was increased to $125 million, and by 1938 the sum had increased to more than $300 million, but by 1941 it had dropped to $125 million. World War II brought a temporary halt to the federal-aid program for highways.

Before the termination of World War II the Federal-Aid Highway Act of 1944 was passed. This measure extended national aid to the devel-

[12] Henry J. Bittermann, *State and Federal Grants-in-Aid* (Chicago: Mentzer, Bush & Co., 1938), p. 508.

opment of certain secondary roads and city streets, whereas the federal government previously had confined its aid to the system of primary highways.[13] In the same year the Congress directed the Public Roads Administration in conjunction with the state highway departments to select the major routes that would connect the chief metropolitan areas of the United States and were to be known as the national system of interstate highways. Also in 1944 the Congress commanded the Public Roads Administration to combine the principal secondary and feeder roads, rural free-delivery mail routes, and public school bus routes into a secondary highway system.

The Commission on Intergovernmental Relations, in its report of 1955, reviewed the allocation of responsibilities for highways and stipulated that the primary responsibility for the development of highways rested with the states and their subdivisions. However, it was pointed out that the national interest is of such a nature as to justify the federal government in certain conditions to encourage and supplement state action. The Commission in turn produced the following recommendations:

1. The actual construction and maintenance of highways should be performed by the states and their subdivisions.
2. The present federal-aid highway program should be continued and the appropriation of funds increased. The increase in funds should give recognition to the national responsibility for highways that would be of major importance to the national security, including any special needs for civil defense and to provide for an accelerated improvement of highways in order to insure a balanced program to serve the needs of the expanding economy.
3. The expanded highway program should be financed substantially on a pay-as-you-go basis and that the Congress should provide the additional revenues for this purpose primarily from increased motor fuel taxes.
4. A reduction in the degree and extent of the federal supervision that accompanies highway grants-in-aid.
5. The repeal of the provisions of the Hayden-Cartwright Act that require the states to spend certain amounts of specific taxes for highway purposes.[14]

Roads and highways are classified by both the national and state governments. In many instances the financial system by which a road will be constructed is determined by its classification. In order to establish a uniform basis for discussion, the designation of roads in this chapter will follow basically those categories established under federal grants-in-aid.

[13] Charles L. Dearing and Wilfred Owen, *National Transportation Policy* (Washington: The Brookings Institution, 1949), p. 159.
[14] The Commission on Intergovernmental Relations, *A Report to the President for Transmittal to the Congress* (Washington, D.C.: Government Printing Office, 1955), pp. 216–20.

However, it should be pointed out that states usually produce their own systems of classification.

The national government grants four different types of funds for highway construction but does not provide any money to local units for the maintenance of roads. On the basis of the funds provided, the four types are classified as "federal primary," "federal secondary," "federal urban," and the most recent one, "federal interstate system."

The first three categories comprise a general classification popularly referred to as the ABC system. This system contains approximately 800,000 miles of roads and streets and accounts for approximately 24 per cent of total national mileage and carries about one-half of all traffic. Since this older program continues to receive strong support at the local level, the possibility of diminishing its federal support seems quite unlikely even in spite cf the present-day emphasis on the interstate expressways. It should be noted, however, that the system of classification that is used by the national government is not always followed in the states.

The national government allocates its highway construction funds on a formula based on the number of miles of road, population density, and geography. As a result, the amounts granted to the states on a per-capita basis are not equal, and Arizona, with its smaller population but extensive road mileage, receives far more for its roads per capita than does California. The source of federal funds for highway construction purposes is the federal gasoline tax, but for a number of years the revenue from this tax has not been specifically allocated to road building. Rather, the Congress has designated an amount that bears no immediate relationship to the total collected under the gasoline tax.

The national government determines into which one of the four categories a road will be placed. For the first three classifications—federal primary, federal secondary, and federal urban—the federal government contributes a subsidy that approximates 50 per cent of the cost of construction. For the new interstate system the grant provides for 90 per cent of the construction costs. In order to qualify for a grant from the federal primary or secondary classifications a state must match equally the available funds. For federal urban roads the state and urban community will usually put up 25 per cent each to meet the 50 per cent granted by the national government. Because of the tremendous per-mile cost of the four-lane highways in the interstate system, the national government is requiring the states to contribute only 10 per cent of the construction costs. Although in many states from one-quarter to one-third of the budget will be allocated to highways and roads, only a small percentage is granted for new construction purposes, since most of the funds must be spent on highway maintenance. The total mileage of the federal aid highway system by state is indicated in Table 23–2.

The Federal Aid Highway Act of 1956 provided for the National System of Interstate and Defense Highways to consist of a 41,000-mile network of superhighways. It has been estimated that this new system will carry approximately 21 per cent of all highway traffic in the United States but will account for only slightly more than 1 per cent of all road mileage. By the middle of 1963 almost 15,000 miles of the interstate system were open to traffic, while another 5,000 miles were under construction. The national government has departed from its traditional 50-50 basis for sharing with the states and has agreed to finance 90 per cent of the cost of the new interstate expressway system. The states are free to determine whether the remaining 10 per cent will be financed totally by the state or will be shared with local units. On this basis the national government will be expending about $37 billion, with the total cost estimates at approximately $41 billion or an average of $1 million per mile.[15]

Twenty states have entered into agreements with the Secretary of Commerce to regulate billboard advertising along the interstate system.[16] In the Federal-Aid Highway Amendments Act of 1963 the Congress extended until July 1, 1965, the federal incentive bonus of one-half of 1 per cent of the state's allotment to any state agreeing to regulate billboard advertising along the interstate system. Only three states—Kentucky, Maine, and Virginia—have received the federal bonus payments of their interstate federal-aid allocations for such control.[17] To qualify for the bonus, billboards must be prohibited for a distance of 660 feet on either side of the right-of-way. Many states have refused to enter into the agreement since some state highway officials maintain that it would be more expensive to procure the necessary easements from the landowners for the billboard ban than the federal bonus would produce. Efforts within the Congress to provide for a larger bonus have been unsuccessful.

## HIGHWAY SAFETY

In 1962, 40,900 traffic deaths occurred in the United States, which was an all-time high. Injuries disabled another 1,500,000 Americans. The National Safety Council estimated the total monetary cost of traffic accidents for the year at $6.5 billion.

As traffic miles increase, the accident death problem is certain to grow. By 1969 vehicle miles traveled will reach approximately one trillion, which

[15] Council of State Governments, *The Book of the States, 1962–1963* (Chicago: Council of State Governments, 1962), p. 335.

[16] Connecticut, Delaware, Hawaii, Kentucky, Maine, Maryland, Nebraska, New Hampshire, New Jersey, New York, North Dakota, Ohio, Oregon, Pennsylvania, Rhode Island, Vermont, Virginia, Washington, West Virginia, and Wisconsin.

[17] Council of State Governments, *The Book of the States, 1964–1965* (Chicago: Council of State Governments, 1964), p. 355.

at the 1960 death rate of 5.3 for each 100 million miles would mean a death toll on the nation's highways of 53,000. However, if the present trend of reducing the number of deaths per 100 million miles traveled continues, the mileage death rate should be at 3.9. This progress would save nearly 80,000 lives in the 1960's.

The annual traffic inventory, a program administered by the National Safety Council, measures the extent to which the states and cities have put into effect the action program suggested by the various White House conferences on highway safety. For the year 1960 the inventory revealed that the states were achieving 70 per cent of the minimum action program, while cities were only at 54 per cent.

In order to curb the highway accident rate it is essential that all possible groups work together. The states, cities, and the national government all must take every possible step toward safety on the nation's highways. The major federal activity in highway safety is in providing 90 per cent of the financing of the National System of Interstate and Defense Highways and in supervising its construction according to the most advanced design standards. It is estimated that upon completion it will save nearly 9,000 lives each year. The states must follow the national government's lead in using the same high standards in the construction of the major state highways. Law enforcement by both the state and local governments must be intensified. The reckless driver must be kept from slaughtering the travelers of the highways. Citizen action groups must be encouraged. Research must be increased on traffic safety. The medical profession must continue its increasing degree of interest in traffic accident prevention. Public education in the value of seat belts and other life-saving features must be promoted.[18]

In 1962 approximately 78.6 million vehicles were registered in the United States. This was an increase of 3.7 per cent over the previous year, and the rate of increase each year appeared to be relatively constant. The 1962 travel totaled 767 billion vehicle-miles, again an increase of nearly 4 per cent over the 1961 mileage figure. By 1975 it is estimated that there will be over 100 million vehicles registered in the United States and they will travel more than 1 trillion miles each year.

## STATE CONCERN FOR AVIATION

Aviation is another form of transportation that is receiving a considerable degree of interest not only from state and local governments but also from the national government. On April 24, 1961, the late President

[18] Council of State Governments, *The Book of the States, 1962–1963* (Chicago: Council of State Governments, 1962), pp. 346–49.

Kennedy in a letter to the Speaker of the House, in outlining the major problems facing aviation, maintained that, with respect to airports:

Continuing the program of federal assistance to airports is essential to our national security, passenger safety and economic growth. Air commerce . . . has grown so rapidly that many existing airports are both overburdened and underequipped. The increase in the speed, weight, and capacity of jet age aircraft has already antiquated many existing airports and threatens to outmode many more.

In addition, the expansion in general aviation has created a special need for the development of general aviation airports, particularly where this is necessary to relieve congestion at airports having a high density of traffic and serving other segments of aviation. For this reason, I have recommended that funds be specifically allocated to the development of such airports.

The President recommended that the Congress approve a five-year extension of the Federal Airport Act with a $75 million obligational authority annually.

A national airport survey conducted in 1960 indicated that during the four-year period ending June 30, 1965, a total of 3,579 publicly owned airports planned 1,464 airport projects with an estimated cost of $1,125,-044,435. Of this amount it was anticipated that only $588,065,224 would be available from state and local sources.[19]

The Federal Airport Act, which expired June 30, 1961, was extended by the Congress for three years, until June 30, 1964, rather than five as recommended by the President, the Federal Aviation Agency, and the aircraft industry. The Congress also required that the appropriation of $75 million per year would be approved annually by the appropriations committees. Of the annual appropriation, $49,875,000 was available for distribution to the states on an area-population basis; $1,500,000 to insular areas; and $16,625,000 to the Federal Aviation Agency Administrator's discretionary fund, which could be spent on airport projects in any state; and a $7 million special discretionary fund to develop airports in an effort to serve general aviation and relieve congestion at airports having high density of traffic serving other segments of aviation.

States over the past two decades have appropriated substantial sums for the operation, maintenance, and development of airports. In 1960 the state funds for this purpose totaled approximately $21.3 million.

## BIBLIOGRAPHY

AMERICAN ASSOCIATION OF STATE HIGHWAY OFFICIALS. *Preliminary Report of the Special Committee for the Study of Highway Finance Problems.* Wash-

[19] Council of State Governments, *The Book of the States, 1962–1963* (Chicago: Council of State Governments, 1962), p. 355.

ington, D.C.: American Association of State Highway Officials, September, 1949.

———. *A Policy of Arterial Highways in Urban Areas.* Washington, D.C.: American Association of State Highway Officials, 1957.

BURCH, PHILIP H., JR. *Highway Revenue and Expenditure Policy in the United States.* New Brunswick, N.J.: Rutgers University Press, 1962.

COMMISION ON INTERGOVERNMENTAL RELATIONS. *A Study Committee Report on Federal Aid to Highways.* Washington, D.C.: Government Printing Office, 1955.

CONGRESSIONAL JOINT COMMITTEE ON THE ECONOMIC REPORT. *Highways and the Nation's Economy.* Washington, D.C.: Joint Committee Print, 81st Cong., 1st Sess., 1949.

COUNCIL OF STATE GOVERNMENTS. *Highway Safety, Motor Truck Regulation.* Chicago: Council of State Governments, 1950.

———. *Highway Legislation in 1955.* Chicago: Council of State Governments, 1956.

DEARING, CHARLES L., and OWEN, WILFRED. *National Transportation Policy.* Washington, D.C.: The Brookings Institution, 1949.

———. *Toll Roads and the Problem of Highway Modernization.* Washington, D.C.: The Brookings Institution, 1951.

FEDERAL WORKS AGENCY, PUBLIC ROADS ADMINISTRATION. *Highway Practice in The United States of America.* Washington, D.C.: Government Printing Office, 1949.

FITCH, LYLE C., et al. *Urban Transportation and Public Policy.* San Francisco: Chandler Publishing Co., 1964.

GOMEZ, R. A. *Intergovernmental Relations in Highways.* Minneapolis: University of Minnesota Press, 1950.

HEBDEN, NORMAN, and SMITH, WILBUR S. *State-City Relationships in Highway Affairs.* New Haven: Yale University Press, 1950.

HIGHWAY RESEARCH BOARD. *Urban Research in Highway Planning.* Washington, D.C.: Government Printing Office, 1958.

KURYLO, WALTER. *A Study of Federal Aid Programming with Special Emphasis on Its Budgeting and Planning Aspects.* Washington, D.C.: American University Press, 1960.

LABALUT, JEAN, and LANE, WHEATON J. (eds.). *Highways in Our National Life.* Princeton: Princeton University Press, 1960.

MUMFORD, LEWIS. *The Highway and the City.* Chicago: American Library Association, 1964.

SEBUM, THOMAS J., and MARSH, BERNARD L. *Urban Transportation Administration.* New Haven: Bureau of Highway Traffic, Yale University, 1959.

TYLER, POYNTZ (ed.). *American Highways Today.* New York: The H. W. Wilson Co., 1957.

U.S. DEPARTMENT OF COMMERCE, BUREAU OF PUBLIC ROADS. *Highway Statistics, 1961.* Washington, D.C.: Government Printing Office, 1963.

# 24

# State Regulation of Business

The fifty state governments have wide powers to regulate business and industry. Subject to the limitations of the state and national constitutions, the state, under its police power may regulate any business that is affected with the public interest. As a direct result it is difficult to find many businesses that are not subject to some type of state control or regulation, except those that are strictly engaged in interstate commerce or are established by the federal government itself. This is particularly true of corporations that are incorporated within the state because the state has the right to issue the charter of incorporation and retains the right to take away that charter if the company does not adhere to each and every regulation the state issues.

## THE POWER OF THE STATE TO REGULATE BUSINESS

The police power belongs to the state alone, but it has in every state delegated this power to the local units of government. The police power of the states was verbalized in the famous slaughterhouse cases, (16 Wallace 36, 1873). Since this date the use of this wide-sweeping power has been such that it is difficult, if not impossible, to define it in sharp, concise terms. This doctrine has come to mean that the state may in many ways regulate or restrict individuals and corporations in the rights of both persons and property. At least six different areas of state regulation and control are based upon the exercise of the state police power:[1]

1. Protection of public health
2. Protection of public safety

[1] W. Brooke Graves, *American State Government* (4th ed.; Boston: D. C. Heath & Co., 1950), p. 708.

3. Protection of public convenience
4. Protection of public morals
5. Prevention of fraud
6. Suppression of public nuisance

It should be noted that contrary to some popular beliefs the police power is not an emergency power. It is used daily by state regulatory agencies and referred to constantly in every legislative session as authority that may be tapped to empower legislative action.

A marked difference in the attitude of the business community toward government has prevailed between the nineteenth century and the second half of the twentieth. All segments of the industrial world have asked for favorable treatment by government in both centuries, but in the twentieth century many groups have sought and usually received regulation of various types. It is probably true that the amount of state regulation of business has often exceeded that of the national government. By and large, the national government has done more for the labor groups and the farmers, while the state governments have been more favorably disposed toward business and consumer interests. This is not to imply that the state governments have not been sympathetic toward the cause of the agricultural community and the labor unions, but they have not been granted the generous treatment given to the other segments of the economy.

Each state determines which businesses will be regulated and which will not be so controlled by state law. Free enterprise and laissez-faire are theories under which the states have operated but to which most state governments have given more lip-service than actual practice. Most regulation has been on a hit-or-miss basis, with the local situation the major determinant as to whether or not state governmental regulation will or will not occur.

State regulation was cramped by the commerce clause (of the United States Constitution). Illinois was prevented from limiting railroad transportation charges on interstate traffic in 1886, and Iowa from stopping the sale of intoxicating liquors coming in from neighboring states in 1890, although the United States Congress had not yet expressed a national policy on either subject.[2]

The Intergovernmental Commission has established five guiding principles that it suggests should be followed in the field of regulation:

1. The fact that the National Government has not legislated on a given matter in a field of concurrent powers should not bar state action.
2. National laws should be so framed that they will not be construed to preempt any field against state action unless that intent is stated.

[2] The Commission on Intergovernmental Relations, *A Report to the President, 1956* (Washington, D.C.: Government Printing Office, 1956), p. 26.

3. Exercise of National power on any subject should not bar state action on the same subject unless there is positive inconsistency.
4. When a national minimum standard is imposed in a field where uniformity is not imperative the right of States to set more rigorous standards should be carefully preserved.
5. Statutes should provide flexible scope for administrative cessions of jurisdiction where the objectives of the laws at the two levels are substantially in accord. State legislation need not be identical with the National legislation.[3]

There can be no doubt about the need for complementary actions between the national government and the states in regulations dealing with the economy. This is not intended to mean that for every national action there must be parallel state legislation. Certainly in some cases state action may be redundant. It must be recognized that national control may in some instances be only a stop-gap control or temporary substitute awaiting state action.

It is not sufficient merely to have the state and national legislation in agreement, the administrative arms of the two units of government must also be working in concerted agreement. This may entail joint drafting of regulations, use of common standards, joint inspections, and complete exchange of information between the state regulatory agency and the federal administrators. Unnecessary duplication may be avoided by the federal government empowering the state agencies to make necessary inspections that will be accepted by the state and national governments as certification of compliance. Obviously it makes no sense for both state and national bank inspectors or auditors to check the same bank at different periods.

Lest one gain the impression that the states have proceeded with vigor to regulate everything within their boundaries, it should be noted that some businesses and professions have requested that they be regulated by the state. The reason usually stated is that the established firms desire to assure a high quality of service and merchandise be maintained. Actually the underlying motive may be not quite so altruistic and may be simply that the established firms and practitioners desire to limit the competition of newcomers to their field of endeavor. They desire to avoid unfair competition and ask the state to assist them.

State regulatory power extends to a great number of areas. The regulation of principal interest includes securities, insurance, banking, liquor, public utilities, corporations incorporated within the state, and "foreign" corporations—those incorporated in another state but doing business within the boundaries—licensing of various business activities, such as hotels,

[3] The Commission on Intergovernmental Relations, *A Report to the President, 1956* (Washington, D.C.: Government Printing Office, 1956), p. 70.

motels, and restaurants, licensing of various professions and occupations, and intrastate commerce.

## ADMINISTRATIVE ORGANIZATION FOR REGULATION OF BUSINESS

Probably at the present time no two states use the identical type of administrative organization for regulating business and industry. Not even in the field of public utility regulation is there unanimous agreement, even though a large majority do utilize a public utility commission rather than a single director of a utility department. It would appear that most authorities believe that the commission is better for utility regulation than the single commissioner but that in almost all of the other regulatory fields a single head for a department is to be preferred.

What is needed is a competent administrator who is responsible for the administrative actions of the department. There are relatively few quasi-legislative or quasi-judicial functions in these administrative departments. Most of the rules and regulations are of such a character that they should be enacted into legislation by the state legislature and not made by an administrative unit. If these regulations need to be changed, or modified, or expanded in order to keep pace with changing conditions, this should be the prerogative of the state legislature. The work of the department should be to enforce the rules and regulations established by the legislature, not to create them. Only the details should be made by administrative decree. In other words, the work should be primarily of a routine nature, with a minimum amount of policy making. The head of the department should be an individual of skilled administrative, management ability. He should be selected not because of political qualifications but because of his experience, training, and background. Appointment by the governor is probably the best method for naming the department head with a tenure of at least four years. Frequent changes in personnel both at the top and at all of the other positions within the department should be avoided. Politics should be kept out of the department with only the executive head not under a state-wide civil service merit system. Even he should not be considered a political appointee.

The value of an advisory committee to work with the department head is widely recognized. This group should be empowered to undertake any quasi-legislative or quasi-judicial action that may fall upon the department. This board or committee should be called into session at least quarterly to advise and consult with the top administrative staff of the department. Their pay should be on a per diem basis, with probably not more than ten or fifteen days a year being required. Appointment by the governor for over-lapping terms would be the ideal method of selection. If a vacancy occurs in the head of the department post, the board should be allowed to consult with the chief executive as to a suitable replacement.

Within the department of business and industry, or whatever its title may be, there should be a number of divisions to supervise a variety of business activities that are regulated by the state government. The primary units will consist of the bureau of banking; its companion should be the bureau of insurance. A third unit under the same department head should be a division to enforce the blue-sky laws or investment and securities rules and regulations. Real estate operators and brokers might also be supervised by a bureau within the department. Building and loan associations should be supervised, possibly within the bureau of banking, or under a separate bureau. Pawnbrokers and small loan companies, likewise, should come under regulation within the administrative unit. Public accountants are also usually certified by all states, and their supervision should be included in the list of business activities accountable to the head of the department. A further responsibility should be administering the general incorporation laws. This work of granting incoporation charters is frequently the authority of the secretary of state but might more appropriately fall into the jurisdiction of a trained member of the department's staff. Most of the work involved is of a mechanical and routine nature. Each application must be checked to guarantee that every provision of the state law has been complied with by the applicant.

It is probably a mistake to establish separate agencies to regulate the various business activities. All can be properly handled in one well-organized, integrated department in charge of a competent commissioner or department head. This administrative arrangement should make for the development of one well-organized state agency with consistent, carefully considered policies and with modern methods that inspire confidence and respect of all members of the business community that are subject to its regulation and supervision.

The department of industry and business may also serve as the administrative unit to supervise the regulation of professions and trades. This work is primarily of an examination nature and can best be performed by experts from the various professions and trades doing the actual preparation and grading, but with the administrative details performed by a bureau within the department. The members of the various examining boards should be paid on a per diem basis, appointed by the governor for over-lapping terms. The follow-up work could also be directed from within the bureau.

Those states with business enterprises conducted by the state may also lodge their administrative responsibilities within the department of business and industry, probably each type of state business headed by a bureau chief who would report to the chief executive of the state through the department head. Of course, if the business operation is of gigantic size it may not be administratively feasible to have the unit within the department, and a separate agency may be desirable. Each state must study its own administrative operational schedule before setting down any iron-clad rule that must be followed. A model department of business and industry with its various divisions and bureaus is depicted in Figure 24–1.

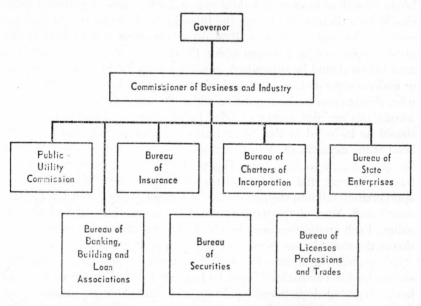

**Fig. 24–1.** Model Department of Business and Industry Organizational Chart.

## STATE REGULATION OF BANKING

Since the enactment of the national banking laws of 1863 the states have exercised an ever-increasing measure of control over state banks. All states, except Hawaii and Idaho, have a separate banking department within the state administrative hierarchy. State banks are those that are chartered under state law as contrasted with national banks that are organized under federal authority and subjected to federal regulation. The number of state banks is far larger than that of national banks, thus making the banking business regulation to a considerable extent under state jurisdiction in terms of numbers.

Several different administrative organizations are used by the various states to administer the state banking laws. By far the most common administrative method is to have the department headed by a superintendent of banking, with more than half of the states utilizing this form of organization, while Virginia has the bureaus of banking and insurance in the state corporations commission. This single director would appear to be the best type of administrative unit for this operation. What is needed is a competent administrator, versed in the banking business and able to supervise its operation. There are few functions of a quasi-legislative or quasi-judicial nature to be exercised by the banking department. The work of the agency should be fairly routine with the emphasis upon accounting and auditing skills. The rules and regulations laid down by the superintendent of banking and his staff supplement the state banking laws. The duties of the personnel are simply to enforce the laws of the state.

A few states have the banking department headed by a commission. There seems no reason to justify this administrative arrangement other than tradition and custom. Several states have combined the banking department with insurance regulation. This seems to be desirable in the smaller states but probably is not feasible in the large ones. A number of states entrust the supervision of the banks to other state officials such as the state treasurer or state auditor. This is of questionable merit because these officials should have sufficient duties without this added responsibility.

The banking laws in every state are designed to safeguard the interests of the public, and they prescribe in great detail the conditions under which the state banking institutions must operate. Regulated are the original incorporation and chartering, the capitalization, reserves, amount and forms of investments, amount and nature of loans permitted, methods of accounting and auditing, and over-all methods of operations. It is a relatively simple ministerial task to enforce most of these requirements assuming that the superintendent has an adequate staff.

One of the few matters of discretion that frequently centers in the banking department is the power to grant a new bank the permission to operate. In matters of this type an advisory banking board, such as operates in several states, is highly useful in advising the banking superintendent. Likewise, the banking board may serve as an appeal agency for a proposed bank that has been denied the privilege of opening its doors.

Other financial institutions located within the state are usually subject to the banking inspectors. These include credit unions, small loan companies, finance companies, building and loan associations, and other financial houses.

The head of the banking department should be appointed by the governor for a term of probably six years. There is no defensible reason for his term coinciding with that of the governor other than to make the chief executive as strong as possible. Since the matters handled by the department are primarily administrative there is no reason that it should be mixed in politics in any way. The inspectors and other functionaries of the office should be under civil service, with tenure when the probationary period has been completed.

In contrast to the insurance commissioner, where twelve states use the elective method for selecting the head of the agency, no superintendent of a state banking department is popularly elected. Coincidentally, not a single banking superintendent is a constitutional officer, with all of the offices being established by state statute.

An examination of the salaries paid to the heads of these two state agencies shows a remarkable similarity, as indicated in Table 24–1. In a

### TABLE 24–1

#### Salaries of Superintendents of Banks and Commissioners of Insurance—July, 1963

| State | Superintendents of Banking | Commissioners of Insurance |
|---|---|---|
| Alabama | $12,000 | $12,000 |
| Alaska | 12,960 | 12,960 |
| Arizona | 12,000 | 10,800 |
| Arkansas | 10,000 | 10,000 |
| California | 19,101 | 19,680 |
| Colorado | 13,536 | 13,536 |
| Connecticut | 13,580 | 17,360 |
| Delaware | 12,000 | 9,000 |
| Florida | – | State Treasurer |
| Georgia | 13,285 | State Controller |
| Hawaii | 12,804 | $18,000 |
| Idaho | 9,600 | 9,600 |
| Illinois | 15,000 | 15,000 |
| Indiana | 11,900 | 11,900 |
| Iowa | 16,000 | 11,900 |
| Kansas | 9,000 | 10,000 |
| Kentucky | 15,000 | 15,000 |
| Louisiana | 12,000 | 17,000 |
| Maine | 12,636 | 11,500 |
| Maryland | 10,000 | 10,000 |
| Massachusetts | 15,000 | 15,000 |
| Michigan | 14,500 | 14,500 |
| Minnesota | 12,000 | 12,500 |
| Mississippi | 12,500 | 12,500 |
| Missouri | 13,500 | 15,000 |
| Montana | 10,000 | Auditor |
| Nebraska | 9,000 | $ 9,000 |
| Nevada | 11,420 | 11,420 |
| New Hampshire | 12,192 | 10,947 |
| New Jersey | 20,000 | 15,053 |
| New Mexico | 10,000 | 9,960 |

## TABLE 24-1 (Continued)

| State | Superintendents of Banking | Commissioners of Insurance |
|---|---|---|
| New York | 28,875 | 28,875 |
| North Carolina | 15,000 | 18,000 |
| North Dakota | 8,400 | 9,000 |
| Ohio | 12,000 | 14,000 |
| Oklahoma | 12,000 | 12,000 |
| Oregon | 11,880 | 11,880 |
| Pennsylvania | 20,000 | 20,000 |
| Rhode Island | 8,658 | 8,658 |
| South Carolina | 11,660 | 14,000 |
| South Dakota | 8,000 | 10,000 |
| Tennessee | 15,000 | 12,500 |
| Texas | 22,500 | 15,000 |
| Utah | 9,600 | 9,600 |
| Vermont | 9,000 | 9,090 |
| Virginia | 13,500 | 13,500 |
| Washington | 10,704 | 12,000 |
| West Virginia | 9,000 | 9,000 |
| Wisconsin | 13,500 | 17,000 |
| Wyoming | 10,000 | 8,400 |

SOURCE: Council of State Governments, *The Book of the States, 1964–1965* (Chicago: Council of State Governments, 1964).

few cases the insurance commissioner receives a lower salary, but the equality is fairly uniform. It should be noted that the heads of these two important units are usually relatively high-paid in comparison with other state non-constitutional heads of departments in the same state governmental hierarchy.[4]

## STATE REGULATION OF INSURANCE COMPANIES

In 1869 the United States Supreme Court held that the insurance business was intrastate and was therefore subject to regulation by the state governments.[5] However, in 1944, the United States Supreme Court declared that insurance was no longer a local matter confined to a single state but that it was subject to the national regulation as well as state control under the interstate commerce clause. The Court also stated that insurance was covered by the federal anti-trust legislation.[6] So disturbed were the insurance executives of America that Congress was persuaded to pass the McCarran Act in 1945 that suspended federal regulation until at least 1948. However, since Congress has still not enacted legislation in

[4] Council of State Governments, *The Book of the States, 1962–1963* (Chicago: Council of State Governments, 1962), p. 146.
[5] *Paul v. Virginia* (8 Wall. 168, 1869).
[6] *United States v. Southeastern Underwriters Association* (322 U.S. 533, 1944).

the insurance field, the state regulations are the rules governing insurance company operations.

All states have detailed statutes concerning the operation of insurance companies and have established administrative mechanisms to enforce these laws. In a vast majority of the states the regulatory agency is a separate state department, but in a few it is combined with the state banking department. In others it is merely an added duty assigned to a state executive officer, such as in Hawaii, where the insurance regulations are enforced under the state treasurer's office.

It is quite apparent that the insurance department, just as the banking department, should be headed by a single commissioner rather than using a board or commission. He should and usually is directly accountable to the chief executive of the state government. In five states—Delaware, Louisiana, North Carolina, North Dakota, and Oklahoma—the insurance commissioner's office is provided for in the state constitution. In Georgia, the comptroller, a constitutional officer, is ex officio the insurance commissioner. In the other states it is a statutory office. Twelve states use the popular election method for securing the head of the insurance department. This is not recognized by students of administration as a desirable method of naming the head of a technical administrative office. States having the office on the popular election ballot for varying terms, usually two or four years, include—Delaware, Florida, Georgia, Kansas, Louisiana, Mississippi, Montana, New Mexico, North Carolina, North Dakota, Oklahoma, and Washington. It might be noted that the states that include the office in their constitutions require the position to be filled by election.[7]

The department in all states is primarily concerned with approving or denying applications for incorporation by insurance companies under the state laws. Secondarily, it must also approve of companies organized in another state that desire to do business within the state. The major work involves the establishment of rules to implement the state laws governing insurance practices. In addition to its own checking of the business methods of the companies, the state insurance departments frequently are authorized to receive and prosecute complaints from private citizens who feel that an insurance company has dealt unfairly with them. If, upon investigation, sufficient grounds are found, the department may be empowered to prohibit the company from continuing to operate within the state. The company, of course, has the right to appeal such a ruling to the state courts in order to gain restoration of its license.

Just as the banking department conducts at least an annual examination of every state bank, the insurance commissioner is required to hold periodic examinations of all insurance companies chartered, incorporated,

---

[7] Council of State Governments, *The Book of the States, 1962–1963* (Chicago: Council of State Governments, 1962), pp. 140–42.

or operating within the state. The objective is to determine the fiscal soundness of the companies operating in the state. The basic premise of all insurance regulations by the states is to assure the public that every insurance company will be able to carry out its contracts with its policyholders and to ascertain that all state laws are being complied with. This has a protective influence or benefit for the stockholders as well as for the policyholders.

The costs of examinations are usually charged against the insurance company receiving the inspection; thus frequently, just as in the case of the banking department, the cost to the state is virtually nil. There is no excuse for the staff of the insurance commissioner being undermanned, nor is there any reason that the qualifications of the agents should be any less than those employed in the banking department.

Just as in the banking department, an advisory board may be useful to the commissioner in determining when licenses should be issued to companies and when they should be revoked. These quasi-judicial decisions will probably be best received if made by more than a single individual.

## STATE REGULATION OF SALE OF SECURITIES

In 1910 both Rhode Island and Kansas began state regulation of the sale of securities. For twenty years or more prior to this state action a ground-swell had been building for governmental protection against swindlers who were defrauding the public. Since no effective federal action had occurred it was left to the states to fill this breach. The laws that were subsequently passed in every state except Nevada are often referred to as blue-sky laws, since it was alleged that some unscrupulous salesmen were even selling blue sky to the public or at least the securities were worth no more to the purchaser than if he had bought rights to blue skies.

The state's attempt to protect the investing public has been upheld by numerous court decisions. One of the first and most important decisions came when the United States Supreme Court ruled on the constitutionality of the Ohio statute allowing the sale of corporate securities only after first being licensed by the state.[8] A similar court decision some thirty-three years later sustained the Virginia state blue-sky law on a similar basis.[9]

The state regulation of securities takes various forms. The most essential feature, if the law is to protect the purchaser effectively, is the registration of the securities with a state agency before they may be sold. This gives the state department, often the department of insurance or possibly the

[8] *Hall v. Geiger-Jones Company* (242 U.S. 539, 1917).
[9] *Travelers Health Association v. Virginia* (339 U.S. 643, 1950).

banking department, an opportunity to check the prospectus and the financial solvency of the corporation or organization offering the securities for sale. Only after the state officials are assured that all of the requirements have been met is sale allowed. A second part of many state blue-sky laws deals with the salesmen of the securities. No sale can be made unless through authorized dealers who have been licensed by the state.

The remedial section of the law ordinarily allows the attorney general of the state to seek an injunction halting the sale of securities that have been suspected of being fraudulent. As worthwhile as are the state attempts to regulate the fraud, it was necessary for the national government to assist, since most companies were engaged in interstate corporate financing. Congress in 1933 finally recognized the limitations of state control and passed the Federal Securities Act and the Securities Exchange Act of 1934. Both laws are administered by the Securities and Exchange Commission which was created in 1934, some twenty-four years after state action began in this field.

Corporations issuing securities to the public, security exchanges, and all over-the-counter sales must be registered with the United States Securities and Exchange Commission. Exchanges, brokers, and dealers are required to keep accounts in accordance with methods prescribed by the commission, and no securities can be sold until commission authorization has been received. This cooperation between the state and national governments has been effective in reducing the number of annual cases of losses by imprudent investors in worthless stock. No longer does the principle of caveat emptor (let the buyer beware) prevail in securities transactions. One loophole that still remains is the sale by dealers from outside of the United States to susceptible clients who reside in the United States. Even in this area, through the postal powers, progress is being made in prosecution of people using the mails to defraud; but the problem is not entirely solved.

## STATE REGULATION OF CORPORATIONS

One of the major responsibilities of the secretary of state in most states is involved with the chartering of corporations by the state government. In the early 1800's most state legislatures passed special statutes granting a charter to each new corporation that sought to organize or do business in the state. Later, with the tremendous growth in the number of corporations, a general incorporation statute was used. This permitted the corporation to be formed or to do business if actually incorporated within another state if it met certain prescribed standards. The United States Supreme Court more than one hundred and thirty years ago assured the states that this authority to approve or disapprove of corporations was a power of the state governments.[10] The Court also guaranteed to corporations in the famous Dartmouth College case that their charters were contracts. This meant that the state government could not change the provisions without the corporation's consent unless the charter itself, when agreed to, waived this right.

The duties of the state official empowered to issue charters, usually the secretary of state but occasionally a special corporation commission, are to check the purposes of the corporation and to inquire into its *modus operandi*. After being satisfied that all state statute requirements are being fulfilled, the state official issues the charter to the corporation. A fee, based on capitalization, is ordinarily charged.

Domestic corporations are those chartered by the state and thereby automatically authorized to do business within the state. Foreign corporations are those that are chartered in another state but after meeting certain statutory requirements are authorized to do business within the state's boundaries.

The state supervision does not end with the issuance of a charter but continues as long as the corporation does business. Annual or even more frequent reports of the business operation must be filed with state agencies for checking. If the corporation fails to comply with any of the state statutes, the charter may be revoked or the license to engage in business canceled.

Some states, including Delaware, have had favorable corporation laws. This means that the state incorporation requirements are easily met, and thus many corporations tend to take out their charters in these states with easy incorporation laws.

## STATE REGULATION OF THE SALE OF LIQUOR

Since the repeal in 1933 of the United States Constitutional amendment which prohibited all alcoholic beverages, each state has had the problem of determining its rules and regulations concerning the sale and use of liquor. The choices have now narrowed actually to three: (1) sale by private persons, under a state licensing system; (2) sale by the state through so-called state monopoly stores; or (3) a combination of the two allowing sale by licensed individuals but forcing these liquor-by-the-drink dispensors to purchase their supply through the state-operated package stores.

Only one state, Mississippi, has retained state-wide prohibition. All of the other forty-nine states make liquor available through one or

[10] *Bank of Augusta v. Earle* (13 Peters 519, 1830).

more of the methods outlined above. Sixteen states, plus Wyoming, which operates a state monopoly on wholesaling of liquor, utilize the state monopoly system. This takes the form of either the state licensing package liquor stores or the state operating the stores themselves. Several of the states combine liquor by the drink with the package system, allowing private merchants to obtain licenses to dispense liquor by the drink but requiring its purchase through the state-owned and -operated liquor stores.[11] Even in states that allow liquor by the glass it is quite common for local governmental units, usually the county but in some states even the municipalities, to decide for themselves whether or not they will permit the sale of liquor.

It is difficult to determine which method is best. The state finds itself in a peculiar position in that it is attempting to control the total consumption of liquor and its "evil" effects but at the same time is using the sale as a source of revenue. Other complications involve establishment of liquor store hours, regulation of who may purchase, and how much may be purchased. Some opposition arises from a state being in the liquor business by elements of the population who assert that this is socialism because it results in a violation of the free enterprise system.

## STATE REGULATION OF PUBLIC UTILITIES

The railroad was the first of the public utilities to be regulated by statewide utility commissions. Shortly after the Civil War the first state public utility commissions came upon the regulatory scene. All of these were either advisory commissions or non-regulatory types. From about 1870 until 1910 a new type of mandatory commission was created by a number of states. Its power was primarily over railroads with a few state commissions being allowed to regulate other utilities. About 1910 an entirely modern concept of state public utility regulatory commission entered the picture. For example, the Wisconsin commission, created in 1907, was granted power over light, power, gas, water, telephone, and telegraph companies. This authority extended to passing upon the issuance of stocks, bonds, and other securities; to prescribe accounting procedures, to fix rates; and to require service at a minimum standard.

Since 1910 the growth both in numbers and in powers of state public utilities has been such that by 1963 all states had some type of state-wide utility regulatory body, with the Texas commission having the least power and regulating the fewest types of public utilities. The typical state com-

---

[11] States with a monopoly system include: Alabama, Idaho, Iowa, Maine, Michigan, Montana, New Hampshire, North Carolina, Ohio, Oregon, Pennsylvania, Utah, Vermont, Virginia, Washington, and West Virginia.

mission has three members, appointed by the governor, usually with senate approval, for terms of six years, with one commissioner's term expiring each two years. Rhode Island and Oregon do not use a commission but employ a single commissioner to regulate the public utilities. The methods of selecting the members of state public utility commissions, both constitutional and statutory, and the number of members on each is indicated in Table 24–2.

### TABLE 24–2

Selection of Public Utility Commissioners—July, 1963
State and Number of Members

| Popularly Elected Public Utility Commissions in Fourteen States | |
|---|---|
| Constitutional Office | Statutory Office |
| Arizona (3) | Alabama (3) |
| Georgia (5) | Florida (3) |
| Louisiana (3) | Minnesota (3) |
| Nebraska (3) | Mississippi (3) |
| North Dakota (3) | Montana (3) |
| Oklahoma (3) | South Dakota (3) |
| Texas (3) | Tennessee (3) |

| Statutory Public Utility Commissions Appointed by the Governor* | | |
|---|---|---|
| Alaska (3) | Kentucky (3) | Ohio (3) |
| Arkansas (3) | Maine (3) | Oregon† (1) |
| California (5) | Maryland (3) | Pennsylvania (5) |
| Colorado (3) | Massachusetts (7) | Rhode Island† (1) |
| Connecticut (3) | Michigan (3) | South Carolina (7) |
| Delaware (3) | Missouri (5) | Utah (3) |
| Hawaii (5) | Nevada (3) | Vermont (3) |
| Idaho (3) | New Hampshire (3) | Virginia (3) |
| Illinois (5) | New Jersey (3) | Washington (3) |
| Indiana (3) | New Mexico (3) | West Virginia (3) |
| Iowa (3) | New York (5) | Wisconsin (3) |
| Kansas (3) | North Carolina (5) | Wyoming (3) |

* All are appointed by the governor with the exception of South Carolina and Virginia which are constitutional officers and appointment is made by the legislature.
† Single commissioner rather than a commission.

SOURCE: Council of State Governments, *The Book of the States, 1964–1965* (Chicago: Council of State Governments, 1964).

The public utilities regulated by these state commissions commonly include: electrical light and power, manufactured and natural gas, street railways, motor buses, motor trucks, water, telephone, and oil pipe lines. A few states allow regulation of all public utilities which have the following common features:

1. Produce commodities or render service of general importance (vital) to the public

2. Are a natural monopoly

3. Have exclusive right to service an area because of a franchise

The impossibility of a city regulating a public utility that has operations all over the state or even in several states is obvious. A fundamental principle found in controlling the rates and services of public utilities is that the regulatory agency to be effective must be exercised by a unit of government whose jurisdiction is as extensive as the operation of the utility regulated.[12]

In several states the state public utility commission has jurisdiction over the rates charged by municipally owned utilities, but most state legislatures have not granted that far-reaching authority.

The primary problem involved in regulating public utilities is the determination of a rate that will bring to the utility a fair return. Before the actual rate can be established, agreement upon the valuation of the utility's holdings must be made. The United States Supreme Court in 1898 said,

Original cost of construction, the amount of permanent improvements, the amount and market value of bonds and stocks, the present as compared with the original cost of construction, the probable earning capacity of the property under particular rates prescribed by statute, and the sum required to meet operating expenses, are all matters for consideration in an effort to set a rate schedule.[13]

In a second series of decisions in 1909 and 1923 involving the same problem the Supreme Court placed greater emphasis upon the reproduction costs as a basis for rate-making decisions.[14] A third basis for establishing the valuation of public utility companies was introduced in 1944, when the court used the "prudent investment theory" as to the proper method of valuation determination.[15] Three factors are considered: the original investment, value of additions, and the amount of depreciation of the property involved. The state courts have been guided by the United States Supreme Court decisions but have followed their own economic theories from time to time. A few states have put great weight upon the reproduction costs, while placing only limited emphasis upon depreciation and original cost of the utility property.

The second problem that naturally follows the establishment of the valuation base is what constitutes a fair return. The utility executives have desired this figure to be as large as possible, believing that anything less

[12] H. H. Trachsel, *Public Utility Regulation* (Homewood, Ill.: Richard D. Irwin, Inc., 1947), p. 113.

[13] *Smythe v. Ames* (169 U.S. 466, 1898).

[14] *Wilcox v. Consolidated Gas Co.* (212 U.S. 19, 1909); and *Southwestern Bell Telephone Co. v. Missouri* (262 U.S. 276, 1923).

[15] *Federal Power Commission v. Hope Natural Gas Co.* (320 U.S. 591, 1944).

than 7 per cent would not be satisfactory. The general public has not held the 7 per cent figure as mandatory and generally favored a figure of 6 or even less as being equitable. The ultimate decision is usually made by the courts as the regulatory agency's decision is subject to judicial review, if the question is raised by the utility.

The technical details involved in rate making require that the public utility commission have a staff of experts who are trained in this specialized field. The number of legal entanglements also makes it mandatory that the staff include lawyers with specialized training in utility operations.

The importance of public utility regulation, both on the national and state levels, to the economy of the entire United States was emphasized by President John F. Kennedy in a message of April 13, 1961, to the Congress in which he said:

The responsibilities with which [the regulatory agencies] have been entrusted permeate every sphere and almost every activity of our national life. . . . These agencies and their performance have a profound effect upon the direction and pace of our economic growth. It is in the public interest to maintain an industry, it is clearly not in the public interest by the impact of regulatory authority to destroy its otherwise viable way of life. Furthermore, the industries subject to their jurisdiction are intertwined with our national defense to such a degree that the health of these industries can well be regarded as an index of both our strength and our power to survive. Thus, the capacity of these regulatory agencies to meet their responsibilities, and the efficiency with which they dispatch their business, became a subject of tremendous significance to the entire nation.

## REGULATION OF PROFESSIONS AND TRADES

The Tenth Amendment of the United States Constitution reserves to the states the authority to establish standards and to prescribe qualifications for the various professions and trades. As a direct result, all of the states have enacted legislation that sets the requirements for various professions and trades and provides administrative machinery to ascertain if the applicants possess the required education and experience.

Probably no two states license the same complete list of professions or trades. Nor do the states agree upon the qualifications that are required to secure authorization to practice their occupation within the state. It has been universally recognized that the states have a right to prescribe standards for professions and trades as long as the prerequisites meet the test of reasonableness. The test of reasonableness has been one that numerous state licensing requirements have been unable to satisfy.[16] Most

[16] *Smith v. Texas* (233 U.S. 630, 1914); and *Dent v. West Virginia* (129 U.S. 114, 1889).

states require more than one hundred different types of licenses for the various professional and trade occupations of its citizens. The less-industrialized states may have only about one hundred different licensing provisions on the statute books, while California has probably the highest number with more than three hundred.[17] No complete listing is probably possible since each session of almost every state legislature finds new licensing arrangements for some new "profession."

The ordinary or original purpose for licensing was to protect the public from unqualified persons practicing certain professions or trades. Now it is not uncommon for a group to request that they be licensed, with their petition to the legislature usually affirming their desire to protect the public from inferior service by newcomers in the area who do not have the high qualifications that the group desiring licenses possesses. This type of appeal to the state legislature merits serious study as it may be based not upon the alleged reason but rather upon a desire to stifle new competition in the profession or trade.

The state statutes usually provide for each licensed profession or group to have its own examining board that passes upon the qualifications of new applicants. The board is usually appointed by the governor, normally without consent of the senate. Some state statutes require the governor to make his selections from names submitted by the professional association of the licensed group. The average number of examining boards for the fifty states is now over fifteen.[18]

The following list of professional and vocational licenses as issued in Ohio is typical of those to be found in other states:[19]

| | |
|---|---|
| Accountants | Distilling manufacturers |
| Architects | Dry cleaners |
| | |
| Barbers | Elevator inspectors |
| Beer distributors | Engineers and surveyors |
| Brewery manufacturers | |
| Brokers | Fair concessionaires |
| | Fish buyers |
| Chauffeurs | Frozen dessert manufacturers |
| Chiropractors | Fur buyers |
| Cocktail dealers | |
| Cold storage warehousemen | Highball manufacturers |
| Commercial canners | Hospital service agents |
| Cosmotologists | Hotel keepers |
| | |
| Dental hygienists | Insurance agents |
| Dentists | Insurance brokers |

[17] Council of State Governments, *Occupational Licensing Legislation in the States* (Chicago: Council of State Governments, 1952), pp. 26–28.

[18] James W. Fesler, *The Independence of State Regulatory Agencies* (Chicago: Public Administration Service, 1942), chap. vii., p. 46.

[19] Francis Aumann and Harvey Walker, *Government and Administration of Ohio* (New York: Thomas Y. Crowell Co., 1956), p. 395.

Lawyers
Liquid fuel dealers
Livestock agents
Livestock dealers
Livestock weighers

Manicurists
Midwives

Milk and cream dealers
Milk weighers
Milk samplers
Milk testers
Mine fire bosses
Mine foreman
Minnow dealers
Motor transportation agents
Motor vehicle dealers
Motor vehicle agents
Movie film exhibitors

Notary Publics
Nursery stock dealers
Nurses

Optometrists

Pawnbrokers
Pharmacists
Physicians
Plumbing inspectors

Real estate brokers
Real estate salesman
Restaurant keepers

Sacramental wine distributors
Sales tax vendors
Security brokers
Security salesmen
Soft drink manufacturers
Soft drink bottlers
Steam & engine boiler inspectors
Steam & engine operators

Teachers

Veterinarians

Wine dealers
Wine bottlers
Wine distributors

More than one-fourth of the states have adopted either in whole or in part the Model State Administrative Act dealing with the licensing process. The model act provides six major safeguards to insure the principles of justice and fairness:

1. A requirement that each licensing board or unit adopt essential procedural rules and that all rule-making, both procedural and substantive shall be accompanied by notice of hearing to all interested personnel.
2. Assurance of proper publicity for administrative rules that affect the general public.
3. Provision for advance determination of "declaratory judgments" on the validity of administrative rules, and for "declaratory rulings" affording advanced determination of the application of administration to particular cases.
4. Assurance of fundamental fairness in administrative hearings, particularly in regard to rules of evidence and the taking of official notice in quasi-judicial proceedings.
5. Provisions assuring personal familiarity on the part of the responsible deciding officers and agency heads with the evidence in the quasi-judicial cases decided by them.
6. Assurance of proper scope of judicial review of administrative orders to guarantee correction of administrative errors.[20]

[20] Council of State Governments, *Model State Administrative Procedures Act* (Chicago: Council of State Governments, 1946), sections 2–12.

## STATE OWNERSHIP OF BUSINESS OPERATIONS

Probably no state has engaged in business enterprises to the extent that North Dakota has since 1922. Four major business ventures of the state include banking, insurance, land, and mill and elevator operations. Included in the mill and elevator operations in North Dakota are mills capable of processing thousands of barrels of grain each day, branch warehouses, and elevators with a grain capacity of several million bushels. In the banking field North Dakota has a state bank. The Bank of North Dakota, while in the insurance field three insurance enterprises are state-owned and operated. In addition to these usually private enterprise operations more than three million acres of state-owned land are either directly managed by the state or leased to private operators with the payments received held in trust for the common schools of the state.

The states of New York and New Jersey and a few other states with sea-water ports operate sizable businesses in the form of port authorities. Similarly, Louisiana operates the port of New Orleans as a state enterprise.


## STATE INDUSTRIAL DEVELOPMENT PROGRAMS

By 1963 all fifty states were for the first time committed to broad programs of development. Various agencies have been created in every state and, supported by state tax funds, have endeavored to stimulate industrial growth. Usually the agency was given the title of development commission or board.

Every state developmental agency has the responsibility of gathering certain types of information believed to be useful to industrialists that determine where new plants and expansion of existing plants will be built. Included in the types of information almost universally collected are water resources, waste disposals facilities, transportation, fuel and labor resources, financing, industrial sites available, and market analyses.

A prime function of most of the developmental agencies is advertising in appropriate periodicals, while in thirty-nine states direct-mail advertising is used to attract new industry. A new dimension of this state activity is found in twenty-eight states that make available financial assistance to new or expanding enterprises.

The size of the staffs in the state promotional agencies vary from the three full-time employees of the Delaware staff to more than 325 employees in the New York state agency. The budget for New York is more than $4 million and the Florida budget is nearly $3 million. A recent survey shows that seven states have staffs of less than ten persons as contrasted with the large operation in New York and the 284 persons employed in the Florida development agency.

In addition to the traditional emphasis upon attracting new industries and tourists, the state promotional agencies are being called upon for higher levels of professional services. The economic feasibility studies, requiring graduate engineers and economists and techno-economic studies, are replacing the idle claims and boasts of former years. The state agencies are interested in international markets, and several have sent missions overseas to stimulate promotion functions.

The trend continues toward providing incentives or subsidies to attract new industry. The most common programs include:

1. Issuance of bonds or revenue certificates. Between fifteen and twenty states are now active in this approach.
2. State industrial development authorities, which usually have money available to support industrial plant development or expansion. At least seven states use this method, with Pennsylvania being the first to enter this field.
3. State development credit corporations, whereby private financial institutions pool their resources to finance ventures. Some twenty-five states have enacted legislation permitting this type of developmental operation.
4. Direct tax concessions. At least twenty states offer varying tax exemptions, with Louisiana allowing a ten-year tax-forgiving system to new industrial developments.[21]

Since the release of the President's Outdoor Recreation Resources Review Commission report in 1962, the states have promoted on an unprecedented scale programs for outdoor recreational facilities. During the fiscal years 1963 and 1964 state programs involving hundreds of millions of dollars were started. Recreational administration, study, and planning also were advanced in most states.

One of the outstanding programs was the expenditure in Pennsylvania of $70 million. Pennsylvania's Project 70 was passed by the general assembly in 1962 and again in 1963, since it was a constitutional amendment, and was approved by a majority of 100,000 voters in November, 1963. The program includes: (1) $40 million for regional parks and reservoirs in forty-three counties, (2) $20 million for matching grants to regional, county, or municipal authorities for local park, recreation, and open-space purposes, and (3) $10 million for important fish, wildlife, or boating areas threatened by impending private development.[22]

[21] Council of State Governments, *The Book of the States, 1964–1965* (Chicago: Council of State Governments, 1964), p. 487.
[22] Council of State Governments, *The Book of the States, 1964–1965* (Chicago: Council of State Governments, 1964), p. 518.

Tourism each year appears to become a larger industry in most states. During the winter season of December through March of 1961 and 1962 Florida, for example, recorded a high of 3,413,678 persons who visited within the state. Even states that are not well-known for outstanding recreational or scenic attractions are attempting to utilize new approaches to tourist attractions. In 1964 the states of Illinois, Wisconsin, Minnesota, and Iowa opened a tourist route entitled "The Hiawatha Trail," which covers scenic and historical sites in the four states. The developmental commissions of the four states have published booklets describing the different features that may be viewed, and special highway signs have been posted to mark the state and federal highways included in the trail. The highway marking was done with the cooperation of the United States Bureau of Public Roads.

## BIBLIOGRAPHY

ANDERSON, RONALD A. *Government Regulation of Business.* Cincinnati: South-Western Publishing Co., Inc., 1950.

ARNOLD, THURMAN. *Democracy and Free Enterprise.* Norman: University of Oklahoma Press, 1942.

BAUER, JOHN. *The Public Utility Franchise: Its Functions and Terms Under State Regulation.* Chicago: Public Administration Service, 1946.

——— and COSTELLO, PETER. *Public Organization of Electric Power.* New York: Harper & Row, Inc., 1949.

BAUM, ROBERT D. *The Federal Power Commission and State Utility Regulation.* Washington, D.C.: American Council on Public Affairs, 1942.

BERNSTEIN, MARVER H. *Regulating Business by Independent Commission.* Princeton: Princeton University Press, 1955.

COTTER, CORNELIUS P. *Government and Private Enterprise.* New York: Holt, Rinehart & Winston, Inc., 1960.

COUNCIL OF STATE GOVERNMENTS. *Occupational Licensing Legislation in the States.* Chicago: Council of State Governments, 1952.

DIMOCK, MARSHALL E. *Business and Government,* 4th ed. New York: Holt, Rinehart & Winston, Inc., 1961.

EDELMAN, J. M. *Securities Regulation in the Forty-eight States.* Chicago: Council of State Governments, 1942.

FAINSOD, MERLE, LINCOLN, GORDON, and PALAMOUNTAIN, JOSEPH C. *Government and the American Economy.* New York: W. W. Norton & Co., Inc., 1959.

FEDERAL POWER COMMISSION AND NATIONAL ASSOCIATION OF RAILROAD AND UTILITIES COMMISSIONERS. *State Commission Jurisdiction and Regulation of Electric and Gas Utilities.* Washington, D.C.: Government Printing Office, 1948.

FESLER, JAMES W. *The Independence of State Regulatory Agencies.* Chicago: Public Administration Service, 1942.

GRAHAM, GEORGE A., and REINING, HENRY, JR. (eds.). *Regulatory Administration.* New York: John Wiley & Sons, Inc., 1943.

HALL, FORD P. *The Concept of a Business Affected with a Public Interest.* Bloomington, Ind.: The Principa Press, Inc., 1940.

———. *Government and Business,* 3d ed. New York: McGraw-Hill Book Co., Inc., 1949.

———. *State Control of Business Through Certificates of Convenience & Necessity.* Bloomington: Bureau of Gov't Research, U. of Indiana, 1947.

KOONTZ, HAROLD, and GRABLE, RICHARD W. *Public Control of Economic Enterprise.* New York: McGraw-Hill Book Co., Inc., 1956.

LANE, ROBERT E. *The Regulation of Businessmen.* New Haven: Yale University Press, 1954.

MARKETING LAWS SURVEY, U.S. Department of Commerce. *State Occupational Legislation.* Washington, D.C.: Government Printing Office, 1942.

———. *State Liquor Legislation.* Washington, D.C.: Government Printing Office, 1941.

MULLER, FREDERICK W. *Public Rural Electrification.* Washington, D.C.: American Council on Public Affairs, 1944.

MUND, V. A. *Government and Business,* 3d ed. New York: Harper & Row, Inc., 1960.

ROHLFING, CHARLES C., and OTHERS. *Business and Government.* Brooklyn, N.Y.: Foundation Press, Inc., 1949.

THOMPSON, C. W., and SMITH, WENDELL. *Public Utility Economics.* New York: McGraw-Hill Book Co., Inc., 1941.

TRACHSEL, HERMAN H. *Public Utility Regulation.* Chicago: R. D. Irwin, 1947.

WILCOX, CLAIR. *Public Policies Toward Business,* rev. ed. Homewood, Ill.: Richard D. Irwin, Inc., 1960.

WILSON, G. LLOYD, HERRING, JAMES, and EUSTLER, R. B. *Public Utility Regulation.* New York: McGraw-Hill Book Co., Inc., 1938.

# 25

# The State and Labor

The growth of industrialism and commerce has changed the type of relationship that exists between the individual laborer and his government. When the factory system was very small the vast proportion of craftsmen or artisans was self-employed and therefore did not require governmental assistance in arranging for the terms of employment. As corporations assumed a larger degree of control over the instruments of production and began to employ workers in larger numbers, controversies gradually arose with respect to the terms and conditions of employment. With employees at first having no voice or major control over these two items, and in the absence of national and state laws of a regulatory nature, abuses and problems arose which eventually were to call for some type of governmental regulation.

The states were called upon to enact our earliest labor laws. The authority of the states in the field of labor law stems from two considerations. First of all, the national constitution is silent with respect to labor, and therefore, under the Tenth Amendment, that power which is not delegated to the national government is reserved to the states or to the people. Secondly, the state has been able to use its police power to regulate in the interest of public health, safety, morals, and welfare of its citizens. The national government, particularly since the advent of the New Deal, has enacted a large body of labor legislation basically under the power of the Congress to regulate interstate or foreign commerce and to establish labor standards for those agencies supplying services or goods under contract to the national government. As a result, both the national and state governments have passed many laws pertaining to the laborer. In spite of the fact that national labor laws have had a tendency to attract wide-spread public attention, it must be recognized that the state is still called upon to legislate in very vital areas of concern to the worker—his safety, health, security, and even general welfare.

## HISTORY OF LABOR ORGANIZATIONS

While the early beginnings of organized labor can be traced to the last decades of the eighteen century, some local unions did exist before 1800. No doubt the growth of labor unions was delayed by the prevalent philosophy that these organizations were some type of illegal conspiracy in restraint of trade. However, the decision of the Massachusetts State Supreme Court in 1842, which recognized the legality of labor unions, did much to dispel the old ideas with respect to such organizations.[1] The Knights of Labor, which began as a secret society in 1869, was the first labor organization to attain any national importance and by the 1880's its membership, open to all workers, reached 700,000. By the turn of the century this union was almost ineffective due perhaps to its inability to attract strong political support and to win certain key strikes.

The present-day American Federation of Labor and Congress of Industrial Organizations began in 1881 as the Federation of Trades and Labor Unions. The Federation, which was in bitter opposition to the Knights of Labor, was instrumental in gaining the support of other unions for the forming of the American Federation of Labor in 1886. The AFL was a federation of craft unions, each of which contained members possessing the same skills. The question of receiving industrial unions—those composed of all workers, skilled or unskilled, in a single industry—eventually created dissatisfaction with the federation. In 1938 a group of labor leaders established the Congress of Industrial Organizations after being expeled from the AFL. In 1955 the breach was healed, and these two powerful unions were united as the AFL-CIO. At the present time approximately one-fourth of our total labor force of slightly over 70,000,000 workers are members of labor unions. In 1962 the AFL-CIO alone reported a membership of 12,500,000.

The organization along union lines of state and local employees has occurred primarily since 1910. Undoubtedly the presence of the spoils system within the states and municipalities delayed the organization of state and local employees. In the state and local field the American Federation of State, County, and Municipal Employees, an AFL-CIO affiliate, is the primary national union with general coverage. In addition, some national organizations concerned with a particular type of local workers, such as the International Association of Fire Fighters, are also affiliated with the AFL-CIO. After reviewing the role of the national organizations, the scene becomes quite confused. In some states there are general statewide employee organizations, but many times these are not as active or effective as the national unions. In many of the large municipalities local

[1] *Commonwealth v. Hunt* (45 Mass. 111, 1842).

employee organizations or associations exist. In addition, several craft unions may also operate in local jurisdictions.

Perhaps indicative of the changing philosophy within state governments, the governor of Rhode Island in 1963 signed a one-year agreement with the American Federation of State, County, and Municipal Employees. By this arrangement the union was recognized as the spokesman for state employees. In addition, negotiations were stipulated to cover hours and working conditions in items pertaining to the salary adjustment fund. Also the state agreed that seniority would apply to promotions, layoffs, rehirings, vacations, shifts, and choice of work. The agreement also established a grievance procedure.

## LABOR STANDARDS

### Hours of Work

The determination of the number of hours of work was initially left to the employer, who arrived at the decisions following some degree of consultation with his employees. The original attempts by the state to limit the number of hours that could be demanded from an employee were viewed by federal and state courts alike as constituting a violation of the freedom of employer and employee to contract without due process of law. However, the early position of the United States Supreme Court in the matter of the determination of working hours was not always a consistent one. As early as 1898, the Court upheld a statute of Utah which limited the work within mines to eight hours a day.[2] Seven years later the Court ruled a New York law invalid that limited bakery employment to ten hours per day.[3]

Following the decision of the United States Supreme Court in 1917 in *Bunting v. Oregon*, which upheld a state law prescribing a maximum number of hours for industrial workers, every state enacted some legislation concerning the hours of work.[4] It must be recognized that many of these laws apply to only particular classes of persons, such as women or children, or to labor that could be classified as hazardous in nature or dangerous to the health of the laborers. At the present time all states strictly regulate the number of hours a minor may work, and over forty states have established maximum hours for women.

In most state laws a man is not covered by regulations with respect to a maximum number of working hours unless: (1) he is employed in a business subject to national regulation, (2) he is filling a hazardous position, and

[2] *Holden v. Hardy* (169 U.S. 366, 1898).
[3] *Lochner v. New York* (198 U.S. 45, 1905).
[4] 243 U.S. 426, 1917.

(3) his job poses the danger of an occupational disease or his work is classified as dangerous to public health.

National hour legislation, which is applicable to all employees in interstate commerce, was established by the Fair Labor Standards Act as passed by the Congress in 1938. This measure, as upheld by the United States Supreme Court in 1941, and later amended by the Congress, limits hours of work to eight per day and forty per week.[5] While most state laws are less restrictive than this national measure, virtually all of our states have accepted the eight-hour day for their own use and in many instances for local governmental employees.

## Minimum Wages

As soon as states attempted to enact any type of statute respecting the establishment of minimum wages, they encountered the old constitutional demand of due process, as had been the situation with regard to hours of work. While it was recognized that the state might determine the pay of those individuals employed on public works, the fixing of wages within private employment was an entirely different proposition. The first state laws providing for minimum wages were applicable only to women and children. While the Congress and some state legislatures had passed this type of law prior to 1920, it was not until 1937 that the concept of a minimum wage law was accepted by the United States Supreme Court. In that year the Court sustained a State of Washington law setting the minimum wages to be paid women and minors.[6] At the present time approximately two-thirds of the states have minimum wage statutes, but some only apply to women or to women and children. Since only four states have minimum wage laws applicable to both sexes, adult males are not covered by these provisions in many states unless their employment is in an industry subject to national control.[7]

The Fair Labor Standards Act of 1938, as amended, fixes $1.25 as a minimum hourly wage. It provides for overtime but at a compensatory rate of one and one-half times the hourly wage. State laws regulating minimum wages vary from less than 75¢ to $1.50 per hour. A survey of state minimum wage laws indicates a general concern also for the following items: (1) the times or intervals at which wages must be paid, (2) that the payment of wages must be in legal tender, and (3) for the payment of wages upon termination of employment. In addition, each state provides for the mechanics lien by which specified categories of laborers, usually mechanics and construction workers, can secure unpaid wages through proceedings against the value of the employers' property.

[5] *U.S. v. Darby Lumber Co.* (321 U.S. 100, 1941).
[6] *West Coast Hotel v. Parrish* (300 U.S. 379, 1937).
[7] Connecticut, Massachusetts, New York, and Rhode Island.

Within the states the minimum wage laws are administered usually by one of two accepted practices: (1) through a wage commission or board which is given the responsibility to set minimum wages, or (2) by statutes which definitely and specifically determine the minimum wages, as in the case of Arkansas, and in the national Fair Labor Standards Act.

## Workmen's Compensation

All of our states by 1948 had enacted laws providing for some phase of workmen's compensation. While this form of social legislation had received widespread acceptance in many European countries prior to 1900, it was not until 1902 that the first state workmen's compensation act was passed by Maryland. This experiment was to be of only brief duration since a Baltimore court declared this pioneer law unconstitutional in 1904. The subsequent attempts in Montana and New York were to meet a similar fate by also being declared unconstitutional. These early statutes were declared invalid on the grounds that they resulted in the taking of property without due process of law in contravention of the Fourteenth Amendment. In addition, the courts held that these early laws were not a proper exercise of the state police power.[8]

The turning point for the acceptance of state workmen's compensation laws occurred in 1911 when four states—California, New Jersey, Washington, and Wisconsin—passed such acts which were upheld by the courts. Since that time, gradually over the years, the states have passed measures that have provided for workmen's compensation for injuries as a result of accidents on the job, for the contracting of an occupational disease, or for damages arising out of employment.

Under current workmen's compensation laws, when an accident occurs or an employee develops an occupational disease, collections can be made, since the employer is presumed to be at fault. This philosophy is almost in direct opposition to that which prevailed years ago under common law, when it was almost impossible for the employee to receive any compensation. Before workmen's compensation laws, the injured employee could sue for damages in a court of law, but the employer could in most instances utilize one of the following rules or doctrines: (1) that the employee in accepting employment had assumed the risk of the job and therefore, under the *assumption of risk* philosophy, the employer was freed from any claim for damages; (2) that the accident occurred as the result of the fault of a fellow employee, and under the *fellow-servant* rule collection of damages was prevented; or (3) that the injury occurred as a result, either in whole or part, of the employee's own negligence or care-

---

[8] *Cunningham v. Northwestern Improvement Co.* (119 Pac. 554, 1911); *Ives v. South Buffalo Railroad Co.* (201 N.Y. 271, 1911).

lessness, and therefore the employer's plea was contributory negligence. Workmen's compensation laws generally abolished these old common-law protections for the employer and granted safeguards to the employee in the form of payments for injuries incurred, regardless of blame.

Workmen's compensation laws vary, and no state law covers all types of employment, all kinds of injuries, or all hazardous or occupational diseases. Some state laws are very liberal, and yet in eleven states these statutes apply only to hazardous occupations. Casual laborers, domestic servants, and farm laborers are usually excluded from coverage of such measures as are individuals or firms employing fewer than a certain number of workers.

The method of financing workers' compensation involves the establishment of some type of an insurance fund. Three different forms of insurance plans are possible depending upon individual state requirements: (1) most states permit employers to insure their risks with a private insurance concern, (2) in seven states the employer must insure with the state fund, and (3) some states will permit those employers who can exhibit a strong financial position to self-insure.

## Unemployment Compensation

The movement for some system of unemployment compensation has its roots both in private organizations and in governmental operations. Some labor unions had provided for unemployment compensation shortly after the turn of the nineteenth century. In the United States as early as 1894 an employer-employee plan in the wallpaper industry established some out-of-work benefits. On the European continent the city of Ghent, Belgium, in 1900, granted payments to labor unions and other private agencies which paid unemployment benefits. The Ghent Plan was not received with much enthusiasm in the United States but was rather widely adopted in many European cities. In 1911, in England, a compulsory unemployment compensation insurance law was adopted. No similar plan was enacted in the United States until 1934, when the Wisconsin Act of 1932 went into effect.

During the first years of the Great Depression many unemployment compensation measures were introduced in several state legislatures. These early state proposals failed to win legislative support, no doubt as the result of two basic factors: (1) the legislatures were not willing to impose an additional tax upon home industries and thereby place these firms in an unfair position while competing for business with out-of-state concerns, and (2) many states were fearful that the additional tax might further delay industrial recovery. As the intensity of the depression increased, with unemployment rising from three to twelve million workmen, and the states continued to postpone the enactment of any unemployment compensation laws, the national government was forced into action. President Franklin D. Roosevelt, in June, 1934, appointed the members of the Committee on Economic Security to study problems relating to the economic security of our citizens and to make a report with recommendations by December 1 of the same year. This report became the basis for the Social Security Act of 1935 which, as one of its main features, established the current cooperative federal-state program.

The primary stimulus for the universal acceptance by the states of the unemployment compensation plan is the tax credit device. Under the current law a national payroll tax of 3 per cent is assessed against certain categories of employers.[9] Actually, the law provides that the tax, while it may not exceed 3 per cent, is levied only upon that part of the payroll equal to $3,000 per employee per year or less, to the extent that certain employees did not earn that amount. These proceeds are placed in a federal unemployment insurance fund. However, a credit up to 90 per cent of this tax is granted to an employer in a state that enacts a tax for unemployment compensation purposes. This tax credit convinced the states to accept the provisions of the federal Social Security Act and to adopt their own individual laws, since a federal subsidy covers the cost of state administration. If a state has failed to pass its own unemployment compensation measure, the employer still must make a payment to the national government, so no advantage accrues to the state that would elect to remain out of the system. In actual practice most of the states have levied a 2.7 per cent tax, and the employer then is given credit for this amount against the national account, thereby owing the national government only 0.3 per cent. These proceeds from the state tax of 2.7 per cent are not retained in the state but are sent to the national treasury and held in earmarked accounts to be released to the states as claims arise.

While each state actually administers its own phase of the national act, it is subject to some federal requirements before employers can use the tax credit offsets. The most outstanding of these federal standards are: (1) certain reserve requirements must be met, (2) state personnel administering the act must be chosen by a merit system, (3) employees who are denied compensation must be able to appeal to a state tribunal, and (4) state funds must be deposited with the United States Secretary of the Treasury. If a state meets these and certain other national specifications, its costs for the administration of unemployment compensation is borne by the national government.

The number of weeks of duration of payment and the specific amounts paid vary, with some states actually exceeding, on their own initiative, the federal minimums. The tax on employers is based on an experience rating

---

[9] The use of the national government's taxing powers and the tax offset or credit device was upheld as being constitutional in *Steward Machine Company v. Davis* (301 U.S. 548, 1937).

system which permits those employers who can show low rates of unemployment to be taxed at reduced rates. While benefits are determined by the use of different formulas, all states have a tendency to follow one acceptable principle: a percentage of the wages earned weekly or quarterly during a given period of employment. In addition, an eligible employee must have earned a certain minimum wage for a stipulated period in order to qualify for benefits. Most state laws also require a waiting period of from one to two weeks before unemployment compensation can be paid.

The number of weeks of payment vary from as few as 18 in Virginia to as many as 39 in Oklahoma. The most common figure is 26 weeks of compensation. The weekly benefits range from a low of from $3 to $16 per week to a maximum varying from $26 to $70. Since the major purpose of unemployment compensation payments is to assist an unemployed worker until he can find new employment, the number of eligible weeks is naturally limited, and in all instances this type of compensation ceases when suitable work is found.

## Temporary Unemployment Benefit Programs

The Temporary Extended Unemployment Compensation Act of 1961 (TEUC) provided that state employment security agencies could act as agents of the United States, under agreements with the Secretary of Labor, in taking claims and paying temporary extended benefits to individuals who exhausted their unemployment benefits under the state law after June 30, 1960, and before approximately April 1, 1962. No extended benefits were to be payable for any week of unemployment beginning after June 30, 1962. All of the states chose to participate in this program.

This program permitted states to pay extended benefits up to half of the total amount of benefits originally payable on the exhausted claim but not in excess of thirteen times the weekly benefit amount paid on that claim. Also, the law provided for federal re-imbursement to a state for benefits paid to an individual in excess of twenty-six times the weekly benefit amount. The total amount of state benefits plus federal extended benefits which might be paid in a compensation period was thirty-nine times the individual's weekly benefit amount.

During the period of its operation, from April 8, 1961, to June 30, 1962, approximately 2.8 million individuals were paid about $817 million in benefits under this federal program. Of this total amount some $46 million were in the form of reimbursements to states for payments in excess of 26 weeks under regular state programs to those claimants who were not entitled to TEUC benefits.[10]

[10] Council of State Governments, *The Book of the States, 1964–1965* (Chicago: Council of State Governments, 1964), p. 551.

## Fair Employment Practices

There seemingly has been popular acceptance in our American democracy of the general principle that there should exist no discrimination in hiring and firing practices with particular respect to color, creed, national origin, race, or religion. For many years certain segments of our population have maintained that too many citizens have been content to pay mere lip service to this general principle and have thereby permitted employers, employees, and even in some instances labor unions too much freedom in exercising discrimination. Our society is still divided on the question as to the best means by which discrimination in employment can be curbed or eliminated. Some maintain that education and good conscience are the most effective methods. Others believe that a law prohibiting discrimination is a step in the right direction but caution that the effectiveness of such a measure is conditioned by the actual degree of acceptance on behalf of our citizens. Those opposed to what are popularly referred to as fair employment practices laws do so primarily on the grounds that these measures merely increase the antagonisms rather than eliminate the problems, and, in addition, violate the freedom of an employer to manage his business as he so desires.

The national government made certain attempts to prevent employment discrimination during World War II. Following the war, states began to enact FEP measures, with New York passing its law in 1945, followed by New Jersey in the same year. By 1964 twenty-five states had enacted mandatory laws which prohibited discrimination in employment practices on the basis of race, creed, or color.[11] In seventeen states discrimination on the basis of age is also prohibited.[12]

In most of the states that have passed mandatory fair employment practices acts and included penalty for violations, a board or commission is the usual administrative agency created. This board or commission is generally clothed with the following powers or responsibilities: (1) to initiate enforcement proceedings either on the basis of complaints filed with the board or commission or on its own initiative, (2) to conduct an investigation that may involve a public hearing, and (3) to issue orders, usually in the form of a cease and desist order, that will stop the discriminatory practice and compel compliance with the provisions of the state law. While refusal to obey such an order may lead to court action on behalf of the

[11] Alaska, California, Colorado, Connecticut, Delaware, Hawaii, Idaho, Illinois, Indiana, Iowa, Kansas, Massachusetts, Michigan, Minnesota, Missouri, New Jersey, New Mexico, New York, Ohio, Oregon, Pennsylvania, Rhode Island, Vermont, Washington, and Wisconsin.

[12] Alaska, California, Colorado, Connecticut, Delaware, Hawaii, Louisiana, Massachusetts, Nebraska, New Jersey, New York, Ohio, Oregon, Pennsylvania, Rhode Island, Washington, and Wisconsin.

board or commission, most employers will comply and only infrequently will such cases get into the court system. Also, in those states providing for this type of a board or commission, these orders are subject to judicial review.

## Employment Services

For years the time-honored practices in the field of employment involved the individual worker in finding suitable employment on his own initiative or utilizing the services of a private employment agency that charged a substantial fee. Unethical practices and excessive fee-charging on behalf of some of these private agencies undoubtedly prodded a few states to create employment agencies as early as the 1890's. The states attempted to regulate the fees charged by private employment agencies, but it was not until 1941 that the United States Supreme Court sustained such state regulations as constituting a valid exercise of the police power of the state.[13] The national government became interested in federal employment services at the time of World War I, but very little cooperation existed between the state employment offices and the national government before 1933.

With increasing unemployment in the United States to approximately 13 million workers by the spring of 1933, the national government was forced to establish a federal-aid program to cope with the problem of large-scale unemployment and to assist the states in creating more employment agencies. The Congress in 1933 passed the Wagner-Peyser Act which eventually was to draw every state into the program, which provided grants to the states that would match federal appropriations and maintain certain standards in the organization and administration of their state employment offices. This act established the United States Employment Service as a unit of the Bureau of Employment Security in the Department of Labor to work with a nation-wide network of state employment offices in such matters as promoting the use of public employment services, dissemination of labor market information, and in the selection and training of office staffs.

With the advent of World War II, the national government took over the management and supervision of all such agencies in an effort to cope with the manpower shortage created by the wartime situation. In 1946 the United States Employment Service returned control to the state agencies and centered its operating services directly for veterans and farm workers.

## Child Labor

The employment of children for excessive hours of work was a common practice until fairly recent times. Even the first hour-and-wage laws passed

[13] *Olsen v. Nebraska* (313 U.S. 236, 1941).

supposedly in their behalf did little to ease the problem. Various groups, including reform organizations, enlightened employers, and organized labor, worked strenuously for measures that would cease or at least curb the continued exploitation of children in industry. The United States Supreme Court in 1918 and 1922 voided legislation that had been passed by the Congress.[14] The Congress in 1924 proposed an amendment to the United States Constitution that would have delegated the authority to regulate child labor to the national government. Before the necessary number of state ratifications could be secured, the Supreme Court upheld the Fair Labor Standards Act that forbade employers in interstate commerce from employing anyone under the age of sixteen or anyone under eighteen in hazardous occupations.[15]

Every one of the states has now passed laws protecting children in the area of employment. Most of the child labor laws prohibit children from participating in any type of employment that could be classified as potentially harmful to them, with hazardous jobs not being held by anyone under sixteen or eighteen years of age. The minimum age for employment is not uniform among the states but is often fixed at fourteen, fifteen, or sixteen. Usually the state laws establish the daily and weekly maximum number of hours of work for child laborers, with night work being restricted in every state. Certain exceptions are made, particularly with respect to farm labor or for circumstances of extreme necessity. During 1962 and 1963 about one-third of the states enacted changes in their child labor laws. Steps were taken in a number of states to aid school drop-outs and to assist them in remaining in school.[16]

## LABOR UNION ACTIVITIES

### Collective Bargaining

In labor relations the term "collective bargaining" has been used to refer to a method of negotiation through which representatives of management and labor organizations work out agreements with respect to terms and conditions of employment. This process is usually regarded as strengthening the position of organized labor, for a union is in a favorable bargaining position if it can represent all or a large percentage of an employer's workers.

Unions have not always been effective labor organizations. Not only have they been deprived of some of their effectiveness as the result of fac-

---

[14] *Hammer v. Dagenhart* (247 U.S. 251, 1918); and *Bailey v. Drexel Furniture Company* (259 U.S. 20, 1922).

[15] *United States v. Darby Lumber Company* (312 U.S. 100, 1941).

[16] Council of State Governments, *The Book of the States, 1964–1965* (Chicago: Council of State Governments, 1964), p. 529.

tional fighting within the ranks, but for years employers were not required by law to bargain collectively. In addition, many union leaders were placed on the "black list" and could not find employment, and individual workers were forced to sign "yellow-dog" contracts that provide for employment only as long as they did not join the union. Many times the employers established company unions to prevent any recruitment among the workers by the labor unions. The strike, one of labor's most potent weapons, was often prevented by injunctions.

State action on behalf of labor did not actually occur until the national government began to enact labor laws during the 1930's. In 1932 the Congress passed the Norris-LaGuardia Act, which prohibited the use of the injunction as a means of enforcing yellow-dog contracts. The Supreme Court negated both the National Industrial Recovery Act of 1933, which provided that workers "shall have the right to organize and bargain collectively," and the Guffey Coal Act of 1935, which contained similar language. The Wagner Act of 1935 not only contained the provision for collective bargaining but also prohibited a series of "unfair labor practices," which included the refusal by employers to bargain with the recognized representatives of organized employees. While this measure pertains only to interstate commerce, about one-fourth of the states have enacted miniature Wagner Acts that are applicable to intrastate labor relations. In addition, many states have passed various laws dealing with a variety of unfair labor practices.

## Mediation, Conciliation, and Arbitration

In virtually every state some type of machinery has been established that can be used by labor and management to assist in the settlement of their disputes. Three different forms of assistance are usually provided: (1) mediation, (2) conciliation, and (3) arbitration.

*Mediation* utilizes the presence of an impartial third party who attempts to suggest a possible solution to the problem facing the disputants. No effort is made on the part of the mediator to force or coerce the parties to accept any particular solution. The emphasis is placed upon the role of the mediator to propose or suggest possible solutions. In *conciliation*, which is quite similar to mediation and sometimes used as a synonymous term, the third party, who is referred to as a conciliator, performs a major duty of keeping the disputants present at the negotiating table until a final agreement or compromise is reached. In most states the services of the mediator or conciliator must be requested by the disagreeing parties and is not an automatic service of the labor section of state government.

*Arbitration* is also conducted by a neutral third party. It is different from mediation and conciliation in these respects. First, the disputants agree before negotiations begin to accept the decision of the arbitrator. Secondly, the parties to the dispute agree to abide by the decision of the arbitrator as binding and final. While arbitration in most states is a voluntary process, six states have provided for some phase of compulsory arbitration, even in the face of considerable opposition not only from management but also from organized labor.[17] It must be pointed out, however, that the provisions for compulsory arbitration have been upheld in a few state court cases but only when applied to the area of public utilities. The United States Supreme Court in 1923 held compulsory arbitration to be unconstitutional when applied outside the public utility field. In this instance, the meat-packing business, the application of compulsory arbitration was viewed as a deprivation of the employee's and the employer's liberty under due process of law.[18] In 1951 the decision of the United States Supreme Court that the Wisconsin statute was unconstitutional was on the grounds that it conflicted with the national authority to regulate interstate commerce.[19]

## The Right To Strike

The strike is usually viewed as the ultimate or final tool placed at the disposal of a union. Labor's right or ability to use this potent and drastic weapon has received widespread acceptance, especially when the process of collective bargaining has not succeeded. The more generally accepted objectives for the strike involve questions of higher pay, shorter hours or a reduced working week, and improved working conditions. Under most state laws a strike must meet two major requirements: (1) the purposes must be legal, and (2) the methods or tactics used in conducting the strike must be lawful or proper.

The definition as to what constitutes a lawful or proper purpose and a legal method have been the subject of considerable state legislation, in addition to many court decisions. Many states have passed laws that declare certain specific labor objectives to be unlawful and also condemn as illegal particular types of strikes. As an example, a strike designed to compel an employer to hire only members of a union would be declared unlawful or illegal in a state that has outlawed the closed shop. In turn, a strike will usually be declared unlawful if techniques involving coercion, intimidation, or violence have been utilized by the union, even when the purposes sought are completely legal and proper. The difference between legal and illegal practices, methods, or tactics has usually centered around

[17] Florida, Indiana, Missouri, Nebraska, New Jersey, and Pennsylvania.
[18] *Wolff Packing Co. v. Court of Industrial Relations* (262 U.S. 522, 1923).
[19] *Amalgamated Association v. Wisconsin Employment Relations Board* (340 U.S. 383, 1951).

the distinction between intimidation and persuasion. In Wisconsin a jurisdictional strike is listed by law as an unlawful labor practice while sympathetic strikes are held by many courts to be illegal. In those states that have copied the cooling off provisions of the Taft-Hartley Act, strikes may not be called during the compulsory waiting period. The United States Supreme Court has held the sit down strike to be unlawful in those conditions covered by national laws, and several states have specifically outlawed this type of strike.[20]

The strike, which permits employees to work together to achieve certain goals, actually results in a temporary halt of the processing of goods or services. Two practices closely associated with the strike are: (1) picketing, and (2) the boycott. *Picketing* involves the stationing of representatives of the union at the place of employment as a means of informing the public that a labor dispute exists. It also gives indication that the union plans to use every legal and proper method to halt temporarily the operation of the plant or business until a satisfactory settlement is reached. Within the states, as a general rule, peaceful picketing for legal purposes has been declared lawful and proper. The United States Supreme Court has ruled that action by a state to declare peaceful picketing unlawful is probably an unconstitutional interference with the freedom of speech. This court, in holding as unconstitutional an Alabama law which prohibited picketing or loitering, maintained that the dissemination of information relating to the facts of a labor dispute must be regarded as "within that area of free discussion that is guaranteed by the Constitution."[21] In many states where picketing involves coercion it is held to be unlawful and injunctions can be issued to restrain this practice. Since over the years the injunction has served as an effective device in breaking strikes, almost every state, no doubt in response to the demand of organized labor, has passed laws limiting the use of the injunction in labor relations cases.

The situation with respect to mass picketing is not so clear cut. In some states this form of picketing has been declared legal while other states have classified it as an illegal practice. It must be noted that even the position of the United States Supreme Court with respect to mass picketing has not been consistent. In 1921 the Court declared mass picketing to be unlawful since the number of pickets in the groups constituted intimidation.[22] Just two decades later the United States Supreme Court upheld mass picketing, when not accompanied by violence, as an exercise of free speech as guaranteed by the Fourteenth Amendment.[23] The states are also

[20] *National Labor Relations Board v. Fansteel Metallurgical Corporation* (306 U.S. 204, 1939).

[21] *Thornhill v. Alabama* (310 U.S. 88, 1940).

[22] *American Steel Foundries Co. v. Tri-City Central Trades Council* (257 U.S. 184, 1921).

[23] *American Federation of Labor v. Swing* (312 U.S. 321, 1941).

divided with regard to the problem of secondary picketing, with some declaring it illegal, while the New York Court of Appeals accepted the practice where no fraud or violence was proven.[24]

The *boycott* constitutes a refusal to carry on business relations or to patronize a firm or, in some instances, another individual. Two forms of the boycott, primary and secondary, are generally recognized. The *primary boycott* exists when employees refuse to patronize their employer. It is also present when a union group agrees not to buy from an employer who is labeled as unfair. This type of the boycott is now recognized as a legitimate labor weapon, although this was not always the situation. However, it is possible that a primary boycott may be declared illegal if its objective is unlawful under the state law.

The *secondary boycott* involves the concerted action of the union or employees to prevent third parties, or those individuals not directly involved in the labor dispute, from patronizing an employer. A number of states, following the Taft-Hartley Act, have classified the secondary boycott as an unfair union practice. Other states have passed statutes outlawing the secondary boycott or otherwise declaring it illegal. In some states the courts have held that those individuals who participate in a secondary boycott are guilty of unlawful conspiracy and are subject to certain penalties imposed against such conduct. This is even true in some states where the secondary boycott is not definitely forbidden by law.

## Open, Closed, and Union Shops

For several years regulations have been in effect in many states that have determined the hiring practices that could be followed by management. Organized labor has maintained an interest in these laws as a means of increasing what is referred to as union security. With respect to hiring practices, a firm is often referred to as having an *open, closed,* or *union shop.*

An *open shop* exists where an employer is free to hire anyone he desires, irrespective of the prospective employee's union status. The employee is free to join the union or not, depending entirely on his own desires. The *closed shop* is one in which membership in a union serves as a definite prerequisite for employment, and as a result this system provides the union with a monopoly, many will maintain, since only union members may be employed. The *union shop* permits the initial employment of non-union workers but provides that such employees must join the union within a certain time period, usually from thirty to ninety days.

At the present time approximately one-fourth of our states prohibit both the closed and union shops. On the national scene the Taft-Hartley Act outlaws the closed shop in those businesses subject to federal regulation.

[24] *Labor Course* (Englewood Cliffs, N.J.: Prentice-Hall, Inc., 1952), par. 11, p. 166.

Union shops are permitted when approved by a majority of the workers within a business or establishment except in those states that have outlawed this type of shop.

In twenty states either statutes or constitutional amendments have been passed which have been referred to as right-to-work measures.[25] While varying in detail, these laws basically prevent the union from compelling management to hire only members of unions. Most of these state laws have been adopted since 1947, but a few were in effect before the passage of the Taft-Hartley Act. Organized labor has been bitterly opposed to such laws on the grounds that any employee who benefits from the gains secured by union action should make a contribution to the union, and that such laws are designed, therefore, to weaken the position of the union. The advocates of the right-to-work law maintain that this statute will have a tendency to force unions to strive constantly to offer better programs and to seek self-improvement in order to attract new members, while still retaining the concept of individual freedom with respect to the choice of union membership. Most of these laws are in operation in Southern or rural (agricultural) states, with Indiana being the only one that could be classified in the heavily industrial category. The state elections of 1958 provided the right-to-work movement with a very serious setback; the proposition was accepted only in Kansas while going down to defeat in five states, including California.

Two other devices closely associated with unions are (1) the *check-off* and (2) *maintenance of membership* provisions. The *check-off* is a means by which an employer withholds or deducts union dues from the wages of employees and pays these sums to the union. This system is authorized in some states when agreed to by the employer and yet is directly forbidden in other states. The *maintenance of membership* provision is actually an agreement between management and the union by which those individuals who decide on their own to join the union must remain a member of the union during the life of the contract or lose their jobs. Once again there is division within the states with respect to this provision, with some states listing it is a lawful practice while others will not permit it.

## STATE ADMINISTRATIVE ORGANIZATION

The first state labor laws had a tendency not to establish any special administrative enforcement offices, and as a result the administration of these

[25] Alabama, Arizona, Arkansas, Florida, Georgia, Indiana, Iowa, Kansas, Mississippi, Nebraska, Nevada, North Carolina, North Dakota, South Carolina, South Dakota, Tennessee, Texas, Utah, Virginia, and Wyoming. A law that pertains only to agricultural labor or those employed in the processing of particular agricultural products is in force in Louisiana.

measures fell to the general law-enforcement officers of the state. Many times the enforcement was carried on in a very aimless style. In many states the first administrative agencies in this field were bureaus of labor statistics, which were only fact-finding bodies charged with the collecting and publishing of labor information. Eventually these bureaus were given the responsibility of enforcing certain sections of the labor laws of the state. Later, the position of factory inspector was established in many states, and the regulatory functions previously placed in bureaus of labor statistics or local officials were transferred to this type of officer. However, as new state laws were passed, additional and separate enforcement officials were provided until the responsibility for labor law enforcement was scattered among many state and local officers. Beginning in the 1920's the states started to work toward an integrated administration of labor laws by establishing a central authority.

At the present time the primary agency for administering state labor laws is a department of labor or industrial relations under a commission, a director, or a secretary. The popular election of the top labor officials occurs in only five states—Georgia, North Carolina, North Dakota, Oklahoma, and Oregon. The more prevalent pattern of selection of state labor officials is one of appointment by the governor with senatorial confirmation. This is the course of action followed in twenty states. The governor is granted the complete power of appointment, without any type of confirmation necessary, in only thirteen states. In Connecticut the labor office is filled by gubernatorial appointment with approval by either house of the state legislature, while in Maine, Massachusetts, and New Hampshire the appointment is made by the governor and council. The Alaska arrangement calls for appointment by the governor with the approval of both legislative houses.[26]

## A Case Study: California Department of Industrial Relations

The department of industrial relations of the state of California typifies, with perhaps a few exceptions, the organization of state activities within this field under the direction of a statutory officer who is appointed by the governor. Since the establishment of the department in 1927 by the state legislature, this agency has grown in its efforts to meet the demands of a state labor force of over 6.5 million workers. At the present time the department consists of ten divisions and is staffed with approximately 2,300 employees. The California labor code provides that the philosophy of this agency is to "foster, promote, and develop the welfare of wage earners in

[26] The information contained in this paragraph is taken from Council of State Governments, *The Book of the States, 1964–1965* (Chicago: Council of State Governments, 1964), p. 148.

California, improve their working conditions, and advance their opportunities for profitable employment."

The department is headed by a director who, with the consent of the governor, coordinates and administers the various operations. The director has the control over and is responsible for all moneys allocated to the department and its divisions for the purpose of carrying on its work, including personnel, materials, supplies, and property. In addition, it is imperative that the director make certain that each division understands the aims and problems of the other sections. In Figure 25–1 the administrative organization of the California department of industrial relations is presented. The activities of some of the divisions of this department are discussed in the following paragraphs.

*Division of Fair Employment Practices.* California, in 1959, became the sixteenth state to establish an agency to protect the right and opportunity of all persons to seek, obtain, and hold employment without discrimination on account of race, religious creed, color, national origin, or ancestry. The fair employment practice commission, consisting of five members appointed by the governor, was given the dual responsibility of enforcing the law and of bringing about the widest possible voluntary compliance. The division of fair employment practices was organized to provide essential staff services for the commission.

The fair employment practices act generally forbids private employers, employment agencies, labor organizations, and state and local government bodies to make any discrimination with regard to the following employment practices: hiring; upgrading; terms of employment; conditions of discharge; job application forms or interviews; help-wanted advertising, classification of applicant by employment agencies and referral to openings; and admission to union membership or dispatch to jobs. A few categories of employers are exempted from the requirements of the FEP law. A complaint of unlawful employment practices may be filed by the person claiming to be aggrieved, by the state attorney general, or by employers whose employees refuse to cooperate with the law. The commission may initiate investigations of apparent unlawful practices and seek to eliminate them by conference, conciliation, and persuasion. Each case received is assigned to a member of the commission who, with the assistance of the staff, conducts an investigation. If the complaint is found to lack probable cause the commissioner dismisses it. If unlawful discrimination is found, the commissioner seeks to bring about voluntary acceptance by the parties of a just and practicable remedy. The law provides that there shall be no disclosure of what has transpired in the endeavors at conciliation and persuasion. If settlements are not reached through these informal processes, the assigned commissioner may call a public hearing. Such hearings are conducted before a panel of at least three members of the commission ex-

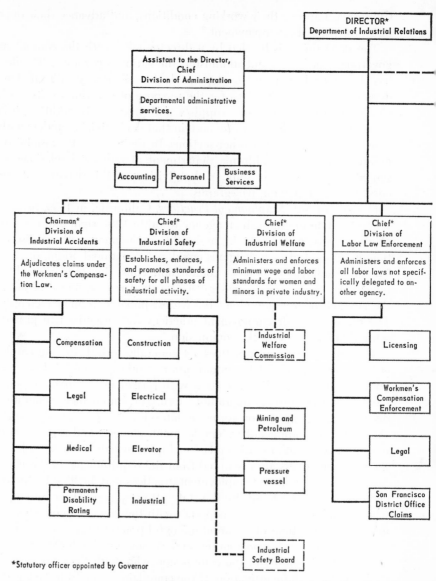

Fig. 25–1. Organizational Chart, Department of Indus fornia Department of Industrial Relations, January 1, 1963.)

clusive of the assigned commissioner, who may appear only as a witness and may not participate in the deliberations of the commission with regard to the case. If, after a hearing, the commission makes a finding of unlawful discrimination, it may serve upon the respondent an order re-

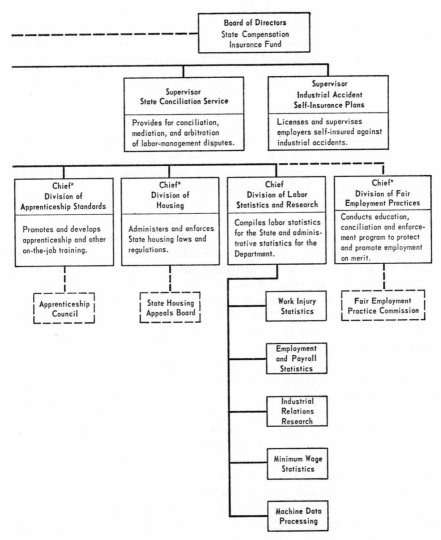

trial Relations, State of California. (Source: State of Cali-

quiring him to take such action necessary to correct the practice complained about. If he refuses to comply with the order, the commission may seek a superior court injunction. Every final order or decision of the commission is subject to judicial review.

A second major responsibility of the division of fair employment practices relates to the promotion of good will and understanding among all segments of the state's population and for educational programming designed to minimize or eliminate discrimination. The commission is authorized to create advisory or conciliation councils to foster good will and cooperation and to study problems of discrimination. These councils are to consist of representative citizens who will serve without pay. The commission is also empowered to issue such publications, including results of investigations and research, as in its judgment will promote good will and minimize or eliminate discrimination.

*Division of Apprenticeship Standards.* The division of apprenticeship standards is the administrative agency of the department of industrial relations that is designated to carry out the provisions of the Shelley-Maloney Apprentice Labor Standards Act. This measure, which became effective in 1939, established within the department of industrial relations the California apprentice council to promote, foster, and develop the training of young men and women who desire, through apprenticeship, to become fully skilled journeymen in trades taking from one to six years to learn. The council is composed of sixteen members, fourteen of whom are appointed by the governor. Of the fourteen, six representatives each are selected from employer and employee organizations, with two representatives from the general public. The ex-officio members are the director of industrial relations and the chief of the bureau of industrial education, state department of education.

The apprenticeship consultants, or field staff, promote and maintain apprenticeship training through: (1) the development of labor-management committees; (2) establishment of apprenticeship standards and other on-the-job training programs; (3) analysis of occupational job training and advice on the establishment, registration, content, and operation of apprenticeship programs; (4) advice with regard to recruitment, testing, evaluation of apprentice applicants; (5) mediation of disputes relating to apprenticeship (6) reporting on the establishment and administration of training agreements and programs in the various apprenticeable trades; (7) addressing meetings and conferences of labor, management, civic, and other public groups; and (8) gathering and disseminating information on current trends, practices, and techniques for the improvement of apprentice training, and other duties as may be required. In addition, the division serves as the registration agency and depository of training standards and apprenticeship agreements, issues certificates of completion of apprenticeship under the authority of the California apprenticeship council, issues certificates of meritorious service to personnel of joint apprenticeship committees, does research work on special problems of apprentice training,

and compiles data and publishes materials relating to apprenticeship training.

The apprenticeship Council carries on the following functions: (1) aids
the administrator of apprenticeship in the formulating of policies; (2) establishes standards for minimum wages, maximum hours, and working
conditions for apprentice agreements; (3) issues rules and regulations
necessary to carry out the intent of the act; (4) fosters, promotes, and
develops the welfare of the apprentice and industry; (5) improves the
working conditions of apprentices and advances their opportunities for
profitable employment; and (6) holds hearings on appeals from determi-
nations of the administrator with respect to alleged violations of the terms
of apprentice agreements.

*The Division of Labor Law Enforcement.* This division originated in the
bureau of labor statistics which was created by the state legislature in
1883 for the purpose of investigating conditions of employment and the
job opportunities within the state. When the bureau was brought into the
department of industrial relations its name was changed to division of
labor statistics and law enforcement in an effort to project its two major
responsibilities. In 1945 the agency was divided into two sections, one of
labor statistics and research and the division of labor law enforcement.

The administrative staff consists of a chief, who is also known as the
state labor commissioner, the assistant chief (assistant labor commissioner), an administrative assistant, a licensing section, and a clerical com-
plement. The enforcement staff is composed of five supervising deputy
labor commissioners, with each one in charge of a designated area; forty-
nine deputy labor commissioners, who have major responsibility for all of
the division's functions in their respective districts; eleven special investi-
gators, who are concerned not only with the general work of the division
but more particularly in the areas of workmen's compensation, child labor
investigations, employment agencies, and farm labor contractors.

At the present time the division administers more than sixty laws, which
are concerned with almost every phase of employee-employer relations.
These are usually classified into the following nine categories: (1) wage
payment laws, (2) laws relating to contributions to health and welfare
funds, (3) child labor laws, (4) statutes regulating private employment
agencies, (5) farm labor contracts, (6) labor on public works, (7) the
produce unloaders act, (8) compulsory workmen's compensation insurance, and (9) hours of employment in specified industries and other miscellaneous laws relating to employment practices and working conditions.

*Division of Industrial Welfare.* The division is responsible for the enforcement and administration of state laws covering the employment of
women and minors in California, with the exception of agriculture, gov-

ernment, and domestic service. There are some fifty-three different labor standards relating to the employment of women and minors which can be categorized under the following headings: minimum wage, hours of work, records, working conditions, plant facilities, industrial homework, defense production, and equal pay. The primary responsibility of the division is to work with employers and employer organizations to prevent violations of the labor standards. The division also engages in some selective investigations. The minimum wage act of 1913 provided for a five-member commission to be appointed by the governor. This commission was to determine cost of living and fix minimum wage, maximum hours of labor, and proper working conditions for women and minors employed in any industry or occupation. Originally this commission not only possessed the power to make mandatory orders regulating the wages, hours, and working conditions of women and minors but also to enforce and administer these orders. In 1927 the legislative function of the commission was separated from the administrative and enforcement functions. As a result the division of industrial welfare was established as the administrative and enforcement unit while the industrial welfare commission continued with its legislative powers. In recent years the commission has devoted major portions of its time to the study of hours, wages, and working conditions of women and minors in agriculture. The division personnel consists of the chief, assistant chief, special information officer, four area supervisors, two payroll auditors, and thirty-three enforcement officers assigned to sixteen district offices throughout the state.

*Division of Labor Statistics and Research.* This division is concerned with recording a wide variety of statistics that in turn reveal the many changing facets of the California economy. Also this division works very closely with other state agencies: (1) compiling quarterly and annual statistics for the industrial accident commission which summarize original and supplemental decisions of the commission; (2) assisting the division of industrial safety in scheduling their inspection services and in utilizing data processing equipment; (3) preparing monthly, quarterly, and annual statistics for the division of housing with respect to inspections of labor camps and various other dwelling units; (4) providing semiannual and annual tabulations of conciliation service cases and assisting in preparing annual reports; (5) preparing statistical material for the California conference on apprenticeship; and (6) producing annual statistics of placement made and fees collected by private employment agencies in California licensed by the division of labor law enforcement.

The division is also responsible for issuing certain publications including the annual reports in the series *Union Labor in California,* monthly estimates of work stoppages as a part of the department's *Report to the Governor's Council,* annual reports on *Wage Settlements* and *California*

*Union Agreements,* and issues of *California Industrial Relations Reports.*

In addition to measuring current developments, the division is called upon to conduct various surveys. As an example, the division, jointly with the research and statistics section of the department of employment, prepared projections of the California labor force to the year 1975 for the use of the governor in long-range planning for the state. At the request of the industrial welfare commission the division conducted wage and hour surveys in industries in which women and minors are employed.

## BIBLIOGRAPHY

COHEN, SANFORD. *State Labor Legislation: 1937–1947.* Columbus: Bureau of Business Research, Ohio State University, 1948.

DIAMOND, NORENE M. *A Guide to State Mediation Laws and Agencies.* (U.S. Bureau of Labor Standards, Bulletin No. 176). Washington, D.C.: Government Printing Office, 1958.

DULLES, FOSTER RHEA. *Labor in America.* New York: Thomas Y. Crowell Co., 1949.

GREGORY, CHARLES O. *Labor and Law.* New York: W. W. Norton & Co., Inc., 1946.

KILLINGSWORTH, C. C. *State Labor Relations Acts.* Chicago: The University of Chicago Press, 1948.

LEEKS, JOHN H. *Government and Labor in the United States.* New York: Holt, Rinehart & Winston, Inc., 1952.

LESTER, RICHARD A. *As Unions Mature.* Princeton: Princeton University Press, 1958.

MAGNUSSON, LEIFUR. *Government and Labor in the United States.* Chicago: Public Administration Service, 1945.

MILLU, HARRY A., and MONTGOMERY, ROYAL E. *Organized Labor.* New York: McGraw-Hill Book Co., Inc., 1945.

MUELLER, S. J. *Labor Law and Legislation.* Cincinnati: South-Western Publishing Co., Inc., 1949.

ROBERTS, B. C. *Unions in America.* Princeton: Industrial Relations Section, Princeton University, 1959.

SOMERS, HERMAN M., and SOMERS, ANNE R. *Workmen's Compensation.* New York: John Wiley & Sons, Inc., 1954.

TAYLOR, G. W. *Government Regulation of Industrial Relations.* Englewood Cliffs, N.J.: Prentice-Hall, Inc., 1949.

TURNBULL, JOHN G., WILLIAMS, C. ARTHUR, JR., and CHEIT, EARL F. *Economic and Social Security—Public and Private Measures Against Economic Insecurity.* New York: The Ronald Press Co., 1962.

U.S. Bureau of Labor Standards. *State Labor Relations Acts.* Washington, D.C.: Government Printing Office, 1961.

# 26

# The States and
# Their Future

The national government has gained power at the expense of the state governments. Whether or not this is desirable has been discussed by serious students of government and politicians as well as the average citizen for a number of years. It is obvious, however, that even if the national government has expanded at the expense of the states, the states are now assuming more power than ever before: spending more money, raising more taxes, and employing more people. Yet this expansion in most states has been largely unplanned.

Two types of federalism have become recognized by political scientists —legal and functional federalism. Legal federalism is usually defined as two separate entities dealing with each other on more or less equal terms, with the Supreme Court of the United States as the final arbitrator. Functional federalism is an operational understanding that certain problems must be solved, work performed, and needs satisfied, with the governmental unit best equipped to perform the task being allowed by mutual consent to take the necessary steps.

In the former definition the courts have tended to build up the jurisdiction of the national government and to limit the sphere of influence of the states. The interpretations of what may be included under the national government's commerce power, for example, has broadened the scope of power granted to the federal government. The functional federalism, however, has tended to give the states increased functional activities.

The basic problem has become one of allocating the work of government to the governmental unit that can best perform the needed service or regulation rather than restraining a governmental unit from exercise of power. It should be the will of the people that determines which unit should perform a specific function, if democracy and government of the people, by the people, and for the people is to prevail.

The governmental unit that can best perform the function usually is interpreted to mean the one which can most efficiently and economically do the job. Each function has to be examined in light of its own peculiarities. In some instances the government closest to the problem is best able to handle the situation; in others only a government with wide territorial powers can efficiently deal with the problem. One axiom that seems to prevail is that the unit of government must have territorial jurisdiction over a large enough area to include all of the geographic aspects of the function. For example, it is not feasible for each city to regulate the rates and service of a light and power company that serves a hundred cities within the state. It is necessary for the entire state to be under a regulatory agency. Likewise, it is necessary for the national government to regulate telephone and telegraph rates and service when the company performing the service operates in all of the fifty states and is constantly engaged in interstate commerce.

Every state in the Union has a government that is similar to that of every other in many ways. The differences are more a matter of degree. The basic organizations are fundamentally the same. Each state has its own written document, the state constitution, which is the basis for the governmental structure if not its functions. Each of the state constitutions divides the governmental power into three branches; a legislative, judicial, and executive-administrative. All three branches check and balance one another so that no one division has total power and authority.

The common denominators of state government are a written constitution, a theory of separation of power, and a reverence for custom and traditions of the past. To be sure within these common denominators many variations are found: Nebraska has a unicameral legislature rather than a bicameral as do the other forty nine states; only North Carolina does not allow its governor to have the veto power; only New Hampshire does not permit the legislature to amend the state constitution.

Experts do not agree as to one proper way of organizing state services. There is agreement on some features but disagreement on many others. State governments do many things, but all fall into certain categories: protection of its citizens, regulation and promotion of activities, and operation of certain state services deemed necessary by the state for the public welfare.

If good government is to prevail three essential features must be present:

1. Good structure and organization
2. Honest and competent personnel
3. Intelligent, informed, and an interested electorate

## STATES VS. REGIONAL GOVERNMENTAL UNITS

In recent years not too much has been written about replacing the states by regional governmental units, but in the 1930's several leading political scientists made proposals of this nature. Professor Roy V. Peel in 1932 suggested:

It is my proposal that the states be divested of all the political attributes which they now have, except those which are of an historical or purely ceremonial character. These attributes, whether of status or function, I would redistribute among a series of political units, beginning with the neighborhood or community, at the base, and proceeding to the nation, at the top. Midway between the units which I have named stands the region, by which is meant that area within which geographic fact, economic organization, social custom, and political interest have established and fostered a sense of cohesiveness and community of interest which distinguishes it from any other area.[1]

An even more far reaching suggestion was made a year later by Professor Simeon Leland. His recommendation would have the federal government take over all matters of more than local concern and place all truly local affairs in the hand of the state (eliminating counties and townships), and giving all urban affairs to the cities.[2]

A Harvard University political scientist, William Y. Elliott in 1935, spelled out in concrete terms his regional proposal. He would divide the United States into eleven regions:

1. New England
2. Central Atlantic
3. New York
4. Eastern Mid-West
5. Central Mid-West
6. South Atlantic Seaboard
7. Eastern Southern "Border" Area
8. Deep South
9. Western Prairie
10. Rocky Mountain Region
11. Pacific Coast Region

These regional commonwealths would have regional legislative bodies and governors. The judicial system would be a single one for the entire United States. The Elliott plan was patterned upon the Canadian provinces, with

[1] Roy V. Peel, *The Displacement of States by Political Regions: An Address Before the Conference of Metropolitan Government, New York City, October 19, 1932*, as reported by Brooke Graves, *American State Government* (Boston: D. C. Heath & Co., 1946), pp. 953–54.

[2] Simeon E. Leland, "The Coordination of Federal, State and Local Fiscal Systems," *Municipal Finance*, August, 1933, pp. 35–46.

autonomous units for local functions, but contemplated the consolidation of counties. It should be noted that the states would still perform as do English counties.[3]

Two other regional plans, neither as radical a departure from the present system as the other programs, were proposed a few years later. Professor William B. Munro in 1936 suggested that a regional plan be interposed between the states and the federal government. The proposed nine or ten regions would be not merely federal administrative areas but would possess autonomy.[4]

Professor Alexander Hehmeyer in 1943 suggested that the same approach that was used in the TVA, of establishing regional governmental units for certain basic problems that ordinarily cut across state boundaries, be installed. This would not displace state governments but merely shift some of the regulatory burdens from the states to a regional government composed of combined federal and state officials.[5]

What was at one time thought to be the forerunner of extensive dependence upon regionalism was the compact entered into by twelve Southern states in 1948 for higher education. This compact, which was given impetus by various Supreme Court decisions of the late 1930's and 1940's, established a board of control for Southern regional education. This method of pooling resources of the Southern states in order to give equal educational opportunities to the Negroes who sought higher education would still continue segregated schooling. More recent decisions of the Supreme Court, which have ruled that equal but separate education is unconstitutional, have tended to lessen the utility of the Southern regional education program as far as maintaining segregation. The value of pooling facilities and faculties still remains an important educational step.

Even though the idea may no longer be viewed as of use in the segregation problem, it still may have important implications for regional government, as it allows less affluent states to meet various problems by cooperative action. It is a method of deterring over-centralization by enabling states with limited means to find a financial way other than appealing to the federal government for aid and assistance.

## CONSTITUTIONAL REVISIONS

The late Senator Richard L. Neuberger of Oregon wrote, "Most of the circumstances which have put state government on the toboggan can be

[3] William Y. Elliott, *The Need for Constitutional Reform* (New York: McGraw-Hill Book Co., Inc., 1935), pp. 191–204.
[4] William B. Munro, "Regional Governments for Regional Problems," *The Annals of the American Academy of Political and Social Science,* Vol. CLXXXV pp. 129–30.
[5] Alexander Hehmeyer, *Time for Change* (New York: Farrar, Straus & Co., Inc., 1943), pp. 123–31.

rectified through a wholesale overhauling of state constitutions."[6] This statement applies to a vast majority of the fifty states. In the last twenty years the only new constitutions that have been framed have been in Hawaii, Alaska, Connecticut, Georgia, Missouri, New Jersey, and Michigan.

Almost all of the others, and possibly even some of these seven new constitutions, have provisions that not only do not fit present times and needs but actually hinder governmental agencies and officials in the performance of their assigned duties. Complete constitutional revision, or at least examination, probably should occur in every state once in every twenty-five years, but seldom is such a schedule followed. It might be noted that the New Jersey Constitution of 1947 did not contain a provision for periodic constitutional revision. The proposal was considered and rejected by the delegates not so much on its merits but owing to the political pressures in the convention.[7]

This is evidence that even the best of the newer state constitutions are beset by shortcomings. It is generally conceded that periodic review is needed, or at least the people should be given the opportunity to review the supreme law. At least fifteen states have to contend with a cumbersome amending process that frequently requires at least two years or more to amend their state constitutions because two successive legislative sessions must approve of a constitutional amendment before it can be sent to the people for their decision.

No one contends that a new constitution will automatically give a state good government, any more than a change in organizational structure guarantees efficiency and economy. However, a new, flexible constitution, fashioned on the pattern of the Model State Constitution, will in all probability allow a legislative majority the opportunity to handle problems with greater ease and at less cost. New constitutions should allow the majority to prevail and not permit the minority to prevent progress, economy, and efficiency.

A new constitution is not a guarantee that civil rights will prevail for all groups in the state, but it will probably give the elected officials a better chance of obtaining proper machinery to accomplish equality of treatment and opportunity. However, in this area as in so many others, it is the personnel and their dynamic quality that must be present to assure success of the governmental operation.

The Commission on Intergovernmental Relations suggested that

[6] Richard L. Neuberger, "The Decay of State Governments," *Harper's Magazine* (October, 1953), p. 41.

[7] Bennett M. Rich, *Government and Administration of New Jersey* (New York: Thomas Y. Crowell & Co., 1957), p. 393.

Self-imposed constitutional restrictions have been often the underlying causes of state and municipal pleas for federal assistance. One way to arrest the trend is to make sure that our state constitutions provide for vigorous and responsible government, not forbid it.[8]

## STATE LEGISLATURES

During the next decade the one item of state government that over-shadows all others is the apportionment problem that exists in the state legislatures. Since the *Baker v. Carr* decision the present apportionment of all state legislatures has been questioned. There can be no denial that this is a basic problem that must be solved before other aspects of state government will be given proper attention. At the current time it would appear that the United States Supreme Court will be the ultimate authority. When it outlines what it is willing to accept as proper representation, the fifty states will have a guide-line established to work out this perplexing problem. There is no question that if population is ruled as the only factor that can be considered in apportioning state legislatures, virtually every state legislature will have to be reapportioned along this line. The arguments pro and con for population as the factor are well known and have been discussed elsewhere in this volume.

Beyond the apportionment problem other needed reforms involving the legislature need to be considered. The age-old question of bicameral vs. unicameral legislative bodies is still current and may become more important if population is to be represented in each house on an equal basis. The major arguments for bicameral legislatures will have been diluted if not voided.

The need for annual sessions of the legislature is also a pressing change that is undergoing considerable scrutiny in many states. A reduction in the number of committees and the use of joint committees to speed up the consideration of legislation also must be given proper attention.

The compensation paid legislators in a majority of the states is so low that many qualified persons are unable to afford to serve in the state general assembly. This too must be weighed and proper decisions made as to what constitutes adequate remuneration for legislative service. Adequate research and legislative assistance for members of state policy-making bodies in another serious problem that must be given increasing attention in many states. Archaic legislative procedures, such as time-consuming roll calls answered by voice and three readings of bills, should also be seriously questioned in the years ahead with appropriate reforms taken.

[8] The Commission on Intergovernmental Relations, *A Report to the President* (Washington, D.C.: Government Printing Office, 1955), pp. 38, 56.

## THE GOVERNORS

State governors can realize their full potential only when the entire constitutional framework within which they operate has been remodeled. The dynamic leadership which the people want and expect from their chief executives, and which the future requires, can be realized to the full only under optimum conditions. The first of these is a short and simple state constitution.[9]

In the immediate years ahead the institutional features and the powers of the governor in the states must be improved if maximum results from the leadership of the state's chief executives are to be achieved. Best results will probably be attained when all governors are elected for a four-year term, and are permitted to succeed themselves, administrative elective offices are eliminated from state constitutions, the powers of appointment and removal are made commensurate with the responsibilities of the governor for administrative management, appropriate authority over budgetary matters is given to the governors including the item veto power, and adequate staff made available to all governors. Every governor should be not only the chief executive in name but also in fact. His authority to enforce the law must be supported by control over all law enforcement agencies of the state government.

The salary of the governor in many states is still not adequate to allow the best qualified persons to afford contesting for this highest state public office. He must be given all of the management tools known to the art and science of administration if he is to have half a chance to carry out an aggressive dynamic program.

## STATE ADMINISTRATIVE ORGANIZATION

Even the states that have in theory been administratively reorganized usually fall far short of the standards established by the students of administration. The nearly twenty-five states that have not undergone reorganization within the last thirty years have an antiquated administrative system to cope with the problems of the second half of the twentieth century.

Every state administrative reorganization is inevitably predicated upon the theory that more economical and efficient state government must be attained. In the rare instances in which complete reorganization has taken place there is some evidence to demonstrate that to a degree improvements have accompanied the change, probably not as much as the re-

[9] Bennett M. Rich, *State Constitutions: The Governor* (New York: National Municipal League, 1960), p. 33.

formers had hoped but more than the opponents had believed possible. Usually the ballot has been shortened, more modern administrative techniques have been utilized, such as better accounting procedures, better purchasing methods, and executive budgeting, and there has been some reduction in costs. Most reorganizations have also included a greater use of modern personnel methods of employment, retirement, and promotion, usually with a state-wide civil service system.

The use of boards as administrative units and commissions has been abandoned in some states where complete administrative reorganization has taken form. Single-headed departments, with advisory boards to perform quasi-legislative and quasi-judicial tasks, have resulted in greater accountability and centralization of responsibility, less buck-passing, and greater efficiency.

The consolidating of state agencies to be supervised by the chief executive into a number compatible with span of control is usually another feature of complete state administrative changeover. This results in a minimum number of major departments, usually not over fifteen or twenty, with all functional activities in one major component.

The state governments of the future must, if the increasing number of state problems are to be solved, grant increasing authority to the governor. The administrative hierarchy must be clarified, with the chief executive truly in command of the entire structure. Greater reliance upon staff and auxiliary agencies, both within the governor's office and throughout the entire administrative organization, will become indispensable.

Coordinated financial powers in one administrative agency will go far to assure maximum use of every revenue dollar produced by the state tax system. It is imperative that all taxes be collected and then properly spent. Pre-auditing of all expenditures, with the comptroller directly accountable to the governor, should be accepted as a regular part of the state's administrative organization. Post-audit also should be standardized, with the auditor appointed by the legislative branch and reporting to it on a periodic basis, with timely audits of all funds.

## PERSONNEL ADMINISTRATION

Reform in state personnel administration in both those states that now are assumed to have complete civil service programs for all employees and those who admittedly have only a merit system for employees who receive a portion of their compensation from the federal government is a "must" of the future.

Just as a government can be no better than those who work in the system no matter what form of administrative hierarchy is utilized, a civil service system can be no better than the men who administer it. They can help it to succeed or can make it a total failure. Not only must the legislation that authorizes the civil service be sound, but the people who are appointed to the civil service commissions must also be individuals who believe in the system and work effectively to have it serve the purpose of contributing to good government.

In the future, state and local government must be made as attractive as possible. The stature of the government service must be elevated, and the stigma of working for these units must be erased. Career opportunities must be expanded so that young men and women of talent, training, and dynamic ability will not only be attracted to the jobs but retained for years in governmental employment. This means that the working conditions must be as good if not better than in private industry, that the pay scales, the opportunities for advancement, the fringe benefits, including retirement programs, must be made enticing. Most of all, the idea that public service is not only a public trust but is an opportunity to contribute to the welfare of the people must be enhanced and emphasized.

The development of political dynasties at any level of government, and particularly state and local government, must be curbed. Machine politics that depend so largely upon corrupt personnel practices must be abolished. The integrity of the personnel system of the last quarter of the present century will do much to increase the chances of state and local government to continue as an important force in the American government pattern. If it is not placed on a high plain, it can easily contribute to the total destruction of the sacred American dependency upon local government. Personnel systems of the future must be geared to attracting competent personnel rather than having as their main objective the negative approach of keeping incompetents out of the public employment. Not only must recruitment be based on ability but the merit motive must permeate the entire operation.

## STATE JUDICIARY

This is an area in which genuine progress has been made in recent years. The Missouri plan, which provides that state judges be appointed by the governor from a list supplied him by a judicial selection commission, has been accepted by a number of states. The electorate is allowed at periodic intervals to express their approval or disapproval of the judicial activities of individual judges before they are allowed to complete the term to which they were originally appointed, and before re-appoinment. This promises to elevate the quality of the men serving in the judicial branch of state government.

The plan of a unified state court is also being accepted in various states and likewise appears to be a step forward for justice in state courts. The gradual elimination of the justice of the peace court and other truly inferior courts will probably come in years ahead. The unified court would require that the chief justice of the highest state court be appointed on a long-term basis and become an administrative leader for the courts of the state.

All states in the foreseeable future will probably find it desirable to establish judicial councils or their counterparts. These councils should be given power to make rules for the administration of the courts and regulations regarding pleadings and court procedures, as well as administrative duties.

State courts will probably become more active in the fields of conciliation and arbitration. A development of the future may also be the establishment of administrative courts and claims courts to rule upon claims filed against the state, rather than to require individuals and corporations to file special bills with the state legislature. Time- and expense-saving reforms, such as a more extensive use of declaratory judgments and advisory opinions by the state courts, may well be two other developments in the state judicial fields.

Re-examination of the indictment process and the jury system is far overdue in most of the states. Too many states exempt from jury service a large part of the better-qualified members of the state community. Remuneration for members of juries is ridiculously low in all but a few of the fifty states. Too many cases are tried before juries that should be heard by a panel of judges. Justice delayed is still justice denied and most state court dockets are falling farther and farther behind. Frequently at least a year will pass before a case will be settled, and it is not unknown in some judicial jurisdictions for several years to be consumed with settlement of relatively simple cases.

## LOCAL GOVERNMENT

Improvements in the organization of local governmental units must continue in the years remaining in the twentieth century. Both municipalities and counties throughout the country need to re-examine their administrative organizations. Gradually state constitutional restrictions on forms of government that may be used by these local units are being eased. Modernized local governmental machinery, with responsibility more clearly focused, is probably the greatest need. The boards and commissions that perform strictly administrative duties are slowly being abolished and single-headed divisions formed. Use of trained, full-time administrators in both municipalities and counties is still sorely needed.

A reduction in the number of local governmental units is problematical. There is no question that the number of school districts will be reduced in many states, but this gain may easily be offset by the rapidly expanding number of special districts. Various county government reforms are available. City-county consolidation would appear to be a distinct possibility in some areas. County functional consolidation, by which several counties would use the same individual to perform the same service in more than one county is advocated by some experts. The establishment of a county administrator to centralize administrative functions is a third suggested reform. Some states will no doubt find it best to eliminate the county as a governmental unit. All will soon conclude that the township government is a vestigal unit that can offer no service that cannot be more efficiently and economically performed by a larger territorial unit. The idea that the degree of democracy is in direct proportion to the number of local governmental units will eventually be abandoned.

Home rule, both constitutional and legislative, for local governments, particularly municipalities and to a lesser extent for counties, should again in the immediate future receive more extensive utilization. County and municipal officials, who have in several states had the opportunity to utilize home-rule provisions but who have not done so because of court litigation, will no doubt see the wisdom of accepting the opportunity of having a greater amount of authority over their local institutions as afforded by the home-rule charters. In a number of states eligible municipalities have not exercised this option of forming their governments under home-rule provisions established either through the state constitution or state statutes. While to a large extent relatively small communities have exercised the privilege of home rule more enthusiastically than the metropolitan areas, it would certainly seem that these urban centers are likely to be the focal point in the future growth of home rule. Self-determination of local government should be one of the best remedies for citizen apathy that any governmental unit could embrace. Its possibilities are almost unlimited. Where malapportionment has deprived proper representation, it serves as at least a partial remedy. Where antiquated constitutional and statutory provisions prevail, it allows for circumvention of these handicaps.

## STATE AND LOCAL REVENUES

Most of the states have already given up reliance upon the general property tax as a revenue source for state operations and have turned it over to the local governmental units as their primary tax base. The few states that have not taken this step will probably do so soon. Further tax developments must be forthcoming. Additional revenue sources for both state and local units must be found if the continuing expansion of governmental services is to persist, as it inevitably will.

Probably every state will be forced to a general sales tax, possibly as high as 5 per cent. The major cities within the state will undoubtedly be allowed to use an additional sales tax as a major revenue source. Similarly, all states will in the future find that a withholding income tax will have to be resorted to in order to balance the budget. The cities, and possibly the counties, will require a portion of the state's income tax or an independently imposed income tax. Excise taxes of various types will no doubt continue to increase in numbers in almost every state. City excise taxes also will become an important part of the total revenue pattern.

Local governments, and possibly even state governments, may, before the end of this century, be charging for many services that have been given by the governmental units in the past. Garbage collection and similar types of services can be charged on a per-call basis to help defray some governmental expenses.

The Commission on Intergovernmental Relations concluded in its 1955 report that:

> . . . a fundamental objective of our system of government should be to keep centralization to a minimum and State-local responsibility to a maximum. The fiscal resources available to the National and State governments are adequate for the needs of a federal system responsive to the people. If States are to assume a larger share of governmental activities in the future, however, changes will have to be made to help overcome serious financial problems.[10]

Furthermore, the commission acknowledged that there was no grand solution to the intergovernmental fiscal problems, but suggested that what was needed in the future was a consistent and sustained attack at all levels of government with improved coordination of fiscal policies through greater separation of revenue sources and administrative cooperation.

This need for constant re-examination of taxation measures with particular attention to constitutional and statutory limitations on revenue powers and debt limitations of local governments must be followed in future years. All planning in the revenue area should focus on the impact on state and local finances of population growth, migration, and urbanization, not for just the next five or six years but for the next twenty to fifty years.

The states must expect national government action whenever any one of the following five conditions prevail:

    1. When the national government is the only agency that can summon the resources needed for an activity

[10] The Commission on Intergovernmental Relations, *A Report to the President* (Washington, D.C.: Government Printing Office, 1955), p. 116.

2. When the activity cannot be handled within the geographic and jurisdictional limits of smaller governmental units, *including those created by compacts*
3. When the activity requires a nationwide uniformity of policy that cannot be achieved by interstate action
4. When a state through action or *inaction* does injury to the people of other states
5. When states fail to respect or to protect basic political and civil rights that apply throughout the United States[11]

These guidelines should encourage further development of interstate compacts in the future. Recent years have again seen more interest and more action in this area, encouaged to a great extent by the Council of State Governments. Future years undoubtedly will see even greater expansion in the number of interstate compacts consummated. One of the future means of at least slowing down the drift toward national centralization and depletion of powers among the states will be the full utilization of interstate agreements on many different functional activities.

## CONCLUSIONS

What is to be the future of the states? The increasing affluence of the national government in matters of policy cannot be seriously questioned. Furthermore, as to its major functions, the national government is free, if it so desires, to ignore the states and to set up its own complete administration. Its regulation can be made to override those of the states. By its control in the field of taxation, and to satisfy its own tremendous needs, it might force the states into progressive diminution of their own revenues and a reduction of their own activities. This would bring about rapid strangulation, or at best a slow atrophy of the states.

It is one of the tasks of political scientists and statesmen for the next generation to work out a constructive and autonomous role for the states within the national framework. The current formula has not yet been discovered. The value to the whole nation of preserving the states can hardly be questioned. To keep the states alive and strong they must be kept active in the performance of functions over which they have their own control. They should not be allowed to die of sheer inactivity or to become mere administrative districts of the national government. The question is: How can the national government without impairing its power, achieve national purposes promptly and effectively and render public services on a national scale in such a manner as to preserve the advantage of state and local self-government?

[11] *Ibid.*, p. 64.

To prove their value in the future, the states must show beyond a shadow of doubt that they can be effective and economical in their operations and also demonstrate that they can be responsive to local needs and sensitive to regional as well as national opinions.

What is needed is a deliberate reappraisal and demonstration of the role of the states in the national social order that now exists, and an attempt to re-educate the people in the values of self-government in state and local communities.[12]

## BIBLIOGRAPHY

ALLEN, ROBERT S. (ed.). *Our Sovereign State.* New York: Vanguard Press, 1949.

———. *Our Fair City.* New York: The Vanguard Press, 1947.

ANDERSON, WILLIAM. *The Nation and the States, Rivals or Partners?* Minneapolis: University of Minnesota Press, 1957.

BROGAN, D. W. *Politics in America.* New York: Harper & Row, Inc., 1954.

BROWN, HARRISON. *The Next Hundred Years; Man's Natural and Technological Resources.* New York: The Viking Press, Inc., 1957.

DEWHURST, J. F., and ASSOCIATES. *America's Needs and Resources.* New York: 1955.

DRUCKER, PETER F. *America's Next Twenty Years.* New York: Harper & Row, Inc., 1957.

GOLDWIN, ROBERT A. (ed.). *A Nation of States.* Chicago: Rand McNally & Co., 1963.

GOSNELL, HAROLD F. *Democracy—the Threshold of Freedom.* New York: The Ronald Press Co., 1948.

JEWELL, MALCOLM E. (ed.). *The Politics of Reapportionment.* New York: Atherton Press, 1962.

JOINT COMMITTEE ON THE ECONOMIC REPORT, 83d CONGRESS. *Potential Economic Growth of the United States During the Next Decade.* Washington, D.C.: Government Printing Office, 1954.

LOCKARD, DUANE. *The Politics of State and Local Government.* New York: The Macmillan Co., 1963.

LUBELL, SAMUEL. *The Future of American Politics.* New York: Harper & Row, Inc., 1952.

MAAS, ARTHUR (ed.). *Area and Power: A Theory of Local Government.* New York: The Free Press of Glencoe, Inc., 1959.

MACMAHON, ARTHUR W. (ed.). *Federalism Mature and Emergent.* Garden City, N.Y.: Doubleday & Co., Inc., 1955.

PEEL, ROY V. *State Government Today.* Albuquerque: University of New Mexico Press, 1948.

RICH, BENNETT M. *State Constitutions: The Governor.* New York: National Municipal League, 1960.

STEIN, MAURICE R. *The Eclipse of Community: An Interpretation of American Studies.* Princeton: Princeton University Press, 1960.

[12] William Anderson, "Federalism—Then and Now," *State Government,* Vol. XVI, No. 5, (May, 1940), pp. 107–12.

STIEBER, JACK (ed.). *United States Industrial Relations: The Next Twenty Years.* East Lansing: Michigan State University, 1958.

VILE, M. J. C. *The Structure of American Federalism.* Fair Lawn, N.J.: Oxford University Press, 1961.

WERNETTE, J. P. *The Future of American Prosperity.* New York: The Macmillan Co., 1955.

WHITE, LEONARD D. *The States and the Nation.* Baton Rouge: Louisiana State University Press, 1953.

WHITE, WALTER. *How Far the Promised Land?* New York: The Viking Press, Inc., 1955.

WOOD, ROBERT C. *Suburbia: Its People and Their Politics.* Boston: Houghton Mifflin Co., 1959.

# APPENDIX

# Model State Constitution*

## PREAMBLE

We, the people of the state of _____, recognizing the rights
and duties of this state as a part of the federal system of government,
reaffirm our adherence to the Constitution of the United States of America; and in order to assure the state government power to act for the good
order of the state and the liberty, health, safety and welfare of the people,
we do ordain and establish this constitution.

## Article I
### BILL OF RIGHTS

Section 1.01 *Freedom of Religion, Speech, Press, Assembly and Petition.* No law shall be enacted respecting an establishment of religion, or
prohibiting the free exercise thereof, or abridging the freedom of speech
or of the press, or the right of the people peaceably to assemble and to
petition the government for a redress of grievances.

Section 1.02. *Due Process and Equal Protection.* No person shall be
deprived of life, liberty or property without due process of law, nor be
denied the equal protection of the laws, nor be denied the enjoyment of
his civil rights or be discriminated against in the exercise thereof because
of race, national origin, religion or ancestry.

Section 1.03. *Searches and Seizures and Interceptions.*
(a) The right of the people to be secure in their persons, houses, papers
and effects against unreasonable searches and seizures shall not be violated, and no warrants shall issue, but upon probable cause, supported by
oath or affirmation, and particularly describing the place to be searched
and the persons or things to be seized.
(b) The right of the people to be secure against unreasonable interception of telephone, telegraph and other electronic means of communi-

* National Municipal League: *Model State Constitution*, 6th ed.

669

cation [, and against unreasonable interception of oral and other communications by electric or electronic methods,] shall not be violated, and no orders and warrants for such interceptions shall issue but upon probable cause supported by oath or affirmation that evidence of crime may be thus obtained, and particularly identifying the means of communication and the person or persons whose communications are to be intercepted.

(c) Evidence obtained in violation of this section shall not be admissible in any court against any person.

Section 1.04. *Self-Incrimination.* No person shall be compelled to give testimony which might tend to incriminate him.

Section 1.05. *Writ of Habeas Corpus.* The privilege of the writ of habeas corpus shall not be suspended unless when in cases of rebellion or invasion the public safety may require it.

Section 1.06. *Rights of Accused Persons.*

(a) In all criminal prosecutions the accused shall enjoy the right to a speedy and public trial, to be informed of the nature and cause of the accusation, to be confronted with the witnesses against him, to have compulsory process for obtaining witnesses in his favor, to have the assistance of counsel for his defense, and to the assignment of counsel to represent him at every stage of the proceedings unless he elects to proceed without counsel or is able to obtain counsel. In prosecutions for felony, the accused shall also enjoy the right of trial by an impartial jury of the county [or other appropriate political subdivision of the state] wherein the crime shall have been committed, or of another county, if a change of venue has been granted.

(b) All persons shall, before conviction, be bailable by sufficient sureties, but bail may be denied to persons charged with capital offenses or offenses punishable by life imprisonment, giving due weight to the evidence and to the nature and circumstances of the event. Excessive bail shall not be required, nor excessive fines imposed, nor cruel or unusual punishment inflicted.

(c) No person shall be twice put in jeopardy for the same offense.

Section 1.07. *Political Tests for Public Office.* No oath, declaration or political test shall be required for any public office or employment other than the following oath or affirmation: "I do solemnly swear [or affirm] that I will support and defend the Constitution of the United States and the constitution of the state of _____ and that I will faithfully discharge the duties of the office of _____ to the best of my ability."

## Article II

## POWERS OF THE STATE

Section 2.01. *Powers of Government.* The enumeration in this constitution of specified powers and functions shall be construed neither as a grant nor as a limitation of the powers of state government but the state government shall have all of the powers not denied by this constitution or by or under the Constitution of the United States.

## Article III

## SUFFRAGE AND ELECTIONS

Section 3.01. *Qualifications for Voting.* Every citizen of the age of _____ years and a resident of the state for three months shall have the right to vote in the election of all officers that may be elected by the people and upon all questions that may be submitted to the voters; but the legislature may by law establish: (1) Minimum periods of local residence not exceeding three months, (2) a reasonable literacy test to determine ability, except for physical cause, to read and write English, and (3) disqualifications for voting for mental incompetency or conviction of felony.

Section 3.02. *Legislature to Prescribe for Exercise of Suffrage.* The legislature shall by law define residence for voting purposes, insure secrecy in voting and provide for the registration of voters, absentee voting, the administration of elections and the nomination of candidates.

## Article IV

## THE LEGISLATURE

Section 4.01. *Legislative Power.* The legislative power of the state shall be vested in the legislature.

Section 4.02. *Composition of the Legislature.* The legislature shall be composed of a single chamber consisting of one member to represent each legislative district. The number of members shall be prescribed by law but shall not be less than _____ nor exceed _____. Each member of the legislature shall be a qualified voter of the state and shall be at least _____ years of age.

> BICAMERAL ALTERNATIVE: Section 4.02. *Composition of the Legislature.* The legislature shall be composed of a senate and an assembly. The number of members of each house of the legislature shall be prescribed by law but the number of assemblymen shall not be

less than _____ nor exceed _____, and the number of senators shall not exceed one-third, as near as may be, the number of assemblymen. Each assemblyman shall represent one assembly district and each senator shall represent one senate district. Each member of the legislature shall be a qualified voter of the state and shall be at least _____ years of age.

Section 4.03. *Election and Term of Members.* The members of the legislature shall be elected by the qualified voters of the state for a term of two years.

BICAMERAL ALTERNATIVE: Section 4.03. *Election and Terms of Members.* Assemblymen shall be elected by the qualified voters of the state for a term of two years and senators for a term of six years. One-third of the senators shall be elected every two years.

Section 4.04. *Legislative Districts.*
(a) For the purpose of electing members of the legislature, the state shall be divided into as many districts as there shall be members of the legislature. Each district shall consist of compact and contiguous territory. All districts shall be so nearly equal in population that the population of the largest district shall not exceed that of the smallest district by more than _____ per cent. In determining the population of each district, inmates of such public or private institutions as prisons or other places of correction, hospitals for the insane or other institutions housing persons who are disqualified from voting by law shall not be counted.
(b) Immediately following each decennial census, the governor shall appoint a board of _____ qualified voters to make recommendations within ninety days of their appointment concerning the redistricting of the state. The governor shall publish the recommendations of the board when received. The governor shall promulgate a redistricting plan within ninety to one hundred and twenty days after appointment of the board, whether or not it has made its recommendations. The governor shall accompany his plan with a message explaining his reasons for any changes from the recommendations of the board. The governor's redistricting plan shall be published in the manner provided for acts of the legislature and shall have the force of law upon such publication. Upon the application of any qualified voter, the supreme court, in the exercise of original, exclusive and final jurisdiction, shall review the governor's redistricting plan and shall have jurisdiction to make orders to amend the plan to comply with the requirements of this constitution or, if the governor has failed to promulgate a redistricting plan within the time provided, to make one or more orders establishing such a plan.

BICAMERAL ALTERNATIVE:    Section 4.04.    *Legislative Districts.*

(a) For the purpose of electing members of the assembly, the state shall be divided into as many districts as there shall be members of the assembly. Each district shall consist of compact and contiguous territory. All districts shall be so nearly equal in population that the district with the greatest population shall not exceed the district with the least population by more than _____ per cent. In determining the population of each district, inmates of such public or private institutions as prisons or other places of correction, hospitals for the insane or other institutions housing persons who are disqualified from voting by law shall not be counted.

(b) For the purpose of electing members of the senate, the state shall be divided into as many districts as there shall be members of the senate. Each senate district shall consist of a compact and contiguous territory. All districts shall be so nearly equal in population that the district with the greatest population shall not exceed the district with the least population by more than _____ per cent. In determining the population of each district, inmates of such public or private institutions as prisons or other places of correction, hospitals for the insane or other institutions housing persons who are disqualified from voting by law shall not be counted.

(c) Immediately following each decennial census, the governor shall appoint a board of _____ qualified voters to make recommendations within ninety days of their appointment concerning the redistricting of the state. The governor shall publish the recommendations of the board when received. The governor shall promulgate a redistricting plan within ninety to one hundred and twenty days after appointment of the board, whether or not it has made its recommendations. The governor shall accompany his plan with a message explaining his reasons for any changes from the recommendation of the board. The governor's redistricting plan shall be published in the manner provided for acts of the legislature and shall have the force of law upon such publication. Upon the application of any qualified voter, the supreme court, in the exercise of original, exclusive and final jurisdiction, shall review the governor's redistricting plan and shall have jurisdiction to make orders to amend the plan to comply with the requirements of this constitution or, if the governor has failed to promulgate a redistricting plan within the time provided, to make one or more orders establishing such a plan.

Section 4.05.    *Time of Election.* Members of the legislature shall be elected at the regular election in each odd-numbered year.

Section 4.06. *Vacancies.* When a vacancy occurs in the legislature it shall be filled as provided by law.

Section 4.07. *Compensation of Members.* The members of the legislature shall receive an annual salary and such allowances as may be prescribed by law but any increase or decrease in the amount thereof shall not apply to the legislature which enacted the same.

Section 4.08. *Sessions.* The legislature shall be a continuous body during the term for which its members are elected. It shall meet in regular sessions annually as provided by law. It may be convened at other times by the governor or, at the written request of a majority of the members, by the presiding officer of the legislature.

> BICAMERAL ALTERNATIVE: Section 4.08. *Sessions.* The legislature shall be a continuous body during the term for which members of the assembly are elected. The legislature shall meet in regular sessions annually as provided by law. It may be convened at other times by the governor or, at the written request of a majority of the members of each house, by the presiding officers of both houses.

Section 4.09. *Organization and Procedure.* The legislature shall be the final judge of the election and qualifications of its members and may by law vest in the courts the trial and determination of contested elections of members. It shall choose its presiding officer from among its members and it shall employ a secretary to serve for an indefinite term. It shall determine its rules of procedure; it may compel the attendance of absent members, discipline its members and, with the concurrence of two-thirds of all the members, expel a member, and it shall have power to compel the attendance and testimony of witnesses and the production of books and papers either before the legislature as a whole or before any committee thereof. The secretary of the legislature shall be its chief fiscal, administrative and personnel officer and shall perform such duties as the legislature may prescribe.

> BICAMERAL ALTERNATIVE: Section 4.09. *Organization and Procedure.* Each house of the legislature shall be the final judge of the election and qualifications of its members and the legislature may by law vest in the courts the trial and determination of contested elections of members. Each house of the legislature shall choose its presiding officer from among its members and it shall employ a secretary to serve for an indefinite term, and each house shall determine its rules of procedure; it may compel the attendance of absent members, discipline its members and, with the concurrence of two-thirds of all the members, expel a member, and it shall have power to compel

Section 4.06. *Vacancies.* When a vacancy occurs in the legislature it shall be filled as provided by law.

Section 4.07. *Compensation of Members.* The members of the legislature shall receive an annual salary and such allowances as may be prescribed by law but any increase or decrease in the amount thereof shall not apply to the legislature which enacted the same.

Section 4.08. *Sessions.* The legislature shall be a continuous body during the term for which its members are elected. It shall meet in regular sessions annually as provided by law. It may be convened at other times by the governor or, at the written request of a majority of the members, by the presiding officer of the legislature.

> BICAMERAL ALTERNATIVE: Section 4.08. *Sessions.* The legislature shall be a continuous body during the term for which members of the assembly are elected. The legislature shall meet in regular sessions annually as provided by law. It may be convened at other times by the governor or, at the written request of a majority of the members of each house, by the presiding officers of both houses.

Section 4.09. *Organization and Procedure.* The legislature shall be the final judge of the election and qualifications of its members and may by law vest in the courts the trial and determination of contested elections of members. It shall choose its presiding officer from among its members and it shall employ a secretary to serve for an indefinite term. It shall determine its rules of procedure; it may compel the attendance of absent members, discipline its members and, with the concurrence of two-thirds of all the members, expel a member, and it shall have power to compel the attendance and testimony of witnesses and the production of books and papers either before the legislature as a whole or before any committee thereof. The secretary of the legislature shall be its chief fiscal, administrative and personnel officer and shall perform such duties as the legislature may prescribe.

> BICAMERAL ALTERNATIVE: Section 4.09. *Organization and Procedure.* Each house of the legislature shall be the final judge of the election and qualifications of its members and the legislature may by law vest in the courts the trial and determination of contested elections of members. Each house of the legislature shall choose its presiding officer from among its members and it shall employ a secretary to serve for an indefinite term, and each house shall determine its rules of procedure; it may compel the attendance of absent members, discipline its members and, with the concurrence of two-thirds of all the members, expel a member, and it shall have power to compel

BICAMERAL ALTERNATIVE:   Section 4.04.   *Legislative Districts.*

(a) For the purpose of electing members of the assembly, the state shall be divided into as many districts as there shall be members of the assembly. Each district shall consist of compact and contiguous territory. All districts shall be so nearly equal in population that the district with the greatest population shall not exceed the district with the least population by more than _____ per cent. In determining the population of each district, inmates of such public or private institutions as prisons or other places of correction, hospitals for the insane or other institutions housing persons who are disqualified from voting by law shall not be counted.

(b) For the purpose of electing members of the senate, the state shall be divided into as many districts as there shall be members of the senate. Each senate district shall consist of a compact and contiguous territory. All districts shall be so nearly equal in population that the district with the greatest population shall not exceed the district with the least population by more than _____ per cent. In determining the population of each district, inmates of such public or private institutions as prisons or other places of correction, hospitals for the insane or other institutions housing persons who are disqualified from voting by law shall not be counted.

(c) Immediately following each decennial census, the governor shall appoint a board of _____ qualified voters to make recommendations within ninety days of their appointment concerning the redistricting of the state. The governor shall publish the recommendations of the board when received. The governor shall promulgate a redistricting plan within ninety to one hundred and twenty days after appointment of the board, whether or not it has made its recommendations. The governor shall accompany his plan with a message explaining his reasons for any changes from the recommendation of the board. The governor's redistricting plan shall be published in the manner provided for acts of the legislature and shall have the force of law upon such publication. Upon the application of any qualified voter, the supreme court, in the exercise of original, exclusive and final jurisdiction, shall review the governor's redistricting plan and shall have jurisdiction to make orders to amend the plan to comply with the requirements of this constitution or, if the governor has failed to promulgate a redistricting plan within the time provided, to make one or more orders establishing such a plan.

Section 4.05.   *Time of Election.* Members of the legislature shall be elected at the regular election in each odd-numbered year.

the attendance and testimony of witnesses and the production of books and papers either before such house of the legislature as a whole or before any committee thereof. The secretary of each house of the legislature shall be its chief fiscal, administrative and personnel officer and shall perform such duties as each such house of the legislature may prescribe.

Section 4.10. *Legislative Immunity.* For any speech or debate in the legislature, the members shall not be questioned in any other place.

Seciton 4.11. *Special Legislation.* The legislature shall pass no special or local act when a general act is or can be made applicable, and whether a general act is or can be made applicable shall be a matter for judicial determination.

Section 4.12. *Transaction of Business.* A majority of all the members of the legislature shall constitute a quorum to do business but a smaller number may adjourn from day to day and compel the attendance of absent members. The legislature shall keep a journal of its proceedings which shall be published from day to day. The legislature shall prescribe the methods of voting on legislative matters but a record vote, with the yeas and nays entered in the journal, shall be taken on any question on the demand of one-fifth of the members present.

BICAMERAL ALTERNATIVE: Section 4.12. *Transaction of Business.* Refer to "each house of the legislature" instead of "the legislature" wherever appropriate.

Section 4.13 *Committees.* The legislature may establish such committees as it may deem necessary for the conduct of its business. When a committee to which a bill has been assigned has not reported on it, one-third of all the members of the legislature shall have power to relieve it of further consideration. Adequate public notice of all committee hearings, with a clear statement of all subjects to be considered at each hearing, shall be published in advance.

BICAMERAL ALTERNATIVE: Section 4.13. *Committees.* Refer to "each house of the legislature" instead of "the legislature" wherever appropriate.

Section 4.14. *Bills; Single Subject.* The legislature shall enact no law except by bill and every bill except bills for appropriations and bills for the codification, revision or rearrangement of existing laws shall be confined to one subject. All appropriation bills shall be limited to the subject of appropriations. Legislative compliance with the requirements of this section is a constitutional responsibility not subject to judicial review.

Section 4.15. *Passage of Bills.* No bill shall become a law unless it has been printed and upon the desks of the members in final form at least three days prior to final passage and the majority of all the members has assented to it. The yeas and nays on final passage shall be entered in the journal. The legislature shall provide for the publication of all acts and no act shall become effective until published as provided by law.

BICAMERAL ALTERNATIVE: Section 4.15. *Passage of Bills.* Refer to "each house of the legislature" instead of "the legislature" wherever appropriate.

Section 4.16. *Action by the Governor.*

(a) When a bill has passed the legislature, it shall be presented to the governor and, if the legislature is in session, it shall become law if the governor either signs or fails to veto it within fifteen days of presentation. If the legislature is in recess or, if the session of the legislature has expired during such fifteen-day period, it shall become law if he signs it within thirty days after such adjournment or expiration. If the governor does not approve a bill, he shall veto it and return it to the legislature either within fifteen days of presentation if the legislature is in session or upon the reconvening of the legislature from its recess. Any bill so returned by the governor shall be reconsidered by the legislature and, if upon reconsideration two-thirds of all the members shall agree to pass the bill, it shall become law.

(b) The governor may strike out or reduce items in appropriation bills passed by the legislature and the procedure in such cases shall be the same as in case of the disapproval of an entire bill by the governor.

BICAMERAL ALTERNATIVE: Section 4.17. *Post-Audit.* The legislature Refer to "each house of the legislature" instead of "the legislature" wherever appropriate.

Section 4.17. *Post-Audit.* The legislature shall appoint an auditor to serve at its pleasure. The auditor shall conduct post-audits as prescribed by law and shall report to the legislature and to the governor.

BICAMERAL ALTERNATIVE: Section 4.17. *Past-Audit.* The legislature shall, by joint resolution, appoint. . . .

Section 4.18. *Impeachment.* The legislature may impeach the governor, the heads of principal departments, judicial officers and such other officers of the state as may be made subject to impeachment by law, by a two-thirds vote of all the members, and shall provide by law procedures for the trial and removal from office, after conviction, of officers so impeached. No officer shall be convicted on impeachment by a vote of less than two-thirds of the members of the tribunal hearing the charges.

BICAMERAL ALTERNATIVE:   Section 4.18.   *Impeachment.* Refer to "by a two-thirds vote of all the members of each house."

# Article V
# THE EXECUTIVE

Section 5.01.   *Executive Power.* The executive power of the state shall be vested in a governor.

Section 5.02.   *Election and Qualifications of Governor.* The governor shall be elected, at the regular election every other odd-numbered year, by the direct vote of the people, for a term of four years beginning on the first day of [December] [January] next following his election. Any qualified voter of the state who is at least _____ years of age shall be eligible to the office of governor.

Section 5.03.   *Governor's Messages to the Legislature.* The governor shall, at the beginning of each session, and may, at other times, give to the legislature information as to the affairs of the state and recommend measures he considers necessary or desirable.

Section 5.04.   *Executive and Administrative Powers.*

(a) The governor shall be responsible for the faithful execution of the laws. He may, by appropriate action or proceeding brought in the name of the state, enforce compliance with any constitutional or legislative mandate, or restrain violation of any constitutional or legislative power, duty or right by an officer, department or agency of the state or any of its civil divisions. This authority shall not authorize any action or proceeding against the legislature.

(b) The governor shall commission all officers of the state. He may at any time require information, in writing or otherwise, from the officers of any administrative department, office or agency upon any subject relating to the respective offices. He shall be commander-in-chief of the armed forces of the state, except when they shall be called into the service of the United States, and may call them out to execute the laws, to preserve order, to suppress insurrection or to repel invasion.

Section 5.05.   *Executive Clemency.* The governor shall have power to grant reprieves, commutations and pardons, after conviction, for all offenses and may delegate such powers, subject to such procedures as may be prescribed by law.

Section 5.06.   *Administrative Department.* All executive and administrative offices, agencies and instrumentalities of the state government, and their respective functions, powers and duties, shall be allocated by law among and within not more than twenty principal departments so as to group them as far as practicable according to major purposes. Regulatory, quasi-judicial and temporary agencies established by law may, but need not, be allocated within a principal department. The legislature shall by law prescribe the functions, powers and duties of the principal departments and of all other agencies of the state and may from time to time reallocate offices, agencies and instrumentalities among the principal departments, may increase, modify, diminish or change their functions, powers and duties and may assign new functions, powers and duties to them; but the governor may make such changes in the allocation of offices, agencies and instrumentalities, and in the allocation of such functions, powers and duties, as he considers necessary for efficient administration. If such changes affect existing law, they shall be set forth in executive orders, which shall be submitted to the legislature while it is in session, and shall become effective, and shall have the force of law, sixty days after submission, or at the close of the session, whichever is sooner, unless specifically modified or disapproved by a resolution concurred in by a majority of all the members.

BICAMERAL ALTERNATIVE: Section 5.06. *Administrative Departments.* Change the last phrase to read "majority of all the members of each house."

Section 5.07. *Executive Officers; Appointment.* The governor shall appoint and may remove the heads of all administrative departments. All other officers in the administrative service of the state shall be appointed and may be removed as provided by law.

Section 5.08. *Succession to Governorship.*
(a) If the governor-elect fails to assume office for any reason, the presiding officer of the legislature shall serve as acting governor until the governor-elect qualifies and assumes office or, if the governor-elect does not assume office within six months, until the unexpired term has been filled by special election and the newly elected governor has qualified. If, at the time the presiding officer of the legislature is to assume the acting governorship, the legislature has not yet organized and elected a presiding officer, the outgoing governor shall hold over until the presiding officer of the legislature is elected.
(b) When the governor is unable to discharge the duties of his office by reason of impeachment or other disability, including but not limited to physical or mental disability, or when the duties of the office are not being discharged by reason of his continuous absence, the presiding officer of the legislature shall serve as acting governor until the governor's disability or absence terminates. If the governor's disability or absence

does not terminate within six months, the office of the governor shall be vacant.

(c) When, for any reason, a vacancy occurs in the office of the governor, the unexpired term shall be filled by special election except when such unexpired term is less than one year, in which event the presiding officer of the legislature shall succeed to the office for the remainder of the term. When a vacancy in the office of the governor is filled by special election, the presiding officer of the legislature shall serve as acting governor from the occurrence of the vacancy until the newly elected governor has qualified. When the presiding officer of the legislature succeeds to the office of governor, he shall have the title, powers, duties and emoluments of that office and, when he serves as acting governor, he shall have the powers and duties thereof and shall receive such compensation as the legislature shall provide by law.

(d) The legislature shall provide by law for special elections to fill vacancies in the office of the governor.

(e) The supreme court shall have original, exclusive and final jurisdiction to determine absence and disability of the governor or governor-elect and to determine the existence of a vacancy in the office of governor and all questions concerning succession to the office or to its powers and duties.

BICAMERAL ALTERNATIVE: Section 5.08. *Succession to Governorship.* For "presiding officer of the legislature" substitute "presiding officer of the senate."

## Article VI
## THE JUDICIARY

Section 6.01. *Judicial Power.* The judicial power of the state shall be vested in a unified judicial system, which shall include a supreme court, an appellate court and a general court, and which shall also include such inferior courts of limited jurisdiction as may from time to time be established by law. All courts except the supreme court may be divided into geographical departments or districts as provided by law and into functional divisions and subdivisions as provided by law or by judicial rules not inconsistent with law.

Section 6.02. *Supreme Court.* The supreme court shall be the highest court of the state and shall consist of a chief judge and _____ associate judges.

Section 6.03. *Jurisdiction of Courts.* The supreme court shall have appellate jurisdiction in all cases arising under this constitution and the Constitution of the United States and in all other cases as provided by law. It shall also have original jurisdiction in cases arising under subsections 4.04(b) and 5.08(e) of this constitution and in all other cases as provided by law. All other courts of the state shall have original and appellate jurisdiction as provided by law, which jurisdiction shall be uniform in all geographical departments or districts of the same court. The jurisdiction of functional divisions and subdivisions shall be as provided by law or by judicial rules not inconsistent with law.

Section 6.04. *Appointment of Judges; Qualifications; Tenure; Retirement; Removal.*

(a) The governor, with the advice and consent of the legislature, shall appoint the chief judges and associate judges of the supreme, appellate and general courts. The governor shall give ten days' public notice before sending a judicial nomination to the legislature or before making an interim appointment when the legislature is not in session.

ALTERNATIVE: Subsection 6.04(a). *Nomination by Nominating Commission.* The governor shall fill a vacancy in the offices of the chief judges and associate judges of the supreme, appellate and general courts from a list of nominees presented to him by the appropriate judicial nominating commission. If the governor fails to make an appointment within sixty days from the day the list is presented, the appointment shall be made by the chief judge or by the acting chief judge from the same list. There shall be a judicial nominating commission for the supreme court and one commission for the nomination of judges for the court sitting in each geographical department or district of the appellate court. Each judicial nominating commission shall consist of seven members, one of whom shall be the chief judge of the supreme court, who shall act as chairman. The members of the bar of the state in the geographical area for which the court or the department or district of the court sits shall elect three of their number to be members of such a commission, and the governor shall appoint three citizens, not members of the bar, from among the residents of the same geographical area. The terms of office and the compensation for members of a judicial nominating commission shall be as provided by law. No member of a judicial nominating commission except the chief judge shall hold any other public office or office in any political party or organization, and no member of such a commission shall be eligible for appointment to a state judicial office so long as he is a member of such a commission and for [five] [three] [two] years thereafter.

(b) No person shall be eligible for judicial office in the supreme court, appellate court and general court unless he has been admitted to practice law before the supreme court for at least _____ years. No person who holds judicial office in the supreme court, appellate court or general court shall hold any other paid office, position of profit or employment under the state, its civil divisions or the United States. Any judge of the supreme court, appellate court or general court who becomes a candidate for an elective office shall thereby forfeit his judicial office.

(c) The judges of the supreme court, appellate court and general court shall hold their offices for initial terms of seven years and upon reappointment shall hold their offices during good behavior. They shall be retired upon attaining the age of seventy years and may be pensioned as may be provided by law. The chief judge of the supreme court may from time to time appoint retired judges to such special assignments as may be provided by the rules of the supreme court.

(d) The judges of the supreme court, appellate court and general court shall be subject to impeachment and any such judge impeached shall not exercise his office until acquitted. The supreme court may also remove judges of the appellate and general courts for such cause and in such manner as may be provided by law.

(e) The legislature shall provide by law for the appointment of judges of the inferior courts and for their qualifications, tenure, retirement and removal.

(f) The judges of the courts of this state receive such salaries as may be provided by law, which shall not be diminished during their term of office.

Section 6.05. *Administration.* The chief judge of the supreme court shall be the administrative head of the unified judicial system. He may assign judges from one geographical department or functional division of a court to another department or division of that court and he may assign judges for temporary service from one court to another. The chief judge shall, with the approval of the supreme court, appoint an administrative director to serve at his pleasure and to supervise the administrative operation of the judicial system.

Section 6.06. *Financing.* The chief judge shall submit an annual consolidated budget for the entire unified judicial system and the total cost of the system shall be paid by the state. The legislature may provide by law for the reimbursement to the state of appropriate portions of such cost by political subdivisions.

Section 6.07. *Rule-making Power.* The supreme court shall make and promulgate rules governing the administration of all courts. It shall make and promulgate rules governing practice and procedure in civil and criminal cases in all courts. These rules may be changed by the legislature by a two-thirds vote of all the members.

## Article VII
## FINANCE

Section 7.01.  *State Debt.* No debt shall be contracted by or in behalf of this state unless such debt shall be authorized by law for projects or objects distinctly specified therein.

Section 7.02.  *The Budget.* The governor shall submit to the legislature, at a time fixed by law, a budget estimate for the next fiscal year setting forth all proposed expenditures and anticipated income of all departments and agencies of the state, as well as a general appropriation bill to authorize the proposed expenditures and a bill or bills covering recommendations in the budget for new or additional revenues.

Section 7.03.  *Expenditure of Money.*

(a) No money shall be withdrawn from the treasury except in accordance with appropriations made by law, nor shall any obligation for the payment of money be incurred except as authorized by law. The appropriation for each department, office or agency of the state, for which appropriation is made, shall be for a specific sum of money and no appropriation shall allocate to any object the proceeds of any particular tax or fund or a part or percentage thereof, except when required by the federal government for participation in federal programs.

(b) All state and local expenditures, including salaries paid by the legislative, executive and judicial branches of government, shall be matters of public record.

## Article VIII
## LOCAL GOVERNMENT

Section 8.01.  *Organization of Local Government.* The legislature shall provide by general law for the government of counties, cities and other civil divisions and for methods and procedures of incorporating, merging, consolidating and dissolving such civil divisions and of altering their boundaries, including provisions:

(1) For such classification of civil divisions as may be necessary, on the basis of population or on any other reasonable basis related to the purpose of the classification;

(2) For optional plans of municipal organization and government so as to enable a county, city or other civil division to adopt or abandon an authorized optional charter by a majority vote of the qualified voters voting thereon;

(3) For the adoption or amendment of charters by any county or city

for its own government, by a majority vote of the qualified voters of the city or county voting thereon, for methods and procedures for the selection of charter commissions, and for framing, publishing, disseminating and adopting such charters or charter amendments and for meeting the expenses connected therewith.

ALTERNATIVE PARAGRAPH: Section 8.01(3). *Self-Executing Home Rule Powers.* For the adoption or amendment of charters by any county or city, in accordance with the provisions of section 8.02 concerning home rule for local units.

Section 8.02. *Powers of Counties and Cities.* A county or city may exercise any legislative power or perform any function which is not denied to it by its charter, is not denied to counties or cities generally, or to counties or cities of its class, and is within such limitations as the legislature may establish by general law. This grant of home rule powers shall not include the power to enact private or civil law governing civil relationships except as incident to an exercise of an independent county or city power, nor shall it include power to define and provide for the punishment of a felony.

ALTERNATIVE PROVISIONS FOR SELF-EXECUTING HOME RULE POWERS: Section 8.02. *Home Rule for Local Units.*

(a) Any county or city may adopt or amend a charter for its own government, subject to such regulations as are provided in this constitution and may be provided by general law. The legislature shall provide one or more optional procedures for nonpartisan election of five, seven or nine charter commissioners and for framing, publishing and adopting a charter or charter amendments.

(b) Upon resolution approved by a majority of the members of the legislative authority of the county or city or upon petition of ten per cent of the qualified voters, the officer or agency responsible for certifying public questions shall submit to the people at the next regular election not less than sixty days thereafter, or at a special election if authorized by law, the question "Shall a commission be chosen to frame a charter or charter amendments for the county [or city] of _____?" An affirmative vote of a majority of the qualified voters voting on the question shall authorize the creation of the commission.

(c) A petition to have a charter commission may include the names of five, seven or nine commissioners, to be listed at the end of the question when it is voted on, so that an affirmative vote on the question is a vote to elect the persons named in the petition. Otherwise, the petition or resolution shall designate an optional election procedure provided by law.

(d) Any proposed charter or charter amendments shall be published by the commission, distributed to the qualified voters and submitted to them at the next regular or special election not less than thirty days after publication. The procedure for publication and submission shall be as provided by law or by resolution of the charter commission not inconsistent with law. The legislative authority of the county or city shall, on request of the charter commission, appropriate money to provide for the reasonable expenses of the commission and for the publication, distribution and submission of its proposals.

(e) A charter or charter amendments shall become effective if approved by a majority vote of the qualified voters voting thereon. A charter may provide for direct submission of future charter revisions or amendments by petition or by resolution of the local legislature authority.

Section 8.03. *Powers of Local Units.* Counties shall have such powers as shall be provided by general or optional law. Any city or other civil division may, by agreement, subject to a local referendum and the approval of a majority of the qualified voters voting on any such question, transfer to the county in which it is located any of its functions or powers and may revoke the transfer of any such function or power, under regulations provided by general law; and any county may, in like manner, transfer to another county or to a city within its boundaries or adjacent thereto any of its functions or powers and may revoke the transfer of any such function or power.

Section 8.04. *County Government.* Any county charter shall provide the form of government of the county and shall determine which of its officers shall be elected and the manner of their election. It shall provide for the exercise of all powers vested in, and the performance of all duties imposed upon, counties and county officers by law. Such charter may provide for the concurrent or exclusive exercise by the county, in all or in part of its area, of all or of any designated powers vested by the constitution or laws of this state in cities and other civil divisions; it may provide for the succession by the county to the rights, properties and obligations of cities and other civil divisions therein incident to the powers so vested in the county, and for the division of the county into districts for purposes of administration or of taxation or of both. No provision of any charter or amendment vesting in the county any powers of a city or other civil division shall become effective unless it shall have been approved by a majority of those voting thereon (1) in the county, (2) in any city containing more than twenty-five per cent of the total population of the county, and (3) in the county outside of such city or cities.

Section 8.05. *City Government.* Except as provided in sections 8.03 and 8.04, each city is hereby granted full power and authority to pass laws and ordinances relating to its local affairs, property and government; and no enumeration of powers in this constitution shall be deemed to limit or restrict the general grant of authority hereby conferred; but this grant of authority shall not be deemed to limit or restrict the power of the legislature to enact laws of statewide concern uniformly applicable to every city.

FURTHER ALTERNATIVE: A further alternative is possible by combining parts of the basic text of this article and parts of the foregoing alternative. If the self-executing alternative section 8.02 is preferred but not the formulation of home rule powers in alternative sections 8.03, 8.04 and 8.05, the following combination of sections will combine the self-executing feature and the power formulation included in the basic text:

Section 8.01. *Organization of Local Government,* with alternative paragraph (3).
Alternative Section 8.02. *Home Rule for Local Units.*
Section 8.02, renumbered 8.03. *Powers of Counties and Cities.*

## Article IX
## PUBLIC EDUCATION

Section 9.01. *Free Public Schools; Support of Higher Education.* The legislature shall provide for the maintenance and support of a system of free public schools open to all children in the state and shall establish, organize and support such other public educational institutions, including public institutions of higher learning, as may be desirable.

## Article X
## CIVIL SERVICE

Section 10.01. *Merit System.* The legislature shall provide for the establishment and administration of a system of personnel administration in the civil service of the state and its civil divisions. Appointments and promotions shall be based on merit and fitness, demonstrated by examination or by other evidence of competence.

## Article XI
## INTERGOVERNMENTAL RELATIONS

Section 11.01. *Intergovernmental Cooperation.* Nothing in this constitution shall be construed: (1) To prohibit the cooperation of the gov-

ernment of this state with other governments, or (2) the cooperation of
the government of any county, city or other civil division with any one
or more other governments in the administration of their functions and
powers, or (3) the consolidation of existing civil divisions of the state. Any
county, city or other civil division may agree, except as limited by general
law, to share the costs and responsibilities of functions and services with
any one or more other governments.

## Article XII
## CONSTITUTIONAL REVISION

Section 12.01.  *Amending Procedure; Proposals.*

(a) Amendments to this constitution may be proposed by the legislature or by the initiative.

(b) An amendment proposed by the legislature shall be agreed to by
record vote of a majority of all of the members, which shall be entered
on the journal.

(c) An amendment proposed by the initiative shall be incorporated by
its sponsors in an initiative petition which shall contain the full text of
the amendment proposed and which shall be signed by qualified voters
equal in number to at least _____ per cent of the total votes cast for
governor in the last preceding gubernatorial election. Initiative petitions
shall be filed with the secretary of the legislature.

(d) An amendment proposed by the initiative shall be presented to the
legislature if it is in session and, if it is not in session, when it convenes
or reconvenes. If the proposal is agreed to by a majority vote of all the
members, such vote shall be entered on the journal and the proposed
amendment shall be submitted for adoption in the same manner as amendments proposed by the legislature.

(e) The legislature may provide by law for a procedure for the with-
drawal by its sponsors of an initiative petition at any time prior to its
submission to the voters.

Section 12.02.  *Amendment Procedure; Adoption.*

(a) The question of the adoption of a constitutional amendment shall
be submitted to the voters at the first regular or special statewide election
held no less than two months after it has been agreed to by the vote of the
legislature and, in the case of amendments proposed by the initiative
which have failed to receive such legislative approval, not less than two
months after the end of the legislative session.

(b) Each proposed constitutional amendment shall be submitted to
the voters by a ballot title which shall be descriptive but not argumenta-
tive or prejudicial, and which shall be prepared by the legal department
of the state, subject to review by the courts. Any amendment submitted

to the voters shall become a part of the constitution only when approved by a majority of the votes cast thereon. Each amendment so approved shall take effect thirty days after the date of the vote thereon, unless the amendment itself otherwise provides.

Section 12.03.   *Constitutional Conventions.*

(a) The legislature, by an affirmative record vote of a majority of all the members, may at any time submit the question "Shall there be a convention to amend or revise the constitution?" to the qualified voters of the state. If the question of holding a convention is not otherwise submitted to the people at some time during any period of fifteen years, it shall be submitted at the general election in the fifteenth year following the last submission.

(b) The legislature, prior to a popular vote on the holding of a convention, shall provide for a preparatory commission to assemble information on constitutional questions to assist the voters and, if a convention is authorized, the commission shall be continued for the assistance of the delegates. If a majority of the qualified voters voting on the question of holding a convention approves it, delegates shall be chosen at the next regular election not less than three months thereafter unless the legislature shall by law have provided for election of the delegates at the same time that the question is voted on or at a special election.

(c) Any qualified voter of the state shall be eligible to membership in the convention and one delegate shall be elected from each existing legislative district. The convention shall convene not later than one month after the date of the election of delegates and may recess from time to time.

(d) No proposal shall be submitted by the convention to the voters unless it has been printed and upon the desks of the delegates in final form at least three days on which the convention was in session prior to final passage therein, and has received the assent of a majority of all the delegates. The yeas and nays on any question shall, upon request of one-tenth of the delegates present, be entered in the journal. Proposals of the convention shall be submitted to the qualified voters at the first regular or special statewide election not less than two months after final action thereon by the convention, either as a whole or in such parts and with such alternatives as the convention may determine. Any constitutional revision submitted to the voters in accordance with this section shall require the approval of a majority of the qualified voters voting thereon, and shall take effect thirty days after the date of the vote thereon, unless the revision itself otherwise provides.

Section 12.04.   *Conflicting Amendments or Revisions.* If conflicting constitutional amendments or revisions submitted to the voters at the same election are approved, the amendment or revision receiving the highest number of affirmative votes shall prevail to the extent of such conflict.

BICAMERAL ALTERNATIVE: Appropriate changes to reflect passage by two houses must be made throughout this article.

## Article XIII
## SCHEDULE

Section 13.01. *Effective Date.* This constitution shall be in force from and including the first day of _____, 19 _____, except as herein otherwise provided.

Section 13.02 *Existing Laws, Rights and Proceedings.* All laws not inconsistent with this constitution shall continue in force until they expire by their own limitation or are amended or repealed, and all existing writs, actions, suits, proceedings, civil or criminal liabilities, prosecutions, judgments, sentences, orders, decrees, appeals, causes of action, contracts, claims, demands, titles and rights shall continue unaffected except as modified in accordance with the provisions of this constitution.

Section 13.03. *Officers.* All officers filling any office by election or appointment shall continue to exercise the duties thereof, according to their respective commissions or appointments, until their offices shall have been abolished or their successors selected and qualified in accordance with this constitution or the laws enacted pursuant thereto.

Section 13.04. *Choice of Officers.* The first election of governor under this constitution shall be in 19 _____. The first election of members of the legislature under this constitution shall be in 19 _____.

Section 13.05. *Establishment of the Legislature.* Until otherwise provided by law, members of the legislature shall be elected from the following districts: The first district shall consist of [the description of all the districts from which the first legislature will be elected should be inserted here].

BICAMERAL ALTERNATIVE: Section 13.05. *Establishment of the Legislature.* Refer to "assembly districts" and "senate districts."

Section 13.06. *Administrative Reorganization.* The governor shall submit to the legislature orders embodying a plan for reorganization of administrative departments in accordance with section 5.06 of this constitution prior to [date]. These orders shall become effective as originally issued or as they may be modified by law on [a date three months later] unless any of them are made effective at earlier dates by law.

Section 13.07.  *Establishment of the Judiciary.*

(a) The unified judicial system shall be inaugurated on September 15, 19 _____. Prior to that date the judges and principal ministerial agents of the judicial system shall be designated or selected and any other act needed to prepare for the operation of the system shall be done in accordance with this constitution.

(b) The judicial power vested in any court in the state shall be transferred to the unified judicial system and the justices and judges of the [here name all the courts of the state except justice of the peace courts] holding office on September 15, 19 _____, shall become judges of the unified judicial system and shall continue to serve as such for the remainder of their respective terms and until their successors shall have qualified. The justices of the [here name the highest court of the state] shall become judges of the supreme court and the judges of the other courts shall be assigned by the chief judge to appropriate service in the other departments of the judicial system, due regard being had to their positions in the existing judicial structure and to the districts in which they had been serving.

# Index

Abrams, Charles, 558
Accounting, 448–49, 455–56
Administration (state)
  departments of, 358–67
  organization, 379–81
  position of strong governor, 372–73
  position of weak governor, 367–72
  reorganization, 373–79, 381–83
Administrative agencies, influence on legislation, 346, 358–59
Administrative control (over local government)
  advice and assistance, 61–62
  approval and review, 56–60
  extent, 60–62
  grants-in-aid, 60–61
  inspections, 53–54
  merits, 53–54
  substitute administration, 157–59
Administrative offices of courts, 321–22
Administrative organization (state)
  constitutional offices, 358–61
  proposed changes in, 660–61
  reorganization, 373–79
  statutory agencies, 361
  traditional, 358–60
Administrative reorganization (state)
  by executive order, 382
  by legislature, 359–60
  departments under, 375–77
  fiscal control, 380
  in Illinois, 375–76
  in Missouri, 376–77
  in New Jersey, 374, 377
  in New York, 376–77
  integrated, 380
  Little Hoover Commissions, 378–79
  movements for, 373–78, 381–83

  partial, 380
  plural executive, 380–81
Advertising (state), 573–74, 626–27
Advisory Commission on Intergovernmental Relations, 137
Advisory opinions
  by state judges, 320
  distinguished from declaratory judgments, 320
Aged, medical assistance for, 527–28
Agricultural extension work
  county agent, 575–77
  experiment stations, 577–78
  farmers' institutes, 575
  home-demonstration agent, 577
Agriculture
  agricultural statistics, 572
  animal industry division, 570–71
  control of animal and plant disease, 574–75
  dairy and food division, 567–70
  department of, 565–75
  entomology division, 574–75
  market-news division, 572–73
  marketing, 573–74
  organization (state), 565–75
  soil conservation, 578–79
  state botanist, 571–72
  weather division, 567
Agriculture, Secretary of (state), 367, 565–66
Air transportation, 604–5
Alabama, 6, 78, 130, 191, 195, 254, 263, 345, 348, 351, 380, 413, 415, 539
Alaska, 9, 10, 28, 29, 43, 67, 68, 114, 146, 174, 178, 182, 184, 185, 191, 194, 253, 263, 289, 290, 294, 306, 307, 317, 321, 332, 335, 337, 380, 415,

Alaska (*Continued*)
  421, 424, 427, 431, 433, 440, 455,
  460, 502, 512, 533, 598, 599, 646,
  658
Allotment system of budget control, 449
Almshouses, 99
*Amalgamated Association v. Wisconsin
  Employment Relations Board,* 642
Amendment of state constitutions, 180–91
*American Federation of Labor v. Swing,*
  643
American Political Science Committee on
  American Legislatures, recommenda-
  tions of, 279–80
*American Steel Foundries Co. v. Tri-City
  Central Trades Council,* 643
Anderson, William, 44–45
Appellate courts (state), 308–9
Appointing power
  of city managers, 132–36
  of governor, 339–41
  of mayors, 123–26
Apportionment of seats in state legisla-
  tures, 249–53
Appropriations
  itemized, 447
  lump sum, 447
Arbitration of labor disputes, 641–42
Arkansas, 11, 81, 115, 182, 194, 195, 222,
  225, 263, 294, 332, 427, 444, 445,
  514, 515, 534, 539, 565
Arizona, 10, 74, 150, 225, 294, 307, 317,
  423, 449, 512, 515, 598, 602
Arraignment in criminal proceedings, 312
Arrest, 90, 464
Articles of Confederation
  acceptance, 3
  characteristics of government, 3–4
  Congress, 4
  Continental Congress, 3–4
  defects of, 4
Assessment of property for taxation, 95–
  96
Assessor (county), 95–96
Assigned counsel (for the indigent), 467
Attainder, bill of, 177, 246
Attorney
  county, 90–91
  prosecuting, 90–91
Attorney general, 279, 365–66, 459–60
Auditing
  post audit, 379, 453–54
  pre-audit, 379
Auditor
  county, 95
  state, 364–65
Australian ballot, 240–41

Authorities
  functions of, 109–10
  organization of, 111
  reasons for creation, 110
Aviation, state concern for, 604–5

Bail, 177
*Bailey v. Drexel Furniture Co.,* 640
*Baker v. Carr,* 252
Ballot
  Australian, 240–41
  Indiana (party column), 224, 241
  Massachusetts (office-group), 224, 241
*Bank of Augusta v. Earle,* 619
Banking, state regulation of, 612–14
Bicameralism (in state legislatures)
  arguments for, 247–48
  defects of, 247
Bills (in state legislature)
  committee procedures, 284–85
  drafting, 279–80
  introduction of, 280–81
  number of, 283
  steps in enactment, 280–87
  vetoes of, 288–89
Bills of rights (in state constitutions),
  177–78
Bishop, Donald G., 79
Blind, aid to, 523–25
Blue-sky laws, 617–18
Board of education, 499–500
Boards and commissions, 368, 382
  education, 494–96
Bollens, John C., 106–7, 161
Bookmobiles, 516–17
Borrowing, 415–16, 432–33
Bosses, political, 212–14
Boycott, primary and secondary, 644
Brown, Edmund G., 238–39
*Brown v. Topeka Board of Education,* 514
Buck, A. E., 368
Budget
  allotments, 449
  budget bills, 446
  budget message, 342
  budget periods, 444, 445, 446
  definition (the document), 443–44
  essential characteristics, 445
  execution of, 444, 448–49
  legislative action on, 448
  preparation, 448
  types of budget-making authority, 445
Building codes, 142–43
*Bunting v. Oregon,* 632
Business
  administrative organization, 610–12
  banking regulation, 612–14

insurance regulation, 615–17
liquor regulation, 619–20
local government enterprises, 620
local licensing, 625
public utility regulation, 620–23
sale of securities regulation, 617–18
state-owned enterprises, 626
state regulation of corporations, 618–19
state regulation of professions and trades, 623–25
Businessmen in state legislatures, 261–62
Butler, George D., 581

California, 5, 28, 44, 69, 70, 83, 84, 85, 106, 108, 129, 150, 166, 182, 187, 189, 199, 227, 238, 244, 262, 276, 283, 295, 307, 317, 321, 332, 345, 376, 380, 381, 387, 389, 415, 416, 421, 424, 427, 428, 431, 434, 448, 462, 489, 507, 508, 509, 511, 512, 528, 533, 534, 539, 551, 557, 560, 579, 580, 598, 602, 624, 634, 646, 647, 650, 651, 652, 653
Campaigns (political)
headquarters, 231–32
local, 239–40
press relationships, 233
schedules, 229
techniques, 229–31
use of TV, 228
Campaigns (political) expenditures
amounts spent, 238–39
state limitations, 235–36
Capital budgeting, 447
Caucus, nominating, 225
Centralized purchasing, 449–53
Certiorari, writ of, 299
Charters, local, 70–72, 116–17
Checkoff of union dues, 645
Checks and balances, 23–25
Child labor, 639–40
Children, aid to dependent, 525–26
Chisholm v. Georgia, 29
Cigarette taxes, 423
Cincinnati and city manager form of government, 113
City-county consolidation, 164–66
City-county separation, 163–64
City government
commission, 129–32
council-manager, 132–36
mayor-administrative assistant, 127–29
New England Town, 118–22
principal forms, 117–36
relative prevalence, 118
strong-mayor council, 125–27
weak-mayor council, 122–25

City manager, 132–36
City-state, 163
Civil Administrative Code of Illinois, 375–76
Civil defense
continuity of government in relation to, 480–82
expenditures for, 480
federal role in, 477–78
organization for, 479–82
Civil rights, 177–78
Civil rights acts (federal), voting rights, 195
Civil service (state), 386–90
Clerk, county, 93
Closed primary, 222
Closed shop, 644–45
Codification of state law, 289
Collective bargaining, 640–41
Colleges and universities
community and junior, 505
enrollments in, 9
municipal, 506–7
state, 502–4
Colonial governments
charter, 2
proprietary, 1–2
royal, 1–2
Colorado, 68, 153, 187, 223, 236, 252, 263, 294, 318, 320, 381, 416, 418, 433, 497, 504, 505, 512, 513, 539, 565, 579
Commission government (in cities), 129–32
Commission on Efficiency and Economy, 375
Commission on Intergovernmental Relations, 54, 665
Commission on Organization of the Executive Branch of the Government (Hoover Commission), 377–78
Commission on Uniform State Laws, 40
Commissioners of Hamilton County v. Mighels, 104
Common law, nature of, 302
Commonwealth v. Hunt, 631
Commutation of sentence by governor, 350
Compacts, 37–38, 512–14
Comptroller
role in budget-making, 445–46
role in pre-audit, 449
Compulsory voting, 200
Conciliation, 321, 641
Conference committee in state legislatures, 286–87
Conference of Chief Justices, 313

Connecticut, 2, 14, 37, 51, 66, 67, 114, 118, 175, 181, 184, 224, 253, 254, 304, 311, 376, 380, 388, 427, 461, 467, 491, 515, 557, 560, 565, 598, 646, 658
Conservation (of natural resources), 578–79
Consolidation (in local government)
  city-county, 164–66
  county, 79
  functional, 161–63
  school, 500–502
Constable, town, 119, 468
Constitution (U.S.)
  bill of rights, 5
  distribution of powers, 23–25
  establishment of, 4, 5
  federal obligations to states, 26–29
  limitations on states, 24–25
  powers denied states and national government, 25
  ratification of, 5
Constitutional conventions, 184–87
Constitutional revisory commission, 187–90
Constitutions (state)
  approval of amendments, 182–83
  by initiative and referendum, 181–82
  contents, 177
  distributive provisions, 178–79
  evolution of, 174–77
  frequency of amendments, 190–91
  how first made, 3
  methods of amending, 180–81
  need for orderly methods of change, 180
  powers of government, 179–80
  purposes of, 172–73
  recommended changes in, 657–59
Contracts, states forbidden to impair, 179
Conventions (nominating), combined with primary, 223, 224
Cooley v. Board of Wardens Port of Philadelphia, 34
Cooperation between nation and states, 29–33
Coroner, 94–95
Corporations, state regulation of, 618–19
Corrupt-practices legislation, 289–90
Council (city)
  under commission plan, 129–32
  under manager plan, 132–36
  under strong mayor, 125–27
  under weak mayor, 122–25
Council-manager government (in cities)
  advantages, 135
  alleged defects, 135–36

appointment of manager, 132–33
duties of manager, 133–35
extent of utilization, 132
organization, 136
origin, 132–33
manager-council relations, 133
Council of State Governments
  affiliated organizations, 40
  board of control, 39
  founding, 38
  objectives and purposes, 38–39
  publications, 39–40
Council of State Governments Committee on Legislation Procedures, 292–93
County
  future of, 105–6
  merit systems, 389
  new county functions, 97–104
  non-county government areas, 67–68
  number and organization, 67–69
  proposed reorganization, 79–88
  urban, 104–5
County agricultural agent, 575–77
County almshouse, 99
County central committee (political), 209–10
County commissioners and supervisors, 72–78
County courts, 309
County executive
  appointive, 83–84
  clerk as, 80–81
  elective, 81–83
County governing boards
  compensation, 78
  organization, 75–76
  powers, 76–78
  selection and terms, 73–74
  sessions, 76
  size of, 74
  types of governing bodies, 73
County government officers
  assessor, 95–96
  attorney, 90–91
  auditor, 95
  clerk, 93
  coroner, 94–95
  executive officers, 79–88
  other officials, 96–97
  sheriff, 88–90
  superintendent of schools, 96
  treasurer, 92–93
County highways, 595
County home rule, 70–72
County jail, 475–77
County libraries, 516–18
County manager, 84–88

County officers, 88–97
County superintendent of schools, 96, 500
Courts, state and federal, relationship of, 299–301
Crime, 464–65
Criminal law, 302
*Cunningham v. Northwestern Improvement Co.*, 634

Dade County (Florida) plan, 167–68
Davidson County (Tennessee), 165, 168
de Tocqueville, Alexis, 34, 326
Debt (state), 415–16, 432–33
Declaratory judgments, 320
Delaware, 5, 47, 100, 116, 181, 182, 184, 236, 253, 272, 295, 306, 362, 415, 424, 431, 433, 449, 530, 533, 585, 587, 588, 590, 598, 616, 619, 626
*Dent v. West Virginia*, 623
Depository laws for state funds, 456–57
Des Moines Plan (commission government), 130–32
Dillon, John F., 49
Dillon's Rule (definition of municipal power), 49
Direct primary
closed, 222
open, 222
origin and spread, 221–24
post primary conventions, 223
pre-primary conventions, 223
Disability of governor, 334–36
Disabled, aid to, 526–27
Disaster aid by governor, 348–49
Disease control in public health programs, 544–45
Dishman, Robert, 172–73
District of Columbia, voting in, 198
Divorce and "full faith and credit," 30–31
Dodd, Walter F., 362
Domicile in suffrage qualifications, 195
Dorr's Rebellion, 28
Due process of law, 177–78, 537–39, 607–8

Earmarking, 429, 447
of revenues, 419–21
Education
consolidation movements, 500–502
and the county, 101
county units of, 500
district system, 499
higher education, 502–9
local government and, 498–502
major problems of, 509–16

municipal colleges, 506–7
national role, 492–94
number of school districts, 489–92
public school units, 489–92
school finance, 440–41
state board of, 494–96
state departments of, 497–98
state organization for, 494–98
state universities, 502–4
town or township unit of, 499–500
Elections
administrative officers, 240–41, 337, 339
ballot forms, 224, 241
cost of, 223
Electorate, role of, 193
Electrical voting in state legislatures, 286
*Elliot v. City of Detroit*, 51
Eminent domain, power of, 177–78
Employee organizations, 401–4
Employees, number of federal and state, 13
Employment agencies, 639
*Engle v. Vitale*, 515–16
Equal protection of the laws
and legislative apportionment, 249–53
and school segregation, 514–15
Equalization of property assessment, 95–96
Equity (law), 302, 309–10
Ex post facto law, 177–78
Executive
leadership, 344–47
nature of the function, 325–29
Executive budget, 342
Executive councils, composition and powers, 380–81
Expenditures
distribution by functions (state), 442
distribution by functions (state and local), 440
major purposes, 440
per capita (state and local), 440
reasons for increased, 442
trends, 439–42
Experience rating
in public personnel, 399–400
in unemployment compensation, 636–37
Extradition, 30, 350–51

Fair employment practices, 638–39
Fair Labor Standards Act, 633
Farmers' institutes, 575
Faust, Martin, 364
Federal aid as state and local revenue source, 430–32
Federal Aid Highway Act (1956), 603

Federalism
    American system, 22–23, 32–33
    defined, 22
    legal and functional, 654
    merits of, 32–33
*Federalist, The,* 23
Fee compensation
    of county sheriff, 89–90
    of justice of the peace, 310
    of New England town officials, 120
Fifteenth Amendment, 194
Finance committees, 210
Financial aid by state to local units, 60–61
Fines and justice of the peace courts, 310–11
Fire administration
    municipal, 140, 484–88
    national government, 482–83
    state fire marshal, 483–84
Fiscal management
    accounting, 455–56
    basic elements of, 443
    centralized purchasing, 449–53
    financial reporting, 454–55
    post-audit, 453–54
Fiscal officers, 455–56
Fiscal services, 443
Fiscal year, 413–14
Fisher, Marguerite J., 79
Floor leader, 271
Florida, 10, 47, 51, 116, 150, 167, 190, 238, 254, 277, 320, 421, 433, 444, 445, 551, 561, 616, 626, 627, 628
Forests (conservation), 579
Fourteenth Amendment, 194
Franchise, 622
"Full faith and credit" clause, 30
Functional consolidation (in local government), 161–63

Gasoline taxes, 421–23
General property tax, 427
General trial courts, 309
Georgia, 3, 29, 51, 74, 191, 194, 199, 263, 266, 272, 321, 336, 350, 376, 472, 561, 616, 646, 658
Gerrymandering, 249–50
*Gibbons v. Ogden,* 34
Government ownership, 626
Governor
    appointive power, 339–41
    authority to investigate state agencies, 343–44
    budget power, 342
    call for reports, 342–43
    call of special sessions, 347–48
    colonial, 1–2
    compensation, 332–34
    daily and weekly schedule, 353–55
    executive office of, 351–55
    judicial powers of, 344–51, 472–73
    legal qualifications, 328
    and legislature, 282–83
    messages to legislature, 345–47
    military power, 348–49, 463, 646
    nomination and election, 330–31
    ordinance-making, 343
    original role, 325–26
    political qualifications, 328–30
    political role, 329
    as presidential "timber," 326–27
    proposed changes in office of, 660
    removal and succession, 334–36
    removal power, 341–42
    role in civil defense, 349
    staff of, 351–53
    supervision of administration, 336–44
    term, 331–32
    veto power, 344–45
Governors' Conference, 355
Grand jury, 312–13, 468, 471
Grants-in-aid, 430–32
Graves, W. Brooke, 454–55
*Guinur v. United States,* 196

Habeas corpus, 177–78, 299
*Hall v. Geiger-Jones Company,* 617
Hamilton, Alexander, 23
*Hammer v. Dagenhart,* 640
Hart, James P., 178
Hawaii, 29, 43, 44, 68, 114, 133, 174, 181, 194, 307, 328, 355, 362, 380, 421, 427, 428, 449, 450, 460, 462, 489, 491, 502, 512, 560, 612, 658
Health
    federal role, 537
    state authority in, 537
    state expenditures for, 550–51
    trends, 537–38
Health departments
    communicable disease control, 544–45
    dental health care, 547–48
    early organization of, 539
    health education, 544
    industrial public health, 547
    maternal and child care, 548
    municipal, 140–41
    public health nursing, 546–47
    public health labs, 548–49
    pure food and drug division, 549–50
    sanitary engineering, 545
    state organization of, 539–50
Health education, 544
Herring, E. Pendelton, 550

Highway departments
  state, 584–87
  typical, 587–94
Highway officers, 584–85
Highways
  administration (state), 584–87
  classification of, 601–2
  county responsibility, 595
  federal financing, 599–603
  financing (state), 596–603
  local responsibility for, 594–96
  municipal responsibility for, 594–95
  organization (state), 587–94
  safety on, 603–4
  town and township role, 595–96
Hiscock, Ira V., 541
Holden v. Hardy, 632
Home rule (constitutional), 49–50, 70–72
Home rule (legislative), 51–52
Home-rule charters, 70–72, 116–17
Hoover Commission, 377–78, 381
Hospitals (government), 553–54
Hours of work, 639–48
Housing, 557–61
Housing authorities, 561
Houston, E & W Texas Railway v. United
  States, 34
Hume, Alexander, 153

Idaho, 31, 68, 184, 199, 222, 236, 263,
  294, 376, 380, 381, 417, 419, 425,
  427, 512, 529, 598, 612
Illinois, 44, 82, 114, 150, 187, 191, 236,
  317, 318, 326, 345, 375, 376, 380,
  381, 386, 389, 404, 416, 418, 421,
  434, 455, 504, 515, 560, 608, 628
Impeachment
  of governor, 335
  of judges, 307
  general aspects, 291
Income taxes
  corporation, 425–27
  personal, 423–25
  state, 416
Incorporated towns, 116–17
Indebtedness
  local, 433
  state, 415–16, 432–33
Indeterminate sentence, 473
Indiana, 10, 57, 81, 133, 184, 224, 416,
  431, 444, 445, 489, 497, 534, 561,
  565
Indictment, 312–13, 470–71
Indoor public assistance, 520–21
Industrial development programs (state),
  626–28
"Information," 312–13, 470–71

Inheritance tax, 430
Initiative, 180–82
Injunction, 299
Inquest, 94
Insurance, state regulation of, 615–17
Intergovernmental agreements, 37–38,
  512–14
Intergovernmental tax immunity, 413
Interim committees and commissions, 276
Interlocal relations, 161–63
International City Managers' Association,
  134
Interstate citizenship, 31
Interstate compacts, 37–38, 512–14
Interstate cooperation, voluntary, 39–41,
  161–63
Interstate highways, 603
Interstate relations
  compacts, 37–38, 512–14
  cooperation, 38–39
  "full faith and credit," 30
  interstate citizenship, 31
  rendition, 30
Interstate rendition, 30, 350–51
Interstate trade barriers, 4
Iowa, 51, 114, 116, 130, 132, 184, 235,
  236, 270, 272, 276, 306, 313, 317,
  318, 345, 369, 372, 380, 414, 418,
  425, 429, 449, 450, 467, 479, 480,
  503, 551, 566, 567, 571, 573, 574,
  608, 628
Item veto by governor, 344–45
Ives v. South Buffalo Co., 634

Jails, 90, 475–77
Jones, Victor, 105
Judges (state)
  compensation, 305–11
  qualifications, 302–4
  removal, 307
  retirement, 307, 318
  selection, 305, 306, 309, 310
  terms, 305–10
Judicial administration
  conference of judicial officials, 313–14
  judicial conference, 313
  recommended reforms, 662–63
Judicial conferences, 313
Judicial control, 319
Judicial councils, 314, 321–22
Judicial functions, 299–301
Judicial review of legislation, 319
Judicial system
  criticisms of, 314–16
  reforms, 322–23
  reorganization of, 316–18

Judiciary
  court of last resort, 305–8
  equity courts, 309–10
  general trial courts, 309
  intermediate appellate courts, 308–9
  justice of the peace, 310–12
  state court organization, 304–12
Junior colleges, 505
Jury
  coroner's, 94–95
  grand, 312–13
  trial, 312–13
Justices of the peace, 310–12

Kansas, 44, 190, 225, 236, 263, 277, 307,
    318, 379, 388, 418, 421, 425, 490,
    501, 503, 505, 506, 533, 534, 616,
    617, 645
Kentucky, 5, 26, 29, 184, 190, 194, 304,
    318, 331, 336, 376, 380, 423, 434,
    489, 506, 507, 603
Kentucky Whip & Collar Co. v. Illinois
    Central Railway, 34
Kerr-Mills Act, 527–28
Key, V. O., Jr., 204, 205
Kidnapped persons, 64
Kilpatrick, Wylie, 56

Labor
  collective bargaining, 640–41
  history of labor organizations, 631–32
  hours of work, 632–33
  mediation, conciliation, and arbitration,
    641–42
  minimum wages, 633–34
  open, closed, and union shops, 644–45
  right to strike, 642–44
  state organization, 645–53
  unemployment compensation, 635–37
Labor departments, 645–53
Labor relations acts, 639–41, 644–45
Labor unions, 631–32
Lancaster, Lane W., 100–101
Land-grant colleges, 502–3
Laski, Harold J., 7–8
Law, 302
Law enforcement, 100–101
  local agencies, 466–72
  role of governor, 459
  state agencies, 459–65
  treatment of criminals, 472–77
Legal aid bureaus, 99
Legislation (direct)
  initiative, 294–95
  referendum, 295
Legislation (state)
  enactment procedure, 280–87

item veto, 288
sources of bills, 280–82
veto, 288–89
Legislative address, 307
Legislative calendar, 286
Legislative committees
  bills, action on, 280–87
  conference, 286–87
  improvement of, 273–74
  interim, 276
  joint, 272–73
  number and size, 274–75
  procedure, 284–85
  research assistance, 277–80, 293
  role of, 271
  standing, 272, 284
Legislative councils
  advantages of, 278
  bill-drafting role, 278
  nature and functions, 277–78
  research agencies, 278
Legislative employees, 270–71
Legislative functions
  general reference to, 268
  policy determination, 244–45
  supervision of administration, 245
Legislative officers
  house majority floor leader, 271
  minor officials, 271
  presiding officer of senate, 270
  president pro tem of senate, 271
  speaker of the house, 268–70
Legislative procedure
  calendars, 286
  engrossment, 286
  introduction of bills, 280–81
  origin of bills, 280–82
  readings, 284–86
  relations with governor, 282–83
Legislative reference bureaus, 280
Legislative reorganization, 292–93
Legislators
  characteristics of, 262
  compensation, 262–66
  election, 254
  non-partisan, 255
  occupations, 261–62
  privileges and immunities, 267
  prototype, 261
  qualifications, 260–62
  retirement plans, 266
  tenure, 254–55
Legislatures (state)
  apportionment, 249–53
  bicameral and unicameral, 246–48
  descriptive features, 261
  improvement, 292–93

initiation of constitutional amendments, 244
legal designations, 244
length of sessions, 258–60
lobbying, regulation of, 289–91
non-legislative functions, 291–92
party control, 287–88
powers, 244–45
proposed revisions, 659
sessions of, 256–58
size, 253–54
state constitutional restrictions on, 246
terms, 254–55
urban underrepresentation, 249–53
U.S. Constitutional limitations, 245–46
Levin, Murray, 234
Liability of legislators, 267
Libraries, 516–18
Library Services Act, 517–18
Licensing (state)
  hunting and fishing, 429–30
  professions and trades, 623–25
Lieutenant governor
  duties of, 270, 358
  as presiding officer, 270
  successor to governor, 335–36
Lindbergh Kidnapping Law, 64
Liquor control, 429, 619–20
Liquor stores, 429
Liquor taxes, 429
Literacy tests, 196
Little Hoover Commissions, 378, 410
Lobbying (in state legislatures), 289–91
Local "federalism," 166–68
Local government
  characteristics of, 42–43
  expenditures of, 440
  number of units, 43–44
  powers of legislature over, 52–53
  proposal for reorganization of, 44–46
  recommended reforms in, 663–64
Local option (charters), 70–72
Local revenues, 433–35
Lochner v. New York, 632
Los Angeles County, 69, 84, 86–87
Louisiana, 68, 106, 184, 190, 199, 254, 263, 318, 336, 349, 428, 434, 489, 539, 560, 616
Luther v. Borden, 27

McAnaw, Richard L., 360
McCulloch v. Maryland, 34, 107, 413
McKean, Dayton D., 217
Magistrate court (inferior courts), 310–12
Maine, 5, 114, 118, 272, 294, 317, 328, 331, 362, 376, 380, 460, 491, 517, 529, 539, 565, 603, 646

Manager government
  city, 132–36
  county, 84–88
Mandamus, writ of, 299
Marbury v. Madison, 34
Martial law, 348
Maryland, 66, 70, 83, 184, 244, 254, 294, 304, 311, 362, 386, 388, 404, 448, 489, 491, 497, 534, 539, 555, 599, 634
Massachusetts, 2, 55, 66, 68, 114, 118, 166, 175, 182, 184, 223, 238, 244, 253, 258, 266, 272, 276, 306, 321, 345, 347, 381, 386, 388, 389, 411, 428, 461, 491, 497, 505, 517, 524, 527, 528, 539, 560, 562, 563, 575, 646
Mayers, Lewis, 398
Mayor
  administrative assistant, 127–29
  strong, 125–27
  weak, 122–25
Mayor-council government, 122–27
Mediation, 641
Medical care, 527–28
Medical examiner, 94
Mental health, 554–57
Merit system, 386–89
Messages of governor to legislature, 345–47
Messick, Charles P., 405
Metropolitan areas
  annexation, 159–61
  city-county consolidation, 164–66
  city-state proposal, 163
  definition of, by U.S. Census, 146–47
  development of standard, 146–47
  federation, 166–69
  intergovernmental cooperation, 161–63
  planning, 142–43
  population trends in, 147–55
  urban region theory, 155
Metropolitan federation, 166–69
Metropolitan problems, 155–57
  proposed solutions of
    city-county consolidation, 164–66
    city-county separation, 163–64
    city-state, 163
    intergovernmental arrangements, 161–63
    metropolitan federation, 166–69
    municipal annexation, 159–61
    substitute national administration, 157–58
Michigan, 51, 55, 70, 74, 150, 177, 184, 185, 189, 222, 248, 276, 277, 294, 318, 339, 349, 367, 380, 413, 416,

Michigan (*Continued*)
    418, 436, 455, 462, 497, 503, 504,
    539, 580, 658
Militia, 348–49
Milk control, 570
Millspaugh, Arthur C., 366
Minimum wage laws, 633–34
Minnesota, 44, 55, 57, 70, 187, 189, 190,
    222, 253, 254, 287, 375, 379, 425,
    427, 490, 534, 539, 561, 628
Misdemeanor, 302
Mississippi, 11, 14, 15, 51, 115, 195, 199,
    222, 236, 254, 331, 449, 514, 524,
    527, 560, 616, 619
Missouri, 68, 70, 78, 83, 166, 182, 184,
    191, 291, 294, 311, 313, 317, 328,
    364, 415, 421, 434, 475, 476, 505,
    513, 514, 529, 539, 557, 598, 658,
    662
*Missouri ex rel. Gaines v. Canada,* 514
*Missouri v. Holland,* 34
Mitau, G. Theodore, 190
Model Defender Act, 467
Model State Civil Service Law, 407–11
Model state constitution, *see Appendix*
Moderator, 119
Montana, 68, 70, 187, 222, 244, 294, 425,
    512, 616, 634
Morrill Act, 502–3
Motor fuel taxes, 421–23
Motor vehicle license taxes, 428–29
*Moyer v. Peabody,* 464
*Mueller v. Thompson,* 51
*Mulford v. Smith,* 34
Mumford, Lewis, 154
Municipal administration    expenditures,
    138–39
    fire, 140
    local functions, 137–38
    parks and recreation, 142
    police, 139–40
    public health, 140–41
    public utilities, 143
    public welfare, 141
    streets, 141–42
    zoning and planning, 142–43
Municipal corporation
    contrasted with quasi-corporation, 46–
    47
    dissolution of, 48
    incorporation of, 116–17
    legal position, 46–48
    methods of creation, 47–48
    sources of municipal powers, 49
Municipal courts, 310–12
Municipal government
    commission, 129–32

council-manager, 113, 132–36
    forms of, 117–18
    functions, 136–43
    mayor–administrative assistant, 127–29
    New England town, 118–22
    strong-mayor council, 125–27
    weak-mayor council, 122–25
Municipal police, 471–72
Munro, William B., 172
Mustard, Harry S., 551–52
Myrdal, Gunnar, 220

National Civil Service League, 407
National committee (political), 211–12
National Defense Education Act, 493
National government,    immunity    from
    state tax, 413
National Guard, 348–49, 462–64
National Labor Relations Act, 641
*National Labor Relations Board v. Fan-
    stall Metallurgical Corporation,* 643
*National Labor Relations Board v. Jones
    Laughlin Steel Corp.,* 34
National-local relations
    contacts between, 62–63
    direct relationships, 63–64
    future relations, 64
    services rendered by national govern-
    ment, 63
National Municipal League, 131, 132, 407
National power, 23–29
National Recreational Association, 581
Natural gas, 621
Natural resources, 578–79
Nebraska, 182, 184, 244, 248, 254, 268,
    287, 291, 317, 319, 335, 381, 417,
    418, 427, 433, 448, 490, 491, 506,
    513, 655
Negro disfranchisement, 196
Nelson, Gaylord, 559
Neuberger, Richard L., 657–58
Nevada, 10, 31, 50, 53, 114, 150, 236,
    244, 253, 254, 255, 256, 266, 277,
    283, 294, 307, 337, 351, 416, 430,
    500, 512
New England towns, 118–27
    modifications of, 121–22
New Hampshire, 5, 37, 47, 114, 116, 118,
    146, 180, 182, 187, 191, 205, 226,
    244, 253, 263, 272, 304, 347, 362,
    380, 388, 416, 418, 423, 427, 428,
    460, 497, 517, 560, 563, 646, 655
New Jersey, 59, 62, 82, 83, 129, 150, 174,
    175, 177, 181, 182, 184, 189, 191,
    244, 260, 307, 311, 317, 337, 339,
    344, 345, 362, 367, 372, 373, 376,
    380, 389, 417, 424, 435, 460, 491,

497, 500, 502, 515, 525, 533, 539, 546, 549, 557, 560, 565, 626, 634, 638, 658

New Mexico, 6, 180, 223, 257, 294, 427, 500, 512, 616

New York Bureau of Municipal Research, 373

New York City, 89, 128, 156

New York State, 8, 50, 55, 70, 82, 85, 114, 178, 184, 185, 189, 190, 191, 224, 244, 263, 276, 280, 283, 291, 304, 307, 309, 332, 335, 347, 362, 376, 380, 386, 388, 389, 390, 414, 415, 416, 417, 418, 420, 424, 428, 434, 441, 448, 452, 462, 496, 497, 502, 516, 517, 528, 533, 551, 556, 560, 561, 579, 580, 599, 626, 627, 632, 634, 638

Nineteenth Amendment, 194

Nixon, Richard, 227, 238–39

*Nixon v. Herndon*, 198

Nomination, methods
by caucus, 225
by convention, 224
by petition, 224
by self-announcement, 224–25

Non-partisan elections, 287–88

Non-partisan primary, 224

Norris, George W., 246

North Carolina, 26, 31, 47, 51, 59, 70, 81, 84, 100, 116, 190, 236, 288, 317, 337, 344, 347, 351, 376, 423, 477, 489, 491, 539, 585, 616, 646, 655

North Dakota, 70, 182, 184, 194, 222, 244, 263, 294, 319, 332, 335, 336, 380, 424, 444, 445, 452, 557, 560, 565, 616, 626, 646

Occupational disease, 634

Occupations, 624–25

Office consolidation, 79, 106

Ohio, 50, 55, 70, 114, 132, 254, 262, 266, 277, 294, 319, 321, 380, 389, 434, 444, 489, 506, 524, 533, 545, 549, 556, 557, 560, 579, 580, 599, 617, 624

Oklahoma, 182, 184, 205, 263, 294, 306, 307, 308, 335, 425, 427, 532, 559, 560, 616, 637, 646

Old-age assistance, 521–23

*Olsen v. Nebraska*, 639

Open primary, 222

Oregon, 14, 15, 70, 182, 190, 191, 226, 244, 294, 307, 318, 373, 423, 425, 448, 512, 560, 621, 632, 646

Original cost, 622

Outdoor public assistance, 521–28

"Overseers of the poor," 99, 120

*Pacific States Telephone and Telegraph Co. v. Oregon*, 27

Pardon, 349–50, 472

Parishes, 68

Parks
federal activity, 579–80
municipal, 581–82
state, 580–81

Parole, 350, 473–74

Parole board, 477

Parties (political)
bosses, 212–14
defined, 202–3
finance, 235–39
national organization, 211–12
and pressure groups, 214–17
state and local organizations, 205–11
two-party system, 204–5
types of, 203–4

*Paul v. Virginia*, 34, 615

Peel, Roy V., 656

Penal institutions (state), 464–65
number of prisoners, 474

Pennsylvania, 3, 44, 68, 114, 129, 150, 166, 184, 190, 221, 287, 362, 380, 381, 414, 416, 421, 434, 456, 460, 461, 490, 497, 500, 515, 524, 529, 551, 560, 580, 585, 598, 627

Performance budget, 444

Personnel agencies (state) types of, 388–89, 404–8

Personnel management organization
bipartisan commission, 388
director-commission, 407–8
single director, 404–7

Petition, 224
in primary election, 222

Phillips, Jewell Cass, 106, 110

"Pigeonholing" of bills in committees, 284

Planning, city, 142–43

Playgrounds, municipal, 142

*Plessy v. Ferguson*, 514

Pocket veto, 345

Police (state), 460–62

Police magistrates, 311–12

Police power
public health as an exercise of, 537–39
regulation of business, 607–8

Poll tax, 195–97, 428

Polls, public opinion, 234–35

Population
characteristics of, 11–12
employed by government, number of, 13, 14

Population (*Continued*)
 mobility of, 12–13
 urban components, 115
Porter, Kirk H., 8, 342, 363, 504
 541
*Posse comitatus,* 90
Precinct committeemen, 206–9
Preprimary conventions, 223–24
Prescott, Frank W., 344–45
Presentment, 469
President of the senate, 270
President pro tem, 270
Primary, presidential, 225–27
Prison labor, 475–76
Privileges and immunities, 267
Probation, 350–51, 473–74
Property taxes, 427
Prosecuting attorney
 county, 90–91, 466–67
 state, 459–60
Prudent investment, 622
Public assistance, 520–28
Public defender, 99, 467
Public employees
 attitude of public toward, 385–86
 certification, 396–97
 classification systems, 392–93
 current personnel trends, 410–11
 eligible lists, 396
 employee organizations, 401–4
 evaluation of, 399–400
 examinations, 393–95
 initial appointments, 396–97
 legislative employees, 271
 organization for central personnel management, 404–10
 political patronage, 387
 probationary period, 397
 promotions, 398–99
 recommended reform in systems, 661–
  62
 recruitment, 390–92
 removal processes, 400–401
 retirement systems, 411–12
 right to strike, 403–4
 "rule of three," 396
 state distribution of, 389–90
 veteran preference, 395–96
Public health
 development, 539
 local organization for, 552–53
 state expenditures, 550–51
 state-local relations, 551–53
Public health nursing, 546–47
Public housing, 557–61
Public utilities
 municipal, 143

 regulation of, 620–23
Public utility commissions, 620–23
Public works administration, municipal,
 141–42
Purchasing, 449–53

Quasi-corporations, 97
Quasi-judicial powers, 291
Quasi-manager, 83

Rankin, Robert S., 178
Ransone, Coleman B., Jr., 204–5, 330
Ratification
 amendments, 182–84
 constitutions, 187–90
Reapportionment of state legislatures,
 249–53
Recall, 335
Recreation
 municipal, 142, 581–82
 state, 580–81
Reed, Thomas H., 163
Referendum, 182–84
Regionalism, 656
Register of deeds, 93
Removal power, of governor, 341–42
Rendition, 30, 350–51
Representative town meeting, 121
Reprieve by governor, 350, 473
Reproduction cost, 622
Republican government guaranteed to
 states, 26–27
Reston, James, 202
Revenues, 420–30
 intergovernmental, 430–32, 433–35
 property, 427
 revisions of system, 664–65
 trends, 413–18
*Reynolds v. Simms,* 253
Rhode Island, 2, 5, 37, 50, 66, 67, 114,
 118, 175, 184, 187, 223, 236, 263,
 306, 336, 380, 388, 411, 448, 467,
 491, 517, 617, 621, 632
Rich, Bennett M., 54
"Right-to-work" laws, 645
Roads, 584–96
Robson, W. A., 147
Rockefeller, Nelson A., 8
Roosevelt, Franklin D., 153
Root, Elihu, 33
Rule on parliamentary questions, 269
Run-off primary, 223

Sales taxes, 420–21
Sanitation, 545
Schattschneider, E. E., 217

*Schechter Poultry Corporation v. United States*, 34
Schlesinger, Joseph, gubernatorial study by, 329
School boards, 494–96, 499–500
School consolidation, 500–502
School districts, 489–92
School finance, 509–12
*Scott v. Sanford*, 34
Secretary of state, 362–63
Securities regulation, 617–18
Segregation in public schools, 514–15
Selectmen, 119
Seligson, Harry, 385
Senate (state), 244
Service charges, 665
Severance taxes, 428
Sheriff, 88–90, 466
*Sherrer v. Sherrer*, 31
Short ballot, trend toward, 360
Smillie, Wilson G., 541, 543, 551
Smith, Bruce, 466
*Smith v. Texas*, 623
*Smythe v. Ames*, 622
Snider, Clyde F., 77, 500
Social Security Act, 522, 525–26, 529
Soil conservation, 578–79
Solomons, Samuel R., gubernatorial study by, 326–27, 345
Soule, George, 154
South Carolina, 51, 132, 181, 191, 194, 199, 221, 222, 225, 277, 336, 440, 444, 445, 489
South Dakota, 44, 50, 68, 78, 257, 294, 320, 376, 380, 433, 490, 534
*Southwestern Bell Telephone v. Missouri*, 622
Speaker of the house, 268–70
Special districts
 definition of, 106–7
 functions, 108–9
 organizational patterns, 108
 organizational procedures, 107
Special legislation, 283
Special sessions of state legislature, 347–48
State aid to local governments, 433–35
State central committee (political), 210–11
State control (state-local relations), 52–62
 constitutional, 52–53
 finance, 56–57
 governor's supervision, 55–56
 highways, 59–60
 indebtedness, 58
 local budgeting, 57–58
 personnel, 58, 59

supervision by state administration, 53–55, 61–62
State government
 changing nature of, 7–8
 expansion of, 9
 functional activities, 8–9
State party systems, 202–11
State police, 460–62
*State v. Common School District No. 87*, 501
*State v. Hines*, 501
States
 admission, 6–7
 constitutional limitations on, 24–25
 equality of, 28
 federal protection, 27–28
 obligations to each other, 30–31
 obligations to nation, 29
 suits between, 28–29
 territorial integrity, 26
States' rights
 moderate position, 35–36
 philosophy of, 33–34
Steering (sifting) committee, 284
*Sterling v. Constantin*, 464
*Steward Machine Company v. Davis*, 636
Streets, 141–42
Substitute administration, 158–59
Suffrage
 age, 194
 citizenship, 194
 compulsory voting, 200
 in District of Columbia, 198
 literacy, 195
 nature, 197
 negro, 196, 198
 non-voting, 199–200
 poll tax, 195–96
 qualifications, 197
 registration, 195
 residency, 195
 voting patterns, 201–2
Superintendent of public instruction
 county, 96
 state, 366–67, 496–97
Supreme Court (U.S.), 299–301
Supreme courts (state), 305–8
Surveyor, 97–98

Taft-Hartley Act, 644–45
Tax administration, 435–36
Tax commission, 435–36
Tax limits, 413
Tax sharing, 433–35
Taxation
 characteristics of system, 419–20
 classification of, 413

Taxation (*Continued*)
    constitutional limitations on, 413
    defined, 413
    general sales, 420–21, 422
    income, personal, 423–26, 427
    miscellaneous, 429–30
    motor fuels, 421–23
    per capita collection, 415
    property, 427
    tobacco, 423
Tennessee, 5, 26, 50, 57, 68, 71, 74, 78, 165, 168, 189, 191, 248, 249, 250, 262, 335, 362, 380, 427, 460, 491, 534
Tenth Amendment, 23–24, 492, 623, 630
Territorial governments, constitutions of, 6
Texas, 5, 44, 69, 70, 129, 150, 160, 184, 190, 191, 194, 195, 198, 306, 308, 329, 335, 362, 414, 416, 421, 423, 428, 461, 498, 532, 556, 575, 587, 588, 589, 592, 593, 598, 620
*Thornhill v. Alabama*, 643
Tobacco taxes, 423
Toronto, metropolitan federation of, 166–68
Toll roads, 585–87
Town managers, 121
Town meeting (New England), 119
Towns (New England), 118
Township boards, supervisors of, 73
Trade barriers, 4
*Travelers Health Association v. Virginia*, 617
Treasurer
    county, 92
    state, 363–64, 449, 456–57
Twenty-fourth Amendment, 196
Twenty-third Amendment, 198


Unemployment compensation, 635–37
Unicameralism in state legislatures, 246–47
Uniform state laws, 40
Union shop, 644–45
United States Housing Acts, 558–59
United States Office of Education, 493–94
*United States v. Butler*, 34
*United States v. Classic*, 198
*United States v. Darby Lumber Company*, 633, 640
*United States v. Southeastern Underwriters Association*, 34, 615
Universities, 502–4
Urban Affairs (HUD), U.S. Department of, 158

Urban renewal, 558–59
Urban underrepresentation in state legislatures, 249–53
Use taxes, 420–21
Utah, 31, 50, 222, 223, 294, 295, 433, 500, 512, 534, 539, 559, 560, 632

Vermont, 5, 26, 37, 57, 71, 118, 180, 184, 205, 236, 253, 321, 381, 431, 491, 502, 517
Veteran preference, 395–96
Veto power of governor
    item, 288, 344–45
    over-riding, 288–89, 345
    pocket, 345
    suspensory, 344
    time allowed, 345
Virginia, 26, 68, 70, 85, 100, 150, 160, 195, 199, 244, 304, 311, 345, 362, 380, 428, 477, 489, 491, 502, 539, 585, 603, 617, 637
*Virginia v. Tennessee*, 37
Vital statistics in public health, 546
Voter registration, 195
Voting
    Negro, 196, 198
    non-voting, 220–21
    participation, 198–202
    state requirements, 194–96
    U.S. Constitutional requirements, 194

Wager, Paul W., 105
Wages, regulation of, 633–34
Wagner-Peyser Act, 639
Wahlke, John C., *et al.*, study by, 262
Wallace, Schuyler, 53
Warrant, 90, 468
Washington, D.C., suffrage in, 198
Washington State, 70, 80, 81, 222, 263, 295, 306, 380, 423, 512, 524, 527, 533, 557, 560, 598, 616, 634
Weidner, Edward W., 80
Welfare
    aid to blind, 523–25
    aid to dependent children, 525–26
    aid to permanently disabled, 526–27
    categorial outdoor assistance, 521–28
    definition of, 520
    medical assistance to aged, 527–28
    old-age assistance, 521–23
    programs for the aged, 530–35
    state agencies, 528–30
    types of programs, 520–21
Welfare department, typical (Delaware), 530
Welfare institutions, 528–30
*West Coast Hotel v. Parrish*, 633

West Virginia, 5, 11, 26, 100, 115, 190,
    226, 244, 304, 420, 423, 424, 444,
    445, 448, 462, 475, 513, 528, 529,
    534, 585
*West Virginia v. Sims*, 37
Wheeler, John P., 174
White, Leonard D., 369, 385, 404
White primary, 198
*Wilcox v. Consolidated Gas Co.*, 622
*Williams v. North Carolina*, 31
Willoughby, W. F., 299, 392
Wilson, Woodrow, 325
Wisconsin, 50, 51, 55, 57, 114, 222, 244,
    271, 280, 290, 307, 317, 321, 380,
        386, 416, 424, 433, 514, 529, 557,
        559, 560, 628, 634
*Wolff Packing Co. v. Court of Industrial
    Relations*, 642
Workmen's compensation, 634–35
Wyoming, 31, 68, 146, 277, 283, 329,
    390, 421, 431, 433, 460, 497, 512,
    513, 559, 560, 599

Yellow-dog contracts, 641

Zeller, Belle, 273–74
Zoning regulation, 103–4, 142–43

West Virginia, 5, 11, 26, 100, 115, 190, 226, 244, 304, 420, 423, 424, 444, 445, 448, 462, 475, 513, 528, 529, 534, 585
*West Virginia v. Sims*, 37
Wheeler, John P., 174
White, Leonard D., 369, 385, 404
White primary, 198
*Wilcox v. Consolidated Gas Co.*, 622
*Williams v. North Carolina*, 31
Willoughby, W. F., 299, 392
Wilson, Woodrow, 325
Wisconsin, 50, 51, 55, 57, 114, 222, 244, 271, 280, 290, 307, 317, 321, 380, 386, 416, 424, 433, 514, 529, 557, 559, 560, 628, 634
*Wolff Packing Co. v. Court of Industrial Relations*, 642
Workmen's compensation, 634–35
Wyoming, 31, 68, 146, 277, 283, 329, 390, 421, 431, 433, 460, 497, 512, 513, 559, 560, 599

Yellow-dog contracts, 641

Zeller, Belle, 273–74
Zoning regulation, 103–4, 142–43